KU-545-724

SCOTLAND

Touring Guide to Scotland

CONTENTS

INTRODUCTION

HOW TO USE THIS GUIDE 3

SCOTLAND IN BRIEF 3

SCOTLAND BY REGION 4

TRANSPORT AND ACCOMMODATION 5

NATIONAL TOURIST ROUTES 7

TOURIST INFORMATION 9

LOCATION MAPS 12

VISITOR ATTRACTIONS 26

INDEX 294

HarperCollins*Publishers*

Published by Collins
An imprint of HarperCollins*Publishers*
77-85 Fulham Palace Road
London W6 8JB

www.fireandwater.com
www.bartholomewmaps.com

First published 1998
New edition 2000
Text © HarperCollins*Publishers* 2000
Maps © Bartholomew Ltd 2000

Collins® is a registered trade mark of
HarperCollins*Publishers* Limited

All rights reserved. No part of this publication may be reproduced, stored in a retrieval system, or transmitted in any form or by any means, electronic, mechanical, photocopying, recording, or otherwise, without the prior written permission of the Publisher and copyright owners.

The information quoted in this publication is as supplied to HarperCollins*Publishers*, and to the best of the Publisher's knowledge was correct at the time of going to press. While every care has been taken in the preparation of this guide, the Publisher accepts no responsibility whatsoever for any loss, damage, injury or inconvenience sustained or caused as a result of using this guide.

Typeset by Bob Vickers

The Publisher would like to thank everyone who has helped in the provision of information for this publication, particularly the Scottish Tourist Board, staff of the Area Tourist Boards and Tourist Information Centres throughout Scotland, Historic Scotland, the National Trust for Scotland, Forest Enterprise, the Royal Society for the Protection of Birds, and all of the visitor attractions which provided information.

Printed in Italy
ISBN 000 448 942 X
98/2/28

INTRODUCTION

HOW TO USE THIS GUIDE

This brand new edition of the *Touring Guide to Scotland* features over 1500 visitor attractions and is one of the most comprehensive gazetteers of places to visit and things to do in Scotland.

Attractions are listed alphabetically, according to the name of the attraction. The location is only given when it is part of the attraction name, eg Alloa Tower. The exceptions to this are attractions in the cities of Aberdeen, Dundee, Edinburgh and Glasgow – as there are so many attractions close together, they are listed together under the name of the city, to make planning a day out easier.

Each attraction is numbered (eg **56**) and the numbers appear on the location maps (see pages 12–25). The number is also used for reference in the index (see pages 294–304). Please note that attractions are indexed within subject areas. Each attraction also has a map reference (eg **2 E4**) to help you pinpoint the location of each attraction on the maps. The first number (**2**) refers to the location map, the letter and number (**E4**) refer to the grid square in which the attraction is located.

Many of the properties listed in this guide are owned or managed by charities or statutory bodies. We have indicated where an attraction is under the care of Historic Scotland (HS), the National Trust for Scotland (NTS), Forest Enterprise (FE) and the Royal Society for the Protection of Birds (RSPB).

The following information is given on each attraction: address/location; how to get to the attraction by public transport (if relevant); opening times; admission charge (if free, stated thus, otherwise, based on the adult admission price – up to £3 indicated by £, £3–£5 indicated by ££, £5 and over indicated by £££); facilities such as refreshments and parking; followed by a brief description of what the attraction has to offer. We assume that guided tours (where available) are in English. If they are provided in other languages, or if translated material is available, this is stated.

For disabled visitors, we have used three categories to describe access: *wheelchair access* (most or all of the site is accessible, no more than one step, no rough terrain, but not all the footpaths may be suitable); *wheelchair access with assistance* (two or more steps, but not as many as a flight); *limited wheelchair access* (easy access to part of the site, but the rest may not be possible because of stairs, rough ground). Where no access is indicated this is because it is strenuous or dangerous. We assume that all attractions welcome guide dogs. Where dogs are not admitted, this is mentioned in the text. Special facilities for deaf and blind visitors are mentioned.

Finally, visitor attraction opening and closing times, and other details, often change. It is always advisable to check the details of your visit in advance.

SCOTLAND IN BRIEF

Rich in history and heritage, this ancient nation can trace its origins back over 14 centuries when the Scots tribe from Ireland, who had carved out their new Kingdom of Dalriada from land held by the Picts in the 5th century, eventually gave their name to the united nation of Picts and Scots – Scotland.

Prehistoric sites can be found in almost every corner of Scotland, and ancient standing stones have long been a fascination for curious visitors.

Far from being stuck in the past, though, Scotland boasts cosmopolitan cities throbbing with life and vitality. Edinburgh has its striking setting, impressive architecture, imposing castle and the new Scottish Parliament. Glasgow combines the sophistication of a major European cultural capital with the history, heritage and scenic splendour of Scotland.

Getting around is easy with a modern transport infrastructure and communications befitting a nation whose sons invented the telephone, television and tarmacadam!

The glorious natural environment remains one of Scotland's most attractive features, offering endless options for sports, including walking, cycling, sailing, riding and climbing. The home of golf, fishing and the Highland games, Scotland is an outdoor enthusiast's dreamland.

Scotland's stunning scenic splendour acts as a magnet for visitors from all over the globe and each region of Scotland has its individual character and appeal.

SCOTLAND BY REGION

We have split Scotland into eight regions and a brief description of each is given below. For further information on the areas highlighted, contact the relevant Area Tourist Board (see page 9).

The South of Scotland

The softly rolling landscape and richly historic past of the **Scottish Borders** make it a uniquely inviting place to explore. Friendly towns and charming villages all have their own distinctive character, and there are a large number of historic houses, abbeys and gardens throughout the area. **Ayrshire and Arran** offer all the contrasts of mainland and island life. Visit the Burns National Heritage Park, Culzean Castle near Ayr and Brodick Castle on Arran. The beautiful natural surroundings of **Dumfries and Galloway** are ideal for fishing, golfing, walking and cycling. From lochs and craggy hills to rugged cliffs and long sandy beaches, you are surrounded by dramatic scenery. Here, too, you will find many historic castles, abbeys, gardens and museums.

Edinburgh – City, Coast and Countryside

Edinburgh, Scotland's capital, needs little introduction. You'll get a feel for the past just by walking through its famous streets, but if you want to know more, you'll find museums and historic buildings that bring to life every aspect of its history. The surrounding **Lothians** ring Edinburgh with country houses and ruined castles and offer space for outdoor activities as well as a variety of nature and heritage-based attractions.

Greater Glasgow and the Clyde Valley

One of Scotland's most diverse and dynamic visitor destinations, **Greater Glasgow and the Clyde Valley** combines the excitement of a great cultural capital of Europe with some of Scotland's most breathtaking scenery: from the panoramic views of the Clyde Estuary to the Victorian splendour of the City of Glasgow; and from the verdant gardens of the Clyde Valley to the unspoilt and remote Lowther Hills.

West Highlands and Islands, Loch Lomond, Stirling and the Trossachs

From the islands of Coll and Tiree, lying in the Hebridean Sea to the west, to the green slopes of the Ochil Hills east of Stirling, this area of Scotland straddles Highland and Lowland. Peaceful glens, shapely peaks and clear blue lochs contrast vividly with the gentle hills and historic towns of the lowlands. Visit Stirling, which played a leading role in Scotland's past, or travel by ferry from Oban to the Isle of Mull, and on to Iona, cradle of Scottish Christianity.

Perthshire, Angus and Dundee, and the Kingdom of Fife

This is an area offering plenty of contrasts. **Perthshire** has fine mountains, deep lochs and ancient castles, and is an ideal touring centre, located just 80 miles (129km) north of Edinburgh and Glasgow. **Angus and Dundee** offer mountainous glens and rugged coastline, and the bustle of a waterfront city. The old **Kingdom of Fife** has plenty of character. St Andrews has the oldest university in Scotland and is, of course, the home of golf. The attractive East Neuk fishing villages are well worth a visit.

Grampian Highlands, Aberdeen and the North East Coast

This quiet corner of Scotland has varied mountain, rural and coastal scenery. As a major Scottish centre and gateway to Royal Deeside, the city of **Aberdeen** has much to offer the visitor. You can follow the Castle Trail which is steeped in history, or take the Royal Road along the beautiful Dee valley and visit Balmoral Castle. The **North East Coast** offers picturesque fishing villages, spectacular cliff scenery and unrivalled birdlife.

The Highlands and Skye

No single image can capture the scale and diversity of this region. From the soaring crags of Glen Coe to the wide rolling moors of Caithness, from the old pinewoods of upper Speyside to the spectacular Cuillin mountains of Skye, the north and west offer unmatched scenic splendour. **The Highlands of Scotland** is rich in places to visit, with castles, battlefields and forts to remind you of a turbulent past, while distilleries, woollen mills and other crafts contribute to today's diverse Highland economy. Inverness, often called the capital of the Highlands, is a natural gateway to the north. At the other end of the Great Glen, Fort William stands in the shadow of Ben Nevis.

The Outer Islands

The Outer Islands are for those looking for a totally different experience. **Orkney** is made up of 70 islands, rich in historical and archaeological remains. Here you will find villages, burial chambers and standing stones built before the Great Pyramids of Egypt. **Shetland**, a cluster of islands set between Scotland and Scandinavia, shares something of the character of both, while guarding a rich local identity. Magnificent seascapes and fine seabird colonies are among the many features of these untamed islands. The **Western Isles**, a 130-mile long chain of islands lying to the north west of Scotland, offer a unique experience. The combinations of land, sea and inland water have produced landscapes which have been designated areas of outstanding scenic value.

TRANSPORT AND ACCOMMODATION

Driving

Many visitors choose to see Scotland by road – distances are short and roads are generally uncrowded. If you want to get to your destination quickly, the motorways and trunk roads are generally fast and efficient, with plenty of services en route. If, on the other hand, you are not in a hurry, take time out to follow one of the many designated routes and trails. National Tourist Routes (see page 7) take the visitor off the motorways and main trunk roads along attractive routes passing a variety of things to see and do. There are also varied special interest trails – from the Malt Whisky Trail in Speyside to the Castle Trail in Aberdeen. Contact the Scottish Tourist Board (see page 9) for further information.

Comprehensive touring and leisure information can be found on the companion *Touring Map of Scotland*. Collins also publish a range of Scottish maps and atlases to help you find your way around.

As you travel around Scotland look out for the tourist signposting – distinctive brown signs bearing the thistle symbol. These signs will direct you to a wide variety of things to do and places to visit, including attractions in the care of Historic Scotland and the National Trust for Scotland. They are also used to indicate the National Tourist Routes and the tourist trails mentioned above.

In common with the rest of the UK, all driving in Scotland is on the left and overtaking is permissible only on the right. Particular care is needed at roundabouts (priority is given to traffic from the right, and you should go round the roundabout in a clockwise direction) and on single track roads, where passing places must be used to overtake.

Speed limits are as follows: dual carriageways 70mph (112kph); single carriageways 60mph (96kph); built-up areas (unless otherwise signposted) 30mph (48kph). The maximum speed limit for camper vans and caravans is 50mph (80kph).

Fuel is generally available in all parts of Scotland and all filling stations provide unleaded petrol and diesel. In remote areas distances between stations may be greater and opening hours shorter. Note that there is Sunday closing in the West Highlands and Islands.

It is compulsory to wear seatbelts at all times. Small children and babies must be restrained with an appropriate child seat or carrier.

Public Transport

There is a good internal rail network in Scotland. All major towns are linked by rail and there are also links to the western seaboard at Mallaig and Oban (for ferry connections to Skye, Mull and the Western Isles) and to Inverness, Thurso and Wick (for ferries to Orkney and Shetland). Multi-journey tickets and discount cards allow you to save on fares. Local bus companies in Scotland offer explorer tickets and discount cards. Post buses (normally minibuses) take passengers on over 130 rural routes throughout Scotland.

Ferries to and around the islands are regular and reliable; most ferries carry vehicles, although some travelling to smaller islands convey only passengers.

Contact the Scottish Tourist Board (see page 9), or call in to any Tourist Information Centre for information. Alternatively, contact the following travel companies direct:

Airlines
British Airways (0345) 222111
British Midland (0870) 6070555
Easy Jet (0990) 292929
Gill Air 0191 214 6666
KLM UK (0870) 5074074
Ryanair (0541) 569569

Bus Companies
National Express Coaches (0990) 808080
Scottish Citylink Coaches (0990) 505050

Rail Companies
National Rail Enquiries (0345) 484950
Great North Eastern (0345) 225225
Scotrail 0141 335 4260
Virgin Trains (0345) 222333

Ferry Companies
Caledonian Macbrayne
Hebridean and Clyde Ferries
enquiries (01475) 650100
reservations (0990) 650000
Orkney Islands Ferries Ltd (01856) 872044
P&O Scottish Ferries (01224) 572615
Serco Denim (Isle of Jura Ferry) (01496) 840681
Western Ferries (Clyde) (01369) 704452

Where to stay

There is an extensive choice of bed and breakfast (B&B) accommodation in Scotland, and somewhere to stay for all budgets – hotels, guest houses, youth hostels, caravan and camping parks and self-catering accommodation. The Scottish Tourist Board produces four accommodation guides, revised annually, covering all types of accommodation and including the Scottish Tourist Board's star system, the first in the world to show the quality of accommodation by using one to five stars. The more stars, the better the quality. Accommodation listings can be obtained from Area Tourist Boards (see page 9) and local Tourist Information Centres can book all kinds of accommodation for you. Many operate the national Book-a-Bed-Ahead Service, booking accommodation at your next port of call (a fee is usually required for this service).

Information for visitors with disabilities

The Scottish Tourist Board (see page 9) produces a useful fact sheet on accessible accommodation in Scotland. Practical advice and information can also be obtained from:

Holiday Care Service
2nd Floor
Imperial Buildings
Victoria Road
Horley
Surrey
RH6 7PZ
Telephone (01293) 774535

Radar
Information Department
12 City Forum
250 City Road
London EC1V 8AF
Telephone 020 7250 3222

NATIONAL TOURIST ROUTES

Scotland has 12 National Tourist Routes designed to provide the travelling holidaymaker with an alternative to the main trunk roads and motorways. Varying in length and as diverse as the Scottish landscape itself, these routes also offer a variety of things to see and do on the way to your chosen destination. They are all well signposted and easy to follow.

Angus Coastal Route *(58 miles/93km)*
Begins in Dundee, with its fascinating industrial heritage and maritime traditions, and takes you north towards Aberdeen. Along the way you will discover a spectacular coastline with picturesque seaside resorts, sandy beaches, championship golf courses, nature reserves, country parks and a fertile countryside reaching inland through the Mearns and the Vale of Strathmore to the scenic splendour of the Angus Glens and the Grampians.

Argyll Coastal Route *(149 miles/238km)*
From Tarbet on the bonny banks of Loch Lomond, climb steadily to a famous beauty spot called, aptly, Rest-and-be-Thankful. Descend to Inveraray and continue to follow the shores of Loch Fyne to Lochgilphead. Turning north, pass the lovely Crinan Canal and proceed to the bustling holiday town of Oban. Here there is an exceptionally fine view across the Firth of Lorn and the Sound of Mull to the Inner Hebrides. From Oban, cross the impressive Connel Bridge and journey on up through Ballachulish to Fort William at the foot of Ben Nevis.

Borders Historic Route *(95 miles/152km)*
Travelling in either direction between the great border city of Carlisle and Scotland's capital, Edinburgh, savour the area which has been at the heart of Scotland's history and culture for centuries and a major inspiration for Sir Walter Scott's romantic novels. Follow in the footsteps of the Reivers by crossing the border between England and Scotland at Scots Dyke and explore Royal Burghs, woollen mills and market towns, historic houses and visitor centres. Sample true Borders hospitality, local goods, crafts and culture in an outstanding environment making this journey a memorable start or finish to your visit to Scotland.

Clyde Valley Route *(42 miles/67km)*
Turn off the M74 at Abington (or Hamilton from the opposite direction) to follow the River Clyde through an area of contrasting landscapes, rich in historical interest. Attractions include the nominated World Heritage village of New Lanark, the model community brainchild of philanthropist, Robert Owen, founded by his father-in-law David Dale. Visit the magnificently restored Chatelherault, the David Livingstone Centre at Blantyre or the cluster of fascinating museums around the market town of Biggar. Or take advantage of the extensive watersport facilities, theme park and nature trails at Strathclyde Country Park.

Deeside Tourist Route *(107 miles/171km)*
From Perth all the way to Aberdeen. The area around Blairgowrie has long been associated with soft fruit growing, and Blairgowrie itself is a popular touring base. Thereafter, the Highland landscape takes over as the route climbs to 2182 feet (665m) on Britain's highest main road. Enjoy spectacular views in every direction as you pass through the Glenshee Ski Centre

before descending to Braemar. In Royal Deeside drive past Balmoral Castle, summer residence of the Royal family. Continue through the delightful villages of Ballater, Aboyne and Banchory before finally reaching Aberdeen.

Fife Coastal Route *(70 miles/112km)*
Between the Firths of Forth and Tay lies the historic Kingdom of Fife. Best known is St Andrews, home of golf and seat of Scotland's oldest university. Just to the south of St Andrews are the picturesque villages of the East Neuk with their distinctive pan-tiled roofs and unspoilt beaches. More golden sands can be enjoyed at Burntisland and Aberdour. Dunfermline is the country's ancient capital, the Westminster of the North and final resting place of Robert the Bruce. Don't miss Deep Sea World at North Queensferry where the longest underwater safari will take you exploring far beneath the waves. Further west is Culross, an outstanding example of a 16th-century town.

Forth Valley Route *(39 miles/62km)*
This short route from Edinburgh to Stirling takes in the attractive old burgh of South Queensferry, dominated by the mighty Forth Bridges. Nearby are Dalmeny House and the elegant Hopetoun House, one of Scotland's finest mansions. Alternatively, take a trip on the Union Canal from Ratho or delve into the Lothians' clay mining heritage. Visit the bustling town of Falkirk, with its impressive Callendar House, or take a nostalgic ride on the Bo'ness and Kinneil Steam Railway.

Galloway Tourist Route *(96 miles/154km)*
This route, stretching from Gretna to Ayr, links the Robert Burns attractions in both Dumfries and Ayr. En route, it gives you an introduction to the Galloway Forest Park and the industrial heritage of the Doon Valley. Look out for the Old Blacksmith's Shop at Gretna Green, the award-winning Robert Burns Centre and Bridge House Museum in Dumfries, or the Carsphairn Heritage Centre. Enjoy the peace and tranquility of colourful Threave Garden, or ponder over the bloody history of Threave Castle, ancient stronghold of the Black Douglas. The Galloway Tourist Route connects with the Solway Coast Heritage Trail at Dalbeattie, providing an opportunity to visit the castles, abbeys, gardens and harbours further west.

Highland Tourist Route *(118 miles/189km)*
From Aberdeen to Inverness, passing the Grampian Transport Museum at Alford. Continue through the lovely valley of Upper Donside and on up the heather-clad slopes of the Lecht to Tomintoul in the fringes of the Cairngorms, at the heart of whisky country. Take a guided tour round one of the many distilleries and continue on through Grantown-on-Spey, a popular salmon fishing centre, to Inverness, capital of the Highlands.

Moray Firth Route *(80 miles/128km)*
A semi-circular route around three of the most beautiful inlets on the east coast of Britain – the Beauly, Cromarty and Dornoch Firths – north from Inverness in to the heart of the northern Highlands. On the way you can enjoy wonderful scenery (the Struie viewpoint over the Dornoch Firth will take your breath away), seals and clan history at Foulis Ferry, salmon leaping at Shin Falls, whisky being made at Glen Ord and Highland wine at Moniack Castle. You can walk to the Fyrish Monument, visit Beauly Priory or learn about the archaeology of the north at Ferrycroft, Lairg – or you can enjoy shopping for crafts and woollens in the towns and villages along the route.

North and West Highlands Route *(140 miles/224km)*
This route boasts some of the wildest and most magnificent scenery in Europe – wild mountains and lochs, foaming salmon rivers, rugged coastlines with mighty sea cliffs and secluded sandy bays, isolated crofts and large farms, small fishing villages and bustling towns. Starting at the thriving fishing village of Ullapool, the route wends its way north through magnificent

mountain country to Durness in the north west corner of Scotland. From Durness, the route heads east through gradually softening scenery to John o' Groats, taking you from one end of Scotland's north coast to the other.

Perthshire Tourist Route *(45 miles/72km)*
Beginning just north of Dunblane and ending at Ballinluig near Pitlochry. An attractive alternative to the main A9, the route runs through fertile, rolling farmland before arriving at the peasant hillside town of Crieff. Beyond Crieff the lush cultivated landscape changes dramatically and gives way to the rugged splendour of the Sma' Glen, associated with Bonnie Prince Charlie. Descend to Aberfeldy and skirt the fast flowing River Tay on the A827, rejoining the A9 near Pitlochry.

TOURIST INFORMATION

Scottish Tourist Board
For further information on any aspect of your visit to Scotland, contact the Scottish Tourist Board at the following addresses:

Scottish Tourist Board
23 Ravelston Terrace
Edinburgh
EH4 3TP
Telephone 0131 332 2433
(*telephone and written enquiries only*)
www.holiday.scotland.net

Scottish Tourist Board
19 Cockspur Street
London
SW1Y 5BL
Telephone 020 7930 8661/2/3
(*telephone enquiries and personal callers*)

Area Tourist Boards and Tourist Information Centres
There are 14 Area Tourist Boards in Scotland (addresses and telephone numbers are given below). They can provide you with accommodation listings and information on what to see and do in the area. They will also give you locations and telephone numbers of local Tourist Information Centres (look out for the symbol) – of which there are over 150 throughout Scotland. Tourist Information Centres are the best place to go for a wide range of services which include: free information and advice on places to visit; an accommodation booking service, either in the local area or, if you are planning ahead, in any other part of Scotland and throughout the rest of the UK; tickets for events and activities; maps, guide books and reference material; bureau de change (in the larger centres).

Aberdeen and Grampian
Tourist Board
27 Albyn Place
Aberdeen AB10 1YL
Telephone (01224) 632727
www.agtb.org

Angus and City of Dundee
Tourist Board
21 Castle Street
Dundee DD1 3AA
Telephone (01382) 527527
www.angusanddundee.co.uk

Argyll, the Isles, Loch
Lomond, Stirling and
Trossachs Tourist Board
7 Alexandra Parade, Dunoon
Argyll PA23 8AB
Telephone (01369) 701000
www.scottish.heartlands.org

Ayrshire and Arran
Tourist Board
Burns House
Burns Statue Square
Ayr KA7 1UP
Telephone (01292) 262555
www.ayrshire-arran.com

Dumfries and Galloway
Tourist Board
64 Whitesands
Dumfries DG1 2RS
Telephone (01387) 245550
www.galloway.co.uk

Edinburgh and Lothians
Tourist Board
3 Princes Street
Edinburgh EH2 2QP
Telephone 0131 473 3800
www.edinburgh.org

Greater Glasgow and
Clyde Valley Tourist Board
11 George Square
Glasgow G2 1DY
Telephone 0141 204 4400
www.seeglasgow.com

The Highlands of Scotland
Tourist Board
Peffery House
Strathpeffer
Ross-shire IV14 9HA
Telephone (01997) 421415

Kingdom of Fife
Tourist Board
70 Market Street
St Andrews
Fife KY16 9NU
Telephone (01334) 472021
www.standrews.co.uk

Orkney Tourist Board
6 Broad Street
Kirkwall
Orkney KW15 1NX
Telephone (01856) 872856
www.orkney.com

Perthshire Tourist Board
Lower City Mills
West Mill Street
Perth PH1 5QP
Telephone (01738) 627958
www.perthshire.co.uk

Scottish Borders
Tourist Board
Tourist Information Centre
Murray's Green
Jedburgh TD8 6BE
Telephone (01835) 863435
www.scot-borders.co.uk

Shetland Tourist Board
Shetland Islands Tourism
Market Cross
Lerwick
Shetland ZE1 0LU
Telephone (0990) 168209
www.shetland-tourism.co.uk

Western Isles Tourist Board
26 Cromwell Street
Stornoway
Isle of Lewis
HS1 2DD
Telephone (01851) 703088
www.witb.co.uk

Visitor Attraction Quality Assurance

The Scottish Tourist Board operates an inspection scheme for visitor attractions. The scheme provides you with an assurance that the condition and standard of the facilities and services have been assessed, alongside the all important warmth of welcome, efficiency and friendliness of service, level of cleanliness and standard of the overall visitor services including the toilets, restaurant and shop, if provided.

The scheme does not attempt to grade the quality of the experience at the attraction but is a helpful indicator of the quality of facilities provided for visitors. A world famous castle or a small local museum can attain high grades if their services for the visitor are of a high standard. The standards you can expect are:

★★★★★ Exceptional

★★★★ Excellent

★★★ Very good

★★ Good

★ Fair and acceptable

In addition to the star grades, every attraction is categorised under one of the following types to help give you an indication of the type of experience on offer:

Activity centre
Arts venue
Castle
Garden
Historic attraction
Historic house
Leisure centre
Museum
Tour
Tourist shop
Visitor attraction

Association of Scottish Visitor Attractions (ASVA)

As you travel round Scotland, you may see the ASVA symbol displayed at visitor attractions. The Association of Scottish Visitor Attractions aims to improve the quality and viability of visitor attractions in Scotland through training, advice and marketing. ASVA can be contacted at:

20-22 Torphichen Street
Edinburgh
EH3 8JB
Telephone 0131 623 6630

Welcome Host

When you visit an attraction in Scotland, you may see the Welcome Host badge being worn by staff who have taken part in the Scottish Tourist Board's Welcome Host training programme, and who have given a personal commitment to providing quality service during your visit. Many organisations display the Welcome Host certificate to demonstrate their commitment to the provision of this quality service.

Other Useful Addresses

British Waterways Scotland
Canal House
Applecross Street
Glasgow G4 9SP
Telephone 0141 332 6936

Forestry Commission
231 Corstorphine Road
Edinburgh EH12 7AT
Telephone 0131 334 0303

Historic Houses Association
(over 40 houses and gardens in Scotland)
Heritage House
PO Box 21
Baldock
Herts SG7 5SH
Telephone (01462) 896688

Historic Scotland
Longmore House
Salisbury Place
Edinburgh EH9 1SH
Telephone 0131 668 8800

Landmark Trust
Shottesbrooke
Maidenhead
Berkshire SL6 3SW
Telephone (01628) 825925

National Cycle Network
(Sustrans)
3 Coates Place
Edinburgh EH3 7AA
Telephone 0131 623 7600

National Trust for Scotland
5 Charlotte Square
Edinburgh EH2 4DU
Telephone 0131 226 5922

Royal Society for the Protection of Birds
Dunedin House
25 Ravelston Terrace
Edinburgh EH4 3TP
Telephone 0131 311 6500

Scotland's Gardens Scheme
31 Castle Terrace
Edinburgh EH1 2EL
Telephone 0131 229 1870

Scotland's Churches
Dunedin
Holehouse Road
Eaglesham
Glasgow G76 0JF
Telephone (01355) 302416

Scottish Natural Heritage
12 Hope Terrace
Edinburgh EH9 2AS
Telephone 0131 447 4784

Scottish Tourist Guides Association
Old Town Jail, St John Street
Stirling FK8 1EA
Telephone (01786) 447784

Scottish Wildlife Trust
16 Cramond Glebe Road
Edinburgh EH4 6NS
Telephone 0131 312 7765

Scottish Youth Hostels Association
7 Glebe Crescent
Stirling FK8 2JA
Telephone (01786) 891400

Taste of Scotland
33 Melville Street
Edinburgh EH3 7JF
Telephone 0131 220 1900

LOCATION MAPS

These maps show the locations of the numbered visitor attractions listed in this guide. The country has been split into six areas as shown. Each attraction has a map reference (eg 6 E4). The first number (6) refers to the location map, the letter and number (E4) refer to the grid square in which the attraction is located.

Comprehensive touring and leisure information can be found on the companion *Touring Map of Scotland.*

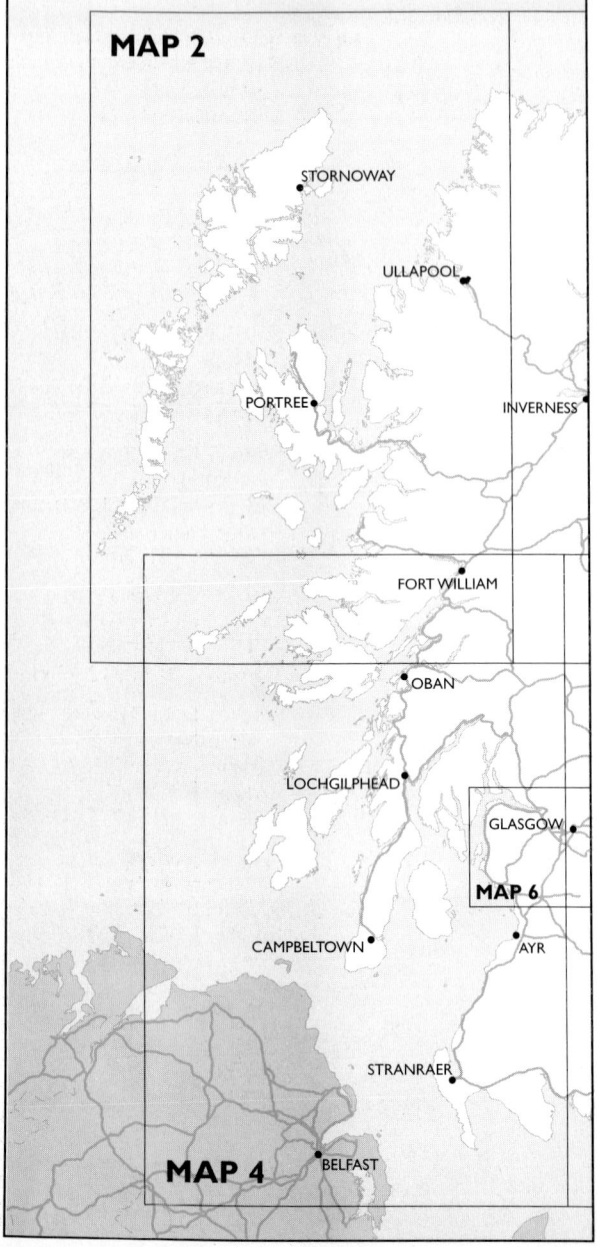

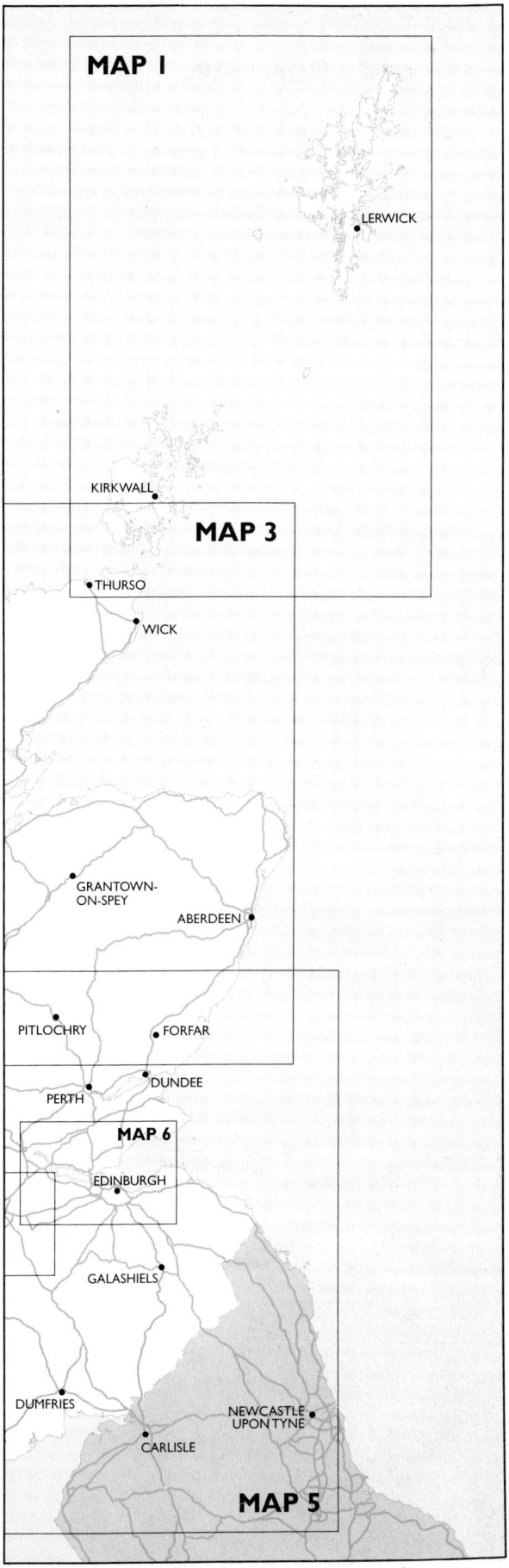
MAP 1
LERWICK
KIRKWALL
MAP 3
THURSO
WICK
GRANTOWN-
ON-SPEY
ABERDEEN
PITLOCHRY
FORFAR
DUNDEE
PERTH
MAP 6
EDINBURGH
GALASHIELS
DUMFRIES
NEWCASTLE
UPON TYNE
CARLISLE
MAP 5

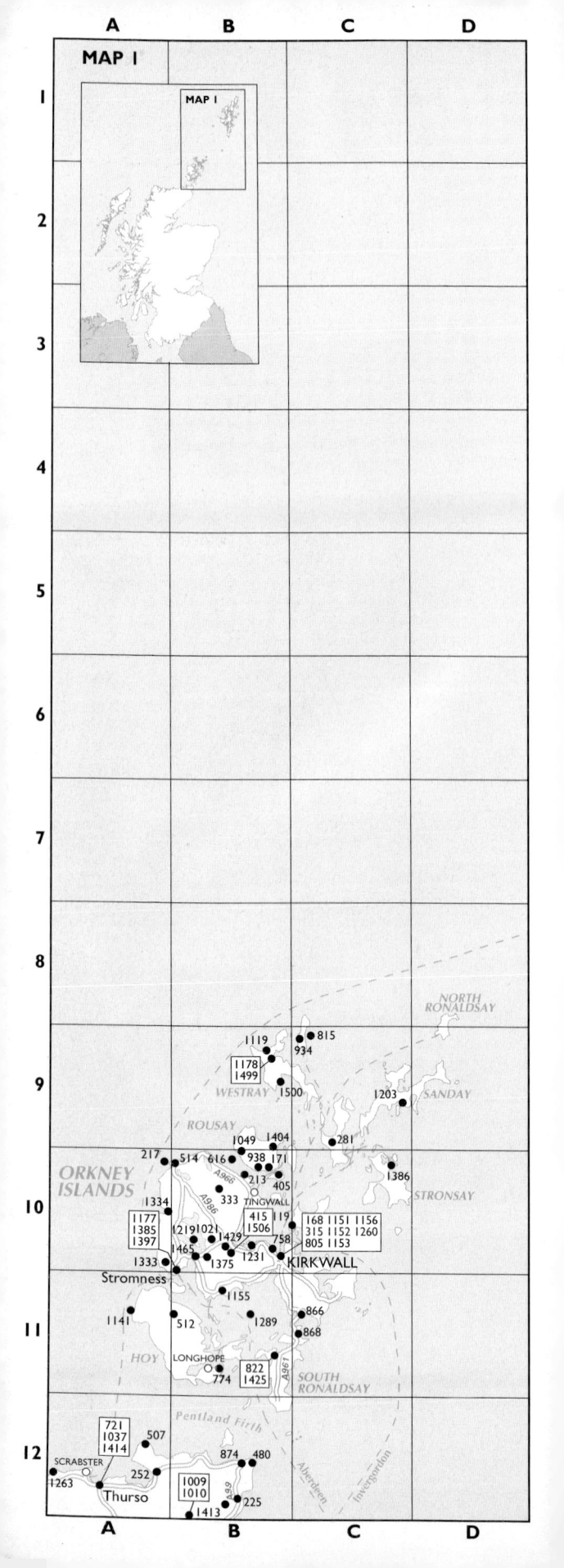
MAP 1
MAP 1
A
B
C
D
1
2
3
4
5
6
7
8
9
10
11
12
NORTH RONALDSAY
815
934
1119
1178
1499
WESTRAY
1500
1203
SANDAY
ROUSAY
1049
1404
281
217
514
616
938
171
213
405
1386
ORKNEY ISLANDS
A966
333
TINGWALL
STRONSAY
A986
1334
1177
1385
1397
415
1506
119
168 1151 1156
315 1152 1260
805 1153
1219
1021
1429
758
1465
1231
1333
1375
KIRKWALL
Stromness
1155
1141
512
1289
866
868
HOY
LONGHOPE
774
822
1425
A961
SOUTH RONALDSAY
Pentland Firth
721
1037
1414
507
874
480
SCRABSTER
1263
252
Thurso
1009
1010
A99
225
1413
Aberdeen
Invergordon

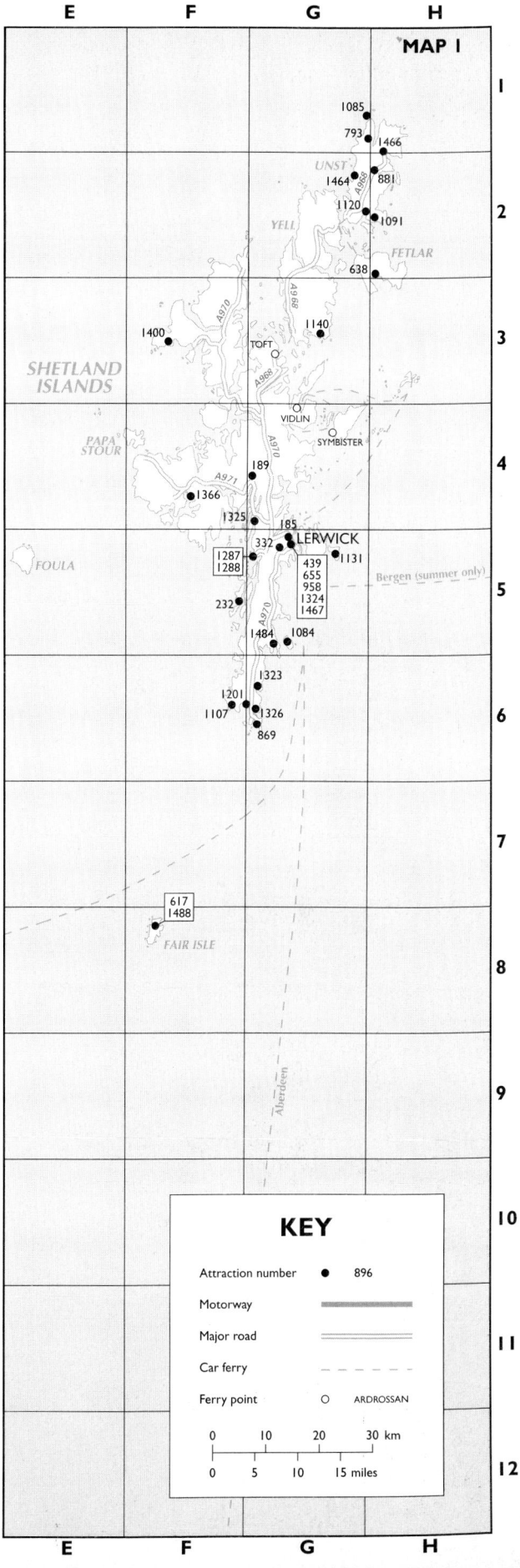
MAP 1
E
F
G
H
1
2
3
4
5
6
7
8
9
10
11
12
1085
793
1466
UNST
1464
A968
881
1120
1091
YELL
FETLAR
638
A970
A968
1140
1400
TOFT
SHETLAND ISLANDS
A968
VIDLIN
SYMBISTER
PAPA STOUR
A970
189
A971
1366
1325
185
LERWICK
332
1287
1288
1131
FOULA
439
655
958
1324
1467
Bergen (summer only)
232
A970
1484
1084
1323
1201
1107
1326
869
617
1488
FAIR ISLE
Aberdeen
KEY
Attraction number
896
Motorway
Major road
Car ferry
Ferry point
ARDROSSAN
0
10
20
30 km
0
5
10
15 miles

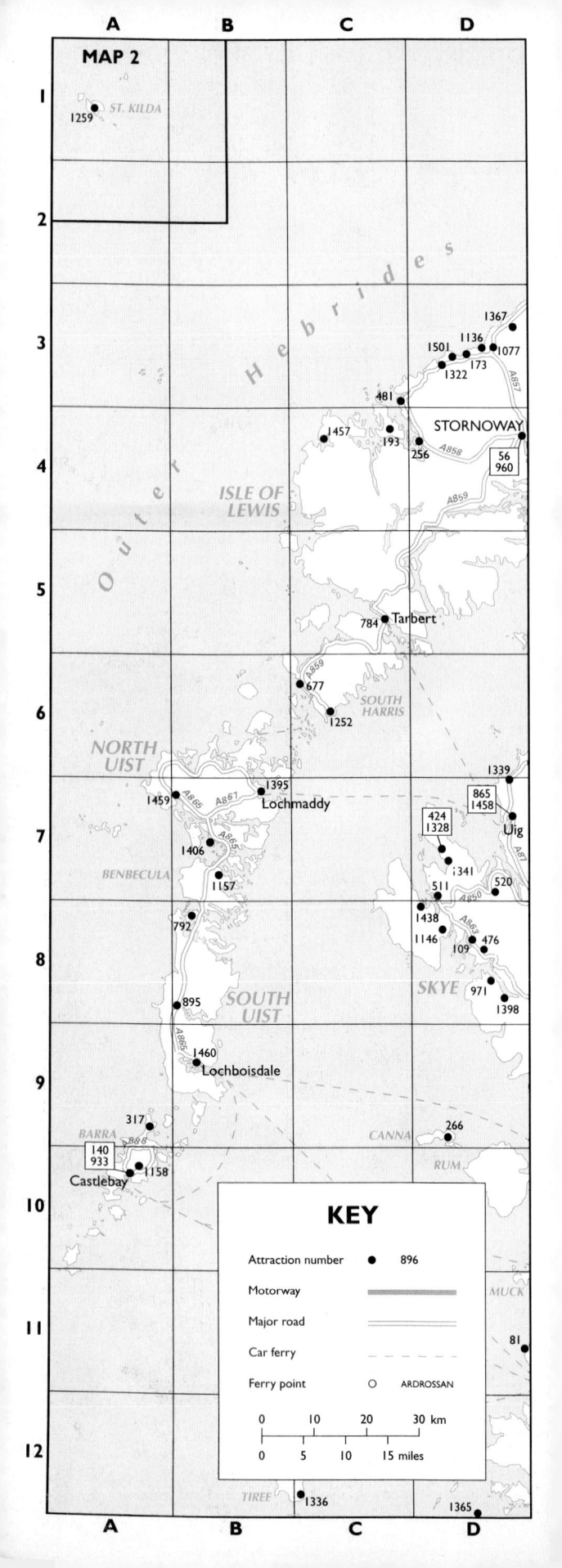
MAP 2
A
B
C
D
1
2
3
4
5
6
7
8
9
10
11
12
ST. KILDA
1259
Outer Hebrides
1367
1136
1077
1501
173
1322
A857
481
1457
193
256
STORNOWAY
A858
56
960
ISLE OF LEWIS
A859
784
Tarbert
677
1252
SOUTH HARRIS
NORTH UIST
1339
1459
A865
A867
1395
Lochmaddy
865
1458
424
1328
Uig
A87
1406
A865
1341
BENBECULA
1157
511
520
A850
1438
792
A865
1146
476
109
SKYE
971
1398
895
SOUTH UIST
A865
1460
Lochboisdale
317
BARRA
A888
CANNA
266
140
933
1158
Castlebay
RUM
MUCK
81
TIREE
1336
1365
KEY
Attraction number
896
Motorway
Major road
Car ferry
Ferry point
ARDROSSAN
0
10
20
30 km
0
5
10
15 miles

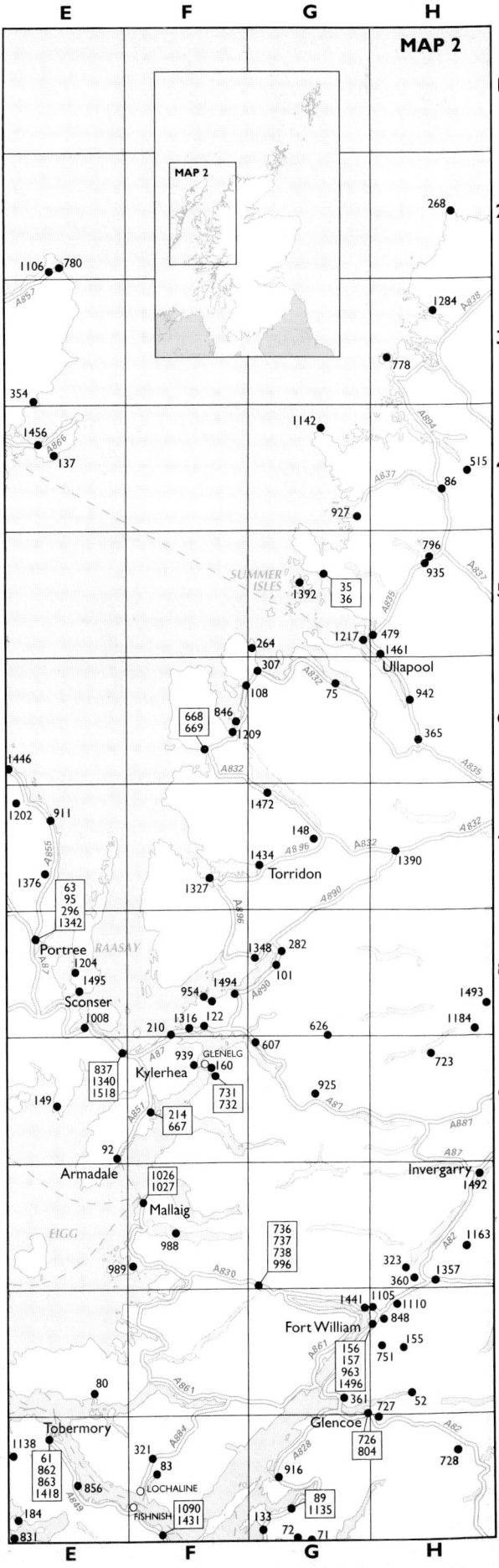
MAP 2
MAP 2
E
F
G
H
1
2
3
4
5
6
7
8
9
10
11
12
268
1106
780
A857
1284
A838
778
354
1142
A894
1456
A866
137
515
A837
86
927
796
935
A837
SUMMER ISLES
1392
35
36
A835
1217
479
1461
Ullapool
264
307
A832
108
75
942
668
669
846
1209
365
1446
A832
A835
1472
1202
911
148
A832
A832
A855
1434
A896
1390
1376
Torridon
1327
A896
A890
63
95
296
1342
Portree
RAASAY
1348
282
1204
101
1495
A890
954
1494
Sconser
1493
1008
1316
122
1184
210
626
607
A87
939
GLENELG
160
723
837
1340
1518
Kylerhea
925
149
731
732
A87
A857
214
667
A887
92
A87
Armadale
1026
1027
Invergarry
1492
Mallaig
EIGG
736
737
738
738
996
988
A82
1163
989
A830
323
360
1357
1441
1105
1110
848
Fort William
A861
155
751
156
157
963
1496
80
A861
361
727
52
Glencoe
Tobermory
A884
A82
726
804
1138
61
862
863
1418
321
A828
728
83
916
856
LOCHALINE
A849
184
FISHNISH
1090
1431
133
89
1135
72
71
831

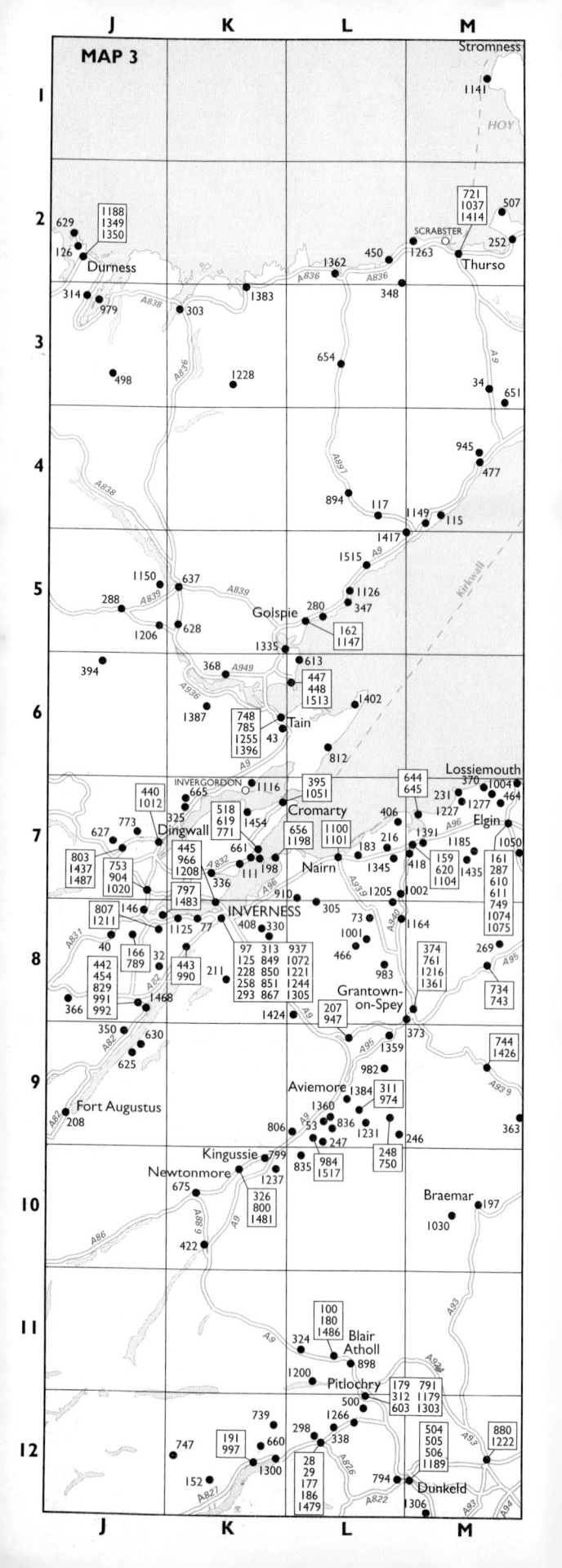
MAP 3
J
K
L
M
1
2
3
4
5
6
7
8
9
10
11
12
Stromness
1141
HOY
721
1037
1414
507
SCRABSTER
1263
252
Thurso
450
1362
348
1383
303
1228
498
314
979
629
126
1188
1349
1350
Durness
654
34
651
945
477
894
117
1149
115
1417
1515
1126
347
Golspie
280
162
1147
1150
637
288
1206
628
1335
613
394
368
447
448
1513
1387
1402
748
785
1255
1396
43
Tain
812
Lossiemouth
370
1004
464
644
645
231
1277
1227
Elgin
1391
1185
1050
INVERGORDON
1116
395
1051
440
1012
665
325
Cromarty
406
518
619
771
1454
773
627
Dingwall
656
1198
1100
1101
183
216
803
1437
1487
753
904
1020
445
966
1208
661
111
198
Nairn
1345
418
159
620
1104
1435
161
287
610
611
749
1074
1075
336
797
1483
910
305
1205
1002
807
1211
146
INVERNESS
408
330
73
1001
1164
40
166
789
32
1125
77
466
983
269
442
454
829
991
992
443
990
211
97
125
228
258
293
313
849
850
851
867
937
1072
1221
1244
1305
374
761
1216
1361
734
743
366
1468
1424
207
947
Grantown-
on-Spey
373
350
630
625
1359
744
1426
982
Aviemore
1384
311
974
1360
Fort Augustus
208
806
53
836
1231
246
363
247
248
750
Kingussie
799
835
984
1517
Newtonmore
675
1237
326
800
1481
Braemar
197
1030
422
100
180
1486
324
Blair
Atholl
898
1200
Pitlochry
179
312
603
791
1179
1303
500
1266
739
298
338
747
191
997
660
1300
28
29
177
186
1479
504
505
506
1189
880
1222
152
794
Dunkeld
1306
A836
A838
A837
A9
A839
A949
A936
A832
A96
A939
A940
A95
A82
A831
A835
A99
A889
A86
A93
A826
A822
A821
A94

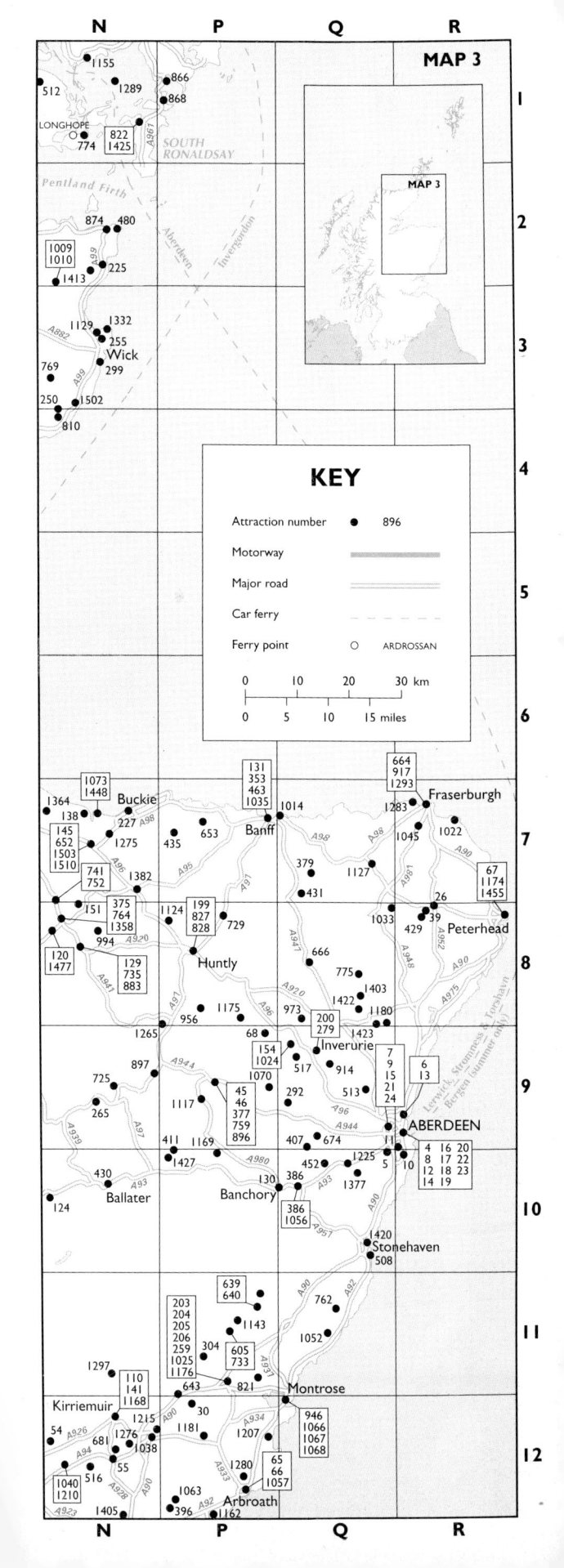
MAP 3
N
P
Q
R
1
2
3
4
5
6
7
8
9
10
11
12
1155
512
1289
866
868
LONGHOPE
774
822
1425
A961
SOUTH RONALDSAY
Pentland Firth
874
480
1009
1010
A99
225
1413
Aberdeen
Invergordon
1129
1332
A882
255
Wick
299
769
A99
250
1502
810
KEY
Attraction number
896
Motorway
Major road
Car ferry
Ferry point
ARDROSSAN
0
10
20
30 km
0
5
10
15 miles
1073
1448
Buckie
1364
138
227
A98
145
652
1503
1510
1275
741
752
1382
151
375
764
1358
994
120
1477
129
735
883
A941
A920
A96
A95
435
653
131
353
463
1035
Banff
1014
A98
1124
199
827
828
729
Huntly
956
1175
1265
A97
664
917
1293
Fraserburgh
1283
1022
1045
A90
379
1127
431
A98
67
1174
1455
26
1033
429
39
A982
Peterhead
A947
666
775
1403
1422
1180
A948
A90
A975
973
200
279
1423
68
154
1024
Inverurie
517
914
897
A944
725
1070
1117
45
46
377
759
896
265
292
513
6
13
Lerwick, Stromness, Torshavn
Bergen (summer only)
A939
A97
A96
A944
ABERDEEN
411
1169
407
674
11
4 16 20
8 17 22
12 18 23
14 19
1427
A980
452
1225
5
10
430
Ballater
124
130
386
1377
Banchory
386
1056
A957
1420
Stonehaven
508
639
640
203
204
205
206
259
1025
1176
1143
304
605
733
762
1052
1297
110
141
1168
643
821
Montrose
Kirriemuir
1215
30
1181
1207
946
1066
1067
1068
54
681
1276
1038
55
516
1040
1210
1280
65
66
1057
1063
396
Arbroath
1162
1405
A90
A92
A93
A934
A926
A94
A928
A923
A932

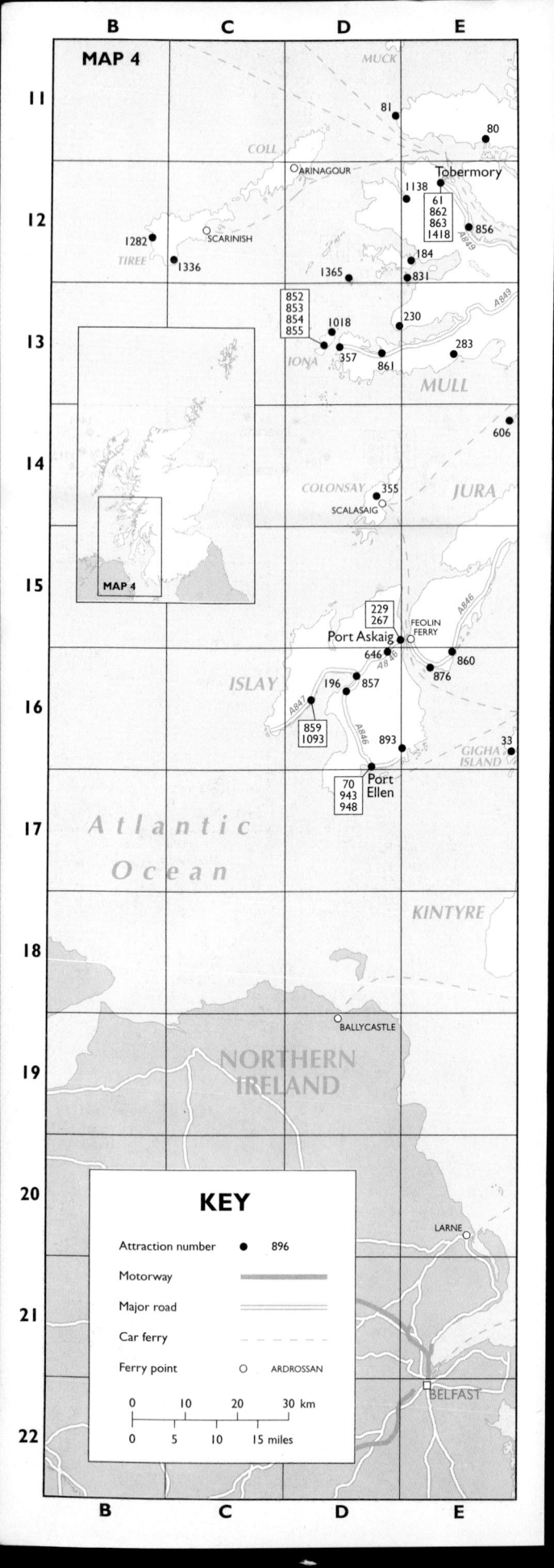
MAP 4
B
C
D
E
11
12
13
14
15
16
17
18
19
20
21
22
MUCK
81
80
COLL
ARINAGOUR
Tobermory
1138
61
862
863
1418
856
A849
1282
SCARINISH
TIREE
1336
184
1365
831
852
853
854
855
1018
230
A849
283
IONA
357
861
MULL
606
COLONSAY
355
JURA
SCALASAIG
MAP 4
229
267
FEOLIN FERRY
Port Askaig
A846
646
860
876
ISLAY
196
857
A847
859
1093
A846
893
33
GIGHA ISLAND
70
943
948
Port Ellen
Atlantic Ocean
KINTYRE
BALLYCASTLE
NORTHERN IRELAND
KEY
Attraction number
896
Motorway
Major road
Car ferry
Ferry point
ARDROSSAN
0
10
20
30 km
0
5
10
15 miles
LARNE
BELFAST

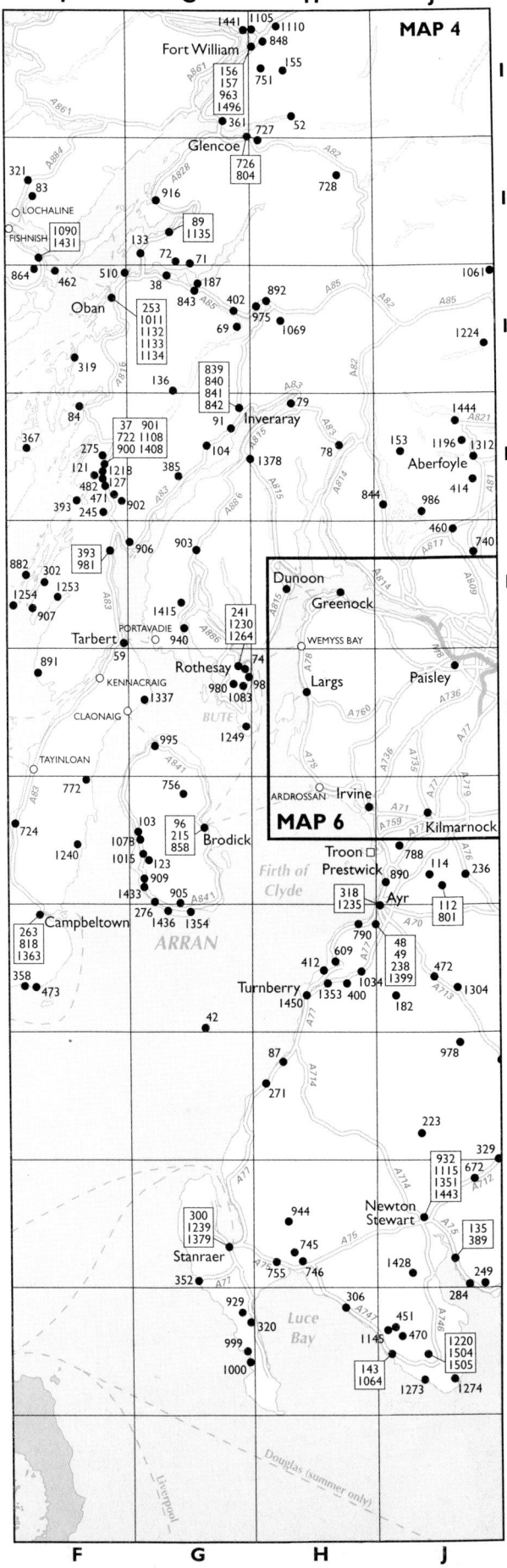
MAP 4
F
G
H
J
11
12
13
14
15
16
17
18
19
20
21
22
Fort William
156
157
963
1496
Glencoe
726
804
LOCHALINE
FISHNISH
1090
1431
89
1135
Oban
253
1011
1132
1133
1134
839
840
841
842
Inveraray
37 901
722 1108
900 1408
Aberfoyle
393
981
Dunoon
Greenock
PORTAVADIE
Tarbert
241
1230
1264
WEMYSS BAY
Rothesay
KENNACRAIG
Largs
Paisley
CLAONAIG
BUTE
TAYINLOAN
ARDROSSAN
Irvine
MAP 6
Kilmarnock
Brodick
96
215
858
Troon
Prestwick
Firth of Clyde
Ayr
112
801
318
1235
Campbeltown
263
818
1363
ARRAN
48
49
238
1399
Turnberry
Newton Stewart
932
1115
1351
1443
135
389
300
1239
1379
Stanraer
Luce Bay
143
1064
1220
1504
1505
Douglas (summer only)
Liverpool

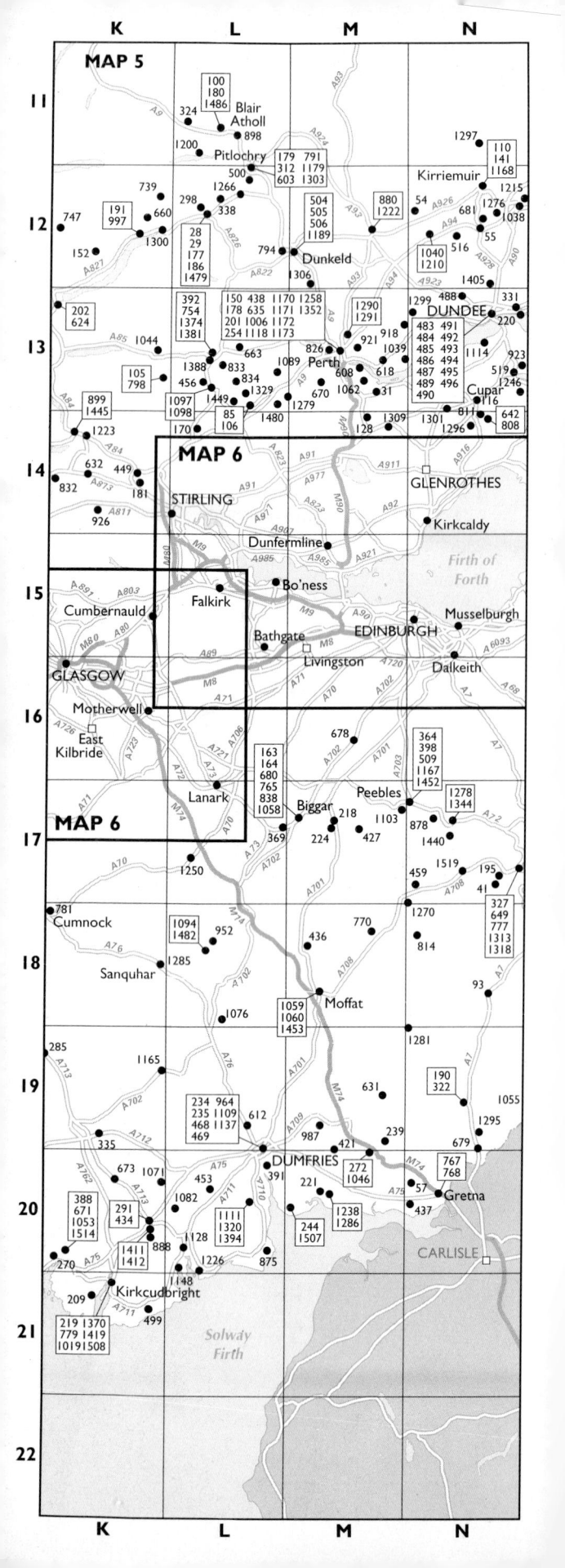
K
L
M
N
MAP 5
MAP 6
MAP 6
11
12
13
14
15
16
17
18
19
20
21
22
Blair Atholl
Pitlochry
Kirriemuir
Dunkeld
DUNDEE
Perth
Cupar
GLENROTHES
STIRLING
Kirkcaldy
Dunfermline
Firth of Forth
Falkirk
Bo'ness
Cumbernauld
Musselburgh
Bathgate
EDINBURGH
Livingston
Dalkeith
GLASGOW
Motherwell
East Kilbride
Lanark
Peebles
Biggar
Cumnock
Sanquhar
Moffat
DUMFRIES
Gretna
CARLISLE
Kirkcudbright
Solway Firth

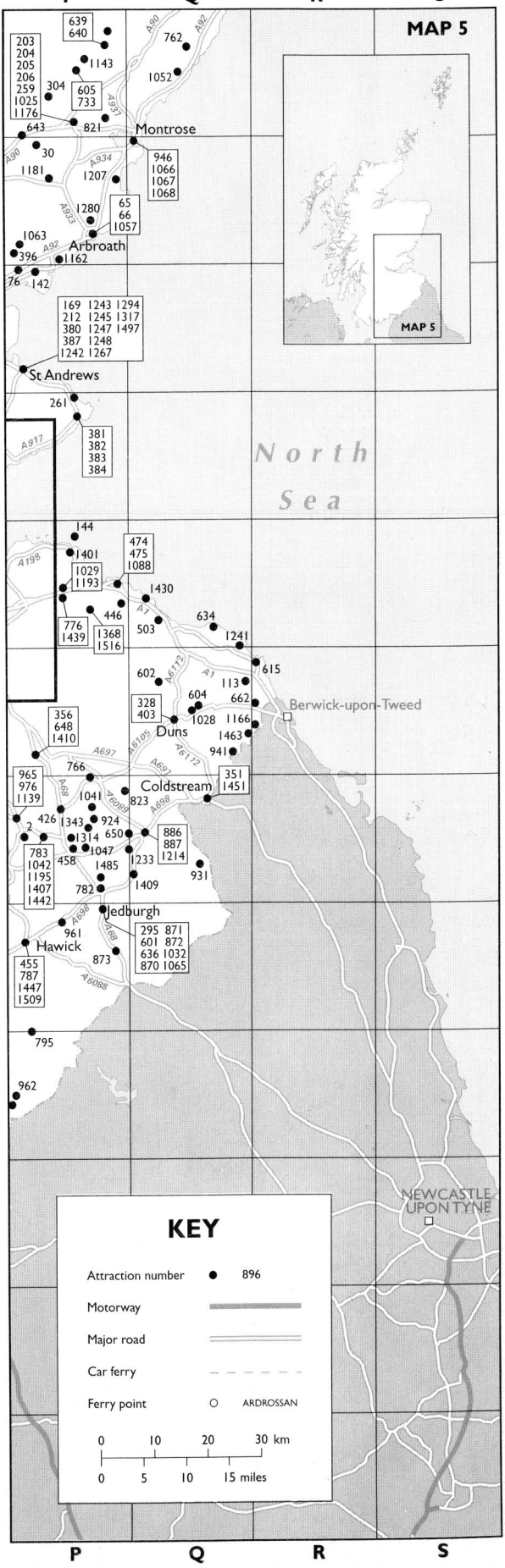
MAP 5
P
Q
R
S
11
12
13
14
15
16
17
18
19
20
21
22
Montrose
Arbroath
St Andrews
North Sea
Berwick-upon-Tweed
Duns
Coldstream
Jedburgh
Hawick
NEWCASTLE UPON TYNE
639 640
203 204 205 206 259 1025 1176
1143
605 733
304
762
1052
643
821
30
1181
946 1066 1067 1068
1207
1280
65 66 1057
1063
396
1162
76
142
169 1243 1294 212 1245 1317 380 1247 1497 387 1248 1242 1267
261
381 382 383 384
144
1401
474 475 1088
1029 1193
1430
446
776 1439
1368 1516
503
634
1241
615
602
113
604
662
328 403
1028
1166
1463
941
356 648 1410
766
965 976 1139
351 1451
823
1041
426
1343
924
2
1314
650
886 887 1214
783 1042 1195 1407 1442
458
1047
1233
931
1485
782
1409
961
295 871 601 872 636 1032 870 1065
873
455 787 1447 1509
795
962
KEY
Attraction number
896
Motorway
Major road
Car ferry
Ferry point
ARDROSSAN
0 10 20 30 km
0 5 10 15 miles

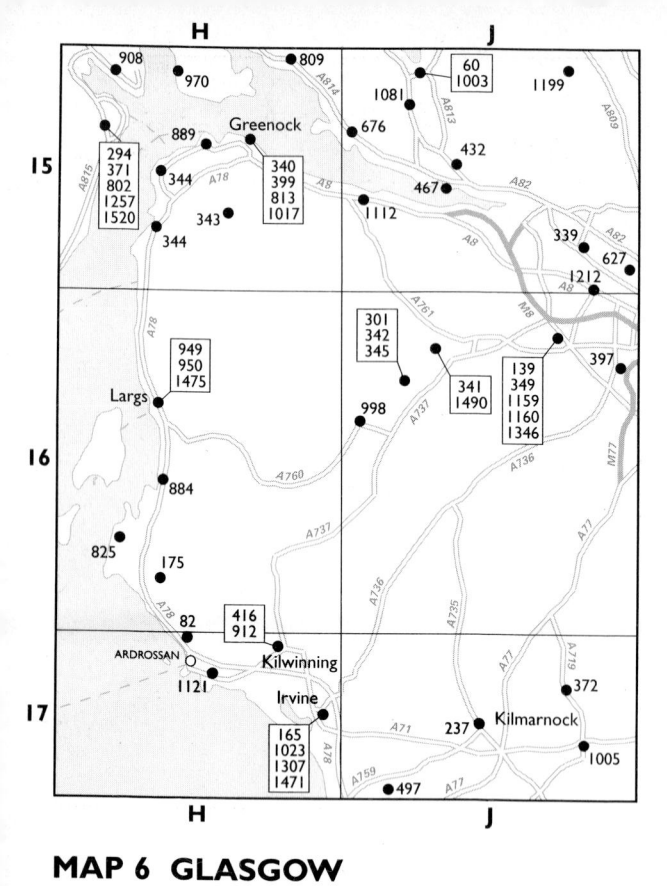

MAP 6 GLASGOW

MAP 6 EDINBURGH

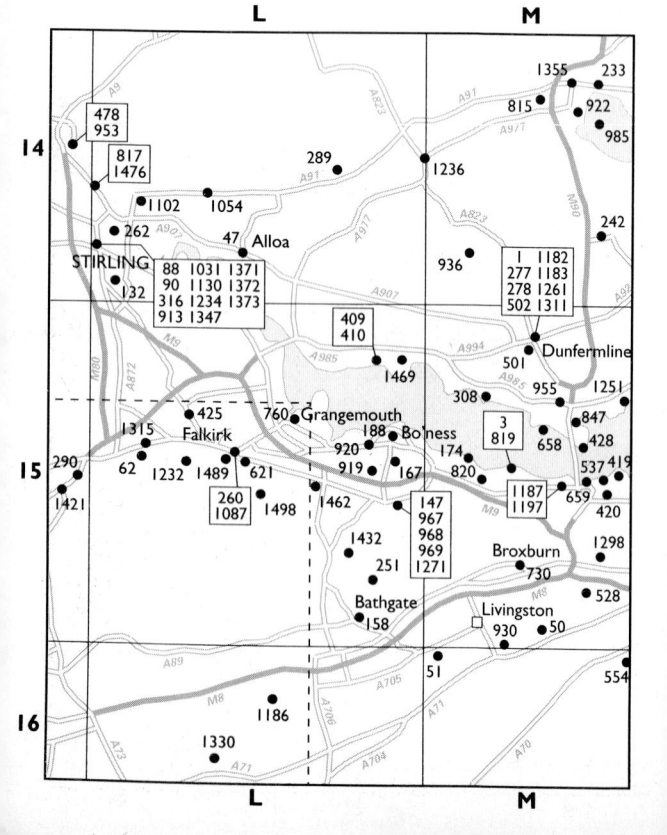

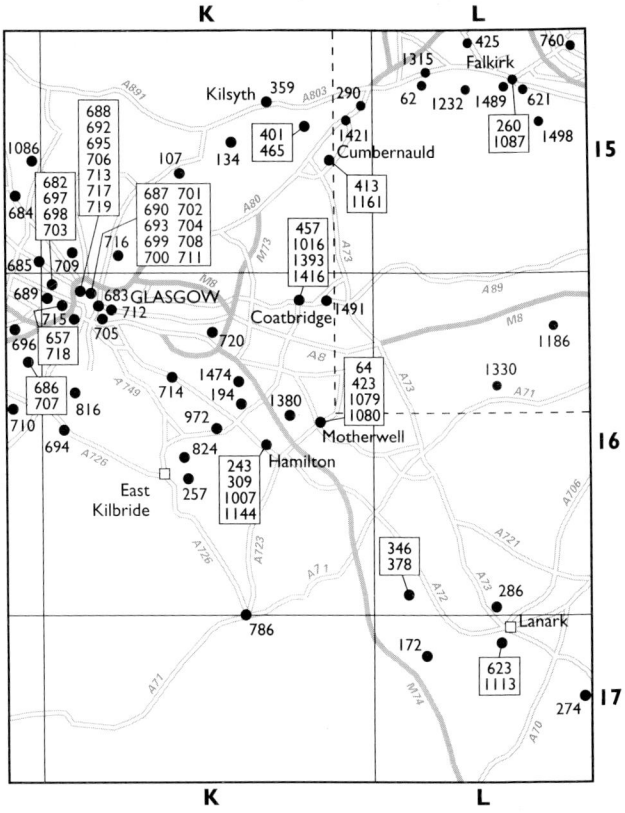
K
L
Falkirk
Kilsyth
Cumbernauld
GLASGOW
Coatbridge
Motherwell
Hamilton
East Kilbride
Lanark
15
16
17
688 692 695 706 713 717 719
682 697 698 703
687 701 690 702 693 704 699 708 700 711
401 465
413 1161
457 1016 1393 1416
260 1087
657 718
686 707
64 423 1079 1080
243 309 1007 1144
346 378
623 1113
A891
A803
A80
A73
A89
A8
A749
A726
A723
A71
A72
A721
A706
A70
M8
M73
M74

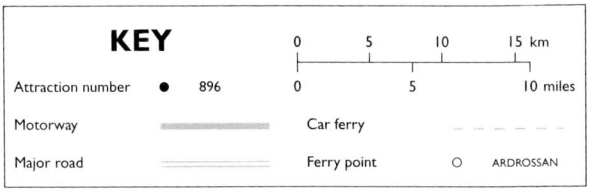
KEY
0 5 10 15 km
0 5 10 miles
Attraction number
896
Motorway
Car ferry
Major road
Ferry point
ARDROSSAN

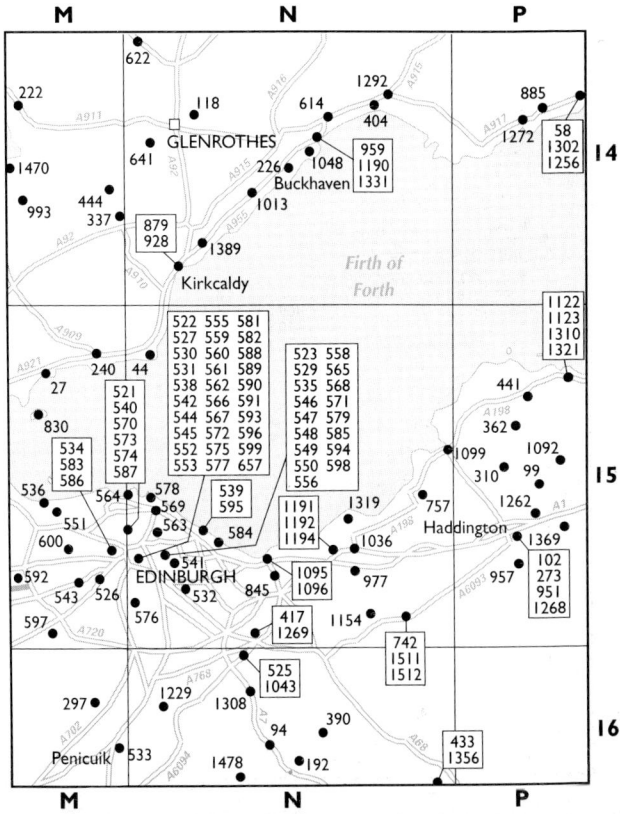
M
N
P
GLENROTHES
Buckhaven
Kirkcaldy
Firth of Forth
EDINBURGH
Haddington
Penicuik
14
15
16
959 1190 1331
58 1302 1256
879 928
522 555 581 527 559 582 530 560 588 531 561 589 538 562 590 542 566 591 544 567 593 545 572 596 552 575 599 553 577 657
523 558 529 565 535 568 546 571 547 579 548 585 549 594 550 598 556
1122 1123 1310 1321
521 540 570 573 574 587
534 583 586
539 595
1191 1192 1194
1095 1096
417 1269
525 1043
742 1511 1512
102 273 951 1268
433 1356
A916
A915
A911
A917
A92
A965
A910
A909
A921
A198
A1
A6093
A720
A768
A702
A6094
A68

1 ABBOT HOUSE HERITAGE CENTRE 6 M15

Maygate, Dunfermline, Fife. 2 miles (3 km) from M90 (signposted). Walking distance from Dunfermline railway and bus station. Coach parking nearby. Open all year (except Christmas and New Year's Day), daily 1000–1700. Charge £. Garden and all ground floor free. Group concessions. Guided tours (French, German, Spanish and Korean available). Explanatory displays. Gift shop. Restaurant with outside seating in garden. Garden. WC. Wheelchair access to ground floor (with video display) and gardens. Disabled WC. Car parking. Telephone (01383) 733266.

This award-winning heritage centre is in the restored 15th-century residence of the Abbot of Dunfermline. Learn Scotland's story from Pictish to modern times and find out about King Robert the Bruce, St Margaret and other important figures who played a role in the history of Scotland's ancient capital. Attractive art work by Alasdair Gray and other artists. Enjoy the garden with access to Dunfermline Abbey next door.

---

2 ABBOTSFORD 5 P17

Abbotsford, Melrose, Roxburghshire. On the B7060 between Galashiels and Melrose, 2 miles (3km) from Melrose. Bus from Galashiels or Melrose to within 0.25 mile (0.5km). Open Mar–Oct, Mon–Sat 1000–1700; Jun–Sep, Sun 1000–1700; Mar, Apr, May and Oct, Sun 1400–1700. Charge ££. Group concessions. Guided tours (French available). Gift shop. Tearoom. Garden. WC. Wheelchair access with assistance via private entrance. Disabled WC. Car and coach parking. Telephone (01896) 752043.

The house which Sir Walter Scott built in 1822, on the site of the Cartley Hole farmhouse, and where he lived until he died in 1832. Features Scott's collection of historical relics, including armour and weapons, Rob Roy's gun and Montrose's sword; his library with over 9000 rare volumes, and other rooms including the chapel.

---

3 ABERCORN CHURCH AND MUSEUM 6 M15

Hopetoun Estate, South Queensferry. 6 miles (10km) west of South Queensferry off the A904. Open all year daily. Free. Wheelchair access. Car parking. Telephone 0131 331 1869.

There has been a church on this site for 1500 years. Abercorn was the first bishopric in Scotland, dating from 681AD. The present church (dedicated to St Serf) developed from the Reformation to the present day – the present building, on the site of a 7th-century monastery, dates from the 12th century. The museum contains Viking burial stones.

---

4 ABERDEEN ART GALLERY 3 R9

Schoolhill, Aberdeen. City centre, off Union Street. 15 minute walk from Aberdeen railway and bus stations. Open all year, Mon–Sat 1000–1700, Sun 1400–1700. Free. Guided tours. Explanatory displays. Gift shop. Tearoom. WC. Wheelchair access with assistance. Disabled WC. Telephone (01224) 523700.

Aberdeen Art Gallery houses one of the finest public collections in the United Kingdom from from the 18th to the 20th century including British works by Spencer, Nash and Bacon. Paintings include Sir John Lavery's *The Tennis Party* and Sir James Guthrie's *To Pastures New*. Varied exhibition programme.

---

5 ABERDEEN, BRIDGE OF DEE 3 G10

Access at all times. Free.

Built in the 1520s by Bishop Gavin Dunbar in James V's reign. It's seven arches span 400 feet (122m) and it formerly carried the main road south. The medieval solidity of the structure is enlivened by heraldic carvings.

6 ABERDEEN, BRIG O' BALGOWNIE 3 R9

At Bridge of Don, north of Aberdeen, upstream of main A92 bridge. Access at all times. Free.

Also known as the Auld Brig o'Don, this massive arch, 62 feet (19 m) wide, spans the deep pool of the river and is backed by fine woods. It was completed circa 1320 and repaired in 1607. In 1605 Sir Alexander Hay endowed the bridge with a small property. This so increased in value that it built the New Bridge of Don downstream (in 1830 at a cost of £26,000), bore most of the cost of the Victoria Bridge, and contributed to many other public works. Now closed to motor vehicles.

---

7 ABERDEEN, CATHEDRAL CHURCH OF ST MACHAR 3 Q9

The Chanonry, Old Aberdeen. Bus from centre. Open all year, daily 0900–1700 (except during weddings, funerals and unscheduled special events). Free. Guided tours by arrangement. Explanatory displays. Gift shop. WC. Induction loop system during services. Wheelchair access. Car and coach parking. Telephone (01774) 485988.

On an ancient site of worship dating from 580AD, becoming a cathedral church in 1140, the present building dates from 1350–1520. It is a twin-towered granite building with stone pillars inside, an impressive heraldic ceiling of panelled oak dating from 1520 depicting notable sovereigns of Europe and the nobles and ecclesiastical households of Scotland, and impressive stained glass windows on three sides. There is also a collection of medieval charters in the Charter Room. Outside, the tomb of Bishop Gavin Dunbar.

---

8 ABERDEEN COLLEGE PLANETARIUM 3 R9

Gallowgate, Aberdeen. Nearest railway and bus stations Aberdeen, then 5 minute walk. Public shows Wed 1830 and Sat 1100, telephone to confirm. Charge £. Group concessions. Guided tours. Explanatory displays. Canteen in college. WC. Wheelchair access. Disabled WC. Car and coach parking. Telephone (01224) 641122 or 612323.

Aberdeen College Planetarium was built in 1977 as part of the college facilities for teaching navigation. It is now open to the general public and holds a varied programme of shows and events. The Planetarium is one of the best in Scotland – a unique plaster dome and 2500 stars.

---

9 ABERDEEN, CRUICKSHANK BOTANIC GARDEN 3 Q9

Old Aberdeen Campus, Aberdeen University, Aberdeen. Nearest railway station Aberdeen, bus service number 20 from city centre. Open all year, Mon–Fri 0900–1630; May–Sep, Sat and Sun 1400–1700. Free. Guided tours. Limited wheelchair access. Telephone (01224) 272704.

Originally founded in 1898 as the University of Aberdeen's teaching and research garden. The 11 acres (4.5 ha) are laid out in an ornamental style. Rock garden and ponds, herbaceous border, rose garden, terrace and arboretum. The museum is part of the Conoco Natural History Centre which caters for educational groups (pre-booking essential).

---

10 ABERDEEN, DOONIES FARM 3 R10

Coast Road, Nigg, Aberdeen. Off A956 to village of Cove, signposted from there, look for golf course. Bus from centre to Torry or Cove then walk 1 mile (2km). Open all year, daily 1000–1830 summer and 1000–1600 winter. Charge £. Children under 5 free. Group concessions. Guided tours. Explanatory displays. Picnic area. Play area. WC. Wheelchair access. Disabled WC. Car and coach parking. Telephone (01224) 522771.

A 182 acre (74ha) working farm populated with rare breeds (animals and birds). Visitors can wander around freely.

11 ABERDEEN, DUTHIE PARK WINTER GARDENS AND RESTAURANT 3 R9

Duthie Park, Polmuir road, Aberdeen. By bus from centre. Open daily, Jan–Mar 0930–1630; Apr 0930–2000; May–Sep 0930–2100; Oct–Nov 0930–1630; Dec 0930–1630. Free. Guided tours (charge £). Explanatory displays. Gift shop. Restaurant. WC. Wheelchair access. Disabled WC. Car and coach parking. Telephone (01224) 585310.

One of Britain's most popular attractions. 2 acres (1ha) of covered gardens (the largest in Europe) displaying plants from around the world. Features entrance hall and Bromeliad house, cacti and succulent hall, Victorian corridor and outside gardens, floral hall, corridor of perfumes and fern house.

---

12 ABERDEEN, GALLERY HEINZEL 3 R9

21 Spa Street, Aberdeen. In centre, behind Her Majesty's Theatre. 10 minute walk from railway station. Open all year, Tue–Sat 1000–1730. Free. No guide dogs. Wheelchair access. Car parking. Telephone (01224) 625629.

An art gallery with permanent and monthly exhibitions of the best of contemporary art, paintings, watercolours, sculpture and ceramics by emerging and established Scottish artists.

---

13 ABERDEEN, GLOVER HOUSE 3 R9

79 Balgownie Road, Aberdeen. Bridge of Don, north of Aberdeen. Local bus service passes the entrance. Open all year, Tue–Sat 1030–1630; Sun 1330–1630 by appointment only. Charge £. Guided tours (available in Japanese, other languages by appointment). Explanatory displays. Gift shop. Garden. WC. Limited wheelchair access. Disabled WC. Telephone (01224) 709303.

Family home of Thomas Blake Glover, the early industrial pioneer who introduced modern coal mining and shipbuilding methods to 19th-century Japan. Glover commissioned new ships for the Emperor in his struggle against the Shogun and thus became the founder of the Japanese navy. The house has been restored to its original Victorian splendour, showing connections with the Far East.

---

14 ABERDEEN, GORDON HIGHLANDERS MUSEUM 3 H9

St Luke's, Viewfield Road, Aberdeen. Bus from city centre. Open Apr–Oct, Tue–Sat 1030–1630, Sun 1330–1630. Other times by arrangement. Charge £. Group concessions by arrangement. Explanatory displays, both audio-visual and interactive. Temporary exhibitions. Gift shop. Tearoom. Gardens. WC. Induction loop system in audio-visual room, handling area. Wheelchair access. Disabled WC. Car parking. Telephone (01224) 311200.

The regimental museum of the Gordon Highlanders. Striking displays of the regiment's unique collection recalling 200 years of service and gallantry. Housed in the former home and studio of the famous Victorian artist Sir George Reid PRSA.

---

15 ABERDEEN, KINGS COLLEGE CENTRE 3 Q9

College Bounds, Old Aberdeen, Aberdeen. In the University of Aberdeen campus, 2 miles (3km) from the centre. Open all year (except Christmas and New Year), Mon–Sat 1000–1700, Sun 1200–1700. Free. Explanatory displays. Gift shop. Coffee shop. WC. Wheelchair access. Disabled WC. Car parking. Telephone (01224) 273702.

A multi-media centre giving history of the university.

---

16 ABERDEEN, KIRK OF ST NICHOLAS 3 R9

Back Wynd, Aberdeen. In churchyard bounded by Union Street, Back Wynd, Schoolhill and Correction Wynd, 0.25 mile (0.5 km) from bus and rail stations. Open May–Sep (except local holidays) Mon–Fri 1200–1600, Sat 1300–1500. Other times by arrangement. Free. Donations. Guided tours. Guide book available in English, French, German, Dutch and Spanish. Explanatory displays. Churchyard. WC. Wheelchair access with assistance. Disabled WC. Car parking. Telephone (01224) 643494.

A complex building of Aberdeen's original parish church. Main features – 12th-century transept, refurbished in 1990, 15th-century vaulted lower church (variously used as a chantry chapel, witches' prison, soup kitchen, place of worship for Gaelic and Russian Orthodox services and presently as a Third World centre), 18th-century West Kirk, retaining its characteristic reformed layout, 19th-century East Kirk, medieval effigies, medieval and 17th-century carved woodwork, 17th-century needlework, 48-bell carillon, 20th-century Scottish stained glass.

---

17 ABERDEEN, MARISCHAL MUSEUM 3 R9

Marischal College, Broad Street, Aberdeen. In city centre, opposite Tourist Information Centre. Nearest railway station Aberdeen, then 10 minute walk. Local buses stop nearby. Open all year, Mon–Fri 1000–1700, Sun 1400–1700. Free. Explanatory displays. WC. Disabled WC. Telephone (01224) 274301.

Lying inside a spectacular granite building, Marischal Museum displays the collections of graduates and friends of Aberdeen University over 500 years. Exhibitions include the Enclyclopedia of the Northeast, containing objects from all periods and parts of the region, exploring its character; and Collecting the World, which includes objects from Africa, Australia, America, India and the Pacific, ancient Egyptian mummies and much more.

---

18 ABERDEEN, MARITIME MUSEUM 3 R9

Shiprow, Aberdeen. City centre, off Union Street. 15 minute walk from Aberdeen railway and bus stations. Open all year, Mon–Sat 1000–1700, Sun 1200–1500. Charge ££. Group concessions. Guided tours. Explanatory displays. Gift shop. Restaurant. WC. Induction loop system in auditorium. Wheelchair access. Disabled WC. Telephone (01224) 337700.

Aberdeen Maritime Museum tells the story of the city's long and fascinating relationship with the sea through a unique collection of ship models, paintings, artefacts, computer interaction and set-piece exhibitions. A major display about the offshore oil industry features an 8.5 metre high model of the Murchison oil platform. Situated on four floors and incorporating the 16th-century Provost Ross's House, the complex is linked by a modern glass structure to Trinity Church.

---

19 ABERDEEN, PROVOST SKENE'S HOUSE 3 R9

Guestrow, Aberdeen. City centre, off Broad Street. 15 minute walk from Aberdeen railway and bus stations. Open all year, Mon–Sat 1000–1700, Sun 1300–1600. Charge £. Group concessions. Guided tours. Explanatory displays. Coffee shop. WC. Telephone (01224) 641086.

One of Aberdeen's few remaining examples of early burgh architecture. Splendid room settings including a suite of Georgian rooms, an Edwardian nursery, magnificent 17th-century ceilings and wood panelling. The painted gallery houses the most important cycle of religious painting in north-east Scotland. Archaeological and social history displays.

---

20 ABERDEEN, ST ANDREW'S CATHEDRAL 3 R9

28 King Street, Aberdeen. At the junction of Union Street and Kine Street. Railway and bus stations close by. Open May–Sep, daily 1100–1600. Free. Explanatory displays. Gift shop. Tearoom (Fri am only). Induction loop. Wheelchair access. Disabled WC. Car parking. Telephone (01224) 640119.

Birthplace of the Anglican Communion. The first Anglican Bishop outside of the UK, Bishop Samuel Stabury of Connecticut, was consecrated here in 1784. He sought consecration in England but was refused. Three Scottish Bishops intervened to form a link with the American Episcopal Church which is strongly maintained to this day.

21 ABERDEEN, ST MACHAR'S CATHEDRAL TRANSEPTS **3 Q9**

HS. In Old Aberdeen. Nearest railway station Aberdeen, bus from city centre. Access at all times. Free. Telephone 0131 668 8800.

The nave and towers of the cathedral remain in use as a church, and the ruined transepts are in care. The fine tomb of Bishop Dunbar is in the south transept.

---

22 ABERDEEN, SATROSPHERE **3 R9**

19 Justice Mill Lane, Aberdeen. In Aberdeen, 0.5 miles (1km) from the railway and bus stations. Open daily (except Christmas and New Year) Mon–Sat 1000–1600, Sun 1330–1700; closed Tue in winter. Charge ££. Group concessions. Explanatory displays. Gift shop. Snack bar. Baby change. WC. Wheelchair access. Disabled WC. Car parking. Telephone (01224) 213232.

An interactive science centre with more than 70 exciting exhibits covering all aspects of science and technology. Science gifts, kits and books on sale.

---

23 ABERDEEN, TOLBOOTH **3 R9**

Castle Street, Aberdeen. City centre, continuation of Union Street. 15 minute walk from Aberdeen railway and bus stations. Open Apr–Sep, Mon–Sat 1000–1700, Sun 1230–1530. Charge £. Group concessions. Guided tours. Explanatory displays. Limited wheelchair access. Telephone (01224) 621167.

Aberdeen's museum of civic history housed in the city's 17th-century Tolbooth Prison. It charts the development of local government and the history of crime and punishment through the ages in Aberdeen. Visit the old cells and watch the interactive displays bring the city's past to life. Learn how Jacobite prisoners spent their days after 1745.

---

24 ABERDEEN, UNIVERSITY ZOOLOGY MUSEUM **3 R8**

Zoology Building, Tillydrone Avenue, Aberdeen. In Old Aberdeen adjacent to the Cruickshank Botanic Garden. Bus from centre. Open all year, Mon–Fri 0900–1700. Free. Explanatory displays. Vending machine. WC. Wheelchair access. Disabled WC. Car parking. Telephone (01224) 272850.

A collection of zoological specimens ranging from flies to whales. The museum contains the Conoco Natural History Centre which caters for educational groups; pre-booking essential, telephone (01224) 493288.

---

25 ABERDEEN, WINTER GARDENS

See 11 Aberdeen, Duthie Park Winter Gardens and Restaurant.

---

26 ABERDEENSHIRE FARMING MUSEUM **3 R8**

Aden Country Park, Mintlaw, Peterhead. 10 miles (16km) east of Peterhead on A92. Bus from Aberdeen to Mintlaw. Open May–Sep, daily 1100–1630, open at other times, telephone to check. Free. Guided tours. Explanatory displays. Gift shop. Tearoom and picnic area. WC. Limited wheelchair access. Disabled WC. Car and coach parking. Telephone (01771) 622906.

Visitors can relive the story of our famous farming past. Unique semi-circular Home Farm steading where visitors can explore the Aden Estate Story, and the Weel Vrocht Grun exhibitions and visit Hareshowe, a working farm set in the 1950s. Features award-winning displays and audio-visual show, guided tours and costumed guides. Temporary exhibitions.

---

27 ABERDOUR CASTLE **6 M15**

HS. Aberdour, Fife. In Aberdour, 5 miles (8km) east of the Forth Bridges on the A921. Nearest railway station Aberdour, bus from Kirkcaldy and Inverkeithing. Open Apr–Sep, daily 0930–1830; Oct–Mar, Mon–Sat

0930–1630 (closed Thu pm and Fri), Sun 1400–1630. Charge £. Group concessions. Explanatory displays. Gift shop. Tearoom. WC. Limited wheelchair access. Car parking. Telephone (01383) 860519.

A 13th-century fortified residence overlooking the harbour. Extended in the 15th, 16th and 17th centuries with splendid residential accommodation and a terraced garden and bowling green. There is a fine circular dovecot.

---

28 ABERFELDY DISTILLERY **5 L12**

Aberfeldy, Perthshire. 20 miles north of Perth on A827, off A9. Bus service from Pitlochry or Perth. Open Easter–Oct, Mon–Fri 1000–1600; Nov–Easter by appointment. Charge £. Guided tours. Gift shop. Forest walk and nature trail. WC. Car and coach parking. Telephone (01887) 822000.

The distillery was opened in 1898 by John and Thomas Dewar, sons of John Dewar, one of the early pioneers of whisky blending. Guided tours illustrate the process of malt whisky distillation and maturation. Visitor centre.

---

29 ABERFELDY RECREATION CENTRE **5 L12**

Crieff Road, Aberfeldy, Perthshire. 12 miles (19km) south of Pitlochry on B827. Nearest railway station Pitlochry, bus from Pitlochry to Perth. Open all year, Mon–Fri 0900–2100, Sat–Sun 0900–1800. Charge £. Group concessions. Explanatory displays. Café and picnic area. Crèche (by appointment). WC. Wheelchair access. Disabled WC. Car and coach parking. Telephone (01887) 820922.

Sport and recreation activities including a 25 metre swimming pool, two squash courts, snooker room, fitness room, sauna, sunbed and spa pool.

---

30 ABERLEMNO SCULPTURED STONES **5 P12**

HS. At Aberlemno on the B9134, 6 miles (9.5 km) northeast of Forfar, Angus. Nearest railway station Arbroath, bus from Arbroath to Forfar. Access at all times. Free. Telephone 0131 668 8800.

A magnificent upright cross-slab sculptured with Pictish symbols stands in the churchyard. Three other stones (covered in winter) stand beside the B9134 road.

---

31 ABERNETHY ROUND TOWER **5 M13**

HS. In Abernethy on the A913, 9 miles (14.5 km) southeast of Perth. Nearest railway station Perth, bus from Perth to Kintillo. Open summer only. For access apply to key holder. Free. Telephone 0131 668 8800.

One of two round towers of the Irish style surviving in Scotland and dating from the end of the 11th century. Beside it is a Pictish stone.

---

32 ABRIACHAN GARDEN NURSERY **3 J8**

Loch Ness side, Inverness. North shore of Loch Ness, 9 miles (14.5 km) southwest of Inverness on the A82. Bus services from Inverness, Fort William and Fort Augustus. Open Feb–Nov, daily 0900–1900 (or dusk if earlier). Charge £. Group concessions on application. Guided tours. Explanatory displays. Picnic area. Limited wheelchair access. Car and coach parking. Telephone (01463) 861232.

Exciting garden on Loch Ness side. A combination of native and exotic plants in a beautiful woodland setting. Hardy perennial plantings are a speciality. The adjacent nursery sells many unusual plants. Catalogue available.

---

33 ACHAMORE GARDENS **4 E16**

Isle of Gigha, Argyll. Car and passenger ferry (20 mins) from Tayinloan. Bus from Glasgow to Tayinloan. Open all year, daily dawn to dusk. Charge £. Pets corner. WC. Limited wheelchair access. Car and coach parking. Telephone (01583) 505254.

Rhododendrons, camellias, azaleas and many semi-tropical shrubs and plants may be seen at these gardens developed over the past 40 years. There is also a spring bank and a viewpoint with fine views of Islay and Jura. There are two self-guided garden routes; one takes 40 minutes, the other 90 minutes.

---

34 ACHAVANICH STANDING STONES **3 M3**

Caithness. Situated approximately 5 miles (8km) from Latheron on the A895 to Thurso.

The stones are set in an unusual U shape and are thought to date from the Bronze Age. Today 36 stones survive out of a possible 54.

---

35 ACHILTIBUIE HYDROPONICUM **2 G5**

Achiltibuie, Ross-shire. North of Ullapool in the Coigach Peninsula. Open Apr–Sep, daily 1000–1800. Charge ££. Group concessions. Guided tours. Gift shop. Café and Picnic area. Access to shore. WC. Limited wheelchair access, easy access to lower level; wheelchair provided if required. Disabled WC. Car parking. Telephone (01854) 622202.

A pioneering indoor garden created for the 21st century, overlooking the beautiful Summer Isles. Guided tours take visitors around three growing houses, each with different climatic zones. Here lush, sub-tropical fruit trees, exotic flowers, vegetables and herbs all grow without soil.

---

36 ACHILTIBUIE SMOKEHOUSE **2 G5**

The Smokehouse, Achiltibuie, Ullapool, Ross and Cromarty. At Altandhu, 5 miles (8km) northwest of Achiltibuie village, 25 miles (40km) northwest of Ullapool. Open Easter–Oct, Mon–Sat 0930–1700. Free. Explanatory displays. Gift shop. No guide dogs. Car parking. Telephone (01854) 622353.

A smokehouse where visitors can view the work areas and see fish being prepared for smoking and other processes.

---

37 ACHNABRECK CUP AND RING MARKS **4 F14**

HS. Kilmartin Glen. 1.5 miles (2.5 km) northwest of Lochgilphead, Argyll. Nearest railway station Oban, then Lochgilphead bus to Kilmartin. Access at all times. Free. Telephone 0131 668 8800.

The exposed crest of a rocky ridge with well-preserved cup and ring marks. Bronze Age.

---

38 ACHNACLOICH GARDENS **4 G13**

Connel, Oban, Argyll. Off the A85, 8 miles (13km) east of Oban. Bus from Oban. Open Apr–Oct, daily 1000–1800. Charge £. WC. Limited wheelchair access. Car parking. Telephone (01631) 710221.

A woodland garden of around 35 acres (14 ha) developed over a period of about 130 years. Small walled garden. Planted ponds. Wide variety of shrubs, many from Southern Hemisphere.

---

39 ADEN COUNTRY PARK **3 R8**

Mintlaw, Aberdeenshire. 10 miles (16km) east of Peterhead on A92. Bus to Mintlaw, 1.5 mile (2.5 km) walk to Park. Open daily Apr–Oct, 0700–2200; Nov–Mar 0700–1900. Free. Gift shop. Restaurant, picnic and barbeque area. WC. Sensory garden. Limited wheelchair access. Disabled WC. Car and coach parking. Telephone (01771) 622857.

A 230 acre (93ha) country park containing Wildlife Discovery Centre, woodland walks, nature trails, ranger service with special events run throughout the year, orienteering course, sensory garden, adventure play area, lake and caravan park. Aden is also the home of the award-winning Aberdeenshire Farming Museum. See also 26 Aberdeenshire Farming Museum.

40 AIGAS DAM **3 J8**

Inverness-shire. By A831, between Beauly and Struy.

This dam, part of the River Beauly Hydro scheme, is by-passed by a fish lift which allows the salmon to migrate upstream.

---

41 AIKWOOD TOWER **5 N17**

Aikwood Tower, Selkirk. On B7009, 4 miles (6.5km) west of Selkirk. Bus service to Selkirk but no public transport between Selkirk and Aikwood. Open Apr–Sep, Tue, Thu and Sun 1400–1700. Charge £. Free access for wheelchair users. Limited wheelchair access. Disabled WC. Car parking. Telephone (01750) 52253.

A 16th-century tower house restored in the 1990s by the Steel family to a standard that has resulted in many architectural awards. It houses a permanent exhibition relating to the life and work of James Hogg, the Ettrick Shepherd (1770–1835), and temporary exhibitions of art and sculpture.

---

42 AILSA CRAIG **4 G18**

Island in the Firth of Clyde, 10 miles (17km) west of Girvan. To arrange a visit telephone the Lighthouse Attendant on (01465) 713219.

A granite island rock, 1114 feet (339.5m) high with a circumference of 2 miles (3km). The rock itself was used to make some of the finest curling stones and the island has a gannetry and colonies of guillemots and other seabirds.

---

43 ALDIE WATER MILL AND THE TAIN POTTERY **3 K6**

Tain, Ross-shire. Off the A9, 0.5 mile (1km) south of Tain, 30 miles (48km) north of Inverness. Open Apr–Sep, daily 0930–1730; Oct–Mar, Mon–Sat 1100–1600. Charge £. Group concessions. Explanatory displays. Gift shop. WC. Limited wheelchair access. Disabled WC. Car and coach parking. Telephone (01862) 893786.

There has been a water mill on the Aldie Estate since 1552. The present mill dates from 1860 and has been restored to working order. Tain pottery is for sale, together with other products produced locally, including baskets, weaving and carving.

---

44 ALEXANDER III MONUMENT **6 N15**

By A921, south of Kinghorn at Pettycur Promontory. Access at all times. Free. Car parking.

On the King's Crag, a monument marks the place where Alexander III was killed in a fall from his horse in 1286.

---

45 ALFORD HERITAGE CENTRE **3 P9**

Mart Road, Alford, Aberdeenshire. 25 miles (40km) west of Aberdeen on A944 Highland Tourist Route. Local bus from Aberdeen. Open Apr–Oct, Mon–Sat 1000–1700, Sun 1300–1700. Charge £. Group concessions. Guided tours for parties by arrangement. Explanatory displays. Gift shop. WC. Wheelchair access. Disabled WC. Car and coach parking. Telephone (01975) 562906.

Housed in the unique auction mart building, the Alford Heritage Centre features the greatest collection of rural bygones in northeast Scotland. The exhibition is designed to give the visitor an insight into the rural life of the ordinary working people of Donside. There is also a room dedicated to local poet, Charles Murray. Hear the local dialect called Doric. Special events programme.

---

46 ALFORD VALLEY RAILWAY **3 P9**

Alford Station, Main Street, Alford, Aberdeenshire. At Alford Station. Alford is 25 miles (40km) west of Aberdeen on the A944 Highland Tourist

Route. Nearest railway station Insch 11 miles (18km), bus service to Alford from Aberdeen (Stagecoach). Open Apr, May and Sep, Sat and Sun; Jun, Jul and Aug daily. 30 minute service from 1300, last train at 1630. Charge £. Explanatory displays. Gift shop. WC. Wheelchair access. Disabled WC. Car and coach parking. Telephone (01975) 562811.

Narrow gauge railway running a 30 minute trip from the restored Alford Station to Haughton Caravan Park, which is approximately 1 mile (1.5km) away. Train collection includes a former Aberdeen suburban tram, a steam locomotive from Durban in South Africa and three diesel Simplex locomotives.

---

47 ALLOA TOWER 6 L14

NTS. Alloa Park, Alloa. On A907 in Alloa. Bus from Alloa centre. Open Apr–Sep, daily 1330–1730. Charge £. Children free. Group concessions. Explanatory displays. WC. Limited wheelchair access. Disabled WC. Car parking. Telephone (01259) 211701.

Alloa Tower was the ancestral home of the Earls of Mar and Kellie for four centuries. The present building dates from 1497 and was built by the 3rd Lord Erskine. In the early 18th century, the 6th Earl remodelled the tower to tie in with the adjoining mansion house, which was destroyed by fire in 1800. Impressive parapet walk round the tower's battlements offering spectacular views of the Forth. Fine collection of family portraits, including works by Jamesone and Raeburn.

---

48 ALLOWAY OLD KIRK 4 H18

Alloway, Ayrshire. 2.5 miles (4km) south of Ayr on B7024. Bus from Ayr. Open all year. Free. Guided tours by arrangement. Explanatory displays. Gift shop. Garden. WC. Car and coach parking. Telephone (01292) 441252.

Ancient church, a ruin in Burns' day. William Burnes, the poet's father, is buried in the churchyard. In the poem, *Tam o' Shanter*, Burns described the 'warlocks and witches in a dance, within Alloway's auld haunted kirk'.

---

49 ALLOWAY PARISH CHURCH 4 H18

Alloway, Ayrshire. 2.5 miles (4km) south of Ayr. Bus from Ayr. Open Jun–Sep Mon–Fri 1000–1600. Sunday services 0945 and 1115. Free. Guided tours fortnightly on Wed, Jun–Sep. Explanatory displays. Gift shop. Picnic area. WC. Limited wheelchair access. Car and coach parking. Telephone (01292) 441252.

Built between 1858 and 1890 by architect Campbell Douglas, this church has a very fine collection of stained glass including works by Adam Small, W. and J. J. Kier, Whall, Webster, Clayton, Bell and two by Susan Bradbury in 1996, The Seasons and Robert Burns Memorial Window.

---

50 ALMONDELL AND CALDERWOOD COUNTRY PARK 6 M15

Broxburn, West Lothian. On B7015 (A71) at East Calder or off A89 at Broxburn. 12 miles (19km) south southwest of Edinburgh. Park open all year. Visitor centre open Apr–Sep, Mon, Tue and Thu 0930–1700, Wed 0930–1630, Sat 1000–1700 (Sun 1730); Oct–Mar, Mon–Thu 0915–1700, Sat and Sun 1000–1630. Closed for lunch 1200–1300. Free. Guided tours cost £. Explanatory displays. Refreshments in visitor centre. Garden. WC. Wheelchair access to visitor centre. Disabled WC. Car and coach parking. Telephone (01506) 414957.

Extensive riverside and woodland walks in former estate, with large picnic and grassy areas. The visitor centre, housed in old stable block, has a large freshwater aquarium, displays on local and natural history, and a short slide show. Ranger service, guided walks programme.

51 ALMOND VALLEY HERITAGE CENTRE 6 M15

Millfield, Livingston Village, West Lothian. Off A705, 2 miles (3km) from Junction 3 on M8, 15 miles (24km) west of Edinburgh. Bus from Edinburgh. Open all year, daily 1000–1700. Charge £. Group concessions. Explanatory displays. Gift shop. Tearoom. WC. Wheelchair access. Disabled WC. Car and coach parking. Telephone (01506) 414957.

The history and environment of West Lothian brought to life in an exciting and innovative museum combining a working farm, restored watermill and museum of social and industrial history. Award-winning interactive displays for children, indoor play areas, nature trail, trailer rides and a narrow-gauge railway.

---

52 THE ALUMINIUM STORY LIBRARY AND VISITOR CENTRE 2 H11

Linnhe Road, Kinlochleven. 7 miles (11km) from Glencoe and 21 miles (34km) from Fort William at the head of Loch Leven. Bus service from Fort William. Open Apr–Oct, Mon–Fri 1000–1800. Free. Group concessions. Explanatory displays. Gift shop. WC. Wheelchair access. Disabled WC. Car and coach parking. Telephone (01855) 831663.

The Aluminium Story uses audio-visual displays and a video presentation system to tell the story of the British Aluminium Company which opened a smelter here in 1908. Visitors can learn how the industry and the company's hydro scheme altered the life of the area.

---

53 ALVIE ESTATE 3 L9

Kincraig, Kingussie, Inverness-shire. On the B9152, 4 miles (6.5km) south of Aviemore. Bus from Aviemore. Open daily (except Christmas Day and New Year's Day), 0900–1700. Entrance to estate free, charges for activities. Guided tours. Gift shop. Picnic area. Play area. WC. Limited wheelchair access. Car and coach parking. Telephone (01540) 651249.

A traditional Highland sporting estate which has been in the same family since 1927. Now diversified into tourism – clay pigeon shooting, fishing, horse riding, 4x4 off-road driving, estate tours and corporate entertainment. Spectacular views across the Spey Valley to the Cairngorms.

---

54 ALYTH MUSEUM 5 N12

Commercial Street, Alyth, Perthshire. In Alyth centre. Bus from Perth or Dundee. Open May–Sep, Wed–Sun 1300–1700. Free. Explanatory displays. Car parking. Telephone (01738) 632488.

Displays of local history relating to Alyth and the surrounding agricultural area.

---

55 ANGUS FOLK MUSEUM 5 N12

NTS. Kirkwynd, Glamis. Off A94, 5 miles southwest of Forfar. Buses from Dundee, Forfar and Kirriemuir. Open Apr–Sep, daily 1100–1700; weekends in Oct. Charge £. Children free. Group concessions. Explanatory displays (information sheets in French, German, Italian and Spanish). WC. Wheelchair access, wheelchair available. Disabled WC. Car parking. Telephone (01307) 840288.

The museum is within Kirkwynd Cottages, a row of six reconstructed early 18th-century cottages with stone-slabbed roofs. The interiors display one of the finest folk collections of domestic relics in Scotland. There is an exhibition, Life on the Land, in a separate reconstructed Angus farm steading, showing rural life in Angus over the last 200 years.

---

56 AN LANNTAIR 2 E4

Town Hall, South Beach, Stornoway, Isle of Lewis. On the seafront in Stornoway adjacent to ferry and bus station. Open all year, Mon–Sat 1000–1730. Free. Gift shop. Tearoom. WC. Wheelchair access. Car and coach parking. Telephone (01851) 703307.

The main public arts facility in the Western Isles since 1985. A forum for local, national and international arts, promoting a diverse year-round programme of exhibitions and events.

---

57 ANNAN ACTIVITIES **5 N20**

Westlands, Annan, Dumfriesshire. On the B6357 between Annan and Kirkpatrick Fleming, 2 miles (3.5km) from junction 21 on the M74. Open Easter–Oct, daily 0930–1700; after 1700 and during winter by appointment. Charge per activity. Group concessions. Explanatory displays. WC. Limited wheelchair access. Car and coach parking. Telephone (01461) 800274.

The 70 acre (29ha) site has activities for all the family: quad bike tracks and safari, crazy golf, paintball, fishing pond, fly fishing lochans, clay pigeon shooting. See emus and red deer stags. Activities suitable for all ages. All equipment available for hire.

---

58 ANSTRUTHER PLEASURE TRIPS TO THE ISLE OF MAY **6 P14**

The Harbour, Anstruther, Fife. Buses from Edinburgh, Glasgow or Kirkcaldy. Open May–Sep; telephone for sailing times. Charge £££. Children under 3 years free. Group concessions midweek only. Explanatory displays. Snack bar on board. Visitor centre and picnic area on Isle of May. WC. Limited wheelchair access. Car and coach parking. Telephone (01333) 310103.

Daily boat trips to the Isle of May nature reserve to view large numbers of sea birds, including puffins. Also colony of grey seals, remains of a 12th-century monastery and light houses. Five hour trip, including three hours ashore and a cruise around the island. Boat carries 100 passengers.

---

59 AN TAIRBEART HERITAGE CENTRE **4 F15**

Tarbert, Argyll. 0.5 mile (0.8 km) south of Tarbert on main A83 Campbeltown Road. Glasgow to Campbeltown bus stops in Tarbert. Open Easter–Oct, daily 1000–1800. Other times by arrangement. Free. Charges for special events. Guided tours. Explanatory displays. Gift shop. Restaurant and picnic area. WC. Limited wheelchair access. Disabled WC. Car and coach parking. Telephone (01880) 820190.

An Tairbeart explores the rich heritage of this unique coastline. Eighty-six acres (35ha) of native woodland with hill and pasture and wonderful views plus a wealth of wildlife. There is a varied programme of events, such as children's activities, local food tastings, rural skills demonstrations, storytelling, art exhibitions and ceilidhs. An Tairbeart is also a shop window for local produce, stocking a wide range of fresh and smoked produce and local delicacies.

---

60 ANTARTEX VILLAGE **6 J15**

Lomond Industrial Estate, Heather Avenue, Alexandria. 1 mile (2km) from A82, 15 miles (24km) north of Glasgow. Bus and rail service from Glasgow. Open daily all year 1000–1800 except Christmas and New Year. Free. Explanatory displays and sheepskin cutting demonstrations. Gift shop. Restaurant. WC. Wheelchair access. Disabled WC. Car and coach parking. Telephone (01389) 752393.

Watch the famous Antartex sheepskins being made and choose from a vast selection of sheepskin and leather goods. Also golfing equipment and whisky tasting. Restaurant offers traditional Scottish dishes.

---

61 AN TOBAR ARTS CENTRE, GALLERY AND CAFÉ **4 E12**

Argyll Terrace, Tobermory, Isle of Mull. Ferry from Oban to Craignure, then bus to Tobermory. Open Mar–Jun and Sep–Dec, Tue–Sat 1000–1600; Jul–Aug, Mon–Sat 1000–1800, Sun 1300–1600. Free. Explanatory displays. Gift shop. Café. WC. Wheelchair access. Disabled WC. Car parking. Telephone (01688) 302211.

Based in a renovated Victorian primary school, the building has retained its historic detail and atmosphere and commands breathtaking views over Tobermory Bay. Monthly touring local art and craft exhibitions. The best of traditional and contemporary music. Concerts and informal ceilidhs, usually on Tuesday and Friday evenings. Art, craft and music workshops with local and visiting artists.

---

62 ANTONINE WALL **6 L15**

HS. From Bo'ness to Old Kilpatrick, best seen off A803 east of Bonnybridge, 12 miles (19km) south of Stirling. Access at all reasonable times. Free. Explanatory board. Telephone 0131 668 8800.

This Roman fortification stretched from Bo'ness on the Forth to Old Kilpatrick on the Clyde. Built about 142–3AD, it consisted of a turf rampart behind a ditch, with forts about every two miles. It was probably abandoned around 163AD. Remains are best preserved in the Falkirk/Bonnybridge area. See also Bar Hill Fort, Castlecary, Croy Hill, Dullatur, Glasgow Bearsden Bathhouse, Rough Castle, Seabegs Wood, Tollpark and Garnhall, and Watling Lodge.

---

63 AN TUIREANN ARTS CENTRE **2 E8**

Struan Road, Portree, Isle of Skye. On the B885, 0.5 mile (1km) from Portree centre. Open all year, daily Mon–Sat 1000–1700. Free. Explanatory displays. Gift shop. Restaurant/café. WC. Induction loop system. Wheelchair access. Disabled WC. Car parking. Telephone (01478) 613306.

An exhibition gallery for the visual arts and crafts and related educational events.

---

64 AQUATEC **6 K16**

1 Menteith Road, Motherwell. 5 minutes walk from Motherwell railway station. Open daily all year 1000–2200 except Christmas Day and New Year's Day. Charge £. Children under 3 years free. Group concessions. Gift shop. Café and vending machines. WC. Wheelchair access. Disabled WC. Car and coach parking. Telephone (01698) 276464.

The Aquatec is a leisure facility with a free form leisure pool with tyre ride, wild water channel and outdoor pool, children's beach area and lagoon. A leisure ice rink and ice cavern, snow machines and video wall. Health suite and conditioning gym.

---

65 ARBROATH ABBEY **5 P12**

HS. Abbey Street, Arbroath, Angus. In Arbroath town centre. Nearest railway station Arbroath, bus services from Dundee and Montrose to Arbroath. Open Apr–Sep, Mon–Sat 0930–1830, Sun 1400–1830; Oct–Mar, Mon–Sat 0930–1630. Charge £. Group concessions. Guided tours. Explanatory displays. Telephone (01241) 878756.

The substantial ruins of a Tironesian monastery founded by William the Lion in 1178 and intended as his own burial place. Parts of the Abbey Church and domestic buildings remain, notably the gatehouse range and the abbot's house. This was the scene of the signing of the Declaration of Arbroath in 1320, which asserted Scotland's independence from England.

---

66 ARBROATH MUSEUM **5 P12**

Signal Tower, Ladyloan, Arbroath. 16 miles (26km) north of Dundee on A92.. Six minutes walk from Arbroath bus and railway stations. Open all year (except 25,26 Dec and 1,2 Jan), Mon–Sat 1000–1700; in Jul and Aug also Sun 1400–1700. Free. Guided tours (booking required). Explanatory displays. Gift shop. Garden. WC. Limited wheelchair access. Car and coach parking. Telephone (01241) 875598.

Housed in the shore station for the Bell Rock lighthouse, the museum features displays devoted to this renowned lighthouse as well as exhibits exploring the fishing community with life-size models which converse in the local dialect. Recreated 1950s schoolroom, Victorian parlour and wash house complete with noises and smells. Displays on Arbroath's linen and engineering industries plus maritime wildlife tableaux.

---

67 ARBUTHNOT MUSEUM **3 R8**

St Peter Street, Peterhead. In Peterhead town centre. Bus from Aberdeen. Open Mon–Sat (except Wed and public holidays) 1030–1330 and 1430–1700, Wed 1030–1300. Free. Guided tours. Explanatory displays. Gift shop. Car and coach parking. Telephone (01771) 622906.

One of Aberdeenshire's oldest museums, once private. Features Peterhead's maritime history, Inuit art, Arctic whaling and animals, one of the largest coin collections in northern Scotland. Temporary exhibitions and changing programme.

---

68 ARCHAEOLINK PREHISTORY PARK **3 P9**

Oyne, Insch, Aberdeenshire. At Oyne village, 1 mile (1.5km) off the A96 Aberdeen to Inverness road, 25 miles (40km) west of Aberdeen. Railway station Insch (2.5 miles/4km), bus service to Insch from Aberdeen. Open Apr–Oct, daily 1000–1700. Charge ££. Children under 5 years free. Group concessions. Guided tours by arrangement. Explanatory displays. Gift shop. Restaurant. WC. Wheelchair access. Disabled WC. Car and coach parking. Telephone (01464) 851500.

Discover Scotland's prehistoric past – from Stone Age to Iron Age. Indoor and outdoor displays make it a unique living history experience for all ages.

---

69 ARDANAISEIG GARDENS **4 G13**

Ardanaiseig Hotel, Kilchrenan, Taynuilt, Argyll. On the B845, 10 miles (11.5km) east of Taynuilt. Nearest railway station Taynuilt. Open all year except Jan, and first two weeks of Feb, 0900–dusk. Charge £. Explanatory displays. Refreshments and WC in hotel. Car parking. Telephone (01866) 833333.

A wild woodland garden laid out in the 1820s before the hotel was built. Many exotic shrubs and trees.

---

70 ARDBEG DISTILLERY VISITOR CENTRE **4 D16**

Port Ellen, Isle of Islay. 3 miles (5km) east of Port Ellen on the southern tip of Islay. Ferry from Kennecraig; by air from Glasgow to Islay. Open Jun–Aug, daily 1000–1700; Sep–May, Mon–Fri 1000–1600. Charge £. Guided tours. Explanatory displays. Gift shop. Restaurant. WC. No guide dogs. Limited wheelchair access. Disabled WC. Car parking. Telephone (01496) 302244.

Take a step back in time and experience the history and mystique of the Ardbeg Distillery. Visitors enjoy a personal guided tour and a dram of Ardbeg's extraordinary malt whisky.

---

71 ARDCHATTAN GARDENS **4 G13**

Ardchattan Priory, Connel, Oban. On the north shore of Loch Etive, 5 miles (8km) east of Connel. Bus from Oban. Open Apr–Oct, daily 0900–1800. Charge £. Children under 14 free. Explanatory displays. WC. Wheelchair access. Disabled WC. Car and coach parking. Telephone (01796) 481355.

Four acres (1.6ha) of garden surrounding Ardchattan Priory, a private home, with a ruined chapel and interesting stones. Herbaceous borders and extensive lawn facing the loch. Rose, sorbus and many varieties of hebe.

---

72 ARDCHATTAN PRIORY **4 G12**

HS. On the north side of Loch Etive, 6.5 miles (10.5km) northeast of Oban, Argyll. Nearest railway station Oban. Access at all times. Free. Telephone 0131 668 8800.

The ruins of a Valliscaulian priory founded in 1230 and later converted to secular use. The meeting place in 1308 of one of Robert the Bruce's parliaments. Burned by Cromwell's soldiers in 1654. The remains include some carved stones.

---

73 ARDCLACH BELL TOWER **3 L8**

HS. Off A939, 8.5 miles (13.5km) southeast of Nairn. Nearest railway station Nairn, then post bus to Ardclach (no bus for return). Access at all times. For access apply to keyholder. Free. Telephone 0131 668 8800.

A remarkable little two-storey fortified bell tower built in 1655 on the hill above the parish church of Ardclach. It summoned worshippers to the church and warned in case of alarm.

---

74 ARDENCRAIG GARDENS **4 G16**

Ardencraig Lane, Rothesay, Isle of Bute. 2 miles from Rothesay. Bus service from Rothesay. Open May–Sep, Mon–Fri 0900–1630, Sat and Sun 1300–1630. Free. Gift shop. Tearoom. WC. Wheelchair access. Car and coach parking. Telephone (01700) 504644.

A working greenhouse and garden which produces plants for floral displays on Bute. Built from 1919 to 1923 and developed over the years, they now house a collection of rare plants, an aviary with many foreign bird species and ornamental fish ponds.

---

75 ARDESSIE FALLS **2 G6**

Beside the A832 at Dundonnel, Ross and Cromarty.

Waterfalls offering impressive views of Little Loch Broom.

---

76 ARDESTIE AND CARLUNGIE EARTH HOUSES **5 P13**

HS. Ardestie, about 6 miles (9.5km) east of Dundee and 1.25 miles (2km) north of Monifieth, at junction with B962. Nearest railway station Dundee, bus to Monifieth. Carlungie is 1 mile (1.5km) north on an unclassified road. Open all year. Free. Telephone 0131 668 8800.

Two examples of large Iron Age earth houses attached to surface dwellings (both now uncovered). At Ardestie the gallery is curved and 80 feet (24m) in length. The Carlungie earth house is 150 feet (45.5m) long and most complex.

---

77 ARDFEARN NURSERY **3 K8**

Bunchrew, Inverness. 4 miles (6.5km) west of Inverness on A862. Nearest railway and bus stations Inverness. Open all year, daily 0900–1700 (except Christmas Day and New Year's Day). Free. Guided tours if pre-booked. WC. Wheelchair access with assistance. Car and coach parking. Telephone (01463) 243250.

Horticultural adviser and broadcaster Jim Sutherland and his son Alasdair have created a large family nursery on the shores of the Beauly Firth. Huge variety of plants of extreme hardiness, attractive display beds containing over 1000 species and cultivars, with easy access for all including wheelchair users. Sales area with a wide selection of plants including the nursery's speciality, alpines. Panoramic views.

---

78 ARDGARTAN VISITOR CENTRE **4 H14**

FE. Glen Croe, Arrochar, Argyll. On A83 west of Arrochar on Cowal Peninsula. Nearest railway station Tarbet then local bus service. Open daily Apr–Oct 1000–1700. Free. Explanatory displays. Gift shop. Picnic area. Forest walks and cycleways. Wheelchair access. Car and coach parking. Telephone (01301) 702432.

Situated in Argyll Forest Park and close to the Arrochar Alps, the visitor centre is a good access point for the forest and its surroundings. Many special events are held throughout the year (nominal charge) and include Deer Watch, guided walks on the hills to see local wildlife and archaeology, and barbecues.

---

79 ARDKINGLAS WOODLAND GARDEN **4 H14**

Ardkinglas Estate, Cairndow, Argyll. In Cairndow, on the A83, 8 miles (13km) north of Inveraray. Buses from Glasgow, Oban or Campbeltown. Open daily dawn to dusk. Charge £. Group concessions. Guided tours for groups. Explanatory displays. Picnic area. WC. Limited wheelchair access. Car and coach parking. Telephone (01499) 600263.

One of the finest collections of rhododendrons and conifers in the British Isles. Established about 1875 by the Callender family. Contains five champion trees (tallest or broadest of the species in the UK).

---

80 ARDNAMURCHAN NATURAL HISTORY CENTRE **2 E11**

Glenmore, Acharacle, Argyll. On the B8009 9 miles (14.5km) west of Salen. Open Easter–Oct, Mon–Sat 1030–1730, Sun 1200–1730. Charge £. Group concessions. Explanatory displays. Gift shop. Tearoom. WC. Limited wheelchair access. Disabled WC. Car parking. Telephone (01972) 500209.

An introduction to the peninsula's wealth of wildlife. The Living Building is designed to attract as much wildlife as possible and offers a chance to come face to face with birds, butterflies and even pine martens. Tells the story of Ardnamurchan.

---

81 ARDNAMURCHAN POINT VISITOR CENTRE **2 D11**

Kilchoan, Acharacle, Argyll. On B8007, 6 miles (10km) west of Kilchoan. Ferry terminal at Kilchoan. Open Apr–May and Oct, daily 1000–1700; Jun–Sep, daily 1000–1730. Charge £. Group concessions. Guided tours. Explanatory displays. Gift shop. Picnic area. WC. Wheelchair access. Disabled WC. Car parking. Telephone (01972) 510210.

Ardnamurchan lighthouse is set amongst spectacular scenery on mainland Britain's most westerly point, embracing world-class views of the Hebrides and the Small Isles. Listen to the keepers' radio conversations, learn how the light tower was built, join in the centre's Whale Watch, visit the beautifully restored original room and trace the history of Ardnamurchan through anecdotes of people past and present.

---

82 ARDROSSAN CASTLE **6 H17**

Ardrossan, on a hill overlooking Ardrossan Bay. Access at all reasonable times. Free.

Mid 12th-century castle on a hill with fine views of Arran and Ailsa Craig. Castle was destroyed by Cromwell and only part of the north tower and two arched cellars remain.

---

83 ARDTORNISH ESTATE **4 F12**

Morvern, by Oban, Argyll. 40 miles (64km) southwest of Fort William via the Corran Ferry. Open Mar–Oct, daily 0900–1800. Market garden open all year, daily (except Thu) 0900–1800. Charge £. Market garden free. Explanatory displays. Gift shop. Picnic area. Garden. WC. Car and coach parking. Telephone (01967) 421288.

Ardtornish estate is a 35,000 acre (14,164ha) Highland estate with 24 acres (10ha) of established gardens around the Grade A listed Ardtornish House. Fly fishing for brown trout, sea trout and salmon on three rivers and 16 hill lochs. Free loch fishing to residents of estate's self catering properties.

84 ARDUAINE GARDEN 4 F14

NTS. Arduaine, Argyll. On A816, 20 miles (32km) south of Oban. Infrequent bus service from Oban. Open all year, daily 0930–sunset. Charge £. Children free. Explanatory displays (information sheets in French and German). Plant sales. WC. Wheelchair access, wheelchair available. Disabled WC. Car and coach parking. Telephone (01852) 200366.

Twenty acre (8ha) garden on promontory with fine views overlooking Loch Melfort. Noted for rhododendrons, azaleas, magnolias and other interesting trees and shrubs. The garden also has a series of ponds and watercourses and many beautiful herbaceous perennials flowering throughout the season.

---

85 ARDUNIE ROMAN SIGNAL STATION 5 L13

HS. At Trinity Gask, 4 miles (6.5km) north of Auchterarder, Perthshire. Nearest railway station Perth, bus from Perth to Crieff, then bus to Kinkell Bridge. Access at all times. Free. Telephone 0131 668 8800.

The site of a Roman watchtower, one of a series running between Ardoch and the River Tay. First century AD. See also 1089 Muir O'Fauld Signal Station.

---

86 ARDVRECK CASTLE 2 H4

A837, 11 miles (18km) east of Lochinver, on Loch Assynt. Access at all reasonable times. Free.

Built by the MacLeods, who in the mid-13th century obtained Assynt by marriage, the three-storeyed ruins stand on the shores of Loch Assynt. After his defeat at Culrain, near Bonar Bridge, in 1650, the Marquess of Montrose fled to Assynt but was soon captured and confined here before being sent to Edinburgh and executed.

---

87 ARDWELL GARDENS 4 H19

Ardwell Estate, Ardwell, Stranraer, Wigtownshire. On the A716, 10 miles (16km) south of Stranraer. Nearest railway station Stranraer, bus from Stranraer. Open Mar–Sep, daily 1000–1700. Charge £. Guided tours by arrangement. Gift shop. Plant sales. Picnic area. WC. Limited wheelchair access. Disabled WC. Car and coach parking. Telephone (01776) 860227.

Gardens surrounding an 18th-century country house (not open to the public) with the formal layout round the house blending into the informality of woods and shrubberies. Daffodils, azaleas, camellias, rhododendrons. Walled garden and herbaceous borders. Walks and fine views over Luce Bay. Plants for sale and pick-your-own.

---

88 ARGYLL AND SUTHERLAND HIGHLANDERS REGIMENTAL MUSEUM 6 K14

Stirling Castle, Stirling. In Stirling centre. Nearest railway station Stirling, buses from Glasgow and Edinburgh. Open Easter–Sep, Mon–Sat 1000–1745, Sun 1100–1645; Oct–Easter, daily 1000–1615. Free. Fee for entry to castle. Explanatory displays. Gift shop. Refreshments and WC in castle. Car and coach parking. Telephone (01786) 475165.

A fine museum which brings alive the history of the Regiment from 1794 to the present. Features weapons, silver, colours, uniforms, medals, pictures, music, First World War trench. See also 1371 Stirling Castle.

---

89 ARGYLL POTTERY 4 G12

Barcaldine, Oban, Argyll. On the A828, on the south shore of Loch Creran. Bus from Oban. Open all year, Mon–Fri 1000–1800, Sat 1300–1800. Free. Explanatory displays. Gift shop. Wheelchair access. Car parking. Telephone (01631) 720503.

A pottery producing mostly domestic ware, including a full range of ovenware and some individual pieces.

90 ARGYLL'S LODGING 6 L14

HS. Castle Wynd, Stirling. At the top of Castle Wynd in centre of the town. Nearest railway station Stirling, buses from Glasgow and Edinburgh. Open Apr–Sep, daily 0930–1830; Oct–Mar, Mon–Sat 0930–1830, Sun 1400–1630. Charge £. Joint ticket with Stirling Castle available. Group concessions. Explanatory displays. Gift shop. WC. Limited wheelchair access. Disabled WC. Car and coach parking. Telephone (01786) 450000.

A superb mansion built around an earlier core in about 1630 and further extended by the Earl of Argyll in the 1670s. It is the most impressive town house of its period in Scotland. The principal rooms are now restored to their former glory.

---

91 ARGYLL WILDLIFE PARK 4 G14

Dalchenna, Inverary, Argyll. On the A83, 1.25 miles (2km) from Inveraray. Bus from Glasgow. Open daily, Easter–Oct 1000–1700. Charge ££. Group concessions. Guided tours. Explanatory displays. Gift shop. Tearoom and picnic area. Baby changing. WC. Limited wheelchair access. Disabled WC. Car and coach parking. Telephone (01499) 302264.

A 55 acre (22ha) park with many animals wandering freely. Ponds with water birds. Natural surroundings.

---

92 ARMADALE CASTLE GARDENS AND MUSEUM OF THE ISLES 2 E9

Armadale Castle, Sleat, Isle of Skye. 0.5 mile (1km) north of Armadale ferry terminal, 21 miles (34km) south of the Skye Bridge at Kyle of Lochalsh on A851. Car and passenger ferry from Mallaig to Armadale. Bus from Kyle of Lochalsh. Open Apr–Oct, daily 0930–1730. Charge ££. Carers of disabled visitors. Group concessions. Guided tours. Also tour of gardens by head gardener for small groups. Gift shop. Restaurant and tearoom. Children's play area. WC. Wheelchair access; wheelchairs available for use. Disabled WC. Car and coach parking. Telephone (01471) 844305.

Probably one of the best gardens in the highland region, a 40 acre (16ha) garden set within the 20,000 (8094ha) Armadale Estate where some of the flora otherwise associated with warmer climes can be grown because of the gulf stream passing close to our shores. Woodland walks and meadows ablaze with wild flowers, seascapes round every corner. Museum explaining the sometimes complex story of Highland history. See also 1495 West Highland Heavy Horse Tours.

---

93 JOHNIE ARMSTRONG OF GILNOCKIE MEMORIAL 5 N18

Carlanrig, Teviothead. Take the A7 south from Hawick for 9 miles (14.5km) then turn right on to unclassified road. Memorial is 100 yards (91m) south on left next to churchyard. Access at all times. Free. Information plaque. Wheelchair access via nearby field gate. Car parking.

A stone marker marks the mass grave of Laird of Gilnockie and his men, hanged without trial by King James V of Scotland in 1530.

---

94 ARNISTON HOUSE 6 N16

Gorebridge, Midlothian. On the B6372, 1 mile (2km) from the A7 and 10 miles (16km) from Edinburgh. Bus on A7. Open Jul–Sep, Tue, Thu and Sun 1400–1700. Guided tours Apr–Jun, Tue 1400 and 1530. Charge ££. Children under 5 years free. Gardens free. Guided tours. Garden. WC. Limited wheelchair access. Disabled WC. Car and coach parking. Telephone (01875) 830230.

An outstanding example of the work of William Adam, built in the 1720s. Contains an important collection of furniture, Scottish portraiture and other fascinating items.

95 AROS EXPERIENCE 2 E8

Viewfield Road, Portree, Isle of Skye. On A850 south of Portree. Bus service from Portree. Open daily, Apr–Sep 0900–2100; Oct–Mar 1000–1700. Charge ££. Children under 12 free. Group concessions. Guided tours (Gaelic, European languages and Japanese available). Explanatory displays. Gift shop. Restaurant and café. Crèche, play area and forest walks. WC. Infra-red headsets for deaf people. Wheelchair access. Disabled WC. Car and coach parking. Telephone (01478) 613649.

The exhibition tells the story of Skye from 1700 to the present day. An audio-visual presentation introduces the scenery of Skye and a purpose-built auditorium is the location for regular shows on the Gaelic arts, including step dancing, singing and theatre.

---

96 ARRAN HERITAGE MUSEUM 4 G17

Rosaburn, Brodick, Isle of Arran. 1.5 miles (2.5km) north of Brodick Pier. Bus from Brodick Pier. Open Easter–Oct daily, 1030–1630. Charge £. Children under 5 free. Group concessions. Guided tours. Explanatory displays. Gift shop. Tearoom and picnic area. Garden. WC. Wheelchair access. Car and coach parking. Telephone (01770) 302636.

An original 18th-century croft farm with smiddy, cottage, coach house and stables. Extensive garden and special display area which is changed annually. Exhibits on shipping, geology, archaeology and local history.

---

97 ART.TM GALLERY 3 K8

20 Bank Street, Inverness. In the centre of Inverness, on the river front. 5 minutes from bus and railway stations. Open all year, Tue–Fri 1100–1800. Free. Guided tours. Explanatory displays. Gift shop. Tea and coffee available. WC. Wheelchair access. Disabled WC. Telephone (01463) 712240.

Houses three galleries for contemporary art, including the Edward Marshall Gallery for applied art – the only Crafts Council selected gallery in the north of Scotland. It hosts a changing exhibition programme showing a wide range of artists, both national and Highland.

---

98 ASCOG HALL, FERNERY AND GARDENS 4 G16

Ascog Hall, Ascog, Isle of Bute. 3 miles (5km) south of Rothesay on A886. Nearest railway station Wemyss Bay, then ferry (30 minutes) to Rothesay. Bus service from Rothesay to Ascog Hall (request stop). Open Apr–Oct, Wed–Sun 1000–1700, closed Mon and Tue. Charge £. Children free. Group concessions. Guided tours. Explanatory displays. Wheelchair access with assistance. Car and coach parking. Telephone (01700) 504555.

Built circa 1870, this magnificent Victorian fernery, with beautiful rock work and water pools, has been restored and refurnished with an impressive collection of subtropical ferns. The only surviving fern from the original collection is said to be around 1000 years old. The large and partly restored gardens are attractively laid out with paths meandering through flower-carpeted banks and beds.

---

99 ATHELSTANEFORD, FLAG HERITAGE CENTRE 6 P15

Athelstaneford, East Lothian. Behind Athelstaneford Church. Off B1347, 3 miles (4.5km) off the A1, 2.5 miles (4km) east of Haddington off B1343. Nearest railway station Drem, 2.5 miles (4km). Bus from North Berwick to Haddington stops in village. Open Apr–Sep, daily 1000–1700. Free. Explanatory displays. WC. Wheelchair access. Disabled WC. Car and coach parking. Telephone (01620) 880378.

A 16th-century dovecot restored to house an audio-visual dramatisation of the battle in 832AD at which an army of Picts/Scots encountered a larger force of Saxons under Athelstan. The appearance of a cloud formation of a white saltire (the diagonal cross on which St Andrew had been martyred) against a blue sky inspired the Scots to victory. Since that time, the St Andrew's Cross has been the national flag of Scotland. There is a viewpoint overlooking the battle site, and visitors can also inspect the Saltire Memorial, the Book of the Saltire, and walk through the historic churchyard.

---

100 ATHOLL COUNTRY COLLECTION **3 K11**

Blair Atholl, Perthshire. In Blair Atholl on A924. Nearest railway station Blair Atholl. Bus from Pitlochry. Open Easter, then Jun–Oct, daily 1330–1700; Jul–Sep, Mon–Fri 1000–1700. Charge £. Group concessions. Explanatory displays. Gift shop. Picnic area. WC. Wheelchair access. Car and coach parking. Telephone (01796) 481232.

Folk museum with lively displays showing village and glen life in the past, including blacksmith's smiddy, crofter's stable, byre and living room. Road, rail and postal services, the school, the kirk, the vet and gamekeeper are all featured. Attractions include the Trinafour post office and shop, the Caledonian Challenge Shield for Rifle Shooting and a photographic display of wildflowers.

---

101 ATTADALE GARDEN AND WOODLAND WALKS **2 G8**

Strathcarron, Ross and Cromarty. On south shore of Loch Carron, 2 miles (3km) south of Strathcarron on A890. Nearest railway station Attadale on main Inverness to Kyle of Lochalsh line, then walk 0.5 mile (1km). Open Apr–Oct, Mon–Sat 1000–1730. Charge £. Group concessions. Guided tours by arrangement. Explanatory displays. WC. Limited wheelchair access. Disabled WC. Car and coach parking. Telephone (01520) 722217.

Attadale House was built in 1755 by Donald Matheson. The gardens and woodlands were started in 1890 by Baron Schroder and planted with rhododendrons, azaleas and specimen trees. Since the storms of the 1980s, more old paths have been revealed, bridges have been built and water gardens have been planted with candelabra primulas, gunnera, iris and bamboo. Restored sunken garden, vegetable and herb gardens. Visitors are advised to wear waterproof shoes.

---

102 AUBIGNY SPORTS CENTRE **6 P15**

Mill Wynd, Haddinton. In Haddington, 5 minutes walk from High Street. Bus from Edinburgh. Open daily all year except Christmas and New Year, Mon–Fri 0900–2200, weekends 0900–1700. Charges dependent on activity. Group concessions. Café. Crèche. WC. Wheelchair access. Disabled WC. Car and coach parking. Telephone (01620) 826800.

A sports centre with a swimming pool with toddlers pool, sauna, steam room, activity hall, gym, aerobics studio, soft play area and a variety of coached activities.

---

103 AUCHAGALLON STONE CIRCLE **4 G17**

HS. Isle of Arran. 4 miles (6.5km) north of Blackwaterfoot on the Isle of Arran. By ferry from Ardrossan to Brodick. Bus from Brodick to Blackwaterfoot. Access at all times. Free. Telephone 0131 668 8800.

A Bronze Age burial cairn surrounded by a circle of 15 standing stones.

---

104 AUCHINDRAIN TOWNSHIP OPEN AIR MUSEUM **4 G14**

By Inveraray, Argyll. 6 miles (10km) southwest of Inveraray on A83. Open Apr–Sep, daily 1000–1700. Charge £. Group concessions. Explanatory displays. Gift shop. Light refreshments available. Picnic area. WC. Car and coach parking. Telephone (01499) 500235.

Auchindrain is an original West Highland township of great antiquity and the only communal tenancy township in Scotland to have survived on its centuries-old site, much of it in its original form. The various township buildings and surrounding lands look as they would have done at the end of the 19th century and give visitors a fascinating glimpse of Highland life.

105 AUCHINGARRICH WILDLIFE CENTRE 5 K13

Comrie, Perthshire. 2 miles (3km) south of Comrie on B827. Open all year, daily 1000–dusk. Charge ££. Children under 4 free. Group concessions. Guided tours. Explanatory displays. Gift shop. Restaurant, tearoom and picnic/barbecue area. Indoor play barn. WC. Handling facilities for blind people. Limited wheelchair access. Disabled WC. Car and coach parking. Telephone (01764) 679469.

Wildlife centre set in 100 acres (40ha) of scenic Perthshire countryside. Abundance of animals and birds including foxes, otters, meerkats, deer, Highland cattle, birds of prey and wildcats. Hatchery where visitors can handle newly born chicks. Covered walkway.

---

106 AUCHTERARDER HERITAGE 5 L13

Auchterarder Tourist Office, 90 High Street, Auchterarder, Perthshire. Nearest railway stations Perth and Gleneagles. Bus from Perth. Open Apr–Oct, Mon–Sat 0930–1700, Sun 1200–1630; Nov–Mar, Mon–Fri 0930–1230. Free. Explanatory displays. Telephone (01764) 663450.

History of the town and area told in descriptive panels using old photographs. Information on the railway, local history, the territorial army and church history.

---

107 AULD KIRK MUSEUM 6 K15

The Cross, Kirkintilloch, Glasgow. Take A803 from Glasgow to Kirkintilloch Cross. Bus service to Kirkintilloch Cross from Buchanan Street Bus Station, Glasgow. Open all year, Tue–Sat 1000–1300 and 1400–1700. Closed Sun and Mon. Free. Explanatory displays. Gift shop. Wheelchair access. Disabled WC. Car parking. Telephone 0141 578 0144.

The Auld Kirk Museum dates back to 1644 when it was the parish church of Kirkintilloch. It is now a museum describing the domestic and working life of people in the area. Temporary exhibition programme of crafts, photography and local history throughout the year.

---

108 AULTBEA WOODCRAFT AND HARDWOOD CAFE 2 F6

Drumchork, Aultbea, Achnasheen, Ross and Cromarty. Off the A832, 6 miles (9.5km) north of Inverewe Garden (see 846). Bus from Inverness. Open all year Mon–Sat 0930–1800. Free. Gift shop. Tearoom. Garden. WC. Wheelchair access. Disabled WC. Car parking. Telephone (01445) 731394.

A wood-turning workshop with craft shop and tearoom with superb views over loch and mountains. Large display of wood-turning in native and exotic woods. Wood-turning tuition available.

---

109 AURORA CRAFTS 2 D8

2 Ose, Struan, Isle of Skye. In Ose, 0.25 mile (0.5km) off the A863, 6 miles (9.5km) south of Dunvegan. Open Apr–Oct, daily 0900–1900. Free. Gift shop. Wheelchair access. Car parking. Telephone (01470) 572208.

A craft shop where visitors can see demonstrations of lace-making most days. Lace, embroidery, knitwear, spinning, wood-turned articles and other crafts made on the premises.

---

110 AVIATION MUSEUM 5 N12

Bellies Brae, Kirriemuir. Off the A90, near Forfar. Local bus service. Open Apr–Sep, Mon–Thu and Sat 1000–1700, Fri and Sun 1100–1700. Entry by donation. Guided tours. Explanatory displays. Picnic area nearby. Wheelchair access with assistance. Car and coach parking. Telephone (01575) 573233.

Open since 1983, the museum displays a huge and varied collection of ephemera associated with flight, from radar and radio equipment, model planes, to photographs, uniforms and operation manuals.

111 AVOCH HERITAGE EXHIBITION 3 K7

Old Post Office Buildings, High Street, Avoch, Ross-shire. In Avoch on the A832, 12 miles (19km) from Inverness. Bus from Inverness. Open Jul–Sep, Mon–Sat 1330–1700. Charge £. Group concessions. Explanatory displays. WC. Wheelchair access. Car and coach parking. Telephone (01381) 621125.

An exhibition displaying the heritage and history of Avoch and area. Different theme each year. A village model with commentary recreates the atmosphere of 1900.

---

112 AYR GORGE WOODLANDS 4 J17

At Failford, south of A758 Ayr-Mauchline road. Access at all times. Free. Viewing platform. Car parking.

Gorge woodland, semi-natural, dominated by oak and some coniferous plantation. Situated by the River Ayr. Historic sandstone steps and extensive network of well-maintained footpaths.

---

113 AYTON CASTLE 5 Q16

Ayton, Eyemouth, Berwickshire. 7 miles (11km) north of Berwick on A1. Nearest railway station Berwick. Open May–Sep, Sundays only 1400–1700. Other times by appointment. Charge £. Under 15s free. Guided tours. Explanatory displays. WC. Wheelchair access with assistance. Disabled WC. Car and coach parking. Telephone (01890) 781212.

Historic castle, built in 1846 and an important example of the Victorian architectural tradition. Ayton Castle has been restored in recent years and is lived in as a family home.

---

114 BACHELORS' CLUB 4 J17

NTS. Sandgate Street, Tarbolton, South Ayrshire. A77 south of Kilmarnock and off A76 at Mauchline. Bus from Ayr. Open Apr–Sep, daily 1330–1730, weekends in Oct 1330–1730. Charge £. Children free. Group concessions. Explanatory displays. Limited wheelchair access. Car parking. Telephone (01292) 541940.

Robert Burns and his friends founded a debating society here in 1780. Period furnishings.

---

115 BADBEA OLD VILLAGE 3 M4

Caithness. North of Ousdale on A9. Footpath leads from the lay-by to groups of ruined crofthouses perched above cliffs.

Tenants evicted from inland straths during the infamous Clearances founded this lonely settlement. The site is very exposed – tradition has it that children and livestock had to be tethered to prevent them being blown over the cliffs. Many of the inhabitants emigrated to America or New Zealand, as the monument, erected in 1911, testifies.

---

116 SIR DOUGLAS BADER DISABLED GARDEN 5 N13

Duffus Park, Carslogie Road, Cupar, Fife. In Cupar at junction of A913. Nearest railway station Cupar, on local bus route. Open daily all year, summer months 0800–2000, winter 0800–1630. Free. Picnic site. Wheelchair access. Disabled WC. Car parking. Telephone (01334) 412820.

The Sir Douglas Bader Garden was opened in 1982 and was designed specifically for disabled visitors. There is a small public garden with raised flower borders, raised ponds, an aviary and a shelter with picnic facilities.

---

117 BAILLE AN OR, GOLDRUSH TOWN 1869 3 L4

Sutherland. 4 miles (6.5km) north west of Helmsdale, on A897 Strath of Kildonan road.

Gold panning still takes place and you can get all the necessary equipment from the craft shop in Helmsdale.

118 BALBIRNIE CRAFT CENTRE 6 N14

Balbirnie Park, Markinch, Fife. On eastern outskirts of Glenrothes in Markinch. Nearest railway station Markinch, bus service from Glenrothes. Open all year, Mon–Sat 1000–1700, Sun 1400–1700. Individual workshop times may vary. Park open all year round. Free. Guided tours by appointment. Gift shop. Restaurant and WC in park. Limited wheelchair access. Car and coach parking. Telephone (01592) 753743.

Independently owned craft workshops producing leather goods, wrought ironwork, paintings and prints, gold and silver jewellery and glass blowing. The craft centre is located in the centre of Balbirnie park with woodland walks, specimen trees and rhododendrons. Bronze Age stone circle, golf course, picnic area and children's play area.

---

119 BALFOUR CASTLE 1 C10

Shapinsay Island, Orkney. 25 minute car ferry journey from Kirkwall. Open all year for resident guests, May–Sep for guided tours Wed only, 1415 from Kirkwall (buy tickets from tourist information office). Charge £££. Guided tours. Gift shop. Picnic area. Garden. WC. No guide dogs. Car and coach parking. Telephone (01856) 711282.

Personally guided tours by member of family of this Victorian castle with original furnishings and 3 acre (1.2ha) walled garden. One of the tour highlights is a traditional Orkney tea with home produce from the island, inclusive in tour price.

---

120 BALLINDALLOCH CASTLE 3 N8

Near Aberlour, Banffshire. On the A95, 13 miles (20km) northeast of Grantown-on-Spey. Open Easter–Sep, daily 1000–1700. Charge £££. Children under 6 free. Grounds only, £. Group concessions. Explanatory displays in French, German, Italian and Spanish. Gift shop. Tearoom and picnic area. WC. Limited wheelchair access. Disabled WC. Car and coach parking. Telephone (01807) 500205.

One of the few privately owned castles to be lived in continuously by its original family, the Macpherson-Grants, since 1546. Ballindalloch exemplifies the transition from the stark tower house, necessary for survival in 16th-century Scotland, to the elegant and comfortable country house so beloved of Victorians in the Highlands. Ballindalloch is also the home of the famous Aberdeen Angus herd of cattle founded by Sir George Macpherson-Grant in 1860, and now the oldest herd in continuous existence.

---

121 BALLYGOWAN CUP AND RING MARKS 4 F14

HS. Kilmartin Glen. 1 mile (2km) southwest of Kilmartin, near Poltalloch, Argyll. Nearest railway station Oban, then bus to Kilmartin. Access at all times. Free. Telephone 0131 668 8800.

Bronze Age cup and ring marks on natural rock faces.

---

122 BALMACARA ESTATE AND LOCHALSH WOODLAND GARDEN 2 F8

NTS. Lochalsh House, Balmacara, Ross and Cromarty. On A87, 3 miles (4.8km) east of Kyle of Lochalsh. By bus from Inverness and Glasgow. Open all year, daily 0900–sunset; information kiosk (unstaffed) open Apr–Sep, daily 0900–1700. Charge £. Honesty box. Explanatory displays. Car parking. Telephone (01599) 566325.

A beautiful Highland estate where traditional crofting is still carried out. Includes the village of Plockton, an outstanding conservation area and location for the television series Hamish Macbeth. The garden provides sheltered lochside walks among pine, ferns, fuchsias, hydrangeas and rhododendrons.

123 BALMICHAEL VISITOR CENTRE 4 G17

Shiskine, Isle of Arran. 7 miles (11km) from Brodick on B880. Bus service from Blackwaterfoot or Brodick. Open Apr–Oct, Mon–Sat 1000–1700, Sun 1200–1700; Nov–Mar, Wed–Sat 1000–1700, Sun 1200–1700. Free. Charge for activities. Group concessions. Gift shop. Tearoom and picnic area. WC. Wheelchair access. Disabled WC. Car and coach parking. Telephone (01770) 860430.

Converted farm buildings and courtyard including three craft shops, working pottery, antique and tapestry shops. Adventure playground and indoor play barn. Quad biking for all ages. Heritage area with working mill wheel.

---

124 BALMORAL CASTLE 3 N10

Balmoral, Ballater, Aberdeenshire. 8 miles (13km) west of Ballater off A93. Nearest railway station Aberdeen, bus service from Aberdeen to Ballater (some buses to Braemar) stop at Crathie for Balmoral. Open daily mid Apr–Jul, 1000–1700. Charge ££. Explanatory displays. Gift shop. Café. WC. Wheelchair access. Disabled WC. Car and coach parking. Telephone (01339) 742334.

The Highland holiday home of the Royal Family since 1852. Queen Victoria visited the earlier castle in 1848 and Prince Albert bought the estate in 1852. The new castle was designed by Prince Albert and William Smith of Aberdeen and was completed in 1855. Exhibition of paintings, works of art and royal tartans in the Castle Ballroom. Wildlife, travel and carriage exhibition in the carriage hall. Grounds and garden with country walks. Pony trekking and pony cart rides. Wheelchairs available free of charge from estates office.

---

125 BALNAIN HOUSE 3 K8

40 Huntly Street, Inverness. On the banks of the River Ness, 5 minutes walk from the town centre. 5 minutes walk from Inverness railway and bus stations. Open Jul and Aug, Mon–Fri 1000–2200, Sat and Sun 1000–1800; Sep–Jun, Mon–Sat 1000–1700. Charge £. Group concessions. Explanatory displays. Gift shop. Licensed café bar. Garden. WC. Limited wheelchair access. Disabled WC. Telephone (01463) 715757.

This beautiful Georgian building by the River Ness contains a superb audio-visual exhibition charting Scotland's music from pre-history to present times. Visitors can play the clarsach, fiddle and Highland bagpipe. Balnain House also holds ceilidhs with some of the top names in traditional music.

---

126 BALNAKEIL CRAFT VILLAGE 3 J2

Balnakeil, Durness, Sutherland. 1 mile (1.5km) west of Durness, off the single track road to Balnakeil Bay. Nearest railway station Lairg, post bus from Lairg to Durness. Bookshop open all year; Easter–Oct, Tue–Thu 1000–1730, Fri–Mon 1000–2030; Nov–Easter, Wed, Thu 1000–1700, Fri–Sun 1000–2030. Craft shops open Easter or May–Oct. Free. Licensed restaurant. Baby changing facilities. WC. Wheelchair access. Disabled WC. Car and coach parking. Telephone (01971) 511277 or (01971) 511777 for bookshop.

Craft village including print and painting galleries, embroidery, weaving, spinning and feltwork, enamelwork, basketry and leatherwork, woodwork, stonemason and bookshop. The bookshop stocks a wide range of general titles and features a restaurant serving everything from a pot of tea to a three-course dinner. Theme nights, occasional live music and other events.

---

127 BALUACHRAIG CUP AND RING 4 F14

HS. Kilmartin Glen. 1 mile (2km) south southeast of Kilmartin, Argyll. Nearest railway station Oban, then bus to Kilmartin. Access at all times. Free. Telephone 0131 668 8800.

Several groups of Bronze Age cup and ring marks on natural rock faces.

128 BALVAIRD CASTLE 5 M14

HS. About 6 miles (9.5km) southeast of Bridge of Earn, Perthshire. Nearest railway station Perth, bus from Perth to Glenfarg. Limited opening; confirm by telephone. Charge £. Limited wheelchair access. Car and coach parking. Telephone (01786) 450000.

A late 15th-century tower on an L-plan, extended in 1581 by the addition of a walled courtyard and gatehouse. Refined architectural details.

---

129 BALVENIE CASTLE 3 N8

HS. Dufftown, Banffshire. At Dufftown on the A941, 16 miles (25.5km) south southeast of Elgin. Nearest railway stations Elgin or Keith, then bus to Dufftown. Open Apr–Sep, daily 0930–1830. Charge £. Group concessions. Gift shop. Picnic area. WC. Limited wheelchair access. Car parking. Telephone (01340) 820121.

Picturesque ruins of a 13th-century moated stronghold originally owned by the Comyns. Additions in the 15th and 16th centuries. Visited by Edward I in 1304 and Mary, Queen of Scots in 1562. Occupied by Cumberland in 1746.

---

130 BANCHORY MUSEUM 3 Q10

Bridge Street, Banchory. In the centre of Banchory. Car and coach parking nearby. Bus service from Aberdeen. Open Jun–Sep, Mon–Sat 1000–1300 and 1400–1730, Sun 1400–1800; Easter–May and Oct, telephone for details. Closed Nov–Easter. Free. Guided tours. Explanatory displays. Gift shop. Wheelchair access. Telephone (01771) 622906.

Features the life of Banchory-born musician and composer J. Scott Skinner, the 'Strathspey King', royal commemorative china, 19th-century tartans, Deeside natural history.

---

131 BANFF MUSEUM 3 P7

High Street, Banff. In the centre of Banff. Car and coach parking nearby. Bus service from Aberdeen. Open Jun–Sep, Fri–Wed 1400–1715. Free. Guided tours. Explanatory displays. Gift shop. Limited wheelchair access. Telephone (01771) 622906.

One of Scotland's oldest museums, founded in 1828. Feature electrotype copy of the Deskford Carnyx, a unique 2000-year-old Iron Age war trumpet, award-winning natural history display, local geology, nationally-important collections of Banff silver, arms and armour.

---

132 BANNOCKBURN HERITAGE CENTRE 6 L14

NTS. Glasgow Road, Stirling. 2 miles (3.2km) south of Stirling, off M80/M9 at junction 9. By bus from Stirling. Open daily, Mar and Nov–Christmas 1100–1630; Apr–Oct 1000–1730. Charge £. Children free. Group concessions. Explanatory displays, audio-visual programme and guidebook in French and German. Gift shop. Café. WC. Induction loop system, Braille guidebook. Wheelchair access, wheelchair available. Disabled WC. Car and coach parking. Telephone (01786) 812664.

Site of the famous battle in 1314 when Robert the Bruce, King of Scots, defeated the English army of Edward II. Colourful exhibition with life-size figures of Bruce and William Wallace, heraldic flags. Equestrian statue of Bruce outside.

---

133 BARCALDINE CASTLE 4 G12

Ledaig, Oban, Argyll. 9 miles (14.5km) north of Oban off A85. Open May–Sep, daily 1100–1730; Jun, Sep closed Sat. To visit at other times, please telephone. Charge ££. Group concessions. Explanatory displays (in English, French, German and Italian). Souvenirs available for purchase. Tearoom. Garden with toys. B&B accommodation. WC. No guide dogs. Car parking. Telephone (01631) 720598.

The oldest intact castle on the Argyll mainland open to the public. Family home of the Campbells of Barcaldine and last of Black Duncan's seven castles remining in Campbell hands. Historically associated with the massacre of Glencoe and the Appin Murder. Explore secret passages, view the bottle dungeon. Unique and haunted.

---

134 BAR HILL FORT **6 K15**

HS. 0.5 mile (1km) east of Twechar, Stirlingshire (signposted from the village). Nearest railway station Glasgow, bus from Glasgow (Buchanan Street). Access at all times. Free.

The highest on the line of the Antonine Wall, containing the foundations of the headquarters building and bath-house. A small Iron Age fort lies to the east. See also 62 Antonine Wall.

---

135 BARHOLM MAINS OPEN FARM **4 J20**

Barholm Mains, Creetown. Off A75, 0.25 mile (.5km) west of Creetown and 5.5 miles (9km) from Newton Stewart. Local bus service. Open May–Sep, daily 1030–1600. Charge £. Group concessions. Explanatory displays. Gift shop. Ice-cream and cold drinks available, picnic area. WC. Wheelchair access. Car and coach parking. Telephone (01671) 820346.

An all-weather attraction, Barholm Mains is a working farm. Visitors can see, feed and touch all types of farm animals including rare breeds and exotic animals.

---

136 BARNALINE WALKS **4 G13**

Dalavich, on an unclassified road along west shore of Loch Awe. Access at all times. Free. Car parking.

Three walks starting from Barnaline car park and picnic site, taking in Dalavich Oakwood Forest Nature Reserve (an interpretive trail with old stable information point), Avich Falls and Loch Avich. Panoramic views of Loch Awe.

---

137 BARN GALLERY **2 E4**

2 Eagleton, Lower Bayble (Pabail Iarach), Isle of Lewis. 6 miles (10km) from Stornoway on the Eye Peninsular. Coach parking by arrangement. Infrequent bus service from Stornoway. Open all year, Mon–Sat; visitors welcome any time (telephone to confirm). Free. Explanatory displays. Spanish spoken. Wheelchair access with assistance. Car parking. Telephone (01851) 870704.

A small gallery displaying the original work of four artists, in watercolour, oil, pastel, acrylic and liquid wax.

---

138 BARNYARD STUDIOS, GALLERY AND TEAROOM **3 N7**

Garmouth, Fochabers, Moray. On B9015, 4.5 miles (7km) northwest of Fochabers (signposted on the A96 at Mosstodloch). Bus from Elgin and on long distance Aberdeen–Inverness cycle route. Open mid Jun–mid Sep, Wed–Mon 1300–1600; mid Sep–mid Jun, Sat and Sun 1300–1600 (closed Christmas and New Year). Telephone to confirm opening. Free. Gift shop. Tearoom and picnic area. Dog tethering hooks, pond and woodland walks. WC. Limited wheelchair access. Disabled WC. Car and coach parking. Telephone (01343) 870599.

Located in a beautiful rural setting, the gallery displays local art and design, including textiles, painting, pottery, jewellery, stained glass, collector bears and furniture.

---

139 BAROCHAN CROSS **6 J16**

HS. In Paisley Abbey, in the centre of Paisley. Nearest railway station Paisley Gilmour Street. For access see 1159 Paisley Abbey. Free. Telephone 0131 668 8800.

A fine free-standing Celtic cross that formerly stood in Houston parish, west of Paisley.

140 BARRA HERITAGE AND CULTURAL CENTRE **2 A10**

Dualchas, Castlebay, Isle of Barra. 0.3 mile (0.5km) west of Castlebay pier. Bus service from Castlebay. Open Apr–Sep, Mon–Fri 1100–1700. Charge £. Explanatory displays. Gift shop. Tearoom. WC. Wheelchair access. Disabled WC. Car and coach parking. Telephone (01871) 810413.

Also known as Dualchas. Local history exhibition in Gaelic and English in a high tech environment. Art exhibitions. Local artefacts and old photographs. The centre also runs an attraction known as the Dubharaidlt Thatched Cottage Museum. This is a restored house in a magnificent secluded location only ten minutes walk from Craigston village which is 3 miles (5km) northwest of Castlebay. No cars. Charge £.

---

141 BARRIE'S BIRTHPLACE AND CAMERA OBSCURA **5 N12**

NTS. 9 Brechin Road, Kirriemuir, Angus. On A90/A926 in Kirriemuir, 6 miles (10km) northwest of Forfar. By bus from Dundee. Open Apr–Sep, Mon–Sat 1100–1730, Sun 1330–1730; Oct, Sat 1100–1730, Sun 1330–1730. Charge £. Children free. Charge for Camera Obscura £. Group concessions. Explanatory displays (information in Dutch, German, French, Italian, Spanish, Swedish and Japanese). Tearoom. WC. Induction loop, Braille information sheets. Limited wheelchair access. Car and coach parking. Telephone (01575) 572646.

Birthplace of J. M. Barrie, creator of Peter Pan. Exhibition about his work, with his first theatre – an outside washhouse – also on display. Camera Obscura: within the cricket pavillion on Kirrie Hill, presented to Kirriemuir by the author.

---

142 BARRY MILL **5 P13**

NTS. Barry, Carnoustie, Angus. North of Barry village between A92 and A930, 2 miles (3km) west of Carnoustie. By bus from Dundee or Arbroath (stop in Barry 0.5 mile from the Mill). Open Apr–Sep, daily 1100–1700; weekends in Oct. Charge £. Children free. Group concessions. Guided tours. Explanatory displays. Picnic area. Waymarked walks. WC. Wheelchair access. Disabled WC. Car and coach parking. Telephone (01241) 856761.

A working 19th-century meal mill. Full demonstrations on weekend afternoons and by prior arrangement. Attractive country walk to mill lade.

---

143 BARSALLOCH FORT **4 J21**

HS. off A747, 7.5 miles (12km) west northwest of Whithorn, Wigtownshire. Nearest railway station Stranraer, bus from Stranraer or Newton Stewart to Whithorn. Above Barsalloch Point, 0.75 mile (1km) west of Monreith. Telephone 0131 668 8800.

Remains of an Iron Age hill fort on the edge of a raised beach bluff. Defended by a deep ditch in horseshoe form.

---

144 BASS ROCK **5 P15**

Off North Berwick. Boat trips from North Berwick go round the Bass Rock. Telephone (01620) 892838 (boat trips) or (01620) 892197 (tourist information centre). Car parking.

A massive 350-feet (106.5m) high rock whose many thousands of raucous seabirds include the third largest gannetry in the world.

---

145 BAXTERS VISITOR CENTRE **3 N7**

Fochabers, Moray. 1 mile (1.5km) west of Fochabers on the A96. Nearest railway stations Keith and Elgin. Local bus service. Open daily Apr–Oct, 0900–1800, Nov–Mar, 1000–1700. Free. Explanatory displays and audio-visual presentation, cooking demonstrations. Gift shop. Restaurant. WC. Wheelchair access (visitor centre only). Disabled WC. Car and coach parking. Telephone (01343) 820666.

The story of the Baxter family began in 1868. George Baxter, their founder, opened a small grocery shop in Fochabers. The fame of their products spread and their reputation was firmly established. See the Baxters Story and cookery demonstrations in the visitor centre, then browse through a range of shops and restaurants.

---

146 BEAULY PRIORY **3 J8**

HS. The Square, Beauly, Inverness-shire. On A9 in Beauly, 12 miles (19km) west of Inverness. Nearest railway and bus station Inverness, bus to Beauly. Telephone 0131 668 8800 to confirm opening times. Charge £. Group concessions. Guided tours. Gift shop. WC. Limited wheelchair access. Car and coach parking. Telephone (01463) 782141.

Ruins of a Valliscaulian priory founded in about 1230, although much of the building was later reconstructed. Notable windows and window-arcading.

---

147 BEECRAIGS COUNTRY PARK **6 L15**

The Park Centre, Linlithgow, West Lothian. 2 miles (3km) south of Linlithgow. Nearest railway station Linlithgow. Open all year, daily. Park centre closes only for Christmas and New Year. Free. Guided tours. Explanatory displays. Gift shop. Restaurant and refreshments. WC. Braille map of park. Wheelchair access to park centre. Disabled WC. Car and coach parking. Telephone (01506) 844516.

Nestled high in the Bathgate hills, Beecraigs offers a wide range of leisure and recreational pursuits within its 370 hectares. Archery, orienteering, fly-fishing, walks and trails. Trim course, play area, all-terrain bicycle trail, picnic areas, barbecue sites, fish farm, horse route, deer farm, caravan and camping site. Ranger service.

---

148 BEINN EIGHE NATIONAL NATURE RESERVE **2 G7**

South of Loch Maree near Kinlochewe, Ross and Cromarty. No dogs allowed in the reserve.

The first National Nature Reserve in Britain, acquired primarily to protect an important remnant of Scotland's ancient pinewood. Red deer, roe deer, pinemarten and wildcat all inhabit this area. Golden eagle, buzzard and other birds of prey may occasionally be seen. The mountain slopes of Beinn Eighe are also of great geological and botanical interest. Woodland and mountain trail.

---

149 BELLA JANE BOAT TRIPS **2 E9**

Elgol, by Broadford, Isle of Skye. 15 miles (24km) from Broadford on B8083. Post bus from Broadford twice a day, Mon–Fri. Sailings Apr–mid Oct daily. Nov–Mar by arrangement. Booking essential, telephone between 0730–1000 or 1930–2200. Charge £££. Group concessions. Guided tours. Refreshments on trip. WC. Limited wheelchair access. Car and coach parking. Telephone (01471) 866244.

Bella Jane run a three-hour trip from Elgol which sails to Loch Coruisk in the Cuillin Mountains, pausing to see a seal colony then landing ashore. Hot drinks and shortbread on the return journey. Knowledgeable skipper and crew. Award winning. Also day excursions to Isle of Rum National Nature Reserve.

---

150 BELL'S CHERRYBANK GARDENS **5 M13**

Cherrybank, Perth. On western outskirts of Perth. Open Easter–Sep, daily 0900–1700. Charge £. Group concessions. Guided tours. Explanatory displays. Gift shop. Tearoom. WC. Wheelchair access. Disabled WC. Car and coach parking.

The gardens contain the Bell's National Heather Collection. This is the largest collection in the UK and has over 900 varieties from all over the world, with plants flowering every month of the year. Other features include a dovecot, aviary, play area and putting green, mosaic, sundial, acoustic pool, hidden pool, pond, the Rocky Island, natural burn, sculpture collection, and a fountain.

---

151 BEN AIGAN CYCLE TRAILS **3 N8**

FE. Moray Forest District Office, Balnacoul, Fochabers, Moray. Off A95, 1.5 miles (2km) south of Mulben to eastern end; or from north of Craigellachie, follow the Speyside Way via Arndilly to western end. Open all year except when timber harvesting – contact District Office. Free. Leaflet available. Car parking. Telephone (01343) 820223.

Two forest mountain bike trails giving excellent views over the winding River Spey. Colour-coded routes: the red trail of 4.5 miles (7km) follows part of the Speyside Way, the blue trail of 6 miles (10km) covers demanding terrain.

---

152 BEN LAWERS **5 K12**

NTS. Off A827, 6 miles (9.5km) northeast of Killin. Office at Lynedoch, Main Street, Killin, Perthshire. Visitor centre open Apr–Sep, daily 1000–1700. Charge for audio-visual programme £ (honesty box). Explanatory displays, special audio-visual programme for children. Guided walks by rangers, nature trails. WC. Induction loop. Wheelchair access to visitor centre. Disabled WC. Car and coach parking. Telephone (01567) 820397.

Perthshire's highest mountain (3984 feet/1214m) with views from the Atlantic to the North Sea. Noted for the rich variety of mountain plants and the bird population – birds include raven, ring-ouzel, red grouse, ptarmigan, dipper and curlew. Nature trail. Extensive information on site at the visitor centre. Ranger service.

---

153 BEN LOMOND **4 J14**

NTS. Ardess Lodge, Rowardennan, by Drymen, Stirlingshire. By B837, 11 miles (17.5km) beyond Drymen off A811. By bus from Glasgow to Drymen, then to Balmaha. Open all year. Free. Explanatory displays. Guided walks by rangers. WC. Car and coach parking. Telephone (01360) 870224.

Rising from the east shore of Loch Lomond to 3194 feet (973.5m), the mountain offers exhilarating walking and spectacular views. It is part of the Ben Lomond National Memorial Park commemorating war dead.

---

154 BENNACHIE CENTRE **3 Q9**

Esson's Car Park, Chapel of Garioch, Inverurie. Nearest bus and railway stations Inverurie. Open Apr–Sep, Tue–Sun 1030–1700; Oct–Mar, Tue–Sun 1000–1630. Free. Explanatory displays and leaflets. Gift shop. Refreshments available. WC. Wheelchair access. Disabled WC. Car and coach parking. Telephone (01467) 681470.

The centre describes the local social and natural history through visual displays, CD-Rom presentations and video. A wide range of activities take place throughout the year, including guided walks, bat and bird box building, fungal forays and classes for beginners on painting, bodging, drystone dyke building and other countryside skills.

---

155 BEN NEVIS **2 H11**

2 miles (3km) from Fort William.

Britain's highest (4406 feet/1344m) and most popular mountain for both rock climber and hill walker. It is best seen from the north approach to Fort William, or from the Gairlochy Road, across the Caledonian Canal (see 258).

---

156 BEN NEVIS DISTILLERY VISITOR CENTRE **2 H11**

Lochy Bridge, Fort William. On the A82, 2 miles (3km) north of Fort William. Nearest railway station Fort William, bus from Fort William.

Open all year Mon–Fri 0900–1700, Sat 1000–1600; Jul and Aug closes at 1900, also open Sun 1200–1600. Charge £. Admission refunded upon whisky purchase. Guided tours (leaflets in French, German and Italian). Explanatory displays. Gift shop. Tearoom. WC. Guide dogs welcome in visitor centre. Limited wheelchair access. Disabled WC. Car and coach parking. Telephone (01397) 702476.

Visitors can tour distillery and taste the famous whisky, the Dew of Ben Nevis. Exhibition and video programme.

---

157 BEN NEVIS WOOLLEN MILL **2 H11**

Belford Road, Fort William, Inverness-shire. 0.5 mile (1km) outside Fort William town centre at entrance to Glen Nevis. Railway station in town centre, regular bus service. Apr–Oct, daily 0900–1730; Nov–Mar, daily 1000–1600. Free. Gift shop. Restaurant. WC. Wheelchair access. Disabled WC. Car and coach parking. Telephone (01397) 704244.

At the end of the West Highland Way, Ben Nevis Woollen Mill stocks fleeces, waterproofs and accessories. Also knitwear, tweeds and Scottish gifts.

---

158 BENNIE MUSEUM **6 L15**

9-11 Mansefield Street, Bathgate, West Lothian. 3 miles (5km) east of Livingston off M8. Nearest railway station Bathgate. Bus service from Edinburgh. Open Apr–Sep, Mon–Sat 1000–1600; Oct–Mar, Mon–Sat 1100–1530. Closed Christmas and New Year. Free. Guided tours on request. Gift shop. WC. Limited wheelchair access. Disabled WC. Car parking. Telephone (01506) 634944.

Local heritage museum with almost 5000 artefacts illustrating the social, industrial, religious and military history of Bathgate, a former burgh town. Displays of postcards and photographs from the 1890s onwards. Fossils, Roman glass and coins, relics from Prince Charles Edward Stuart and the Napoleonic Wars.

---

159 BEN ROMACH DISTILLERY **3 M7**

Invererne Road, Forres. Off A96, 0.33 mile (0.5km) on north side of Forres bypass. Nearest railway station Forres. Open Apr–Sep, Mon–Sat 0930–1700, also Jun–Aug, Sun 0930–1600; Oct–Mar, Mon–Fri 1000–1600. Charge £. Group concessions. Guided tours (available in French and German). Explanatory displays. Picnic area. WC. Limited wheelchair access. Disabled WC. Car and coach parking. Telephone (01343) 545111.

Benromach distillery and malt whisky centre is Moray's smallest distillery, re-opened by Prince Charles in 1998. The attractive wood panelled malt whisky centre, sited in the former drier house, describes 100 years of history and tradition in whisky making.

---

160 BERNERA MUSEUM **2 F9**

Bernera, Lewis. On B8059, 2 miles (3km) from Bernera Bridge. Bus on request to local operator (01851) 612224/350. Open May–Sep, Mon–Sat 1100–1700. Charge £. Group concessions. Explanatory displays. Gift shop. Café. WC. No guide dogs. Wheelchair access. Disabled WC. Car and coach parking. Telephone (01851) 612331.

Opened in 1995 as part of a community centre, the museum displays information on genealogy, archaeology and historical sites, also archives, old photographs and a lobster fishing exhibition in summer.

---

161 BIBLICAL GARDEN **3 M7**

King Street, Elgin, Moray. At Cooper Park in Elgin by the cathedral. Nearest railway station Elgin, then bus. 5 minute walk from bus station. Open daily, May–Sep 1000–1930. Free. Explanatory displays. Wheelchair access. Car and coach parking.

A 3 acre (1.2ha) garden created using the Bible as a reference. A desert area depicts Mount Sinai and the cave of resurrection and there is an area of marsh contained with the garden. An impressive central walkway is laid in the shape of a Celtic cross. Planted with every species of plant mentioned in the Bible. Also life-size statues depicting various parables.

---

162 BIG BURN WALK **3 L5**

Start point of walk in Golspie, Sutherland.

One of the finest woodland walks in Sutherland. The extensive and well-maintained paths cross the burn by a series of bridges and allow access up to a waterfall.

---

163 BIGGAR GASWORKS MUSEUM **5 M17**

HS. On the A702 in Biggar, Lanarkshire. Nearest railway station Lanark, bus from Lanark and Edinburgh. Open daily, Jun–Sep 1400–1700. Charge £. Group concessions. Guided tours. Explanatory displays. Picnic area. Wheelchair access with assistance. Car parking. Telephone (01899) 221050.

Typical of a small town coal-gas works, the only surviving example in Scotland (dates from 1839). Managed by the Biggar Museum Trust.

---

164 BIGGAR KIRK **5 M17**

The Manse, High Street, Biggar, Lanarkshire. In the centre of Biggar, 28 miles (45km) southwest of Edinburgh, 12 miles (19km) east of M74 junction 13. Nearest railway station Lanark, bus service from Lanark and Edinburgh. Open daily during summer months. Free. Explanatory displays. Induction loop for church services. Car parking. Telephone (01899) 221050.

Cruciform 16th-century church with fine examples of modern stained glass.

---

165 BIG IDEA **6 H17**

Irvine Harbourside, Irvine, Ayrshire. Nearest railway station Irvine, then 1 mile (1.5km) walk. Open all year, daily 1000–1800 (closed Christmas Day). Charge £££. Guided tours (available in French, German and Spanish). Explanatory displays. Café. WC. Induction loop in auditorium. Wheelchair access. Disabled WC. Car and coach parking. Telephone (01294) 461999.

The world's first centre devoted to invention and discovery. Take a mind-blowing journey through the history of inventions with over 30,000 square feet (9144 square metres) of attractions to explore. Experience a ride through the history of explosions, interact with exhibits through unique technology and construct inventions in the inventors workshop.

---

166 BIRCH HOUSE HERBS **3 J8**

Tigh Bea, Kiltarlity, Inverness-shire. 12 miles (19km) west of Inverness on A862, then A833. Nearest railway station Inverness; local bus service from Inverness stops 0.5 miles (1km) away. Open May–Sep, Mon–Thu 1000–1700, usually Fri–Sun but telephone to confirm. Optional charity box for garden. Gift shop. Wheelchair access with assistance. Car parking. Telephone (01463) 741425.

A small family-run nursery set within a developing garden, specialising in herbs, wild flowers and native trees. The garden consists of an informal herb garden, various areas of formal beds, ponds and wild gardening. There is also a potager style vegetable garden. The whole garden is developed with wildlife in mind and non-chemical sprays or weedkillers are used. Advice is freely given on all aspects of wildlife gardening. See also 789 Stephen Hayward Woodcarving.

167 BIRKHILL FIRECLAY MINE **6 L15**

c/o Bo'ness Development Trust, 17–19 North Street, Bo'ness, West Lothian. 3 miles (5km) west of Bo'ness. Accessed by the Bo'ness and Kinneil Railway, no bus service. Open Jul and Aug, daily except Mon; Apr, May, Jun, Sep and Oct weekends only. Charge £. Joint ticket with Bo'ness and Kinneil Railway available. Group concessions. Guided tours. Explanatory displays. Picnic area. WC. No guide dogs. Car parking. Telephone (01506) 825855.

The caverns of Birkhill Fireclay Mine are set in the picturesque Avon Gorge. A mine guide takes visitors on a tour of the mine workings where you can discover how fireclay was mined. There are also fossils which are over 300 million years old. The mine can only be reached by descending 130 steps into the Avon Gorge so access for the disabled and elderly is difficult. See also 188 Bo'ness and Kinneil Railway.

---

168 BISHOP'S AND EARL'S PALACES **1 B10**

HS. Watergate, Kirkwall, Orkney. In Kirkwall. Open Apr–Oct, daily 0930–1830. Charge £. Group concessions. Guided tours. Explanatory displays. Gift shop. Telephone (01856) 875461.

The Bishop's Palace is a 12th-century hall house, later much altered with a round tower built by Bishop Reid 1541–8. A later addition was made by the notorious Patrick Stewart, Earl of Orkney, who built the adjacent Earl's Palace in 1600-7 in a splendid Renaissance style.

---

169 BLACKFRIARS CHAPEL **5 P13**

HS. In South Street, St Andrews, Fife. Nearest railway station Leuchars 4 miles (6.5km), connecting bus to St Andrews. Buses from Dundee and Edinburgh. Access at all times. Free. Telephone 0131 668 8800.

The vaulted side apse of a church of Dominican friars. Rebuilt about 1516.

---

170 BLACKHALL ROMAN CAMPS **5 L14**

HS. Ardoch. 0.5 mile (1km) north of Braco, Perthshire. Nearest railway station Dunblane, bus from Dunblane to Braco (ask driver for Ardoch Roman Fort). Access at all times. Free. Telephone 0131 668 8800.

Parts of the defences of two Roman marching camps, probably dating from the early third century AD.

---

171 BLACKHAMMER CAIRN **1 B10**

HS. North of the B9064 on the south coast of the island of Rousay, Orkney. Bus from Kirkwall to Tingwall then ferry to Rousay. Access all year. Free. Telephone 0131 668 8800.

A long Neolithic cairn bounded by a retaining wall with a megalithic burial chamber divided into seven compartments.

---

172 BLACK HILL **6 L17**

NTS. South Lanarkshire. Off B7018 between Kirkfieldbank and Lesmahagow, 3 miles (5km) west of Lanark. Open all year. Free. Explanatory displays.

This is the site of a Bronze Age burial cairn, Iron Age hill fort, and outlook point over the Clyde Valley.

---

173 BLACK HOUSE **2 D3**

HS. 42 Arnol, Barvas, Isle of Lewis. At Arnol, on the A858. 15 miles (24km) northwest of Stornoway. Ferry from Ullapool to Stornoway, bus from Stornoway. Open Apr–Sep, Mon–Sat 0930–1830; Oct–Mar, Mon–Thu and Sat 0930–1630. Charge £. Group concessions. Guided tours. Explanatory displays. Gift shop. WC. Limited wheelchair access. Car and coach parking. Telephone (01851) 710395.

A traditional Hebridean thatched house with byre, attached barn and stackyard, complete and furnished.

174 BLACKNESS CASTLE 6 M15

HS. Blackness, West Lothian. On the B903, 4 miles (6.5km) northeast of Linlithgow, West Lothian. Nearest railway station Linlithgow, buses from Bo'ness and Linlithgow to Blackness. Open Apr–Sep, daily 0930–1830; Oct–Mar, Mon–Sat 0930–1630 (except Thu pm and Fri), Sun 1400–1630. Charge £. Group concessions. Explanatory displays. Gift shop. WC. Limited wheelchair access. Car parking. Telephone (01506) 834807.

A 15th-century stronghold, once one of the most important fortresses in Scotland and one of the four castles which the Articles of Union left fortified. A state prison in Covenanting times; a powder magazine in the 1870s. More recently, for a period, a youth hostel.

---

175 BLACKSHAW FARM PARK 6 H16

West Kilbride, Ayrshire. 2 miles (3km) east of West Kilbride on B781 (road to Dalry). Rail service to West Kilbride (2 miles/3km). Limited bus service to Farm Park. Free bus service on Wed and Sun from Irvine, Kilwinning, Stevenson, Saltcoats, Ardrossan. Open Mar–Sep, daily 1030–1700. Also open weekends and Mon during Oct and Oct school holidays. Charge ££. Children under 2 free. Group concessions. Guided tours on request. Explanatory displays. Gift shop. Tearoom and refreshments, picnic area. WC. Wheelchair access. Disabled WC. Car and coach parking. Telephone (01294) 823014.

Working farm with seasonal demonstrations. Large and small animals, tractor and trailer rides. Extensive indoor and outdoor play areas, grass sledging, four wheel all terrain motorbikes, nature trails, cup and ring stones of historic interest.

---

176 BLACKSMITHS SHOP, GRETNA GREEN

See 767 Gretna Green.

---

177 BLACK WATCH MONUMENT 5 L12

Taybridge Drive, Aberfeldy. In Aberfeldy, 10 miles (16km) west of A9 at Ballinluig. Nearest railway station Pitlochry, local bus service. Free. WC. Wheelchair access. Disabled WC. Car parking.

A cairn surmounted by a statue of Private Farquhar Shaw dressed in the original uniform of the Black Watch Regiment. The monument was unveiled in 1887 by the Marquess of Breadalbane to commemorate the first muster of the regiment in May 1740. The muster took place on the north bank of the Tay, in what is now part of the golf course.

---

178 BLACK WATCH REGIMENTAL MUSEUM 5 M13

Balhousie Castle, Hay Street, Perth. Entrance from Hay Street and North Inch. Public transport by summer city bus tour only. Open May–Sep, Mon–Sat (including public holidays) 1000–1630, (closed last Sat in Jun); Oct–Apr, Mon–Fri 1000–1530. Closed Dec 23–Jan 4 inclusive. Other times by appointment. Free. Explanatory displays and audio tour. Gift shop. WC. Car parking. Telephone 0131 310 8530.

Balhousie Castle houses the Regimental Headquarters and Museum of the Black Watch Regiment, describing its history from 1740 to the present day. Displays of silver, colours, uniforms and medals.

---

179 BLAIR ATHOL DISTILLERY 5 L12

Perth Road, Pitlochry, Perthshire. 1 mile (1.5km) south of Pitlochry town centre on A924. Pitlochry railway station 1.5 miles (2.5km), bus service. Open Easter–Sep, Mon–Sat 0900–1700, Sun 1200–1700, last tour 1600; Oct–Easter, Mon–Fri 0900–1700, last tour 1530; Nov–Feb restricted opening hours, telephone for appointment. Charge £. Group concessions by arrangement. Guided tours (German and French available for groups). Explanatory displays. Gift shop. Coffee shop (Easter–Sep). Banqueting suite available for private parties. WC. Limited wheelchair access. Disabled WC. Car and coach parking. Telephone (01796) 482003.

Established in 1798 in the popular Highland resort of Pitlochry, Blair Athol distillery is the home of Bell's 8 Year Old Extra Special, the biggest selling blended whisky in the UK. Exhibition.

---

180 BLAIR CASTLE **3 L11**

Blair Atholl, Pitlochry, Perthshire. 7 miles (11km) north of Pitlochry off A9. Railway station 874 yards (800m), bus stop 765 yards (700m). Open 1 Apr or Easter (whichever is earlier) to last Friday in Oct, daily 1000–1800, last entry at 1700. Charge £££. Group concessions. Guided tours for groups. Explanatory displays. Gift shop. Licenced restaurant, tearoom and picnic areas. Children's play area. WC. Limited wheelchair access. Disabled WC. Car and coach parking. Telephone (01796) 481207.

A white turreted baronial castle, the traditional seat of the Dukes and Earls of Atholl. The oldest part, Cumming's Tower, dates back to 1269. Visited by Mary, Queen of Scots, Prince Charles Edward Stewart and Queen Victoria. The last castle in Britain to be besieged (1746). The present Duke of Atholl maintains the only private army in Europe – the Atholl Highlanders. Fine collections of furniture, portraits, lace, china, arms, armour, Jacobite relics and Masonic regalia. Deer park, pony trekking, caravan park, woodland, riverside and mountain walks. Admission to grounds allows access to the 18th-century walled garden restoration project.

---

181 BLAIR DRUMMOND SAFARI AND LEISURE PARK **5 K14**

Blair Drummond, Stirling. 4 miles (6.5km) towards Doune on A84, take junction 10 off M9. Nearest railway and bus stations Stirling. There is transport around the park for visitors without vehicles. Open Apr–Oct, daily 1000–1730, last admission 1630. Charge £££. Children under 3 free. Group concessions. Explanatory displays. Gift shop. Restaurant, bar, picnic and barbeque areas. WC. Wheelchair access. Disabled WC. Car and coach parking. Telephone (01786) 841456.

Drive through wild animal reserves, boat safari around chimpanzee island, pets' farm, adventure playground. Giant astra-glide and flying-fox cable slide across lake. Five-seater pedal boats. Amusement arcade, bouncy castle, dodgem cars.

---

182 BLAIRQUHAN **4 J18**

Blairquhan Estate Office, Maybole, Ayrshire. 14 miles (22.5km) south of Ayr. Bus service from Maybole (7 miles/11km) and Ayr. Open mid Jul–mid Aug, daily (except Mon) 1400–1730, telephone to check dates. Gardens open 1400–1800. Charge £. Guided tours (French available). Explanatory displays. Gift shop. Tearoom. Garden. WC. Wheelchair access with assistance. Disabled WC. Car and coach parking. Telephone (01655) 770239.

Four families have lived at Blairquhan. The first tower-house was built in 1346. The new house was designed by Scottish architect William Burn between 1821 and 1824. Walled garden with original glasshouse. Pinetum. Sir James Hunter Blair's Collection of Scottish Colourists.

---

183 BOATH DOOCOT **3 L7**

NTS. Auldearn, Nairn, Highland. 2 miles (3km) east of Nairn, off A96. Nearest railway station Nairn. Open all year. Charge £. Honesty box. Explanatory displays.

A 17th-century doocot on the site of an ancient motte. Montrose defeated the Covenanters nearby in 1645; battle-plan on display.

---

184 BOATHOUSE VISITOR CENTRE **4 E12**

Ardalum House, Isle of Ulva. On the northwest side of Mull; from Salen take B8035 then B8073 to Ulva Ferry. Post bus service. Open Apr–Oct,

Mon–Fri; Jun–Aug also Sun. Charge ££. Charge for mountain bikes. Group concessions. Explanatory displays. Gift shop. Tearoom/Oyster bar. Waymarked walks. WC. Limited wheelchair access. Telephone (01688) 500264.

Provides information on the history of Ulva and also the local natural history. There is a restored thatched croft house and five waymarked walking trails.

---

185 BØD OF GREMISTA **1 G5**

Gremista, Lerwick, Shetland. 1.5 miles (2.5km) north of Lerwick town centre. Open Jun–Sep, Wed–Sun 1000–1300 and 1400–1700. Charge £. Charge includes guidebook. Group concessions. Guided tours. Explanatory displays. WC. Limited wheelchair access. Car and coach parking. Telephone (01595) 694386.

A restored 18th-century fishing booth, the birthplace of local shipowner and politician Arthur Anderson. Displays tell the story of Anderson's life and service to Shetland, and of the fisheries 200 years ago. Also recreated room interiors of the kitchen and bedroom, including many original objects such as furniture, models, utensils, fishing gear and paintings.

---

186 BOLFRACKS GARDEN **5 L12**

Aberfeldy, Perthshire. 2 miles (3km) west of Aberfeldy on A827. Nearest railway station Pitlochry, buses to Aberfeldy. Open Apr–Oct, daily 1000–1800. Charge £. Under 16s free. Guided tours by appointment. No guide dogs. Car and coach parking. Telephone (01887) 820207.

A garden overlooking the Tay Valley with spectacular views. A wide range of trees, plants, shrubs, perennials and bulbs. Specialities are rhododendrons, mecanopsis, old and rambling roses, all contained within a walled garden and a less formal wooded garden with stream.

---

187 BONAWE IRON FURNACE **4 G13**

HS. Taynuilt, Argyll. At Bonawe, close to Taynuilt on the A85, 12 miles (19km) east of Oban. Nearest railway station Taynuilt, bus to Oban via Taynuilt then 15 minute walk. Open Apr–Sep, Mon–Sat 0930–1830, Sun 1400–1830. Charge £. School parties free. Group concessions. Guided tours (leaflets in French and German). Explanatory displays. Gift shop. Picnic area. WC. Wheelchair access with assistance. Disabled WC. Car parking. Telephone (01866) 822432.

The restored remains of a charcoal furnace for iron smelting. Established in 1753, it functioned until 1876. The most complete example of its type. Displays illustrate how iron was made here.

---

188 BO'NESS AND KINNEIL RAILWAY **6 L15**

Bo'ness Station, Bo'ness. On A904 and A706. Buses from Edinburgh, Glasgow and Falkirk, nearest railway station Linlithgow. Open Apr–Oct (weekends) and Jul–Aug daily except Monday; exhibition 1130–1700, steam train journeys between 1100 and 1615. Charge ££. Children under 5 free (except for special events). Group concessions. Explanatory displays. Gift shop. Tearoom and picnic area. WC. Wheelchair access and adapted coach. Disabled WC. Car and coach parking. Telephone (01506) 822298.

An exhibition tells the story of the movement of goods and people in the days before motorway travel. See locomotives, carriages and wagons, some over 100 years old. Take the steam train to Birkhill Fireclay Mine (see 167).

---

189 BONHOGA GALLERY **1 G4**

Weisdale, Shetland. 12 miles (19km) west of Lerwick. Bus service from Lerwick, Scalloway and Westside. Open all year, Tue–Sat 1030–1630, Sun 1200–1630. Free. Guided tours. Gift shop. Tearoom. WC. Wheelchair access. Disabled WC. Car and coach parking. Telephone (01595) 830400.

Bonhoga Gallery displays local, national and international art and craft exhibitions. Plus the Shetland Textile Working Museum. Café in conservatory overlooking the Weisdale Burn.

---

190 BORDER FINE ARTS GALLERY **5 N19**

Townfoot, Langholm. 20 miles (32km) north of Carlisle, 7 miles (11km) from the Border. Open all year, Mon–Fri 0900–1700, Sat 1000–1600. Free. Explanatory displays. Gift shop. WC. Wheelchair access. Car parking. Telephone (01387) 383033.

Border Fine Arts have been producing high quality ceramic figurines for over twenty-five years and have many collectors throughout the world. Visitors can see an extensive display of long-retired sculptures which collectors find enthralling.

---

191 BORELAND RIDING CENTRE AND SCOTTISH FARM PARK **3 K12**

Boreland Farm, Fearnan, Aberfeldy, Perthshire. On A827, 10 miles (16km) west of Aberfeldy. Nearest railway station Pitlochry, 22 miles (35km); nearest bus station Aberfeldy. Farm Park and coffee shop open Mar–Oct, daily 0930–1830; riding centre open all year. Charge £. Guided tours. Explanatory displays. Picnic area. Children's play barn. WC. Limited wheelchair access. Car and coach parking. Telephone (01887) 830212.

On the shores of Loch Tay with superb views, the Riding Centre caters for all ages and experience. The Farm Park is varied and interesting for all ages. Children's play barn

---

192 BORTHWICK PARISH CHURCH **6 N16**

Borthwick, Gorebridge, Midlothian. 13 miles (21km) southeast of Edinburgh. Nearest railway station Edinburgh, local bus service to North Middleton on A7. Open all year, daily. Free. Garden. WC. Induction loop during church services. Wheelchair access. Car and coach parking.

This church, which is largely Victorian, has an aisle and a vault dating from the 15th century, an apse originating in the 12th century, 18th- and 19th-century memorials (particularly the Dundas family), and two 15th-century effigies thought to be the best preserved in Scotland. Associated also with the Borthwick family and clan. Commemorates the birthplace of the great 18th-century Scottish Enlightenment figure, Principal William Robertson.

---

193 BOSTA IRON AGE HOUSE **2 C4**

Great Bernera, Lewis. At the end of B8059, northwest Lewis. Bus by request to local operator (01851) 612224/350. Open May–Sep, Tue–Sat 1200–1600. Charge £. Group concessions. Guided tours. Explanatory displays. Refreshments available in community centre. WC. Disabled WC. Car and coach parking. Telephone (01851) 612331.

The adjacent archaeological site was excavated in 1996 and revealed a complex of several iron-age houses. To protect the original structures the site has been back-filled with sand, leaving only outlines visible. A full-scale replica of one house has been built nearby, using authentic construction methods, and gives a fascinating insight into the way of life of the inhabitants 1500 years ago.

---

194 BOTHWELL CASTLE **6 K16**

HS. Uddingston, near Glasgow. At Uddingston off the B7071, 7 miles (11km) southeast of Glasgow. Nearest railway station Uddingston, bus from Glasgow or Hamilton. Open Apr–Sep, daily 0930–1830; Oct–Mar, Mon–Sat (except Thu pm and Fri) 0930–1630, Sun 1400–1630. Charge £. Group concessions. Guided tours. Explanatory displays. Gift shop. WC. Car and coach parking. Telephone (01698) 816894.

In a picturesque setting above the Clyde valley, the largest and finest 13th-century stone castle in Scotland. Much fought over during the Wars of Independence. Most of the castle dates from the 14th and 15th centuries.

---

195 BOWHILL HOUSE AND COUNTRY PARK **5 N17**

Bowhill, Selkirk. 3 miles (5km) west of Selkirk on A708. Nearest bus at Selkirk. Park open May–Aug, daily (except Fri) 1200–1700; house and park open 1–31 Jul 1300–1630. Also open all year for educational groups by appointment. Charge ££. Free to wheelchair users. Group concessions. Guided tours. Explanatory displays. Gift shop. Licensed restaurant, tearoom and picnic area. Garden. WC. Personal guided tours for blind visitors. Wheelchair access. Disabled WC. Car and coach parking. Telephone (01750) 22204.

For many generations Bowhill has been the Border home of the Scotts of Buccleuch. Inside the house, begun in 1812, there is an outstanding collection of pictures, including works by Van Dyck, Reynolds, Gainsborough, Canaletto, Guardi, Claude Lorraine, Raeburn. There is also a selection of the world-famous Buccleuch collection of portrait minatures. Also porcelain and furniture, much of which was made in the famous workshop of André Boulle in Paris. Restored Victorian kitchen. In the grounds are an adventure woodland play area, a riding centre, garden nature trails, bicycle hire. Audio-visual presentation, theatre and visitor centre.

---

196 BOWMORE DISTILLERY VISITOR CENTRE **4 D16**

School Street, Bowmore, Isle of Islay. Bus service to Bowmore from ferry terminals and airport. Open May–Sep, Mon–Fri, guided tours at 1030, 1130, 1400 and 1500, Sat 1030, closed Sun; Oct–Apr, Mon–Fri 1030 and 1400. Charge £. Under 18s free. Group concessions. Guided tours (Foreign language video). Explanatory displays. Gift shop. Visitors receive a dram of whisky. WC. Wheelchair access. Disabled WC. Car and coach parking. Telephone (01496) 810441.

Malt whisky distillery, licensed since 1779 with guided tours explaining the process of whisky making. Traditional floor maltings are a major feature. Across the entrance yard, a former warehouse, gifted to the local community, is now a swimming pool heated by waste energy from the distillery.

---

197 BRAEMAR CASTLE **3 M10**

Braemar, Aberdeenshire. 0.5 mile (1km) northeast of Braemar on A93. Daily bus service from Aberdeen to Braemar. Special transport available from two local hotels, Fife Arms and Invercauld Arms. Open Easter–Oct, Sat–Thu 1000–1800; Jul, Aug also Fri. Charge £. Group concessions. Guided tours (available in French, German and Italian). Explanatory sheets. Gift shop. Refreshments and picnic area. WC. Car and coach parking. Telephone (01339) 741219.

A turreted stronghold, built in 1628 by the Earl of Mar, Braemar Castle was burned in 1689 by the Black Colonel (John Farquharson of Inverey). Repaired by the Government after the 1745 Rising, it was garrisoned by Hanoverian troops. Later transformed into a private residence by the Farquharsons of Invercauld who had purchased it in 1732. L-plan with a central round tower and spiral stair. Barrel vaulted ceilings, massive iron gate (yett), underground prison. Star-shaped defensive curtain wall. Fully furnished residence.

---

198 BRAHAN SEER PLAQUE, CHANONRY POINT **3 K7**

On the shore near Chanonry Lighthouse, Fortrose, Black Isle.

Commemorating the burning at the stake of Kenneth MacKenzie (Coinneach Odhar) – the Brahan Seer. This cruel act was instigated by the Countess of Seaforth when the Brahan Seer, on the insistence of the Countess, told of the 'goings on' of her husband who was on state business in Paris and was away longer than his wife thought necessary. The famous Brahan Seer, who lived in the first half of the 17th century, made many prophecies about the Highlands, some of which are still coming true.

---

199 BRANDER MUSEUM **3 P8**

The Square, Huntly. In centre of Huntly. Nearest railway station and bus services Huntly. Open all year, Tue–Sat 1000–1200 and 1400–1600. Free. Explanatory displays. Gift shop. Wheelchair access with assistance. Car and coach parking. Telephone (01771) 622906.

A display about Huntly-born author George Macdonald. Also extensive collection of communion tokens, finds from archaeological excavations at Huntly Castle, and arms and armour from 19th-century Sudan.

---

200 BRANDSBUTT SYMBOL STONE **3 Q9**

HS. About 1 mile (2km) northwest of Inverurie, Aberdeenshire. Bus from Aberdeen to Inverurie then 1 mile (2km) walk. Access at all times. Free. Telephone 0131 668 8800.

An early Pictish symbol stone with an ogham inscription.

---

201 BRANKLYN GARDEN **5 M13**

NTS. 116 Dundee Road, Perth. On A85 near Perth city centre, 25 minutes walk from Perth railway station. Buses from Perth and Dundee stop near the garden. Open Mar–Oct, daily 0930–sunset. Charge £. Children free. Group concessions. Guided tours of the garden. Explanatory displays. Gift shop. WC. Limited wheelchair access. Disabled WC. Car and coach parking. Telephone (01738) 625535.

Started in 1922 on the site of a former orchard, Branklyn is an outstanding 2 acre (0.8ha) garden with rhododendrons, alpines, herbaceous and peat garden plants.

---

202 BREADALBANE FOLKLORE CENTRE **5 K13**

Falls of Dochart, Killin, Perthshire. 2 miles (3km) along A827 from A85 at Lix Toll junction. 12 miles (19km) east of Crianlarich, 20 miles (32km) northwest of Callander. Post and school bus from Callander, Mon–Fri, term–time only. Open Mar–May, daily 1000–1700; Jun, daily 1000–1800; Jul–Aug, daily 0900–1800; Sep, daily 1000–1800; Oct, daily 1000–1700; closed Nov–Jan; Feb open weekends only 1000–1600. Charge £. Group concessions. Guided tours by request. Explanatory displays. Gift shop. WC. Induction loop. Limited wheelchair access. Disabled WC. Car and coach parking. Telephone (01567) 820254.

Centre includes a tourist information centre, water wheel and healing stones. History of local clans (MacLaren, MacNab, Campbell and MacGregor). Artefacts on Killin heritage. Display boards and visual display units tell the story of Breadalbane. Visitors can also learn about St Fillan, the local patron saint and healer, a 6th-century Celtic monk who preached from the original mill building.

---

203 BRECHIN BRIDGE **3 P11**

In Brechin, Angus.

Known locally as the Auld Brig, this is one of the oldest stone bridges in Scotland. Until the 1780s it was the only bridge over the South Esk.

---

204 BRECHIN CASTLE CENTRE **3 P11**

Haughmuir, Angus. At the Brechin junction off A90, 25 miles (40km) north of Dundee. Nearest railway station Montrose (9 miles/14.5km) bus service to Brechin (1 mile/2km). Minibus service runs from Stonehaven to centre daily. Open summer months, Mon–Sat 0900–1800, Sun 1000–1800; winter months, Mon–Sat 0900–1700,

Sun 1000–1700; closed Christmas and New Year. Charge £. Group concessions. Guided tours by prior arrangement. Gift shop. Restaurant and picnic areas. Play area for under fives and main play area in country park. WC. Disabled WC. Car and coach parking. Telephone (01356) 626813.

Brechin Castle Centre is part of the Dalhousie Estates. Scottish breeds of domestic animals, pets corner and pheasantry, farm buildings and display of traditional agricultural machinery and implements. Garden centre.

---

205 BRECHIN CATHEDRAL ROUND TOWER **3 P11**

HS. In Brechin, Angus. Nearest railway station Montrose, bus to Montrose. View exterior only. Access at all times. Free. Telephone 0131 668 8800.

One of the two remaining round towers of the Irish type in Scotland. Built in the late 11th century with a remarkable carved doorway. Capped by a stone roof added in the 15th century. Now attached to the Cathedral. See also 1159 Paisley Abbey.

---

206 BRECHIN MUSEUM **3 P11**

St Ninians Square, Brechin, Angus. 9 miles (15km) from Montrose on A935, two miles from turn-off on A94. Bus service from Montrose, Caledonian steam railway. Open all year (except Christmas and New Year), Mon–Thu 0930–1830 (Mon and Wed closes 2000), Fri and Sat 0930–1700. Free. Explanatory displays. WC. Wheelchair access. Car parking. Telephone (01356) 622687.

Local collections tell the story of the development of Brechin from the Celtic church of the 10th century to the last days of the burgh in 1975. There is a small display of some of the works of D. Waterson, etcher and colourist.

---

207 BRIDGE OF CARR **3 L9**

Carrbridge. Access at all times. Free.

High and narrow single-arch bridge. Built by John Niccelsone, mason, in summer 1717, for Sir James Grant.

---

208 BRIDGE OF OICH **3 J9**

HS. On the A82, 4 miles (6.5km) south of Fort Augustus, Inverness-shire. Bus service from Inverness or Fort William. Telephone 0131 668 8800.

A splendid suspension bridge designed by James Dredge in 1854. It employs a patented design of double cantilevered chains with massive granite pylon arches at each end.

---

209 BRIGHOUSE BAY TREKKING PONIES **5 K21**

Brighouse Bay, Borgue, Kirkcudbright. 6 miles (10km) southwest of Kirkcudbright off the B727 Borgue road. Open Easter–Oct, telephone to confirm times. Charge £££. Gift shop. Bistro, licensed lounge, take-away food and picnic area. WC. Disabled riders telephone in advance. Wheelchair access. Disabled WC. Car and coach parking. Telephone (01557) 870222.

Approved by the British Horse Society, the Trekking Centre offers riding for all abilities. Hard hats are provided. Riding is within the 1200 acre (486ha) holiday/farm complex. Also holiday park.

---

210 BRIGHT WATER VISITOR CENTRE **2 F8**

The Pier, Kyleakin, Isle of Skye. Approximately 1 mile (1.5km) left of Skye Bridge on the Isle of Skye. Nearest railway station Kyle of Lochalsh then bus to Kyleakin; or coach to Kyleakin/Skye. Open Mar–Dec, Mon–Sat 0900–1730. Donation box, charge for boat trip. Guided tours (available in French, Gaelic, German, Italian and Spanish). Explanatory displays. Gift shop. Wheelchair access. Disabled WC. Car and coach parking. Telephone (01599) 530040.

Due to open April 2000, the centre is located on the island Eilean Ban, and will focus on the Stephenson lighthouse; the story of the island's previous owner, the naturalist and writer Gavin Maxwell; and the splendours of the area's natural heritage.

---

211 BRIN HERB NURSERY **3 K8**

Flichty, Farr, Inverness-shire. 7 miles (11km) from A9 on Daviot-Fort Augustus road. Infrequent local bus service from Inverness. Open Mar–Oct, Mon–Sat 0930–1800, Sun 1400–1700. Free. Guided tours (small groups by arrangement). Explanatory displays. Gift shop. Tearoom. Garden. WC. Wheelchair access. Disabled WC. Car parking. Telephone (01808) 521288.

Over 300 varieties of herb and wild flower plants are grown on the nursery at 700 feet (213m) above sea level. Display gardens give planting ideas. Shop sells herb related products, books, cards and gifts.

---

212 BRITISH GOLF MUSEUM **5 P13**

Bruce Embankment, St Andrews, Fife. 10 minutes walk from town centre, opposite the Royal and Ancient Golf Club. Nearest railway station Leuchars 4 miles (6.5km), connecting bus to St Andrews. Buses from Dundee and Edinburgh. Open Easter–Oct, daily 0930–1730; Nov–Mar, daily (except Tue and Wed) 1100–1500. Charge ££. Children under 5 free. Group concessions. Explanatory displays. Gift shop. Braille guide available. Wheelchair access. Disabled WC. Car and coach parking. Telephone (01334) 478880.

At the British Golf Museum visitors encounter many famous professionals and amateurs of status. Touch screen videos allow visitors to look deeper into the lives of champions and to test their skills and knowledge of the game of golf. Exhibits display the evolution of golf equipment as well as fun features of the game.

---

213 BROCH OF GURNESS **1 B10**

HS. Evie, Orkney. Off the A966 at Aikerness, about 14 miles (22.5km) northwest of Kirkwall. Tour bus from Kirkwall. Open Apr–Sep, daily 0930–1830. Charge £. Group concessions. Explanatory displays. Gift shop. Car and coach parking. Telephone (01831) 579478.

An Iron Age broch over 10 feet (3m) high, surrounded by stone huts, deep ditches and ramparts.

---

214 LAURENCE BRODERICK SCULPTURE EXHIBITION **2 F9**

Gallery An Talla Dearg, Eilean Iarmain, Isle Ornsay, Isle of Skye. On the A851 between Broadford and Armadale, 8 miles (13km) from Broadford. Nearest railway station Kyle of Lochalsh; bus from Armadale or Broadford. Open Aug and Sep, Mon–Fri 0930–1830, Sat 0930–1300. Free. Guided tours on request. WC. Wheelchair access with assistance. Disabled WC. Car and coach parking. Telephone (01767) 650444.

A gallery displaying the work of the sculptor, especially carvings of otters. Work in various stones, including Skye marble. Also in bronze. Sculptor usually available to discuss his work and do demonstrations.

---

215 BRODICK CASTLE **4 G17**

NTS. Isle of Arran, Bute. 2 miles (3km) north of Brodick. By ferry from Ardrossan to Brodick, by bus from Brodick. Open Apr–Jun and Sep–Oct, daily 1100–1630; Jul–Aug daily 1100–1700. Charge £££. Children free. Garden and grounds only, £. Group concessions. Guided tours by arrangement. Explanatory displays. Guidebook in French and German. Text in eight languages. Gift shop. Restaurant with terrace overlooking sea, picnic area. WC. Braille information sheet. Limited wheelchair access, wheelchairs available. Disabled WC. Car and coach parking. Telephone (01770) 302202.

Mainly Victorian castle, but original parts date from the 13th century. Fine collections of furniture, paintings, porcelain and silver collected by the Dukes of Hamilton.

Beautiful walled garden, and woodland garden with famous rhododendron collection. The castle occupies a fine site overlooking Brodick Bay, on the slopes of Goatfell (2866 feet/873m). Nature trail and other walks in country park.

---

216 BRODIE CASTLE **3 L7**

NTS. Brodie, Forres, Moray. Off A96, 4.5 miles (7km) west of Forres. By bus from Inverness. Open Apr–Sep (and weekends in Oct), Mon–Sat 1100–1730, Sun 1330–1730. Charge ££. Children free. Grounds only, £ (honesty box). Group concessions. Guided tours (with information sheets in six languages). Explanatory displays. Gift shop. Tearoom and picnic area. Garden and adventure playground. WC. Braille guides and personal audiotape for blind visitors. Limited wheelchair access, wheelchair available. Disabled WC. Car and coach parking. Telephone (01309) 641371.

The oldest parts of the castle are 16th century, with 17th- and 19th-century additions. Fine collections of furniture and porcelain and a major art collection. Woodland walk, 4 acre (1.6ha) pond with wildlife observation hides. Famous daffodil collection in spring.

---

217 BROUGH OF BIRSAY **1 A10**

HS. On the island of Birsay, at the north end of mainland Orkney. 20 miles (32km) northwest of Kirkwall. Tourist bus from Kirkwall to Birsay. Telephone to confirm opening times. Charge £. Group concessions. Explanatory displays. Car parking. Telephone (01856) 721205.

The remains of a Romanesque church and a Norse settlement.

---

218 BROUGHTON GALLERY **5 M17**

Broughton, Biggar, Lanarkshire. On the A701 just north of Broughton village. Bus from Peebles or Biggar. Open Apr–mid Oct and mid Nov–Christmas, Thu–Tue 1030–1800. Free. Gift shop. Garden. WC. Wheelchair access with assistance. Access for small coaches only. Car parking. Telephone (01899) 830234.

Sells paintings and crafts by living British artists and makers in Tower House, designed in 1937 by Sir Basil Spence.

---

219 BROUGHTON HOUSE AND GARDEN **5 K21**

NTS. 12 High Street, Kirkcudbright. Off A711/A755. By bus from Dumfries and Castle Douglas. Open Apr–Oct, daily 1300–1730. Charge ££. Children free. Group concessions. Explanatory displays (information sheets in French and German). Small hall-table shop, garden. WC. Limited wheelchair access. Car parking. Telephone (01557) 330437.

Eighteenth-century town house, home and studio 1901–33 of artist E. A. Hornel, one of the Glasgow Boys. Permanent exhibition of his work. Extensive collection of Scottish books including Burns' works. Attractive Japanese-style garden, added by Hornel, leading down to River Dee estuary.

---

220 BROUGHTY CASTLE **5 N13**

HS. In Broughty Ferry, east of Dundee. Nearest railway station Dundee, bus service from Dundee. Open all year, Mon 1100–1700, Tue–Thu and Sat 1000–1700, closing between 1300–1400. Sun in Jul, Aug and Sep 1400–1700. Closed Fri, Christmas and New Year. Free. Explanatory displays. Telephone (01382) 776121.

A 16th-century tower adapted for changing defence needs during the 19th century. Now houses a branch of Dundee Arts and Heritage Department.

---

221 BROW WELL **5 M20**

On B725, 1 mile (1.5km) west of Ruthwell. Access at all times. Free.

Ancient mineral well visited by Robert Burns in July 1796, when at Brow sea bathing under his doctor's orders.

222 MICHAEL BRUCE'S COTTAGE

6 M14

The Cobbles, Kinnesswood, Kinross. 4 miles (6.5km) east of Milnathort. Bus from Kinross. Open Apr–Sep, daily 1000–1800. Free. Donations welcome. Guided tours by appointment. Garden. No guide dogs. Telephone (01542) 840203.

An 18th-century pantiled weaver's cottage and a museum since 1906. Houses collection relating to the life of the poet, and local history including the manufacture of vellum and parchment.

---

223 BRUCE'S STONE

4 J19

North side of Loch Trool, unclassified road off A714, 13 miles (21km) north of Newton Stewart. Access at all times. Free.

A massive granite memorial to Robert the Bruce's first victory over the English, which led to his subsequent success at Bannockburn. Fine views of Loch Trool and the hills of Galloway. Start of hill climb to the Merrick (2764 feet/842.5m), the highest hill in southern Scotland.

---

224 JOHN BUCHAN CENTRE

5 M17

Broughton, Biggar, Lanarkshire. On the A703, 6 miles (9.5km) east of Biggar and 28 miles (45km) from Edinburgh. Bus service from Edinburgh. Open Easter and May–Sep, daily 1400–1700. Charge £. Explanatory displays. Second-hand books for sale. Bookshop. WC. Wheelchair access with assistance. Car and coach parking. Telephone (01899) 221050.

The Centre tells the story of John Buchan, 1st Lord Tweedsmuir, author of *The Thirty Nine Steps* and also lawyer, politician, soldier, historian, and Governor-General of Canada. Broughton village was his mother's birthplace, and a much-loved holiday home.

---

225 BUCHOLIE CASTLE

3 N2

Caithness. South of Freswick on the A9 John O' Groats to Wick road.

The 12th-century stronghold of Sweyn Asliefson, the Norse pirate. The Mowats brought the present name of Bucholie with them from their estates in Aberdeenshire.

---

226 BUCKHAVEN MUSEUM

6 N14

College Street, Buckhaven. 8 miles (13km) east of Kirkcaldy. Bus service stops outside museum. Open all year, Mon 1400–1700 and 1730–1900, Tue 1000–1300 and 1400–1700, Thu 1000–1300, 1400–1700 and 1730–1900, Fri 1400–1700, Sat 1000–1230. Closed Wed, Sun and public holidays. Free. Explanatory displays. Gift shop. Wheelchair access with assistance. Car and coach parking. Telephone (01592) 412860.

Museum displays Buckhaven's history with a focus on the fishing industry. Stained glass windows made by local people with the help of a community artist. Recreation of a 1920s kitchen. Changing exhibitions of local interest.

---

227 BUCKIE DRIFTER

3 N7

Freuchny Road, Buckie. 18 miles (29km) east of Elgin on A98. Bus service from Aberdeen or Elgin. Nearest railway station Keith, regular local bus service from station. Open Apr–Oct, Mon–Sat 1000–1700, Sun 1200–1700. Other times by arrangement. Charge £. Group concessions. Guided tours for pre-booked groups. Explanatory displays. Gift shop. Restaurant. Baby changing facilities. WC. Wheelchair access. Disabled WC. Car and coach parking. Telephone (01542) 834646.

A journey back in time to discover why thousands of northeast Scotland's fisherfolk spent their lives following the herring. Clamber on board a Buckie drifter and catch a glimpse of life on a recreated 1920s quayside. Explore a 37 foot (11m) retired Oakley class lifeboat.

228 BUGHT FLORAL HALL AND VISITOR CENTRE 3 K8

Bught Lane, Inverness. In Bught Park, off the A82, 1.5 miles (2.5km) from the centre. Open Apr–Oct, Mon–Sun 1000–1830; Nov–Mar, daily 1000–1630 (closed Christmas–New Year). Charge £. Children free. Guided tours. Explanatory displays. Coffee shop. WC. Wheelchair access. Disabled WC. Car and coach parking. Telephone (01463) 222755.

The Floral Hall, Cacti House and gardens are part of a working horticultural nursery with professional staff. Visitors can stroll along winding paths through a sub-tropical landscape enhanced with a grotto, waterfall, fountain and tropical fish. Ferns and orchids flourish. Rare and fascinating tropical plants. Demonstration gardens outside consist of a number of landscaped areas.

---

229 BUNNAHABHAIN DISTILLERY 4 E15

Port Askaig, Isle of Islay. Limited post bus service from Bowmore. Telephone Mundalls (01496) 840273 from ferry terminals and airport. Open all year (except Christmas and New Year), Mon–Fri 1000–1600. Free. Guided tours by arrangement. Gift shop. WC. Car and coach parking. Telephone (01496) 840646.

Visitors can see the malt whisky distillation process. Individuals and groups welcome.

---

230 BURG 4 D13

NTS. Isle of Mull. 7 miles (11km) west of Tiroran, off B8035, then rough path. Car parking at Tiroran. Access at all times. Free. Telephone (01631) 570000.

Covering a distance of 1405 acres (568.5ha), this is a spectacular and remote part of Mull. The high cliffs here are known as the Wilderness. MacCulloch's Fossil Tree is 50 million years old, and can be reached by a steep iron ladder down to the beach at low tide.

---

231 BURGHEAD WELL 3 M7

HS. In King Street, Burghead, Moray. Nearest railway station Elgin, bus from Elgin to Burghead. Access at all times. Free. Telephone 0131 668 8800.

A rock-cut well, identified by some as an early Christian baptistry associated with the local cult of St Ethan.

---

232 BURLAND CROFT TRAIL 1 F5

Burland, Trondra, Shetland. 3 miles (5km) from Scalloway. Open May–Sep, Mon–Sat 1000–1800. Donation. Charge for school and nursery groups. Group concessions. Guided tours by arrangement. Explanatory displays. WC. Limited wheelchair access. Car and coach parking. Telephone (01595) 880430.

Follow the way-marked route through this working croft. See the croft animals such as sheep, Shetland cattle, Tamworth pigs, and Shetland ducks and geese which have been re-introduced as a result of detailed research. All donations contribute to the cost of animal feed.

---

233 BURLEIGH CASTLE 6 M14

HS. Near Milnathort, off the A911, 2 miles (3km) northeast of Kinross, Perthshire. Nearest railway station Perth, bus from Perth to Milnathort. Open Apr–Sep, Mon–Sat 0900–1830, Sun 1400–1830. Keys collected from 16 Burleigh Road, Milnathort, (01577) 862408. Free. Telephone 0131 668 8800.

The roofless but otherwise complete ruin of a tower house of about 1500 with a section of defensive barmkin wall and a remarkable corner tower with a square cap-house corbelled out. The seat of the Balfours of Burleigh; much visited by James IV.

234 ROBERT BURNS CENTRE 5 L19

Mill Road, Dumfries. Situated on the west bank of the River Nith. 15 minutes walk from Dumfries railway station, 5 minutes walk from Whitesands bus station. Open Apr–Sep, Mon–Sat 1000–2000, Sun 1400–1700; Oct–Mar, Tue–Sat 1000–1300 and 1400–1700. Charge £ (for audio-visual presentation only). Explanatory displays. Leaflet guides in European languages, Russian and Japanese. Gift shop. Gallery café bistro. WC. Induction loop. Wheelchair access. Disabled WC. Car and coach parking. Telephone (01387) 264808.

Award-winning centre illustrates the connection between Robert Burns, Scotland's national poet, and the town of Dumfries. Situated in the town's 18th-century watermill, the centre tells of Burns' last years spent in the busy streets and lively atmosphere of Dumfries in the 1790s. Film theatre shows feature films in the evening.

---

235 BURNS HOUSE 5 L19

Burns Street, Dumfries. 5 minutes walk from Dumfries town centre. Dumfries railway station 15 minutes walk, Loreburn Centre bus stance 2 minutes walk. Open Apr–Sep, Mon–Sat 1000–1700, Sun 1400–1700; Oct–Mar, Tue–Sat 1000–1300 and 1400–1700. Free. Explanatory displays. Gift shop. Leaflets in European languages and Japanese. Limited wheelchair access. Car parking. Telephone (01387) 255297.

It was in this ordinary sandstone house that Robert Burns, Scotland's national poet, spent the last years of his brilliant life. Now a place of pilgrimage for Burns enthusiasts around the world. The house retains much of its 18th-century character and contains many relics of the poet. Visitors can see the chair in which he wrote his last poems and many original letters and manuscripts. The famous Kilmarnock and Edinburgh editions of his work are also on display.

---

236 BURNS HOUSE MUSEUM 4 J17

Castle Street, Mauchline, Ayrshire. 11 miles (18km) from Ayr and Kilmarnock. Nearest railway and bus stations Ayr and Kilmarnock, bus stop close to museum. Open Easter then May–Sep, Tue–Sun, otherwise by appointment only. Telephone for opening hours. Charge £. Guided tours by appointment. Explanatory displays. Gift shop. Garden available for picnics. WC. Limited wheelchair access. Disabled WC. Car and coach parking. Telephone (01290) 550045.

A museum with a gallery devoted to Burns memorabilia. On the upper floor is the room Burns took for Jean Armour in 1788. It has remained intact and is furnished in the style of the period. Models of Jean and Robert plus a full video presentation. Visitors can also see a large collection of Mauchline boxware and an exhibition devoted to curling and curling stones. Nearby is Mauchline churchyard in which are buried four of Burns' daughters and a number of his friends and contemporaries.

---

237 BURNS MONUMENT 6 J17

Kay Park, Kilmarnock. 0.5 mile (1km) from centre of Kilmarnock. View from outside only.

Victorian red sandstone monument with statue of Burns by W. G. Stevenson. Set in an attractive park with boating, pitch and putt, and children's play area.

---

238 BURNS NATIONAL HERITAGE PARK 4 J18

Murdochs Lane, Alloway, Ayr. 2 miles (3km) south of Ayr on B7024. Nearest railway station Ayr. Bus service to Alloway from Ayr. Summer open-top bus service from Ayr bus station. Open all year except Christmas and New Year. Tam o'Shanter Experience Apr–Oct 0900–1800; Nov–Mar 0900–1700. Burns Cottage Apr–Oct 0900–1800; Nov–Mar Mon–Sat 1000–1600, Sun 1200–1600. Charge ££. Group concessions. Explanatory displays (with translations in French, German and Japanese). Gift shop. Restaurant, tea-room and picnic area. Gardens and children's play area. WC. Wheelchair access. Disabled WC. Car and coach parking. Telephone (01292) 443700.

The Burns National Heritage Park was established in 1995. It embraces Burns' Cottage, Museum, Monument, Auld Brig o' Doon and Alloway Kirk together with the Tam o' Shanter Experience. The old and new are linked in time by a 5-minute walk which transports the visitor from 1759 (when Burns was born) to the exciting, humorous and action-filled Tam o' Shanter Experience (see 1399).

---

239 BURNSWARK HILL **5 M19**

By unclassified road, 1.5 miles (2.5km) north of B725, Ecclefechan to Middlebie road. Access at all reasonable times. Free.

A native hill fort (around 6th century BC) with extensive earthworks, flanked by a Roman artillery range. Thought to have been a series of Roman practice seige works, best seen from the hilltop. The excavated ditches and ramparts of Birrens Fort are nearby.

---

240 BURNTISLAND EDWARDIAN FAIR MUSEUM **6 M15**

102 High Street, Burntisland, Fife. 7 miles (11km) west of Kirkcaldy. Nearest railway station Burntisland. Open all year, Mon, Fri and Sat 1000–1300 and 1400–1900, Tue and Thu 1000–1300 and 1400–1900. Closed Wed, Sun and public holidays. Free. Explanatory displays. WC. Telephone (01592) 412860.

Permanent display about the Edwardian Fair that visited Burntisland every year, plus displays on the local history of Burntisland.

---

241 BUTE MUSEUM **4 G16**

Stuart Street, Rothesay, Isle of Bute. Located in the centre of Rothesay. Car ferry from Wemyss Bay to Rothesay Pier or from Colintraive to Rhubodach at north end of Bute. Open Apr–Sep, Mon–Sat 1030–1630, Sun 1430–1630; Oct–Mar, Tue–Sat 1430–1630. Charge £. Groups normally admitted with a donation. Guided tours by arrangement. Explanatory displays. Gift shop. WC. Touch table. Wheelchair access with assistance. Car and coach parking. Telephone (01700) 505067.

Custom-made museum, gifted by the fourth Marquis of Bute in 1926. A recognised source of information on the Island of Bute. Archaeology, natural history, geology, photography, archives and social history.

---

242 BUTTERCHURN AND SCOTTISH FOOD AND CRAFT CENTRE **6 M14**

Cocklaw Mains Farm, Kelty, Fife. By junction 4 of M90, on B914. Open all year, daily (except Christmas and New Year) 0900–2100 (telephone to confirm winter opening hours). Free. Explanatory displays. Gift shop. Restaurant (telephone to book). Children's play area. Garden. Farmyard pets. WC. Disabled WC. Car parking. Telephone (01383) 830169.

Courtyard setting with quality food and craft centre. Taste of Scotland restaurant

---

243 CADZOW CASTLE **6 K16**

HS. Chatelherault Country Park, Hamilton. In the grounds of Chatelherault Country Park, Hamilton, Lanarkshire. Nearest railway and bus stations Hamilton, bus from Hamilton. Access at all times. View exterior only. Free. Telephone 0131 668 8800.

Constructed between 1500 and 1550, the castle was known as 'the castle in the woods of Hamilton'. See 309 Chatelherault.

---

244 CAERLAVEROCK CASTLE **5 M20**

HS. Glencaple, Dumfries. Off the B725, 9 miles (14.5km) south of Dumfries. Bus from Dumfries to Shearington. Open Apr–Sep, daily 0930–1830; Oct–Mar, Mon–Sat 0930–1630, Sun 1400–1630. Charge £. Group concessions. Guided tours. Explanatory displays and visitor

centre. Gift shop. Tearoom and picnic area. Children's park and nature trail to old castle. WC. Wheelchair access with assistance. Car and coach parking. Telephone (01387) 770244.

One of the finest castles in Scotland – its remarkable features are the twin-towered gatehouse and the Nithsdale Lodging, a splendid Renaissance range dating from 1638.

---

245 CAIRNBAAN CUP AND RING MARKS **4 F14**

HS. Kilmartin Glen. Near to the Cairnbaan Hotel on the A841, 2.5 miles (4km) northwest of Lochgilphead, Argyll. Nearest railway station Oban, then bus to Lochgilphead. Access at all times. Free. Telephone 0131 668 8800.

Cup and ring marks on a natural rock surface.

---

246 CAIRNGORM CHAIRLIFT **3 L9**

Aviemore, Inverness-shire. 10 miles (16km) east of Aviemore on B970. Nearest railway station Aviemore, regular bus service from Aviemore. Open all year, daily, weather permitting. Charge £££. Group concessions. Explanatory displays and Ranger service. Gift shop. Café bar, Ptarmigan Café. WC. Limited wheelchair access (assistance with advance notice). Disabled WC. Car and coach parking. Telephone (01479) 861261.

A two-stage journey from the Cairngorm Day Lodge at 2150 feet (655m) up to the Ptarmigan Café at 3600 feet (1097m) – Britain's highest restaurant, just below the summit of Cairngorm. Suitable for all ages, the chairlift journey takes 25 minutes from bottom to top.

---

247 CAIRNGORM GLIDING CLUB **3 L9**

Feshie Airstrip, Feshiebridge, Kincraig, Inverness-shire. 2 miles (3km) east of Kincraig. Nearest railway stations Kingussie and Aviemore, bus to Kincraig or taxi. Open all year dependant on weather, telephone to confirm. Charge £££. Group concessions. Explanatory displays. WC. Wheelchair access. Disabled WC. Car and coach parking. Telephone (01540) 651317.

Founded in 1966 by a group of ten pilots and would-be pilots, this members club offers trial lessons, half- and full-day courses and week (5 day) courses.

---

248 CAIRNGORM REINDEER CENTRE **3 L9**

Reindeer House, Glenmore, Aviemore, Inverness-shire. 6 miles (10km) east of Aviemore on A951. Nearest railway station Aviemore, bus service to Glenmore. Open all year. Tours to the reindeer Easter–Oct 1100 and 1430; Nov–Easter 1100 only. Centre open 1000–1700. Charge ££. Group concessions. Guided tours. Explanatory displays. Gift shop. No guide dogs. Limited wheelchair access. Car and coach parking. Telephone (01479) 861228.

Britain's only free-ranging herd of reindeer. Visitors join the guide for a walk to the reindeer's hillside grazing. For visitors unable to make the walk, reindeer can also be seen at the centre. Exhibition and gift shop. Opportunity to adopt your own reindeer.

---

249 CAIRN HOLY CHAMBERED CAIRNS **4 J20**

HS. 6.5 miles (10.5km) southeast of Creetown, Kirkcudbrightshire. Nearest railway station Dumfries, buses from Dumfries, Newton Stewart or Stranraer. Car parking. Telephone 0131 668 8800.

Two remarkably complete Neolithic burial cairns situated on a hill giving good views over Wigtown Bay.

---

250 CAIRN O' GET **3 N4**

HS. 5 miles (8km) northeast of Lybster, Caithness. Dunnet's buses to Ulbster (request stop for Cairn o' Get), then 2 miles (3km) walk. Access at all times. Free. Telephone 0131 668 8800.

A horned and chambered burial cairn.

251 CAIRNPAPPLE HILL 6 L15

HS. Near Torphichen, off the B792, 3 miles (5km) north of Bathgate, West Lothian. Bus from Linlithgow to Bathgate via Torphichen, then a 3 mile (5km) walk. Open Apr-Sep, daily 0900-1830; Oct-Mar, daily 0900-1630. Charge £. Group concessions. Guided tours. Explanatory displays. Car parking. Telephone (01506) 634622.

One of the most important prehistoric monuments in Scotland. It was used as a burial and ceremonial site from around 3000–1400BC. Excellent views.

---

252 CAITHNESS AND SUTHERLAND NATURAL HISTORY DISPLAY 3 M2

Dunnet Pavilion, Dunnet, Castletown, Caithness. On the A836, 7 miles (11km) east of Thurso, next to caravan site. Nearest railway station Thurso, bus from Thurso. Open May–Sep, Tue–Fri and Sun 1400–1700. Free. Explanatory displays and guided walks. Picnic area. WC. Limited wheelchair access. Car and coach parking. Telephone (01847) 821531.

A display illustrating the natural history of Caithness and Sutherland. National nature reserve nearby.

---

253 CAITHNESS GLASS VISITOR CENTRE, OBAN 4 F13

The Waterfront, Railway Pier, Oban. Located in the centre of Oban beside the railway station, ferry terminal and bus stops. Open Mar–Oct, Mon–Sat 0900–1700, and Easter–Oct, Sun 1100–1700; Nov–Feb, Mon–Sat 1000–1700. Free. Explanatory displays. Gift shop. Wheelchair access. Telephone (01631) 563386.

Audio-visual presentation and interpretive exhibition on Caithness Glass and how glass is designed and made. Factory shop, Royal Doulton seconds shop and craft section.

---

254 CAITHNESS GLASS VISITOR CENTRE, PERTH 5 M13

Inveralmond Industrial Estate, Perth. On A9 north of Perth. Nearest railway and bus stations Perth, bus service to site Mon–Fri. Visitor centre open all year, Mon–Sat 0900–1700 (Sun, Mar–Nov 1000–1700 then Dec–Feb 1200–1700). Glassmaking all year, Mon–Fri 0900–1630 (except Christmas and New Year). Free. Explanatory displays and factory viewing. Gift shop. Licenced restaurant. Baby change facilities. WC. Wheelchair access. Disabled WC. Car and coach parking. Telephone (01738) 492320.

See the fascinating process of glass making. Also paperweight collectors gallery, audio-visual theatre and children's play area.

---

255 CAITHNESS GLASS VISITOR CENTRE, WICK 3 N3

Airport Industrial Estate, Wick, Caithness. On outskirts of Wick. Nearest railway station Wick. Bus service from Wick passes visitor centre. Open all year, Mon–Sat 0900–1700; Easter–Dec, Sun 1100–1700. Free. Explanatory displays. Gift shop. Licensed restaurant. Baby change facilities. WC. Wheelchair access. Disabled WC. Car and coach parking. Telephone (01955) 602286.

Visitors can see glass making and watch glass cutting, engraving and jewellery making. Factory shop and exhibition telling the history of the company.

---

256 CALANAIS STANDING STONES 2 D4

HS. At Calanais, off A858, 12 miles (19km) west of Stornoway, Isle of Lewis (Western Isles). Ferry from Ullapool to Stornoway, then bus from Stornoway to Calanais. Site open all year. Visitor centre operated by Western Isles Council, telephone (01851) 621422 for details; open in summer from 1000–1900; winter from 1000–1600, closed Sun. Free. Charge for visitor centre. Explanatory displays. Gift shop. Tearoom. WC. Wheelchair access with assistance. Disabled WC. Car and coach parking. Telephone (01851) 621422.

A unique cruciform setting of megaliths second in importance only to Stonehenge. Erected about 3000BC. An avenue of 19 monoliths leads north from a circle of 13 stones, with rows of more stones fanning out to the south, east and west. Inside the circle is a small chambered tomb.

257 CALDERGLEN COUNTRY PARK 6 K16

Strathaven Road, East Kilbride, South Lanarkshire. 1 mile (1.5km) from East Kilbride town centre on A726/Strathaven Road. Nearest railway and bus station East Kilbride. Country park open all year at all times. Visitor centre open summer Mon–Fri 1030–1700, weekends and public holidays 1130–1830; winter months daily 1130–1600. Free. Guided tours by arrangement. Explanatory displays. Gift shop. Courtyard café, snack bar and picnic area. WC. Large print text leaflet. Wheelchair access to buildings. Partial access to nature trails. Disabled WC. Car and coach parking. Telephone (01355) 236644.

The park consists of over 440 acres (180ha) of attractive wooded gorge and parkland, including several fine waterfalls. All are accessible by an extensive network of paths and nature trails. Visitor centre, conservatory, ornamental garden, children's zoo, toddler's play area, adventure and special needs play area centred around the historic Torrance House. Horticultural staff, animal keepers and a countryside ranger service run a year-round programme of activities and events.

---

258 CALEDONIAN CANAL 3 K8

Contact Canal Office, Seaport Marina, Muirtown Wharf, Inverness. Access at all times. Free. Limited wheelchair access. Car parking. Telephone (01463) 233140.

Designed by Thomas Telford and completed in 1822, the Caledonian Canal links the lochs of the Great Glen (Loch Lochy, Loch Oich and Loch Ness). It provides a coast to coast shortcut between Corpach near Fort William and Clachnaharry at Inverness. The canal has been described as the most beautiful in Europe – the spectacular Highland scenery of lochs, mountains and glens is unusual for a canal. A wide variety of craft use the canal throughout the year and can usually be seen at close quarters as they pass through locks and bridges. There are a number of pleasure cruises available on the canal and small boats are available. See also 1105 Neptune's Staircase.

---

259 CALEDONIAN RAILWAY, BRECHIN 3 P11

The Station, 2 Park Road, Brechin, Angus. Near Brechin town centre, follow road signs. Nearest railway station Montrose, bus or tour bus from Montrose. Open Easter, May–Sep and Dec, Sun only; telephone to confirm. Charge ££. Group concessions. Guided tours by prior arrangement. Explanatory displays. Gift shop. Light refreshments, picnic area at Bridge of Dun. Baby changing facilities at Brechin. WC. Wheelchair access with assistance. Disabled WC. Car and coach parking. Telephone (01561) 377760 publicity, (01356) 622992 station.

From the unique Victorian terminus at Brechin, board a steam train and journey back in time as you travel the falling grade to Bridge of Dun. The station at Bridge of Dun was a junction on the former Strathmore main line and a frequent stopping point for Royal Trains. A short distance from the station, visitors can take interesting walks along both banks of the South Esk and part of the Montrose Basin bird sanctuary.

---

260 CALLENDAR HOUSE 6 L15

Callendar Park, Falkirk. 1 mile (2km) east of town centre. Railway and bus station, 10 minutes walk. Open all year, Mon–Sat 1000–1700 (also Suns from Apr–Sep 1400–1700 and most public holidays). Charge £. Group concessions. Guided tours by arrangement (£££). Explanatory displays. Gift shop. Tearoom. Garden and children's play area, leisure facilities in park. WC. Braille map of exhibition. Wheelchair access. Disabled WC. Car and coach parking. Telephone (01324) 503770.

Callendar House encapsulates 600 years of Scotland's history from medieval times to the 20th century and was visited by great historical figures like Mary, Queen of Scots, Cromwell and Bonnie Prince Charlie. Permanent attractions include displays on the Story of Callendar House, and on the Falkirk area during the great social revolution of 1750–1850. Costumed interpretations bring this history to life, while a programme of temporary exhibitions provides for a wide range of interests. The house's research centre contains an extensive archive and other material on the area's history.

---

261 CAMBO GARDENS **5 P14**

Cambo Estate, Kingsbarns, St Andrews. 1 mile (1.5km) south of Kingsbarns on A917, 2.5 miles (4km) north of Crail. Nearest railway station Leuchars. Open all year, daily 1000–1700. Charge £. Children free. Group concessions. Guided tours by arrangement. Picnics allowed. WC. Wheelchair access. Car and coach parking. Telephone (01333) 450313.

Walled garden full of romantic charm designed around the Cambo burn, which is spanned by ornamental bridges and a greenhouse. Carpets of snowdrops and bulbs in spring, a lilac walk, magnificent herbaceous borders, an extensive rose collection and ornamental potager are highlights in summer. There is a September border and a colchicum meadow in autumn. Woodland walks follow the burn to a secluded sandy beach.

---

262 CAMBUSKENNETH ABBEY **6 L14**

HS. 1 mile (2km) east of Stirling. Nearest railway station Stirling, bus from Glasgow and Edinburgh. Access at all times. View exterior only. Free. Telephone 0131 668 8800.

Ruins of an abbey founded in 1147 as a house of Augustinian canons. Scene of Robert the Bruce's parliament in 1326 and the burial place of James III and his queen. The fine detached tower is the only substantial survivor, but extensive foundations remain of the rest.

---

263 CAMPBELTOWN MUSEUM **4 F18**

Hall Street, Campbeltown, Argyll. 38 miles (61km) south of Tarbet, Loch Fyne on A83. Daily bus service from Glasgow. Open all year, Tue and Thu 1000–1300, 1400–1700 and 1730–1930, Wed, Fri and Sat 1000–1300 and 1400–1700. Closed Sun and Mon. Free. Explanatory displays. WC. Wheelchair access with assistance. Car parking.

Listed building (A), designed by the renowned Scottish architect J J Burnet. The collections are mainly archaeology and natural history with some local history and maritime material. Natural history displays and a diorama depicting the landscape and birdlife of Kintyre.

---

264 CAMUS A CHARRAIG **2 G5**

Ross and Cromarty. On the main road to Mellon Udrigle, north of Gairloch on A832.

A beautiful white sand beach which borders a broad sandy bay of sparkling blue-green waters surrounded by mountains.

---

265 CANDACRAIG GARDENS, GALLERY AND NURSERY **3 N9**

Strathdon, Aberdeenshire. 20 miles (32km) west of Alford on A944 (Aberdeen to Inverness Highland Tourist Route). Nearest railway station Huntly, bus service from Aberdeen. Coach parking by arrangement. Open May–Sep, daily 1000–1800. Charge £. Children free. Honesty box. Guided tours by arrangement. Explanatory displays. Barbecue and picnic area for hire on hourly or daily basis. Garden marquees available. WC. Wheelchair access. Disabled WC. Car parking. Telephone (01975) 651226.

An 1830s listed walled garden and a Gothic summerhouse. Recently restored, it now serves as a gallery and marriage room. There is a display garden featuring specialist hardy plants, some from the Himalayas and the Far East. Visitors are offered a wide selection of the plants grown and propagated in the garden nursery which was formerly a kitchen garden adjacent to Candacraig House.

266 CANNA

2 D9

NTS. Inner Hebrides. Access by ferry (no cars) from Mallaig. Open all year. Free. Telephone (01687) 462466.

This beautiful Hebridean island offers spectacular views, interesting archaeological remains and fascinating birdlife. The small farming population still uses traditional crofting systems. There is a post office, but no shops, pubs or roads. For details of work camps and holiday accommodation, contact the NTS Head Office in Edinburgh on 0131 243 9300.

---

267 CAOL ILA DISTILLERY

4 E15

Port Askaig, Isle of Islay. On the A846, on the east side of Islay, just by Port Askaig. Bus on island, 0.5 mile (2km) walk to distillery. Open all year, Mon–Fri by appointment. Visitor centre. Charge £. Guided tours by arrangement. Gift shop. WC. Car parking. Telephone (01496) 840207.

A distillery built in 1846 by Hector Henderson. It stands in a picutresque setting at the foot of a steep hill with its own small pier overlooking the Sound of Islay and paps of Jura.

---

268 CAPE WRATH

2 H2

12 miles (19.5km) northwest of Durness. Ferry: telephone (01971) 511376. Minibus: telephone (01971) 511287 or 511343.

The most northerly point of Scotland's northwest seaboard. A passenger ferry (summer only) connects with a minibus service to the cape. Also mainland Britain's highest sea cliffs at Clo Mor which stand 920 feet (280.5m) high.

---

269 CARDHU DISTILLERY VISITOR CENTRE

3 M8

Knockando, Aberlour. From Elgin take the A941 south to Rothes, continue for 3 miles (5km) then travel west on the B9102 for approximately 7 miles (11km). From Grantown-on-Spey take the B9102 northeast for approximately 17 miles (27km). Open Mar–Nov, Mon–Fri 0930–1630; Jul–Sep also Sat 0930–1630 and Sun 1100–1600. Dec–Feb, Mon–Fri (except between Christmas and New Year) 1000–1600. Charge £. Guided tours. Explanatory displays. Gift shop. Picnic area. WC. Limited wheelchair access. Disabled WC. Car parking. Telephone (01340) 872555.

The origins of Cardhu go back to the heyday of illicit distilling, when farmers made use of their own barley and local water. Licensed since 1824, the Cumming family expanded and improved the distillery over many years. Now a major element in the Johnnie Walker brand. Visitor centre, shop with gifts and souvenirs.

---

270 CARDONESS CASTLE

5 K20

HS. Gatehouse of Fleet, Kirkcudbrightshire. On A75, 1 mile (2km) southwest of Gatehouse of Fleet. Situated on main bus route from Stranraer to Dumfries. Open Apr–Sep, daily 0930–1830; Oct–Mar, Sat and Sun 0930–1630. Charge £. Group concessions. Guided tours. Explanatory displays. Gift shop. Carvings can be touched. Car and coach parking. Telephone (01557) 814427.

The well-preserved ruin of a 15th-century tower house, the ancient home of the McCullochs of Galloway. Four storeys with a vaulted basement. Features include the original stairway, stone benches and elaborate fireplaces.

---

271 CARLETON CASTLE

4 H19

Off A77, 6 miles (9.5km) south of Girvan. Access at all reasonable times. Free.

One in a link of Kennedy watchtowers along the coast. Now a ruin, it was famed in a ballad as the seat of a baron who got rid of seven wives by pushing them over the cliff, but who was himself disposed of by May Culean, his eighth wife.

272 CARLYLE'S BIRTHPLACE **5 M20**

NTS. The Arched House, Ecclefechan, Lockerbie. On A74 in Ecclefechan, 5.5 miles (9km) southeast of Lockerbie. Bus from Lockerbie. Open May–Sep, Fri–Mon 1330–1730. Charge £. Children free. Group concessions. Explanatory displays. WC. Car and coach parking. Telephone (01576) 300666.

Birthplace of writer Thomas Carlyle (born 1795). Furnished to reflect domestic life in his time, with an important collection of family portraits and belongings.

---

273 JANE WELSH CARLYLE MUSEUM **6 P15**

2 Lodge Street, Haddington, East Lothian. Located at west end of Haddington High Street. Bus service from Edinburgh. Open Apr–Sep, Wed–Sat 1400–1700. Charge £. Group concessions. Guided tours. Explanatory displays. Garden. WC. Wheelchair access to garden. Car and coach parking. Telephone (01620) 823738.

The childhood home of Jane Baillie Welsh has been restored to perpetuate her memory. Jane was the only child of Dr John Welsh, a 19th-century Haddington medical practitioner. In 1821, she met and was courted by Thomas Carlyle, writer and philosopher who was to become the 'sage of Chelsea'.

---

274 CARMICHAEL HERITAGE CENTRE **6 L17**

Carmichael Estate Office, Westmains, Carmichael, Biggar. 4 miles (6.5km) south of Lanark on A73. Nearest railway and bus stations Lanark, bus to Biggar. Open all year except Jan and Feb, daily 0930–1730. Farm and gift shop open all year, daily (except Christmas and New Year) 0930–1730. Charge ££. Group concessions. Guided tours by prior arrangement (available in French and German). Explanatory displays. Gift shop. Restaurant and picnic area. WC. Wheelchair access. Disabled WC. Car and coach parking. Telephone (01899) 308336.

Scotland's only wax model collection tells Scotland's and Carmichael's story using Madame Tussaud quality models. The Clan Centre for southern Scotland concentrates on the Carmichaels who have lived here throughout the millennium. It also includes information on many other southern Scottish families and clans as well as the history of the estate's agriculture and environment. Wind energy exhibit. Deerpark. Venison farm shop. Adventure playground. Animal farm. Horse and pony trekking. Clydesdale horse and cart rides. Heritage walks. Orienteering and way-finding.

---

275 CARNASSERIE CASTLE **4 F14**

HS. Off A816, 9 miles (14.5km) north of Lochgilphead, 2 miles (3km) north of Kilmartin, Argyll. Nearest railway station Oban, then bus to Kilmartin. Open at all times. Free. Picnic area. Car and coach parking. Telephone 0131 668 8800.

A handsome combined tower house and hall, home of John Carswell, first Protestant Bishop of the Isles and translator of the first book printed in Gaelic. Fine architectural details of the late 16th century. The castle was captured and partly blown up during Argyll's rebellion in 1685.

---

276 CARN BAN **4 G17**

HS. 3.5 miles (5.5km) northeast of Lagg on the south coast of the Isle of Arran. By ferry from Ardrossan to Brodick, bus from Brodick to Corriecravie. Access at all times. Free. Telephone 0131 668 8800.

One of the most famous Neolithic long cairns of southwest Scotland.

---

277 ANDREW CARNEGIE BIRTHPLACE MUSEUM **6 M15**

Moodie Street, Dunfermline, Fife. 18 miles (29km) from Edinburgh on A823 off M90. Nearest railway and bus stations Dunfermline. Frequent service all year. Open Apr–Oct, Mon–Sat 1100–1700, Sun 1400–1700;

Jun–Aug, Mon–Sat 1000–1700; Nov–Mar, daily 1400–1600. Charge £. Children free. Group concessions. Guided tours by arrangement. Explanatory displays. Gift shop. WC. Wheelchair access. Photo album of cottage (inaccessible) available. Disabled WC. Car and coach parking Telephone (01383) 724302.

Weaver's cottage and the birthplace of Andrew Carnegie who was born here in 1835. The adjoining memorial hall was provided by his widow in 1928. The displays tell the extraordinary rags to riches story of Andrew Carnegie, the weaver's son who emigrated to America and forged a fortune from the furnaces of the American steel industry. He went on to endow a range of trusts which still operate today. Weaving demonstrations on the first Friday of the month from May to October.

---

278 CARNEGIE LEISURE CENTRE **6 M15**

Pilmuir Street, Dunfermline, Fife. Situated in the centre of Dunfermline. Railway station less than 1 mile (1.5km), bus station 5 minutes walk. Open all year, Mon–Fri 0700–2200, Sat, Sun and bank holidays 0800–2200. Charge £. Group concessions. Guided tours by prior arrangement only. Explanatory displays. Café and vending machines. Crèche. WC. Wheelchair access with lift to upper floors. Disabled WC. Car parking. Telephone (01383) 314200.

Listed building dating from 1904. Donated by Andrew Carnegie to the town of his birth. The building is now a fully equipped leisure centre. It caters for a wide variety of wet and dry activities and is open throughout the year.

---

279 CARNEGIE MUSEUM **3 Q9**

The Square, Inverurie. In Inverurie. Nearest railway and bus service Inverurie. Open all year, Mon–Fri (not Wed) 1400–1700, Sat 1000–1300 and 1400–1600. Free. Explanatory displays. Gift shop. Car and coach parking. Telephone (01771) 622906.

Local archaeology including Beaker folk and Pictish carved stones and transportation.

---

280 CARN LIATH **3 L5**

HS. By the A9, 3 miles (5km) east northeast of Golspie, Sutherland. Nearest railway station Dunrobin. Bus service from Inverness, alight past Dunrobin Castle. Access at all times. Free. Car parking. Telephone 0131 668 8800.

A typical broch, surviving to first-floor level, with associated settlement.

---

281 CARRICK HOUSE **1 C9**

Eday, Orkney Islands. 20 miles (32km) north of Kirkwall by ferry. Ferry runs twice daily, air service from Kirkwall on Wed. Taxis and bicycles available from pier, 7 miles (11km) to house. Open mid Jun–mid Sep, Sunday afternoons. Other times by arrangement. Charge £. Concessions for large groups. Guided tours (available in French and German). Explanatory displays. Postcards for sale. Picnic area. Garden. WC. Limited wheelchair access. Car parking. Telephone (01857) 622260.

Historic private house dating from the 17th century, built by John Stewart, Earl of Carrick, younger brother of Patrick Stewart, Earl of Orkney. The house was the scene of the capture of Pirate Gow in 1725. It was renovated into a larger house incorporating earlier buildings in the mid 19th century. It is built of local sandstone and is harled and crow-stepped in the traditional Orkney style. The guided tours take in the house, garden and other parts of the island. Spectacular views.

---

282 CARRON POTTERY, CRAFT AND ART GALLERY **2 G8**

Cam-Allt, Strathcarron, Ross and Cromarty. 1 mile (1.5km) south of Strathcarron railway station on A890. Open Mar–Dec, Mon–Sat 0900–1800. Closed Sun. Free. Gift shop. Restaurant next door. WC.

Wheelchair access with assistance. Disabled WC. Car and coach parking. Telephone (01520) 722321.

Well-established craft shop selling a wide range of Scottish and local crafts. Visitors can view the pottery attached to the shop. Art Gallery with work by local and professional artists. Occasional solo exhibitions. Sculptures and ceramics.

---

283 CARSAIG ARCHES **4 E13**

On shore 3 miles (5km) west of Carsaig, South Mull. Access at all times. Free.

A 3-mile (5km) walk from Carsaig leads to these remarkable tunnels formed by the sea in the basaltic rock. Reached only at low tide. On the way is the Nun's Cave; it is said that nuns driven out of Iona at the time of the Reformation sheltered here. The west wall bears numerous incised carvings, including crosses of various shapes, some of which could be as old as the late 6th-9th centuries.

---

284 CARSLUITH CASTLE **4 J20**

HS. On A75, 7 miles (11km) west of Gatehouse of Fleet, Kirkcudbrightshire. Nearest railway station Dumfries, buses from Dumfries, Newton Stewart or Stranraer. Open at all times. Free. Car parking. Telephone 0131 668 8800.

The delightful and well-preserved ruin of a 16th-century tower house with 18th-century ranges of outhouses still in use by the farmer. One of its owners was the last abbot of Sweetheart Abbey.

---

285 CARSPHAIRN HERITAGE CENTRE **5 K19**

Carsphairn. On A713, 25 miles (40km) south of Ayr and 25 miles (40km) north of Castle Douglas. Limited bus service from Castle Douglas and Ayr. Open Easter–May and early Oct, Sat 1030–1700, Sun and bank holidays 1400–1700; Jun–Sep, Mon–Sat (except Wed) 1030–1700, Sun 1400–1700. Free. Explanatory displays. Gift shop. Picnic area. Garden. WC. Wheelchair access. Disabled WC. Car and coach parking. Telephone (01644) 460653.

Carsphairn Heritage Centre houses a permanent display on the parish together with a temporary annual exhibition, featuring local history. There is also a reference section which pays particular attention to family history records relevant to the area and a small display of locally made articles for sale together with other relevant momentos of the area.

---

286 CARTLAND BRIDGE **6 L16**

On A73 west of Lanark. Access at all times. Free.

An impressive bridge built by Telford in 1822 over a gorge, carrying the Mouse Water. It is one of the highest road bridges in Scotland.

---

287 CASHMERE VISITOR CENTRE **3 M7**

Newmill, Elgin, Moray. 45 miles (72.5km) east of Inverness on A96 near Elgin Cathedral. Rail and bus service to Elgin from Inverness and Aberdeen. Open all year, Mon–Sat 0900–1730; Jul–Sep, Mon–Fri closes at 1800; Jun–Sep, Sun 1100–1700. Free. Guided tours (also available in German and French). Explanatory displays. Gift shop. Audio-visual in European languages and Japanese. WC. Wheelchair access. Disabled WC. Car and coach parking. Telephone (01343) 554099.

The only British mill to transform cashmere from fibre to garment. Knitwear, travel rugs and fabrics are dyed, spun, woven, knitted and finished using traditional skills and the latest technology. The story of luxury fine fibres interwoven with the 200-year history of the Johnstons (who started manufacturing on this site) is told through an audio-visual presentation, hands-on displays and information boards.

288 CASSLEY FALLS 3 J5

At Invercassley, Sutherland, on A837.

An attractive falls and walkway by Rosehall. Salmon can be seen leaping during the summer months.

---

289 CASTLE CAMPBELL 6 L14

HS. Dollar, Clackmannanshire. In Dollar Glen, 1 mile (2km) north of Dollar. Bus via Dollar from Stirling of St Andrews then 20 minute walk. Open Apr–Sep, daily 0930–1830; Oct–Mar, Mon–Sat (except Thu pm and Fri) 0930–1630, Sun 1400–1630. Charge £. Group concessions. Guided tours. Explanatory displays. Gift shop. Tearoom. Garden. WC. Car parking. Telephone (01259) 742408.

Once known as Castle Gloom, the castle was built towards the end of the 15th century by the first Earl of Argyll. Located on a steep mound with extensive views to the plains of the Forth. Burned by Cromwell in the 1650s. The original tower is well preserved. The 60 acres (24ha) of woodland in the Glen make an attractive walk to the castle.

---

290 CASTLECARY 6 K15

HS. On the B816, east of Castlecary village, Stirlingshire. Nearest railway and bus stations Falkirk. Access at all times. Free. Telephone 0131 668 8800.

The reduced earthworks of a fort on the Antonine Wall (see 62).

---

291 CASTLE DOUGLAS ART GALLERY 5 K20

Market Street, Castle Douglas. Adjacent to Castle Douglas library at the east end of the town. Nearest railway station Dumfries, bus to Castle Douglas. Open Mar–Dec, Mon–Sat 1100–1600; telephone to confirm. Free. Charge for some exhibitions. Wheelchair access. Telephone (01557) 331643.

First opened in 1938, having been gifted to the town by Mrs Ethel Bristowe, a talented artist in her own right. The gallery now forms an excellent venue for an annual programme of temporary exhibitions from Easter to Christmas, ranging from fine art and craft to photography.

---

292 CASTLE FRASER 3 Q9

NTS. Sauchen, Inverurie. Off A944, 16 miles (25.5km) west of Aberdeen. Bus from Aberdeen. Open Easter–May and Sep, daily 1330–1730; Jun–Aug, daily 1100–1730; weekends in Oct 1330–1730. Garden and grounds open all year, daily 0930–1800 (grounds close at sunset). Charge ££. Children free. Garden and grounds only, £. Group concessions. Guided tours by arrangement. Explanatory displays (information sheets in six languages). Gift shop. Tearoom and picnic area. Garden and grounds, adventure playground. WC. Limited wheelchair access. Disabled WC. Car and coach parking. Telephone (01330) 833463.

Magnificent castle completed in 1636, one of the most sophisticated Scottish buildings of the period – particularly fine Great Hall. Notable paintings and furnishings. Peaceful walled garden and interesting woodland walks.

---

293 CASTLE GARRISON ENCOUNTER 3 K8

Inverness Castle, Castle Hill, Inverness. In Inverness town centre. 0.25 miles (0.5km) from Inverness railway station, local bus service. Open Mar–Nov, Mon–Sat 1030–1730. Charge £. Group concessions. Guided tours. Explanatory displays. Gift shop. Limited wheelchair access.

Based at the imposing Inverness castle, Castle Garrison Encounter portrays life as it was during the Jacobite rebellion period of 1745. Actors depict life as soldiers and tell of conditions while garrisoned at the castle. Visitors sign on as new recruits to the regiment and are taken through the castle basements and into the round tower.

294 CASTLE HOUSE MUSEUM 6 H15

Castle Gardens, Dunoon, Argyll. Opposite the pier in Dunoon. Open Easter–mid Oct, Mon–Sat 1030–1630, Sun 1400–1630. Charge £. Accompanied children free. Group concessions. Guided tours. Explanatory displays and audio-visual presentation. Gift shop. WC. Wheelchair access. Disabled WC. Car parking. Telephone (01369) 701422.

The museum illustrates the history of Dunoon and district from pre-history to the recent past. Four rooms have been set aside to give the visitor a reflection of life in Victorian times. Set in pleasant gardens, opposite Dunoon's beautiful Victorian Pier with excellent views of the surrounding area.

---

295 CASTLE JAIL 5 P18

Castle Gate, Jedburgh, Roxburghshire. Short walk from town centre up the Castlegate. Nearest railway station Edinburgh; bus from Edinburgh. Open late Mar–Oct, Mon–Sat 1000–1645, Sun 1300–1600. Open on bank holidays. Last entry 30 minutes before closing time. Charge £. Scottish Borders residents admitted free. Group concessions. Guided tours if pre-booked. Explanatory displays. Gift shop. Picnic area; drinks available. Children's play area. WC. Limited wheelchair access. Disabled WC. Car and coach parking. Telephone (01835) 863254.

Jedburgh Castle, which was built in 1824, is one of the few remaining examples of a Howard Reform prison. It stands on the site of the old Jedburgh Castle, which was razed to the ground in the mid 1400s. It takes its architectural appearance from the earlier castle.

---

296 CASTLE KEEP 2 E8

Unit 7B1, Portree Industrial Estate, Portree, Isle of Skye. On the outskirts of Portree on the Dunvegan Road. 1 mile (1.5km) from the town centre. Open all year, Mon–Fri 1000–1630. Free. Explanatory displays. Gift shop. WC. Car parking. Telephone (01478) 612114.

Bladesmith making hand-forged swords, knives, dirks and traditional Scottish weaponry.

---

297 CASTLELAW HILL FORT 6 M16

HS. 1 mile northwest of Glencorse, Midlothian, off the A702, 7 miles (11km) south of Edinburgh. Nearest railway station Edinburgh, bus from Edinburgh then 1 mile (2km) walk. Open at all times. Free. Car and coach parking. Telephone 0131 668 8800.

A small Iron Age hill fort consisting of two concentric banks and ditches. An earth-house is preserved in the older rock-cut ditch. Occupied in Roman times.

---

298 CASTLE MENZIES 5 L12

Weem, Aberfeldy, Perthshire. 1.5 miles (2.5km) west of Aberfeldy. Nearest railway station Pitlochry (12 miles/19km). Bus service to Aberfeldy. Coach parking by prior arrangement. Open Apr–Oct, Mon–Sat 1030–1700, Sun 1400–1700. Last entry 1630. Charge £. Group concessions. Explanatory displays and self-guided leaflet (also available in French and German). Gift shop. Tearoom. Walled garden. WC. Limited wheelchair access. Disabled WC. Car parking. Telephone (01887) 820982.

Imposing 16th-century castle restored by the Menzies Clan Society, a fine example of the transition between a Z-plan clan stronghold and a later mansion house. Seat of the clan chiefs for over 400 years, Castle Menzies was involved in a number of historic occurrences. Bonnie Prince Charlie stayed here on his way to Culloden in 1746. Small clan museum.

---

299 CASTLE OF OLD WICK 3 N3

HS. 1 mile (2km) south of Wick, Caithness. Nearest railway station Wick, bus service from Wick. Free. Telephone 0131 668 8800.

The ruin of a very early Norse tower house on a spectacular site on a spine of rock, known as the Brig O' Trams, projecting into the sea between two deep narrow gulleys. Great care required when visiting site.

---

300 CASTLE OF ST JOHN **4 G20**

Charlotte Street, Stranraer, Wigtownshire. In Stranraer centre. Nearest railway station Stranraer, bus from Glasgow or ferry from Belfast. Open Easter–mid Sep, Mon–Sat 1000–1300 and 1400–1700. Charge £. Explanatory displays. Gift shop. Telephone (01776) 705088.

Medieval tower house built circa 1500. Houses an exhibition which tells its story, highlighting its use by Government troops during the suppression of the Covenanters and its Victorian use as a prison. Family activities.

---

301 CASTLE SEMPLE COLLEGIATE CHURCH **6 J16**

HS. At Castle Semple, Ayrshire, 4 miles (6.5km) west of Howwood. Access at all times, view exterior only. Telephone 0131 668 8800.

A late gothic church with a three-sided east end with windows of an unusual style. See also 342 Clyde Muirshiel Castle Semple Visitor Centre.

---

302 CASTLE SWEEN **4 F15**

HS. On the east shore of Loch Sween, 15 miles (24km) southwest of Lochgilphead, Argyll. Bus from Lochgilphead to Achanamara, then 14 mile (22.5km) walk. Access at all times. Free. Telephone 0131 668 8800.

Probably the oldest stone castle on the Scottish mainland. Built in the mid 12th century with later towers in addition to now vanished wooden structures. Destroyed by Sir Alexander Macdonald in 1647.

---

303 CASTLE VARRICH **3 K3**

Tongue, Sutherland. Ruin located above Kyle of Tongue on a promintory. Steep path to castle accessible from the gate beside the Royal Bank of Scotland.

A 14th-century MacKay stronghold. Beautiful views along Kyle of Tongue

---

304 CATERTHUNS **3 P11**

HS. Near the village of Menmuir about 5 miles (8km) northwest of Brechin, Angus. Nearest railway station Montrose, bus to Brechin. Open all year. Free. Telephone 0131 668 8800.

Two spectacular large Iron Age hill forts standing either side of the road from Balrownie to Pitmundie. The Brown Caterthun has four concentric ramparts and ditches; the White Caterthun is a well-preserved fort with a massive stone rampart, defensive ditch and outer earthworks.

---

305 CAWDOR CASTLE **3 L7**

Nairn. 5 miles (8km) southwest of Nairn on B9090 off the A96. Bus service from Inverness and Nairn. Open May–mid Oct, daily 1000–1730, last admission 1700. Charge £££. Free to blind visitors. Group concessions. Explanatory displays. Gift shop. Licensed restaurant, snack bar and picnic area. WC. Limited wheelchair access. Disabled WC. Car and coach parking. Telephone (01667) 404615.

Cawdor Castle is the name romantically associated by Shakespeare with Macbeth. The medieval tower and drawbridge are still intact and generations of art lovers and scholars are responsible for the eclectic collection of paintings, books and porcelain to be found in the castle. There are beautiful gardens, five nature trails, a nine-hole golf course and putting green, gift and bookshop and woolshop with a wide range of Scottish knitwear and children's clothes.

306 CHAPEL FINIAN **4 H21**

HS. 5 miles (8km) northwest of Port William, Wigtownshire. Nearest railway station Stranraer, then bus to Port William. Access at all times. Free. Telephone 0131 668 8800.

The foundation remains of a small chapel or oratory, probably dating from the 10th or 11th century, in an enclosure about 50 feet (15m) wide.

---

307 CHAPEL OF SAND **2 G6**

In Laide, north of Gairloch, Ross and Cromarty.

Said to have been constructed by St Columba in the 6th century. Parts of the intricately carved windows of the chapel are still intact and a large remnant of an arch can be seen.

---

308 CHARLESTOWN LIME HERITAGE TRUST **6 M15**

Granary Building, Rocks Road, Charlestown. Off A985, 4 miles (6.5km) south of Dunfermline. Nearest railway station Dunfermline, local bus service. Open May–Sep, guided walks Sun 1400 and Wed 1900; groups by arrangement. Charge £. Group concessions. Guided tours. Explanatory displays. Gift shop. Restaurant and tearoom. WC. Wheelchair access. Car and coach parking. Telephone (01383) 872006.

Charlestown is a very early example of a planned village and has a fascinating unique story to tell. Established in 1756 by Charles Bruce, 5th Earl of Elgin and 9th of Kincardine. The village was a self-sufficient complete industrial complex based on the large deposits of limestone surrounding the village. Today there are 14 kilns. The works closed in 1956.

---

309 CHATELHERAULT COUNTRY PARK **6 K16**

Carlisle Road, Ferniegair, Hamilton. Nearest railway station Hamilton, bus from Hamilton. Visitor centre open all year, daily 1000–1700 (Apr–Sep, Sun closes 1730). Oct–Mar lodge closed Fri. Free. Guided tours. Explanatory displays. Gift shop. Tearoom and picnic area. Garden, children's play area. WC. Limited wheelchair access. Disabled WC. Car and coach parking. Telephone (01698) 426213.

A magnificent hunting lodge and kennels built in 1732 by William Adam for the Duke of Hamilton, since restored. Extensive country walks. Exhibition on the Clyde Valley, geology and natural history of the park, 18th-century gardens, terraces and parterre. See also 243 Cadzow Castle.

---

310 CHESTERS HILL FORT **6 P15**

HS. 1 mile (2km) south of Drem on unclassified road to Haddington, East Lothian. Nearest railway station Drem, bus from Edinburgh to North Berwick, then bus to Drem, then walk 1 mile (2km). Open all year. Free. Telephone 0131 668 8800.

One of the best examples of an Iron Age hill fort with multiple ramparts. A souterrain is built into one of the ditches.

---

311 CHILDHOOD MEMORIES TOY MUSEUM **3 L9**

Coylumbridge, Aviemore. 2 miles (3km) from Aviemore off ski road, look for Nethybridge junction. Bus service from Aviemore. Open summer months, daily 1000–1700, for other times please check. Charge £. Group concessions. Guided tours. Explanatory displays. Gift shop. Picnic area. WC. Artefacts can be handled by blind visitors. Wheelchair access with assistance. Car and coach parking. Telephone (01479) 812022.

A small white cottage by the banks of the River Druie is home to over 2500 toys, dolls, teddy bears, working train sets. Displays of 3D holograms. Children's quizzes. Attractions for all ages.

312 CHILDREN'S AMUSEMENT PARK — 5 L12

Armoury Road, Pitlochry, Perthshire. In the centre of Pitlochry, off the main street on road to dam and fish ladder. 546 yards (500m) from railway station. Open Easter–Oct, daily 1000–2100. Free. Charge £ per ride. Group concessions. Picnic area and snack bar. WC. Wheelchair access. Car parking. Telephone (01796) 472876.

Amusement park with remote control boats, cars and trucks, bumper cars and boats, racing cars and bikes, water blasters, children's roundabout, football and basketball. Family amusement arcade, driving, shooting and skill games.

---

313 CHISHOLMS HIGHLAND DRESS — 3 K8

47–51 Castle Street, Inverness. Inverness town centre. 10 minutes walk from railway and bus stations. Open all year, Mon–Sat 0900–1730 and 0700–2100 during summer. Free. Guided tours by request. Explanatory displays. Gift shop. WC. Limited wheelchair access. Telephone (01463) 234599.

Display of kilt-making and of Scottish Highland dress. There are also models in Highland dress and uniforms from the period of 1745 to the present day. Tartans, swords and other weapons on show.

---

314 CHORAIDH CROFT FARM PARK — 3 J3

94 Laid, Loch Eribollside, Altnaharra, Sutherland. On the western shore of Loch Eriboll on A838 between Durness (7 miles/11km), and Tongue (22 miles/35.5km). Post bus from Lairg via Altnaharra. Open Easter–Oct, daily 1030–1830. Charge £. Group concessions. Explanatory displays. Gift shop. Restaurant, tearoom and picnic area. Evening meals in restaurant by arrangement. Pets corner. B&B accommodation available. WC. Limited wheelchair access. Disabled WC. Car and coach parking. Telephone (01971) 511235.

Britain's most northerly farm park with over 40 different breeds of friendly animals, a pets corner and museum showing crofting life over the last 150 years. Good location for artists, photographers and bird and animal enthusiasts of all ages.

---

315 CHURCH OF ST MAGNUS — 1 B10

HS. On the Isle of Egilsay, Orkney. Bus from Kirkwall to Tingwall, ferry from Tingwall to Egilsay. Access at all times. Free. Telephone 0131 668 8800.

The complete, but roofless, ruin of a 12th-century church with a remarkable round tower of the Irish type. Dramatically sited.

---

316 CHURCH OF THE HOLY RUDE — 6 L14

St John Street, Stirling. Nearest railway and bus station Stirling. Open all year Sunday services; May–Sep, Mon–Sun 1000–1700. Free. Explanatory displays. Induction loop system. Wheelchair access. Telephone (01786) 475275.

Reputed to be the only church in Scotland still in use which has witnessed a coronation, that of James VI in 1567. John Knox preached here. Many Scottish kings and queens worshipped here, most notable Mary, Queen of Scots. Magnigicent pipe organ, extensive restoration.

---

317 CILLE BHARRA — 2 A9

At Eolaigearraidh (Eoligarry), at the north end of Isle of Barra. Access at all times. Free. Telephone 01871 810336 (Castlebay Tourist Office).

The ruined church of St Barr, who gave his name to the island, and the restored chapel of St Mary formed part of the medieval monastery. Among the gravestones preserved there was a unique stone carved with a Celtic cross on one side and Norse runes on the other. A replica of this stone now stands in Cille Bharra.

318 CITADEL LEISURE CENTRE, AYR 4 J17

South Harbour Street, Ayr. Situated at north end of the sea front. Nearest railway and bus stations Ayr. Open all year, daily until 2200. Check timetables for facilities. Charges depend on activity. Café. Limited Crèche facilities. WC. Wheelchair access. Disabled WC. Car and coach parking. Telephone (01292) 269793.

The centre has a 25-metre lane pool, teaching and diving pool sauna suite, steam room and plunge pool. Sports hall, squash courts, meeting rooms and fitness suite which incorporates several units of resistant equipment compatible for wheelchair users.

---

319 CLACHAN BRIDGE 4 F13

B844 off A816, 12 miles (19k) southwest of Oban. Access at all times. Free.

This picturesque single-arched bridge, built in 1792 and linking the mainland with the island of Seil, is often claimed to be the only bridge to span the Atlantic (although there are others similar). The waters are actually those of the narrow Seil Sound, which joins the Firth of Lorne to Outer Loch Melfort, but they can, with some justification, claim to be an arm of the Atlantic.

---

320 CLACHANMORE GALLERY AND TEAROOM 4 H21

Ardwell, Stranraer. 10 miles (16km) south of Stranraer, between Sandhead and Ardwell. Open Easter–Oct, Wed–Sun 1100–1700. Free. Guided tours. Explanatory displays. Gift shop. Tearoom. Walled garden with tables. WC. Wheelchair access. Disabled WC. Car parking. Telephone (01776) 860200.

Changing exhibitions, many featuring the best of Dumfries and Galloway artists. Outside are sculptures by Jeff White.

---

321 CLAGGAN CRAFTS 4 F12

Claggan, by Lochaline, Morvern, Argyll. 4 miles (6.5km) from Lochaline on A884. Open Mar–Dec daily (except Tue and Sat) 1100–1700; Jan, Feb by arrangement. Free. Gift shop. Wheelchair access with assistance. Car parking. Telephone (01967) 421240.

Knitwear workshop producing an extensive range of made-to-measure garments using varied designs with themes taken from wildlife, animals and sport. Pet markings can be matched from photograph and knitted on a sweater. High quality, locally produced crafts – glass, ceramics, leatherwork plus cards and prints featuring local views.

---

322 CLAN ARMSTRONG MUSEUM 5 N19

Lodge Walk, Castleholm, Langholm, Dumfriesshire. Off the A7 in Langholm, north of Carlisle. Regular bus service from Edinburgh to Carlisle passes on A7. Open Easter–mid Oct, Tue–Sun 1330–1630. Charge £. Clan Armstrong Trust members free on production of card. Guided tours. Explanatory displays. Gift shop. Picnic area nearby. Wheelchair access. Car and coach parking. Telephone (01387) 381610.

The world's largest Armstrong Museum, containing the most extensive Armstrong archives and displaying the history of this formidable Borders' family from the reiving days of the 15th and 16th centuries to the present.

---

323 CLAN CAMERON MUSEUM 2 H10

Achnacarry, Spean Bridge, Inverness-shire. 5 miles (8km) from the Commando Memorial on B8005. Signposted. Open Easter–Oct, daily 1330–1700; Jul–Aug, daily 1100–1700. Charge £. Children free. Group concessions. Guided tours if requested. Explanatory displays. Gift shop. Garden. WC. Wheelchair access. Car and coach parking. Telephone (01397) 712480.

The history of the Cameron Clan, its involvement in the Jacobite Risings and the subsequent resurgence of the clan.

Visitors can also learn about the story of Achnacarry and its wildlife. There are sections on the Queen's Own Cameron Highlanders and the Commandos who trained at Achnacarry during WWII. The building is on the site of a croft burned by Cumberland's soldiers in 1746.

---

324 CLAN DONNACHAIDH MUSEUM **3 L11**

Bruar, by Pitlochry, Perthshire. 4 miles (6.5km) north of Blair Atholl, 328 yards (300m) from A9. Nearest railway station Blair Atholl, local bus service. Open Easter–Oct, Mon–Sat 1000–1730, Sun 1100–1730. Charge £. Group concessions. Guided tours on request. Explanatory displays. External seating area and garden. Wheelchair access. Car and coach parking. Telephone (01796) 483264.

Clan Donnachaidh history and artefacts from the 14th century to the present day.

---

325 CLANLAND AND SEALPOINT **3 K7**

Foulis Ferry, Evanton, Ross and Cromarty. 16 miles (26km) north of Inverness on A9, 1 mile (1.5km) north of Cromarty Bridge. Nearest railway station and bus service Inverness. Open all year daily, 0930–1730; closed Christmas and New Year's Day. Charge ££. Group concessions. Explanatory displays. Gift shop. Restaurant and picnic area. WC. Wheelchair access. Disabled WC. Car and coach parking. Telephone (01349) 830000.

Discover the secret of the Munro clan and explore the stories of seven centuries of land and people brought to life in the rogue's gallery. Son et lumiere shows. Sealpoint explains the behaviour of seals, which you might see from the shore.

---

326 CLAN MACPHERSON MUSEUM **3 K10**

Clan House, Main Street, Newtonmore. 15 miles (24km) south of Aviemore on A86. Nearest railway station 0.5 mile (1km), Citylink bus service stops outside. Open Apr–Oct, Mon–Sat 1000–1700, Sun 1430–1700. Free. Donations. Guided tours. Explanatory displays. Gift shop. WC. Wheelchair access. Disabled WC. Car parking. Telephone (01540) 673332.

Museum depicting the history of the Clan Macpherson with portraits, photographs and other Macpherson memorabilia.

---

327 ROBERT CLAPPERTON'S DAYLIGHT PHOTOGRAPHIC STUDIO **5 P17**

The Studio, 28 Scotts Place, Selkirk. 15 minutes walk from Selkirk market place. Open May–Aug, Fri–Sun 1400–1600. Telephone for other times. Charge £. Group concessions. Guided tours. Explanatory displays. Wheelchair access. Telephone (01750) 20523.

One of the oldest surviving daylight photographic studios in the UK. The Studio is set up as a working museum and photographic archive, in the building originally used by Robert Clapperton in 1867. Photographic equipment, cameras and prints. Demonstrations of black and white print processing in the original dark room can be arranged. Archive photographs and postcards for sale.

---

328 JIM CLARK ROOM **5 Q16**

44 Newtown Street, Duns, Berwickshire. 15 miles (24km) west of Berwick upon Tweed. Nearest railway station Berwick upon Tweed, bus service to Duns. Open Easter–Sep, Mon–Sat 1030–1300 and 1400–1630, Sun 1400–1600; Oct Mon–Sat 1300–1600. Charge £. One child free with each paying adult. Free admission for Scottish Borders residents. Group concessions. Explanatory displays. Gift shop. Wheelchair access with assistance. Car parking. Telephone (01361) 883960.

A museum devoted to the twice world motor racing champion, Jim Clark. A collection of trophies, photographs and memorabilia including a video presentation and souvenirs.

329 CLATTERINGSHAWS FOREST WILDLIFE CENTRE **4 J20**

FE. New Galloway, Castle Douglas. Open daily Apr–Oct. Free. Explanatory displays. Gift shop. Tearoom and picnic area. WC. Wheelchair access. Disabled WC. Car and coach parking. Telephone (01644) 420285.

Situated in Galloway Forest Park. Forest wildlife exhibition. Guided walks. Fishing (by permit). Waymarked walks and cycle trails.

---

330 CLAVA CAIRNS **3 K8**

HS. Near Culloden, Inverness-shire, off B9006, 6 miles (10km) east of Inverness. Nearest railway station Inverness, bus from Inverness to Culloden Battlefield, then walk 2 miles (3km). Access at all times. Free. Telephone 0131 668 8800.

Two chambered cairns and a ring cairn in a row, each surrounded by a circle of stones. Of late Neolithic or early Bronze Age date. An extensive and well-preserved site in a beautiful setting.

---

331 CLAYPOTTS CASTLE **5 N13**

HS. South of A92, near Broughty Ferry, Angus. Nearest railway station Dundee, bus service from Dundee. Opening hours limited; telephone to check. Charge £. Group concessions. Explanatory displays. WC. Telephone (01382) 731640.

An unusually complete tower house with circular towers at diagonally opposite corners corbelled out to form overhanging cap houses. Built in the late 16th century for the Strachan family and later the property of Bonnie Dundee, John Graham of Claverhouse.

---

332 CLICKIMIN BROCH **1 G5**

HS. About 1 mile (2km) southwest of Lerwick, Shetland. Bus from Lerwick. Access at all times. Free. Telephone 0131 668 8800.

A good example of a broch tower with associated secondary buildings of Iron Age date.

---

333 CLICK MILL **1 B10**

HS. At Dounby, on mainland Orkney. Bus from Kirkwall. Access at all times. Free. Telephone 0131 668 8800.

The last surviving and working horizontal water mill in Orkney, a type well represented in Shetland and Lewis.

---

334 CLOCH LIGHTHOUSE **6 H15**

A770, 3 miles (4.5km) southwest of Gourock. View exterior only.

This notable landmark stands at Cloch Point with fine views across the upper Firth of Clyde estuary. The white-painted lighthouse was constructed in 1797.

---

335 CLOG AND SHOE WORKSHOP **5 K19**

Balmaclellan, Dumfries and Galloway. 13 miles (21km) north of Castle Douglas in Balmaclellan. Bus service from Castle Douglas or Dalmellington. Open Easter–Dec, Mon–Fri 1000–1700. Workshop available to view all year round, but telephone in advance out of season. Free. Guided tours by appointment (charge £££). Explanatory displays. Gift shop. Wheelchair access. Disabled WC. Car parking. Telephone (01644) 420456.

Rural workshop where visitors can watch ongoing work which includes the making of modern and traditional clogs, boots, sandals, baby footwear, bags and purses. Footwear can be made to measure.

---

336 CLOOTIE WELL **3 K7**

Munlochy, south of Fortrose, Black Isle.

Wishing well dedicated to St Boniface (or Curidan). Although no trace of it can now be found there is said to have been a chapel on this site. The trees and fence around the well are draped with thousands of rags. To have your wish granted you must spill a small amount of water three times on the ground, tie a rag on a nearby tree, make the sign of the cross and then drink from the well. Tradition states that anyone removing a rag will succumb to the misfortunes of the original owner.

---

337 CLUNY CLAYS **6 M14**

Cluny Mains, Cluny, Kirkcaldy, Fife. 2 miles (3km) north of Kirkcaldy on B922. Nearest railway station Kirkcaldy. Visitors can be collected if pre-arranged. Open daily except Christmas and New Year. There is no clay target shooting on Sundays except for Scottish Team Selection Shoots or by arrangement. Charges (£-££) dependent on activity. Gift shop. Licensed restaurant, tearoom, snack bar and picnic area. Outdoor seating and parkland. WC. Wheelchair access. Disabled WC. Car and coach parking. Telephone (01592) 720374.

Scotland's national clay pigeon shooting and archery centre. Comprehensive clay target shooting ranges covers all disciplines. Indoor and outdoor target archery ranges; also field archery courses, set in 140 acres (57ha) of woodland. Indoor air rifle ranges. Children's playpark and electric trikes. Off-road driving, falconry, highland games and other group activities by arrangement. Set in beautifully landscaped surroundings in open rolling countryside.

---

338 CLUNY HOUSE GARDENS **5 L12**

Aberfeldy, Perthshire. 3.5 miles (5.5km) northeast of Aberfeldy on the minor road between Weem and Strathtay. Nearest railway station Pitlochry (13 miles/21km), occasional bus service from Aberfeldy and Pitlochry. Open Mar–Oct, daily 1000–1800. Charge £. Under 16s free. Guided tours. Explanatory displays. Picnic area. Plant stall. Limited wheelchair access. Car parking. Telephone (01887) 820795.

Cluny is a Himalayan woodland garden created and planted by the late Mr and Mrs Robert Masterton from 1950 onwards. It is situated on a slope in the Strathtay valley where the climate and soil provide perfect conditions for growing a profusion of primulas, mecanopsis, rhododendrons, lilies, trilliums and spring bulbs. Cluny is at its most colourful in spring and autumn, but at all times of the year there is much of interest.

---

339 CLYDEBANK MUSEUM **6 J15**

Town Hall, Dumbarton Road, Clydebank. 2 miles (3km) northwest of Glasgow on A814. Nearest railway stations Clydebank Central and Singer, frequent bus service. Open all year, Mon and Wed–Fri 1400–1630, Tue and Sat 1000–1630. Closed public holidays. Other times by appointment. Free. Guided tours. Explanatory displays. Gift shop. audio-visual presentation. WC. Wheelchair access. Car and coach parking. Telephone (01389) 738702.

Community museum on local social and industrial history. Small collection on the story of ship building and engineering, major displays of sewing machines including the Singer Collection with technical documentation on Singer production. Display on World War II munitions.

---

340 CLYDE MARINE CRUISES **6 H15**

Princes Pier, Campbell Street, Greenock. 25 miles (40km) west of Glasgow. Nearest railway station Greenock Central. Sailings all year (Kenilworth), May–Sep (Second Snark). Charges variable. Group concessions. Licensed bar with refreshments. Commentary in English. WC. Car and coach parking. Telephone (01475) 721281.

Cruises, with accommodation for up to 120 persons, to all the scenic lochs and resorts of the Upper Firth of Clyde. Pickups from Greenock, Helensburgh, Kilcreggan, Dunoon, Rothesay, Largs and Millport. Special day and evening charters can be arranged from Glasgow or Greenock.

341 CLYDE MUIRSHIEL REGIONAL PARK, BARNBROCK FARM 6 J16

Kilbarchan, Renfrewshire. 3 miles (5km) north of Lochwinnoch just off B786. Nearest railway and bus service Lochwinnoch. Open all year, Mon–Fri 0900–1630; campsite open at all times Apr–Oct. Free. Guided tours. Explanatory displays. Picnic area. WC. Limited wheelchair access. Car and coach parking. Telephone (01505) 614791.

Barnbrock Farm incorporates the headquarters of the Clyde Muirshiel Regional Park. Campsite, picnic area and easy access to nearby Locherwood Community Woodland.

---

342 CLYDE MUIRSHIEL REGIONAL PARK, CASTLE SEMPLE VISITOR CENTRE 6 J16

Lochlip Road, Lochwinnoch, Renfrewshire. Just off A760 in Lochwinoch. Nearest railway station Lochwinnoch, bus from Glasgow or Largs. Open summer months daily, 1000–dusk; winter months Mon–Fri 1200–1600, Sat and Sun 1000–1600. Free. Guided tours. Explanatory displays. Gift shop. Café, picnic area and barbeque facilities. WC. Wheelchair access. Disabled WC. Car and coach parking. Telephone (01505) 842882.

Castle Semple Loch offers sailing, canoeing and wind surfing. Craft available for hire. Mountain bike hire. Coarse fishing. Tuition in canoeing, dinghy sailing, archery. Woodland walks at Parkhill Wood which was formerly part of Castle Semple estate. Historical landmarks include Peel Castle, Collegiate Church, grotto, maze and fishponds. Local and natural history displays. Ranger service. See also 301 Castle Semple Collegiate Church.

---

343 CLYDE MUIRSHIEL REGIONAL PARK, CORNALEES VISITOR CENTRE 6 H15

Loch Thom, Inverkip. Nearest railway and bus service Greenock (Branchton or Inverkip stations) 3 miles (5km). Open Apr–Oct, Mon–Fri 1230–1800, Sat and Sun 1200–1800. Free. Guided tours. Explanatory displays. Gift shop. Picnic and Barbeque areas. WC. Wheelchair access. Disabled WC. Car and coach parking. Telephone (01475) 521458.

Woodland walks in Shielhill Glen. Greenock Cut and Kelly Cut walks with scenic views of the Clyde estuary. Natural and local history exhibitions. Indoor games with environmental themes. Navigation and orienteering courses. Children's nature club, children's activities in the summer, guided walks, ranger service.

---

344 CLYDE MUIRSHIEL REGIONAL PARK, LUNDERSTON BAY 6 H15

Lunderston Bay, Inverkip, Renfrewshire. On A78 Gourock to Inverkip road. Nearest railway station Inverkip 2 miles (3km). Open all year, daily. Free. Guided tours. Picnic area. Children's play area. WC. Sensory garden. Wheelchair access. Disabled WC. Car and coach parking. Telephone (01475) 521458.

Beach and picnic area on the Clyde coast. Panoramic views of Cowal peninsula. Coastal walks, rock pools, marine birds and plants. Children's activities and ranger service.

---

345 CLYDE MUIRSHIEL REGIONAL PARK, MUIRSHIEL VISITOR CENTRE 6 J16

Lochwinnoch, Renfrewshire. 4 miles (6.5km) northwest of Lochwinnoch, off B786. Nearest railway and bus service Lochwinnoch. Open Apr–Sep, daily 1200–1630. Free. Guided tours. Explanatory displays. Gift shop. Picnic and barbeque areas. WC. Wheelchair access. Disabled WC. Car and coach parking. Telephone (01505) 842803.

Muirshiel was originally a Victorian sporting estate. It has woodland, riverside and waterfall walks, picnic and barbecue sites and boardwalk access to the scenic viewpoint, Windyhill. An area rich in archaeological sites with much to offer the botanist and ornithologist. Orienteering and navigation courses throughout the year. Ranger service.

346 CLYDE VALLEY COUNTRY ESTATE 6 L16

Crossford, Carluke, Lanarkshire. Nearest railway stations Lanark or Carluke; bus from Lanark. Open daily all year, garden centre 0900–1700; craft shops open at various times, telephone to check. Charge for activities £. Explanatory displays at bird of prey centre. Gift shop. Restaurant, coffee shop and picnic area. Adventure playground. WC. Wheelchair access. Disabled WC. Car and coach parking. Telephone (01555) 860691.

Garden centre, narrow gauge railway, bird of prey centre, putting green. Trekking centre offers pony rides. Crystals and aromatherapy products, children's wear, various craft shops. Also woodland walks.

---

347 CLYNELISH DISTILLERY 3 L5

Brora, Sutherland. 58 miles (93km) north of Inverness on A9. Rail and bus service to Brora. Open Mar–Oct, Mon–Fri 0930–1600; Nov–Feb, Tue–Thu 0930–1530 or by appointment. Charge £. Children free. Guided tours. Gift shop. Picnic area. Garden. WC. No guide dogs. Limited wheelchair access. Disabled WC. Car and coach parking. Telephone (01408) 623000.

The original Clynelish Distillery was built in 1819 by the Marquis of Stafford, later to become Duke of Sutherland. The superb quality of Clynelish whisky was so much in demand that only private customers at home and abroad could be supplied. Trade orders were refused. The distillery was extended in 1896 by the Leith Whisky blenders, Ainslie and Co. In 1967 the new Clynelish Distillery was built alongside the original building with three times the production capacity. Clynelish is available as a 14-year old single malt and is the heart of Johnnie Walker's Gold Label blend.

---

348 CNOC FREICEADAIN LONG CAIRNS 3 L2

HS. 6 miles (9.5km) west southwest of Thurso, Caithness. Nearest railway and bus stations Thurso. Access at all times. Free. Telephone 0131 668 8800.

Two unexcavated Neolithic long-horned burial cairns, set at right angles to each other.

---

349 COATS OBSERVATORY 6 J16

49 Oakshaw Street West, Paisley. 7 miles (11km) west of Glasgow. Nearest railway station Paisley Gilmour Street. Open all year, Sat 1000–1700, Sun 1400–1700. Last entry 15 mins before closing. Free. Explanatory displays. Telephone 0141 889 2013.

Designed by John Honeyman, Coats Observatory continues a tradition of astronomical, meteorological and seismic observing which started in 1883. Displays relate to the history and architecture of the building, astronomy and astronautics, meteorology and seismicity.

---

350 COBB MEMORIAL 3 J9

Between Invermoriston and Drumnadrochit by A82. Access at all times. Free.

A cairn commemorates John Cobb, the racing driver, who lost his life near here in 1952 when attempting to beat the water speed record, with his jet speedboat, on Loch Ness.

---

351 COLDSTREAM MUSEUM 5 Q17

12 Market Square, Coldstream. 15 miles (24km) west of Berwick upon Tweed. Nearest railway station Berwick, bus from Berwick. Open Easter–Sep, Mon–Sat 1000–1600, Sun 1400–1600; Oct, Mon–Sat 1300–1600. Charge £. One child free with paying adult. Free admission for Scottish Borders residents. Group concessions. Explanatory displays. Gift shop. Picnic area. Children's corner within museum. WC. Wheelchair access. Disabled WC. Car and coach parking. Telephone (01890) 882630.

Local history displays and section on the Coldstream Guards. Temporary exhibition gallery with displays such as needlework, local artists work and information on the Border Reivers.

---

352 COLFIN SMOKEHOUSE **4 G20**

Colfin Creamery, Portpatrick, Stranraer. 2 miles (3km) from Portpatrick on A77. Bus service from Stranraer passes close (200m). Open all year, Mon–Sat 0900–1700, Sun 1000–1500, closed Christmas and New Year. Free. Guided tours. Explanatory displays. Gift shop. WC. Wheelchair access. Disabled WC. Car and coach parking. Telephone (01776) 820622.

Visitors can observe the salmon smoking process in detail and purchase the product or use mail order.

---

353 COLLEONARD SCULPTURE GARDEN AND GALLERY **3 P7**

Sandyhill Road, Banff. In Banff on the A97, 1 mile (2km) from the tourist information office. Nearest railway station Huntly, bus to Banff. Open all year by appointment. Free. Guided tours. Explanatory displays. Wheelchair access. Car and coach parking. Telephone (01261) 818284.

A 5.5 acre (2ha) sculpture garden in a sylvan setting. Figurines sculptured in wood and stone.

---

354 COLL POTTERY **2 E3**

Fear an Eich, Back, Isle of Lewis, Western Isles. In township of Coll on the B895, 6 miles (9.5km) northeast of Stornoway. Bus from Stornoway. Open Apr–Sep, Mon–Sat 0900–1800; Oct–Mar, Mon–Sat 0900–1700. Free. Explanatory displays. Gift shop. Tearoom. WC. Wheelchair access. Disabled WC. Car and coach parking. Telephone (01851) 820219.

A working pottery making a wide range of items, from the unique marbled ware of the Hebridean range and the traditional figurines of the Highlands and Islands, to the collectible range of MacKatts of Glen Kitloch.

---

355 COLONSAY HOUSE GARDENS **4 D14**

Kiloran, Isle of Colonsay, Argyll. 2 miles (3km) from pier. Car ferry from Oban. Open Easter–Sep, Wed 1200–1700 and Fri 1500–1730. Charge £. Group concessions. Explanatory displays. Gift shop. Tearoom and picnic area. Children's play area. WC. Limited wheelchair access. Car and coach parking. Telephone (01951) 200211.

Famous rhododendron garden of 20 acres (8ha), adjacent to Colonsay House, home of Lord Strathcona. In the woods surrounding the house, rocks, streams and contours of land have been used to create a natural woodland garden where native trees and rare rhododendrons, bluebells and mecanopsis flourish together. Due to the mildness of the climate and the shelter of the woods, many tender and rare shrubs from all parts of the world grow happily including mimosa, eucalyptus and palm trees.

---

356 COLOUR BOX SCOTLAND **5 P16**

Whitlaw Road, Lauder, Scottish Borders. 25 miles (40km) south of Edinburgh on A68. Local bus service and taxis. Open all year, Mon–Thu 1000–1700, Fri 1000–1530; closed Christmas and New Year. Free. Guided tours. Gift shop. Refreshment area. WC. Wheelchair access. Disabled WC. Car and coach parking. Telephone (01578) 722725.

The Colour Box studios produce hand-painted ceramic sculpture of teddy bears, cats and wildlife. Visitors can visit the workshop.

---

357 COLUMBA CENTRE **4 D13**

Fionnphort, Isle of Mull, Argyll. 38 miles (61km) from Craignure and situated near ferry terminal for Iona. Ferry from Oban to Craignure, then bus to Fionnphort. Open Easter–Sep, Mon–Sat 1000–1700, Sun 1100–1700. Charge £. Group concessions. Explanatory displays. Gift shop. Refreshments available. Wheelchair access. Disabled WC. Car and coach parking. Telephone (01681) 700660.

Exhibition on St Columba, Iona and Celtic heritage of interest to all visitors. Opportunities to practice script writing.

---

358 COLUMBA'S FOOTSTEPS **4 F18**

West of Southend at Keil, Mull of Kintyre.

Traditionally it is believed that St Columba first set foot on Scottish soil near Southend. The footsteps are imprinted in a flat topped rock near the ruin of an old chapel.

---

359 COLZIUM ESTATE **6 K15**

Colzium Lennox Estate, Stirling Road, Kilsyth. From Glasgow follow A803 to Kilsyth from where Colzuim House is well signposted. Bus from Kilsyth. Open daily between dawn and dusk. Free. WC. Limited wheelchair access. Car and coach parking.

Outstanding collection of conifers and rare trees in a beautifully designed small walled garden. All trees well labelled – excellent for learning the difference between varieties of conifers. Fabulous display of snowdrops and crocuses in spring. Other attractions include a 17th-century ice house, glen walk, 15th-century tower house, arboretum, curling pond, clock theatre and pitch and putt course.

---

360 COMMANDO MEMORIAL **2 H10**

Off A82, 11 miles (17.5km) northeast of Fort William. Access at all times. Free. Car parking.

An impressive sculpture by Scott Sutherland, erected in 1952 to commemorate the commandos of World War II who trained in this area. Fine views of Ben Nevis and Lochaber.

---

361 CONFECTIONARY FACTORY VISITOR CENTRE **2 G11**

Old Ferry Road, North Ballachulish, Fort William. On the A82, 13 miles (20km) south of Fort William. Local bus service from Fort William to Oban, Glasgow or Kinlochleven. Open all year. Free. Explanatory displays. Gift shop. Picnic area. WC. Limited wheelchair access. Car and coach parking. Telephone (01855) 821277.

Displays of products and an explanation of the history of Islay tablet, its origins on Islay and reason for the use of goats' milk. Also speciality Scottish food shop. Scenic views of loch Ballachulish bridge.

---

362 JANE CONNACHAN GOLF CENTRE **6 P15**

Fenton Barns, North Berwick, East Lothian. On the B1345, between Drem and North Berwick. Nearest railway station Drem. Open daily all year (except Christmas Day) 0900–2100. Free. Charge for balls. Restaurant. Playground. WC. Wheelchair access with assistance. Disabled WC. Car and coach parking. Telephone (01620) 850475.

A floodlit driving range and nine-hole 3-par golf course. Part of a retail and leisure village, including a farm shop, coffee shop and archery centre.

---

363 CORGARFF CASTLE **3 M9**

HS. Corgarff, Strathdon, Aberdeenshire. Off A939, 15 miles (24km) northwest of Ballater, Aberdeenshire. Bus from Aberdeen to Strathdon only, then 9 mile (14.5km) walk. Open Apr–Sep, daily 0930–1830; via keyholder in winter at weekends only, 0930–1630. Charge £. Group concessions. Guided tours. Explanatory displays. Gift shop. Car and coach parking. Telephone (01975) 651460.

A 16th-century tower house converted into a barracks for government troops in 1748 by being enclosed within a star-shaped loopholed wall. The castle was burned in 1571 by Edom o' Gordon, killing the family and household of Alexander Forbes, the owner.

364 CORNICE MUSEUM OF ORNAMENTAL PLASTERWORK **5 N17**

Innerleithen Road, Peebles. Near Peebles town centre, opposite the Park Hotel. Nearest railway station Edinburgh, bus service with stop close to museum. Open all year, Mon–Thu 1030–1200 and 1400–1600, Fri 1030–1200 and 1400–1530; closed weekends and holiday periods such as Easter, 2 weeks in summer and 2 weeks at Christmas, telephone to check. Entrance charges by donation. Guided tours. Explanatory displays. Some items for sale. WC. Limited wheelchair access. Telephone (01721) 720212.

The museum is a plasterer's casting workshop virtually unchanged since the turn of the century and illustrates the main methods of creating ornamental plasterwork in Scotland at that time. It also displays probably the largest surviving collection of 'masters' in Scotland.

---

365 CORRIESHALLOCH GORGE **2 H6**

NTS. Braemore, by Ullapool, Ross-shire. 12 miles (19.5km) southeast of Ullapool, on A835. Open all year. Charge £. Honesty box. Explanatory displays. Car and coach parking. Telephone (01445) 781200.

Here is one of the finest examples of a box canyon in Britain, forming a spectacular 200 feet (61m) deep, mile-long gorge. A viewing platform stretched across the gorge looks up towards the Falls of Measach.

---

366 CORRIMONY CAIRN **3 J8**

HS. In Glen Urquhart, 8.5 miles (13.5km) west of Drumnadrochit, Inverness-shire. Bus service from Inverness to Cannich, then walk from Cannich. Open all year. Free. Telephone 0131 668 8800.

A chambered burial cairn surrounded by a kerb of stone slabs, outside of which is a circle of standing stones.

---

367 CORRYVRECKAN WHIRLPOOL **4 F14**

Between the islands of Jura and Scarba.

This treacherous tide race, very dangerous for small craft, covers an extensive area and may be seen from the north end of Jura or from Craignish Point. The noise can sometimes be heard from a considerable distance.

---

368 COTTON MILL, SPINNINGDALE **3 K6**

In Spinningdale, between Dornoch and Bonar Bridge, Sutherland.

The ruins of an 18th-century cotton mill destroyed by fire in 1808.

---

369 COULTER MOTTE **5 L17**

HS. Off A72, 2 miles (3km) north of Coulter, 1.5 miles (2.5km) south-west of Biggar, Lanarkshire. Nearest railway station Lanark, bus from Edinburgh or Lanark to Biggar.

Early medieval castle mound, originally moated and probably surrounded by a palisade enclosing a timber tower.

---

370 COVESEA GOLF COURSE **3 M7**

Covesea, Lossiemouth. On the B9040, 2 miles (3km) west of Lossiemouth. Open Mar–Oct or Nov, daily 0900–2000; telephone to confirm times. Charge ££. Cold drinks available. WC. Disabled WC. Car and coach parking. Telephone (01343) 814124.

A links course, 12-hole 3-par short course and set on the spectacular Moray Firth coast. Equipment for hire.

---

371 COWAL BIRD GARDEN **6 H15**

Locan Wood, Sandbank Road, Dunoon, Argyll. 1 mile (2km) north of Dunoon on A855. Reliable and inexpensive taxi service from Dunoon.

Open Easter–Oct, daily 1030–1800. Charge ££. Children under 4 free. Group concessions. Explanatory displays. Gift shop. Picnic areas (one covered). Garden. Pets corner. WC. Limited wheelchair access. Disabled WC. Car and coach parking. Telephone (01369) 707999.

Attraction with a wide range of animals such as donkeys, macaws, parrots, rabbits, guinea pigs, pot-bellied pigs, aviary birds, all set in mature woodland. Nature trail through native woodland.

---

372 COWANS LAW TROUT FISHING AND COUNTRY SPORTS — 6 J17

Hemphill Road, Moscow, Galston, Ayrshire. From A77 take A719 to Moscow, signposted. Nearest railway and bus station Kilmarnock. Special transport from local hotels. Open summer months, daily 0800–dusk; winter months, daily 1000–1600. Charge £££. Group concessions. Restaurant and clubhouse. WC. Staff have sign language. Wheelchair access. Disabled WC. Car and coach parking. Telephone (01560) 700666.

Cowans Law is set in the heart of Ayrshire's farming country with a 4 acre (1.7ha) trout loch. Clay shooting, archery and air rifle range. Families and beginners welcome.

---

373 CRAGGAN FISHERY AND GOLF COURSE — 3 M8

Craggan, Grantown-on-Spey, Moray. 1 mile (2km) south of Grantown-on-Spey on A95. Bus service from Grantown, Aviemore and Carrbridge. Open Apr–Oct, daily 0900–1800 and also 1800–2200 on Thu. Golf open all year daily, weather permitting. Charge £. Charges dependant on activity. Group concessions. Tearoom and picnic area. WC. Limited wheelchair access. Disabled WC. Car and coach parking. Telephone (01479) 873283.

Two nine-hole golf courses suitable for individuals and families of all levels. Fly fishing loch, children's and adult's bait fishing loch stocked with rainbow and brown trout. Also falconry and archery.

---

374 CRAGGAN MILL RESTAURANT, CRAFTS AND ART GALLERY — 3 M8

Grantown-on-Spey, Moray. 1 mile (1.5km) south of Grantown-on-Spey on A95. Bus service from Grantown, Aviemore and Carrbridge. Open all year, summer daily 1030–2200; winter, Mon–Fri 1830–2200, occasional weekends, telephone to check. Closed for two weeks in Oct. Free. Gift shop. Restaurant and beer garden. WC. Limited wheelchair access. Car and coach parking. Telephone (01479) 872288.

Old converted water mill displays local crafts and paintings, wooden sculptures, dried flowers and wrought iron work in art gallery.

---

375 CRAIGELLACHIE BRIDGE — 3 N8

Near A941, just north of Craigellachie, 12 miles (19km) south southeast of Elgin. Access at all times. Car parking.

One of Thomas Telford's most beautiful bridges. Opened in 1814, it carried the main road until 1973 when a new bridge was built alongside. It has a 152 feet (46m) main span of iron, cast in Wales, and two ornamental stone towers at each end.

---

376 CRAIG HIGHLAND FARM — 2 F8

Plockton, Ross and Cromarty. Situated between Plockton and Achmore on shore road. Nearest railway station Duncraig, request stop. Postbus from Kyle of Lochalsh. Open Easter–Oct, daily 1000–dusk. Charge £. Group concessions. Explanatory displays. Picnics or barbeques welcome on beach. WC. Car parking. Telephone (01599) 544205.

Rare breeds farm and animal sanctuary situated in bay on shore of Loch Carron. Visitors can feed the llamas, ponies, donkeys, goats and poultry and observe the owls, pigs and rabbits. Low tide gives access to Scottish Wildlife Trust island via Coral Beach heronry.

377 CRAIGIEVAR CASTLE 3 P9

NTS. Alford, Aberdeenshire. On A980, 26 miles (42km) west of Aberdeen. Open May–Sep, daily 1330–1730. Charge £££. Children free. Grounds only, £ (honesty box). Explanatory displays. Information sheets in four languages. Gift shop. Picnic area. Woodland walk. Car parking. Telephone (013398) 83635.

A 'fairytale' castle, a masterpiece of Scottish Baronial architecture, which seems to grow out of the hillside. Much of the building is still as it was when completed in 1626. Fine collection of family portraits and 17th- and 18th-century furniture.

---

378 CRAIGNETHAN CASTLE 6 L16

HS. Blackwood, Lesmahagow, Lanarkshire. 2.5 miles (4km) west of A72 at Crossford, 5 miles (8km) northwest of Lanark. Nearest railway station Carluke then bus to Lanark. Bus from Lanark or Hamilton to Crossford then 15 minute walk. Open Mar–Oct, daily 0930–1830. Charge £. Group concessions. Guided tours by arrangement. Explanatory displays. Gift shop. Tearoom, open at weekends only. WC. Limited wheelchair access. Car and coach parking. Telephone (01555) 860364.

An extensive and well-preserved ruin of an unusual and ornate tower house built by Sir James Hamilton of Finnart in the 16th century. It is defended by an outer wall pierced by gun ports, also by a wide and deep ditch with a most unusual caponier (a stone vaulted chamber for artillery). Attacked and dismantled by the Protestant party in 1579. In a very picturesque setting overlooking the River Nethan.

---

379 CRAIGSTON CASTLE 3 Q7

Turriff, Aberdeenshire. 5 miles (8km) from Turriff on the B9105. Nearest bus station Turriff. Open Jul or Aug, telephone for exact dates. Other times by appointment. Charge £. Guided tours. Explanatory displays. Picnic area. Garden. WC. Car and coach parking. Telephone (01888) 551228.

Craigston Castle was built from 1604-7 and is still owned by the original family. Few changes have been made to the castle's exterior in 400 years. The main exterior feature is a sculpted balcony unique in Scottish architecture. It depicts a piper, two grinning knights, and David and Goliath. The interior decoration dates mainly from the early 19th century. Remarkable carved wood panels. Library. Beautiful mixed woodland.

---

380 CRAIGTOUN COUNTRY PARK 5 P13

St Andrews, Fife. 2.5 miles (4km) southwest of St Andrews on the B939. Nearest railway station Leuchars 10 miles (16km), connecting bus to St Andrews. Buses from Dundee and Edinburgh. Infrequent bus service from St Andrews, then 0.5 mile (1km) walk to main entrance. Open Easter–Oct, daily 1030–1830. Park open all year for garden, other facilities available in main season only. Telephone to confirm charge. Group concessions. Gift shop. Tearoom and picnic area. Baby changing facilities. WC. Wheelchair access with assistance. Disabled WC. Car and coach parking. Telephone (01334) 473666.

Craigtoun Country Park was formerly the grounds of Mount Melville House. In 1947 the grounds were purchased by Fife Council. The park consists of 50 acres (20ha) including formal gardens, two ponds (with boating pond), landscaped areas, Dutch village and cypress walk. Also putting, crazy golf, trampolines, bouncy castle, bowling green, train, adventure playground, glasshouses, countryside centre, pets corner, and aviaries.

---

381 CRAIL GUIDED WALKS 5 P14

Crail Museum & Heritage Centre, Marketgate, Crail. On A917, 4 miles (6.5km) from Anstruther, 10 miles (16km) from St Andrews. Local bus route from Leven to Dundee passes Crail. Guided walks late Jun–late Aug, Sun 1430. Charge £. Group concessions. Guided tours. WC. Car and coach parking. Telephone (01333) 450869.

Walking tours (lasting 1.5–2 hours) of the oldest parts of Crail, taking in buildings of architectural and historic interest.

---

382 CRAIL MUSEUM **5 P14**

62–64 Marketgate, Crail, Fife. 10 miles (16km) south of St Andrews in the centre of Crail. Bus service from Edinburgh and St Andrews. Open Easter, weekends and holidays, then Jun–Sep, Mon–Sat 1000–1300 and 1400–1700, Sun 1400–1700. Free. Guided tours on request. Explanatory displays. Gift shop. WC. Limited wheelchair access. Car and coach parking. Telephone (01333) 450869.

The museum provides an insight into the past life of this ancient Royal Burgh. Visitors can learn about the seafaring tradition, 200-year-old golf club and HMS Jackdaw, a WWII Fleet Air Arm Station. Museum also doubles as a tourist information centre.

---

383 CRAIL POTTERY **5 P14**

75 Nethergate, Crail, Fife. In centre of Crail, down Rose Wynd. Nearest railway station Leuchars, connecting bus to St Andrews and Crail. Bus service from St Andrews. Open all year, Mon–Fri 0800–1700, Sat and Sun 1000–1700. Closed Christmas and New Year. Free. Explanatory displays. Showroom. Limited wheelchair access. Car and coach parking. Telephone (01333) 451212.

Tucked away in a flower and pot-filled medieval yard, three generations of potters produce a huge variety of hand-thrown pottery from porcelain to gardenware, sculpture, teapots and jardinières.

---

384 CRAIL TOLBOOTH **5 P14**

Marketgate, Crail. 9 miles (14.5km) southeast of St Andrews.

The Tolbooth, now a library and town hall, dates from the early 16th century, displaying a fish weather vane, and a coat of arms dated 1602. In the striking Dutch Tower is a bell dated 1520, cast in Holland. There have been 18th- and 19th-century additions. Elsewhere in this picturesque fishing village see the Collegiate Church dating back to the 13th century, the Mercat Cross topped by a unicorn, the harbour and the crowstepped, red-tiled houses.

---

385 CRARAE GARDENS **4 G14**

Crarae, Inveraray, Argyll. 10 miles (16km) south of Inveraray on A83. Bus service from Inveraray to Lochgilphead. Open all year daily, summer months 0900–1800; winter months daylight hours only. Charge £. Free to visitors in wheelchairs. Group concessions. Guided tours by prior arrangement. Explanatory displays. Gift shop. Refreshments and picnic area. WC. Limited wheelchair access. Disabled WC. Car and coach parking. Telephone (01546) 886388.

A superb natural gorge with a series of waterfalls and extensive walks through a unique collection of rhododendrons, azaleas, conifers and eucalyptus.

---

386 CRATHES CASTLE **3 Q10**

NTS. Banchory. On A93, 3 miles (5km) east of Banchory and 15 miles (24km) west of Aberdeen. Bus from Aberdeen. Open Apr–Oct, daily 1030–1730 (timed ticket system). Garden and grounds open all year, daily 0900–sunset. Charge ££. Children free. Joint ticket available, £££. Guided tours by arrangement. Explanatory displays. Information sheets in twelve languages. Gift shop. Restaurant and picnic area. Plant sales, garden and adventure playground. WC. Leaflet lists facilities available to disabled visitors. Audio guide for blind visitors. Limited wheelchair access, wheelchairs available. Disabled WC. Car and coach parking. Telephone (01330) 844525.

Sixteenth-century castle built on lands granted to the Burnett family in 1323 by King Robert the Bruce. Remarkable original painted ceilings and a collection of

Scottish furniture; some of it contemporary with the castle building. Famous walled garden contains eight separate gardens designed for colour combinations.

---

387 CRAWFORD ARTS CENTRE **5 P13**

93 North Street, St Andrews, Fife. In centre of St Andrews opposite police station. Nearest railway station Leuchars 6 miles (10km), connecting bus to St Andrews. Buses from Dundee, Edinburgh and Glasgow. Open all year, Mon–Sat 1000–1700, Sun 1400–1700. Closed Christmas and New Year. Free. Guided tours by prior arrangement. Gift shop. Coffee available. WC. Wheelchair access. Telephone (01334) 474610.

Founded in 1977, the centre provides exciting exhibitions of all kinds of visual art from sculpture and painting to photography, design and architecture.

---

388 CREAM O'GALLOWAY **5 K20**

Rainton, Gatehouse of Fleet, Castle Douglas. 4 miles (6.5km) south of Gatehouse of Fleet off A75.. Open Easter–Sep, daily 1100–1800; Oct, daily 1100–1700. Free. Adventure playground £. Explanatory displays. Tearoom and picnic area. WC. Limited wheelchair access. Disabled WC. Car and coach parking. Telephone (01557) 814040.

Cream o' Galloway is a small farm-based ice cream manufacturer specialising in traditional quality ice cream and frozen yoghurt with unusual flavours. There is a farm shop and a viewing gallery where visitors can watch the manufacturing process. There are illustrated nature walks as well as an extensive adventure playground, treasure hunt and nature quizzes.

---

389 CREETOWN GEM ROCK MUSEUM **4 J20**

Chain Road, Creetown, Newton Stewart. 7 miles (11km) east of Newton Stewart on A75. Bus service from Dumfries or Stranraer. Open Easter–Sep, daily 0930–1700; Oct–Nov, daily 1000–1600; Dec–Feb, weekends only 1000–1600; Mar–Good Friday, daily 1000–1600; closed Christmas and New Year. Charge £. Group concessions. Explanatory displays. Gift shop. Tearoom. WC. Wheelchair access. Disabled WC. Car and coach parking. Telephone (01671) 820357.

The museum houses one of the finest collections of privately owned gemstones, crystals, minerals and fossils in Europe. Visitors can witness the spectacular volcanic eruption display, the Crystal Cave and a 15-minute audio-visual programme.

---

390 CRICHTON CASTLE **6 N16**

HS. Crichton, Pathhead, Midlothian. Off the A68, 2.5 miles (4km) south southwest of Pathhead. Bus from Edinburgh to Pathhead then 2.5 mile (4km) walk. Open Apr–Sep, daily 0930–1830. Charge £. Group concessions. Guided tours. Carvings can be touched. Limited wheelchair access. Car and coach parking. Telephone (01875) 320017.

A large and sophisticated castle built around a 14th-century keep. The most spectacular part is the arcaded range erected by the Earl of Bothwell between 1581 and 1591. This has a façade of faceted stonework in an Italian style. The small Collegiate Church nearby dates from 1499 and is notable for its tower and barrel vaulting.

---

391 CRICHTON ROYAL MUSEUM **5 L20**

Easterbrook Hall, Bankend Road, Dumfries. 1.5 miles (2.5km) south of Dumfries centre on Bankend road, enter site via Crichton Church Gate. Nearest railway station Dumfries, local bus service. Open all year (except Christmas and New Year) Thu and Fri, 1330–1630; Easter–Sep, Sat 1330–1630. Other times by appointment. Free. Guided tours on request. Tearoom, meals may be booked in dining room. Gardens, church. WC. Wheelchair access. Disabled WC. Car and coach parking. Telephone (01387) 244228.

The Museum tells the story of mental health care in south-west Scotland over a period of more than 200 years, a story featuring the part played by Dumfries Infirmary in the 18th century; the Crichton family and its wealth; stylish architecture; elegant furniture; stained glass; beautiful gardens; operating theatre and medical equipment; exhibits accruing from the various therapies, especially art therapy; and topical health-related exhibitions.

---

392 CRIEFF VISITOR CENTRE **5 L13**

Muthil Road, Crieff. On the A85 Crieff to Comrie road. Bus service from Perth. Open all year daily 0900–1730. Free. Guided tours of pottery, weekdays only. Explanatory displays. Gift shop. Licensed restaurant with outside terrace. Baby changing. Children's play area. WC. Wheelchair access. Car and coach parking. Telephone (01764) 654014.

Traditional whisky flagons, tableware and glass paperweights. Visitors can view production process and see craftsmen at work. Factory showroom and video presentation. Plant centre. Collection of cacti from all over the world and experts to give advice. Large children's play area.

---

393 CRINAN CANAL **4 F14**

Crinan to Ardrishaig, by Lochgilphead. Nearest bus station Ardrishaig. Open all year daily, 0830–1700. Telephone to confirm times. Free. Explanatory displays. Picnic area. Limited wheelchair access. Car parking. Telephone (01546) 603210.

Constructed between 1793 and 1801 to carry ships from Loch Fyne to the Atlantic without rounding Kintyre. The 9-mile (14.5km) stretch of water with 15 locks is now almost entirely used by pleasure craft. The towing path provides a pleasant, easy walk with the interest of canal activity. There are magnificent views to the Western Isles from Crinan. The Crinan basin, coffee shop, boatyard and hotel make a visit well worthwhile.

---

394 CROICK CHURCH **3 J6**

At Croick, Sutherland, 9 miles (14.5km) west of Ardgay.

Made famous in 1845, during the Highland clearances, when many of the tenants of nearby Glencalvie were evicted to make way for sheep. They took refuge in the churchyard and even now names scratched on the east window bear witness to their distress.

---

395 CROMARTY COURTHOUSE MUSEUM **3 K7**

Chruch Street, Cromarty. 25 miles (40km) north of Inverness on A832. Bus service from Inverness. Open Apr–Oct, daily 1000–1700. Telephone to check winter opening hours. Charge £. Group concessions. Guided tours (tape tour in French and German). Explanatory displays. Gift shop. Induction loop. Car and coach parking. Telephone (01381) 600418.

The courthouse, which dates from 1773, has been converted into an award-winning museum interpreting the history of the well-preserved town of Cromarty. Displays include a reconstructed trial in the courtroom, prison cells, animated figures and costumes. A personal tape tour of the town is included in the admission price.

---

396 CROMBIE COUNTRY PARK **5 P12**

Monikie, Broughty Ferry, Angus. Follow A92 to Muirdrum then clearly signposted at crossroads. Nearest railway station Dundee, bus service from Dundee to Monikie then 2.5 mile (4km) walk. Open May–Aug, daily 0900–2100; Sept–Apr, daily 0900–1700. Free. Parking £ (disabled free). Guided tours by prior arrangement. Explanatory displays. Vending machine, picnic and barbeque area (two free marquees available

Apr–Sep). WC. Wheelchair access. Disabled WC. Car and coach parking. Telephone (01241) 860360.

A Victorian reservoir with the appearance of a natural loch. Set in 250 acres (101ha). Wildlife hide, trails, displays and interpretation centre, ranger service, guided walks, child play park. Barbecue area. Also angling, telephone Monikie Angling Club (01382) 370300.

---

397 CROOKSTON CASTLE **6 J16**

HS. Off Brockburn Road, Pollock, 4 miles (6.5km) southwest of Glasgow city centre. Nearest railway station Glasgow Central, bus from Union Street. Open at all times; see keyholder. Free. Telephone 0131 668 8800.

The altered ruin of an unusual 15th-century castle. It consists of a central tower with four square corner towers, set within 12th-century earthworks. Affords excellent views of southwest Glasgow.

---

398 CROSS KIRK **5 N17**

HS. In Cross road, Peebles. Open at all times. Key from custodian in nearby house. Free. Telephone 0131 668 8800.

The remains of a Trinitarian friary founded in the late 13th century. Consists of nave, west tower and foundations of domestic buildings.

---

399 CROSS OF LORRAINE **6 H15**

Lyle Hill, Greenock. Access via Newton Street. Access at all reasonable times. Free. Car parking.

Monument to the contribution made by the Free French Navy during World War II. The Cross of Lorraine is situated at a popular viewpoint overlooking the Clyde.

---

400 CROSSRAGUEL ABBEY **4 H18**

HS. Maybole, Ayrshire. On the A77, 2 miles (3km) southwest of Maybole. Nearest railway station Maybole, bus service via Maybole from Ayr to Girvan. Open Apr–Sep, daily 0930–1830. Charge £. Group concessions. Guided tours. WC. Wheelchair access with assistance. Car and coach parking. Telephone (01655) 883113.

A Cluniac monastery built in 1244 by the Earl of Carrick. Inhabited by Benedictine monks until the end of the 16th century. Extensive and remarkably complete remains of high quality, including the church, cloister, chapter house and much of the domestic premises.

---

401 CROY HILL **6 K15**

HS. Between Croy and Dullatur, Stirlingshire. Nearest railway station Croy. Access at all times. Free. Telephone 0131 668 8800.

The site of a Roman fort (not visible) on the Antonine Wall. Part of the Wall ditch can be seen, beside two beacon platforms on the west side of the hill. See also 62 Antonine Wall.

---

402 CRUACHAN POWER STATION **4 G13**

Dalmally, Argyll. 18 miles (29km) east of Oban on A85. Nearest railway station Cruachan, bus service from Oban and Glasgow. Open Easter–Nov, daily 0930–1700. Jul and Aug closes at 1800. Charge £. Group concessions. Guided tours. Explanatory displays. Gift shop. Café and picnic area. WC. Wheelchair access with assistance. Disabled WC. Car and coach parking. Telephone (01866) 822518.

A guided tour takes visitors 0.5 mile (1km) inside Ben Cruachan to see a reversible pumped storage scheme. An exhibition houses touch screen and computer video technology.

403 CRUMSTANE FARM PARK **5 Q16**

Duns, Berwickshire. On the A6105, 1.5 miles (2.5km) east of Duns. Bus from Duns or Berwick-upon-Tweed. Open Easter–Sep, Wed–Mon 1000–1800. Charge £. Group concessions. Explanatory displays. Picnic area. WC. Limited wheelchair access. Car and coach parking. Telephone (01361) 883268.

A farm park with a collection of rare British farm animals.

---

404 ROBINSON CRUSOE STATUE **6 N14**

Lower Largo. Bus from Edinburgh or St Andrews. Access at all times. Free.

Bronze statue of Alexander Selkirk, the real life mariner on whom Daniel Defoe based his famous character. The statue has stood on the site of his home for over 100 years.

---

405 CUBBIE ROW'S CASTLE **1 B10**

HS. On the island of Wyre, Orkney. Bus from Kirkwall to Tingwall and ferry from Tingwall to Wyre. Access at all times. Free. Telephone 0131 668 8800.

Probably the earliest stone castle authenticated in Scotland. Built circa 1145 by Norseman Kolbein Hruga, it consists of a small rectangular tower enclosed in a circular ditch. Nearby are the ruins of St Mary's Chapel, late 12th-century in the Romanesque style.

---

406 CULBIN FOREST **3 L7**

FE. Moray. A96 from Nairn to Brodie, then unclassified road to Cloddymoss; or A96 from Forres to Findhorn bridge then Kintessack road for 3 miles (5km) to Wellhill car park. Nearest bus at Nairn, 1 mile (2km) to Kingsteps (western end of forest); or Brodie on A96, 1.5 miles (3km) to Cloddymoss (centre of forest); nearest railway stations Nairn and Forres. Open daily all year. Free. Leaflet available. Picnic areas. Guided walks and events. Public and disabled toilets at Cloddymoss. Wheelchair access with assistance. Car parking. Telephone (01343) 820223.

An extensive pine forest, from Nairn to Findhorn Bay. Planted from the 1920s to stabilise the drifting sands. Unique natural history. Botanical trail. Five waymarked low level walks, from 1 to 3.5 miles (5.5km) from Wellhill car park; one walk of 2 miles (4km) from Kingsteps (western forest). Informal walks throughout the forest. Ranger service.

---

407 CULLERLIE STONE CIRCLE **3 Q10**

HS. Near Echt, off the A944, 1 mile (2km) south of Garlogie, Aberdeenshire, 13 miles (21km) west of Aberdeen. Nearest railway station Aberdeen, bus from Aberdeen to Garlogie then 0.5 mile (1km) walk. Access at all times. Free. Car parking. Telephone 0131 668 8800.

A stone circle enclosing an area on which eight small cairns were later constructed. About 4000 years old.

---

408 CULLODEN **3 K8**

NTS. Visitor Centre, Culloden Moor, Inverness. On B9006 5 miles (8km) east of Inverness. Bus from Inverness. Visitor Centre open Feb–Mar and Nov–Dec, daily 1000–1600; Apr–Oct, daily 0900–1800. Site of battle open all year. Charge ££. Children free. Group concessions. Guided tours in summer. Explanatory displays, audio-visual programme in five languages. Guidebook in French and German. Gift shop. Restaurant. WC. Braille guide, raised maps and audio tape for blind visitors. Induction loop, subtitled audio-visual programme and special audio-visual channel for hard of hearing. Wheelchair access, wheelchairs available. Disabled WC. Car and coach parking. Telephone (01463) 790607.

Site of the battle on 16 April 1746, when the forces of Bonnie Prince Charlie were defeated by the Hanoverian army, so ending the Forty-Five Jacobite uprising. Visitor centre with Jacobite exhibition, displays, audio-visual programme and bookshop.

409 CULROSS 6 L15

NTS. West Green House, Culross, Fife. Off A985, 12 miles (19km) west of Forth Road Bridge. Bus from Glasgow or Dunfermline. Palace and Town House open Apr–May and Sep, daily 1330–1700; Jun–Aug, daily 1100–1700. Study open Apr–Sep, daily 1330–1630. Village open all year. Charge ££. Children free. Group concessions. Explanatory displays. Guidebook and video programme in French and German, information sheets in seven languages. Tearoom. Town trail, palace garden. WC. Induction loop and Braille guide. Limited wheelchair access. Disabled WC. Car and coach parking. Telephone (01383) 880359.

Many buildings from the 16th and 17th centuries survive in this ancient royal burgh on the north shore of the River Forth. Most spectacular is the Palace, built 1597–1611 for local entrepreneur Sir George Bruce. Visitor reception in Town House, with exhibition and video.

---

410 CULROSS ABBEY 6 L15

HS. In Culross, Fife. Off A985, 12 miles (19km) west of Forth Road Bridge. Bus from Dunfermline. Open daily, summer 1000–dusk; winter 1000–1600. Sunday service 1130. Free. Telephone 0131 668 8800.

The remains of a Cistercian monastery founded in 1217. The eastern parts of the Abbey Church form the present parish church. There are also ruins of the nave, cellars and other domestic buildings.

---

411 CULSH EARTH HOUSE 3 P9

HS. On B919 at Culsh, 1 mile (2km) east of Tarland, Aberdeenshire. Nearest railway station Aberdeen, bus from Aberdeen, access by Culsh Farmhouse at all times. Free. Telephone 0131 668 8800.

A well-preserved underground passage with roofing slabs intact over the large chamber and entrance. About 2000 years old.

---

412 CULZEAN CASTLE AND COUNTRY PARK 4 H18

NTS. Maybole. On A719, 12 miles (19km) south of Ayr. Bus from Ayr. Open Apr–Oct, daily 1030–1730. Country Park open all year, daily 0930–sunset. Charge £££. Children free. Country park only, ££. Group concessions. Guided tours of castle by arrangement; guided walks by rangers in park. Explanatory displays. Information sheets in six languages, guidebook in French and German. Gift shop. Two restaurants and several snack-bars and picnic areas. Gardens, adventure playground. WC. Induction loop and basic language audio tape tour. Braille guidebooks and tactile models. Wheelchair access, wheelchairs and batricars available. Disabled WC. Car and coach parking. Telephone (01655) 884455.

High on a cliff above the Firth of Clyde, Robert Adam's Culzean Castle is one of the most romantic in Scotland. Designed at the end of the 18th century, the elegant interior includes the spectacular Oval Staircase and the Circular Saloon. Fascinating associated buildings in the 563 acre (227ha) Country Park include the Fountain Court and the Camellia House. Swan pond, deer park, woodland and beach walks.

---

413 CUMBERNAULD MUSEUM 6 K15

Cumbernauld Library, 8 Allander Walk, Cumbernauld. In Cumbernauld town centre. Nearest railway station Cumbernauld, local bus service. Open all year, Mon–Fri 0900–1900 (Wed closes 1200), Sat 0900–1700. Free. Guided tours. Explanatory displays. WC. Wheelchair access. Car and coach parking. Telephone (01236) 725664.

Telling the history of Cumbernauld from the setting of a Roman camp, past the fireside chat of a medieval lord, to the parlour of a 1930s miner. Audio-visual techniques bring the past to life.

---

414 CUNNINGHAME GRAHAM MEMORIAL 4 J14

NTS. Gartmore, Stirling. 2 miles (3km) southwest of Aberfoyle, off A81. Access at all times. Free. Explanatory displays. Wheelchair access with assistance. Car and coach parking.

A cairn commemorates the extraordinary life of R. B. Cunninghame Graham (1852–1936). He was a radical politician, writer, traveller and renowned horseman. An interpretive panel gives details of his life and the estate of Gartmore, his family home.

---

415 CUWEEN HILL CAIRN **1 B10**

HS. On A965, 0.5 mile (1km) south of Finstown, Orkney. Bus service from Kirkwall or Stromness then 1 mile (2km) walk. Access at all times. Free. Car parking. Telephone 0131 668 8800.

A low mound covering a Neolithic chambered tomb with four cells. When discovered, it contained the bones of men, dogs and oxen.

---

416 DALGARVEN MILL AND MUSEUM OF COUNTRY LIFE AND COSTUME **6 H17**

Dalry Road, Kilwinning, Ayrshire. On the A737 between Dalry and Kilwinning. Bus from Dalry or Kilwinning (or express bus from Glasgow). Open Apr–Oct, Tue–Sun and bank holidays, 1000–1700; Nov–Mar, Wed–Sun 1100–1600. Charge £. Group concessions. Guided tours by prior arrangement. Explanatory displays. Antiques shop. Gift shop. Coffee shop and picnic area. Riverside walk and wild flower meadow. WC. Limited wheelchair access. Disabled WC. Car and coach parking. Telephone (01294) 552448.

A 17th-century restored water mill, set in a secluded hollow, housing an exhibition of traditional flour production. In the adjoining granary there is a museum of Ayrshire country life, with collections of farming and domestic memorabilia and local costume, including some good examples of Ayrshire whitework. Room reconstructions of 1880 lifestyle.

---

417 DALKEITH COUNTRY PARK **6 N15**

Dalkeith, Midlothian. In Dalkeith High Street, off A68, 7 miles (11km) south of Edinburgh. Bus from Edinburgh. Open Apr–Sep, daily 1000–1800. Charge £. Children under 5 free. Group concessions. Guided tours. Explanatory displays. Gift shop. Restaurant, tearoom and picnic area. WC. Wheelchair access. Disabled WC. Car and coach parking. Telephone 0131 654 1666.

The extensive grounds of Dalkeith Palace (not open to the public), an 18th-century planned landscape. Farm animals, including working Clydesdale horses, adventure woodland play area, nature trails, woodland walks, 18th-century bridge, orangery and ice house. Ranger service.

---

418 DALLAS DHU HISTORIC DISTILLERY **3 M7**

HS. Mannachie Road, Forres, Morayshire. Off the A940, 2 miles (3km) south of Forres, Moray. Nearest railway station Forres, bus from Inverness or Aberdeen, then 2 mile (3km) walk. Open Apr–Sep, daily 0930–1830; Oct–Mar, Mon–Sat 0930–1630, Sun 1400–1630, closed Thu pm and Fri. Charge £. Guided tours. Explanatory displays. Visitor centre. Audio-visual presentation in several languages. Gift shop. Picnic area. WC. Limited wheelchair access. Disabled WC. Car and coach parking. Telephone (01309) 676548.

A picturesque small distillery built in 1898 to supply malt whisky for Wright and Greig's Roderick Dhu blend. Video on the history of Scotch whisky. Visitors may sample whisky.

---

419 DALMENY HOUSE **6 M15**

South Queenferry, West Lothian. Off the B924, 7 miles (11km) west of Edinburgh. Bus or rail (Dalmeny station) from Edinburgh. Open Jul and Aug, Sun, Mon and Tue 1400–1730; groups by special arrangement at other times. Charge ££. Group concessions. Guided tours. Tearoom. WC. Wheelchair access with assistance. Disabled WC. Car and coach parking. Telephone 0131 331 1888.

The home of the Earls of Rosebery for over 300 years, but the present Tudor Gothic building, by William Wilkins, dates from 1815. Interior Gothic splendour of hammer-beamed hall, vaulted corridors and classical main rooms. Works of art include a magnificent collection of 18th-century British portraits, 18th-century furniture, tapestries, porcelain from the Rothschild Mentmore collection and the Napoleon collection. Lovely grounds and a 4.5 mile (7km) shore walk.

---

420 DALMENY PARISH CHURCH **6 M15**

Main Street, Dalmeny, West Lothian. 10 miles (16km) west of Edinburgh. A90 to South Queensferry then follow signs to Dalmeny. Nearest railway station Dalmeny then 1 mile (1.6km) walk, bus service from Edinburgh. Open Apr–Sep, Sun 1400–1630; other times by request. Free. Donation box. Guided tours by arrangement. Leaflets (available in French and German). Gifts available. WC. Wheelchair access. Car and coach parking. Telephone 0131 331 1479.

The best preserved Romanesque (Norman) church in Scotland, dating from the 12th century. Coach tours should book in advance.

---

421 DALTON POTTERY **5 M20**

Meikle Dyke, Dalton, Dumfriesshire. On the B725, 1 mile (2km) towards Dalton from Carrutherstown (off A75 between Dumfries and Annan). Bus from Dumfries. Open all year, daily 0900–1700 (closed Christmas, Boxing Day and New Years Day). Free. Explanatory displays. Gift shop. Tearoom and picnic area. Indoor clay play area, outdoor play area. WC. Wheelchair access. Disabled WC. Car parking. Telephone (01387) 840236.

A working potte·y where visitors can see a range of porcelain giftware being made and hand decorated. Showroom.

---

422 DALWHINNIE DISTILLERY VISITOR CENTRE **3 K10**

Dalwhinnie, Inverness-shire. Off the A9, 50 miles (80km) north of Perth. Nearest railway station Dalwhinnie, bus from Inverness or Perth stops 2 miles (3km) on new A9 road. Open Apr–Nov, Mon–Fri 0930–1630 (Jun–Oct, also Sat 0930–1630, Jul–Aug, also Sun 1230–1630); Dec–Mar, appointment advisable (closed Christmas to New Year). Charge £. Group concessions. Guided tours. Explanatory displays. Leaflets available in Dutch, French, German, Italian, Japanese and Spanish. Gift shop. WC. Limited wheelchair access. Disabled WC. Car and coach parking. Telephone (01540) 672219.

The highest distillery in Scotland, opened in 1898. Tour guides explain the secrets of distilling. The exhibition features the history and geography of the area, and the Classic Malts.

---

423 DALZELL PARK **6 K16**

Adele Street, Motherwell. Nearest railway station Motherwell, bus from Glasgow. Open from dawn–dusk. Free. Limited wheelchair access. Car and coach parking. Telephone (01698) 266155.

Peaceful woodland with spectacular scenery and heritage monuments such as Dalzell House and Lord Gavin's Temple. Wildlife includes woodpeckers, roedeer and squirrels. Ranger service

---

424 DANDELION DESIGNS AND IMAGES GALLERY **2 D7**

The Captain's House, Stein, Waternish, Isle of Skye. On the B886, Waternish Road, betwen Edinbane and Dunvegan. By bus from Portree or Dunvegan (limited service). Open Mar–Oct, daily 1100–1700. Nov–Feb by arrangement. Free. Gift shop. Wheelchair access. Car and coach parking. Telephone (01470) 592218 or 592223.

A craft workshop and gallery. A local artist demonstrates craft work and painting techniques. Situated in a fine listed building on the shore of Loch Bay with spectacular views.

425 BARBARA DAVIDSON POTTERY 6 L15

Muirhall Farm, Larbert, Stirlingshire. On the A88 north side of Larbert, 9 miles (14.5km) south of Stirling, signposted from the A9. Nearest railway station Larbert (12 minutes walk away), bus from Stirling or Falkirk. Open all year, Mon–Sat 1000–1700, Sun 1200–1700; closed Christmas and New Year. Free. Guided tours and demonstration by arrangement (£). Gift shop. Wheelchair access. Car parking. Telephone (01324) 554430.

A working pottery in a picturesque converted 17th-century farm steading. Products are hand-thrown stoneware, mostly functional. In July and August, visitors can try their hand at making a pot (small charge).

---

426 TOM DAVIDSON GALLERY 5 P17

High Street, Earlston, Berwickshire. On the A68, 14 miles (22km) north of Jedburgh, 38 miles (61km) south of Edinburgh. Bus from Edinburgh, Jedburgh, Galashiels or Berwick-upon-Tweed. Open all year, including bank holidays, but not Sun. Free. Explanatory displays. Gift shop. Wheelchair access with assistance. Car and coach parking. Telephone (01896) 848898.

A gallery featuring mostly landscape paintings, etchings and linocuts. Davidson is known as one of Scotland's leading exponents of the linocut and he can be seen at work either cutting or printing the block. Time is given to explain the process to visitors.

---

427 DAWYCK BOTANIC GARDEN 5 M17

Stobo, Peeblesshire. On the B712, 8 miles (13km) southwest of Peebles. Bus from Peebles. Open Mar–Oct, daily 0930–1800. Charge £. Group concessions. Guided tours by arrangement. Explanatory displays. Gift shop. Tearoom and picnic area. WC. Limited wheelchair access. Car and coach parking. Telephone (01721) 760254.

A specialist garden of the Royal Botanic Garden, Edinburgh (see 574). A historic arboretum with landscaped walks. The mature trees include the unique Dawyck Beech. There are also many varieties of flowering trees, shrubs and herbaceous plants. Visitors can explore Heron Wood and the world's first Cryptogamic Sanctuary and Reserve to see non-flowering plants. Other notable features include the Swiss Bridge, stonework and terracing created by Italian craftsmen in the 1820s.

---

428 DEEP SEA WORLD 6 M15

North Queensferry, Fife. In village of North Queensferry. Nearest railway station North Queensferry, bus services (Fife Scottish). Take junction 1 off M90 and follow signs. Open Mar–Oct, daily 1000–1800; Jul–Aug daily 1000–1830; Nov–Mar, Mon–Fri 1100–1700, Sat, Sun and public holidays 1000–1800. Charge £££. Reduced rates for carers on request. Group concessions. Guided tours. Explanatory displays. Gift shop. Café and picnic area. WC. Wheelchair access. Disabled WC. Car and coach parking. Telephone 0930 100 300 (calls cost 50p per minute).

A triple award-winning aquarium. Visitors can enjoy a spectacular diver's eye view of our marine environment on an underwater safari through the world's longest underwater tunnel – come face to face with Europe's largest collection of sand tiger sharks and watch divers hand feed a spectacular array of sea life; touch the live exhibits in the large rockpools; and visit the stunning Amazonian Experience which features ferocious piranhas and electrifying eels. Other exhibits include the dangerous animals tank, sea-horses, octopus, wolf-fish and many many more fascinating creatures. New exhibits include the Amazing Amphibians display featuring the world's most poisonous frog, and animal handling sessions including snakes. Free behind the scenes tours.

429 DEER ABBEY 3 R8

HS. Off A950 at Old Deer, 10 miles (16km) west of Peterhead, Aberdeenshire. Bus to Mintlaw then 1.5 miles (2.5km) walk. Access at all times. Free. Car parking. Telephone 0131 668 8800.

Scant remains of a Cistercian monastery founded in 1218.

---

430 DEE VALLEY CONFECTIONERS 3 N10

Station Square, Ballater, Aberdeenshire. 44 miles (70km) west of Aberdeen. Bus service from Aberdeen. Shop open Apr–Oct, Mon–Thu 0900–2000; factory open to visitors Apr–Oct, Mon–Thu 0900–1200 and 1400–1630. Free. Gift shop. WC. Wheelchair access. Car and coach parking. Telephone (01339) 755499.

The visitor can observe sweets being made from a viewing area. Watch the process of colours and flavours being added to the candy, followed by the stretch and pull methods for stripes and lettering. The old-fashioned machines form the sweets and cool the candy. Free samples.

---

431 DELGATIE CASTLE 3 Q7

Delgatie, Turriff, Aberdeenshire. Off the A947, on the B9170. 3 miles (5km) northeast of Turriff. Nearest railway and bus station Aberdeen. Open Apr–Oct, daily 1000–1700. Charge £. Group concessions. Guided tours. Explanatory displays. Gift shop. Tearoom and picnic area. WC. Wheelchair access to ground floor and tearoom. Car and coach parking. Telephone (01888) 562750.

An 11th-century tower house, the home of Captain Hay of Delgatie who has restored it over the last 50 years. It contains late 16th-century painted ceilings and has the widest turnpike stair in Scotland. Mary, Queen of Scots stayed here after the Battle of Corrichie.

---

432 DENNY SHIP MODEL EXPERIMENT TANK 6 J15

Castle Street, Dumbarton, Dunbartonshire. 200 yards (182m) east of Dumbarton town centre. Bus or rail from Glasgow. Open all year (except Christmas and New Year), Mon–Sat 1000–1600. Charge £. Group concessions. Guided tours on request. Explanatory displays. Gift shop. Tearoom and picnic area. WC. Limited wheelchair access. Car and coach parking. Telephone (01389) 763444.

A ship model experiment tank constructed in 1882 and retaining many of its original features. Fully restored to working order by the Scottish Maritime Museum so that the original process can be demonstrated.

---

433 DERE STREET ROMAN ROAD 6 N16

HS. On the B6438 (off the A68) beside Soutra Aisle, Midlothian. Bus from Edinburgh to Jedburgh, alight at top of Soutra Hill then 0.6 mile (1km) walk. Access at all times. Free. Telephone 0131 668 8800.

A good stretch of the Roman road which ran from Corbridge beside Hadrian's Wall to Cramond on the Firth of Forth. Beside the road are scoops, pits from which the gravel for building the road was taken.

---

434 DESIGNS GALLERY AND CAFE 5 K20

179 King Street, Castle Douglas, Dumfries and Galloway. On the A75, 18 miles (29km) west of Dumfries. Bus from Castle Douglas. Open all year (except Christmas and New Year), daily 0930–1730. Free. Gift shop. Restaurant. Sculpture garden. WC. Limited wheelchair access. Disabled WC. Telephone (01556) 504552.

A focal point for arts and crafts in southwest Scotland. Changing exhibitions of high quality crafts. Adjacent shop sells cards, prints, ceramics, knitwear, studio glass and jewellery.

435 DESKFORD CHURCH 3 P7

HS. Off B9018, 4 miles south of Cullen, Banffshire. Nearest railway station Elgin, bus from Elgin the 0.5 mile (1km) walk. Access at all times. Free. Telephone 0131 668 8800.

Ruin of a small, late medieval church with a richly carved sacrament house characteristic of northeast Scotland.

---

436 DEVIL'S BEEF TUB 5 M18

A701, 6 miles (9.5km) north of Moffat. Access at all times. Free. Car parking.

A huge, spectacular hollow among the hills, at the head of Annandale. In the swirling mists of this out-of-the-way retreat, Borders reivers hid cattle lifted in their raids. Can be seen from the road.

---

437 DEVIL'S PORRIDGE 5 N20

St John's Church, Eastriggs, Dumfriesshire. Off A75 between Gretna and Annan. Nearest railway station Annan 3 miles (5km), bus from Carlisle and Dumfries. Open late May–Oct, Wed–Sat 1000–1600, Sun 1200–1600. Charge £. Accompanied children under 12 free. Group concessions. Guided tours by arrangement. Explanatory displays. Gift shop. Coffee and tea available. WC. Wheelchair access. Car and coach parking. Telephone (01461) 40460.

An exhibition on the fascinating story of the 30,000 women and men who worked in HM Factory Gretna in World War I. Women munition workers mixed the Devil's Porridge, the name coined by Sir Arthur Conan Doyle for the highly explosive mixture of gun cotton and nitro-glycerine which was made into cordite for British shells and bullets. Photographs, video, murals, artifacts and supporting exhibitions.

---

438 DEWARS CENTRE 5 M13

Glover Street, Perth. In centre of Perth. Within walking distance of bus and railway stations. Open Sep–Apr, daily 0800–0000; May–Aug, daily 0800–1800. Skating at scheduled times, telephone to confirm. Free. Charge by activity, equipment hire. Group concessions. Explanatory displays. Restaurant/coffee shop. WC. Wheelchair access. Disabled WC. Car and coach parking. Telephone (01738) 624188.

A range of sporting activities are available at the centre: curling, ice skating and indoor bowling are offered in a multi-purpose building housing conference, catering and leisure facilities.

---

439 DIM RIV NORSE LONGSHIP BOAT TRIPS 1 G5

Lerwick, Shetland. Open Jun–Aug, Mon only unless hired privately. Charge ££. Car and coach parking. Telephone (01595) 693097.

This is a working replica of a Norse longship.

---

440 DINGWALL MUSEUM 3 J7

Town House, High Street, Dingwall, Ross and Cromarty. 11 miles (18km) north of Inverness via A9 and A835. Nearest railway station Dingwall; bus service from Inverness, Strathpeffer and the north. Open May–Sep, Mon–Fri 1000–1700. Charge £. Courtyard free. Group concessions. Guided tours. Explanatory displays. Gift shop. Picnic area. Garden and outdoor display area. Amplified hearing units available. Limited wheelchair access. Car and coach parking. Telephone (01349) 865366.

The award-winning museum contains a reconstructed smiddy and kitchen; military room and artefacts relating to the history of the ancient burgh. Special attractions including giant jigsaws for children. Changing exhibitions and activities such as spinning and blanket stamping.

441 DIRLETON CASTLE AND GARDENS 6 P15

HS. Dirleton, North Berwick. Off A198 in Dirleton village, 8 miles (13km) west of North Berwick, East Lothian. Nearest railway station North Berwick, bus to Dirleton from Edinburgh and North Berwick. Open Apr–Sep, daily 0930–1830; Oct–Mar, daily 0930–1630. Charge £. Group concessions. Guided tours. Explanatory displays. Gift shop. Main garden has a selection of scented flowers and plants. Limited wheelchair access. Car and coach parking. Telephone (01620) 850330.

A romantic castle dating from the 13th century with 15th- to 17th-century additions. First besieged in 1298 by Edward I. Destroyed in 1650. The adjoining gardens include an early 20th-century Arts and Crafts garden and a restored Victorian garden. Also a 17th-century bowling green.

---

442 DIVACH FALLS 3 J8

A82 from Inverness through Drumnadrochit, turning right at Lewiston onto Balmacaan road (Falls signposted). Car park at top.

A 100 foot (30.5m) fall above the village of Drumnadrochit. The falls are overlooked by Divach Lodge where J. M. Barrie once stayed.

---

443 DOCHFOUR GARDENS 3 K8

Dochgarroch, Inverness. On the A82, 5 miles (8km) southwest of Inverness. Open Apr–Sep, Mon–Fri 1000–1600. Charge £. Group concessions. Guided tours by prior arrangement. Limited wheelchair access. Car parking. Telephone (01463) 861218.

Fifteen acres (6ha) of Victorian terraced garden at the north end of the Great Glen with panoramic views over Loch Dochfour. Magnificent specimen trees, naturalised daffodils, rhododendrons, water garden and extensive yew topiary.

---

444 DOGTON STONE 6 M14

HS. Off B922, at Dogton farmhouse, near Cardenden. 5 miles (8km) northwest of Kirkcaldy, Fife. 1.5 miles (2.5km) east northeast of Cardenden railway station, bus from Kirkcaldy or Dunfermline.

An ancient Celtic cross with traces of animal and figure sculpture.

---

445 DOLPHINS AND SEALS OF THE MORAY FIRTH 3 K8

Tourist Information Centre, North Kessock, Inverness. Off the A9, just north of the Kessock Bridge. Bus from Inverness. Open Easter–Oct, daily 1000–1700. Charge £. Group concessions. Guided tours (in German by prior arrangement). Explanatory displays. Gift shop. Picnic area. WC. Wheelchair access with assistance. Disabled WC. Car and coach parking. Telephone (01463) 731866.

An exhibition about the local bottle-nosed dolphin population with touch-screen computer programme. Video display. Children's activities. Reference corner and interpretive staff. Visitors may watch the dolphins and also hear them through underwater microphones.

---

446 DOONHILL HOMESTEAD 5 P15

HS. Off the A1, 2 miles (3km) south of Dunbar, East Lothian. Nearest railway station Dunbar, bus from Edinburgh to Dunbar, then walk 2 miles (3km). Access at all times. Free. Car parking. Telephone 0131 668 8800.

The site of a wooden hall of a 6th-century British chief, and of an Anglian chief's hall which superseded it in the 7th century. A rare record of the Anglian occupation of southeast Scotland.

447 DORNOCH CATHEDRAL 3 L6

Dornoch, Sutherland. On A9, 40 miles (64km) north of Inverness. Bus from Inverness or Tain (station). Open all year 0900–dusk. Free. Guided tours in summer after evening service; other times with advance notice. Explanatory displays. Gift shop open in summer, Mon–Fri 1000–1600. Crèche on Sunday during church service. WC. Induction loop and personal radio receivers available on request. Wheelchair access. Car and coach parking. Telephone (01862) 810357.

A small well-maintained cathedral founded in 1224 by Gilbert, Archdeacon of Moray and Bishop of Caithness. Partially destroyed by fire in 1570 and restored in the 17th century, in 1835–37, and again in 1924. The fine 13th-century stonework is still visible.

---

448 DORNOCH LOCHANS 3 L6

Davochfin Farm, Dornoch, Sutherland. 1 mile (2km) west of Dornoch on Cuthill Road. Bus from Dornoch. Open Apr–Nov, Mon–Sat 1000–2200, Sun 1400–1800. Free. Picnic and barbeque area. WC. Wheelchair access with assistance. Disabled WC. Car and coach parking. Telephone (01862) 810600.

A trout fishery with four ponds. Also pitch and putt, croquet and boule, golf driving range.

---

449 DOUNE CASTLE 5 K14

HS. Castle Road, Doune. Off A84 at Doune, 8 miles (13km) northwest of Stirling. Nearest railway station Dunblane, bus via Doune from Stirling or Callander. Open Apr–Sep, daily 0930–1830; Oct–Mar, Mon–Sat 0930–1630, Sun 1400–1630, closed Thu pm and Fri. Charge £. Group concessions. Guided tours. Explanatory displays. Gift shop. Picnic area. Carvings can be touched. Limited wheelchair access. Car parking. Telephone (01786) 841742.

A magnificent late 14th-century courtyard castle built for the Regent Albany. Its most striking feature is the combination of tower, gatehouse and hall with its kitchen in a massive frontal block. Later possessed by the Stuarts of Doune, Earls of Moray.

---

450 DOUNREAY EXHIBITION CENTRE 3 L2

Dounreay, Thurso, Caithness. On A836, 9 miles (14.5km) west of Thurso. Bus service from Thurso. Open May–Oct, daily 1000–1600. Free. Guided tours. Explanatory displays. Tearoom and picnic area. WC. Limited wheelchair access. Car cnd coach parking. Telephone (01847) 802572.

The Dounreay Exhibition Centre tells the story of the remarkable work carried out at the site in the past, the present and looking into the future, which can be easily understood and enjoyed by the whole family. Visitors can also hear how UKAEA Dounreay is developing world-class expertise in decommissioning, waste management and environmental reclaimation of the site.

---

451 DRUCHTAG MOTTE 4 J21

HS. At the north end of Mochrum village, 2 miles (3km) north of Port William, Wigtownshire. Nearest railway station Stranraer, bus from Newton Stewart or Stranraer to Mochrum or Port William. Access at all times. Free. Telephone 0131 668 8800.

A well-preserved Norman motte castle.

---

452 DRUM CASTLE AND GARDENS 3 Q10

NTS. Drumoak, Banchory, Aberdeenshire. Off A93, 10 miles (16km) west of Aberdeen. By bus from Aberdeen. Open Easter–May, Sep and weekends in Oct, daily 1330–1730; Jun–Aug, daily 1100–1730. Grounds open all year, daily 0930–sunset. Charge ££. Children free. Garden and grounds only, £. Group concessions. Guided tours by arrangement. Explanatory displays. Information sheets in five languages. Gift shop. Tearoom. Garden and play area. WC. Wheelchair access with assistance, wheelchair available. Disabled WC. Car and coach parking. Telephone (01330) 811204.

The 13th-century tower of Drum is one of the three oldest tower houses in Scotland and was the work of Richard Cementarius, first Provost of Aberdeen and King's Master Mason. Jacobean and Victorian extensions make this a fine mansion house with notable portraits and furniture, much from the 18th century. Grounds contain 16th-century chapel and a unique Garden of Historic Roses.

---

453 DRUMCOLTRAN TOWER **5 L20**

HS. Off A711, 8 miles (13km) southwest of Dumfries. The tower can be found among farm buildings. Nearest railway station Dumfries, bus services from Dumfries, Stranraer, Dalbeattie then walk. Open at all times, apply to keyholder. Free. Telephone 0131 668 8800.

A well-preserved mid 16th-century tower house. Simple and severe.

---

454 DRUM FARM CENTRE **3 J8**

The Village Green, Drumnadrochit, Loch Ness. 12 miles (19km) south of Inverness on A82. Bus service from Inverness or Fort William stops outside. Open Easter–Oct, Mon–Sat 1000–1630; until 1800 Jul and Aug. Closed Sun. Charge £. Chidren under 2 free. Group concessions. Explanatory displays. Gift shop. Tearoom and picnic area. WC. Staff member trained in British sign language, and information menu in braille. Wheelchair access. Disabled WC. Car and coach parking. Telephone (01456) 450788.

Family-run livestock farm. Lots of play activities including straw barn, indoor sandpit, play tractors and classroom. Feed and stroke the animals. Tractor trailer rides.

---

455 DRUMLANRIG'S TOWER **5 P18**

1 Towerknowe, Hawick. In the centre of Hawick, off the High Street. Bus from Edinburgh or Carlisle. Open Mar–Oct, Mon–Sat 1000–1700, Sun 1200–1700; until 1730 in Jun and Sep and until 1800 in Jul and Aug. Charge £. Group concessions. Guided tours by arrangement. Explanatory displays in visitor centre (touch screen audio-visual). Gift shop. Baby changing and feeding facilities. WC. Wheelchair access. Disabled WC. Car parking. Telephone (01450) 377615.

This 15th-century fortified tower house, stronghold of the Douglases, tells the story of Hawick and Scotland using period sets, costumed figures and audio-visuals. Themes include Border Reivers and Hawick's renowned knitwear industry.

---

456 DRUMMOND CASTLE GARDENS **5 L13**

Drummond Castle, Muthill, Crieff. 2 miles (3km) south of Crieff. Nearest railway station Gleneagles, bus service from Stirling to Crieff. Open Easter, then May–Oct, daily 1400–1800. Charge £. Gift shop. WC. Limited wheelchair access. Disabled WC. Car and coach parking. Telephone (01764) 681257 or 681433 weekends.

One of Scotland's largest formal gardens with magnificent early Victorian parterre, fountains, terracing and topiary. It is laid out in the form of a St Andrews cross. The multi-faceted sundial by John Mylne, master mason to Charles I, has been the centrepiece since 1630.

---

457 DRUMPELLIER COUNTRY PARK **6 K16**

Townhead Road, Coatbridge. 2 miles (3km) from Coatbridge. By rail to Coatbridge Sunnyside or Central stations, then bus to park. Park open all year during daylight. Visitor centre open daily, May and Sep 1100–1730; Jun–Aug 1030–1930; Oct–Apr 1200–1600. Free. Explanatory displays. Ranger guided walks. Gift shop. Tearoom. WC. Limited wheelchair access. Disabled WC. Car and coach parking. Telephone (01236) 422257.

Five hundred acres (202ha) of woodland, heathland and a loch. There is a visitor centre, café, countryside ranger service, road train as well as angling, boating, nature trails, 18-hole golf course and driving range, butterfly house, pets corner, birdwatching and play areas.

458 DRYBURGH ABBEY 5 P17

HS. Dryburgh, St Boswells, Melrose. Near St Boswells on the B6404, 5 miles (8km) southeast of Melrose. Bus service from Newtown to St Boswells, alight at College Stop, 20 minutes walk. Open all year, daily 0930–1830. Charge £. Group concessions. Guided tours. Explanatory displays. Gift shop. Picnic area. WC. Wheelchair access with assistance. Car and coach parking. Telephone (01835) 822381.

The remarkably complete ruins of a Premonstratensian abbey. One of the four famous Border abbeys founded in the reign of David I by Hugh de Morville, Constable of Scotland. Mainly remains of transepts and cloisters. Sir Walter Scott and Field Marshall Earl Haig are buried here.

---

459 DRYHOPE TOWER 5 N17

Off A708 near St Mary's Loch, 15 miles (24km) west of Selkirk. Access at all reasonable times. Free.

A stout tower, now ruinous but originally four storeys high, rebuilt circa 1613. Birthplace of Mary Scott, the Flower of Yarrow, who married the freebooter Auld Wat of Harden in 1576 – ancestors Sir Walter Scott was proud to claim.

---

460 DRYMEN POTTERY 4 J15

The Square, Drymen, Stirlingshire. 20 miles (32km) north of Glasgow. Bus from Glasgow or Balloch (by train to Balloch). Open all year (except Christmas Day and New Year), daily 1000–1600. Free. Gift shop. Coffee shop. WC. Wheelchair access to shop and tearoom only. Car and coach parking. Telephone (01360) 660458.

Pottery studio with a large coffee and gift shop.

---

461 DUALCHAS

See 140 Barra Heritage and Cultural Centre.

---

462 DUART CASTLE 4 F13

Isle of Mull, Argyll. Off the A849 on the east of Mull. By ferry from Oban to Craignure, coach (Mull Experience) from Craignure. By launch from Oban to Castle jetty, weather permitting. Open May–Oct, daily 1030–1800. Charge ££. Grounds free. Group concessions. Guided tours on request. Explanatory displays. Leaflet in French, German and Italian. Gift shop. Tearoom and picnic area. WC. Wheelchair access to shop and tearoom only. Car and coach parking. Telephone (01680) 812309.

One of the oldest inhabited castles in Scotland, built on a cliff overlooking the Sound of Mull and the home of the 28th Chief of Clan Maclean. The keep was built in 1360 adjoining the original courtyard. Because the clan supported the Stewarts, the castle was taken by the Duke of Argyll in 1691. After the 1745 Rising, it was used as a garrison for English troops and then fell into ruin. It was restored by Sir Fitzroy Maclean in 1911. The keep contains dungeons with figures of prisoners from the Spanish Armada and exhibitions of clan history. There are fine views from the wall walk.

---

463 DUFF HOUSE COUNTRY GALLERY 3 P7

Duff House, Banff, Aberdeenshire. Between Banff and Macduff, 47 miles (75km) north of Aberdeen. Nearest railway station Elgin, then bus to Banff from Elgin or Aberdeen, 5 minute walk from bus. Open all year 1000–1700; Oct–Mar, Thu–Sun only, telephone for details. Charge £. Group concessions. Explanatory displays. Gift shop. Tearoom. Children's play area and action playground. WC. Audio guides and induction loops. Wheelchair access. Disabled WC. Car and coach parking. Telephone (01261) 818181.

Constructed between 1735 and 1740 by William Adam for William Braco, the house has been in turn a ducal residence, a hotel, a sanatorium, a prisoner of war camp, and is now a country house gallery of the National Galleries of Scotland. It is one of the finest examples of Georgian baroque architecture in Britain. It contains a fine collection of paintings, furniture, tapestries and artefacts drawn from the National Galleries, the Erskine of Torrie Institute and several private lenders.

---

464 DUFFUS CASTLE **3 M7**

HS. Off B9012, 5 miles (8km) northwest of Elgin, Moray. Nearest railway station Elgin, bus from Elgin then 10 minutes walk. Open at all times. Free. Car parking. Telephone 0131 668 8800.

Massive ruins of a fine motte and bailey castle surrounded by a moat still entire and filled with water. A fine 14th-century tower crowns the Norman motte, the original seat of the de Moravia family, the Murrays, now represented by the dukedoms of Atholl and Sutherland.

---

465 DULLATUR **6 K15**

HS. Dullatur. 0.6 mile (1km) east of Dullatur. Nearest railway station Croy, bus from Glasgow (Buchanan Street).

A well preserved section of ditch. Part of the Antonine wall (see 62).

---

466 DULSIE BRIDGE **3 L8**

Inverness-shire. Off the A939 from Ferness, take the B9007 south, turning right onto an unclassified road to Dulsie.

An old stone bridge dating from 1764 spans the spectacular Findhorn Gorge at this well-known beauty spot.

---

467 DUMBARTON CASTLE **6 J15**

HS. Castle Road, Dumbarton. Off the A814 in Dumbarton on Dumbarton Rock. Nearest railway station Dumbarton East, bus from Glasgow then 20 minute walk. Open Apr–Sep, Mon–Sat 0930–1830, Sun 1400–1830; Oct–Mar, Mon–Sat 0930–1830, Sun 1400–1630, closed Thu pm and Fri. Charge £. Group concessions. Guided tours. Explanatory displays. Gift shop. Picnic area. WC. Car parking. Telephone (01389) 732167.

Spectacularly sited on a volcanic rock, the site of the ancient capital of Strathclyde. The most interesting features are the 18th-century artillery fortifications, with the 19th-century guns. Though mainly a modern barracks, a dungeon, a 12th-century gateway and a sundial gifted by Mary, Queen of Scots are preserved.

---

468 DUMFRIES ICE BOWL **5 L19**

King Street, Dumfries. Nearest railway and bus stations Dumfries. Open all year, 0900–2200 except Christmas and New Year. Charge £. Charge dependent on activity. Group concessions. Gift shop. Restaurant. WC. Wheelchair access. Disabled WC. Car and coach parking. Telephone (01387) 251300.

Curling, skating, ice disco, ice hockey matches and bowls hall.

---

469 DUMFRIES MUSEUM AND CAMERA OBSCURA **5 L19**

The Observatory, Dumfries. 0.5 mile (1km) west of Dumfries centre. 15 minute walk from railway station, 7 minute walk from bus station. Open Apr–Sep, Mon–Sat 1000–1700, Sun 1400–1700; Oct–Mar, Tue–Sat 1000–1300 and 1400–1700 (Camera Obscura closed). Free. Explanatory displays. Leaflet in French, German, Spanish, Italian and Russian. Gift shop. Terraced gardens. WC. Wheelchair access. Disabled WC. Car and coach parking. Telephone (01387) 253374.

Situated in the 18th-century windmill tower on top of Corbelly Hill, the museum is the largest in southwest Scotland, with collections inaugurated over 150 years ago. Exhibitions trace the history of the people and landscape of Dumfries and Galloway. The camera obscura (charge £) was installed in 1836 and gives a table-top panorama of Dumfries and the surrounding area. Note no wheelchair access to camera obscura.

470 DUMTRODDAN CUP AND RING MARKS **4 J21**

HS. Off the A714, 2 miles (3km) northeast of Port William, Wigtownshire. Nearest railway station Stranraer, bus services from Dumfries, Stranraer and Dalbeattie then walk. Access at all times. Free. Telephone 0131 668 8800.

A group of Bronze Age cup and ring markings in bedrock. An alignment of three stones stands 400 yards (365m) south.

---

471 DUNADD FORT **4 F14**

HS. Kilmartin Glen. 1 mile (2km) west of Kilmichael Glassary, Argyll. Nearest railway station Oban, then bus to Lochgilphead. Access at all times. Free. Telephone 0131 668 8800.

A spectacular site occupied since the Iron Age. The well-preserved hill fort is part-Roman, when it was a stronghold of Dalraida, the kingdom of the Scots.

---

472 DUNASKIN OPEN AIR MUSEUM **4 J18**

Dalmellington Road, Waterside, Patna, Ayrshire. Adjacent to A713 Ayr to Castle Douglas/Dumfries road. Nearest railway station Ayr, buses from Ayr and Cumnock. Open Apr–end Oct, daily 1000–1700. Charge ££. Group concessions. Guided tours. Explanatory displays. Gift shop. Coffee shop. Children's play area. WC. Wheelchair access. Disabled WC. Car and coach parking. Telephone (01292) 531144.

Journey back in time at this open-air industrial museum. Local coal, ironstone and limestone was smelted here to make pig iron – the museum describes how the rural valley of Doon was transformed into a busy industrial complex during the 19th century. Craighton Pit Experience contains many original artefacts from local pits and mines. Chapel Row Cottage has been restored to recreate an ironworks cottage of around 1914.

---

473 DUNAVERTY ROCK **4 F18**

At Southend, Mull of Kintyre, dominating beach and golf course. Access at all times. Free.

Formerly the site of Dunaverty Castle, a Macdonald stronghold. In 1647, about 300 people were put to death here by Covenanters under General Leslie. The rock is known locally as Blood Rock.

---

474 DUNBAR LEISURE POOL **5 P15**

Castle Park, Dunbar. Above the harbour in Dunbar. Nearest railway station Dunbar, bus from Edinburgh. Open all year except Christmas and New Year, daily from 1000. Charge dependent on activity. Group concessions. Café. Crèche. WC. Wheelchair access. Disabled WC. Car and coach parking. Telephone (01368) 865456.

Leisure pool with large flume, bubble bed, sprays, tropical temperatures and gently sloping beach. Also sauna, steam room, activity hall, gym and aerobics studio. The café has spectacular views of the harbour and coast.

---

475 DUNBAR TOWN HOUSE MUSEUM **5 P15**

High Street, Dunbar, East Lothian. In Dunbar High Street, at corner of Silver Street. Bus or rail from Edinburgh. Open Apr–Oct, daily 1230–1630. Free. Explanatory displays. Limited wheelchair access. Car and coach parking. Telephone (01368) 863734.

A 16th-century town house now housing a museum of local history and archaeology.

---

476 DUN BEAG BROCH **2 D8**

HS. 1 mile (2km) west of Bracadale, Skye. Bus service from Kyle of Lochalsh to Sligachan or Portree, bus from there past Struan, then short walk. Access at all times. Free. Car parking. Telephone 0131 668 8800.

A fine example of a Hebridean broch, apparently occupied until the 18th century.

---

477 DUNBEATH HERITAGE CENTRE **3 M14**

Old School, Dunbeath, Caithness. Bus from Inverness, Wick or Thurso. Open Apr–Sep, daily 1100–1700. Charge £. Children free. Group concessions. Guided tours. Explanatory displays. Audio-visual programme. Gift shop. Picnic area. WC. Wheelchair access. Disabled WC. Car and coach parking. Telephone (01593) 731233.

Historical tableaux of early settlers, crofting and fishing, Stained glass and a mural bring the environment to life. Ancestral research. Heritage trail, fishing, bookshop. Birthplace of author Neil M. Gunn.

---

478 DUNBLANE CITY CATHEDRAL MUSEUM **6 K14**

The Cross, Dunblane, Perthshire. 6 miles (9.5km) north of Stirling. Bus from Perth, Stirling or Glasgow. Railway station within 500 yards (457m). Open mid May–Sep, Mon–Sat 1000–1230 and 1400–1630. Free. Explanatory displays and video. Gift shop. WC. Limited wheelchair access. Car and coach parking. Telephone (01765) 823440.

A museum located in barrel-vaulted rooms built in 1624. Contents include paintings, books, and artefacts which illustrate the life of the cathedral and its congregation from St Blane to the restoration in 1893. Large collection of communion tokens.

---

479 DUN CANNA **2 H5**

Ardmair, north of Ullapool, Ross and Cromarty.

The site of a Viking Fort. Also a flat pebble beach with good swimming.

---

480 DUNCANSBY HEAD **3 N2**

The northeast point of mainland Scotland, 18 miles (29km) north of Wick. Access at all times. Free.

The lighthouse on Duncansby Head commands a fine view of Orkney, the Pentland Skerries and the headlands of the east coast. A little to the south are the three Duncansby Stacks, huge stone needles in the sea. The sandstone cliffs are severed by great deep gashes (geos) running into the land. One of these is bridged by a natural arch.

---

481 DUN CARLOWAY **2 C3**

HS. On the A858, 1.5 miles (2.5km) south of Carloway and 16 miles (25.5km) west northwest of Stornoway, Isle of Lewis (Western Isles). Ferry from Ullapool to Stornoway, bus service from Stornoway to Carloway road end. Access at all times. Free. Car and coach parking. Telephone 0131 668 8800.

One of the best preserved Iron Age brochs in Scotland.

---

482 DUNCHRAIGAIG CAIRN **4 F4**

HS. Kilmartin Glen. 1.25 miles (2km) south of Kilmartin, Argyll. Nearest railway station Oban, then bus to Lochgilphead. Access at all times. Free. Picnic area. Car parking. Telephone 0131 668 8800.

A Bronze Age cairn excavated in the last century.

---

483 DUNDEE, CAMPERDOWN WILDLIFE CENTRE **5 N13**

Camperdown Country Park, Coupar Angus Road, Dundee. 3 miles (4km) north of Dundee on A923. Nearest railway and bus stations Dundee. Guide Friday tour bus departs from Discovery Quay to the Wildlife Centre every hour. Open Mar–Sep, daily 1000–1630; Oct–Feb, daily 1000–1530. Charge £. Children under 3 free. Group concessions. Explanatory displays. Gift shop. Picnic area. WC. Special needs play area. Wheelchair access. Disabled WC. Car and coach parking. Telephone (01382) 432689.

Over 80 species of native Scottish wildlife; brown bears, lynx, arctic foxes and other more unusual species, such as Britain's rarest mammal, the pine martin. Walkabout map and wildlife trail – complete the wildlife trail and you qualify for a free certificate. Special needs play area. Boating pond, kiddies cars, trampolines and golf course.

---

484 DUNDEE CONTEMPORARY ARTS — 5 N13

152 Nethergate, Dundee. In the centre of Dundee, within 5 minutes walk of railway station and 15 minutes from bus station. Open all year: galleries and shop, Tue–Sun 1030–1730 (Thu and Fri closes 2000); centre and café/bar, daily 1030–1200 (Sun closes 1100). Free. Charge for cinema. Group concessions. Guided tours. Explanatory displays. Gift shop. Café-bar. Baby changing facilities. WC. Induction loop in cinema. Wheelchair access. Disabled WC. Car and coach parking. Telephone (01382) 432000.

Centre for contemporary art and film with two galleries, two screen cinema, print studio, craft shop, visual research centre and activity room. Courses, workshops, talks and tours are offered.

---

485 DUNDEE, DISCOVERY POINT — 5 N13

Discovery Quay, Dundee. In Dundee, beside the railway station. Open daily all year (except Christmas and New Year). Charge ££. Children under 5 free. Group concessions. Guided tours (available in French and German) on request if guides available. Explanatory displays. Gift shop. Café. WC. Limited wheelchair access. Disabled WC. Car and coach parking. Telephone (01382) 201245.

Dundee's flagship attraction centred around Royal Research Ship *Discovery*, Captain Scott's famous polar exploration ship. Spectacular exhibits and special effects recreate the historic voyages of *Discovery* – built in Dundee at the turn of the century to take Scott to the ends of the earth – such as the ship's rescue from the ice by Dundee whaler *Terra Nova* and the *Morning*. Visitors can step on board Discovery herself, experience life below decks and feel the atmosphere of the Ward Room where Scott and his officers talked of the perils of a journey to where no man had gone before. Children's interactive games, giant jigsaws and quiz boards add to the fun and enjoyment for the whole family.

---

486 DUNDEE, HM FRIGATE UNICORN — 5 N13

Victoria Dock, Dundee. Just east of road bridge, 0.5 mile (1km) from rail station. Open Mar–Oct, daily 1000–1700; Nov–Feb, Mon–Fri 1000–1600. Other times by arrangement (closed over Christmas and New Year). Charge ££. Children under 5 free. Group concessions. Guided tours (available in other european languages). Explanatory displays. Gift shop. Tearoom and picnic area. WC. No guide dogs. Limited wheelchair access. Car and coach parking. Telephone (01382) 200900.

Unicorn was launched at Chatham in 1824 and is the third oldest ship, and one of the best preserved, in the world. A navy drill ship in Dundee until 1968. Note port regulations forbid animals entering the docks.

---

487 DUNDEE, THE HOWF — 5 N13

Meadowside, Dundee. In Dundee city centre.

An historic graveyard which was formerly the garden of Greyfriars Monastery, gifted to the people of Dundee by Mary, Queen of Scots. Until 1778 it was the meeting place of the Nine Trades of Dundee and on the great variety of gravestones are seen the signs and symbols of the old craft guilds.

---

488 DUNDEE, JUNGLE KIDS — 5 N13

Dronley Road, Birkhill, Dundee. On the Coupar Angus road, 1.5 miles (2.5km) from Camperdown Park entrance. Bus from Dundee centre.

Open all year, Mon–Fri 1100–1830, Sat 1000–1830, Sun 1100–1830. Charge ££. Group concessions. Café. WC. Wheelchair access. Disabled WC. Car and coach parking. Telephone (01382) 580540.

A large indoor play centre for children up to 12 years including a selection of slides, ball pools, very large climbing frames, soft play area for children under 3. Birthday party rooms. Supervision. Viewing lounge for parents with CCTV monitor.

---

489 DUNDEE LAW **5 N13**

Access at all reasonable times. Free. Car park at top of hill. Floodlit at night.

The Law is the highest point in the city, and takes its name from the old Scots word for a hill. It is the remains of a volcanic plug and was later the site of an ancient hill fort. Atop the Law is Dundee's War Memorial with a beacon which is lit four times a year. Magnificent panoramic views across Dundee and the surrounding countryside to Fife and the northern mountains.

---

490 DUNDEE, MCMANUS GALLERIES **5 N13**

Albert Square, Dundee. In Dundee centre, 10 minute walk from bus and railway stations. Open all year, Mon–Sat 1000–1700 (Thu closes 1900), Sun 1230–1600. Free. Guided tours by arrangement. Explanatory displays. Gift shop. Café. WC. Wheelchair access. Disabled WC. Telephone (01382) 432084.

Victorian Gothic building designed by Sir George Gilbert Scott containing collections of national importance. Features local history, costume, natural history, archaeology, decorative arts, a superb Scottish Victorian art collection and a changing exhibition and events programme throughout the year. Also the magnificent Albert Hall, with its fine stained glass window and vaulted roof.

---

491 DUNDEE, MERCAT CROSS **5 N13**

Nethergate, Dundee. In Dundee city centre. Access at all times.

Standing on the south side of St Mary's Tower, this is a replica of Dundee's old mercat cross which formerly stood in the Seagate. On top of the shaft is a unicorn sculpted by Scott Sutherland, RSA.

---

492 DUNDEE, MILLS OBSERVATORY **5 N13**

Balgay Hill, Dundee. In the heart of Balgay Park, signposted from major routes. Open Apr–Sep, Tue–Fri 1100–1700, Sat and Sun 1230–1600; Oct–Mar, Mon–Fri 1600–2200, Sat and Sun 1230–1600. Free. Guided tours by arrangement. Explanatory displays. Gift shop. WC. Telephone (01382) 435846.

Constructed in 1935 for the people of Dundee, the Mills Observatory is today Britain's only full-time public observatory. Located in picturesque wooded surroundings, it houses a 10-inch (25cm) refracting telescope. Panoramic views over the Tay to Fife.

---

493 DUNDEE, ST ANDREW'S CHURCH AND THE GLASITE HALL **5 N13**

King Street, Dundee. In Dundee city centre.

St Andrew's Church was designed by Samuel Bell and completed in 1772. It was built and paid for entirely by the Nine Trades' Guild of Dundee and there are fine stained glass windows depicting the trades emblems. Immediately to the east is a curious building completed in 1777. Formerly Dundee's Glasite Church – the Rev John Glas left the ministry in the Church of Scotland in 1728.

494 DUNDEE, TAY RAIL BRIDGE **5 N13**

Dundee. Visible on entering the city from the west on A85 or east on A92.

The present bridge, carrying the main line from London to Aberdeen, was completed in 1887. It replaced the first Tay Rail Bridge which was blown down by a storm in 1879 with the loss of 75 lives. At 2 miles and 73 yards long (3.28km) it was the world's longest rail bridge when opened.

---

495 DUNDEE, UNIVERSITY BOTANIC GARDEN **5 N13**

Riverside Drive, Dundee. Nearest railway station Dundee, bus from city centre (numbers 16 and 76). Open daily, Mar–Oct 1000–1630; Nov–Feb 1000–1530. Charge £. Guided tours. Explanatory displays. Gift shop. Tearoom and picnic area. WC. Wheelchair access. Disabled WC. Car and coach parking. Telephone (01382) 566939.

Designed and inaugurated in 1971. Botanic and teaching garden with a fine collection of trees and shrubs, landscaped naturalistically. Two large tropical and temperate plant houses. Award-winning visitor centre.

---

496 DUNDEE, VERDANT WORKS **5 N13**

West Hendersons Wynd, Dundee. 10 minute walk from bus and railway stations. Open daily all year except Christmas and 1–2 Jan. Charge ££. Children under 5 free. Group concessions. Guided tours. Explanatory displays. Gift shop. Café. WC. Loop system. Wheelchair access. Disabled WC. Car and coach parking. Telephone (01382) 225282.

European Museum of the Year 1999. A restored 19th-century jute works surrounding a cobbled courtyard. One of the few surviving and complete examples of the industry. Visitors can view the period office (unchanged since the last century), discover why Dundee became the jute capital of the world and see working machinery processing jute to woven cloth. They can also see a reconstructed tenement balcony, outside loo and the contrasting conditions inside the home of a wealthy jute baron.

---

497 DUNDONALD CASTLE **6 J17**

Dundonald, Kilmarnock, Ayrshire. On the A759, 5 miles (8km) west of Kilmarnock. Bus from Kilmarnock, Irvine or Troon. Open Apr–Sep, daily 1000–1700. Charge £. Explanatory displays. Staff provide information. Visitor Centre with interpretive display. Gift shop. Tearoom. WC. Wheelchair access to Visitor Centre/Interpretive display only. Disabled WC. Car and coach parking. Telephone (01563) 851489.

A prominent large stone castle, built by Robert Stewart in the 1370s, probably to mark his succession to the Scottish throne as Robert II in 1371. Two great feasting halls, one above the other, with great vaults beneath. The third medieval castle to be built on the site, preceded by a hill fort between 500 and 200BC. Remains of an earlier, but equally grand 13th-century castle of the Stewarts are visible.

---

498 DUN DORNAIGIL BROCH **3 J3**

HS. 10 miles (16km) south of Hope, Sutherland. Post bus from Lairg via Altnahara to Hope, alight before Alltnacaillich. Access at all times. Free. Car parking. Telephone 0131 668 8800.

A well-preserved broch standing to a height of 22 feet (6.5m) above the entrance passage.

---

499 DUNDRENNAN ABBEY **5 K21**

HS. Dundrennan, Kirkcudbright. On the A711, 6.5 miles (10.5km) south-east of Kirkcudbright. Bus to Dundrennan from Kirkcudbright or Dalbeattie. Open Apr–Sep, Mon–Sat 0930–1830, Sun 1400–1830; Oct–Mar, Sat and Sun 0930–1630. Charge £. Group concessions. Guided tours. WC. Carvings can be touched. Wheelchair access with assistance. Car and coach parking. Telephone (01557) 500262.

The beautiful ruins, amid a peaceful setting, of a Cistercian abbey founded in 1142 by King David I. Includes much later Norman and transitional work. The east end of the church and the chapter house are of high quality. It is believed that Mary, Queen of Scots spent her last night in Scotland here in May 1568.

---

500 DUNFALLANDY STONE **5 L12**

HS. 1 mile (2km) south of Pitlochry, Perthshire. Nearest railway station Pitlochry, bus from Perth to Pitlochry. Access at all times. Free. Telephone 0131 668 8800.

A fine Pictish sculptured stone with a cross on one face and figures on both faces.

---

501 DUNFERMLINE ABBEY AND PALACE **6 M15**

HS. St Margaret Street, Dunfermline, Fife. Short walk from Dunfermline railway and bus stations. Open Apr–Sep, Mon–Sat 0930–1830, Sun 1400–1830; Oct–Mar, Mon–Sat 0930–1830, Sun 1400–1630, closed Thu pm and Fri. Charge £. Group concessions. Guided tours. Explanatory displays. Gift shop. Telephone (01383) 739026.

The remains of the great Benedictine abbey founded by Queen Margaret in the 11th century. The foundations of her church are under the present nave, built in the 12th century in the Romanesque style. At the east end are the remains of St Margaret's shrine, dating from the 13th century. Robert the Bruce is buried in the choir, now the site of the present parish church (closed during the winter). Of the monastic buildings, the ruins of the refectory, pend and guest house remain. The guest house was later reconstructed as a royal palace where Charles I was born.

---

502 DUNFERMLINE MUSEUM **6 M15**

Viewfield Terrace, Dunfermline, Fife. In Dunfermline centre between the rail and bus stations. Open all year (except Christmas and New Year) by appointment only. Free. Guided tours by arrangement. Explanatory displays. Gift shop. Wheelchair access to ground floor. Car and coach parking. Telephone (01383) 313838.

A 'memory' museum of Dunfermline's social, natural and industrial history, especially damask linen, the industry that made Dunfermline famous in the last century

---

503 DUNGLASS COLLEGIATE CHURCH **5 Q15**

HS. On an estate road west of A1 (signposted Bilsdean), 1 mile (2km) northwest of Cockburnspath, East Lothian. Nearest railway station Dunbar, bus to Cockburnspath, then 1 mile (2km) walk. Access at all times. Free. Telephone 0131 668 8800.

A handsome cross-shaped church with vaulted nave, choir and transepts, all with stone slab roofs. Founded in 1450 for a college of canons by Sir Alexander Hume.

---

504 DUNKELD **5 M12**

NTS. The Ell Shop, Dunkeld, Perthshire. Off A9, 15 miles (24km) north of Perth. By rail (station 1 mile/1.5km from village). NTS shop open Apr–Sep, Mon–Sat 1000–1730, Jun–Aug also Sun 1330–1730; Oct–Christmas, Mon–Sat 1000–1630. Access to village all year. Explanatory displays. Gift shop. Cafés in village (not NTS). WC. Subtitled video. Wheelchair access. Disabled WC. Car and coach parking. Telephone (01350) 727460.

Attractive village with mostly ruined Gothic cathedral on banks of River Tay. The National Trust for Scotland owns many houses dating from the rebuilding of the town in 1689 after the Battle of Dunkeld. They have been carefully restored. NTS shop in restored Ell House; Atholl Memorial Fountain. Many delightful walks.

505 DUNKELD BRIDGE **5 M12**

Over the River Tay at Dunkeld. Parking available. Access at all times. Free. Riverside path not suitable for wheelchairs.

One of Thomas Telford's finest bridges, built in 1809. An attractive riverside path leads from here downstream to the famous Birnam Oak, last relic of Macbeth's Birnam Wood, and then around the village of Birnam. Best view is from riverside garden. Wheelchair users should approach from the square through the archway.

---

506 DUNKELD CATHEDRAL **5 M12**

HS. High Street, Dunkeld, Perthshire. 15 miles (24km) north northwest of Perth. Nearest railway station Birnam, bus from Perth, then 15 minutes walk from Birnam. Open Apr–Sep, Mon–Sat 0900–1830, Sun 1400–1830, Oct–Mar, Mon–Sat 0930–1600, Sun 1400–1600. Closed New Year's Day. Free. Explanatory displays. Picnic area. Cathedral shop. WC. Wheelchair access. Telephone 0131 668 8800.

Beautifully situated on the banks of the River Tay. The restored choir is now the parish church. Originally 12th-century, but nave and great northwest tower from 15th century.

---

507 DUNNET HEAD **3 M2**

B855, 12 miles (19km) northeast of Thurso. Access at all times. Free. Car parking.

This bold promontory of sandstone rising to 417 feet (127m) is the northernmost point of the Scottish mainland. There are magnificent views across the Pentland Firth to Orkney and a great part of the north coast to Ben Loyal and Ben Hope. The windows of the lighthouse are sometimes broken by stones hurled up by the winter seas.

---

508 DUNNOTTAR CASTLE **3 Q10**

Dunnottar Castle Lodge, Stonehaven. On A92, 2.5 miles (4km) south of Stonehaven. Bus from Stonehaven or Montrose. Open Easter–Oct, Mon–Sat 0900–1800, Sun 1400–1700; Nov–Easter, Mon–Fri 0900–sunset. Charge £. Children under 5 free. Group concessions. Picnics welcome. WC. Free entry for blind visitors and companion. Car and coach parking. Telephone (01569) 762173.

A spectacular ruin 160 feet (48.5m) above the sea. An impregnable fortress to the Earls Marischals of Scotland. The site for the successful protection of the Scottish crown jewels against the might of Oliver Cromwell's army.

---

509 DUNNYDEER STUDIO PORCELAIN **6 H15**

Peebles Craft Centre, Peebles. Bus from Edinburgh. Open all year, telephone to confirm times. Free. Studio and shop. WC. Car parking. Telephone (01721) 722875.

Part of a complex of workshops (Peebles Craft Centre). Visitors can see a ceramic artist (Duncan Hood) at work and purchase finished products.

---

510 DUNSTAFFNAGE CASTLE AND CHAPEL **4 F13**

HS. Off the A85 by Loch Etive, 3.5 miles (5km) north of Oban, Argyll. Nearest railway station Oban, bus from Oban to Dunbeg the 1 mile (2km) walk. Open Apr–Sep, Mon–Sat 0930–1830, Sun 1400–1830; Oct–Mar 0930–1630 (closed Thu pm, Fri and Sun am). Charge £. Group concessions. Guided tours. Gift shop. WC. Limited wheelchair access. Car and coach parking. Telephone (01631) 562465.

A fine, well-preserved 13th-century castle built on rock. Nearby, ruins of what was an exceptionally beautiful chapel.

511 DUNVEGAN CASTLE — 2 D7

Dunvegan, Isle of Skye. On A850, 1 mile (2km) north of Dunvegan village. By train to Kyle of Lochalsh or bus from Portree. Open Mar–Oct, daily 1000–1730; in winter 1100–1600. Charge £££. Children under 5 free. Group concessions. Explanatory displays. Gift shop. Restaurant, tearoom and picnic area. WC. Limited wheelchair access. Disabled WC. Car and coach parking. Telephone (01470) 521206.

Historic stronghold of the Clan Macleod, set on the sea loch of Dunvegan, the home of the chiefs of Macleod for nearly 800 years. Possessions on view include books, pictures, arms and treasured relics. Trace the history of the family and clan from the days of their Norse ancestry through 30 generations to the present day. Boat trips from the castle jetty to the seal colony. Castle water gardens, audio-visual room. Clan exhibition with items belonging to Bonnie Prince Charlie.

---

512 DWARFIE STANE — 1 B11

HS. Towards the north end of the island of Hoy, Orkney. Ferry from Stromness to Linkness then 3 mile (5km) walk. Access at all times. Free. Car parking.

A huge block of sandstone in which a Neolithic burial chamber has been cut. No other known example in the British Isles.

---

513 DYCE SYMBOL STONES — 3 Q9

HS. At Dyce Old Church, 5 miles (8km) northwest of Aberdeen. Bus from Aberdeen to Dyce then 1.5 mile (2.5km) walk to Dyce Old Kirk. Access at all times. Free. Car parking. Telephone 0131 668 8800.

Two fine examples of Pictish symbol stones in the ruined parish church, one with the older type of incised symbols, and the other with symbols accompanied by a Celtic cross and decoration.

---

514 EARL'S PALACE — 1 B10

HS. In Birsay at the north end of mainland Orkney, 11 miles (17.5km) north of Stromness. Tour bus from Kirkwall to Birsay. Access at all times. Telephone 0131 668 8800.

The gaunt remains of the courtyard palace built in the 16th century by Robert Stewart, Earl of Orkney.

---

515 EAS COUL AULIN FALLS — 2 H4

At the head of Loch Glencoul, 3 miles (4.5km) west of A894 near Unapool. For boat trips to waterfall telephone Statesman cruises: (01571) 844446.

The tallest waterfall in Britain, dropping 658 feet (200m). Seals and the occasional elusive otter may be seen on the loch.

---

516 EASSIE SCULPTURED STONE — 5 N12

HS. In Eassie churchyard, near Glamis, 7 miles (11km) west southwest of Forfar, Angus. Access at all times. Free. Telephone 0131 668 8800.

A fine elaborately carved monument with richly decorated Celtic cross on one side and Pictish symbols and processional scenes on the reverse.

---

517 EASTER AQUHORTHIES STONE CIRCLE — 3 Q9

HS. About 1 mile (2km) west of Inverurie, Aberdeenshire. Nearest railway station Inverurie. Bus from Aberdeen to Inverurie then 2.5 miles (4km) walk. Access at all times. Free. Car parking. Telephone 0131 668 8800.

A recumbent stone circle about 4000 years old.

518 EATHIE BURN **3 K7**

Rosemarkie, north of Fortrose, Black Isle.

Fossils may be found on the foreshore.

---

519 EDEN ESTUARY CENTRE **5 N13**

Main Street, Guardbridge, Fife. By main entrance for paper mill. Bus from Cupar, Dundee or St Andrews. 1 mile (2km) from Leuchars station. Open daily 0900–1700 (except for Leuchars Air show, Christmas Day and New Year's Day). Free. Explanatory displays. WC. Wheelchair access. Disabled WC. Car parking. Telephone (01334) 429785.

A small centrally-heated hide overlooking Eden Estuary local nature reserve, with displays relating to natural and local history of the site and its management.

---

520 EDINBANE POTTERY **2 D7**

Edinbane, Isle of Skye. Just off the A850, 14 miles (22.5km) from Portree, 8 miles (13km) from Dunvegan. Buses from Portree or Dunvegan. Open Easter–Oct, daily 0900–1800; winter Mon–Fri only. Free. Explanatory displays. Gift shop. Children's play area. Wheelchair access. Car and coach parking. Telephone (01470) 582234.

A pottery where visitors can see work in progress. A wide range of pots, mostly wood-fired.

---

521 EDINBURGH, THE ADAM POTTERY **6 M15**

76 Henderson Row, Edinburgh. In Stockbridge, 1 mile (2km) from centre. Bus from centre. Open Mon–Sat 1000–1800, except Christmas and New Year. Free. Guided tours with advance notice. Gift shop. Telephone 0131 557 3978.

Wheelthrown stoneware and porcelain, with colourful high-fired glazes, functional items. Work by other ceramacists is also available. Visitors may watch work in progress.

---

522 EDINBURGH, BANK OF SCOTLAND MUSEUM **6 N15**

Bank of Scotland Head Office, The Mound, Edinburgh. At the edge of the Old Town, just off the Royal Mile and 3 minute walk from Waverley station. Open Jun–Sep, Mon–Fri 1000–1645. Free. Guided tours on request. Explanatory displays. Telephone 0131 529 1305.

A small but unusual museum telling the 300-year story of Scotland's first bank set against the economic development of the country. Features early adding machines, banknotes and forgeries, bullion chests and gold coins, maps, plans and photographs. Free postcards.

---

523 EDINBURGH, BRASS RUBBING CENTRE **6 N15**

Chalmers Close, 81 High Street, Edinburgh. Just off the Royal Mile opposite the Museum of Childhood (see 558), also access from Jeffrey Street. Nearest railway station Edinburgh Waverley; tour bus from station or 10 minute walk. Open Mar–Oct, Mon–Sat 1000–1700. Free. Charge for making rubbings. Group concessions. Explanatory displays. Gift shop. Limited wheelchair access. Car parking. Telephone 0131 556 4364.

Housed in the historic Trinity Apse, thought to have been founded in 1460 by Queen Mary of Gueldres, consort of King James II of Scotland as a memorial to her husband. Offers a fine collection of replicas moulded from ancient Pictish stones, medieval church brasses and rare Scottish brasses. No experience needed to make a rubbing; instruction and materials provided.

---

524 EDINBURGH, BRITANNIA

See 578 Edinburgh, Royal Yacht Britannia.

525 EDINBURGH BUTTERFLY AND INSECT WORLD 6 N16

Dobbies Garden World, Lasswade, Midlothian. On the A7, near Dalkeith, 5 miles (8km) south of Edinburgh. Bus from Edinburgh. Open all year (except Christmas and New Year's Day), 0930–1730; in winter 1000–1700. Charge ££. Group concessions. Guided tours for groups by arrangement. Explanatory displays. Gift shop. Restaurant, tearooms and picnic areas. Garden centre. Birds of prey centre. Children's play parks. WC. Wheelchair access. Disabled WC. Car and coach parking. Telephone 0131 663 4932.

An exotic rainforest landscaped with tropical plants, cascading waterfalls and lily ponds provides the setting for hundreds of spectacular tropical butterflies to fly freely around. Visitors can watch them feeding and breeding. Also many other insects (spiders, ants, etc). Adjacent to Scotland's largest garden centre.

---

526 EDINBURGH, CALEDONIAN BREWERY VISITOR CENTRE 6 M15

42 Slateford Road, Edinburgh. On A7 Lanark road, 2 miles (3km) from Princes Street. Local bus service. Open all year, Mon–Fri tours at 1100, 1230 and 1430. Parties at evenings and weekends by arrangement. Charge ££. Group concessions. Guided tours. Explanatory displays. Gift shop. WC. No guide dogs. Disabled WC. Car and coach parking. Telephone 0131 623 8066.

A unique reminder of a bygone era when the city boasted over 40 breweries and was one of the great brewing capitals of Europe. Beer is still brewed today using hand selected natural ingredients and the original brewers' equipment – still fired by direct flame and the last of their kind still working in any British brewery.

---

527 EDINBURGH, CAMERA OBSCURA 6 N15

Outlook Tower and Camera Obscura, Castlehill, The Royal Mile, Edinburgh. Adjacent to Edinburgh Castle (see 530) at the top of the Royal Mile. Waverley station 10 minute walk, bus from Princes Street. Open daily (except Christmas Day), summer 0930–1800 (later in high summer); winter 1000–1700. Charge ££. Group concessions. Guided tours (available in other languages by arrangement). Explanatory displays in six languages. Gift shop. WC. Telephone 0131 226 3709.

Edinburgh's oldest attraction. An 1850s camera obscura captures a live panorama of the city below while guides tell Edinburgh's story. Visitors can spy on passers-by or pick vehicles up in the palm of their hand. Three-D hologram display (the biggest in Europe) and photographs of old Edinburgh. Superb views of Edinburgh from the terrace (telescopes free).

---

528 EDINBURGH CANAL CENTRE 6 M15

The Bridge Inn, 27 Baird Road, Ratho, Midlothian. In Ratho, 7 miles (11km) west of Edinburgh off the A8 or A71. Bus from Edinburgh. Open all year, Mon–Thu 1200–2300, Sat 1200–2400, Sun 1230–2300. Charge by facility. Guided tours on canal cruises Apr–Oct. Explanatory displays. Restaurant/bar and restaurants on boats. Garden. Play area. Wildfowl reserve. Towpath for walks and cycling. WC. Wheelchair access to building. Disabled WC. Car and coach parking. Telephone 0131 333 1320.

Built about 1750, the inn became a canalside inn with the opening of the Union Canal in 1822. Canalboat restaurants cater for meals, dances, weddings, etc. Sightseeing cruises and Santa Cruises in December.

---

529 EDINBURGH, CANONGATE KIRK 6 N15

The Kirk of Holyroodhouse, Canongate, Edinburgh. Opposite Huntly House Museum in the Royal Mile. Nearest railway station 15 minutes walk, local bus service and tour buses. Open all year, Sun 1000–1230; also Jun–Sep, Mon–Sat 1030–1630. Free. Guided tours for groups by arrangement. Information sheets in 30 languages. Gift shop. Refreshments. Wheelchair access. Telephone 0131 556 3515.

Historic 300-year-old Church of Scotland, recently renovated and restored. Parish church of the Palace of Holyroodhouse and Edinburgh Castle, with frobenius organ and normandy tapestry.

---

530 EDINBURGH CASTLE **6 N15**

HS. Castlehill, Edinburgh. In the centre of Edinburgh at the top of the Royal Mile. Nearest railway station Waverley. Local bus service and tour buses. Open all year (except Christmas Day and Boxing Day), Apr–Oct, daily 0930–1715; Nov–Mar 0930–1615. Closes 45 minutes later. Charge £££. Guided tours (audio guide in six languages). Explanatory displays. Gift shop. Restaurant. WC. Braille texts and models of Crown Jewels for handling. Wheelchair access. A courtesy vehicle (provided by the Bank of Scotland) takes disabled visitors to the top of the Castle; there are ramps and lift access to the Crown Jewels, Stone of Destiny and associated exhibition; a wheelchair stair climber gives access to the War Memorial. Disabled WC. Car and coach parking. Telephone 0131 225 9846.

One of the most famous castles in the world with battlements overlooking the Esplanade where the floodlit Military Tattoo is staged each year. The oldest part, St Margaret's Chapel, dates from the Norman period. The Great Hall was built by James IV; the Half Moon Battery by the Regent Morton in the late 16th century. The Scottish National War Memorial was erected after the First World War. The Castle houses the Crown Jewels (Honours) of Scotland, the Stone of Destiny and the famous 15th-century gun Mons Meg.

---

531 EDINBURGH, CITY ART CENTRE **6 N15**

2 Market Street, Edinburgh. In centre opposite Waverley station. Open all year (except Christmas and New Year), Mon–Sat 1000–1700, Sun during Festival and special exhibitions. Free. Charge for special exhibitions. Explanatory displays. Gift shop. Licensed restaurant/café. WC. Induction loop. Wheelchair access. Disabled WC. Telephone 0131 529 3993.

Houses the City of Edinburgh's permanent fine art collection and stages a programme of temporary exhibitions from all over the world. Six floors of display galleries (with escalators and lifts). Education programme of workshops, lectures, events and educational publications.

---

532 EDINBURGH, CRAIGMILLAR CASTLE **6 N15**

HS. Craigmillar Castle Road, Edinburgh. Off A68 (Dalkeith road), 2.5 miles (4km) southeast of Edinburgh city centre. Bus from Edinburgh city centre to Little France, stop on Old Dalkeith Road. Open Apr–Sep, Mon–Sat 0930–1830, Sun 1400–1830; Oct–Mar, Mon–Sat (closed Thu pm and Fri) 0930–1830, Sun 1400–1630. Charge £. Group concessions. Guided tours. Explanatory displays and visitor centre. Gift shop. Limited wheelchair access. Disabled WC. Car and coach parking. Telephone 0131 661 4445.

Imposing ruins of massive 14th–century keep enclosed in the early 15th century by an embattled curtain wall. Within are the remains of the stately ranges of apartments dating from the 16th and 17th centuries. The castle was burned by Hertford in 1544. Strong connections with Mary, Queen of Scots.

---

533 EDINBURGH CRYSTAL VISITOR CENTRE **6 M16**

Eastfield, Penicuik, Midlothian. In Penicuik, south of Edinburgh. Regular bus from Edinburgh, free minibus from Waverley Bridge, Edinburgh Apr–Sep. Open all year, Mon–Sat 0900–1700, Sun 1100–1700. Free. Charge for tour £. Group concessions. Guided tours (translations available in other languages). Explanatory displays. Gift shop. Coffee shop and picnic area. WC. Tour synopsis in braille and large print. Wheelchair access. Disabled WC. Car and coach parking. Telephone (01968) 672244.

A glass factory and associated shop. Exhibition showing the story of the factory. Visitors can tour the factory and see glass products being made and engraved. By arrangement groups can try their hand at glass-blowing and decorating, taking their products home.

534 EDINBURGH, DEAN GALLERY 6 M15

Belford Road, Edinburgh. In the centre of Edinburgh, within 15 minutes walk from Princes Street and 10 minutes from Haymarket railway station. Local bus service to Belford Road or Queensferry Road, then walk. Open all year except Christmas, Mon–Sat 1000–1700, Sun 1400–1700. Free. Charge for temporary exhibitions. Group concessions. Guided tours by arrangement. Explanatory displays. Gift shop. Café/brasserie. Gardens. WC. Wheelchair access. Disabled WC. Car parking. Telephone 0131 624 6200.

The Dean Gallery, situated directly opposite the Scottish National Gallery of Modern Art (see 586), houses an extensive collection of Dada and Surrealist art including many celebrated works by Dalí, Duchamp, Ernst, Giacometti, Magritte, Man Ray, Miró, Picasso, Tanguy and Delvaux, among others. The gallery is also home to a large collection of work by Sir Eduardo Paolozzi, including a substantial number of plaster sculptures, prints and drawings, as well as books, toys, machine parts and other items which have inspired his work over the years. Landscaped gardens and commanding views south over Edinburgh.

---

535 EDINBURGH, DYNAMIC EARTH 6 N15

107 Holyrood Road, Edinburgh. Nearest railway station Edinburgh Waverley; local bus or tour bus. Open Easter–Oct, daily 1000–1800; Nov–Easter, Wed–Sun 1000–1700. Charge £££. Carers of disabled visitors free. Group concessions. Explanatory displays. Gift shop. Restaurant and bar. Children's play area, terrace. WC. Large print text. Wheelchair access. Disabled WC. Car parking. Telephone 0131 550 7800.

Through dramatic special effects, stunning wrap-around images and state-of-the-art interactives, visitors discover the story of the planet, from the start of time to an unknown future. See the Restless Earth volcano erupt, walk through the tropical rainforest thunderstorm and meet an ever-changing menagerie of animals. Take a dramatic helicopter flight over the magnificent Scottish mountains and feel the chill of ice in the polar region.

---

536 EDINBURGH, EAGLE ROCK 6 M15

HS. On the shore of the River Forth about 2.5 mile (0.5km) west of Cramond, Edinburgh. Nearest railway station Edinburgh, bus from centre to Cramond, then short walk. Access at all times. Free. Telephone 0131 668 8800.

A much-defaced carving on natural rock, said to represent an eagle.

---

537 EDINBURGH, FORTH RAIL BRIDGE 6 M15

South Queensferry. 10 miles (16km) northwest of Edinburgh. Access at all times. Telephone 0131 319 1699.

Opened on 4 March 1890 by the Prince of Wales. The bridge was designed on the cantilever principle with three towers 340 feet (104m) high. The engineers were Sir John Fowler and Benjamin Baker. See also 658 Forth Bridges Exhibition.

---

538 EDINBURGH, FRUITMARKET GALLERY 6 N15

45 Market Street, Edinburgh. In centre adjacent to Waverley station. Open Mon–Sat 1100–1800, Sun 1200–1700 (later during Festival). Free. Guided tours by arrangement. Explanatory displays. Gift and bookshop. Restaurant. WC. Induction loop. Wheelchair access. Disabled WC. Car and coach parking. Telephone 0131 225 2383.

Originally built in 1938 as a fruit and vegetable market, the gallery is now an acclaimed art gallery with a national and international reputation for diverse and challenging pro-active exhibitions. Exciting and contemporary. Art bookshop and restaurant.

539 EDINBURGH, FUN PARK **6 N15**

Portobello Promenade, Edinburgh. Bus from city centre. Open daily 1000–2300 (except Christmas Day). Free. Charge for entertainments. Explanatory displays. Gift shop. Restaurant and tearoom. WC. Wheelchair access with assistance. Disabled WC. Car and coach parking. Telephone 0131 669 1859.

A family entertainment centre with various amusements – soft play area, dodgems, carousel, juvenile rides (merry-go-round), full-size ten-pin bowling lanes and American pool hall.

---

540 EDINBURGH, GEORGIAN HOUSE **6 M15**

NTS. 7 Charlotte Square, Edinburgh. Near city centre, 10 minute walk from Waverley railway station. Open Apr–Oct, Mon–Sat 1000–1700, Sun 1400–1700. Charge ££. Children free. Group concessions. Guided tours by arrangement. Explanatory displays. Information sheets in twelve languages. Gift shop. WC. Audio-visual programme with induction loop, Braille guidebook. Limited wheelchair access. Telephone 0131 226 3318.

On the north side of Charlotte Square, designed by Robert Adam. A typical house in Edinburgh's New Town, furnished as it would have been by its first owners in 1796. Video programmes on the building of the New Town and A Day in the Life of the Georgian House.

---

541 EDINBURGH, GEOWALKS VOLCANO TOURS **6 N15**

Holyrood Park, Edinburgh. In the centre of Edinburgh, 5 minutes walk from the Royal Mile. Guided walks Mar–Sep, Wed, Fri and Sun, 1400. Charge ££. Group concessions. Guided tours. WC. Car and coach parking. Telephone 0131 555 5488.

Walking tours, led by an expert guide, exploring Holyrood Park and the craggy remains of the extinct Arthur's Seat volcano.

---

542 EDINBURGH, GLADSTONE'S LAND **6 N15**

NTS. 477b Lawnmarket, Edinburgh. Near city centre, 10 minutes walk from Waverley railway station. Open Apr–Oct, Mon–Sat 1000–1700, Sun 1400–1700. Charge ££. Children free. Group concessions. Guided tours by arrangement. Explanatory displays. Information sheets in European languages and Japanese. Gift shop. Tours for blind visitors by arrangement, Braille guidebook. Limited wheelchair access. Car parking. Telephone 0131 226 5856.

Typical example of the 17th-century tenements of Edinburgh's Old Town, clustered along the ridge between the Castle and the Palace of Holyroodhouse – the Royal Mile. Completed in 1620 and originally home to a prosperous Edinburgh merchant, Thomas Gledstanes, the house contains original painted ceilings and some contemporary furniture.

---

543 EDINBURGH, GORGIE CITY FARM **6 M15**

51 Gorgie Road, Edinburgh. On the A71 (to Kilmarnock), 1 mile (2km) southwest of Haymarket station. Bus from centre. Open daily (except Christmas and New Year's Day), summer 0930–1630; winter 0930–1600. Free. Guided tours (charge £). Explanatory displays. Gift shop. Café and picnic area. Baby changing facilities. Play park. WC. Wheelchair access. Disabled WC. Car parking. Telephone 0131 337 4202.

A 2 acre (1ha) farm with various farm animals, commonly kept pets, herbs, vegetables and a wildlife garden. Special events throughout the year, craft classes, educational workshops and tours. Education centre.

---

544 EDINBURGH, GREYFRIARS BOBBY **6 N15**

By Greyfriars churchyard, corner of George IV Bridge and Candlemaker Row. Access at all times. Free.

Statue of Greyfriars Bobby, the Skye terrier who, after his master's death in 1858, watched over his grave in the nearby Greyfriars Churchyard for 14 years.

545 EDINBURGH, GREYFRIARS KIRK 6 N15

2 Greyfriars Place, Edinburgh. In Edinburgh Old Town, 15 minutes walk from Waverley railway station. Bus from centre. Open Easter–Oct, Mon–Fri 1030–1630, Sat 1030–1430; churchyard open every day 0900–1800 (except New Year's Day). Free. Guided tours (available in French and Gaelic by arrangement). Explanatory displays and videos. Gift shop. Refreshments for groups available with advance notice. WC. Tours to suit blind visitors (by arrangement). Loop induction (services and talks). Wheelchair access and disabled parking. Disabled WC. Telephone 0131 225 1900/226 5429.

Edinburgh's first Reformed Church (1620). On display is the National Covenant (signed at the church in 1638), Scotland's finest collection of 17th- and 18th-century funeral monuments, fine 19th-century windows by Ballantyne, Peter Collins' organ (1990) with carvings of Scottish flora and fauna, memorabilia about Greyfriars Bobby (see 163).

---

546 EDINBURGH, HOLYROOD ABBEY 6 N15

HS. At the foot of the Canongate (Royal Mile), Edinburgh, in the grounds of the Palace of Holyroodhouse. Local bus service and tour bus. Access and charges same as Palace of Holyroodhouse. No free entry for Friends of Historic Scotland at this site. Telephone 0131 668 8800.

The ruined nave of the 12th- and 13th-century Abbey church, built for Augustinian canons. The Abbey and palace are administered by the Lord Chamberlain. See also 565 Edinburgh, Palace of Holyroodhouse.

---

547 EDINBURGH, HOLYROOD PARK 6 N15

HS. In Edinburgh, immediately to the east of Holyrood Palace and Abbey. Local bus service and tour buses. Open at all times. Free. Car parking. Telephone 0131 668 8800.

There has probably been a royal park here since the Augustinian Abbey was founded in the early 12th century; but it was formally enclosed in 1541 during James V's reign. Within the park is a wealth of archaeology, including the remains of four hill forts, other settlements and round them a fascinating landscape of prehistoric and early-medieval farming activity.

---

548 EDINBURGH, HUB FESTIVAL CENTRE 6 N15

348 Castlehill, Edinburgh. On the Royal Mile, close to Edinburgh Castle. Nearest railway station Edinburgh Waverley. Open all year except Christmas Day, daily 0800–0100. Charge for performances. Café bar. WC. Wheelchair access. Disabled WC. Telephone 0131 473 2011.

The permanent home for the Edinburgh International Festival housed in the former Tolbooth Church. Many of the original, gothic interiors of the church have been maintained and are complemented by new, comtemporary interior design. The centre offers a booking office, exhibition area and shop.

---

549 EDINBURGH, HUNTLY HOUSE MUSEUM 6 N15

142 Canongate, Edinburgh. In the Royal Mile. Nearest railway station 15 minutes walk, local bus service and tour buses. Open all year (except Christmas and New Year), Mon–Sat 1000–1700. During Festival open Sun 1400–1700. Free. Explanatory displays. Gift shop. WC. Telephone 0131 529 4143.

A restored 16th-century mansion, Huntly House Museum is the city's main museum of local history, with period rooms and reconstructions relating to the city's traditional industries. There are also collections of Edinburgh silver and glass, Scottish pottery, shop signs and relics relating to Field Marshall Earl Haig, the WW1 general.

550 EDINBURGH, JOHN KNOX HOUSE 6 N15

43–45 High Street, Edinburgh. In the Royal Mile within easy walking distance of Waverley railway station. Open all year, Mon–Sat 1000–1700. Also open in evenings if show on at Netherbow Theatre. Charge £. Group concessions. Explanatory displays. Gift shop. Café. WC. Limited wheelchair access. Disabled WC. Telephone 0131 556 9579.

A picturesque 15th-century house associated with John Knox, the religious reformer, and James Mossman, keeper of the Royal Mint to Mary, Queen of Scots. The house contains many original features including the painted ceiling in the Oak Room and an exhibition on the life and times of John Knox and James Mossman.

---

551 EDINBURGH, LAURISTON CASTLE 6 M15

Cramond Road South, Edinburgh. At Davidson's Mains, 3 miles (5km) west of Edinburgh centre. Bus from centre. Open Apr–Oct, Sat–Thu 1100–1700; Nov–Mar, Sat–Sun 1400–1600. Grounds open all year 0900–dusk (admission free). Charge ££. Guided tours – admission to castle by guided tour only. Foreign language guide sheets available. Picnic area. WC. Limited wheelchair access. Disabled WC. Car and coach parking. Telephone 0131 336 2060.

A 16th-century tower house with extensive 19th-century additions. Built about 1590 by Archibald Napier whose son John invented logarithms. In early 18th century it was owned by financier John Law who held high office in the court of pre-revolution France. The last private owners were the Reid family, and the castle contains William Reid's extensive collections of furniture and antiques – a snapshot of the interior of a Scottish country house in the Edwardian era. Thirty acres (12ha) of beautiful gardens and parkland with panoramic views of the Firth of Forth.

---

552 EDINBURGH, MCEWAN'S 80' LITERARY PUB TOUR 6 N15

The Beehive Inn, Grassmarket, Edinburgh. In Edinburgh old town, 10 minutes walk from Princes Street and the Royal Mile. Nearest railway station Edinburgh Waverley, then 15 minutes walk. Tours Jun–Sep, daily 1800 and 2030; Apr–May and Oct, Thu–Sun 1930; Nov–Mar, Fri 1930. Charge £££. Customised tours for groups arranged. Guided tours. Four pubs visited. WC. Limited wheelchair access. Car and coach parking. Telephone 0131 226 6665.

This two hour promenade performance, led by professional actors, begins at the historic Beehive Inn, in the Grassmarket and follows a route through the streets, wynds, courtyards and old taverns of the Old and New Towns of Edinburgh. The lives and work of Scotland's great poets, writers and colourful characters from the past 300 years are described, from Robert Burns and Walter Scott to Muriel Spark and Trainspotting.

---

553 EDINBURGH, MAGDALEN CHAPEL 6 N15

41 Cowgate, Edinburgh. In the centre, 100 yards (91m) from the Grassmarket. Open all year, Mon–Fri 0930–1600. Free. Guided tours. Explanatory displays. Gift shop. WC. Wheelchair access. Disabled WC. Telephone 0131 220 1450.

Built in 1541, the chapel was used by various denominations as an ecclesiastical building and also as a guildhall by the Incorporation of Hammermen until 1862, when it was sold to the Protestant Institute of Scotland. Since 1965, it has been in the possession of the Scottish Reformation Society and used as their headquarters with regular services. Features stained glass (the only medieval examples still in the original setting and situation), bell and clock dating from early 17th century.

554 EDINBURGH, MALLENY GARDEN **6 M16**

NTS. Balerno. Off A70 (Lanark Road) in Balerno near Edinburgh. By bus from Edinburgh centre. Open Apr–Oct, daily 0930–1900; Nov–Mar, daily 0930–1600. House not open to public. Charge £. Honesty box. Group concessions. WC. Limited wheelchair access. Car and coach parking. Telephone 0131 449 2283.

Dominated by four 400-year-old clipped yew trees, this peaceful garden features fine herbaceous borders and a large collection of old-fashioned roses. The National Bonsai Collection for Scotland is also housed here.

---

555 EDINBURGH, MATTHEW ARCHITECTURE GALLERY **6 N15**

20 Chambers Street, Edinburgh. In the centre of the Old Town opposite Royal Museum of Scotland (see 575). Open all year, Mon–Fri 1000–1600, weekends 1030–1430 term time only. Free. Explanatory displays. WC. Wheelchair access with assistance. Disabled WC. Telephone 0131 650 2306.

An ongoing programme of exhibitions bringing the best of contemporary architecture and related arts to the general public.

---

556 EDINBURGH, MERCAT WALKING TOURS **6 N15**

Mercat Cross, City Chambers, High Street, Edinburgh. All tours leave from the Mercat Cross (Royal Mile) beside St Giles Cathedral. 5 minute walk from Waverley railway station. All year, daily 1030–2130. Charge ££. Group concessions. Guided tours (available in Dutch, French, German, Italian). Explanatory displays. Gift shop. WC. Car and coach parking. Telephone 0131 557 6464.

Dramatised history and ghost tours of the Royal Mile. Tours visit the wynds and closes of Old Edinburgh and include a visit to the vaults beneath the South Bridge and the world-famous Mary King's Close. Booking is essential for the latter.

---

557 EDINBURGH, MIDLOTHIAN SKI CENTRE **6 M16**

Hillend, Near Edinburgh. Just south of the city bypass off the A702 at Lothianburn junction. Nearest railway station Edinburgh, bus from city centre. Open winter, Mon–Sat 0930–2100, Sun 0930–1900; summer Mon–Fri 0930–1900, weekends 0930–2100. Charge ££. Chairlift ride £. Group concessions. Explanatory displays. Restaurant/café. WC. Limited wheelchair access. Disabled WC. Car and coach parking. Telephone 0131 445 4433.

Europe's longest and most challenging artificial ski slope. Three slopes and two nursery slopes. Equipment hire, skiing/snowboarding, coaching and instruction for all levels, chair lift and two ski tows. Chairlift open to all visitors, with terrific views.

---

558 EDINBURGH, MUSEUM OF CHILDHOOD **6 N15**

42 High Street, Edinburgh. In the Royal Mile. Open all year, Mon–Sat 1000–1700, sun during Festival 1400–1700. Free. Explanatory displays. Gift shop. WC. Mini-com for the deaf, artefacts to handle. Limited wheelchair access. Disabled WC. Telephone 0131 529 4142.

This unique museum has a fine collection of childhood-related items including toys, dolls, dolls' houses, costumes and nursery equipment. It has a programme of changing exhibitions and activities.

---

559 EDINBURGH, MUSEUM OF FIRE **6 N15**

Brigade Headquaters, Lauriston Place, Edinburgh. In city centre, 20 minutes walk from Waverley station. Bus from station. Open all year (except for first two weeks in Aug, and Christmas and New Year), Mon–Fri 0900–1630. Free. Guided tours. Explanatory displays. WC. Wheelchair access. Disabled WC. Telephone 0131 228 2401.

A museum telling the history of the oldest municipal fire brigade in the United Kingdom. Housed in the historic headquarters building, it shows the development of fire fighting in an exciting and educational way. Displays a range of fire engines from 1806, and many other fire related items.

---

560 EDINBURGH, MUSEUM OF SCOTLAND **6 N15**

Chambers Street, Edinburgh. Within 15 minutes walk of Princes Street; local bus service to South Bridge then turn right onto Chamber Street. Open all year, Mon–Sat 1000–1700 (Tue closes 2000), Sun 1200–1700. Charge £. Children under 18 free. Season ticket available. Free admission Tue, 1630–2000. Joint ticket with Royal Museum of Scotland. Group concessions. Guided tours (also audio tours). Explanatory displays. Gift shop. Restaurant and café. Rooftop garden. WC. Wheelchair access. Disabled WC. Telephone 0131 247 4422.

The Museum of Scotland tells the history of Scotland from its geological beginnings to the present day. A striking piece of architecture to hold the treasured objects of Scotland's past and present.

---

561 EDINBURGH, NATIONAL GALLERY OF SCOTLAND **6 N15**

The Mound, Edinburgh. In city centre, just off Princes Street. Nearest railway and bus stations 10 minute walk. Open all year, Mon–Sat 1000–1700, Sun 1200–1700. Closed Christmas Day and Boxing Day. Free. Small charge for temporary exhibitions. Guided tours by prior arrangement (telephone 0131 624 6506). Room plan. Gift shop. WC. Acoustic guide for visually impaired. Limited wheelchair access. Disabled WC. Telephone 0131 624 6332.

The building was designed by William Henry Playfair and the foundation stone laid by Prince Albert in 1850. The gallery opened to the public in 1859. The collection contains outstanding paintings, drawings and prints by the greatest artists from the Renaissance to Post-Impressionism, including Velásquez, El Greco, Titian, Vermeer, Constable, Monet and Van Gogh. It also houses the national collection of Scottish art featuring works by Taggart, Wilkie, Ramsay and Raeburn.

---

562 EDINBURGH, NATIONAL LIBRARY OF SCOTLAND **6 N15**

George IV Bridge, Edinburgh. In the Old Town just off the High Street. Waverley station 10 minute walk, bus from Princes Street. Open all year (except Easter, Christmas, New Year and Edinburgh autumn holiday in Sep). Exhibitions open (summer only) Mon–Sat 1000–1700, Sun 1400–1700. Free. Guided tours. Explanatory displays. Gift shop. WC. Limited wheelchair access. Disabled WC. Telephone 0131 226 4531.

Founded in 1682, the library is a treasure house of books and manuscripts, with reading rooms open for research to scholars from home and abroad. For the general public and visitors, it has a programme of exhibitions on Scottish themes.

---

563 EDINBURGH, NELSON MONUMENT **6 N15**

32 Calton Hill, Edinburgh. On Calton Hill, above Waterloo Place at the east end of Princes Street. 15 minute walk from Waverley station. Open Apr–Sep, Mon 1300–1800, Tue–Sat 1000–1800; Oct–Mar, Mon–Sat 1000–1500. Charge £. Explanatory displays. Gift shop. Picnic area. WC. Car and coach parking. Telephone 0131 556 2716.

One of the first monuments to Admiral Nelson, built between 1807 and 1815. A telescope-shaped tower with a time-ball on the top. The latter is wound up every day (except Sunday) and dropped at 1300. Nelson's Trafalgar signal is flown every year on 21 October. Good views from top.

---

564 EDINBURGH, NEWHAVEN HERITAGE MUSEUM **6 M15**

24 Pier Place, Edinburgh. Bus service from Princes Street. Open all year, daily 1200–1700. Free. Explanatory displays. Gift shop. Induction loop for video. Wheelchair access. Car and coach parking. Telephone 0131 551 4165.

This museum is situated in the historic fishmarket overlooking the harbour. It tells the story of Newhaven and its people. Find out about fishing and other sea trades, customs and superstitions. Displays tell the stories of the Society of Free Fishermen and the development of this tightly-knit community. Reconstructed sets of fishwives and fishermen, displays of objects and photographs, and first-hand written and spoken accounts of people's lives. Hands-on exhibits, music and video.

---

565 EDINBURGH, PALACE OF HOLYROODHOUSE **6 N15**

Canongate, Edinburgh. At the foot of the Royal Mile, 10 minute walk from Waverley station. By tourist bus. Open all year (except Christmas and Good Friday), Apr–Oct Mon–Sat 0930–1715, Sun 1030–1630; Nov–Mar, Mon–Sat 0930–1545. Closed before, during and after Royal and State visits, also at other times. Charge £££. Group concessions. Guided tours Nov–Mar (available in other languages). Gift shop. Picnic area. Garden in summer. WC. Guide for blind visitors. Wheelchair access. Disabled WC. Car and coach parking. Telephone 0131 556 7371; recorded information on 0131 556 1096.

The official residence of The Queen in Scotland. The oldest part is built against the monastic nave of Holyrood Abbey (see 546), little of which remains. The rest of the palace was reconstructed by the architect Sir William Bruce for Charles II. Here Mary, Queen of Scots lived for six years, here she met John Knox, here Rizzio was murdered and here Prince Charles Edward Stuart held court in 1745. The State Apartments house tapestries and paintings. The Picture Gallery has portraits of over 80 Scottish kings painted by De Wet 1684–6.

---

566 EDINBURGH, PARISH CHURCH OF ST CUTHBERT **6 N15**

5 Lothian Road, Edinburgh. St Cuthbert's Church lies in a graveyard below the Castle just beyond the west end of Princes Street Gardens. Local bus to Princes Street and Lothian Road. Open mid May–mid Sep, Mon–Fri 1000–1600, Sat 1000–1200. Sun open for for worship. Free. Guided tours (leaflets in English, French, German, Italian and Spanish). Explanatory displays. Graveyard. WC. Induction loop during services. Wheelchair access. Disabled WC. Telephone 0131 229 1142.

The seventh church on this site. Tradition has it that St Cuthbert had a small cell church here at the head of the Nor'Loch. Recorded history tells that King David I, gifted lands to 'The Church of St Cuthbert, hard by the Castle of Edinburgh'. Present building built in 1894 to design by Hippolyte Blanc, but retained the 1790 tower. Interior reorganised in 1990 by Stewart Tod. Features Renaissance style stalls, marble communion table, mural, stained glass by Tiffany. Famous names in graveyard.

---

567 EDINBURGH, PARLIAMENT HOUSE **6 N15**

2 Parliament Square, Edinburgh. Behind the High Kirk of St Giles, Royal Mile. Open all year, Tue–Fri 1000–1600. Free. Explanatory displays. Postcards and booklets for sale. Restaurant. Disabled WC. Telephone 0131 225 2595.

Built 1632–9, this was the seat of Scottish government until 1707, when the governments of Scotland and England were united. Now the Supreme Law Courts of Scotland, Parliament Hall has a fine hammer beam roof and portraits by Raeburn and other major Scottish artists. Access (free) to the splendid Signet Library on an upper floor is by prior written request only, to: The Librarian, Signet Library, Parliament House, Edinburgh. Outside is the medieval Mercat Cross, which was restored in 1885 by W. E. Gladstone. Royal proclamations are still read from its platform.

568 EDINBURGH, THE PEOPLES STORY **6 N15**

Canongate Tolbooth, 163 Canongate, Edinburgh. Near the foot of the Royal Mile, 10 minute walk from Waverley station and bus station. Open all year (except Christmas and New Year), Mon–Sat 1000–1700; Jun–Sep 1000–1800; during the Edinburgh Festival, also Sun 1400–1700. Free. Explanatory displays. Gift shop. WC. Induction loop. Limited wheelchair access, to ground and first floor only. Disabled WC. Telephone 0131 529 4057.

In the picturesque Canongate Tolbooth, built in 1591. Tells the story of the life, work and pastimes of the ordinary working people of Edinburgh from the late 18th century. Sights, sounds and smells. Room reconstructions, rare artefacts and everyday objects.

---

569 EDINBURGH, JAMES PRINGLE WEAVERS LEITH MILLS **6 N15**

70–74 Bangor Road, Leith, Edinburgh. In Leith, 2 miles (3km) from Edin- burgh city centre. Bus from Edinburgh centre. Open Apr–Oct, Mon–Sat 0900–1730, Sun 1000–1700; Nov–Mar, Mon–Sat 0900–1700, Sun 1000–1700. Free. Explanatory displays. Gift shop. Restaurant. WC. Wheelchair access. Car and coach parking. Telephone 0131 553 5161.

Large shop selling woollens, tartans, clothing and gifts. Tailor-made outfits. Clan Tartan Centre with an archive computer which will provide visitors with a printed certificate detailing any clan connection, information on the clan chief, its origins, heraldic emblems, plant badge and other historic information.

---

570 EDINBURGH PRINTMAKERS **6 M15**

23 Union Street, Edinburgh. At the east end of Edinburgh near the Playhouse Theatre. Waverley station, bus from centre. Open all year (except Christmas and New Year), Tue–Sat 1000–1800. Free. Guided tours of studios by appointment. Explanatory displays. WC. Limited wheelchair access. Telephone 0131 557 2479.

Edinburgh's main studio for practising artists who make limited edition prints. Visitors can watch artists at work and see the huge range of prints for sale in the gallery. Courses in print-making.

---

571 EDINBURGH, RABBIE'S TRAIL BURNERS **6 N15**

207 High Street, Edinburgh. In the Royal Mile, 5 minutes walk from Waverley station. Open all year, May–Sep 0900–2000; Oct–Apr 0900–1800. Charge £££. Guided tours. Gift shop. Wheelchair access with assistance. Telephone 0131 226 3133.

One, two or three-day tours of the Highlands and Islands by luxury minibus accompanied by guide. Also available are special tours/holidays for groups, chauffeur drive, walking tours. Office located in Celtic Art and Travel Centre.

---

572 EDINBURGH, REGIMENTAL MUSEUM OF THE ROYAL SCOTS **6 N15**

Edinburgh Castle, Edinburgh. In the Castle at the top of the Royal Mile. Car and coach parking in winter only. 10 minute walk from Waverley station. Open daily Apr–Sep, 0930–1730; Oct–Mar, Mon–Fri 0930–1600. Free but charge for entry to Castle. Guided tours by Historic Scotland. Explanatory displays. Gift shop. WC. Wheelchair access. Disabled WC. Telephone 0131 220 4387.

The museum of the oldest regiment in the British Army, housed in Edinburgh Castle. Contains paintings, artefacts, silver and medals which tell the story of the regiment from its formation in 1633 to the present day.

---

573 EDINBURGH, ROBIN'S GHOST AND HISTORY TOURS **6 N15**

c/o Mercat House, Niddry Street South, Edinburgh. Tours begin outside the Tourist Information Centre, Waverley shopping centre, Princes Street.

Tours all year (except seasonal holidays); Grand Tour, daily 1000; Hidden Historic Vaults, daily 1130 (also Oct–Apr at 1430); Ghosts and Witches Tour, daily 1900 (also Apr–Oct at 2100). Charge £££. Group concessions. Guided tours. Gift shop. WC. Limited wheelchair access. Telephone 0131 557 9933.

The tours recreate the dramatic history of Scotland's capital city. The Grand Tour is a journey through the splendours of the Georgian New Town and Edinburgh's medieval heart. The Hidden Historic Vaults tour is a journey down into 18th-century mysterious underground vaults. At night, the Ghosts and Witches tour is a dark journey through streets haunted by the past.

---

574 EDINBURGH, ROYAL BOTANIC GARDEN **6 M15**

20a Inverleith Row, Edinburgh. 1 mile (2km) north of the city centre. Bus from centre. Open daily (except Christmas Day and New Year's Day) from 0930; closes 1600 (Nov–Jan), 1700 (Feb and Oct), 1800 (Mar and Sep), 1900 (Apr–Jun), 2000 (Jul and Aug). Free. Guided tours (available in French, German, Italian and Russian). Explanatory displays. Gift shop. Licensed café and snack bar. Baby changing. WC. Wheelchairs available. Wheelchair access. Disabled WC. Car and coach parking. Telephone 0131 552 7171.

Visitors can discover the wonders of the plant kingdom in Scotland's premier garden. Established in 1670 on an area the size of a tennis court, it now comprises over 70 acres (28ha) of beautifully landscaped grounds. Spectacular features include the world-famous Rock Garden, the Pringle Chinese Collection and a magnificent arboretum. The amazing Glasshouse Experience, featuring Britain's tallest Palm House, leads you on a trail of discovery through Asia, Africa, the Mediterranean and the Southern Hemisphere.

---

575 EDINBURGH, ROYAL MUSEUM OF SCOTLAND **6 N15**

Chambers Street, Edinburgh. In the centre of the Old Town of Edinburgh. Open all year (except Christmas Day), Mon–Sat 1000–1700 (Tue to 2000), Sun 1200–1700. Free. Guided tours (available in French, German and Italian; other languages by prior arrangement). Explanatory displays. Gift shop. Tearoom. Lecture Theatre. Audio Guides. Baby changing. WC. Induction loop. Wheelchair access. Disabled WC. Telephone 0131 225 7534.

The museum houses international collections in a wonderful Victorian glass-topped building. Collections include applied arts, geology and zoology, natural history, social and technical history, jewellery and costume, Egyptian and African treasures, many new permanent galleries as well as exciting temporary exhibition programme. Lectures, concerts and activities for children.

---

576 EDINBURGH, ROYAL OBSERVATORY VISITOR CENTRE **6 M15**

Blackford Hill, Edinburgh. 3 miles (5km) south of city centre. Bus from centre (but walk up steep hill). Open all year except 24 Dec–2 Jan, Mon–Sat 1000–1700, Sun 1200–1700. Charge £. Children under 5 free. Guided tours for groups by prior arrangement. Explanatory displays. Gift shop. Vending machines. WC. Limited wheelchair access. Disabled WC. Car and coach parking. Telephone 0131 668 8405.

A multi-media gallery with ten PCs and CD-ROMs on space and astronomy. Visitors can experiment with light and see one of the largest telescopes in Scotland. Panoramic views of Edinburgh.

---

577 EDINBURGH, ROYAL SCOTTISH ACADEMY **6 N15**

The Mound, Edinburgh. Located on Princes Street at the foot of the Mound. Nearest railway and bus stations 10 minutes walk. Open for temporary exhibitions only, Mon–Sat 1000–1700, Sun 1400–1700. Charges vary, sometimes free. Gift shop. WC. Wheelchair access. Disabled WC. Telephone 0131 225 6671.

The Royal Scottish Academy, established in 1826, is Scotland's oldest art gallery which specialises in showing contemporary art, ranging from works by Academicians and Associates of the Academy (annual exhibition May–June) to works from students at all Scottish Colleges of art and architecture (students exhibition, March).

---

578 EDINBURGH, THE ROYAL YACHT BRITANNIA **6 N15**

Ocean Drive, Leith, Edinburgh. 2 miles (3km) from the centre of Edinburgh, in the port of Leith. Local bus service runs direct from Waverley Bridge. Open all year, daily 1030–1630; during winter telephone to confirm times. Charge £££. Group concessions. Guided tours by audio tape (available in French, German, Italian and Spanish). Explanatory displays. Gift shop. Café and picnic area. WC. Wheelchair access. Disabled WC. Car and coach parking. Telephone 0131 555 5566.

Visitors can view the Royal Family Picture Gallery, learn about life on board for officers and yachtsmen and see the Royal Barge. An audio tour takes visitors around the four main decks of Britannia.

---

579 EDINBURGH, RUSSELL COLLECTION OF EARLY KEYBOARD INSTRUMENTS **6 N15**

Niddry Street, Cowgate, Edinburgh. At the foot of Niddry Street in the Old Town, 8 minutes walk from Waverley station. Bus from centre. Open Wed and Sat 1400–1700; during Edinburgh Festival, Mon–Sat 1030–1230. Charge £. Group concessions. Guided tours. Gift shop. WC. Limited wheelchair access. Telephone 0131 650 2805/2423.

Scotland's oldest concert hall, built to a design by Robert Milne in 1762 for the Edinburgh Musical Society. After many alterations and changes of use, it was acquired by the University of Edinburgh and restored to its original use in 1968. It is the home of the Russell Collection of Early Keyboard Instruments, which is of international importance. Publications, recordings, postcards and technical information available.

---

580 EDINBURGH, ST CECILIA'S HALL

See 579 Edinburgh, Russell Collection of Early Keyboard Instruments.

---

581 EDINBURGH, ST GILES' CATHEDRAL **6 N15**

High Street, Edinburgh. In the Royal Mile, 5 minute walk from Waverley station. Bus from centre. Open all year. Free. Donation box. Guided tours (available in French and German by prior arrangement). Explanatory displays. Gift shop. Restaurant. WC. Wheelchair access with assistance. Telephone 0131 225 9442.

Founded in the 1100s, a triumph of 14th- and 15th-century architecture with a crown spire that has dominated the Edinburgh skyline for 500 years. The church of John Knox during the Reformation. Contains memorials to many great Scots, including the great Covenanting leaders Montrose and Argyll, Robert Louis Stevenson and Robert Burns. Fine Victorian and 20th-century stained glass and a magnificent modern organ. The Thistle Chapel was designed by Lorimer and is a jewel of Scottish craftsmanship.

---

582 EDINBURGH, ST JOHN'S **6 N15**

Princes Street, Edinburgh. Located at the west end of Princes Street. Car park nearby. Nearest railway and bus stations 15 minutes walk. Open all year, Mon–Fri 0730–1600, Sat 0800–1230, Sun for worship. Free. Guided tours by arrangement. Gift shop. Café. Wheelchair access with assistance. Disabled WC. Telephone 0131 229 7565.

St John's, the Church of St John the Evangelist, is one of architect William Burn's finest early 19th-century buildings. It also has one of the finest collections of stained glass in the country. There is a fine collection of modern paintings and sculptures. Outside are the graves of many famous Scots such as Sir Henry Raeburn, Scotland's finest portrait painter, and James Donaldson, the founder of the School for the Deaf.

---

583 EDINBURGH, ST MARY'S CATHEDRAL 6 M15

Palmerston Place, Edinburgh. At the West End, near Haymarket. Haymarket station 5 minute walk. Bus from centre. Open daily 0730–1800 (to 2100 in summer). Free. Guided tours by arrangement. Explanatory displays. Gift shop. Crèche on Sun at 1030. WC. Induction loop. Wheelchair access. Disabled WC. Telephone 0131 225 6293.

An Episcopal cathedral built in 1879, with the western towers added in 1917. The central spire is 276 feet (84m) high. Impressive interior. Nearby is the charming Old Coates House, built in the late 17th century and now the Episcopal Church's Theological Institute.

---

584 EDINBURGH, ST TRIDUANA'S CHAPEL 6 N15

HS. At Restalrig Church, off Restalrig Road South, 1.5 miles (2.5km) east of Edinburgh city centre. Nearest railway station Edinburgh Waverley, bus from centre. Open at all times; contact keyholder. Free. Telephone 0131 668 8800.

The lower part of the chapel built by James III, housing the shrine of St Triduana, a Pictish saint. The hexagonal vaulted chamber is unique.

---

585 EDINBURGH, SCOTCH WHISKY HERITAGE CENTRE 6 N15

354 Castlehill, Edinburgh. At the top of the Royal Mile in Edinburgh. Waverley station within walking distance. Open daily (except 25 Dec) 0930–1730. Charge ££. Reduced admission for disabled. Group concessions. Guided tours (translations in eight languages). Explanatory displays. Gift shop. Tearoom and picnic area. WC. Script available for deaf, braille also available. Wheelchair access. Disabled WC. Telephone 0131 220 0441.

The mystery of Scotch whisky revealed – learn about malt, grain and blended whisky, take a barrel ride through whisky history and meet the resident ghost. Free taste of whisky for adults. Whisky Bond Bar selling over 200 different whiskies.

---

586 EDINBURGH, SCOTTISH NATIONAL GALLERY OF MODERN ART 6 M15

Belford Road, Edinburgh. 20 minutes walk from west end of the city centre. Nearest railway station Edinburgh Haymarket, limited bus service. Open all year, Mon–Sat 1000–1700, Sun 1200–1700. Closed Christmas Day and Boxing Day. Free. Small charge for temporary exhibitions. Guided tours by prior arrangement (telephone 0131 624 6506). Room plan. Gift shop. Restaurant and picnic area. WC. Wheelchair access. Disabled WC. Car and coach parking. Telephone 0131 624 6332.

The building was designed in the 1820s by Sir William Burn and was formerly a school. It has bright spacious rooms and extensive grounds providing the perfect setting for sculptures by Barbara Hepworth, Eduardo Paolozzi, Henry Moore and others. The bulk of the collection, which amounts to almost 4000 works of art, has been amassed since 1960. There are examples of work by Matisse, Kirchner, Picasso, Magritte, Miró, Dali and Ernst. The gallery houses an unrivalled collection of 20th-century Scottish art including work by Charles Rennie Mackintosh, Peploe, Fergusson and Cadell. The greatest strengths of the gallery's modern international collection are works by Surrealist, German Expressionist and French artists.

587 EDINBURGH, SCOTTISH NATIONAL PORTRAIT GALLERY 6 M15

1 Queen Street, Edinburgh. In city centre, 5 minutes walk from Princes Street. Nearest railway and bus stations 10 minutes walk. Open all year, Mon–Sat 1000–1700, Sun 1200–1700. Closed Christmas Day and Boxing Day. Free. Small charge for temporary exhibitions. Guided tours by prior arrangement (telephone 0131 624 6506). Explanatory displays. Gift shop. Restaurant. WC. Wheelchair access. Disabled WC. Telephone 0131 624 6332.

The gallery, built in the 1880s and designed by Sir Robert Rowand Anderson, provides a unique visual history of Scotland, told through the portraits of the figures who shaped it – royalty, poets, philosophers, heroes and rebels. All the portraits are of Scots but not all are by Scots. The collection also holds works by great English, European and American masters such as Van Dyck, Gainsborough, Copley, Rodin, Kokoschka and Thorvaldsen. The gallery also houses the National Photography Collection.

---

588 EDINBURGH, SCOTTISH PARLIAMENT VISITOR CENTRE 6 N15

Committee Chambers (Ground Floor), George IV Bridge, Edinburgh. In the centre of Edinburgh at the junction of George IV Bridge and the Royal Mile. Nearest railway station Edinburgh Waverley, then 5 minutes walk; local bus service. Open all year, Mon–Fri 0930–1700; other times, see press for details. Free. Explanatory displays. Gift shop. Wheelchair access. Disabled WC. Telephone 0131 348 5000.

The visitor centre explains the past, present and future of Scotland's Parliaments through colourful displays, exhibitions and state-of-the-art interactive computer systems. Also historical documents from Scotland's earliest days and a detailed model of the new Parliament building at Holyrood.

---

589 EDINBURGH, SCOTTISH TARTANS MUSEUM 6 N15

The Scotch House, 39–41 Princes Street, Edinburgh. In the New Town near Waverley station. Open all year (except Christmas Day and New Year's Day), Mon–Sat 0900–1730 (Thu to 1800). Charge £. Group concessions. Guided tours (audio available in French, German, Italian, Spanish and Japanese). Explanatory displays. Gift shop. WC. Taped commentary available. Wheelchair access. Telephone 0131 556 1352.

Over 600 examples illustrate the history of tartan from 325AD to the present. Rotating mannequins demonstrate the development of the kilt and the Tartan Room displays over 700 different tartans. Family tartans traced.

---

590 EDINBURGH, SCOTT MONUMENT 6 N15

East Princes Street Gardens, Edinburgh. Open Mar–May and Oct, daily 1000–1800 (or dusk if earlier); Jun–Sep, Mon–Sat 0900–2000, Sun 1000–1800; Nov–Feb, daily 1000–1600 (or dusk if earlier). Charge £. Group concessions. Explanatory displays. Telephone 0131 529 4068.

One of Edinburgh's most famous landmarks, the 150-year-old monument commemorates one of Scotland's greatest writers, Sir Walter Scott. A steep climb to the top rewards the visitor with superb views of Edinburgh and its surroundings.

---

591 EDINBURGH, STILLS GALLERY 6 N15

23 Cockburn Street, Edinburgh. In the Old Town just off the High Street. Waverley station 2 minute walk. Open Tue–Sat 1000–1700. Free. Guided tours on request. Explanatory displays. Café. Book shop. WC. Wheelchair access. Disabled WC. Telephone 0131 622 6200.

A contemporary art gallery, bookshop and café. Open access photography and digital imaging labs open to visitors.

592 EDINBURGH, SUNTRAP GARDEN 6 M15

43 Gogarbank, Edinburgh. Between the A8 and A71, 1 mile (2km) west of city centre. Open daily all year except Christmas and New Year, Mon–Fri 0930–1630. Charge £. Free to NTS members and children. WC. Wheelchair access. Car parking. Telephone (01506) 854387 and 0131 339 2891.

A 3 acre (1.2ha) site with several gardens in one – Italian, rock, rose, peat and woodland. Started in 1957 by philanthropist and keen amateur gardener George Boyd Anderson, bequeathed to the National Trust for Scotland and Lothian region as a centre for gardening advice and horticultural excellence. Now run by Oatridge Agricultural College, with excellent demonstration facilities.

---

593 EDINBURGH, TALBOT RICE GALLERY 6 N15

Old College, South Bridge, Edinburgh. In the Old Town, 0.25 mile (0.5km) from East End of Princes Street and Waverley station. Opens for four weeks at a time; telephone 0131 650 2211 for details. Free. Guided tours (available in other languages by arrangement). Explanatory displays. Book shop. WC. Wheelchair access. Telephone 0131 650 2210.

The Red Gallery shows the University of Edinburgh's Torrie Collection. The White Gallery shows seven contemporary exhibitions each year, mainly by mid-career Scottish artists, but also artists from further afield and occasional historical exhibitions.

---

594 EDINBURGH TARTAN WEAVING MILL AND EXHIBITION 6 N15

555 Castlehill, Edinburgh. Beside Edinbrugh Castle at the top of the Royal Mile. 5 minute walk from Edinburgh Waverley railway station. Open daily all year (except Christmas Day and New Year's Day). Charge ££. Group concessions. Guided tours. Explanatory displays in French, German, Italian and Japanese. Gift shop. Restaurant and café. WC. Wheelchair access with assistance. Disabled WC. Car and coach parking. Telephone 0131 226 1555.

A working mill where visitors can see the production of tartan cloth and try weaving on a 60-year-old pedal loom. Visitors can also have their photo taken in ancient Scottish costume. Clans and tartans information bureau.

---

595 EDINBURGH, TOWER AMUSEMENT CENTRE 6 N15

49 Figgate Lane, Portobello, Edinburgh. On Portobello Promenade, by the A1, 3 miles (5km) east of city centre. Bus from city centre. Open every day 1000–2200, except Christmas Day. Free entrance. Restaurant. WC. Wheelchair access. Car and coach parking. Telephone 0131 669 8418.

Edinburgh's largest amusement centre packed with novelty games, prize bingo, kiddie rides, etc.

---

596 EDINBURGH UNIVERSITY COLLECTION OF HISTORIC MUSICAL INSTRUMENTS 6 N15

Reid Concert Hall, Bristo Square, Edinburgh. Near the McEwan Hall and Students' Union in the southwest corner of Bristo Square. Bus from Waverley railway station. Open Wed 1500–1700, Sat 1000–1300 (and Mon–Fri 1400–1700 during the Edinburgh International Festival); closed Christmas and New Year. Free. Guided tours by arrangement. WC. Wheelchair access with assistance. Car parking. Telephone 0131 650 2423.

Founded circa1850 and opened to the public 1982. The galleries, built in 1859 and still with their original showcases, are believed to be the earliest surviving purpose-built musical museum in the world. On display are 1000 items including stringed, woodwind, brass and percussion instruments from Britain, Europe and from distant lands. The history of the instruments of the orchestra, the wind band, theatre, dance, popular music, domestic music-making and brass bands is shown. The instruments on display include many beautiful examples of the instrument-maker's art over the past 400 years.

597 EDINBURGH, WATER OF LEITH CONSERVATION TRUST **6 M15**

Water of Leith Centre, 24 Lanark Road, Edinburgh. Based in the Heritage Conservation Centre in Slateford (formerly the village school). Bus from city centre. Open Apr–Oct, daily 1000–1600; Nov–Mar limited opening, telephone to check. Charge £. Annual season ticket available. Group concessions. Guided tours. Explanatory displays. Gift shop. Picnic area. Wildlife garden. WC. Wheelchair access. Disabled WC. Telephone 0131 455 7367.

The Trust operates a visitor centre with working models and explanatory displays and provides a central point for information about the river, guided walks and talks. Telephone for details.

---

598 EDINBURGH, WHITE HORSE CLOSE **6 N15**

Off Canongate, Royal Mile.

A restored group of 17th-century buildings off the High Street. The coaches to London left from White Horse Inn (named after Queen Mary's palfrey), and there are Jacobite links.

---

599 EDINBURGH, THE WRITERS' MUSEUM **6 N15**

Lady Stair's Close, Lawnmarket, Edinburgh. City centre. Open all year, Mon–Sat 1000–1700; during Edinburgh Festival only, Sun 1400–1700. Free. Explanatory displays. Gift shop. Baby changing facility. WC. Telephone 0131 529 4901.

Treasure house of portraits, relics and manuscripts relating to Scotland's three great writers – Robert Burns, Sir Walter Scott and Robert Louis Stevenson. Temporary exhibitions on other wirters and literary organisations.

---

600 EDINBURGH ZOO **6 M15**

134 Corstorphine Road, Edinburgh. On the A8, 3 miles (5km) west of the city centre. Bus from city centre. Open daily, Apr–Sep 0900–1800; Oct–Mar 0900–1630. Charge £££. Group concessions. Guided tours if booked. Explanatory displays. Gift shop. Restaurants. Café (spring and summer only) and picnic area. Children's play area. WC. Reduced admission for blind visitors, companion admitted free of charge. Guide dogs allowed into selected areas. No guide dogs. Wheelchair access. Disabled WC. Car and coach parking. Telephone 0131 334 9171.

Established in 1913 by the Royal Zoological Society of Scotland, this is Britain's most popular wildlife attraction with over 1000 animals, many threatened in the wild, all set in 80 acres (32ha) of beautiful hillside parkland. Animals range from tiny blue poison arrow frogs to massive white rhinos. Home to the wonderful Darwin Maze and the world's largest penguin enclosure complete with underwater viewing windows. The famous Penguin Parade takes place April–September, daily at 1400.

---

601 EDINBURGH WOOLLEN MILL, JEDBURGH **5 P18**

Bank End, Edinburgh Road, Jedburgh. Off the A68 in Jedburgh. Bus from Edinburgh. Open daily, Apr–Oct 0900–1730; Nov–Mar 0900–1700; closed Christmas Day and New Year's Day. Free. Gift shop. Restaurant, tearoom and picnic area. WC. Wheelchair access. Disabled WC. Car and coach parking. Telephone (01835) 863773.

A shop selling wool clothing, Scottish gifts and food.

---

602 EDIN'S HALL BROCH **5 Q16**

HS. On the northeastern slope of Cockburn Law, off the A6112 about 4.5 miles (7km) from Grantshouse, Berwickshire. 1 mile (2km) walk from the Duns road. Access at all times. Free. Car parking. Telephone 0131 668 8800.

One of the few Iron Age brochs in the Scottish Lowlands. Unusually large, sitting in a fort defended by ramparts and ditches, partially overlain with a later settlement. Occupied in Roman times.

603 EDRADOUR DISTILLERY 5 L12

Edradour, Pitlochry, Perthshire. On the A294, 2.5 miles (4km) east of Pitlochry. Nearest railway and bus station Pitlochry. Open Mar–Oct, Mon–Sat 0930–1700, Sun 1200–1700; Nov–Feb 1000–1600 (shop only). Closed for two weeks over Christmas and New Year. Free. Guided tours. Explanatory displays. Gift shop. WC. Limited wheelchair access. Disabled WC. Car and coach parking. Telephone (01796) 472095.

The smallest distillery in Scotland, established in 1825. Visitors can taste a hand-crafted single malt whisky.

---

604 EDROM CHURCH 5 Q16

HS. In Edrom churchyard, Berwickshire, off A6015, 3.5 miles (5.5km) northeast of Duns. Access at all times. Free. Car parking. Telephone 0131 668 8800.

A fine Norman chancel arch from the church built by Thor Longus about 1105.

---

605 EDZELL CASTLE AND GARDEN 3 P11

HS. Edzell, by Brechin, Angus. At Edzell, off B966, 6 miles (9.5km) north of Brechin. Nearest railway station Montrose, bus service from Montrose or Brechin to Edzell. Open Apr–Sep, daily 0930–1830; Oct–Mar, Mon–Sat 0930–1630 (closed Thu pm and Fri), Sun 1400–1630. Charge £. Group concessions. Guided tours. Explanatory displays and visitor centre. Gift shop. Picnic area. WC. Limited wheelchair access. Disabled WC. Car and coach parking. Telephone (01356) 648631.

A remarkable and very beautiful complex with a late medieval tower house incorporated into a 16th-century courtyard mansion, and walled garden with a bathhouse and summerhouse laid out by Sir David Lindsay in 1604. The carved decoration of the garden walls is unique in Britain.

---

606 EILACH AN NAOIMH 4 E14

HS. On an island of that name in the Garvellach group, north of Jura, Argyll. Transport by boat on request, dependant on weather; telephone Craobh Haven Boat Trips (01852) 500664 or Ruby Cruises (01852) 500616 for details. Access at all times. Free. Telephone 0131 668 8800.

The ruins of beehive cells, a chapel and a graveyard. Associated by local tradition with St Columba.

---

607 EILEAN DONAN CASTLE 2 G9

Dornie, Kyle of Lochalsh, Ross and Cromarty. On the A87, 8 miles (13km) east of Kyle of Lochalsh. Kyle station, bus from Glasgow or Kyle. Open Apr–Nov, daily 1000–1730. Charge ££. Group concessions. Guided tours (translations available in Dutch, French, German, Italian, Spanish and Japanese). Explanatory displays. Gift shop. Tearoom. WC. Disabled WC. Car and coach parking. Telephone (01599) 555202.

On an islet (now connected by a causeway) in Loch Duich, this picturesque and inhabited castle dates back to 1214. It passed into the hands of the Mackenzies of Kintail who became the Earls of Seaforth. In 1719 it was garrisoned by Spanish Jacobite troops and was blown up by an English man o' war. Now completely restored, it incorporates a war memorial to the Clan Macrae who held it as hereditary Constables on behalf of the Mackenzies.

---

608 ELCHO CASTLE 5 M13

HS. Rhynd, Perth. On the River Tay, 3 miles (5km) southeast of Perth. Nearest railway station Perth, no bus. Open Apr–Sep, daily 0930–1830. Charge £. Group concessions. Guided tours. Explanatory displays. Gift shop. Picnic area. WC. Telephone (01738) 639998.

A handsome and complete fortified 16th-century mansion. Notable for its tower-like jambs or wings and for the wrought-iron grills protecting its windows. An ancestral seat of the Earls of Wemyss.

609 ELECTRIC BRAE **4 H18**

A7, 20 miles (32km) south of Ayr (also known as Croy Brae). Access at all times. Free.

An optical illusion is created so that a car appears to be going down the hill when it is in fact going up.

---

610 ELGIN CATHEDRAL **3 M7**

HS. Elgin, Morayshire. In Elgin on the A96. Nearest railway station Elgin, bus from Aberdeen or Inverness. Open Apr–Sep, daily 0930–1830; Oct–Mar, Mon–Sat 0930–1630, Sun 1400–1630, closed Thu pm and Fri. Charge £. Group concessions. Guided tours. Explanatory displays. Gift shop. Limited wheelchair access . Car and coach parking. Telephone (01343) 547171.

The superb ruin of what was perhaps the most beautiful cathedral in Scotland. It was known as the Lantern of the North. Founded in 1224 but burned in 1390 by the Wolf of Badenoch, after which it was modified. It fell into ruin after the Reformation. The octagonal chapter house is the finest in Scotland. A Pictish slab lies in the choir.

---

611 ELGIN MUSEUM **3 M7**

1 High Street, Elgin, Moray. On the A96, 35.5 miles (57km) east of Inverness. Bus or train from Inverness or Aberdeen. Open Apr–Oct, Mon–Fri 1000–1700, Sat 1100–1600, Sun 1400–1700; in winter by appointment. Charge £. Group concessions. Guided tours occasionally. Explanatory displays. Gift shop. WC. Limited wheelchair access . Disabled WC. Car parking. Telephone (01343) 543675.

An independent museum interpreting the natural and human heritage of Moray. Internationally known for its fossils and Pictish stones.

---

612 ELLISLAND FARM **5 L19**

Holywood, Dumfries. Off the A76, 6.5 miles (10.5km) north northwest of Dumfries. Bus from Dumfries. Open Easter–Sep, Mon–Sat 1000–1300 and 1400–1700, Sun 1400–1700; Oct–Easter same hours but closed Sun and Mon. Charge £. Guided tours. Explanatory displays. Picnic area. Riverside walk. WC. Limited wheelchair access. Car and coach parking. Telephone (01387) 74426.

The farm which Robert Burns took over in 1788, building the farmhouse and trying to introduce new farming methods. Unsuccessful, he became an exciseman in 1789, and when the stock was auctioned in 1791 he moved to Dumfries. Burns wrote some of his most famous works at the Farm, including *Tam o' Shanter* and *Auld Lang Syne*. The Granary houses an audio-visual display.

---

613 EMBO BEACH, ANCHOR **3 L6**

Embo, north of Dornoch, Sutherland.

The anchor probably came from the Prussian barque *Vesta* which was wrecked in 1876. The ship came ashore 300 yards (275m) north of the village and Embo fishermen rescued all 11 crew.

---

614 EMBROIDERY WORKSHOP **6 N14**

Blacketyside Farm, Leven. On A915 coast road to St Andrews, 0.5 mile (1km) north of Leven. Local bus service from Leven to Dundee (via St Andrews), request stop. Open all year, Tue–Sat 1000–1700, Sun 1300–1700. Free. Gift shop. Garden. Wheelchair access. Car parking. Telephone (01333) 423985.

A tiny craft workshop and gift shop, housing an extensive range of original handmade designs. Visitors can watch craftspeople at work. Situated on a farm amid beautiful open countryside, with attractive walks and spectacular views.

615 EYEMOUTH MUSEUM **5 H16**

Old Kirk, Manse Road, Eyemouth. Town centre. Nearest railway station Berwick-upon-Tweed, bus service from Berwick and Edinburgh. Open Apr–Jun and Sep, Mon–Sat 1000–1700, Sun 1300–1500; Jul and Aug, Mon–Sat 1000–1800, Sun 1130–1630; Oct, Mon–Sat 1000–1600. Charge £. Accompanied children free. Group concessions. Guided tours by arrangement. Explanatory displays. Gift shop. Car and Coach parking nearby. Limited wheelchair access . Telephone (01890) 750678.

Magnificent tapestry which was sewn by local ladies to commemorate the Great East Coast Fishing Disaster of 1881, when 189 local fishermen were drowned. Also exhibitions on farming, milling, blacksmith and wheelwright, and of course local fishing heritage.

---

616 EYNHALLOW CHURCH **1 B10**

HS. On the island of Eynhallow, Orkney. Enquire at Kirkwall tourist information centre for private hire to Eynhallow. Access at all times. Free. Telephone 0131 668 8800.

The ruins of a 12th-century church and a group of domestic buildings.

---

617 FAIR ISLE **1 F8**

NTS. Shetland. Between Orkney and Shetland. Flights from Shetland, ferry from Grutness, Shetland. Open all year. Free. Gift shop. Telephone (01463) 232034.

One of Britain's most isolated inhabited islands. It is perhaps most famous for the intricately patterned knitwear which bears its name, a traditional craft which continues today. Fair Isle is important for birdlife, and offers many opportunities for ornithological study. The island also has much of archaeological interest, and traditional crofting is still in evidence. Accommodation is available at the bird observatory (01595) 760258 or in bed and breakfast houses.

---

618 FAIRWAYS HORSE SANCTUARY **5 M13**

Newton Farm, Glencarse, Perth. On the A90, 5 miles (8km) east of Perth. Bus from Perth or Dundee. Open daily, April–Sep 1000–1700, Oct–Mar 1100–1600. Charge £. Disabled and children under 5 free. Group concessions. Guided tours on request (if staffing permits). Explanatory displays. Gift shop. Tearoom and picnic area. WC. Disabled WC. Car and coach parking. Telephone (01738) 860888.

The centre cares for over 30 abandoned or retired working horses.

---

619 FAIRY GLEN, ROSEMARKIE **3 K7**

Rosemarkie, north of Fortrose, Black Isle.

The glen has many tales and ledgends connected with it and is reputed to be the home of a black witch. It is a lovely valley with several waterfalls and rapids situated beneath cliffs of red boulder clay and steep banks covered with wild cherry trees.

---

620 FALCONER MUSEUM **3 M7**

Tolbooth Street, Forres, Moray. On the A96, 11 miles (17.5km) west of Elgin. Nearest railway station Forres. Bus from Inverness or Aberdeen. Open Apr–Oct, Mon–Sat 1000–1700; Nov–Mar, Mon–Fri only. Free. Explanatory displays. Gift shop. Limited wheelchair access. Car and coach parking. Telephone (01309) 673701.

A museum featuring displays on local archaeology, history and climate. Also a display featuring the story of the Corries Folk Group.

---

621 FALKIRK WHEEL **6 L15**

At the interchange between the Union and the Forth and Clyde canals, close to Tomfourhill, south Falkirk. Telephone (01324) 671217.

By mid-2001 a spectacular wheel will reconnect the Union Canal up the 82 feet (25m) to the Forth and Clyde Canal. The wheel will weigh 1300 tonnes and be equivelent in height to a 9 storey block of flats. See also 657 Forth and Clyde Canal, and 1462 Union Canal.

---

622 FALKLAND PALACE, GARDEN AND OLD BURGH **6 N14**

NTS. Falkland, Cupar, Fife. On A912, 10 miles (16km) from junction 8, M90, and 11 miles (17.5km) north of Kirkcaldy. Bus stop in High Street. Palace and garden open Apr–May and Sep–Oct, Mon–Sat 1100–1730, Sun 1330–1730; Jun–Aug, Mon–Sat 1000–1730, Sun 1330–1730. Old Burgh open by appointment only. Charge ££. Children free. Garden only, £. Group concessions. Guided tours by arrangement. Explanatory displays. Guidebook in French and German, text in seven languages. Gift shop. Garden. WC. Tape tour for visually impaired. Limited wheelchair access, wheelchair available. Car and coach parking. Telephone (01337) 857397.

Country residence of the Stewart kings and queens. The gardens contain the original Royal Tennis Court, built in 1539 and the oldest in Britain.

---

623 FALLS OF CLYDE WILDLIFE RESERVE AND VISITOR CENTRE **6 L17**

The Dyeworks, New Lanark, Lanarkshire. 30 miles (48km) southeast of Glasgow. Bus from Lanark. Open Easter–Oct, Mon–Fri 1100–1700, Sat and Sun 1300–1700; Nov–Easter weekends only 1300–1700; closed Jan. Reserve open at all times and free. Free. Guided tours. Explanatory displays. Picnic area. WC. Wheelchair access to visitor centre. Disabled WC. Car and coach parking. Telephone (01555) 665262.

The most spectacular waterfalls in Britain set in ancient gorge woodlands with historical monuments dating from the 15th century. The visitor centre exhibition tells the story of the woods and the wildlife. Ranger service available for guided walks, badger watches, waterfall days and other events.

---

624 FALLS OF DOCHART **5 K13**

Killin. Access to this island and to the graveyard available from Tourist Information Centre in Killin. Free.

Dramatic waterfalls rushing through the centre of this picturesque Highland village. On the island of Inchbuie is the burial ground of Clan McNab.

---

625 FALLS OF FOYERS **3 J9**

Foyers, on the eastern shore of Loch Ness. Car park in village, then walk.

These falls which are particularly spectacular in spate are surrounded by woodland trails. The falls were visited and written about by Robert Burns.

---

626 FALLS OF GLOMACH **2 G8**

NTS. Highland. 18 miles (28km) east of Kyle of Lochalsh, northeast off A87. Open all year. Free. Car and coach parking.

At 370 feet (112m), this is one of the highest waterfalls in Britain, set in a steep narrow cleft in remote countryside. The falls are a 5 mile (8km) walk from the car park at Dorusduain.

---

627 FALLS OF ROGIE **3 J7**

2 miles (3km) west of Strathpeffer. Access at all times. Free. Car parking.

The word Rogie comes from the Norse language and means splashing foaming river. From the suspension bridge which spans the falls, salmon may be seen leaping.

628 FALLS OF SHIN 3 K5

Lairg, Sutherland. Off the A836, 5 miles (8km) north of Bonar Bridge. Bus from Inverness or Lairg. Salmon leap and waterfall open all year. Visitor centre open Mar–Oct, daily 1000–1800; Nov–Christmas, weekends only 1000–1700. Free. Gift shop. Restaurant. Children's play area. WC. Wheelchair access. Disabled WC. Car and coach parking. Telephone (01549) 402231.

Waterfalls in a beautiful wooded section of the Achany Glen. Popular for watching salmon leaping as they migrate upstream. The visitor centre is a popular stop.

---

629 FARAID HEAD AND BALNAKEIL BAY 3 J2

North of Durness, Sutherland.

The Balnakeil area is of outstanding nature conservation interest for its outcrops of Durness limestone and the associated plant communities. Faraid Head, behind the beautiful Balnakeil beach, is a narrow headland with dunes, coastal grasslands and steep cliffs. During the summer months a ranger service is operated from the tourist information centre where advice on guided walks and areas of wildlife interest can be obtained.

---

630 FARIGAIG 3 J9

FE. By Inverfarigaig on south side of Loch Ness, 18 miles (29km) southwest of Inverness. Open daily all year. Free. Forest exhibition. Public toilets open Easter–Sep. Wheelchair access. Car parking. Telephone (01320) 366322.

Farigaig Forest offers excellent views over Loch Ness and across Inverfarigaig to Dum Dearduil, the site of a vitrified Iron Age fort dating from around 500 BC. The forest comprises large specimen conifers, introduced from America during the last century, and a mixture of native trees including birch, rowan, alder, ash, willow, hazel, elm and oak.

---

631 FARM BUGGY TRAILS 5 M19

Cumstone Farm, Corrie, Lockerbie. 5.5 miles (9km) northeast of Lockerbie. Open Apr–Oct during daylight. Charge by activity. Guided trails. Tearoom. Pets corner. WC. Limited wheelchair access. Disabled WC. Car and coach parking. Telephone (01576) 710225.

Guided quad bike tours of various lengths, also go-carts on a custom built track, a small shooting gallery and small-animal shed.

---

632 FARMLIFE CENTRE 5 K14

Dunaverig, Ruskie, Thornhill, Stirling. On the A873, 12 miles west of Stirling, 3 miles (5km) west of Thornhill and 8 miles (13km) east of Aberfoyle. Nearest railway and bus station Stirling. Open daily Easter–Oct, 1000–1800. Charge ££. Group concessions available if booked in advance. Guided tours by prior arrangement. Explanatory displays. Gift shop. Tearoom. WC. Wheelchair access with assistance. Disabled WC. Car and coach parking. Telephone (01786) 850277.

An all-weather attraction. Children can enjoy pony and tractor rides, milk the goat, feed the animals or burn off energy in the outdoor adventure wood playground or indoor activity shed and playbarn. Lots of animals to see and meet. Suitable for children of all ages, from 1 to 100.

---

633 FASQUE 3 P11

Fasque, Fettercairn, Laurencekirk, Kincardineshire. On the B974, 0.5 mile (1km) north of Fettercairn village. Bus from Brechin or Laurencekirk. Open daily May–Sep, 1100–1700 (closes 1730). Charge ££. Guided tours. Explanatory displays. Gift shop. Tearoom and picnic area. WC. Limited wheelchair access. Car and coach parking. Telephone (01561) 320569.

A spectacular example of a Victorian 'upstairs-downstairs' stately home bought by Sir John Gladstone in 1829. Home to Prime Minister William Ewart Gladstone for much of his life. An unspoiled old family home where little has changed. Exhibition of William Gladstone memorabilia. Family church nearby welcomes visitors. Beautiful grounds with deer park.

---

634 FAST CASTLE **5 Q15**

Off A1107, 4 miles (6.5km) northwest of Coldingham. Access at all times. Free. Car parking.

The scant, but impressive remains of a Home stronghold, perched on a cliff above the sea. Care should be taken on the cliffs.

---

635 FERGUSSON GALLERY **5 M13**

Marshall Place, Perth. Corner of Tay Street, beside the river. 5–10 minute walk from bus and train station. Open all year (except Christmas and New Year), Mon–Sat 1000–1700. Free. Explanatory displays. Gift shop. WC. Enlarged label texts, wheelchair available on site. Limited wheelchair access. Disabled WC. Car and coach parking. Telephone (01738) 441944.

An art gallery devoted to the work of the Scottish colourist painter, John Duncan Fergusson (1874–1961) and housing the largest collection of his work. Three galleries, two of which are circular, show changing thematic displays of his paintings, drawings, watercolours and sculpture. An extensive archive is available for consultation by appointment.

---

636 FERNIEHIRST CASTLE **5 P18**

Lothian Estates Office, Jedburgh. On the A86, 2 miles (3km) south of Jedburgh. Nearest bus to Jedburgh, then taxi or transport to castle by prior arrangement with estate office. Open Jul only, Tue–Sun 1100–1600. Charge £. Guided tours. Explanatory displays. Gift shop. Riverside walk. WC. Limited wheelchair access. Disabled WC. Car and coach parking. Telephone (01835) 862201.

A 16th-century Border castle and Scotland's frontier fortress. The ancestral home of the Kerr family; restored by the clan chief, the Marquis of Lothian. Information centre, chapel, Kerr museum and private apartments.

---

637 FERRYCROFT COUNTRYSIDE CENTRE **3 K5**

Lairg, Sutherland. Nearest railway station Lairg. Bus service from Inverness. Open Apr, May and Oct, Mon–Sat 0930–1730; Jun–Sep, also Sun 1000–1700. Free. Explanatory displays. Gift shop. Picnic area. Garden with play equipment. WC. Wheelchair access. Disabled WC. Car and coach parking. Telephone (01549) 402160.

A tourist information centre where visitors can learn about Sutherland. The audio-visual displays show the many changes to Sutherland's landscape from the Ice Age to the present day. Themes include forest cover, inhabitants, hydro-electric schemes, wildlife, conservation and archaeology. There are indoor puzzles and a play area for children. Visitors can also book accommodation, get angling permits, maps and books, and exchange currency. Archaeological trail and forest walks.

---

638 FETLAR INTERPRETIVE CENTRE **1 H2**

Beach of Houbie, Fetlar, Shetland. On the island of Fetlar, 4 miles (6.5km) from the car ferry. Open May–Sep, Tue–Sun 1200–1700. Free. Guided tours (available in French, German and Italian). Explanatory displays. Gift shop. Picnic area. WC. Wheelchair access. Disabled WC. Car and coach parking. Telephone (01957) 207.

A museum and visitor information centre with interpretive displays on Fetlar's history, folklore, flora and fauna and geology. Includes an extensive archive of photographs, audio recordings and videos of film from the 1930s onwards, and interactive multi-media displays.

---

639 FETTERCAIRN ARCH **3 P11**

In Fettercairn. On B9120, 4 miles (6.5km) west of Laurencekirk, Kincardineshire. Access at all times. Free.

Stone arch built to commemorate the visit by Queen Victoria and the Prince Consort in 1861.

---

640 FETTERCAIRN DISTILLERY VISITOR CENTRE **3 P11**

Distillery Road, Fettercairn, Laurencekirk. 0.5 mile (1km) west of Fettercairn. Bus from Brechin or Laurencekirk. Open May–Sep, Mon–Sat 1000–1630. Last tour 1600. Free. Guided tours. Explanatory displays with information sheets in different languages. Gift shop. WC. Limited wheelchair access. Disabled WC. Car and coach parking. Telephone (01561) 340205.

A distillery visitor centre with tours which describe the processes of whisky making. Audio-visual. Includes a free dram of Old Fettercairn (10-year-old malt whisky).

---

641 FIFE AIRPORT **6 N14**

Goatmilk, Glenrothes, Fife. Off the B921, 2 miles (3km) west of Glenrothes. Nearest railway station Kirkcaldy or Thornton, bus from Glenrothes then short walk, taxi or (by arrangement) minibus from bus or rail stations. Open daily, Apr–Oct 0830–2100, Nov–Mar 0830–1800. Explanatory displays. Gift shop. Restaurant and bar (open 1030–1400 and 1830–2100). Beer garden. WC. No guide dogs. Wheelchair access. Disabled WC. Car parking. Telephone (01592) 753792.

A regional airport which is also the home of Fife Flying Club, providing all forms of flying training. Includes the Tipsy Nipper Restaurant, with good views of the airfield.

---

642 FIFE FOLK MUSEUM **5 N14**

The Weigh House, High Street, Ceres, Fife. Bus from Cupar, St Andrews, Dundee or Kirkcaldy. Easter and May–Oct, daily 1400–1700. Charge £. Children under 5 free. Group concessions. Guided tours by arrangement. Explanatory displays. Gift shop. Terraced garden. Limited wheelchair access. Car and coach parking. Telephone (01334) 828180.

A local museum housed in a 17th-century tolbooth and 18th-century cottages overlooking the Ceres Burn. The collection illustrates the social, economic and cultural history of rural Fife and includes an outdoor display of agricultural implements. There is a heritage trail.

---

643 FINAVON DOOCOT **5 P12**

NTS. Angus. 6 miles (10km) north of Forfar, off A90. Open all year. Free. Explanatory displays. Car and coach parking. Telephone (01738) 631296.

A 16th-century dovecot, the largest in Scotland, Finavon Doocot had 2400 nesting boxes. It is believed to have been built by the Earl of Crawford. Visitors should obtain the key from the Finavon Hotel.

---

644 FINDHORN FOUNDATION COMMUNITY **3 M7**

The Park, Findhorn, Forres. Off the A96, 25 miles (40km) east of Inverness. Nearest railway station and coach stop Forres, local bus from Forres. Visitor Centre open Apr–Oct, Mon–Fri 0900–1230 and 1400–1700, Sat and Sun 1400–1700; Oct–Mar, daily 1400–1700. Free. Charge for tour. Group concessions. Guided tours (by arrangement in Dutch, French, German, Italian, Portuguese and Spanish). Explanatory displays. Gift shop. Café. Gardens. WC. Wheelchair access. Disabled WC. Car and coach parking. Telephone (01309) 690311.

The Findhorn Foundation Community was established in 1962 and has grown from a handful of people to more than 400. Visitors can see the ecological village with gardens, ecological barrel houses, turf roofs, innovative architecture, renewable energy sources such as a wind turbine and solar panels, and a Living Machine natural sewage treatment system.

---

645 FINDHORN IN TIME AND TIDE **3 M7**

Northshore, Findhorn, Forres. 5 miles (8km) northeast of Forres, from Kinloss take B9011 to Findhorn. Nearest railway station Forres; local bus service from Forres to Findhorn. Open Easter and Jun–Aug, Wed–Mon 1400–1700; May and Sep, Sat and Sun 1400–1700. Charge £. Group concessions. Guided tours. Explanatory displays. Gift shop. Children's activity area. WC. Wheelchair access. Disabled WC. Car and coach parking. Telephone (01309) 690659.

Based in two salmon fishers' huts and the ice house. One hut is laid out as a salmon fishers' bothy of days gone by, the other is filled with exhibits and illustrated panels which trace the development of Findhorn from prehistoric times to the present. The fascinating ice house (pre-1816) is a particularly fine example of our industrial heritage.

---

646 FINLAGGAN TRUST **4 D16**

The Cottage, Ballygrant, Isle of Islay. 2 miles (3km) off A846 from Port Askaig. Open Apr, Sun, Tue and Thu 1430–1700; May–Sep, Sun–Fri 1430–1700 also Mon–Tue 1000–1300; Oct, Sun, Tue and Thu 1400–1600. Charge £. Group concessions. Explanatory displays. Gift shop. WC. Car and coach parking. Telephone (01496) 840644.

Islay is known as the Cradle of Clan Donald and Finlaggan, as the main headquarters of the Lords of the Isles, is a place of pilgrimmage for clan members today. The interpretive centre describes the history of the area and details the archaeological finds to-date.

---

647 FLAG HERITAGE CENTRE

See 99 Athelstaneford Heritage Centre.

---

648 FLAT CAT GALLERY **5 P16**

2 Market Place, Lauder, Berwickshire. In Lauder town centre, off A68. Bus from Edinburgh to Jedburgh stops in town. Open all year, daily 0930–1700. Free. Explanatory displays. Gift shop. Coffee shop. Children's toy box. WC. Wheelchair access. Disabled WC. Telephone (01578) 722808.

Changing exhibitions of paintings, sculpture, ceramics, jewellery and furniture by artists from the Borders and further afield. Also a resident restorer of middle-eastern rugs and textiles. A good stock of carpets on display.

---

649 FLODDEN MONUMENT **5 N17**

Town centre, Selkirk. Access at all times. Free.

The monument was erected in 1913 on the 400th anniversary of the battle and is inscribed 'O Flodden Field'. The memorial is the work of sculptor Thomas Clapperton, and commemorates the lone survivor of the 80 Selkirk men who marched to Flodden.

---

650 FLOORS CASTLE **5 Q17**

Kelso. In Kelso. Open mid Apr–Oct, daily 1000–1630. Charge ££. Group concessions. Guided tours by prior arrangement. Explanatory displays. Gift shop. Restaurant, tearoom with outdoor seating, and picnic area. Garden Centre. WC. Wheelchair access with assistance. Disabled WC. Car and coach parking. Telephone (01573) 223333.

Floors Castle is the home of the Roxburghe family. The apartments display an outstanding collection of French 17th- and 18th-century furniture, many fine works of art and tapestries, Chinese and Dresden porcelain and a Victorian collection of birds. The extensive parkland and gardens overlooking the River Tweed provide delightful walks and picnic areas. The walled garden contains splendid herbaceous borders and is best seen in July, August and September.

---

651 FLOW COUNTRY **3 M3**

Caithness. At Golticlay, just north of Rumster Forest on the Lybster to Achavanich road.

A view of the open peatlands of central Caithness. To the west, beyond Loch Rangag and Loch Ruard, these ancient peatlands have remained unchanged for thousands of years. Blar nam Faoileag National Nature Reserve is visible and is part of the largest single expanse of actively growing blanket bog remaining in Britain. These peatlands, with their extraordinary surface patterns of pools and ridges, collectively form what is commonly known as the Flow Country.

---

652 FOCHABERS FOLK MUSEUM **3 N7**

High Street, Fochabers, Moray. Nearest railway station Elgin, then bus to Fochabers. Open all year, summer 0930–1300 and 1400–1800; winter, closes 1700. Free. Explanatory displays. Gift shop. Limited wheelchair access. Car and coach parking. Telephone (01343) 821204.

A museum in a former church showing the history of Fochabers over the past 200 years. Includes a large collection of horse-drawn carts and a varied collection of local items.

---

653 FORDYCE JOINER'S WORKSHOP VISITOR CENTRE **3 P7**

Church Street, Fordyce, Banffshire. In Fordyce 4 miles (6.5km) southwest of Portsoy. Open Easter–Sep, Thu–Mon 1000–1800. Free. Explanatory displays. Garden. WC. Wheelchair access. Disabled WC. Telephone (01771) 622906.

Visitors can learn about the importance of the rural carpenter/joiner to the local community over the 150 years, in the days before mass-produced goods. Displays of early tools and machinery, photographs, and an audio-visual presentation. Demonstration by wood craftsman. Victorian style garden. Fordyce is one of Scotland's best conserved small villages and largely traffic-free. It is built around a 16th-century castle and an early church containing splendid canopied tombs.

---

654 FORSINARD NATURE RESERVE **3 L3**

RSPB. Visitor Centre, Forsinard Station, Forsinard, Sutherland. On the A897, 26 miles (41.5km) inland from Helmsdale. Nearest railway station Forsinard (no bus). Open Easter–Oct, daily 0900–1800. Free. Guided tours. Explanatory displays. WC. Wheelchair access to visitor centre. Car and coach parking. Telephone (01641) 571225.

A nature reserve forming 46,950 acres (19,000ha) of rolling peatland in the heart of the world-famous Flow Country. The unique blanket bogs contain thousands of bog pools, with insect-eating plants, dragonflies and many rare birds. Guided walks (in summer) and self-guided pool trail.

---

655 FORT CHARLOTTE **1 G5**

HS. Lerwick, Shetland. In centre of town. Open Apr–Sep, Mon–Sat 0900–1830, Sun 1400–1830. Free. Telephone 0131 668 8800.

A pentagonal artillery fort, with bastions projecting from each corner and massive and high walls. Built in 1665 to protect the Sound of Bressay from the Dutch, but taken by them and burned in 1673. Rebuilt in 1781.

---

656 FORT GEORGE **3 K7**

HS. Visitor Centre, Ardersier, Inverness. Off the A96, by Ardersier, 11 miles (17.5km) east of Inverness. Nearest railway station Inverness, bus service and tour bus from Inverness. Open Apr–Sep, daily 0930–1830; Oct–Mar, Mon–Sat 0930–1630, Sun 1400–1630. Charge ££. Group concessions. Guided tours. Explanatory displays and visitor centre. Gift shop. Tearoom and picnic area. WC. Wheelchair access. Disabled WC. Car and coach parking. Telephone (01667) 462777.

A vast site of one of the most outstanding artillery fortifications in Europe. It was planned in 1747 as a base for George II's army and was completed in 1769. Since then it has served as a barracks. It is virtually unaltered and presents a complete view of the defensive system. There is a reconstruction of barrack rooms in different periods and a display of muskets and pikes. Includes the Regimental Museum of the Queen's Own Highlanders.

---

657 FORTH AND CLYDE CANAL **6 K16**

Between the Rivers Forth and Clyde. Fishing, canoeing, etc by permit. Countryside ranger service. Guided walks and canal events during summer months. Telephone 0141 332 6936.

The Forth and Clyde and the Union Canals formed an important commercial transport corridor across central Scotland for nearly two centuries. They fell victim to the roads culture of the 1960s when they were blocked at more than 30 sites and broken up into short sections. One of the biggest canal restoration projects in Europe, the Millennuim Link will bring the 69 miles (110km) of canal, from Glasgow to Edinburgh, and the Forth to the Clyde back to life. The towing path provides delightful walks through town and country with plenty of interest for both nature and history enthusiasts. Excursions by canal boat are available. See also 621 Falkirk Wheel.

---

658 FORTH BRIDGES EXHIBITION **6 M15**

Queensferry Lodge Hotel, St Margaret's Head, North Queensferry, Fife. On the B981 off the A90, 8 miles (13km) north of Edinburgh. Bus or train from Edinburgh. Open all year (except Christmas) 0900–2100. Free. Explanatory displays. Gift shop. Restaurant and coffee shop. WC. Wheelchair access with assistance. Disabled WC. Car and coach parking. Telephone (01383) 410000.

An exhibition telling the fascinating story of the rail and road bridges. Also a 40 minute video presentation. The bridges can be viewed from a gallery, or travel over the road bridge to South Queensferry for a stunning view of both bridges. See also 156 Edinburgh, Forth Rail Bridge.

---

659 FORTH JET **6 M15**

Hawes Pier, New Halls Road, South Queensferry, West Lothian. Off the A90, 8 miles (13km) northwest of Edinburgh. Nearest railway station Dalmeny. Open Jun–Aug, daily; Apr–May and Sep–Oct, Sat, Sun and Public Holidays. Charge £££. Group concessions. Guided tours. WC. Wheelchair access. Car and coach parking. Telephone 0131 331 4777.

A range of boat tours for all ages. See the Forth Rail Bridge (156) and a wide variety of bird and sealife. The tours include a visit to the seal colonies off Inchcolm island, and the Oxcars lighthouse.

---

660 FORTINGALL YEW **5 K12**

Fortingall, 9 miles (14.5km) west of Aberfeldy. Access at all reasonable times. Car parking.

The surviving part of the great yew in an enclosure in the churchyard is reputedly over 3000 years old, perhaps the oldest tree in Europe. The attractive village, which was rebuilt in 1900 with many thatched cottages, is claimed to be the birthplace of Pontius Pilate and has been a religious centre since St Columban times.

---

661 FORTROSE CATHEDRAL **3 K7**

HS. In Fortrose, Ross and Cromarty, 8 miles (13km) south southwest of Cromarty. Nearest railway and bus stations Inverness, bus to Fortrose. Open at all times. Free. Car parking. Telephone 0131 668 8800.

The surviving fragments consist of the 13th-century vaulted undercroft of the chapter house and the south aisle of the nave, a 14th-century vaulted structure, both finely worked, with two canopied monuments and other memorials.

---

662 FOULDEN TITHE BARN **5 R16**

HS. On the A6105, 4 miles (6.5km) southeast of Chirnside, Berwickshire. Bus from Berwick-upon-Tweed to Duns. View exterior only. Telephone 0131 668 8800.

A two-storey tithe barn with outside stair and crow-stepped gables.

---

663 FOWLIS WESTER SCULPTURED STONE **5 L13**

HS. In the church at Fowlis Wester, 6 miles (9.5km) northeast of Crieff, Perthshire. Nearest railway station Perth; bus from Perth to Fowlis Wester. Access at all times. Free. Telephone 0131 668 8800.

A tall cross-slab carved with Pictish symbols, figure sculpture and Celtic enrichment. A replica stands in the village square.

---

664 FRASERBURGH HERITAGE CENTRE **3 R7**

Quarry Road, Fraserburgh, Aberdeenshire. In Fraserburgh town centre, to the north of the harbour. Open Apr–Oct, Mon–Sat 1000–1700, Sun 1230–1700; Nov–Mar, Tue–Sat 1000–1500, Sun 1300–1600. Charge £. Children under 5 free. Group concessions. Guided tours by prior arrangement. Explanatory displays. Gift shop. Activities. WC. Wheelchair access. Car and coach parking. Telephone (01346) 512888.

The centre describes the history of Fraserburgh and its community over the past 400 years, from the bustling quayside to the haute couture of dress designer Bill Gibb.

---

665 FYRISH MONUMENT **3 K7**

Above village of Evanton on Fyrish Hill, off A9. Access at all times. Free.

Curious monument erected in 1782 by Sir Hector Munro who rose from the ranks and distinguished himself at the relief of Seringapatam. The monument is a replica of the Indian gateway and was built to provide work at a time of poverty and unemployment in the Evanton area.

---

666 FYVIE CASTLE **3 Q8**

NTS. Fyvie, Turriff, Aberdeenshire. Off A947, 8 miles (12.5km) southeast of Turriff and 25 miles (40km) northwest of Aberdeen. Bus from Aberdeen bus station to Fyvie village (1 mile/1.5km). Castle open late Apr–May and Sep, daily 1330–1730; Jun–Aug, daily 1100–1730; weekends in Oct 1330–1730. Grounds open all year, daily 0930–sunset. Charge £££. Children free. Group concessions. Guided tours by arrangement. Explanatory displays. Information sheets in six languages. Gift shop. Tearoom and picnic area. WC. Braille sheet and guidebook. Limited wheelchair access, wheelchair available. Disabled WC. Car and coach parking. Telephone (01651) 891266.

The castle is probably the grandest example of Scottish baronial architecture. The five towers of Fyvie Castle enshrine five centuries of Scottish history, each being named after one of the five families who owned the castle. The oldest part dates from the 13th century. Contemporary decoration, important collection of portraits, arms and armour, and 17th-century tapestries. The grounds and Fyvie Loch were designed around the beginning of the 18th century. Castles of Mar exhibition, restored racquets court, ice house, bird hide, restored patent earth closet, lochside walks.

---

667 GAELIC WHISKIES – WHISKY EXHIBITION **2 F9**

An Oifig, Eilean Iarmain, Sleat, Isle of Skye. On the A851, 8 miles (13km) south of Broadford. Bus from Armadale or Broadford. Open all year, Mon–Fri 0900–1730; Oct–May closed 1300–1400; Jun–Sep, Sat 1000–1400. Free. Explanatory displays and short talk (English or Gaelic). Gift shop. Meals available in Hotel Eilean Iarmain next door. Art Gallery open in summer. WC. Wheelchair access. Car and coach parking. Telephone (01471) 833266.

The only whisky company with its headquarters in the Hebrides. An exhibition about whisky is located in historic buildings, once the Isle Ornsay harbour shop.

---

668 GAIRLOCH HERITAGE MUSEUM **2 F6**

Achtercairn, Gairloch, Ross and Cromarty. In Gairloch, on A832 70 miles (112km) northwest of Inverness. Bus from Inverness or Achnasheen (station). Open Easter–mid Oct, Mon–Sat 1000–1700; mid Oct–end Oct, Mon–Fri 1030–1300. Winter by prior arrangement. Charge £. Group concessions. Explanatory displays. Gift shop. Restaurant. Hands-on activities for children; demonstrations and talks. WC. Wheelchair access. Car and coach parking. Telephone (01445) 712287.

A heritage centre displaying all aspects of life in a typical West Highland parish from the Stone Age to the present day, including archaeology, fishing, agriculture and domestic arts. Reconstructed croft-house room, schoolroom, dairy and shop. Millennuim exhibition with hands-on activities. The local lighthouse and preserved fishing boats are outside. Archive and library.

---

669 GAIRLOCH MARINE LIFE CENTRE AND SAIL GAIRLOCH **2 F6**

Pier Road, Gairloch, Ross-shire. At Gairloch harbour on A832. Infrequent bus service from Inverness. Open May–mid Sep, Mon–Fri 0930–1600, Sat–Sun 1200–1530; Easter and late Sep, Mon–Fri 1000–1400, telephone to confirm. Free. Charge £££ for cruises (duration 2 hours minimum). Guided tours. Explanatory displays. Gift shop. Wheelchair access. Disabled WC. Car parking. Telephone (01445) 712636.

Porpoise, dolphin and whale surveys have been conducted for the Sea Watch Foundation for over ten years. At the centre, visitors can see photo displays, video and computer presentation, maps and charts along with survey records. The whole of marine life is covered, from jellyfish through to birds, seals and whales. Sail Gairloch Cruises take place daily subject to weather conditions and demand.

---

670 GALLERY FORTEVIOT **5 M13**

Forteviot, Perthshire. 5 miles (8km) south of Perth on the B935 Bridge of Earn to Dunning road. Nearest railway station Perth, bus service to Dunning. Open Mar–Dec, Tue–Sun 1030–1730. Free. Explanatory displays. Free coffee. WC. Wheelchair access. Car parking. Telephone (01764) 684319.

Regular exhibitions of contemporary painting, sculpture, photography and printmaking. Also ceramics and furniture.

671 GALLOWAY COUNTRY STYLE **5 K20**

High Street, Gatehouse-of-Fleet. In Gatehouse-of-Fleet. Bus from Dumfries or Stranraer. Open all year except Christmas and New Year, Mon–Sat 1000–1700. Free. Guided tours by arrangement. Explanatory displays. Gift shop. Coffee shop. Children's play area. WC. Wheelchair access. Disabled WC. Car and coach parking. Telephone (01557) 814001.

A kilt-making workshop where visitors can see operations and also learn about the history of kilts and how they are made.

---

672 GALLOWAY DEER RANGE **4 J20**

Laggan O'Dee, New Galloway. 10 miles (16km) from Newton Stewart and 9 miles (14.5km) from New Galloway on A712. Open late Jun–mid Sep, walks Tue and Thu 1100 and 1400, Sun 1430. Charge £. Guided tours. Explanatory displays. No guide dogs. Car and coach parking. Telephone (07771) 748400 or 401.

Created in 1977 to enable visitors to see red deer in a semi-natural habitat of 500 acres (200ha). Good photo opportunities.

---

673 GALLOWAY SAILING CENTRE **5 K20**

Parton, Castle Douglas, Kirkcudbrightshire. On the A713, 10 miles (16km) north of Castle Douglas, on the shore of Loch Ken. Nearest railway station Dumfries, bus from Dumfries/Castle Douglas. Collection from rail station by arrangement. Open Apr–Oct, daily 0900–1800. Free. Charge for activities. Group concessions. Explanatory displays. Gift shop. Café and picnic area. Children's play area. WC. Wheelchair access with assistance. Disabled WC. Car and coach parking. Telephone (01644) 420626.

Provides tuition in sailing, windsurfing and canoeing. Also improvised raft-building, quad bikes and gorge scrambling. Residential courses and boat hire. Groups welcome.

---

674 GARLOGIE MILL POWER HOUSE MUSEUM **3 Q9**

Garlogie, Skene, Aberdeenshire. Near the B9119/B9125 junction, 11 miles (17.5km) west of Aberdeen. Nearest railway station Inverurie, bus from Inverurie. Open May–Sep, Thu–Mon 1230–1700. Free. Explanatory displays. Gift shop. Picnic area. WC. Limited wheelchair access. Disabled WC. Car and coach parking. Telephone (01771) 622906.

Visitors can relive the early days of the industrial revolution and see the rare beam engine which powered the woollen mill, the only one of its type to have survived intact in its original location. Displays feature the history of the mill, with award-winning audio-visual presentation.

---

675 GARVAMORE BRIDGE **3 K10**

6 miles (9.5km) west of Laggan Bridge, 17 miles (27km) southwest of Newtonmore. Access at all times. Free.

This two-arched bridge at the south side of the Corrieyairick Pass was built by General Wade in 1735.

---

676 GEILSTON GARDEN **6 J15**

NTS. Cardross, Dumbarton. On A814 at west end of Cardross, 18 miles (29km) north of Glasgow. Nearest railway station Cardross, then 1 mile (1.5km) walk. Bus from Helensburgh or Dumbarton. Open Apr–Oct, daily 0930–1700. Charge £. Honesty box. Children free. Explanatory displays. WC. Limited wheelchair access. Disabled WC. Car and coach parking. Telephone (01389) 841867.

Small estate typical of those owned on the banks of the Clyde by tobacco barons and factory owners who made their money in 19th-century Glasgow. Charming garden with walled area and wooded glen.

677 GENEALOGY AND EXHIBITION CENTRE, CO LEIS THU? **2 C6**

The Old Schoolhouse, Northton, Isle of Harris. 17 miles (27km) south of Tarbert on A859. Ferry service from Uig and North Uist, bus service from Stornoway or Tarbert. Open all year, Mon–Sat 1000–1800 and by appointment for evenings and bank holidays. Charge £. Group concessions. Guided tours (also available in Gaelic). Explanatory displays. Gift and book shop. Refreshments and picnic area. WC. Wheelchair access with assistance. Disabled WC. Car and coach parking. Telephone (01859) 520258.

Genealogical resource and research centre plus general history exhibitions.

---

678 LADY GIFFORD STATUE **5 M16**

Village clock, in West Linton, 17 miles (27km) south southwest of Edinburgh. Access at all reasonable times.

Statue on the front of the village clock at West Linton, carved in 1666 by the Laird Gifford, a Covenanter and skilled stonemason. The clock is on the site of a well, disused since Victorian times. Laird Gifford also executed panels (1660 and 1678) on a house opposite, depicting Lady Gifford and the entire family genealogy.

---

679 GILNOCKIE TOWER **5 N19**

Hollows, Canonbie, Dumfriesshire. On the A7, 2 miles (3km) north of Canonbie. Bus from Carlisle or Galashiels. Tours Easter–Oct 1000 and 1430; at other times by appointment. Charge £. Group concessions. Guided tours. Explanatory displays. Gift shop. WC. No guide dogs. Car and coach parking. Telephone (01387) 371876.

A tower house built in 1525 by the Border freebooter Johnie Armstrong and originally called Holehouse (from the quarry beside which it stands). Managed by the Clan Armstrong Centre.

---

680 GLADSTONE COURT MUSEUM **5 M17**

North Back Road, Biggar, Lanarkshire. On the A702, 26 miles (41.5km) south of Edinburgh. Bus from Biggar or Edinburgh. Open Easter–Oct, Mon–Sat 1000–1230 and 1400–1700, Sun 1400–1700. Charge £. Group concessions. Guided tours. Explanatory displays. Gift shop. Activity sheets and hands-on sessions for children. WC. Limited wheelchair access. Car and coach parking. Telephone (01899) 221050.

An indoor street museum of shops and windows. Grocer, photographer, dress maker, bank, school, library, ironmonger, chemist, china merchant, telephone exchange.

---

681 GLAMIS CASTLE **5 M12**

Glamis, Angus. On A94, 6 miles (9.5km) west of Forfar. Bus from Dundee. Open daily Apr–Oct, 1030–1730, Jul–Aug opens 1000; Nov 1030–1600. Charge £££. Wheelchair users free admission. Group concessions. Guided tours (by arrangement in French, German, Italian, Spanish or Portuguese, for groups). Explanatory displays. Gift shop. Restaurant, kiosk and picnic area. Playpark, garden. WC. Disabled WC. Car and coach parking. Telephone (01307) 840393.

There has been a building on this site from very early times and Malcolm II is said to have died here in 1034. One of the oldest parts is Duncan's Hall, legendary setting for Shakespeare's Macbeth. The present castle was modified in the 17th century. Famous for being the childhood home of Queen Elizabeth, The Queen Mother, and birthplace of Princess Margaret. Fine collections of china, painting, tapestries and furniture. Two exhibitions, Coach House and Elizabeth of Glamis. Annual events include the Strathmore Vintage Vehicle Club Extravaganza and a Grand Scottish Prom (both in July). Nature trails and pinetum.

682 GLASGOW ART GALLERY AND MUSEUM, KELVINGROVE 6 K16

Kelvingrove, Glasgow. Located in the west end of Glasgow. Nearest railway station Partick, nearest underground station Kelvinhall. Bus service from city centre. Open all year, Mon–Thu and Sat 1000–1700, Fri and Sun 1100–1700. Free. Guided tours. Explanatory displays. Gift shop. Café and picnic area. WC. Wheelchair access. Disabled WC. Car and coach parking. Telephone 0141 287 2700.

This fine national art collection contains superb paintings and sculptures, silver and ceramics, European armour, weapons and firearms, clothing, and furniture. The natural history of Scotland is treated in depth and there are displays of relics from Scotland's history and prehistory. Activities for children and temporary exhibitions.

---

683 GLASGOW, THE BARRAS 6 K16

Gallowgate. 0.25 miles (0.5km) east of Glasgow Cross. Open all year, Sat and Sun 0900–1700, Wed–Fri 1000–1600. Free.

Glasgow's world-famous market, with an amazing variety of stalls and shops. Founded one hundred years ago, the Barras is now home to over 800 traders. Look out for the Barras archways, children's crèche and buskers. Numerous licensed premises and cafés. All markets are covered.

---

684 GLASGOW, BEARSDEN BATHHOUSE 6 J15

HS. On Roman Road, Bearsden, near Glasgow. Nearest railway station Glasgow, bus from centre. Access at all times. Free. Wheelchair access with assistance. Telephone 0131 668 8800.

The well-preserved remains of a bathhouse and latrine built in the 2nd century AD to serve a fort. See also 62 Antonine Wall.

---

685 GLASGOW BOTANIC GARDEN 6 J15

730 Great Western Road, Glasgow. At the west end of Glasgow off the A82, 1.5 miles (2.5km) from the city centre. Bus from city centre or underground to Hillhead station. Open all year, 0700–dusk; glasshouses and Kibble Palace open 1000–1645 (1615 in winter); main range of glasshouses open Mon–Fri as above, Sat 1300–1645 (1615 in winter), Sun 1200–1645 (1615 in winter). Free. Guided tours by arrangement. Explanatory displays. Café. WC. Wheelchair access. Disabled WC. Telephone 0141 334 2422.

The gardens were formed in 1817 to provide a source of plant material for use in teaching medicine and botany. Today they are valued by tourists and as a centre for education, conservation and research. Specialist plant collections include exotic Australian tree and filmy ferns, orchids and tropical begonias.

---

686 GLASGOW, THE BURRELL COLLECTION 6 J16

Pollok Country Park, 2060 Pollokshaws Road, Glasgow. Nearest railway stations, Pollokshaws West or Shawlands, bus service from city centre. Park bus runs every hour, on the half hour, from front entrance of park to the Burrell. Open all year, Mon–Thu and Sat 1000–1700, Fri and Sun 1100–1700. Free. Guided tours (available in French and German). Explanatory displays. Gift shop. Restaurant and café. WC. Audio-guides for visually impaired visitors. Wheelchair access. Disabled WC. Car and coach parking. Telephone 0141 287 2550.

This award-winning building houses a world-famous collection gifted to Glasgow by Sir William Burrell. Visitors can see art objects from Iraq, Egypt, Greece and Italy. Tapestries, furniture, textiles, ceramics, stained glass and sculptures from medieval Europe, and drawings from the 15th to 19th centuries. Regular temporary exhibitions.

687 GLASGOW CATHEDRAL **6 K16**

HS. Cathedral Square, Glasgow. At the east end of Cathedral Street. Nearest railway station Glasgow Queen Street, bus from city centre. Open Apr–Sep, Mon–Sat 0900–1830, Sun 1400–1830; Oct–Mar, Mon–Sat 0900–1630, Sun 1400–1630. Free. Guided tours. Gift shop. Wheelchair access. Telephone 0141 552 6891.

The only Scottish mainland medieval cathedral to have survived the Reformation complete (apart from its western towers). Built during the 12th and 13th centuries over the supposed tomb of St Kentigern. Notable features are the elaborately vaulted crypt, the stone screen and the unfinished Blackadder Aisle. The parish church of Glasgow.

---

688 GLASGOW, CITY CHAMBERS **6 K16**

George Square, Glasgow. In George Square, Glasgow city centre. Nearest railway station Glasgow Queen Street. Open all year, Mon–Fri 0830–1700; tours Mon–Fri 1030 and 1430, telephone to confirm. Free. Guided tours (translations in other languages). Leaflet available. Gift shop. Coffee shop. WC. Wheelchair access. Disabled WC. Telephone 0141 287 2000.

The City Chambers is the headquarters of Glasgow City Council and arguably Glasgow's finest example of Victorian architecture. The building was opened in 1888 by Queen Victoria and to this day has preserved all its original features.

---

689 GLASGOW, CLYDE MARITIME MUSEUM **6 K16**

The Tall Ship at Glasgow Harbour, Clyde Maritime Centre Ltd, 100 Stobcross Road, Glasgow. From Glasgow city centre, follow signs for SECC West off Clydeside Expressway. Nearest railway station Finnieston/ Exhibition Centre; local bus to SECC. Open all year, Mon–Sat 1000–1800. Charge ££. Group concessions. Explanatory displays. Gift shop. Restaurant and café-bar. Children's activities. WC. Limited wheelchair access. Disabled WC. Car and coach parking. Telephone 0141 339 0631.

The principal attraction is an opportunity to board the 103-year-old restored sailing ship *Glenlee*, the only Clyde-built sailing ship afloat in the UK. The Pumphouse Building (1877) also houses exhibitions.

---

690 GLASGOW, COLLINS GALLERY **6 K16**

University of Strathclyde, 22 Richmond Street, Glasgow. Glasgow city centre. Nearest railway station, Glasgow Queen Street, 5 minutes walk. Open all year Mon–Fri 1000–1700, Sat 1200–1600, closed Sun and public holidays and exhibition changeover weeks. Free. Guided tours by arrangement. Explanatory displays. Gift shop. Refreshments. WC. Wheelchair access. Disabled WC. Telephone 0141 548 2558.

Temporary exhibition gallery showing annual programme of ten shows ranging from contemporary, fine and applied art to multi-media installations. Active education programme. Most works are for sale.

---

691 GLASGOW, FOSSIL GROVE **6 J15**

Victoria Park, Glasgow. Nearest railway station Jordanhill, bus from Argyle Street or from Hope Street. Open daily Apr–Sep, 1200–1700. Free. Explanatory displays. Gift shop. WC. Wheelchair access. Disabled WC. Car and coach parking. Telephone 0141 950 1448.

Glasgow's oldest tourist attraction, discovered by accident and now designated a Site of Special Scientific Interest by Scottish Natural Heritage. Fossil stumps and roots of trees which grew here 350 million years ago.

---

692 GLASGOW, GALLERY OF MODERN ART **6 K16**

Queen Street, Glasgow. In Glasgow city centre. Nearest railway stations Glasgow Queen Street and Central Station; or by underground to Buchanan Street. Open all year (except Christmas and New Year),

Mon–Thu and Sat 1000–1700, Fri and Sun 1100–1700. Free. Guided tours. Explanatory displays. Gift shop. Restaurant/tearoom. WC. Wheelchair access. Disabled WC. Telephone 0141 229 1996.

The elegant Royal Exchange building displays works by living artists from across the world. A wide range of contemporary temporary exhibitions plus a programme of events including music, drama, dance and workshops.

---

693 GLASGOW, GEORGE SQUARE **6 K16**

Glasgow city centre. Access at all times. Free.

The heart of Glasgow with the City Chambers and statues of Sir Walter Scott, Queen Victoria, Prince Albert, Robert Burns, Sir John Moore, Lord Clyde, Thomas Campbell, Dr Thomas Graham, James Oswald, James Watt, William Gladstone and Sir Robert Peel.

---

694 GLASGOW, GREENBANK GARDEN **6 K16**

NTS. Flenders Road, Clarkston, Glasgow. Off M77 and A726, 6 miles (10km) south of city centre. By bus from city centre. Open all year except Christmas and New Year, daily 0930–sunset (walled garden closes 1700). Charge ££. Children free. Group concessions. Guided tours of garden. Explanatory displays. Gift shop. Tearoom in summer, picnic area. WC. Gardening advice for disabled. Wheelchair access, wheelchairs available. Disabled WC. Car and coach parking. Telephone 0141 639 3281.

Attractive garden surrounding an elegant Georgian house (only open Sunday 1400–1700 in summer). Wide range of ornamental plants, annuals, perennials, shrubs and trees – especially interesting for owners of small gardens. Fountain garden and woodland walks.

---

695 GLASGOW, HEATHERBANK MUSEUM OF SOCIAL WORK **6 K16**

Glasgow Caledonian University, City Campus, Cowcaddens Road, Glasgow. Near city centre. Nearest railway station Queen Street; by underground to Cowcaddens or bus to Buchanan Street. Open all year except public holidays, Mon–Fri 0900–1645. Free. Guided tours. Explanatory displays. Café. Book shop, sports centre. WC. Wheelchair access. Disabled WC. Car and coach parking. Telephone 0141 331 3000.

Permanent and temporary exhibitions to highlight public awareness of the social welfare needs of society through contemporary and historical issues. Book, picture resources and ephemera. Libraries and archives available for research.

---

696 GLASGOW, HOUSE FOR AN ART LOVER **6 J16**

Bellahouston Park, Glasgow. 3 miles (5km) south of city centre. Bus from city centre, by underground to Ibrox or train to Dumbreck. Open Apr–Sep, Sat–Thu 1000–1600; Oct–Mar, weekends 1000–1600, Mon–Fri by arrangement. Charge ££. Children under 10 free. Group concessions. Guided tours. Explanatory displays. Gift shop. Café. WC. Audio loop with video. Wheelchair access. Disabled WC. Car and coach parking. Telephone 0141 353 4449.

A house designed in 1901 by Charles Rennie Mackintosh but only built between 1989 and 1996. Exhibition and film showing the construction. Sculpture park. Situated in parkland adjacent to magnificent Victorian walled gardens.

---

697 GLASGOW, HUNTERIAN ART GALLERY **6 K16**

82 Hillhead Street, Glasgow. In the west end of Glasgow, near Hillhead underground station. Bus or underground from centre. Open all year, Mon–Sat 0930–1700 (Mackintosh House closed daily 1230–1330). Free. Explanatory displays. Gift shop. Sculpture courtyard. WC. Limited wheelchair access. Disabled WC. Telephone 0141 330 5431.

A prestigious art gallery housing many important works by old masters, impressionists and Scottish paintings from the 18th century to present. The William Hunter collection includes works by Chardin, Rembrandt and Koninck. Many important works by Whistler. The print gallery has a changing display from a collection of 15,000 prints. Also houses the Mackintosh House, a reconstructed interior of the architect's own house in Glasgow, using original furniture, prints and designs.

---

698 GLASGOW, HUNTERIAN MUSEUM **6 K16**

University of Glasgow, University Avenue, Glasgow. In the west end of Glasgow. Nearest underground station Hillhead or Kelvinbridge. Open all year (except public holidays), Mon–Sat 0930–1700. Free. Explanatory displays. Gift shop. Refreshments in visitor centre. WC. Limited wheelchair access. Car parking. Telephone 0141 330 4221.

Scotland's first public museum was established in 1807 based on the vast collections of Dr William Hunter (1718–83). Many items from his valuable collections are on display together with new and exciting additions. See displays of dinosaurs from Scotland, Romans in Scotland, geology, archaeology, the history of science and coins.

---

699 GLASGOW, HUTCHESONS' HALL **6 K16**

NTS. 158 Ingram Street, Glasgow. In city centre near both Central and Queen Street rail stations. Open all year (except public holidays and 24 Dec–6 Jan), Mon–Sat 1000–1700. Free. Explanatory displays and video programme. Gift shop. WC. Induction loop and subtitled video programme. Limited wheelchair access. Disabled WC. Telephone 0141 552 8391.

Built 1802–5, this is one of the most elegant buildings in Glasgow. Its frontage incorporates statues from an earlier building (1641) of local philanthropists George and Thomas Hutcheson. Enlarged in 1876.

---

700 GLASGOW, THE LIGHTHOUSE **6 K16**

11 Mitchell Lane, Glasgow. In Glasgow city centre, between Buchanan and Mitchell Streets. Within walking distance of Glasgow Central and Queen's Street railway stations, St Enochs and Buchanan Street underground stations, and all city centre buses. Open all year, Mon, Wed, Fri and Sat 1030–1730, Tue 1100–1730, Thu 1030–1930 and Sun 1200–1700. Charge £. Charge for Mackintosh Interpretation Centre only. Group concessions. Guided tours. Explanatory displays. Gift shop. Restaurant and café. WC. Induction loop. Wheelchair access. Disabled WC. Car parking. Telephone 0141 225 8414.

Scotland's Centre for Architecture, Design and the City, is the long-term legacy of Glasgow 1999 UK City of Architecture and Design. The Lighthouse is the imaginative conversion of Charles Rennie Mackintosh's first public commission and is located in the heart of the city centre. Mackintosh Interpretation Centre, interactive play environment for young children, IT hotspot, the Young Designers Gallery and temporary exhibitions.

---

701 GLASGOW, LITERARY TOUR **6 K16**

The Scottish Literary Tour Company Ltd, Suite 2, 97B West Bow, Edinburgh. Meet on George Square by the statue of Sir Walter Scott. Nearest railway station Glasgow Queen Street, Buchanan Street bus station 5 minutes walk. Tours Jun and Sep, Thu–Sun 1930; Jul and Aug, daily 1930. No booking required. Charge £££. Group concessions. Guided tours. Wheelchair access with assistance. Telephone 0131 226 6665/7.

This two hour promenade performance, led by professional actors moves between George Square and the Merchant City, past Glasgow Cathedral and other historic streets and buildings, exploring Glasgow's influence on writers and poets, ancient and modern.

---

702 GLASGOW, MCLELLAN GALLERIES **6 K16**

270 Sauchiehall Street, Glasgow. Nearest railway station Queen Street, nearest underground station Cowcaddens. Open for temporary exhibi-

tions only, telephone for details. Charges vary. Explanatory displays. Gift shop. WC. Wheelchair access. Disabled WC. Telephone 0141 332 7521.

This purpose-built exhibition gallery which opened in 1854 provides Glasgow with a superb temporary exhibition venue which is the largest outside London. Currently home of the Contemporary Centre for Art (CCA).

---

703 GLASGOW, MUSEUM OF TRANSPORT **6 K16**

Kelvin Hall, 1 Bunhouse Road, Glasgow. Located in the west end of Glasgow. Nearest railway station Partick, nearest underground station Kelvinhall. Bus service to city centre. Open all year, Mon–Thu and Sat 1000–1700; Fri and Sun 1100–1700. Free. Guided tours. Explanatory displays. Gift shop. Café. WC. Wheelchair access. Disabled WC. Car and coach parking. Telephone 0141 287 2700.

The history of transport on land and sea with vehicles from horse-drawn carriages to motor cycles, fire engines, railway engines, steam and motor cars. The Clyde Room has ship models and there is a recreation of a 1938 Glasgow street and a reconstructed underground station.

---

704 GLASGOW, NECROPOLIS **6 K16**

Behind Glasgow Cathedral. Access restricted: contact Cemeteries and Crematoria, 1st floor, 20 Trongate, Glasgow G1 5ES. Telephone 0141 287 3961.

Remarkable and extensive burial ground laid out in 1833, with numerous elaborate tombs of 19th-century illustrious Glaswegians and others; particularly the Menteith Mausoleum of 1842.

---

705 GLASGOW, PEOPLE'S PALACE **6 K16**

Glasgow Green, Glasgow. Nearest railway station Glasgow Central or Argyll Street, bus from city centre. Open all year, Mon–Thu and Sat 1000–1700, Fri and Sun 1100–1700. Free. Guided tours. Explanatory displays. Gift shop. Café. Winter Garden. WC. Wheelchair access. Disabled WC. Car and coach parking. Telephone 0141 554 0223.

Opened in 1898, this collection displays the story of Glasgow and its people, and its impact on the world from 1175 to the present day. Important collections relating to the tobacco and other industries, stained glass, ceramics, political and social movements including temperance, co-operation, woman's suffrage and socialism. Photographs, film sequences and reminiscences bring to life the city's past.

---

706 GLASGOW, PIPING CENTRE **6 K16**

30–34 McPhater Street, Cowcaddens, Glasgow. In the centre, 5–10 minute walk from rail stations and close to the Royal Scottish Academy of Music and Drama. Open all year, daily: museum 1000–1600; brasserie/bar Jun–Sep, Mon–Fri 0800–2200, Sat and Sun 1000–2200. Charge £. Group concessions. Guided tours (recordings in French, German or Italian). Explanatory displays. Gift shop. Café. WC. Limited wheelchair access. Disabled WC. Telephone 0141 353 0220.

A national and international centre of excellence for the bagpipes and its music, incorporating a school with rehearsal rooms and a performance hall, a museum and interpretation centre, and a reference library and conference facilities. Housed in a fine listed building.

---

707 GLASGOW, POLLOK HOUSE **6 J16**

NTS. Pollok Country Park, 2060 Pollokshaws Road, Glasgow. Off M77, 3 miles (5km) south of Glasgow city centre. Nearest railway stations Pollokshaws West or Shawlands, frequent buses from city centre. Open Apr–Oct, daily 1000–1700; Nov–Mar, daily 1100–1600 (closed Christmas and New Year). Charge ££. Children free. Group concessions. Guided tours by arrangement. Explanatory displays. Gift shop. Restaurant. WC. Limited wheelchair access. Car and coach parking. Telephone 0141 616 6410.

The house was built in 1740 and extended in 1890 by Sir John Stirling Maxwell. Set within the Pollok Country Park (not NTS), the house contains a renowned collection of paintings and furnishings appropriate for an Edwardian country house.

---

708 GLASGOW, PROVAND'S LORDSHIP **6 K16**

3 Castle Street, Glasgow. Opposite Glasgow Cathedral. Nearest railway station Glasgow Queen Street, Buchanan Bus Station nearby. Closed for redevelopment until late 2000. Contact St Mungo Museum for further information, telephone 0141 553 2557. Car and coach parking. Telephone 0141 552 8819.

The oldest dwelling in Glasgow, built in 1471 as a manse for the St Nicholas Hospital, just opposite Glasgow Cathedral. Period displays and furniture. Tranquil recreated medieval herb garden.

---

709 GLASGOW, QUEEN'S CROSS CHURCH **6 K15**

870 Garscube Road, Glasgow. 0.5 mile (1km) west of city centre. Bus from centre. Open all year, Mon–Fri 1000–1700, Sat 1000–1400, Sun 1400–1700; closed some public holidays. Free. Guided tours by arrangement. Gift shop. Refreshments. WC. Wheelchair access with assistance. Car parking. Telephone 0141 946 6600.

The only church designed by Charles Rennie Mackintosh and now the headquarters of the Charles Rennie Mackintosh Society, which has extensively restored the building. Built 1898–9 in a perpendicular Gothic style. Reference library and specialist shop.

---

710 GLASGOW, ROUKEN GLEN **6 J16**

Thornliebank, south Glasgow. Access at all reasonable times. Free. Tearoom.

One of Glasgow's most attractive parks with lovely shaded walks and a waterfall. Children's playground, boating pond, garden centre and butterfly farm.

---

711 GLASGOW, ROYAL HIGHLAND FUSILIERS REGIMENTAL MUSEUM **6 K16**

518 Sauchiehall Street, Glasgow. In Charing Cross area of Glasgow centre. Bus from centre. Open all year, Mon–Thu 0830–1630, Fri 0830–1600. Free. Guided tours. Explanatory displays. Gift shop. WC. Induction loop. Wheelchair access with assistance. Disabled WC. Car parking. Telephone 0141 332 0961.

A museum exhibiting medals, badges, uniforms and records which illustrate the histories of the Royal Scots Fusiliers, the Highland Light Infantry and the Royal Highland Fusiliers, Princess Margaret's Own Glasgow and Ayrshire Regiment.

---

712 GLASGOW, ST MUNGO MUSEUM OF RELIGIOUS LIFE AND ART **6 K16**

2 Castle Street, Glasgow. Next to Glasgow Cathedral. Nearest railway station Glasgow Queen Street, bus from centre. Open daily (except Christmas and New Year), Mon–Thu and Sat 1000–1700, Fri and Sun 1100–1700. Free. Guided tours. Explanatory displays. Gift shop. Restaurant. Zen garden. WC. Wheelchair access. Disabled WC. Telephone 0141 553 2557.

A unique museum exploring the universal themes of life, death and the hereafter through beautiful and evocative art objects associated with different religious faiths. Three galleries focus on art, world religions and religion in Scottish history. Includes Britain's only authentic Japanese Zen garden.

---

713 GLASGOW SCHOOL OF ART **6 K16**

167 Renfrew Street, Glasgow. In Glasgow city centre, 10–15 minute walk from Queen Street and Central railway stations. Open all year (except Christmas to New Year) by guided tour only, Mon–Fri 1100 and 1400, Sat 1030 and 1130; additional tours Jul–Aug Sat 1300, Sun 1030, 1130, 1300. Charge ££. Children under 10 free. Group concessions. Guided tours with brochure. Gift shop. Café. WC. Limited wheelchair access. Disabled WC. Telephone 0141 353 4526.

Glasgow School of Art is Charles Rennie Mackintosh's architectural masterpiece. The Mackintosh Building continues to be admired and respected and has taken its place as one of the most influential and significant structures of the 20th century. Regular guided tours let you experience this famous and fascinating art school.

---

714 GLASGOW, SCOTKART INDOOR KART RACING CENTRE

6 K16

Westburn Road, Cambuslang, Glasgow. 4 miles (6.5km) from city centre (off M74 at Cambuslang exit). Bus from centre or train to Cambuslang. Track open daily (except Christmas Day and New Year's Day), 1000–2200. Booking office open 1000–1800. Charge £££. Group concessions. Snack bar. Viewing gallery and changing rooms. WC. Wheelchair access. Disabled WC. Car and coach parking. Telephone 0141 641 0222.

A large indoor motorsport centre featuring 200cc pro-karts capable of over 40mph. The track can be booked for practice lapping (1100–1700) or visitors can compete in a professionally organised race meeting. All equipment and instruction provided. Also at Clydebank, telephone 0141 641 0222.

---

715 GLASGOW, SCOTLAND STREET SCHOOL

6 K16

225 Scotland Street, Glasgow. 1 mile (2km) south of the city centre, opposite Shields Road underground station. Open daily excluding public holidays, Mon–Thu and Sat 1000–1700, Fri and Sun 1100–1700. Free. Guided tours. Explanatory displays. Gift shop. Café. WC. Limited wheelchair access. Disabled WC. Car and coach parking. Telephone 0141 287 0513.

A magnificent building with twin leaded towers and Glasgow style stone carving designed by Charles Rennie Mackintosh in 1904. Now housing a permanent exhibition on the history of education. There are Victorian, World War II, 1950s and 1960s classrooms, a drill hall and an Edwardian cookery room. Regularly changing exhibitions include subjects such as other cultures, Mackintosh, art, craft, and exhibitions designed for children. Activity sessions.

---

716 GLASGOW, SPRINGBURN MUSEUM

6 K15

Atlas Square, Ayr Street, Glasgow. Off the A803, northeast of centre. Nearest railway station Springburn. Bus from city centre. Open all year except bank holidays, Tue–Fri 1030–1700, Sat 1000–1630. Free. Explanatory displays. Gift shop. Wheelchair access. Telephone 0141 557 1405.

Glasgow's first independent community museum. It preserves the history of an area which was once the greatest centre of railway manufacturing in the world. The story of the rise, decline and rebirth of a typical Glaswegian industrial community is told through photographs and models, objects and graphics and, above all, through the memories of local people. Covers past and present life in tenements and tower blocks, steam locomotive technology and labour history, the Co-operative Society and modern youth clubs. Changing exhibitions.

---

717 GLASGOW, TENEMENT HOUSE

6 K16

NTS. 145 Buccleuch Street, Glasgow. A short walk from Queen Street and Central railway stations. Open Mar–Oct, daily 1400–1700. Charge ££. Children free. Group concessions. Guided tours by arrangement. Explanatory displays. Guidebook available in French and German. WC. Braille guide, audio tour. Disabled WC. Telephone 0141 333 0183.

A typical late Victorian Glasgow tenement flat, retaining many original features. The furniture and possessions of the woman who lived here for 50 years give a fascinating glimpse of life in the early 20th century. Exhibition on ground floor about tenement life.

---

718 GLASGOW WAVERLEY PADDLESTEAMER **6 K16**

Anderston Quay, Glasgow. Nearest railway station, Glasgow city centre. Buses from city centre. Sailings from Easter–Oct, various times. Telephone for full details of departure points and times. Charge £££. Group concessions. Explanatory displays. Some tours have inclusive commentary. Gift shop. Bar meals and light refreshments. Baby changing facilities. WC. Limited wheelchair access. Disabled WC. Car and coach parking. Telephone 0141 221 8152.

Historically one of the most interesting vessels still in operation in the country, the *Waverley* is the last paddle steamer to be built for service on the Clyde, and is now the last sea-going paddle steamer in the world. A variety of cruises from Glasgow and Ayr along the Clyde coast.

---

719 GLASGOW, WILLOW TEA ROOMS **6 K16**

217 Sauchiehall Street, Glasgow. In precinct area above Henderson the Jeweller. Open all year, except public holidays, Mon–Sat 0930–1630, Sun 1200–1615. Free. Gift shop. Restaurant. WC. No guide dogs. Telephone 0141 332 0521.

The Willow Tearooms is an original Charles Rennie Mackintosh building, designed for Miss Cranston 1904–28. Re-opened in 1983, the tearoom still has original glass and mirror work and doors, and functions as a restaurant serving light meals, teas and coffees.

---

720 GLASGOW ZOO **6 K16**

Calderpark, Uddingston, Glasgow. At the M73/M74 junction, 6 miles (9.5km) east of centre. Bus from centre. Open daily all year. Mar–May, Sep and Oct 0930–1700; Jun–Aug 0930–1800; Nov–Feb 0930–1600. Charge ££. Group concessions. Explanatory displays. Gift shop. Tearoom and picnic area. WC. Guide dogs by arrangement. Wheelchair access. Disabled WC. Car and coach parking. Telephone 0141 771 1185.

A medium size zoological park with spacious enclosures set in wooded parkland and featuring a regular programme of animal displays, bird of prey flying displays, parrot displays, and snake handling. Animals include lions, tigers, monkeys, rhinos, bears, lizards and tortoises. Children's farm.

---

721 GLASS CREATIONS **3 M2**

Thurso Glass Studio, Riverside Road, Thurso, Caithness. First right on entry over the bridge to Thurso. Nearest railway station Thurso. Open all year, Tue–Sat 1000–1700. Free. Explanatory displays. Gift shop. Wheelchair access. Car parking. Telephone (01847) 894017.

On the banks of the River Thurso with uninterrupted views of salmon, seals and otters. The studio uses the lampworking method of creating glass items and sculptures. Demonstrations in glass blowing on request. Small orders completed for visitors on holiday.

---

722 GLEBE CAIRN **4 F14**

HS. In Kilmartin Glen, Argyll. Nearest railway station Oban, then bus to Kilmartin. Access at all times. Free. Telephone 0131 668 8800.

An early Bronze Age burial cairn with two burial chambers (cists).

---

723 GLEN AFFRIC **2 H9**

From A831 at Cannich take the unclassified road south to Loch Affric.

Known as one of the most beautiful glens in Scotland, Glen Affric is a mix of high mountains, lochs, rivers and part of the ancient Caledonian pine forest. Main features include Dog Falls in the lower glen, Loch Affric and the wilder West Affric (see 1493).

---

724 GLENBARR ABBEY VISITOR CENTRE **4 F17**

Glenbarr, Tarbert, Argyll. On the A83, 12 miles (19km) north of Campbeltown. Bus from Glasgow. Open Easter–Oct daily (except Tue), 1000–1730. Charge £. Group concessions. Guided tours (available in German). Explanatory displays. Gift shop. Tearoom. Short woodland walk. WC. Limited wheelchair access. Car and coach parking. Telephone (01583) 421247.

A house in the 18th-century Gothic Revival style designed by James Gillespie Graham. The seat of the lairds of Glenbarr since 1796. Tours are conducted by the 5th laird, Angus Macalister, whose home this is. Among items displayed – 19th-century fashions, Spode, Sèvres and Derby china, gloves worn by Mary, Queen of Scots, thimble collection.

---

725 GLENBUCHAT CASTLE **3 N9**

HS. Bridge of Buchat. 14 miles (22.5km) west of Alford, Aberdeenshire. Bus from Aberdeen or Alford to Strathdon. Access at all times. Free. Car parking. Telephone 0131 668 8800.

A fine example of a Z-plan tower house, built in 1590.

---

726 GLENCOE **2 G11**

NTS. Visitor Centre, Glencoe, Ballachulish, Argyll. On A82, 17 miles (27km) south of Fort William. Bus from Edinburgh, Glasgow or Fort William. Site open all year (free). Visitor centre open Mar–Apr and Sep–Oct, daily 1000–1700; May–Aug, daily 0930–1730. Charge £. Children free. Group concessions. Explanatory displays. Guided walks in glen. Gift shop. Snack bar and picnic area. WC. Induction loop. Wheelchair access to visitor centre. Disabled WC. Car and coach parking. Telephone (01855) 811307.

Dramatic and historic glen, scene of the 1692 massacre of part of the MacDonald clan by soldiers of King William. Its steep sided mountains offer superb walking and climbing. Red deer, wild cat, golden eagle and rare arctic plants can be seen among the breathtaking peaks and spectacular waterfalls. Ranger service. Video programme on massacre. Display on history of mountaineering.

---

727 GLENCOE AND NORTH LORN FOLK MUSEUM **4 H12**

Glencoe, Argyll. Off the A82 in Glencoe village. Bus from Glasgow, Inverness, Oban and Fort William. Open Easter and May–Sep, Mon–Sat 1000–1730. Charge £. Explanatory displays. Gift shop. Gift area. Wheelchair access. Car and coach parking. Telephone (01855) 811664.

A local museum in four heather-thatched buildings and two outbuildings. Many exhibits reflecting Highland rural life, history, geology and wildlife.

---

728 GLENCOE SKI CENTRE **4 H12**

Kingshouse, Glencoe, Argyll. On the A82, 30 miles (48km) south of Fort William, 12 miles (19km) from station at Bridge of Orchy. Nearest railway station Bridge of Orchy, bus from Glasgow. Open for skiing Christmas to Apr; chairlift and restaurant open May–Sep. Charge ££. Telephone for winter skiing charges. Group concessions. Explanatory displays. Gift shop. Restaurant (café on plateau). WC. Limited wheelchair access. Disabled WC. Car and coach parking. Telephone (01855) 851226.

Scotland's original ski centre, Glencoe is renowned for its exhilarating skiing and friendly atmosphere. For skiers and boarders of all standards. On-site facilities include ski and snowboard school and hire departments. The chairlift and restaurant are open in summer.

729 GLENDRONACH DISTILLERY 3 P8

Forgue, Huntly, Aberdeenshire. On junction of B9001 and B9024 between Huntly and Inverurie. Open all year, Mon–Fri, tours at 1000 and 1400. Other times by arrangement. Closed Christmas and New Year. Free. Guided tours. Explanatory displays (audio-visual). Gift shop. Picnic areas. Woodland. WC. Limited wheelchair access. Disabled WC. Car and coach parking. Telephone (01466) 730202.

A traditional malt whisky distillery established in 1825 with its own floor maltings, peat fire and kiln. The grounds contain the Gordon Wood in commemoration of the Gordon Highlanders. Highland cattle in the grounds.

---

730 GLENEAGLES CRYSTAL 6 M15

37 Simpson Road, East Mains Industrial Estate, Broxburn, West Lothian. In Broxburn, 4 miles (6.5km) from Newbridge on the M8/M9 junction. Bus from Edinburgh. Open daily except Christmas and New Year, Mon–Sat 1000–1700, Sun 1100–1700. Free. Viewing window. Gift shop. Coffee available. Wheelchair access. Car and coach parking. Telephone (01506) 852566.

A factory shop with viewing area where visitors can watch crystal cutters at work.

---

731 GLENELG BROCHS 2 F9

HS. About 8 miles (13km) southeast of Kyle of Lochalsh, Ross and Cromarty. Nearest railway station Kyle of Lochalsh, limited post bus service to Glenelg. Access at all times. Free. Telephone 0131 668 8800.

Two Iron Age broch towers standing over 30 feet (9m) high, with well-preserved structural features.

---

732 GLENELG CANDLES ARTS AND CRAFTS CENTRE 2 F9

Glenelg, Ross and Cromarty. In Glenelg, 2 miles (3km) from car ferry to Skye and 7 miles (11km) from Shiel Bridge on the A87. By post bus from Kyle of Lochalsh (nearest railway station). Open all year, summer Mon–Fri 0930–1800, Sat and Sun 1000–1700; winter Mon–Fri 1000–1600. Coffee shop open Apr–Oct. Free. Guided tours. Explanatory displays. Gift shop. Licensed coffee shop. Picnic area. Garden and pets' corner. WC. Wheelchair access. Disabled WC. Car and coach parking. Telephone (01599) 522313.

A candle workshop where visitors can see demonstrations of handmade Highland landscape candles, or browse among paintings by local artists, books and gifts.

---

733 GLEN ESK FOLK MUSEUM 3 P11

The Retreat, Glenesk, Brechin, Angus. 18 miles (29km) up Glen Esk off the B966. Open Easter–May, Sat–Mon 1200–1800; Jun–Oct, daily 1200–1800. Charge £. Group concessions. Guided tours for schools and young people's groups only. Explanatory displays. Gift shop. Tearoom. WC. Limited wheelchair access. Disabled WC. Car and coach parking. Telephone (01356) 670254.

A museum housing antiques, documents and artefacts reflecting the history of Glen Esk and surrounding area. Records, costumes, photographs and tools portray the daily life in a close-knit rural community. Shop sells a range of local craft and gift items. The interpretive centre houses a large relief model of Glen Esk, a stable in original form and displays on past and present local life.

---

734 GLENFARCLAS DISTILLERY 3 M8

Glenfarclas, Ballindalloch, Banffshire. On the A95, 4 miles (6.5km) west of Aberlour. Open all year: Apr–Sep, Mon–Fri 0930–1700; Oct–Mar 1000–1600; Jun–Sep, also Sat 1000–1600, Sun 1230–1630. Charge ££. Group concessions. Guided tours. Explanatory displays. Gift shop. WC. Limited wheelchair access. Disabled WC. Car and coach parking. Telephone (01807) 500257.

A distillery with visitor centre. Tours and free tasting.

735 GLENFIDDICH DISTILLERY **3 N8**

Dufftown, Banffshire. On the A941, 0.3 mile (0.5km) north of Dufftown. Bus from Keith or Elgin stations. Open all year (excluding Christmas and New Year), Mon–Fri 0930–1630; Easter–Oct, also Sat 0930–1630 and Sun 1200–1630. Free. Guided tours (in summer in European languages and Japanese). Explanatory displays. Gift shop. Picnic area. WC. Wheelchair access. Disabled WC. Car and coach parking. Telephone (01340) 820373.

A distillery, opened in 1887, producing the only Highland single malt whisky that is distilled, matured and bottled at its own distillery. Visitors can tour the distillery and bottling hall after an audio-visual introduction. Free sample.

---

736 GLENFINNAN MONUMENT **2 G10**

NTS. Information Centre, Glenfinnan, Inverness-shire. On A830, 18.5 miles (30km) west of Fort William. By rail to Glenfinnan Station (1 mile/1.5km). Site open all year. Information Centre open Apr–mid May and Sep–Oct, daily 1000–1700; mid May–Aug, daily 0930–1800. Charge £. Children free. Group concessions. Explanatory displays. Audio programme in French, Gaelic and German. Gift shop. Snack bar and picnic area. WC. Audio tour. Wheelchair access to Information Centre, wheelchair available. Disabled WC. Car and coach parking. Telephone (01397) 722250.

Set amid superb Highland scenery at the head of Loch Shiel, the monument was erected in 1815 in tribute to the clansmen who died for the Jacobite cause. It is on the site where Bonnie Prince Charlie raised his standard in 1745. Displays and audio-visual programme in Information Centre.

---

737 GLENFINNAN STATION MUSEUM **2 G10**

Station Cottage, Glenfinnan, Fort William. At Glenfinnan station. By rail or bus from Fort William or Mallaig. Open Jun–Sep, 0930–1630; winter telephone for details. Charge £. Group concessions. Explanatory displays. Gift shop. Restaurant/tearoom in converted railway carriage (also open in evenings in summer). WC. Wheelchair access with assistance. Car parking. Telephone (01397) 722295.

Restored station containing a museum illustrating the history of the West Highland railway line with objects, displays and photographs. Steam train runs from the station to Fort William and Mallaig during the summer. Woodland walk and viewpoint.

---

738 GLENFINNAN VIADUCT **2 G10**

At Glenfinnan, near Loch Shiel.

Spectacular railway viaduct.

---

739 GLENGOULANDIE DEER PARK **5 K12**

Glengoulandie, Foss, by Pitlochry, Perthshire. On the B846, 8 miles (13km) northwest of Aberfeldy. Open May–Oct, daily 0900 to 1 hour before sunset. Charge £. Group concessions. Gift shop. Picnic area. WC. No guide dogs. Car and coach parking. Telephone (01887) 830261.

Native animals housed in a natural environment. Many endangered species are kept, and there are fine herds of red deer and Highland cattle. Cars can drive through the park, or it can be explored on foot. Dogs must be kept in car at all times.

---

740 GLENGOYNE DISTILLERY **4 J15**

Dumgoyne, Killearn, Glasgow. On the A81, 3 miles (5km) north of Strathblane. Bus from Glasgow or Stirling. Open all year, Mon–Sat 1000–1600, Sun 1200–1600. Charge ££. Children free. Guided tours (available in French, German or Spanish). Explanatory displays. Gift shop. Tearoom. Scenic waterfall walk. WC. Wheelchair access. Disabled WC. Car and coach parking. Telephone (01360) 550254.

First licensed in 1833, this is Scotland's most southerly Highland distillery and the closest to Glasgow. Nestling in the Campsie Hills, it draws water from a waterfall to produce Scotland's only unpeated whisky. Conducted tours show the main process of distilling. Heritage Room houses cooperage display, old artefacts and shop. Visitors taste a dram in reception room, overlooking dam, glen and waterfall.

---

741 GLEN GRANT DISTILLERY AND GARDEN **3 N7**

Rothes, Aberlour, Banff. At the north end of Rothes, about 10 miles (16km) south of Elgin on the A941. Bus from Elgin. Open mid Mar–Oct, Mon–Sat 1000–1600, Sun 1130–1600; Jun–Sep closes at 1700. Charge £. Charge includes voucher for shop. Under 18s free (children under 8 not allowed into production area). Group concessions. Guided tours. Explanatory displays. Gift shop. Garden. WC. Limited wheelchair access. Car and coach parking. Telephone (01542) 783318.

Fine single malt whisky has been produced here since 1840. Founded by brothers John and James Grant, it was inherited by Major James Grant in 1872, whose study has been recreated. Celebrated for his journeys in India and South Africa, he created a romantic woodland garden. The garden has now been restored. Visitors can tour the distillery, sample a dram in the study or heather-thatched pavillion and explore the garden.

---

742 GLENKINCHIE DISTILLERY **6 N15**

Pencaitland, Tranent, East Lothian. 2 miles (3km) from Pencaitland on the A6093 (signposted). Nearest railway station Longniddry, bus from Edinburgh to Pencaitland. Open all year, Mon–Fri 0930–1700; Easter and May holiday weekends and weekends Jun–Oct, Sat 0930–1700, Sun 1200–1700. Last tour 1600. Closed 25/26 Dec and 1/2 Jan. Charge £. Under 18s free. Group concessions. Guided tours (available in French, German, Italian or Spanish). Explanatory displays. Gift shop. WC. Wheelchair access. Disabled WC. Car and coach parking. Telephone (01875) 342004.

Set in a tiny valley, the only remaining malt whisky distillery close to Edinburgh. Visitors can see all aspects of the traditional distilling craft, with sample tasting. Exhibition includes a scale model of a malt distillery made for the British Empire Exhibition of 1924.

---

743 GLENLIVET DISTILLERY **3 M8**

Ballindalloch, Banff. About 10 miles (16km) north of Tomintoul. Nearest railway and bus stations Elgin. Open mid Mar–Oct, Mon–Sat 1000–1600, Sun 1230–1600; Jul and Aug closes at 1800. Charge £. Charge includes voucher for shop. Under 18s free (children under 8 not allowed into production area). Group concessions. Guided tours (translations in French, German, Italian and Spanish). Visitor centre with audio-visual programme and exhibition. Gift shop. Café. WC. Wheelchair access with assistance to visitor centre. Disabled WC. Car and coach parking. Telephone (01542) 783220.

High in the foothills of the Cairngorm Mountains, The Glenlivet Distillery is situated in one of the most scenic and romantic glens in the Scottish Highlands. The Glenlivet has a rich cultural and historical heritage and the visitor centre presents the story of its history and that of the surrounding area. The guided distillery tour also includes the chance to see inside a vast bonded warehouse and to sample a dram.

---

744 GLENLIVET ESTATE **3 M9**

Glenlivet Estate Office, Main Street, Tomintoul, Ballindalloch. On the A939, 14 miles (22km) southeast of Grantown-on-Spey. Open all year. Information centre open Jul and Aug, Mon–Sat 0900–1230; also open at other times but these may vary. Free. Guided tours. Explanatory displays. Picnic areas. Waymarked walks and cycle trails. Ranger service. WC. Audio guide to estate. Wheelchair access to visitor centre. Disabled WC. Car and coach parking. Telephone (01807) 580283.

A large Highland estate in the foothills of the northeast Cairngorms, encompassing some of the finest landscapes of the Grampian Highlands. A network of over 60 miles (96km) of waymarked trails provides access for walkers, mountain bikers and Nordic skiers along forest roads and farm and estate tracks. A variety of ranger services enables visitors to learn about the history, countryside, wildlife and management of the local area. An estate information centre (in Tomintoul) is open (free) when staff are present. Free maps/guides to the walking/cycling trails are available.

---

745 GLENLUCE ABBEY **4 H20**

HS. Glenluce, Newton-Stewart, Wigtownshire. Off the A75, 2 miles (3km) north of Glenluce. Nearest railway station Stranraer (10 miles/16km), bus from Stranraer to Newton Stewart, then 1.5 miles (2.5km) walk. Open Apr–Sep, daily 0930–1830; Oct–Mar, Sat 0930–1630, Sun 1400–1630. Charge £. Group concessions. Guided tours. Explanatory displays. Gift shop. WC. Limited wheelchair access. Disabled WC. Car and coach parking. Telephone (01581) 300541.

The remains of a Cistercian abbey founded circa 1192, including a handsome early 16th-century chapter house. Includes an exhibition of items found on site. Lovely tranquil setting.

---

746 GLENLUCE MOTOR MUSEUM **4 H20**

Glenluce, Wigtownshire. 15 miles (24km) west of Newton Stewart and 10 miles (16km) east of Stranraer on A75. Open Mar–Oct, daily 1000–1900; Nov–Feb, daily 1100–1600. Charge £. Group concessions. Explanatory displays. Gift shop. Tearoom. WC. Wheelchair access. Disabled WC. Car and coach parking. Telephone (01581) 300534.

A collection of vintage and classic cars, motor cycles, memorabilia and an old type garage.

---

747 GLEN LYON GALLERY **5 K12**

Bridge of Balgie, Glen Lyon, Aberfeldy, Perthshire. Off the B846 at Coshieville, 20 miles (32km) from Aberfeldy, 11 miles (17.5km) up Glen Lyon past Fortingall. Clearly signposted. Nearest railway station Pitlochry, bus to Aberfeldy then post bus from Aberfeldy. Open Mar–Dec, daily 1000–1800 (closed most Wed). Free. Explanatory displays. Tearoom and picnic area nearby. Wheelchair access with assistance. Car and coach parking. Telephone (01887) 866260.

A unique gallery. All works of art are by renowned artist Alan B. Hayman who specialises in wildlife art and sculpture. The gallery setting is atmospheric and beautifully Scottish.

---

748 GLENMORANGIE DISTILLERY VISITOR CENTRE **3 K6**

Tain, Ross and Cromarty. On the A9, 0.5 mile (1km) north of Tain. Bus or train from Tain or Inverness. Open all year, Mon–Fri 0900–1700; also Sat in Jun–Oct (restricted hours). Charge £. Guided tours (translations in French, German, Italian or Spanish). Explanatory displays. Gift shop. WC. Limited wheelchair access. Disabled WC. Car and coach parking. Telephone (01862) 892477.

Provides the visitor with 150 years of history of the distillery. Personal and informative tours, and free sample.

---

749 GLEN MORAY DISTILLERY **3 M7**

Bruceland Road, Elgin. Off the A96 to Inverness at the western outskirts of Elgin. Nearest railway station Elgin, local bus stops at Grays Hospital then 0.4 miles (0.5km) walk. Open all year except Christmas and New Year, Mon–Fri. Tours at 0930, 1030, 1130, 1400, 1500 and 1600. Charge £. Guided tours. Explanatory displays. Gift shop. WC. Limited wheelchair access. Car parking. Telephone (01343) 542577.

Originally built as a brewery and converted to a distillery in 1987. Constructed in the classic square layout of a Scottish farm, the distillery features an attractive courtyard surrounded by the buildings where the whisky is produced.

750 GLENMORE VISITOR CENTRE **3 L9**

FE. Ski Road, Glenmore, Aviemore, Inverness-shire. 7 miles (11km) along Ski Road from Aviemore. Bus from Aviemore. Open all year except Christmas and New Year. Free. Guided tours by prior arrangement. Explanatory displays. Gift shop. Restaurant, tearoom and picnic area. Water sports facilities. WC. Wheelchair access to visitor centre. Disabled WC. Car and coach parking. Telephone (01479) 861220.

The Glen More Forest Park is situated in the foothills of the Cairngorm National Nature Reserve. Caravan and camping site, visitor centre, car parks and picnic areas. Waymarked walks, off-road cycle routes, lochside activities, bird watching. Ranger services. Guided walks and tours. Group activities.

---

751 GLEN NEVIS CENTRE **2 H11**

Ionad Nibheis Visitor Centre, Glen Nevis, Fort William. 1.25 miles (2km) up Glen Nevis, located 2 miles (3km) east of Fort William. Nearest railway station Fort William, hourly local bus service to Glen Nevis. Open Easter–mid May and Oct, daily 0900–1700; mid May–Sep, daily 0900–1800. Free. Explanatory displays. Gift shop. Refreshments and picnic area. WC. Wheelchair access. Disabled WC. Car parking. Telephone (01397) 705922.

Information on the history, geology, flora and fauna of Ben Nevis and Glen Nevis. Ranger guided walks during July and August.

---

752 GLEN OF ROTHES TROUT FISHERY **3 N7**

Rothes, Moray. On the A941, 7 miles (11km) south of Rothes. Bus from Elgin. Open all year (except Christmas Day and New Year's Day), daily 0830–2200 or dusk. Free. Charge for fishing. Group concessions. Explanatory displays. Snack shop and picnic area. WC. Limited wheelchair access. Disabled WC. Car and coach parking. Telephone (01340) 831888.

A fishery with 6 acres (2.4ha) of lochs. Visitors can fish for rainbow and brown trout from the banks. Tackle for hire. Free tuition. Heated fishing hut with snacks.

---

753 GLEN ORD DISTILLERY VISITOR CENTRE **3 J7**

Muir of Ord, Ross and Cromarty. Just off the A832 on the outskirts of Muir of Ord, 15 miles (24km) west of Inverness. Bus from Inverness or Dingwall, or rail to Muir of Ord. Open all year, (except Christmas and New Year) Mon–Fri 0930–1700; Jul and Sep, Sat 0930–1700, Sun 1230–1700. Charge £. Children free. Large groups Nov–Feb by appointment; group concessions by arrangement. Guided tours. Explanatory displays. Gift shop. Picnic area. WC. Wheelchair access. Disabled WC. Car and coach parking. Telephone (01463) 872004.

The sole survivor of nine distilleries which once operated around Glen Ord. Licensed in 1838. The tour and exhibition show the history of the Black Isle and the main processes of distilling. Complimentary tasting.

---

754 GLENTURRET DISTILLERY **5 L13**

The Hosh, Crieff, Perthshire. On the A85 towards Comrie, 1.25 miles (2km) from Crieff. Open all year (except 25/26 Dec and 1/2 Jan): Feb–Dec, Mon–Sat 0930–1800, Sun 1200–1800; Jan, Mon–Fri 1130–1600. Charge ££. Children under 12 free. Group concessions. Guided tours (translation sheets in European languages and Japanese). Audio-visual presentation and exhibition. Gift shop. Restaurants and bar. WC. Limited wheelchair access. Disabled WC. Car and coach parking. Telephone (01764) 656565.

The oldest Highland malt distillery in Scotland (established in 1775) where whisky is still produced in the traditional manner. Free tasting. Picturesque setting.

---

755 GLENWHAN GARDENS **4 H20**

Dunragit, Stranraer, Wigtownshire. Off A75, 6 miles (10km) east of Stranraer. Bus from Stranraer. Open Mar–Oct, daily 1000–1700; other times by arrangement. Charge £. Wheelchair users free admission. Group concessions. Guided tours (available in French). Explanatory displays. Licensed restaurant. Garden. WC. Wheelchair access with assistance. Disabled WC. Car and coach parking. Telephone (01581) 400222.

A beautiful 12 acre (5ha) garden overlooking Luce Bay and the Mull of Galloway, begun in 1979 and hewn from the hillside creating two ponds. A rich habitat for many tender species, including alpines, scree plants and conifers. Woodland with bluebells, snowdrops, specie rhododendrons, azaleas and shrub roses. A plantsman's garden. Also rare ducks, guinea fowl and chickens, and Primula Arena.

---

756 GOATFELL **4 G17**

NTS. Isle of Arran. Access from Cladach on A841 Brodick to Lochranza road. Ferry from Ardrossan to Brodick. Open all year. Free. Explanatory displays. Car and coach parking. Telephone (01770) 302462.

At 2866 feet (873m), Goatfell is the highest peak on Arran, dominating the skyline of the island and affording impressive views from the top. The climb includes fine rock-climbing and ridge-walking.

---

757 GOSFORD HOUSE **6 N15**

Longniddry, East Lothian. Off the A198, 1 mile (2km) east of Longniddry. Nearest railway station Longniddry, bus from Edinburgh. Open mid Jul–mid Aug, Wed–Sun 1400–1700; telephone to confirm. Charge ££. Guided tours by prior arrangement. Explanatory displays. Limited wheelchair access. Car and coach parking. Telephone (01875) 870201.

A mansion, in a fine setting overlooking the Firth of Forth, the central part of which is the work of Robert Adam (1800). The north and south wings are by William Young (1890). The south wing contains the celebrated Marble Hall. Extensive grounds, woodland walks, ornamental waters with wildlife, including nesting wild geese.

---

758 GRAIN EARTH HOUSE **1 B10**

HS. At Hatson, about 1 mile (2km) northwest of Kirkwall, Orkney. Open at all times. Key held by Ortak in Kirkwall. Free. Telephone 0131 668 8800.

A well-built Iron Age earth-house with an underground chamber supported on stone pillars.

---

759 GRAMPIAN TRANSPORT MUSEUM **3 P9**

Alford, Aberdeenshire. On the A944, 25 miles (40km) west of Aberdeen. Bus form Aberdeen. Open Apr–Oct, daily 1000–1700. Charge ££. Reduced admission for educational groups. Group concessions. Guided tours for schools by arrangement. Explanatory displays. Gift shop. Tearoom (open Sun Apr–Oct; daily Jul and Aug) and picnic area. Adventure playground. WC. Wheelchair access. Disabled WC. Car and coach parking. Telephone (01975) 562292.

An extensive collection of historic road vehicles housed in a purpose-built exhibition hall. Exhibitions and vehicles are changed regularly. Special events programme. Climb-aboard exhibits for children. Driving simulator, video bus featuring motor sport and road transport history.

---

760 GRANGEMOUTH MUSEUM **6 L15**

Victoria Library, Bo'ness Road, Grangemouth. In town centre. Nearest railway station Falkirk. Bus to Grangemouth from Falkirk. Open all year, Mon–Sat 1230–1700. Free. Explanatory displays. Gift shop. Telephone (01324) 504699.

Display relating to the growth of Grangemouth. Exhibits on local industries, canals, shipping and ship building, and the world's first practical steamship, the *Charlotte Dundas*.

761 GRANTOWN MUSEUM AND HERITAGE TRUST **3 M8**

Burnfield House, Burnfield Avenue, Grantown-on-Spey. Open all year, Tue–Sat 1000–1600. Charge £. Children under 10 free. Group concessions. Explanatory displays. Gift shop. Picnic area. Garden. WC. Induction loop. Wheelchair access. Disabled WC. Car and coach parking. Telephone (01479) 872478.

An exciting permanent display brings to life the history of Grantown-on-Spey with innovative use of audio-visuals. The museum is housed in Burnfield House, a refurbished school built in 1865. Situated in the conservation area of this fine, Highland, planned town, the building has a pleasant setting with spacious grounds.

---

762 GRASSIC GIBBON CENTRE **3 Q11**

Arbuthnott, Laurencekirk, Kincardineshire. On B967, 3 miles (5km) from Inverbervie (A92) or Fordoun (A90). Nearest railway station Montrose or Stonehaven, limited bus service from Stonehaven and school buses. Open Apr–Oct, daily 1000–1630. Charge £. Group concessions. Explanatory displays. Gift shop. Restaurant, tearoom and picnic area. Children's play area. WC. Wheelchair access with assistance. Disabled WC. Car and coach parking. Telephone (01561) 361668.

Visitor centre dedicated to the life and times of the novelist Lewis Grassic Gibbon (James Leslie Mitchell).

---

763 GREAT GLEN FINE FOODS

See 361 Confectionary Factory Visitor Centre.

---

764 GREEN HALL GALLERY **3 N8**

The Green Hall Gallery, 2 Victoria Street, Craigellachie, Aberlour. 12 miles (19km) south of Elgin on A95. Nearest railway station Elgin, bus to Craigellachie. Open all year, Mon–Sat 0900–1300 and 1400–1730, Sun 1400–1730. Free. Gift shop. Wheelchair access. Car parking. Telephone (01340) 871010.

Situated in the old Gospel Hall circa 1890. Featuring over 100 prints and a selection of handmade cards. Original oils and watercolours also on display, featuring local scenes, animals, birds, flowers and fish. Commissions undertaken.

---

765 GREENHILL COVENANTOR HOUSE **5 M17**

Burnbraes, Biggar, Lanarkshire. In Biggar, on the A702, 26 miles (41.5km) from Edinburgh. Bus from Edinburgh or Lanark. Open Easter–Sep, daily 1400–1700. Charge £. Group concessions. Guided tours. Gift shop. Picnic area. Garden. Children's activity sheets. Limited wheelchair access. Car and coach parking. Telephone (01899) 221050.

Farmhouse, rescued in ruinous condition and rebuilt at Biggar, 10 miles (16km) from its original site. Exhibits include relics of local Covenanters, Donald Cargill's bed (1681), 17th-century furnishings, costume dolls.

---

766 GREENKNOWE TOWER **5 P17**

HS. On the A6089, 0.5 mile (1km) west of Gordon on the Earlston road, Berwickshire. Bus from Kelso or Edinburgh to Gordon, then walk. Open at all times; see keyholder. Free. Telephone 0131 668 8800.

A handsome tower house on an L-plan, built in 1581 and still retaining its iron yett (gate).

---

767 GRETNA GREEN, WORLD FAMOUS OLD BLACKSMITH'S SHOP CENTRE **5 L19**

Gretna Green, Dumfriesshire. On the Scottish/English border off A74 or A75, 15 miles (24km) south of Lockerbie. Nearest railway station Gretna Green, bus from Dumfries or Carlisle. Open daily all year, 0900–1700 in winter; Jun and Sep 0900–1900; Jul and Aug 0900–2000; Oct and Nov, Apr and May 0900–1800. Charge £. Children under 10 free. Group concessions. Guided tours (leaflets in 7 languages). Explanatory displays. Gift shop. Restaurant, tearoom and picnic area. Sculpture park. Various art outlets. Animal park. Children's play area. WC. Wheelchair access. Disabled WC. Car and coach parking. Telephone 01461 338441 or 338224.

The Blacksmith's Shop is famous the world over for runaway marriages. The unique Gretna Green Story involves the visitor in the legends of its romantic history and leads into the magnificent anvil and carriage museum. Tartan Shop selling cashmere, tartans, crystal, luxury foods and gifts. Tartan information centre.

---

768 GRETNA HALL BLACKSMITH'S SHOP **5 N20**

Gretna Green. 1 mile (1.5km) north of the border with England. Nearest railway station Gretna Green. Open mid Apr–mid Oct, daily 0900–2000; mid Oct–mid Apr 1000–1600. Charge £. Children under 14 free. Guided tours (leaflets available in Dutch, French, German, Italian and Spanish). Explanatory displays. Gift shop. Restaurant, bar and picnic area. Gardens. WC. Limited wheelchair access. Disabled WC. Car and coach parking. Telephone (01461) 337635.

Built in 1710, the Gretna Hall blacksmiths shop has an interesting history associated with weddings, which are still performed here.

---

769 GREY CAIRNS OF CAMSTER **3 N3**

HS. Off the A9, on the Watten Road, 5 miles (8km) north of Lybster, Caithness. Nearest railway station Wick, bus from Wick to Lybster, request stop at road end for cairns, then walk 8 miles (13km). Access at all times. Free. Car parking. Telephone 0131 668 8800.

Two Neolithic chambered burial cairns. One long with two chambers and projecting horns; one round with a single chamber.

---

770 GREY MARE'S TAIL **5 M18**

NTS. Adjacent to A708, 10 miles (16km) northeast of Moffat, Dumfriesshire. Open all year. Ranger service Apr–Sep. Free. Explanatory displays, remote camera link to waterfall and wildlife. Wheelchair access to reception area. Car and coach parking. Telephone (01556) 502575.

Spectacular 200 foot (61m) waterfall in landscape of geological interest and rich in wild flowers. Herd of wild goats. Marked paths – please keep to these for your safety.

---

771 GROAM HOUSE MUSEUM **3 K7**

High Street, Rosemarkie, Ross and Cromarty. In Rosemarkie on the A832, 15 miles (24km) northeast of Inverness. Bus from Inverness. Open Easter and May–Sep, Mon–Sat 1000–1700, Sun 1400–1630; Oct–Apr, weekends 1400–1600. Charge £. Group concessions. Guided tours by prior arrangement. Explanatory displays and videos. Gift shop. Limited wheelchair access. Car and coach parking. Telephone (01381) 620961.

Award-winning Pictish museum. The centre-piece in a display of locally-found stones is the magnificent 8th-century Rosemarkie cross-slab. Part of the nationally important collection of original work by George Bain, the artist responsible for the revival of Celtic art, is also exhibited. Temporary exhibitions of local history or Pictish interest.

---

772 GROGPORT ORGANIC TANNERY **4 F17**

The Old Manse, Grogport, Carradale, Argyll. On the B842, 4 miles (6.5km) north of Carragale on the east coast of Kintyre. Open daily 0900–1800. Free. Small groups welcome by prior arrangement. Group concessions. Explanatory displays. Gift shop. Wheelchair access. Car parking. Telephone (01583) 431255.

A small rural tannery using an ancient method of tanning skins to make leather. The only organic tannery in the country. Visitors can see skins being processed by hand. Finished sheepskins for sale. Also many small items such as slippers, cushions and gloves.

773 NEIL M GUNN MEMORIAL VIEWPOINT 3 J7

Heights of Brae, Strathpeffer. Access at all reasonable times. Free. Car parking.

Memorial viewpoint for the author Neil M. Gunn, who lived nearby.

---

774 HACKNESS, MARTELLO TOWER 1 B11

HS. At Hackness, at the southeast end of the Island of Hoy, Orkney. Ferry from Stromness to Lyness on Hoy, then 10 miles (16km) walk or passenger ferry to Longhope and a 3 mile (5km) walk. For access, see keyholder. Free. Telephone 0131 668 8800.

An impressive tower (one of a pair) built between 1813 and 1815 to provide defence against the French and American privateers for the British convoys assembling in the sound of Longhope. Renovated in 1866 and used again in World War I.

---

775 HADDO HOUSE 3 Q8

NTS. Ellon, Aberdeenshire. Off B999, 4 miles (6.5km) north of Pitmedden, 19 miles (30km) north of Aberdeen. By bus from Aberdeen. Open Easter–Sep and weekends in Oct, daily 1330–1730. Garden and country park open all year, daily 0930–sunset. Charge ££. Children free. Group concessions. Guided tours by arrangement. Explanatory displays. Information sheets in four languages. Gift shop. Restaurant. Garden and country park. WC. Limited wheelchair access, wheelchairs available. Disabled WC. Car and coach parking. Telephone (01651) 851440.

Elegant house designed by William Adam in 1731 for the Second Earl of Aberdeen. Much of the interior is Adam Revival, dating from the 1880s. Beautiful library, permanent exhibition of James Giles' paintings. Adjacent country park is run by Aberdeenshire Council.

---

776 HAILES CASTLE 5 P15

HS. Off the A1, 1.5 miles (2.5km) southwest of East Linton, East Lothian. Nearest railway station Dunbar, bus to Pencraig (request stop), then 15 minute walk. Access at all times; see keyholder. Free. Picnic area. Car parking. Telephone 0131 668 8800.

A beautifully-sited ruin incorporating a 13th-century fortified manor which was extended in the 14th and 15th centuries. Includes a fine 16th-century chapel and two vaulted pit-prisons.

---

777 HALLIWELL'S HOUSE MUSEUM 5 P17

Market Place, Selkirk. In Selkirk, 35 miles (56km) south of Edinburgh. Bus from Edinburgh, Carlisle or Berwick. Open Apr–Oct, daily 1000–1700, Sun 1400–1600; Jul and Aug 1000–1800, Sun 1400–1700. Free. Explanatory displays. Gift shop. WC. Limited wheelchair access. Disabled WC. Car and coach parking. Telephone (01750) 20096.

A local museum in a row of 19th-century cottages. One of the best collections of domestic ironmongery in the country. Based on local history, it traces the growth of Selkirk, from the Stone Age to its role as an important textile-producing centre.

---

778 HANDA ISLAND FERRY TRIPS 2 H3

Scourie, By Lairg, Sutherland. 6 miles (10km) north of Scourie. Nearest railway station Lairg, post bus from Lairg to Scourie. Open Apr–Sep, Mon–Sat. First ferry 0930 then outward crossings half hourly until 1400; last return crossing 1700. Charge £££. Landing charge £. Guided tours by arrangement (available in German). Explanatory displays. Restaurant and toilets at Tarbet. No guide dogs. Car and coach parking. Telephone (01971) 502340.

Handa Island is internationally famous for its sea-bird colonies including the largest breeding colony of guillemots in Britain. The island is also renowned for its magnificent

Torridonian sandstone cliffs, which rise to a height of 400 feet (122m) along the dramatic northern edge of the island. From this viewpoint you may also see many of the area's marine wildlife such as dolphins, porpoises, seals and the occasional whale. A footpath circles the island. No dogs allowed.

---

779 HARBOUR COTTAGE GALLERY, KIRKCUDBRIGHT **5 K21**

Castlebank, Kirkcudbright. Beside the harbour in Kirkcudbright. Bus from Dumfries. Open Mar–Dec, daily 1030–1230 and 1400–1700; Apr–Oct, also Sun 1400–1700. Charge £. Children free. Group concessions. Limited wheelchair access. Telephone (01557) 330073.

An 18th-century cottage restored and opened in 1957 as a gallery exhibiting the work of local artists.

---

780 HARBOUR VIEW GALLERY **2 E2**

Harbour View Gallery, Port of Ness, Isle of Lewis. Near Butt of Lewis, 28 miles (45km) north of Stornoway on A857. Daily bus service from Stornoway. Open Mar–Oct, Mon–Sat 1030–1700; Nov–Feb by appointment. Free. Wheelchair access with assistance. Car parking. Telephone (01851) 810735.

Artist's studio gallery in a scenic location at the northern tip of the Isle of Lewis, situated above the old harbour and beach at Port of Ness. Contemporary, original watercolours by island based artist Anthony J. Barber. Also prints and cards.

---

781 KIER HARDIE STATUE **5 K18**

Cumnock town centre. Access at all times. Car parking.

Bust outside the Town Hall to commemorate James Keir Hardie (1856–1915), an early socialist leader, and founder of the Independent Labour Party in 1893.

---

782 HARESTANES COUNTRYSIDE VISITOR CENTRE **5 P17**

Ancrum, Jedburgh, Roxburghshire. Off the A68, 3 miles (5km) north of Jedburgh. Buses from Jedburgh, Edinburgh, Kelso, Galashiels, Hawick. Open Apr–Oct, daily 1000–1700. Free. Charges for guided walks and some activities/events. Explanatory displays. Gift shop. Tearoom and picnic area. Outdoor play area. WC. Limited wheelchair access. Disabled WC. Car and coach parking. Telephone (01835) 830306.

Housed in converted farm buildings and comprising both indoor and outdoor attractions. Changing exhibitions, walk routes and guided walks, activities and events. Wildlife garden and wooden games room. Waymarked walks include view of Waterloo Monument. This prominent landmark on the summit of Peniel Heugh (741 ft/226m high) was built after the battle of Waterloo by the Marquess of Lothian and his tenants. No access to interior.

---

783 HARMONY GARDEN **5 P17**

NTS. Melrose, Borders. Opposite Melrose Abbey. Bus from Edinburgh. Open Apr–Sep, Mon–Sat 1000–1730, Sun 1330–1730. Charge £. Honesty box. Explanatory displays. Limited wheelchair access. Car and coach parking. Telephone (01721) 722502.

This attractive walled garden was built in the early 19th century, in a fine conservation area. The garden is lovely throughout the seasons, with a rich display of spring bulbs, colourful herbaceous and mixed borders, and fruiting apricots. The garden is set against the beautiful backdrop of Melrose Abbey ruins, with the Eildon Hills in the distance.

---

784 HARRIS TWEED WEAVING AND KNITTING **2 C5**

4 Plockropool, Isle of Harris, Western Isles. On Golden Road, 5 miles (8km) south of Tarbert. Bus from Tarbert. Open all year, Mon–Sat 0900–1900. Free. Gift shop. WC. Wheelchair access. Car and coach parking. Telephone (01859) 511217.

Visitors can see Harris tweed being woven. Also demonstrations of warping, bobbin winding and wool plying.

---

785 HARTMOUNT WOODTURNING AND CABINET MAKING STUDIO **3 K6**

Tigh an Fhraoich, Hartmount, Tain. Off minor road to Scotsburn, 3 miles (5km) south of Tain. Bus and rail services to Tain. Transport from Tain if required. Open all year including evenings. Free. Guided tours. Explanatory displays. Gift shop. 2 acres (1ha) garden. Wheelchair access. Car parking. Telephone (01862) 842511.

Family business (member of the Guild of Master Craftsman) comprising a custom-built woodworking shop and display area. Courses throughout the year.

---

786 JOHN HASTIE MUSEUM **6 K16**

Threestanes Road, Strathaven, Lanarkshire. On the A726, 6 miles (10km) south of East Kilbride, beside Strathaven Park. Bus from East Kilbride and Hamilton. Open Apr–Sep, daily 1230–1630. Free. Guided tours by arrangement. Explanatory displays. Gift shop. Adjacent to Strathaven Park. Wheelchair access with assistance. Telephone (01357) 521257.

A local history museum with displays on the town, weaving, commerce, Covenanters, ceramics. Temporary display gallery.

---

787 HAWICK MUSEUM AND THE SCOTT GALLERY **5 P18**

Wilton Lodge Park, Hawick, Borders. Bus from Edinburgh or Carlisle. Open Apr–Sep, Mon–Fri 1000–1200 and 1300–1700; weekends 1300–1700; Oct–Mar, Mon–Fri 1300–1600, Sun 1400–1600. Charge £. Group concessions. Guided tours by arrangement. Explanatory displays. Gift shop. WC. Limited wheelchair access. Car and coach parking. Telephone (01450) 373457.

This 200-year-old mansion house set in over 100 acres (40ha) of award-winning parkland houses Hawick's long-established museum and art gallery. A programme of museum and art exhibitions compliments permanent displays on local industrial history, natural history, ethnography, domestic bygones and militaria.

---

788 HAYES GARDEN LAND **4 J17**

Tarbolton Road, Symington, Kilmarnock. On the A77, 4 miles (6.5km) west of Kilmarnock. Open all year (except Christmas to New Year), Mon–Sat 0900–1730, Sun 1000–1730. Free. Gift shop. Tearoom. Garden centre. WC. Wheelchair access. Disabled WC. Car and coach parking. Telephone (01563) 830204.

Garden centre with coffee lounge and home baking.

---

789 STEPHEN HAYWARD WOOD CARVING **3 J8**

Tigh Bea, Kiltarlity, Inverness-shire. 12 miles (19km) west of Inverness on A862 then A833. Nearest railway station Inverness, local bus service to within 0.5 mile (1km). Open all year, Mon–Thu 1000–1700; other times by arrangement. Free. Woodcarving shop and plant sales. Garden. Wheelchair access with assistance. Car parking. Telephone (01463) 741425.

Traditional carving styles and contemporary sculptures in a wide variety of timbers. Wall plaques, bowls, figures and sculptures are all carved on the premises. See also 166 Birch House Herbs.

---

790 HEADS OF AYR FARM PARK **4 H18**

Dunure Road, Ayr. On the A719, 4 miles (6.5km) south of Ayr. Bus from centre. Open daily (except Christmas and New Year), 1000–1700 (limited facilities Oct–Feb). Charge ££. Charge for activities. Group concessions. Guided tours for schools. Explanatory displays. Gift shop. Snack bar barn. WC. Limited wheelchair access. Disabled WC. Car and coach parking. Telephone (01292) 441210.

Park comprising 125 acres (50.5ha) with beautiful views over the Firth of Clyde. Animals include buffalo, wallabies, rhea and rabbits. Reptile house. Pony and buggy rides. Straw barns, toy tractors. Quad biking. Indoor and outdoor play areas.

---

791 HEATHERGEMS **5 L12**

22 Atholl Road, Pitlochry, Perthshire. In Pitlochry, behind the Tourist Office. Open Mar–Oct, daily 0900–1730; winter Mon–Sat 0900–1700. Free. Explanatory displays. Gift shop. Wheelchair access. Car parking. Telephone (01796) 474391.

A Scottish jewellery factory and visitor centre. Visitors can see products being made. Seated video area and a large shop.

---

792 HEBRIDEAN JEWELLERY **2 B8**

Iochdar, South Uist, Western Isles. Located at the north end of South Uist near Benbecula. Bus service from ferry terminals. Open all year, Mon–Fri 0900–1730, Sat 0930–1730, closed Sun. Free. Gift shop. WC. Wheelchair access with assistance. Car and coach parking. Telephone (01870) 610288.

Celtic jewellery shop and workshop. Visitors can see five jewellers at work. Silver, gold and gemstones. Commissions undertaken.

---

793 HERMANESS NATIONAL NATURE RESERVE VISITOR CENTRE **1 G1**

Shorestation, Burrafirth, Unst, Shetland. On the B9086, 3 miles (5km) northwest of Haroldswick. Bus from Lerwick, or air from Sumburgh to Baltasound. Open Apr–Sep, daily 0900–1800. Free. Explanatory displays. WC. Wheelchair access with assistance. Disabled WC. Car parking. Telephone (01957) 711278 when open, otherwise (01595) 693345.

An interpretive display for the neighbouring Hermaness National Nature Reserve. Simulates the sights and sounds of the seabird cliffs. Useful for those unable to visit the reserve.

---

794 THE HERMITAGE **5 L12**

NTS. Off A9, 2 miles (3km) west of Dunkeld, Perthshire. By bus from Perth or Dunkeld. Open all year. Free. Charge for parking. Explanatory displays. Guided walks by rangers. Disabled parking near folly. Car and coach parking. Telephone (01796) 473233 or (01350) 728641.

Interesting walks in mixed conifer and deciduous woodland. The focus is a delightful folly, Ossian's Hall, in a gorge of the River Braan. Ranger service.

---

795 HERMITAGE CASTLE **5 P19**

HS. Hawick, Roxburghshire. In Liddesdale, Roxburghshire, 5.5 miles (9km) northeast of Newcastleton. Bus service from Hawick to Hermitage School House then 1 mile (2km) walk. Open Apr–Sep, daily 0930–1830. Charge £. Group concessions. Guided tours. Gift shop. Car and coach parking. Telephone (01387) 376222.

A vast eerie ruin of the 14th and 15th centuries, consisting of four towers and connecting walls, outwardly almost perfect. Much restored in the 19th century. Associated with the de Soulis family, but with the Douglases after 1341.

---

796 HIGHLAND AND RARE BREEDS FARM **2 H5**

Elphin, Sutherland. On the A835, 15 miles (24km) north of Ullapool. Bus from Ullapool. Open May–Sep, 1000–1700. Charge ££. Children under 3 free. Group concessions. Guided tours (leaflets in five foreign languages). Explanatory displays. Gift shop. Picnic area. WC. Limited wheelchair access. Car and coach parking. Telephone (01854) 666204.

The Scottish Farm Animal Centre which has over 36 breeds of animals, ancient and modern, in 15 acres (6ha) of farmland, river and mountain scenery. A croft has been adapted for education and conservation. A working organic farm has an exhibition of farm tools and farmwork demonstrations.

---

797 HIGHLAND AROMATICS **3 J8**

Inchmore, Kirkhill, Inverness. On the A862, 7 miles (11km) west of Inverness. Open Mon–Thu 1000–1600, Fri 1000–1500 (closed Christmas and New Year). Free. Guided tours. Gift shop. Wheelchair access. Car and coach parking. Telephone (01463) 831625.

Visitors can see the making of high quality soaps in a former church.

---

798 HIGHLAND CATTLE CENTRE **5 K13**

Glascorrie Road, Auchingarrich, Comrie, Perthshire. Two miles (3km) south of Comrie on B827. Open all year, daily 1000–dusk. Charge ££. Disabled visitors free. Group concessions. Guided tours. Explanatory displays. Gift shop. Coffee shop. WC. Limited wheelchair access. Disabled WC. Car and coach parking. Telephone (01764) 679469.

The centre tells the story of the Highland cow's evolution and also shows the 6000 year old head of one of their ancestors. See all the different types of Highland cattle from young calves to huge bullocks with 6 foot (1.8m) long horns. The cattle can be touched. Great photo opportunities.

---

799 HIGHLAND FOLK MUSEUM, KINGUSSIE **3 K10**

Duke Street, Kingussie, Inverness-shire. In Kingussie, 12 miles (19km) southwest of Aviemore off the A9. Nearest railway station Kingussie. Buses from Inverness, Perth or Edinburgh. Open Apr–Oct, telephone to confirm times. Charge £. Group concessions. Guided tours. Explanatory displays. Gift shop. Picnic area. WC. Wheelchair access. Disabled WC. Car and coach parking. Telephone (01540) 661307.

An open air museum, partly housed in an 18th-century shooting lodge. Features a black house from Lewis, a clack mill and exhibits of farming equipment. Indoors, a fine display of barn, dairy, stable and an exhibition of Highland tinkers. Special features on costume, musical instruments and Highland furniture. Special events July and August.

---

800 HIGHLAND FOLK MUSEUM, NEWTONMORE **3 K10**

Aultlarie, Newtonmore, Inverness-shire. In Newtonmore, 15 miles (24km) southwest of Aviemore off the A9. Nearest railway station Newtonmore. Buses from Inverness, Perth or Edinburgh. Open May–Oct, telephone to confirm times. Charge £. Group concessions. Guided tours. Explanatory displays. Gift shop. Café and picnic area. Children's play area. WC. Limited wheelchair access. Disabled WC. Car and coach parking.

In this open air museum whole buildings and their environment have been reconstructed or restored, according to the authentic skills and technology of each period, from the early 18th-century Highland township to the mid-20th-century working croft. A programme of traditional music and a variety of craft activities during July and August.

---

801 HIGHLAND MARY'S MONUMENT **4 J17**

At Failford, on B743, 3 miles (4.5km) west of Mauchline. Access at all times. Free.

The monument commemorates the place where, it is said, Robert Burns parted from his Highland Mary, Mary Campbell. They exchanged vows, but she died the following autumn.

---

802 HIGHLAND MARY'S STATUE **6 H15**

Castle gardens, near Dunoon pier. Access at all times. Car parking.

The statue of Burns' Highland Mary at the foot of the Castle Hill. Mary Campbell was born on a farm in Dunoon and exchanged vows with Burns. However, she died the following autumn and Burns went on to marry Jean Armour.

---

803 HIGHLAND MUSEUM OF CHILDHOOD **3 J7**

The Old Station, Strathpeffer, Ross and Cromarty. On the A834, 5 miles (8km) west of Dingwall. Nearest railway station Dingwall, bus from Dingwall. Open late Mar–Oct, Mon–Sat 1000–1700, Sun 1300–1700; Jul and Aug, Mon–Fri 1000–1900, Sat 1000–1700, Sun 1400–1700. Charge £. Group concessions. Guided tours. Explanatory dist.lays. Gift shop. Tearoom and picnic area. WC. Tape tour for partially sighted. Induction loop. Wheelchair access. Car and coach parking. Telephone (01997) 421031.

Located in part of the old station. Tells the story of childhood in the Highlands over the last century. Regular programme of events and workshops.

---

804 HIGHLAND MYSTERYWORLD **2 G11**

Glencoe, Fort William. On the A82, 1 mile (2km) west of Glencoe. Bus to Ballachulish or rail to Fort William. Open Mar–Oct, daily 1000–1630. Charge ££. Group concessions. Guided tours (leaflets in Gaelic, French, German and Italian). Explanatory displays. Gift shop. Restaurant, tearoom and picnic area. Adventure play area. Swimming pool. WC. Limited wheelchair access. Disabled WC. Car and coach parking. Telephone (01855) 811660.

Visitors can learn about ancient Highland myths and legends as they are brought to life by actors and animatronic effects. There are five different indoor attractions, a lochside trail and a leisure centre.

---

805 HIGHLAND PARK DISTILLERY **1 B10**

Holm Road, Kirkwall, Orkney. 1 mile (2km) outside Kirkwall. Bus from centre. Open Mar–Oct, Mon–Fri 1000–1600 (tours every half hour); Jul and Aug also open Sat and Sun 1200–1600; Nov–Feb, Mon–Fri tour at 1400. Closed Christmas and New Year. Charge £. Children under 12 free. Group concessions. Guided tours (leaflets in French, German and Norwegian). Explanatory displays (and audio-visual in English, French, German and Italian). Gift shop. Tearoom. WC. Wheelchair access. Disabled WC. Car and coach parking. Telephone (01856) 874619.

A 200-year-old distillery and the most northern whisky distillery in the world. Visitors can tour the distillery and traditional floor maltings (still in use). Most days there is also a kiln burning. Visitor centre.

---

806 HIGHLAND WILDLIFE PARK **3 L9**

Kincraig, Kingussie, Inverness-shire. On the B9152, 7 miles (11km) south of Aviemore. Nearest railway station Kingussie. Bus from Inverness, Perth and Edinburgh. Edinburgh. Open daily all year (weather permitting): Apr–Oct 1000–1800; Jun–Aug 1000–1900; Nov–Mar 1000–1600 (shops closed). Last entry 2 hours before closing. Charge £££ per person (reduced rates in winter). Group concessions. Guided tours. Explanatory displays. Gift shop. Coffee shop and picnic area. Baby changing facility. Children's play area. Kennels for pets. WC. No guide dogs. Limited wheelchair access. Disabled WC. Car and coach parking. Telephone (01540) 651270.

Visitors can discover Scottish wildlife, from native species to those creatures long extinct, and explore themed habitats on foot. Cars can be driven around the main reserve (those without a car will be driven by staff). Brightwater Burn is an otter habitat with walkways and pools. Themed special events at weekends and sheepdog demonstrations every Sunday, Tuesday and Thursday (April–October). Managed by the Royal Zoological Society of Scotland.

---

807 HIGHLAND WINERIES **3 J8**

Moniack Castle, Inverness. Off the A862, 7 miles (11km) west of Inverness. Nearest railway station Inverness, bus from Inverness to Inchmore then 1 mile (2km) walk. Open Mar–Oct, daily (except Sun)

1000–1700; Nov–Apr 1100–1600. Charge £. Children free. Group concessions. Guided tours. Gift shop. Picnic area. WC. Limited wheelchair access. Car and coach parking. Telephone (01463) 831283.

A family business in a 16th-century castle producing country wines, liqueurs, meat and game preserves, all made by hand.

---

808 GRISELDA HILL POTTERY **5 N14**

Kirkbrae, Ceres, Cupar, Fife. 3 miles (5km) southeast of Cupar. Nearest railway station Cupar. Open summer, Mon–Fri 0900–1630, Sat 1100–1700, Sun 1400–1700; winter, Sat and Sun 1400–1700. Free. Guided tours. Explanatory displays. Gift shop. WC. Limited wheelchair access. Disabled WC. Car parking. Telephone (01334) 828273.

Wemyss Ware was first produced in Fife in 1882. The beautifully hand-painted cats, pigs and other pottery in bright cheerful colours have a character all their own and soon became highly collectable. The original factory closed in 1932, but in 1985, Wemyss Ware was revived by Griselda Hill Pottery. Visitors can see skilled craftspeople at work.

---

809 HILL HOUSE **6 H15**

NTS. Upper Colquhoun Street, Helensburgh. Off B832, 23 miles (37km) northwest of Glasgow. Nearest railway station Helensburgh, then 1.5 mile (2.5km) walk. Open Apr–Oct, daily 1330–1730. Charge £££. Children free. Groups must pre-book and arrive prior to 1300. Explanatory displays. Gift and design shops. Gift shop. Tearoom. Garden. WC. Braille information sheet. Limited wheelchair access. Disabled WC. Car parking. Telephone (01436) 673900.

Charles Rennie Mackintosh designed this house for the publisher Walter Blackie in 1904. A masterpiece of domestic architecture synthesizing traditional Scottish style with avant-garde innovation, this extraordinary building still looks modern today. Mackintosh, with his wife Margaret, also designed the interiors and most of the furniture.

---

810 HILL O' MANY STANES **3 N4**

HS. At Mid Clyth, 4 miles (6.5km) northeast of Lybster, Caithness. Nearest railway and bus stations Wick, bus form Inverness or Wick to Mid Clyth road end, then 1 mile (2km) walk. Access at all times. Free. Telephone 0131 668 8800.

More than 22 rows of low slabs arranged in a slightly fan-shaped pattern, which may have formed a prehistoric astronomical observatory.

---

811 HILL OF TARVIT MANSION HOUSE AND GARDENS **N14**

NTS. Cupar, Fife. Off A916, 2.5 miles (4km) south of Cupar. By bus to Ceres, then 1 mile (1.5km) walk. Open Apr–May, Sep and weekends in Oct, daily 1330–1730; Jun–Aug, daily 1100–1730. Gardens and grounds open Apr–Sep, daily 0930–2100; Oct–Mar, daily 0930–1630. Charge ££. Children free. Garden and grounds only, £ (honesty box). Group concessions. Guided tours by arrangement. Explanatory displays. Information sheets in four languages. Gift shop. Tearoom and picnic area. Garden. WC. Limited wheelchair access, wheelchair available. Disabled WC. Car and coach parking. Telephone (01334) 653127.

Fine Edwardian house designed by Sir Robert Lorimer and built in 1906 for a Dundee industrialist to provide a setting for his important collection of French, Chippendale-style and vernacular furniture. Superb paintings, including works by Raeburn and Ramsay. Formal gardens also designed by Lorimer. Restored Edwardian laundry in grounds. Woodland walk.

---

812 HILTON OF CADBOLL CHAPEL **3 L6**

HS. At Hilton of Cadboll, 12 miles (19km) northeast of Invergordon, Ross and Cromarty. Nearest railway station Fearn (request stop), bus service from Inverness. Access at all times. Free. Telephone 0131 668 8800.

The foundation remains of a small rectangular chapel.

813 HM CUSTOMS AND EXCISE MUSEUM AND EXHIBITION 6 H15

Custom House, Custom House Quay, Greenock. 25 miles (40km) west of Glasgow, 2 minute walk from Greenock station. Open all year (closed some bank holidays), Mon–Fri 1000–1600. Free. Guided tours. Explanatory displays. WC. Disabled WC. Car parking. Telephone (01475) 726331.

A magnificent building which has been used a customs office since its completion in 1819. The museum shows the diverse and colourful history of the organisation and highlights the great variety of work currently done by the department.

---

814 JAMES HOGG MONUMENT 5 N18

By Ettrick, 1 mile (1.5km) west of B7009. Access at all times. Free. Car parking.

A monument on the site of the birthplace of James Hogg (1770–1835), known as the Ettrick Shepherd, friend of Scott. His grave is in the nearby church.

---

815 HOLM OF PAPA WESTRAY CHAMBERED CAIRN 1 C9

HS. On the island of Holm of Papa Westray, Orkney. Ferry from Kirkwall to Westray, then Papa Westray, then to Holm of Papa. Access at all times. Free. Telephone 0131 668 8800.

A massive tomb with a long narrow chamber divided into three, with 14 beehive cells opening into the walls. There are engravings on the walls.

---

816 HOLMWOOD HOUSE 6 K16

NTS. 61–63 Netherlee Road, Glasgow. Off B767 in Cathcart, Glasgow. Nearest railway station Cathcart, frequent buses from Glasgow city centre. Open Apr–Oct, daily 1330–1730. Charge ££. Children free. Groups must pre-book. Group concessions. Guided tours by arrangement (audio tour in French and German). Explanatory displays. Grounds, riverside walk. WC. Induction loop. Adapted audio tour for visitors with learning difficulties. Wheelchair access. Disabled WC. Car and coach parking. Telephone 0141 637 2129.

Alexander Greek Thomson, Glasgow's greatest Victorian architect, designed this villa for a local mill owner in 1857. Many rooms are richly ornamented in wood, plaster and marble and visitors can see in progress the restoration of Thomson's original stencilled decoration and elaborate friezes.

---

817 HOLY TRINITY CHURCH, STIRLING 6 L14

12 Kier Street, Bridge of Allan, Stirling. 2 miles (3km) south of exit 11 on M9. Nearest railway station Bridge of Allan, then 10 minutes walk. Bus from Stirling. Open Jun–Sep (except during weddings), Sat 1000–1600. Free. Guided tours. Explanatory displays. Gift shop. WC. Wheelchair access. Car and coach parking. Telephone (01786) 834155.

An attractive 19th-century building with fine timbered roof and excellent stained glass windows. The chancel furnishings, consisting of pulpit, communion table, chair, organ screen and choir rail, were designed in 1904 by Charles Rennie Mackintosh in light oak and represent a unique aspect of Mackintosh's style. Four complementing chairs, gifted in 1999, add modern interest.

---

818 HOMESTON FARM TRAIL AND PONY TREKKING 4 F18

Homeston Farm, Campbeltown, Argyll. 1 mile (2km) off the B842, 5 miles (8km) from Campbeltown. Bus from Campbeltown to Southend. Open daily Easter and May–Sep, daily 1030–1800. Charge £. Tearoom and picnic area. WC. Car and coach parking. Telephone (01586) 552437.

Farm trail to see all sorts of farm animals. Children can feed animals. Pony trekking.

819 HOPETOUN HOUSE — 6 M15

South Queensferry, West Lothian. 12 miles (19km) west of Edinburgh. Nearest railway station Dalmeny, bus from Edinburgh to South Queensferry then 2 mile (3km) walk. Open Easter–Sep, daily 1000–1730. Charge £££. Group concessions. Guided tours. Explanatory displays. Gift shop. Restaurant, tearoom and picnic area. WC. Limited wheelchair access. Disabled WC. Car and coach parking. Telephone 0131 331 2451.

A gem of Europe's architectural heritage and the residence of the Marquis of Linlithgow. Set in 100 acres (40ha) of magnificent parkland on the shore of the Firth of Forth with fine views of the famous bridges. Built 1699–1707 by William Bruce and extended by William Adam from 1721. Features original furniture, paintings by famous artists, 17th-century tapestries, rococo ceilings and Meissen ceramics.

---

820 HOUSE OF THE BINNS — 6 M15

NTS. Linlithgow, West Lothian. Off A904, 15 miles (24km) west of Edinburgh, 3 miles (5km) east of Linlithgow. By bus from Linlithgow. Open May–Sep, daily (except Fri) 1330–1730. Charge ££. Children free. Group concessions. Guided tours. Explanatory displays. Information sheets in seven languages. Picnic area. Parkland. WC. Braille information sheets. Photo album of upper rooms available at reception. Limited wheelchair access. Disabled WC. Car and coach parking. Telephone (01506) 834255.

Home of the Dalyell family since 1612. General Tam Dalyell raised the Royal Scots Greys here in 1681. The architecture reflects the early 17th-century transition from fortified stronghold to spacious mansion. Elaborate plaster ceilings dating from 1630. Woodland walk to panoramic viewpoint over Firth of Forth. Famous for snowdrops and daffodils in spring.

---

821 HOUSE OF DUN — 3 P11

NTS. Montrose, Angus. On A935, 3 miles (5km) west of Montrose. By bus from Montrose. Open Apr–May, Sep and weekends in Oct, daily 1330–1730; Jun–Aug, daily 1100–1730. Garden and grounds open all year, daily 0930–sunset. Charge ££. Children free. Garden and grounds only, £ (honesty box). Group concessions. Guided tours by arrangement. Explanatory displays. Gift shop. Restaurant. Adventure playground. WC. Braille information sheets, subtitled video programme. Wheelchair access with assistance, wheelchairs available. Car and coach parking. Telephone (01674) 810264.

Beautiful Georgian house overlooking Montrose Basin, designed in 1730 by William Adam and with superb contemporary plasterwork. Home in 19th century to Lady Augusta Kennedy-Erskine, daughter of William IV and the actress Mrs Jordan. Many of her belongings remain, as well as her woolwork and embroidery. Restored Victorian walled garden and attractive woodland walks.

---

822 HOXA TAPESTRY GALLERY — 1 B11

Neviholm, Hoxa, St Margaret's Hope, Orkney. On mainland 3 miles (5km) from St Margaret's Hope and 18 miles (29km) south of Kirkwall. Open Apr–Sep, Mon–Fri 1000–1730, Sat and Sun 1400–1800. Oct–Mar by appointment. Charge £. Studio free. Group concessions. Guided tours. Explanatory displays. Gift shop. No guide dogs. Wheelchair access with assistance. Car and coach parking. Telephone (01856) 831395.

The gallery shows the work of Leila Thomson who weaves in the High Gobelin technique. Her theme is the life and the landscape of Orkney. Visitors can watch her weaving, view her work or take tuition courses.

---

823 HUME CASTLE — 5 Q17

Hume, Kelso, Roxburghshire. On the B6364, 6 miles (9.5km) north of Kelso. Open daily 0900–2100. Free. Explanatory displays. Car parking.

A ruined castle, destroyed by Cromwell and partially rebuilt by the Earl of Marchmont. Good views of the Tweed valley and beyond.

---

824 HUNTER HOUSE **6 K16**

Maxwelton Road, Calderwood, East Kilbride. 3 miles (4.5km) east of East Kilbride town centre. Nearest railway station East Kilbride, bus from town centre. Open Apr–Sep, daily 1100–1700. Charge £. Group concessions. Guided tours by arrangement. Explanatory displays with interactive computers and touch table. Gift shop. Tearoom. Soft play area. WC. Large-print text. Wheelchair access. Disabled WC. Car and coach parking. Telephone (01355) 261261.

An exhibition about the lives of John and William Hunter, pioneering 18th-century medical surgeons. Audio-visual presentation on East Kilbride new town.

---

825 HUNTERSTON POWER STATION **6 H16**

West Kilbride, Ayrshire. Off the A78, about 5 miles (8km) south of Largs. Coach provided for groups. Open Mar–Sep, daily 0930–1630; Oct–Feb, Mon–Fri 0930–1630, Sat and Sun 1300–1630 (closed Christmas and New Year). Free. Guided tours. Explanatory displays and visitor centre. Gift shop. Refreshments provided (free tea, coffee and soft drinks). WC. Wheelchair access to visitor centre; limited access to power station. Disabled WC. Car and coach parking. Telephone (0800) 838557.

One of Scotland's two nuclear power stations which together produce half of Scotland's electricity. By means of videos, displays and models, the visitor centre explains how electricity is generated.

---

826 HUNTINGTOWER CASTLE **5 M13**

HS. Huntingtower, Perth. Off the A85, 3 miles (5km) northwest of Perth. Nearest railway and bus stations Perth, bus from Perth. Open Apr–Sep, daily 0930–1830; Oct–Mar, Mon–Sat 0930–1630, Sun 1400–1630, closed Thu pm and Fri. Charge £. Group concessions. Guided tours. Gift shop. Picnic area. Car and coach parking. Telephone (01738) 627231.

A 15th-century castellated mansion, until 1600 known as Ruthven Castle. Two fine and complete towers, now linked by a 17th-century range. There are fine painted ceilings.

---

827 HUNTLY CASTLE **3 P8**

HS. Castle Street, Huntly, Aberdeenshire. On the A96 in Huntly. Nearest railway station Huntly, or bus from Aberdeen or Inverness. Open Apr–Sep, Mon–Sat 0930–1830, Sun 1400–1830; Oct–Mar, Mon–Sat 0930–1830, Sun 1400–1630, closed Thu pm and Fri. Charge £. Group concessions. Guided tours. Explanatory displays. Gift shop. Picnic area. WC. Limited wheelchair access. Disabled WC. Car parking. Telephone (01466) 793191.

A magnificent ruin of a castle from the 12th-century motte to the palace erected in the 16th and 17th centuries by the Gordon family. The architectural details and heraldic enrichments are particularly impressive. Beautiful setting in a wooded park.

---

828 HUNTLY NORDIC AND OUTDOOR CENTRE **3 P8**

Hill of Haugh, Huntly, Aberdeenshire. On the outskirts of Huntly by Huntly Castle. Nearest railway station Huntly, bus from Aberdeen or Inverness. Open all year, Mon–Fri 1100–1600, Sat and Sun 1000–1700 (extended hours when snow). Charge ££. Group concessions. Tearoom and picnic area. WC. Limited wheelchair access. Disabled WC. Car and coach parking. Telephone (01466) 794428.

Cross-country ski centre with year-round artificial ski track suitable for all the family. From December–April a fully serviced ski centre offers ski hire and lessons for all abilities. Fifteen miles (25km) of machine-prepared ski trails. Also hire of mountain bikes and rollerblades. Self-guided or accompanied cycle tours, cycling skills courses.

829 ICEBERG GLASSBLOWING STUDIO **3 J8**

Victoria Buildings, Drumnadrochit, Inverness-shire. In Drumnadrochit on the A82. Bus from Inverness. Open daily summer, 1000–2100; winter, 1000–1600 (closed Mon). Free. Explanatory talk given on request. Gift shop. Wheelchair access. Car parking. Telephone (01456) 450601.

A glass-blowing studio manufacturing both solid and hollow glassware including vases, Christmas decorations, animals, and modern jewellery. Visitors can see the manufacturing process.

---

830 INCHCOLM ABBEY **6 M15**

HS. On Inchcolm Island in the Firth of Forth. Nearest railway station Dalmeny, bus from Edinburgh. Reached by ferry (30 minutes) from South Queensferry. Open Apr–Sep, daily 0930–1830. Charge £. Additional charge for ferry. Group concessions. Guided tours. Explanatory displays. Gift shop. Picnic area. WC. Wheelchair access with assistance. Car and coach parking. Telephone 0131 331 4857 or (01383) 823332.

The ruins of an Augustinian house founded circa 1123 and including a 13th-century octagonal chapter house. The best preserved group of monastic buildings in Scotland.

---

831 INCHKENNETH CHAPEL **4 E12**

HS. On the island of Inch Kenneth off the west coast of the Isle of Mull, Argyll. Access at all times. Free. Telephone 0131 668 8800.

A simple building of a distinctive West Highland type, with good medieval monuments in the graveyard.

---

832 INCHMAHOME PRIORY **5 K14**

HS. On an island in the Lake of Mentieth, Perthshire. Access by boat from Port of Menteith, on A81, 4 miles (6.5km) east of Aberfoyle. Bus from Glasgow or Stirling to Port of Menteith, then short walk to ferry. Open Apr–Sep, daily 0930–1830. Charge £. Group concessions. Guided tours. Gift shop. Picnic area. WC. Limited wheelchair access. Disabled WC. Car parking. Telephone (01877) 385294.

The beautifully situated ruins of an Augustinian monastery founded in 1238, with much 13th-century building surviving. Briefly housed Mary, Queen of Scots as an infant in 1547.

---

833 INNERPEFFRAY CHAPEL **5 L13**

HS. Innerpeffray, Crieff. 4 miles (6.5km) southeast of Crieff. Nearest railway station Perth, bus from Perth to Crieff, then bus to Innerpeffray. Car parking. Telephone 0131 668 8800.

A rectangular collegiate church founded in 1508. Still retains its altar and evidence of its furnishings.

---

834 INNERPEFFRAY LIBRARY **5 L13**

Innerpeffray, Crieff, Perthshire. On the B8062, 4 miles (6.5km) southeast of Crieff. Open Apr–Sep, Mon–Sat 1000–1245 and 1400–1645, Sun 1400–1600; Feb, Mar, Oct and Nov closes 1600; closed every Thu. Charge £. Group concessions. Guided tours. Tearoom. WC. Wheelchair access with assistance to chapel; difficult access to library. Car and coach parking. Telephone (01764) 652819.

The first lending library in Scotland, founded in 1680. A collection of 3000 titles printed between 1500 and 1800 now housed in a purpose-built library completed in 1762. Many rare and interesting volumes, including books from the library of The Great Marquis of Montrose. Adjacent collegiate chapel built in 1508, burial place of the Drummond family.

---

835 INSH MARSHES NATURE RESERVE **3 L10**

RSPB. Ivy Cottage, Insh, Kingussie, Inverness-shire. On the B970, 2 miles (3km) south of Kingussie. Nearest railway station and coach stop

Kingussie. Open at all times. Free. Guided tours (charge £) Apr–Aug, Thu pm. Explanatory displays. Picnic area. Bird-watching hides and nature trails. Limited wheelchair access. Car and coach parking. Telephone (01540) 661518.

The most important area of flood plain wetland in Britain with nearly 1000 pairs of wading birds breeding on the marshes, which are an important wintering ground for wildfowl; in winter, these include 200 whooper swans from Iceland. Varied wetland plants. Otters.

---

836 INSHRIACH ALPINE NURSERY **3 L9**

Aviemore, Inverness-shire. On the B970, 4 miles (6.5km) south of Aviemore. Nearest railway station Aviemore. Open mid Feb–mid Nov, Mon–Fri 0900–1700, Sat 0900–1600. Free. WC. Limited wheelchair access. Car and coach parking. Telephone (01540) 651287.

Show garden and alpine plant nursery growing a wide range of alpines, heathers, dwarf shrubs and dwarf rhododendrons.

---

837 INTERNATIONAL OTTER SURVIVAL FUND **2 E9**

Broadford, Isle of Skye. On the A850 near Broadford. Nearest railway station Kyle of Lochalsh, bus form Kyle of Lochalsh and Portree. Open all year. Charge £. Group concessions. Guided tours by arrangement. WC. Wheelchair access with assistance. Car parking. Telephone (01471) 822487.

Guided walks by prior arrangement around the otter pens, with a description of the history, ecology and conservation of the otter.

---

838 INTERNATIONAL PURVES PUPPETS **5 M17**

Biggar Little Theatre, 8 Broughton Road, Biggar, Lanarkshire. Bus from Edinburgh or Hamilton, nearest railway station Lanark. Open all year (except Christmas and New Year) Jan–mid Mar, Sat 1000–1700; mid Mar–Dec, Mon–Sat 1000–1700 (Easter–Aug also Sun). Charge ££. Guided tours £. Group concessions. Guided tours (available in French). Explanatory displays. Gift shop. Tearoom and picnic area. Play area, gardens and pet corner. WC.. Wheelchair access (telephone to confirm for theatre performances). Disabled WC. Car and coach parking. Telephone (01899) 220631.

A unique Victorian puppet theatre seating 100 and set in beautiful grounds. Mysterious glowing scenery, large-scale puppets, secret passages and magical starry ceiling. Regular performances in many languages for all ages. Backstage and museum tours.

---

839 INVERARAY BELL TOWER **4 G14**

The Avenue, Inveraray, Argyll. In centre of town. Bus from Glasgow or Oban. Open May–Sep, daily 1000–1300 and 1400–1700. Charge £. Children under 5 free. Group concessions. Explanatory displays. Gift shop. Picnic area and garden. Limited wheelchair access. Car and coach parking.

This 126 foot (38.5m) high granite tower houses Scotland's finest ring of bells and the world's second-heaviest ring of ten bells. Excellent views, pleasant grounds. Opportunities to see bells and ringers in action. Recordings always available when tower open. Easy staircase to top viewing gallery in bell chamber.

---

840 INVERARAY CASTLE **4 G14**

Inveraray, Argyll. On the A83, 0.5 mile (1km) north of Inveraray. Bus from Glasgow. Open Apr–Jun, Sep and Oct, Mon–Thu and Sat 1000–1300 and 1400–1745, Sun 1300–1745; Jul and Aug, Mon–Sat 1000–1745, Sun 1300–1745. Charge ££. Group concessions. Guided tours (available in French and German by arrangement). Explanatory displays. Gift shop. Tearoom and picnic area. Garden by appointment. WC. Limited wheelchair access. Disabled WC. Car and coach parking. Telephone (01499) 302203.

The Duke of Argyll's family, the senior branch of the Campbell Clan, moved from Loch Awe to Inveraray in the first half of the 15th century. The present building, in the style of a castle, was erected between 1745–90 to replace an earlier traditional fortified keep and marks the start of more settled times. It was designed by Roger Morris and Robert Mylne. On display are the famous collection of armour, French tapestries, fine examples of Scottish and European furniture, a wealth of other works of art together with a genealogical display in the Clan Room. Gardens open by appointment only.

---

841 INVERARAY JAIL **4 G14**

Church Square, Inveraray, Argyll. In Inveraray centre. Bus from Glasgow or Oban. Open Apr–Oct, daily 0930–1700; Nov–Mar, daily 1000–1600 (closed Christmas Day and New Year's Day). Charge ££. Group concessions. Explanatory displays (translated in French, German and Italian). Costumed guides. Gift shop. WC. Induction loop in courtroom. Limited wheelchair access to ground floor, free of charge. Disabled WC. Telephone (01499) 302381.

Voted *Best Scottish Attraction of the Decade*. Visitors can see a medieval punishment exhibition, listen to trials in the superb 1820 courtroom, visit the airing yards, talk with guides dressed as warders, prisoners and matron, experience life inside prison and try the crank machine, whipping table and hammocks, before comparing all this with a new exhibition In Prison Today.

---

842 INVERARAY MARITIME MUSEUM **4 G14**

Arctic Penguin, the Harbour, Inveraray, Argyll. In Inveraray centre. Bus from Glasgow or Oban. Open all year, daily 1000–1800, closed Christmas and New Year's Day. Charge £. Group concessions. Guided tours by prior arrangement. Explanatory displays. Gift shop. Play area. WC. Limited wheelchair access. Disabled WC. Car and coach parking. Telephone (01499) 302213.

A fascinating collection of maritime displays, memorabilia, archive film and entertaining hands-on activities on board one of the last iron ships, built in 1911. Graphic tableaux in the hold depict the hardships suffered on emigrant ships during the Highland clearances. A 'Pepper's Ghost' illusion shows the end of Scotland's most notorious pirate, William Kidd.

---

843 INVERAWE FISHERIES AND SMOKERY EXHIBITION **4 G13**

Inverawe House, Taynuilt, Argyll. Turning off the A85, 14 miles (22.5km) east of Oban. Nearest railway station Taynuilt, bus from Oban then 2.5 miles (4km) walk. Open Mar–Nov, daily 0800–1800. Free but charges for fishing. Explanatory displays. Gift shop. Tearoom and picnic area. Nature trails and wildfowl reserves. WC. Wheelchair access. Disabled WC. Car and coach parking. Telephone (01866) 822446.

Visitors can fish on one of the four stocked lochs, take a look at how the smokery works, and wander around the 50 acre (20ha) estate.

---

844 INVERBEG GALLERIES **4 J14**

Inverbeg, Loch Lomond. At Inverbeg on the A82, 3 miles (5km) north of Luss. Bus from Glasgow. Open daily all year (except Christmas Day), 1000–1800, closed Thu pm. Free. Guided tours. Explanatory displays. Gift shop. Wheelchair access with assistance. Car and coach parking. Telephone (01436) 860277.

An internationally renowned art gallery with one of the largest selections of oil and watercolour paintings and prints in the UK.

845 INVERESK LODGE GARDEN **6 N15**

NTS. Inveresk Village, Musselburgh, East Lothian. On A6124, just south of Musselburgh. By bus from Edinburgh or Musselburgh. Open Apr–Oct, Mon–Fri 1000–1630, Sat–Sun 1400–1700 (Nov–Mar, closed Sat). Charge £. Group concessions. Explanatory displays. WC. Disabled WC. Car and coach parking. Telephone (01721) 722502.

Attractive terraced garden in historic village of Inveresk. Excellent range of roses and shrubs and beautiful display of colour in autumn. The peaceful atmosphere of a secret garden, yet accessible from the centre of Edinburgh.

---

846 INVEREWE GARDEN **2 F6**

NTS. Poolewe, Ross and Cromarty. On A832, 6 miles (10km) northeast of Gairloch. Infrequent bus from Inverness. Open mid Mar–Oct, daily 0930–2100; Nov–mid Mar, daily 0930–1700. Visitor centre closed in winter. Charge ££. Children free. Group concessions. Explanatory displays. Guidebook in French and German, text in four languages. Gift shop. Restaurant. Guided garden walks mid Apr–mid Sep, Mon–Fri 1330. Plant sales. WC. Guide dogs only. Wheelchair access, wheelchairs available. Disabled WC. Car and coach parking. Telephone (01445) 781200.

World-famous garden created from once-barren peninsula on the shore of Loch Ewe by Victorian gardener Osgood Mackenzie. Exotic plants from many countries flourish here in the mild climate created by the North Atlantic Drift. Spectacular lochside setting among pinewoods, with superb views.

---

847 INVERKEITHING MUSEUM **6 M15**

The Friary, Queen Street, Inverkeithing, Fife. In Inverkeithing, 1 mile (2km) from north end of the Forth Road Bridge. Nearest railway station Inverkeithing, then 10 minutes walk. Bus from Edinburgh or Dunfermline. Open all year, Thu–Sun 1200–1600, closed Christmas and New Year. Free. Guided tours. Explanatory displays. Gift shop. Car parking. Telephone (01383) 410495.

Local history of Inverkeithing and Rosyth. Small display on Admiral Greig, founder of the Russian navy.

---

848 INVERLOCHY CASTLE **2 H11**

HS. 2 miles (3km) northeast of Fort William, Inverness-shire. Nearest railway and bus stations Fort William, bus from Fort William, request stop. Limited access due to major consolidation work (telephone for details) – view exterior only. Car parking. Telephone 0131 668 8800.

A fine well-preserved 13th-century castle of the Comyn family in the form of a square with round towers at the corners. The largest tower was the donjon or keep.

---

849 INVERNESS AQUADOME AND SPORTS CENTRE **3 K8**

Bught Park, Inverness. 1 mile (1.5km) west of Inverness town centre off the A82. Nearest railway and bus stations Inverness. Open all year except 25/26 Dec and 1/2 Jan. Charge ££. Children under 18 months free, reduced rates for under 4s. Group concessions. Guided tours. Cafés. WC. Wheelchair access. Disabled WC. Car and coach parking. Telephone (01463) 667500.

A wide variety of activities from basketball to badminton, short tennis to fitness room training, and an adjacent athletics track. The Aquadome has a 25m (82 foot) competition pool, leisure and kiddies pool. Also health suite.

---

850 INVERNESS MUSEUM AND ART GALLERY **3 K8**

Castle Wynd, Inverness. In Inverness centre. Inverness railway and bus stations are 5 minutes walk. Local bus stops nearby. Open all year (except public holidays), Mon–Sat 0900–1700. Free. Explanatory displays. Gift shop. Coffee shop. WC. Wheelchair access. Telephone (01463) 237114.

Displays of natural and human history of Inverness and the Highlands. Features exhibition of Highland and Inverness silver, weapons and musical instruments. Temporary exhibitions and events.

---

851 INVERNESS, JAMES PRINGLE WEAVERS **3 K8**

Holm Mills, Dores Road, Inverness. On the B862, 1.5 miles (2.5km) southwest of Inverness. Nearest railway station Inverness, bus from Inverness. Open daily, Jan–Feb 1000–1700; Mar–Oct 0900–1730; Nov–Dec 0900–1700. Free. Guided tours of weaving factory (information sheets in seven languages). Explanatory displays. Gift shop. Restaurant. WC. Wheelchair access. Car and coach parking. Telephone (01463) 223311.

Tartan is woven in an original mill dating back to 1798. Also cashmere, lambswool and tweeds.

---

852 IONA **4 D13**

NTS. Argyll. An island off the southwest tip of the Isle of Mull. Car and coach parking at Fionnphort. By ferry from Oban to Craignure, bus from Craignure to Fionnphort, by ferry to Iona. Day tours from Oban in summer. Open all year. Free. Explanatory displays. Gift shop. Coffee shop at Abbey (not NTS). WC. Limited wheelchair access. Telephone Telephone NTS Regional Office (01631) 570000.

The island where Columba began to spread the gospel in 563AD. Abbey and other historic sites are owned by Iona Cathedral Trustees, but island is owned by NTS. Superb long sandy beaches and turquoise seas; unrivalled views.

---

853 IONA ABBEY **4 D13**

Isle of Iona, Argyll. On an island off the southwest tip of the Isle of Mull. Car and coach parking at Fionnphort. By ferry from Oban to Craignure, bus from Craignure to Fionnphort, by ferry to Iona. Day tours from Oban in summer. Open all year. Free. Donation. Guided tours. Explanatory displays. Gift shop. Coffee shop. WC. Induction loop for services. Limited wheelchair access. Telephone (01681) 700404.

The site of St Columba's landing in 563AD and his original monastery. From here Christianity spread throughout Scotland and beyond. A Benedictine monastery was founded in 1203, but it fell into ruin at the Reformation in the 16th century. The cathedral was restored in 1910 and has a beautiful interior and carvings. The monastic buildings were later restored by the Iona Community who provide week-long programmes for guests and run a shop and coffee house. The Abbey precincts contain the graves of many kings and chiefs, the restored St Oran's Chapel, and the 10th-century St Martin's Cross.

---

854 IONA HERITAGE CENTRE **4 D13**

Isle of Iona, Argyll. On an island off the southwest tip of the Isle of Mull, 0.3 mile (0.5km) from ferry. By ferry from Oban to Craignure, bus from Craignure to Fionnphort, by ferry to Iona. Day tours from Oban in summer. Open Apr–Oct, Mon–Sat 1030–1630. Charge £. Children under 12 free. Group concessions. Explanatory displays. Gift shop. Tearoom and picnic area. Garden. WC. Wheelchair access via tearoom. Disabled WC. Telephone (01681) 700576.

Located in the old Telford Manse. Displays illustrate the lives of the islanders over the past 200 years.

---

855 IONA POTTERY AND GALLERY **4 D13**

Isle of Iona, Argyll. Beside the Abbey (see 853). By ferry from Oban to Craignure, bus from Craignure to Fionnphort, by ferry to Iona. Day tours from Oban in summer. Open daily Apr–Sep, 0900–1700. Free. Gift shop. Wheelchair access.

A working pottery where visitors can see work in progress. Displays both thrown and hand-built decorative stoneware. Late 19th-century and early 20th-century paintings and etchings, and contemporary landscapes.

---

856 ISLAND ENCOUNTER **4 E12**

c/o Arla Beag Cottage, Arle, Aros, Isle of Mull. Ferry from Oban to Craignure; visitors collected from ferry and other locations on Mull by arrangement. Open Mar–Oct, daily 1030–1700. Charge £££. Group concessions. Guided tours. Picnic lunch provided. Limited wheelchair access. Telephone (01680) 300441.

Day trips for visitors wishing to see and experience wildlife and birds in areas of the island not usually visited. Binoculars and telescopes provided.

---

857 ISLAY WOOLLEN MILL **4 D16**

Bridgend, Islay. On the Askaig Road, 1 mile (2km) from Bridgend. Open Apr–Dec, Mon–Sat 1000–1700; Jan–Mar, Mon–Fri 1000–1700, Sat 1300–1700 (closed Christmas Day and New Year's Day). Free. Guided tours. Explanatory displays. Gift shop. Picnic area. WC. Car and coach parking. Telephone (01496) 810563.

An early Victorian mill containing a tweed and woollen factory which produces tartan. Also a shop.

---

858 ISLE OF ARRAN DISTILLERY VISITOR CENTRE **4 G16**

Lochranza, Isle of Arran. 14 miles (22.5km) north of Brodick. By ferry to Brodick and then by courtesy bus. Open Easter–Oct daily, 1000–1800. Winter, telephone to confirm times. Charge ££. Children 8 years or under cannot take distillery tour. Group concessions. Guided tours. Explanatory displays. Gift shop. Restaurant and picnic area. Garden. WC. Induction loop for audio-visual programme. Wheelchair access with assistance. Disabled WC. Car and coach parking. Telephone (01770) 830264.

This is the newest single malt whisky distillery in Scotland, having been in production since August 1995. Tours explain how whisky is made. Visitor centre has interactive displays and a short film illustrating whisky production on Arran over the last 150 years. Audio-visual room set in mock 18th-century crofter's inn. Shop sells local goods and whisky products.

---

859 ISLE OF ISLAY NATURAL HISTORY TRUST **4 D16**

The Field Centre, Port Charlotte, Isle of Islay. Below the youth hostel in Port Charlotte. Local bus service. Open Easter–Oct, Mon–Sat (closed Wed) 1000–1500, Sun 1400–1700; Nov–Easter by arrangement. Charge £. Children under 5 free. Tickets valid for 1 week. Group concessions. Explanatory displays. Gift shop. Children's room, activities. WC. Wheelchair access. Disabled WC. Car parking. Telephone (01496) 850288.

The Wildlife Information Centre has displays on all aspects of Islay's wildlife and landscape, as well as an extensive reference library, a children's room and a laboratory where children and adults can try a number of hands-on activities such as dissecting owl pellets and making seaweed pictures. Family activity sessions during July and August.

---

860 ISLE OF JURA DISTILLERY **4 E16**

Craighouse, Isle of Jura, Argyll. By ferry from Islay. Open by arrangement. Free. Guided tours. Limited wheelchair access. Car and coach parking. Telephone (01496) 820240.

A distillery built in 1810 on a site where illegal distillation occurred for almost 300 years.

---

861 ISLE OF MULL ANGORA RABBIT FARM **4 D13**

Rehmor Croft, Bunessan, Isle of Mull. On A849, 1 mile (2km) east of Bunessan. By ferry from Oban to Craignure, bus from Craignure. Open Easter–Oct, Sun–Fri 1100–1700. Charge £. Group concessions. Guided tours (available in German). Explanatory displays. Gift shop. Tearoom and picnic area. Nature trail. Children's play area. Viewpoint. WC. Wheelchair access with assistance. Car parking. Telephone (01681) 700507.

A farm with about 30 Angora rabbits bred for their hair (which is used for knitting yarns on sale). Visitors on the tour can hold and stroke rabbits and learn all about them. Clipping and spinning demonstrations daily; treasure hunt every Sunday.

---

862 ISLE OF MULL LANDROVER WILDLIFE EXPEDITIONS **4 E12**

Ulva House Hotel, Tobermory, Isle of Mull. In the centre of Tobermory. Ferry from Oban to Craignure then bus to Tobermory. Tours run all year. Charge £££. Charge includes refreshments and lunch. Guided tours. Explanatory displays. No guide dogs. Car parking. Telephone (01688) 302044.

Explore Mull's wildlife and the island's immensly varied habitats, led by a Hebridean wildlife expert. Visitors usually see otters, sea eagles, golden eagles, seals, deer, porpoises etc.

---

863 ISLE OF MULL MUSEUM **4 E12**

Main Street, Tobermory, Isle of Mull. Main Street, Tobermory, Isle of Mull. By ferry from Oban to Craignure, bus from Craignure. Open Easter–Oct, Mon–Fri 1000–1600, Sat 1000–1300. Charge £. Explanatory displays. Wheelchair access.

An exhibition of items, facts and photos of Mull history.

---

864 ISLE OF MULL WEAVERS **4 F13**

The Steading, Torosay Castle, Craignure, Isle of Mull. On the A849, 1.5 miles (2.5km) south of Craignure ferry. By ferry from Oban to Craignure, bus from Craignure. Miniature railway from Old Pier to Torosay. Open Feb–Easter, Mon–Sat 0900–1700; Easter–Oct, daily 0900–1700; Nov and Dec, Mon–Sat 0900–1700. Free. Guided tours. Gift shop. Environment noisy, guide dogs not advised. Limited wheelchair access. Car and coach parking. Telephone (01680) 812381.

Weaving demonstrations all day.

---

865 ISLE OF SKYE BREWING COMPANY **2 D7**

Uig, Isle of Skye. Adjacent to the pier at Uig (on A856). Nearest railway station Kyle of Lochalsh or Mallaig. Bus from Inverness or Glasgow. Brewery open all year, daily 1000–1800. Shop open May–Sep, Mon–Sat 1000–1800; Jul–Sep, Sun 1200–1700. Charge £. Group concessions. Guided tours. Explanatory displays. Gift shop. WC. Wheelchair access. Disabled WC. Car and coach parking. Telephone (01470) 542477.

A brewery producing several cask-conditioned real ales, most of which have won awards, and its own cold-filtered bottled beers. Visitors can tour the brewery (brewing permitting – please telephone ahead). As well as its own range of beers the company sells a wide range of other Scottish bottled beers, wines and brewery souvenirs.

---

866 ITALIAN CHAPEL **1 C11**

Lambholm, Orkney. On mainland at St Mary's, 7 miles (11km) south of Kirkwall. Bus from Kirkwall. Open daily all year in daylight. Free. Donations. Booklets in English and Italian. Wheelchair access. Car and coach parking. Telephone (01856) 781268.

Two Nissen huts transformed into a chapel by Italian prisoners of war.

---

867 JACOBITE CRUISES **3 K8**

Tomnahurich Bridge, Glenurquhart Road, Inverness. 1 mile (1.5km) west of Inverness town centre on the A82. Local bus service from Church Street, Inverness. Open Easter–Oct, daily; cruises at 1000 and 1400.

Charge £££. Group concessions. Commentary in Dutch, French, German, Italian, Japanese and Spanish. Licensed snack bar on board. WC. Wheelchair access with assistance. Car parking. Telephone (01463) 233999.

A cruise along the Caledonian Canal and on to Loch Ness, through some of Scotland's most beautiful open country.

---

868 STEPHANE JAEGER KNITWEAR **1 C11**

Littlequoy, Burray, Orkney. Near Echnaloch, off the A961, 12 miles (19km) south of Kirkwall. Bus from Kirkwall (2 mile/3km walk). Open Jun–Sep, Mon–Sat 1000–1800; other times by appointment. Free. Wheelchair access. Car and coach parking. Telephone (01856) 731228.

A knitwear workshop in a traditional Orkney building. Garments are made from wool spun and knitted from the undyed natural fibres of the workshop's own sheep and cashmere goats. Hand-spinning demonstrations on request.

---

869 JARLSHOF PREHISTORIC AND NORSE SETTLEMENT **1 G6**

HS. Sumburgh, Shetland. On the A970 at Sumburgh Head, 22 miles (35km) south of Lerwick. Bus from Lerwick. Open Apr–Sep, daily 0930–1830. Charge £. Group concessions. Guided tours. Explanatory displays and visitor centre. Gift shop. WC. Wheelchair access with assistance. Car and coach parking. Telephone (01950) 460112.

An extraordinarily important site with a complex of ancient settlements within 3 acres (1.2ha). The oldest is the Bronze Age village of oval stone huts. Above this there is an Iron Age broch and wheelhouses, and even higher still an entire Viking settlement. On the crest of the mount is a house built around 1600. The displays explain Iron Age life and the history of the site.

---

870 JEDBURGH ABBEY **5 P18**

HS. Abbey Bridgend, Jedburgh. Off the A68 in Jedburgh. Bus service from Edinburgh, Kelso and Galashiels. Open Apr–Sep, daily 0930–1830; Oct–Mar, Mon–Sat 0930–1630, Sun 1400–1630. Charge £. Group concessions. Guided tours. Explanatory displays and visitor centre. Gift shop. Tearoom and picnic area. WC. Limited wheelchair access. Disabled WC. Car and coach parking. Telephone (01835) 863925.

One of the Border abbeys founded by David I circa 1138 for Augustinian canons. The remarkable complete church is mostly Romanesque and early Gothic. The west front has a fine rose window and there is a richly carved Norman doorway. The remains of the cloisters have recently been uncovered and finds from the excavations are displayed. An exhibition portrays life in the monastery.

---

871 JEDBURGH CASTLE JAIL AND MUSEUM **5 P18**

Castle Gate, Jedburgh. In Jedburgh. Nearest railway station Edinburgh or Carlisle, bus from Edinburgh or Carlisle. Open Mon–Sat 1000–1630, Sun 1300–1600. Charge £. Group concessions. Guided tours by arrangement. Explanatory displays. Gift shop. Picnic area. Baby changing. WC. Limited wheelchair access. Disabled WC. Car and coach parking. Telephone (01835) 863254.

Refurbished Reform Prison dating from 1824. Designed by Archibald Elliot to principles advocated by John Howard, prison reformer. New displays in the Jailer's House provide an insight into the development of the Royal Burgh of Jedburgh, while the history of the Jail itself is told in the two adjoining cell blocks. One of the few remaining examples of a Howard Reform Prison in Britain.

---

872 JEDBURGH WOOLLEN MILL **5 P18**

Bankend North, 1 Edinburgh Road, Jedburgh. In Jedburgh on the A68, 10 miles (16km) north of the English border. Bus from Edinburgh or Newcastle. Open all year (except Christmas and New Year's Day):

Apr–Oct, daily 0900–1730; Nov–Mar, daily 0900–1700. Free. Explanatory displays. Gift shop. Picnic area. WC. Limited wheelchair access. Disabled WC. Car and coach parking. Telephone (01835) 863585.

Visitors can trace their clan and tartan at the Clan Tartan Centre – fully authenticated by the Clan Chiefs of Scotland. A world of tartan from small mementoes to full Highland dress, the choice is immense. Also golf equipment.

---

873 JEDFOREST DEER AND FARM PARK 5 P18

Mervinslaw Estate, Camptown, Jedburgh. On the A68, 5 miles (8km) south of Jedburgh. Bus from Jedburgh to Camptown then 0.5 mile (1km) walk. Open May–Aug, daily 1000–1730; Sep and Oct 1100–1630. Charge ££. Group concessions. Guided tours (available in German). Explanatory displays. Gift shop. Tearoom, picnic and barbeque area. WC. Limited wheelchair access. Disabled WC. Car and coach parking. Telephone (01835) 840364.

A Borders working farm with sheep, suckler cows, and red deer. Large display of rare breeds, including sheep, cattle, pigs, goats, poultry and waterfowl. Emphasis on physical contact with animals and involvement with farm activities. Daily bulletin board, coded walks, adventure land, conservation and wet areas. Birds of prey with daily displays, hawk walks and tuition. Tractor rides and commentary can be booked. Educational resources material and guide book. Ranger-led walks and activities. Crazy golf.

---

874 JOHN O' GROATS 3 N2

Caithness. Bus from Wick or Thurso. Tourist office. Gift shop. Refreshments. WC. Car and coach parking.

John o' Groats claims to be the most northerly point of mainland Scotland, but in fact Dunnet Head, to the west, is. Named after Jan de Groot, a Dutch ferryman who settled there in the 16th century. A few miles further east is Duncansby Head (see 480).

---

875 JOHN PAUL JONES COTTAGE MUSEUM 5 L20

Arbigland, Kirkbean, Dumfries. Off the A710, 14 miles (22.5km) south of Dumfries. Nearest railway station Dumfries, bus from Dumfries. Open Apr–Jun and Sep, Tue–Sun 1000–1700; Jul and Aug same hours but also open Mon. Charge £. Group concessions. Guided tours. Explanatory displays (audio-visual). Gift shop. WC. Wheelchair access. Disabled WC. Car and coach parking. Telephone (01387) 880613.

Based around the cottage in which John Paul Jones, the Father of the American Navy, spent his first 13 years before becoming an apprentice in the merchant navy. The original building has been restored to the style of a gardener's cottage of the 1740s, with period furnishings, a replica of the cabin of the *Bonhomme Richard*, and a room containing a model of John Paul Jones and one of the cannons he is known to have used. The cottage gardens have been laid out in period style. Interpretive display and shop in former kennels.

---

876 JURA HOUSE GARDEN 4 E16

Ardfin, Craighouse, Isle of Jura. On the A846, 5 miles (8km) from Feolin Ferry (to Islay). Bus from ferry or from Craighouse. Large parties can request bus. Open all year, daily 0900–1700. Charge £. Under 16s free. Explanatory displays. Plants for sale. Tea tent and picnic area. WC. Wheelchair access with assistance. Car and coach parking. Telephone (01496) 820315.

Interesting woodland and cliff walks with points of local historical interest and, for keen natural historians, abundant wildlife and flowers. The organic garden offers a wide variety of unusual plants and shrubs suited to the protected west coast climate, including a large Australasian collection. The house is not open to visitors.

877 KAGYU SAMYE LING TIBETAN CENTRE

See 1281 Samye Ling Tibetan Buddhist Monastery.

---

878 KAILZIE GARDENS — 5 N17

Kailzie, Kirkburn, Peebles. Near Kirkburn, off the B7062, 2.5 miles (4km) east of Peebles. Bus from Peebles. Open Mar–Oct daily, 1100–1730; in winter during daylight. Charge £. Group concessions. Guided tours. Explanatory displays. Gift shop. Licenced café, picnic area. WC. Wheelchair access with assistance. Car and coach parking. Telephone (01721) 720007.

Seventeen acres (6.8ha) of gardens in the beautiful Tweed valley. The 1812 walled garden is semi-formal, with fine herbaceous borders and shrub roses. Formal rose garden and greenhouses. Woodland and burnside walks. Rhododendrons in season. Duck pond and stocked trout pond. Art gallery. Interpretive area in Old Bothy with video of the Garden Year.

---

879 KARTSTART — 6 N14

Unit 1, Merchant Place, Mitchelston Industrial Estate, Kirkcaldy. Just off A92, Dunfermline to Kirkcaldy link road. Nearest railway and bus stations Kirkcaldy. Open all year, daily 1200–1730 and 1830–2200 (Sat and Sun closes at 2100). Closed Christmas and New Year. Admission free. Charge for driving. Group concessions. Explanatory displays. Café. WC. Wheelchair access. Disabled WC. Car and coach parking. Telephone (01592) 650200.

The largest indoor kart circuit (350-metres) in Scotland. Offers the opportunity to experience the thrill of real motor sport. All weather facility. Mini-quads, cadet karts, senior karts, pro-karts.

---

880 KEATHBANK MILL HERITAGE CENTRE — 5 M12

Balmoral Road, Blairgowrie, Perthshire. On the A93, 1 mile (2km) north of Blairgowrie. Nearest railway station Perth, bus from Dundee or Perth. Open May–Oct, daily 1030–1700. Charge ££. Group concessions. Guided tours (Leaflet available in French, German and Italian). Explanatory displays. Gift shop. Coffee shop. WC. Wheelchair access with assistance. Disabled WC. Car and coach parking. Telephone (01250) 872025.

A mill built in 1864 on the banks of the River Ericht and boasting the largest working water wheel in Scotland. Also an operational steam engine built in the same year. Contains a heraldic museum and workshop which displays clan crests, coats of arms and shields, and an O-gauge model railway.

---

881 KEEN OF HAMAR NATIONAL NATURE RESERVE — 1 H2

Keen of Hamar, Baltasound, Unst, Shetland. On the A968, 1 mile (1.5km) east of Baltasound. Bus from Lerwick or air from Sumburgh to Baltasound. Open daily all year. Free. Guided tours on advertised days. No guide dogs. Car parking.

An important botanical site with unique habitat and landscape. A limited number of specialist plants grow on the serpentine soil.

---

882 KEILLS CHAPEL — 4 F15

HS. 6 miles (9.5km) southwest of Tayvallich, Argyll. Bus from Lochgilphead to Tayvallich, then walk or taxi. Access at all times. Free. Telephone 0131 668 8800.

A small West Highland chapel housing a collection of grave slabs and Keills Cross.

---

883 KEITH AND DUFFTOWN RAILWAY — 3 N8

Dufftown Station, Dufftown. 50 miles (80km) west of Aberdeen on the A96, on B9014 from Keith. Coach parking by arrangement. Open from

Easter. Trains operate Sat and Sun; contact station for details. Charge. Explanatory displays. Gift shop. WC. Wheelchair access. Car parking. Telephone (01340) 821181 Wed and Sat.

The picturesque branch line is 11 miles (18km) in length, connecting the two whisky distilling towns of Keith and Dufftown. Restoration of the line is still taking place. Trains run at Dufftown.

---

884 KELBURN CASTLE AND COUNTRY CENTRE **6 H16**

South Offices, Fairlie, Ayrshire. On the A78, about 2 miles (3km) south of Largs. Bus from Largs and other towns (train to Largs). Free minibus from Largs station weekends and Bank Holidays May and Jun, daily Jul and Aug. Centre open daily, Easter–Oct, 1000–1800; winter 1100–dusk. Castle open Jul and Aug. Riding centre open all year. Charge ££. Group concessions. Guided tours. Explanatory displays. Gift shop. Licensed tea-room, café and picnic areas. WC. Limited wheelchair access. Disabled WC. Car and coach parking. Telephone (01475) 568685.

Historic home of the Earls of Glasgow, and still their home. The original Norman keep is now enclosed in a castle built in 1581. A new mansion (Kelburn House) was added to this in 1700, followed later by a Victorian wing. It is surrounded by spectacular natural scenery and has breath-taking views over the Firth of Clyde. Activities include glen walks, riding, assault and adventure courses, and Scotland's most unusual attraction – the Secret Forest, with fantasy follies and hidden secrets. Exhibitions and ranger centre. Special events most weekends.

---

885 KELLIE CASTLE AND GARDEN **6 P14**

NTS. Pittenweem, Fife. On B9171, 3 miles (5km) north of Pittemweem. Limited bus service. Open Apr–Sep, daily 1330–1730; Oct, Sat and Sun 1330–1730. Gardens open all year, daily 0930–sunset. Charge ££. Children free. Group concessions. Guided tours by arrangement. Explanatory displays in five languages. Gift shop. Tearoom and picnic area. Adventure playground. WC. Induction loop. Limited wheelchair access, wheelchair available. Car and coach parking. Telephone (01333) 720271.

The oldest part of Kellie Castle dates from 1360, and most of the present building was completed around 1606. It was sympathetically restored by the Lorimer family, who lived there, in the 1870s. Late Victorian organic walled garden. Lorimer exhibition in the summerhouse.

---

886 KELSO ABBEY **5 Q17**

HS. In Bridge Street, Kelso, Roxburghshire. Bus service from Edinburgh and Galashiels. Open at all times. Free. Telephone 0131 668 8800.

The west end of the great abbey church of the Tironensians, who were brought to Kelso in 1128 by David I. One of the great Border abbeys. Even in its fragmentary state, this is superb architecture.

---

887 KELSO POTTERY **5 Q17**

The Knowes, Kelso, Roxburghshire. In the centre of Kelso in the large car park behind the Abbey. Open all year, Mon–Sat 1000–1300 and 1400–1700. Free. Explanatory displays. Gift shop. Wheelchair access with assistance. Car and coach parking. Telephone (01573) 224027.

A workshop creating a range of simple, practical stoneware pottery, lately augmented by pit-fired ware.

---

888 KELTON MAINS OPEN FARM **5 K20**

Kelton Mains, Castle Douglas. Off the roundabout on the A75, 1.5 miles (2.5km) west of Castle Douglas. Bus from Castle Douglas (0.5 mile/1km walk). Open Apr–Sep, Sun–Fri. Charge £. Group concessions. Guided tours. Gift shop. Tearoom. WC. No guide dogs. Limited wheelchair access. Disabled WC. Car and coach parking. Telephone (01556) 502120.

A working farm with a variety of breeds of sheep and cattle, poultry and rabbits. Informative and educational tours.

---

889 KEMPOCK STONE **6 H15**

Castle Mansions of Gourock. Access at all reasonable times. Free.

Granny Kempock's stone, of grey schist 6 feet (2m) high, was probably significant in prehistoric times. In past centuries it was used by fishermen in rites to ensure fair weather. Couples intending to wed used to encircle the stone to get Granny's blessing.

---

890 KID'Z PLAY **4 J17**

The Esplanade, Prestwick, Ayrshire. In Prestwick. 5 minute walk from rail and bus stations. By rail or bus from Glasgow. Open daily (except Christmas and New Year's Day): 0930–1900, Fri and Sat 0930–1930. Charge £, adults free. Group concessions. Café. Baby changing facilities. WC. Wheelchair access. Disabled WC. Car and coach parking. Telephone (01292) 475215.

An indoor adventure play area for children up to 12 years. Soft play adventure castle for under 5s.

---

891 KILBERRY SCULPTURED STONES **4 F16**

HS. At Kilberry Castle off the B8024, 17 miles (27km) south southwest of Lochgilphead, on west coast of Knapdale, Argyll. Access at all times. Free. Telephone 0131 668 8800.

A fine collection of late Medieval sculptured stones gather - ed from the Kilberry estate.

---

892 KILCHURN CASTLE **4 H13**

HS. At the northeast end of Loch Awe, 2.5 miles (4km) west of Dalmally, Argyll. Nearest railway station Loch Awe, bus to Loch Awe from Oban or Glasgow. Regular sailings to Kilchurn by steamer from Loch Awe Pier in village. Open at all times, closed in winter. Free. Charge for boat trip. Telephone 0131 668 8800. Ferry company: (01838) 200400 or 200449.

A substantial ruin based on a square tower built by Colin Campbell of Glenorchy circa 1550, but much enlarged in 1693 by Ian, Earl of Breadalbane, whose arms are over the gateway with those of his wife. It incorporates the first purpose built barracks in Scotland. Spectacular views down Loch Awe.

---

893 KILDARTON CROSS **4 D16**

HS. On the island of Islay, 2 miles (3km) east northeast of Port Ellen, Argyll. Limited post bus service. Access at all times. Free. Telephone 0131 668 8800.

The finest intact High Cross in Scotland, carved in the late 8th century.

---

894 KILDONAN CHURCH **3 L4**

10 miles (16km) north of Helmsdale on A897 Strath of Kildonan road, walk up track from Kildonan Farm.

The present church, completed in 1896, contains the old pulpit with the foot marking of Alexander Sage, minister from 1787–1824, a man of 'great bodily weight'. His son, the Rev Donald Sage wrote Memorabilia Domestica, an interesting account of Highland life in 18th- early 19th-centuries.

---

895 KILDONAN MUSEUM **2 B8**

South Uist. 8 miles (13km) north of Lochboisdale on A865 to Lochmaddy. Frequent bus service. Open Apr–Oct, Mon–Sat 1000–1700, Sun 1400–1700. Charge £. School and disabled groups free. Group con-

cessions. Guided tours. Explanatory displays. Gift shop. Tearoom. WC. Wheelchair access. Disabled WC. Car and coach parking. Telephone (01878) 710343.

Recently renovated, the museum displays information on local history. Craft shop.

---

896 KILDRUMMY CASTLE **3 P9**

HS. Kildrummy, by Alford, Aberdeenshire. 10 miles (16km) southwest of Alford on the A97. Nearest railway station Huntly or Aberdeen, local bus service. Open Apr–Sep, daily 0930–1830. Charge £. Group concessions. Guided tours. Explanatory displays. Gift shop. WC. Disabled WC. Car and coach parking. Telephone (01975) 571331.

Called the Queen of Highland Castles, this was the stronghold of the Earls of Mar and headquarters for organising the 1715 Jacobite Rising. Scotland's most complete 13th-century castle.

---

897 KILDRUMMY CASTLE GARDENS **3 N9**

Kildrummy, Alford, Aberdeenshire. Off the A97, 10 miles (16km) west of Alford (via A944). Nearest railway station Aberdeen, bus service to Strathdon. Open Apr–Oct, daily 1000–1700. Charge £. Children free. Guided tours. Explanatory displays. Gift shop. Tearoom and picnic areas. Play area and video room. WC. Disabled WC. Car and coach parking. Telephone (01975) 571277 or 571203.

The shrub and alpine garden in an ancient quarry are of interest to botanists for their great variety. The water gardens lie below the ruins of the 13th-century castle of Kildrummy. Specimen trees are planted below in the Back Den. Interesting old stones. Museum open on request.

---

898 KILLIECRANKIE **3 L11**

NTS. Pitlochry, Perthshire. On the B8079, 3 miles (5km) north of Pitlochry. Bus from Pitlochry. Site open all year, daily (free). Visitor centre open Apr–Oct, daily 1030–1730. Charge £. Children free. Explanatory displays. Guidebook in French and German, information sheets in seven languages. Gift shop. Snack bar and picnic area. WC. Braille guidebook. Remote camera in visitor centre allows viewing of wildlife. Wheelchair access with assistance to visitor centre, wheelchair available. Disabled WC. Car and coach parking. Telephone (01796) 473233.

Site of the 1689 battle of Killiecrankie, won by Highland Jacobites under Bonnie Dundee, this dramatic wooded gorge is now a haven for wildlife. Visitors can see Soldier's Leap, where a fleeing government soldier made a spectacular jump over the River Garry during the battle. The visitor centre exhibition features the battle and natural history of the area.

---

899 KILMAHOG WOOLLEN MILL **5 K14**

Kilmahog, Callander, Trossachs. 1 mile (2km) north of Callander. Open Apr–Sep, Mon–Sat 0900–1700, Sun 1000–1700; Oct–Mar, Mon–Sat 1000–1700, Sun 1200–1600. Free. Gift shop. Restaurant. WC. Limited wheelchair access. Car and coach parking. Telephone (01877) 330268.

A 250-year-old mill with the original waterwheel. Visitors can trace the history of Scottish Clans and tartans. Knitwear, clothing and gifts for sale. Adjacent to 1445 Trossachs Woollen Mill.

---

900 KILMARTIN HOUSE MUSEUM OF ANCIENT CULTURE **4 F14**

Kilmartin, Argyll. On the A816, 9 miles (14.5km) north of Lochgilphead. Nearest railway station Oban, bus from Oban or Lochgilphead. Open all year, daily 1000–1730. Charge ££. Group concessions. Guided tours by arrangement. Explanatory displays (audio-visual). Gift shop. Café. Garden. WC. Wheelchair access. Disabled WC. Car parking. Telephone (01546) 510278.

Award-winning archaeological museum which examines the relationship between Scotland's richest prehistoric landscape and its people over 5000 years. Ancient monuments, local artefacts, audio-visual displays and bookshop.

---

901 KILMARTIN SCULPTURED STONES **4 F14**

HS. In Kilmartin Churchyard, Kilmartin, Argyll. On the A816, 9 miles (14.5km) north of Lochgilphead. Nearest railway station Oban, bus from Oban or Lochgilphead. Access at all times. Free. Car parking. Telephone 0131 668 8800.

Carved West Highland grave slabs housed in a former mausoleum and in the church. One cross dates from the 16th century.

---

902 KILMICHAEL GLASSARY CUP AND RING MARKS **4 F14**

HS. Kilmartin Glen. Near the schoolhouse in village of Kilmichael Glassary, 5 miles north of Lochgilphead, Argyll. Nearest railway station Oban, then bus to Lochgilphead. Access at all times. Free. Telephone 0131 668 8800.

Bronze Age cup and ring carvings on a natural rock outcrop.

---

903 KILMODAN SCULPTURED STONES **F G15**

HS. At Clachan of Glendaruel, on the A886, 8 miles (13km) north of Colintraive, Argyll. Access at all times. Free. Telephone 0131 668 8800.

A group of West Highland carved grave slabs in a churchyard.

---

904 KILMORACK GALLERY **3 J8**

Old Kilmorack Church, Beauly. 2 miles (3km) west of Beauly along the Carrick road. Local bus service. Open Apr–Nov and during Christmas, daily 1100–1730; other times by arrangement. Free. Guided tours. WC. Wheelchair access. Car parking. Telephone (01463) 783230.

Exhibition and sale of work by the Highlands' leading artists. The gallery is housed in a spectacular 18th-century church which remains largely unchanged since it was recast in 1835.

---

905 KILMORY CAIRNS **4 G17**

At south end of Arran, 3.5 miles (5.5km) northeast of Kilmory village, off A841. Access at all times. Free.

Cairn Baan is a notable Neolithic long cairn. Half a mile (0.5km) southwest of A841 at the Lagg Hotel is Torrylin Cairn, a Neolithic chambered cairn.

---

906 KILMORY CASTLE GARDENS **4 G15**

Kilmory, Lochgilphead, Argyll. On A83, 2 miles from centre of Kilmory, by council buildings. Bus service from Glasgow. Open all year, daylight hours. Free. Guided tours by special arrangement only. Explanatory displays. Picnic area. WC. Limited wheelchair access. Car parking. Telephone (01546) 602127.

The garden was started in the 1770s and included around 100 varieties of rhododendron – it supplied plants for Kew Gardens. Now attached to the local council buildings, the gardens have been restored, with woodland walks, nature trails, herbaceous borders and a sensory trail.

---

907 KILMORY KNAP CHAPEL **4 F15**

HS. On the shore between Loch Sween and Loch Caolisport in South Knapdale. Access at all times. Free. Telephone 0131 668 8800.

A small medieval West Highland church with a collection of typical grave slabs. In the church is Macmillan's Cross, a splendid piece of medieval carving.

908 KILMUN (ST MUNN'S) CHURCH **6 H15**

Kilmun, Argyll. 6 miles (10km) from Dunoon on A880. Bus service from Dunoon. Open Easter–Sep, Tue–Thu 1330–1630; Other times by appointment. Free. Donation. Guided tours. Gift shop. Tearoom. WC. Wheelchair access with assistance. Car and coach parking. Telephone (01369) 840342.

On the site of a 7th-century Celtic monastery. Tower of a 15th-century collegiate church. Present building by Thomas Burns dates from 1841, with interior re-modelled in 1899. Important stained glass. Water-powered organ. Ancient graveyard including fine 18th-century carved stones. Mausoleum of Dukes of Argyll. Douglas vault. Grave of Elizabeth Blackwell, the first lady doctor.

---

909 KILPATRICK DUN **4 F17**

HS. 1 mile (2km) south of Blackwaterfoot, Isle of Arran. By ferry from Ardrossan to Brodick, bus from Brodick to Blackwaterfoot. 0.5 mile (1km) walk to site. Free. Telephone 0131 668 8800.

The ruins of a circular drystone homestead of unknown date, with a more recent enclosure wall.

---

910 KILRAVOCK CASTLE **3 L7**

Croy, Inverness-shire. 6 miles (10km) west of Nairn on B9101. Nearest railway station Nairn. Restaurant open all year, daily 1100–1600; gardens open all year, Mon–Sat 1100–1600; tours of castle all year, Wed only. Charge ££. Group concessions. Guided tours (groups by prior arrangement other weekdays). Gift shop. Restaurant and picnic area. Garden. WC. No guide dogs. Limited wheelchair access. Car and coach parking. Telephone (01667) 493258.

The extensive grounds and garden of this 15th-century castle are noted for a large variety of beautiful trees, some centuries old. There are sports facilities and a tree garden; nature trails and river host an abundance of wildlife.

---

911 KILT ROCK **2 E7**

Off A855, 17 miles (27km) north of Portree, Skye. Can be seen from the road. Care should be taken not to go too near the edge of the cliff. Car parking.

The top rock is composed of columnar basalt, the lower portion of horizontal beds, giving the impression of the pleats in the kilt. There is a waterfall nearby.

---

912 KILWINNING ABBEY **6 H17**

HS. In Kilwinning, Ayrshire. Nearest railway station Kilwinning, bus service from Irvine. Access at all times but may be viewed from outside only. Free. Car parking. Telephone 0131 668 8800.

The ruins of a Tironensian–Benedictine abbey. Most of the surviving fragments, which consist of parts of the church and chapter house, appear to date from the 13th century.

---

913 KING'S KNOT **6 L14**

HS. Below the Castle rock in Stirling. Nearest railway station Stirling, buses from Glasgow and Edinburgh. Access at all times. Free. Telephone 0131 668 8800.

The earthworks of a splendid formal garden, probably made in 1628 for Charles I.

---

914 KINKELL CHURCH **3 Q9**

HS. On the east bank of the River Don, off the B993, 2 miles (3km) south of Inverurie, Aberdeenshire. Nearest railway station Inverurie, bus from Aberdeen. Access at all times. Free. Telephone 0131 668 8800.

The ruins of a 16th-century parish church with a fine sacrament house dated 1524 and the grave slab of Gilbert of Greenlaw, killed in battle in 1411.

915 KIN KRAFT CENTRE FOR SCOTTISH CRAFTS **6 M14**

Kinross Services Area, Turfhills, Kinross. Off Junction 6 on the M90. Open all year (except Christmas and New Year), daily 0900–1730. Free. Explanatory displays. Gift shop. WC. Wheelchair access. Car and coach parking. Telephone (01577) 861300.

Visitors can see craftwork demonstrations.

---

916 KINLOCHLAICH GARDENS **4 G12**

Kinlochlaich House, Appin, Argyll. On the A828, entrance beside the police station at Appin. Bus from Oban or Fort William. Open Apr–Oct, Mon–Sat 0930–1730, Sun 1030–1730; Nov–Mar, Mon–Sat 0930–1730. Closed Christmas and New Year. Donation. WC. Guide dogs by arrangement. Wheelchair access with assistance. Disabled WC. Car parking. Telephone (01631) 730342.

A walled garden behind Kinlochlaich House surrounded by mature trees in outstanding Highland scenery. Built with the house at the end of the 18th century by John Campbell. Garden Plant Centre offering an extensive range of plants. Dogs not permitted.

---

917 KINNAIRD HEAD LIGHTHOUSE **3 R7**

HS. On a promontory in Fraserburgh, Aberdeenshire. Nearest railway station Aberdeen, then bus to Fraserburgh. Open all year, daily, telephone for details. Charge £. Joint ticket with Scotland's Lighthouse Museum (see 1293). Explanatory displays in visitor centre. Gift shop. Tearoom. WC. Wheelchair access. Car and coach parking. Telephone (01346) 511022.

A fine 16th-century castle built for the Fraser family but altered to take the first lighthouse built by the Commissioners of the Northern Lighthouses is 1787. The light is still in working order but has been replaced by a small unmanned light nearby.

---

918 KINNAIRD POTTERY **5 M13**

Bankfoot Cottage, Kinnaird, Perthshire. n Kinnaird, above Kinnaird Castle, off the A90 between Perth and Dundee. Open May–Oct, 1400–1800. Telephone for an appointment at other times. Free. Guided tours (available in French). Gift shop. Picnic area. Garden. Car parking. Telephone (01838) 686371.

A small rural pottery manufacturing stone-ware and some slip cast items and, since 1999, specialising in lustred vessels, tiles and architectural ceramics. In a spectacular setting overlooking Carse of Gowrie. Summer courses for young people (7–14 years) available in July each year.

---

919 KINNEIL HOUSE **6 L15**

HS. Bo'ness. On the western outskirts of Bo'ness, West Lothian. Bus from Falkirk. View exterior only. Car parking. Telephone 0131 668 8800.

A 15th-century tower set in a public park. Remodelled by the Earl of Arran between 1546 and 1550 and transformed into a stately home for the Dukes of Hamilton in the 1660s.

---

920 KINNEIL MUSEUM **6 L15**

Duchess Anne Cottages, Kinneil Estate, Bo'ness. 2 miles (3km) west of Bo'ness town centre. Nearest railway station Linlithgow. Open all year, Mon–Sat 1230–1600. Free. Explanatory displays. Gift shop. WC. Limited wheelchair access. Car and coach parking. Telephone (01506) 778530.

Displays on the history of Kinneil Estate and the social history of Bo'ness.

---

921 KINNOULL HILL WOODLAND PARK **5 M13**

FE. c/o Tay Forest District Office, Inverpark, Dunkeld, Perthshire. 1 mile (1.5km) east of Perth. Open at all times. Free. Explanatory displays.

Waymarked walks. Limited wheelchair access. Car parking. Telephone (01350) 727284 or council (01738) 475000.

Comprising five hills (Corsiehill, Deuchny Hill, Barnhill, Binn Hill and Kinnoull Hill). Kinnoull Hill, the highest and most impressive, offers spectacular views over the Ochil and Lomond hills. There are four waymarked forest walks.

---

922 KINROSS HOUSE **6 M14**

Kinross, Tayside. In Kinross, off junction 6 of the M90 motorway. Bus from Edinburgh. Gardens only: open Apr–Oct, daily 1000–1900. View exterior of house only. Charge £. Guided tours for groups by prior arrangement only. Guide dogs welcome by prior arrangement. Wheelchair access. Car and coach parking. Telephone (01577) 862900.

Kinross House was built by the Royal Architect to Charles II, Sir William Bruce, as his own home and is one of the finest examples of late 17th-century architecture in Scotland. It is set in formal walled gardens with rose gardens, yew hedges, topiary and herbaceous borders. On the shore of Loch Leven, opposite the castle where Mary, Queen of Scots was imprisoned in 1567.

---

923 KINSHALDY RIDING STABLES **5 N13**

Kinshaldy Farm, Leuchars. 3 miles (5km) east of Leuchars on unclassified road (signposted to Kinshaldy Beach). Nearest railway station and bus service Leuchars. Open all year, Tue–Thu 1000–1900, Fri–Sun 0900–1630. Charge £££. Explanatory displays. Picnic area. WC. Limited wheelchair access. Car and coach parking. Telephone (01334) 838527.

Horse treks through 4500 acres (1821ha) of scenic woodland, and along 4 miles (6.5km) of sandy beaches. Suitable for children and adults.

---

924 KINSMAN BLAKE CERAMICS **5 P17**

Barn House, Smailholm, Roxburghshire. On the A68, 6 miles (9.5km) east of St Boswells. Open all year, daily 1000–1700 (occasionally open in the evening). Free. Demonstrations given to groups on prior notice (charge). Gift shop. Wheelchair access. Car parking. Telephone (01573) 460666.

A small family pottery where visitors are welcome in the workshop. Demonstrations or explanations as required. Specialists in decorative techniques. Well-stocked showroom.

---

925 KINTAIL AND MORVICH **2 G9**

NTS. Highland. 16 miles (26km) east of Kyle of Lochalsh, north off A87. Bus from Inverness and Glasgow. Open all year. Countryside Centre at Morvich, May–Sep, daily 0900–2200. Charge £. Honesty box. Explanatory displays. WC. Wheelchair access with assistance. Car and coach parking. Telephone (01599) 511231.

A West Highland estate which includes the Falls of Glomach and the Five Sisters of Kintail, four of which are over 3000 feet (914.5m). The site of the Battle of Glen Shiel, which took place in 1719, is within this area, 5 miles (8km) from Morvich. The best access to the mountains is from the Countryside Centre at Morvich.

---

926 KIPPEN PARISH CHURCH **5 K14**

Fore Road, Kippen, Stirling. Off the A811, 9 miles (14.5km) west of Stirling. Bus from Stirling. Open daily 0930–1700. Free. Explanatory displays. Garden. WC. Wheelchair access. Car and coach parking.

A church built in 1824, but 'modernised' in 1924 under the guidance of Sir D. Y. Cameron RA. He and others donated works of art which, with distinguished Webster Windows, make it one of the most beautiful churches in Scotland.

927 KIRKAIG FALLS **2 G4**

Inverkirkaig, south of Lochinver, Caithness.

Popular beauty spot and walk.

---

928 KIRKCALDY MUSEUM AND ART GALLERY **6 N14**

War Memorial Gardens, Kirkcaldy, Fife. Adjacent to the railway station in Kirkcaldy, 10 minute walk from bus station. Open all year except public holidays: Mon–Sat 1030–1700, Sun 1400–1700. Free. Explanatory displays. Gift shop. Café. Garden. WC. Wheelchair access. Disabled WC. Car parking. Telephone (01592) 412860.

An outstanding collection of 18th–20th century Scottish paintings and probably the largest public collection of works (outside the National Galleries of Scotland) by William McTaggart and the Scottish colourist S. J. Peploe. There is also an award-winning permanent museum display, Changing Places, which tells the story of the social, industrial and natural heritage of the area. Lively changing exhibitions programme featuring art, craft, photography, social and natural history.

---

929 KIRKMADRINE EARLY CHRISTIAN STONES **4 G21**

HS. In the Rhinns of Galloway, 2 miles (3km) southwest of Sandhead, Wigtownshire. Nearest railway station Stranraer, bus from Stranraer. Access at all times. Free. Telephone 0131 668 8800.

Three of the earliest Christian memorial stones in Britain, dating from the 5th or early 6th century, displayed in a porch of a former chapel.

---

930 KIRK OF CALDER **6 M15**

Main Street, Mid Calder, West Lothian. 12 miles (19km) west of Edinburgh, off A71 on B7015 in the village of Mid Calder. Nearest railway station Livingston, bus service from Edinburgh. Open May–Sep, Sun 1400–1600. Free. Guided tours. Explanatory displays. Gift shop. Tearoom. WC. Induction loop. Wheelchair access. Car and coach parking.

Sixteenth-century parish church. Famous visitors include John Knox, David Livingstone, Frederick Chopin and James 'Paraffin' Young. Fine stained glass windows. Visitors can learn about four centuries of Scottish history.

---

931 KIRK YETHOLM **5 Q17**

Off B6352, 8 miles (12.5km) southeast of Kelso.

Attractive village, once famous as the home of the Scottish gypsies, now the northern end of the Pennine Way.

---

932 KIRROUGHTREE VISITOR CENTRE **4 J20**

FE. Galloway Forest Park. Open Apr–Sep. Free. Gift shop. Café and picnic area. Adventure play area. WC. Wheelchair access. Disabled WC. Car parking. Telephone (01671) 402165.

Kirroughtree Visitor Centre runs many different activities during the year. Also waymarked cycle trails, walks and a forest drive.

---

933 KISIMUL CASTLE **2 A10**

Castlebay, Isle of Barra, Western Isles. On a tiny island in the bay of Castlebay, Isle of Barra. By air to Barra. Ferry to Castlebay from Oban and Lochboisdale. Open Apr–Sep, Mon, Wed and Sat afternoons. Charge (including boat) £. Telephone (01871) 810336.

For many generations, Kisimul was the stronghold of the Macneils of Barra, widely noted for their lawlessness and piracy, and led by chiefs like Ruari the Turbulent, who boldly seized ships of subjects of Queen Elizabeth I of England. The castle is at least 550 years old. Legend has it that it dates from the 11th century. Restoration was commenced in 1938 by Robert Lister Macneil of Barra and completed in 1972.

---

934 KNAP OF HOWAR **1 C9**

HS. On the west side of the island of Papa Westray, Orkney. Ferry from Kirkwall to Westray then to Papa Westray. Access at all times. Free. Telephone 0131 668 8800.

Probably the oldest standing stone houses in northwest Europe. Two Neolithic dwellings, approximately rectangular with stone cupboards and stalls.

---

935 KNOCKAN STUDIO AND CRAFT CENTRE **2 H5**

Knockan, Elphin, Sutherland. On the A835, 14 miles (22.5km) north of Ullapool. Nearest railway station Lairg, bus from Lairg or Lochinver. Open all year, Mon–Sat 0900–1800. Free. Explanatory displays. Gift shop. Car and coach parking. Telephone (01854) 613365.

A jewellery/lapidary workshop where Scottish gemstones are cut and set. Workshop viewing area. Selection of Scottish crafts, knitwear, pottery, glass. Also at Ullapool.

---

936 KNOCKHILL RACING CIRCUIT **6 M14**

Dunfermline, Fife. On the A823, 6 miles (9.5km) north of Dunfermline. Bus from Dunfermline. Open all year, daily 0900–1700, closed Christmas and New Year. Charges depending on events. Children and OAP's free. Group concessions. Explanatory displays. Gift shop. Restaurant, tearoom and picnic area. WC. Wheelchair access. Disabled WC. Car and coach parking. Telephone (01383) 723337.

Scotland's National Motor Sports Centre with racing events for motor car and motor cycles most weekends from April–October. Visitors can watch or participate. Karts, quadbikes, skid pan and on-road defensive driving.

---

937 KNOCKNAGAEL BOAR STONE **3 K8**

HS. In Highland Council Offices, Glenurquhart Road, Inverness. On ground floor of Council chambers. Nearest railway and bus stations Inverness. Access all year (except public holidays), Mon–Fri, 0900–1700. Free. Telephone (01463) 702000.

A rough slab incised with the Pictish symbols of a mirror-case and a wild boar. Can be viewed at any time through window.

---

938 KNOWE OF YARSO CHAMBERED CAIRN **1 B10**

HS. On the island of Rousay, Orkney. Bus from Kirkwall to Tingwall then ferry to Rousay. Access at all times. Free. Telephone 0131 668 8800.

An oval cairn with concentric walls enclosing a chambered tomb divided into three compartments. Neolithic.

---

939 KYLERHEA OTTER HAVEN **2 F9**

FE. Kylerhea, Isle of Skye. Open daily all year round. Free. Explanatory displays. Summer warden. Public toilets Easter–Sep. Wheelchair access. Car parking.

Kylerhea is a superb place for otters, and from the hide you may be lucky enough to see them. Specially constructed paths are designed to protect the habitat and the wildlife, and visitors should keep to the designated paths and leave the shoreline undisturbed. Success in seeing an otter will be mostly down to your own skills in field craft, an element of luck, and patience. As well as otters, there are falcons, waders, seabirds and seals in the area.

940 KYLES OF BUTE **4 G15**

Narrow arm of the Firth of Clyde, between Isle of Bute and Argyll. Car parking.

A 16 mile (25.5km) stretch of water which presents a constantly changing view of great beauty. It can perhaps be best appreciated from the A8003, Tighnabruaich to Glendaruel road, where there are two view indicators. The western one (Scottish Civic Trust) looks over the West Kyle and identifies many features. The east indicator (NTS) looks over Loch Ridden and the East Kyle.

---

941 LADYKIRK **5 Q16**

Four miles (6.5km) east of Swinton and 0.5 miles ((0.5km) from Norham off B6470. Access at all reasonable times. Car parking.

Ladykirk was built in 1500 by James IV, in memory of Our Lady who had saved him from drowning. As the Border was only 300 yards away and in constant dispute, he ordered it built to withstand fire and flood – hence the all-stone construction of the kirk with no wooden rafters and, until this century, stone pews. The Wardens of East March met regularly in the parish to resolve disputes between Scotland and England. In 1560, a copy of the last peace treaty between them was signed in Ladykirk, marking the end of sporadic warfare.

---

942 LAEL FOREST GARDEN **2 H6**

6 miles (9.5km) south of Ullapool on A835 to Inverness.

Extending to 17 acres (7ha), the garden was set aside in 1933 for interesting and ornamental trees of native and foreign origin. The oldest specimen trees were planted about 1870 and there are now some 150 different trees and shrubs.

---

943 LAGAVULIN DISTILLERY VISITOR CENTRE **4 D16**

Port Ellen, Isle of Islay. 3 miles (5km) from ferry on A846. Air to Islay (airport 5 miles). Bus from Port Askaig to Port Ellen, no transport to Lagavulin. Tours Apr–Oct, Mon–Fri 1000, 1130 and 1430. Charge £. Group concessions. Guided tours. Explanatory displays. Gift shop. WC. No guide dogs. Disabled WC. Car and coach parking. Telephone (01496) 302730.

Home of the famous White Horse blended whisky, established in 1816. Beside the ruins of Dun Naomhaig Castle, ancient stronghold of the Lords of the Isles. Tours and tastings.

---

944 LAGGANGAIRN STANDING STONES **4 H20**

HS. At Killgallioch, New Luce on the Southern Upland Way, Wigtownshire. Nearest railway station Stranraer, bus to New Luce on school days and Tue and Fri only. Difficult access signposted through Forestry Commission land. Free. Telephone 0131 668 8800.

Two stones carved with early Christian crosses.

---

945 LAIDHAY CROFT MUSEUM **3 M4**

Laidhay, Dunbeath, Caithness. On the A9, 1 mile (2km) north of Dunbeath. Nearest railway station Wick, bus from Wick. Open two weeks Mar and Nov; Apr–Oct, daily 1000–1800. Charge £. Group concessions. Guided tours on request. Tearoom and picnic area. WC. Wheelchair access. Disabled WC. Car and coach parking. Telephone (01593) 731244.

An early 18th-century croft complex with stable, dwelling house and byre under one rush thatched roof. Separate cruck barn with winnowing doors. Completely furnished in period style. Crofting hand tools, machinery and harness on view.

946 WILLIAM LAMB MEMORIAL STUDIO **5 Q12**

Market Street, Montrose, Angus. Situated in the Trades Close off the High Street in Montrose. By rail or bus from Aberdeen, Dundee, Edinburgh or Glasgow. Open Jul–mid Sep, daily 1400–1700; other times by appointment. Free. Guided tours. Explanatory displays. Gift shop. WC. Limited wheelchair access. Telephone (01674) 673232.

The working studio of the famous Montrose sculptor includes displays of his sculptures, etchings, paintings and drawings. Also featured are his workroom and tools and his living room with furniture designed by him.

---

947 LANDMARK HIGHLAND HERITAGE AND ADVENTURE PARK **3 L9**

Carrbridge, Inverness-shire. On the B9153 (old A9), 7 miles (11km) north of Aviemore. Nearest railway station Carrbridge, bus from Edinburgh, Inverness or local bus from Aviemore. Open all year (except Christmas Day), 1000–1800 (1700 in winter, 1900 mid Jul–Aug). Charge £££. Group concessions. Explanatory displays. Leaflets in French, German and Italian. Gift shop. Restaurant and snack bar. WC. Wheelchair access with assistance. Disabled WC. Car and coach parking. Telephone 0800 731 3446.

Park contains wild watercoaster ride, red squirrel nature trail, treetop trail, Clydesdale horse, steam-powered sawmill demonstrations, forestry skill area, view tower, maze and adventure play area.

---

948 LAPHROAIG DISTILLERY **4 D16**

Port Ellen, Isle of Islay. Open all year (except Jul and first 2 weeks Aug), Mon–Thu. Tours at 1015 and 1415. All visits by arrangement only. Free. Guided tours. Explanatory displays. Gift shop. WC. Limited wheelchair access. Disabled WC. Car and coach parking. Telephone (01496) 302418.

A working distillery illustrating the whisky making process in depth.

---

949 LARGS MUSEUM **6 H16**

Kirkgate House, Manse Court, Largs, Ayrshire. Nearest railway station Largs, bus from Glasgow and Ayr. Open Jun–Sep, daily 1400–1700. Free. Guided tours. Explanatory displays. Wheelchair access. Telephone (01475) 687081.

The museum holds a small collection of local bygones and a library of local history books and photographs, put together by the local history society. Holds the key to the Skelmorlie Aisle, adjacent, which belongs to Historic Scotland.

---

950 LARGS OLD KIRK **6 H16**

HS. In Bellman's Close, off High Street in Largs, Ayrshire. Nearest railway station Largs, bus from Glasgow and Ayr. Open Apr–Sep, Mon–Sat 1400–1700, Sun 1400–1700. Free. Telephone 0131 668 8800.

A splendid mausoleum with a painted ceiling illustrating the seasons, added to the parish church in 1636 by Sir Robert Montgomerie of Skelmorlie. Contains an elaborate carved stone tomb in Renaissance style.

---

951 LAUDERDALE AISLE, ST MARY'S CHURCH, HADDINGTON **6 P15**

HS. In Haddington, East Lothian. Nearest railway station Drem, bus from Edinburgh. Access at all times. Free. Telephone 0131 668 8800.

The former sacristy of the great 15th-century parish church. Contains a splendid early 17th-century monument in marble with alabaster effigies.

952 LEADHILLS MINERS' LIBRARY AND READING ROOM **5 L18**

15 Main Street, Leadhills, Lanarkshire. On the B797, south of Abington. Open May–Sep, Wed, Sat and Sun 1400–1600. Charge £. Children free. Guided tours. Explanatory displays. WC. Car and coach parking. Telephone (01659) 74216.

The lead miners' subscription library established in 1741 with some rare books, detailed 18th-century mining documents, and local records and history.

---

953 LEIGHTON LIBRARY **6 K14**

Cathedral Square, Dunblane, Perthshire. In the centre of Dunblane, 0.25 mile (0.5km) from the station. By rail or bus from Inverness, Aberdeen, Dundee. Open May–Oct, Mon–Fri 1000–1230 and 1400–1630. Free. Donations. Guided tours (available in European languages and Japanese). Explanatory displays. Wheelchair access with assistance. Car and coach parking.

The oldest (private) library in Scotland, dating from 1684. A collection of 4500 books, mainly first editions, printed in over 90 languages.

---

954 LEISURE MARINE **2 F8**

32 Harbour Street, Plockton, Ross and Cromarty. 6 miles (9.5km) north of Kyle of Lochalsh. Nearest railway station Plockton (train from Inverness). Open Easter–Oct, 0900–late. Charge ££. Group concessions. Guided tours. Gift shop. Refreshments on board. WC. Wheelchair access with assistance. Car parking. Telephone (01599) 544306.

Calum's seal trips at Plockton, made famous by Hamish Macbeth. Views of seals guaranteed, or money back. Spectacular scenery.

---

955 LEISURE ZONE **6 M15**

Primrose Lane, Rosyth, Dunfermline, Fife. On the Dunfermline Road out of Rosyth. 0.25 mile (0.5km), bus from Dunfermline, Edinburgh or Kirkcaldy. Open all year (except Christmas and New Year) Sun–Thu 1100–2300, Fri–Sat 1100–2400. Charge dependent on activity. Group concessions. Restaurants. Play area. WC. Wheelchair access. Disabled WC. Car and coach parking. Telephone (01383) 414000.

A family entertainment complex with ten-pin bowling, snooker, pool, American pool and children's indoor soft play area.

---

956 LEITH HALL AND GARDEN **3 P8**

NTS. Huntly, Aberdeenshire. On B9002, 34 miles (54km) northwest of Aberdeen. By bus from Aberdeen. Open Easter–Sep and weekends in Oct, daily 1330–1730. Garden and grounds open all year, daily 0930–sunset. Charge £££. Children free. Group concessions. Guided tours by arrangement. Explanatory displays. Information sheets in five languages. Tearoom and picnic area. Garden. WC. Limited wheelchair access, wheelchair available. Disabled WC. Car and coach parking. Telephone (01464) 831216.

Mansion house which was home to the Leith family for 300 years. Exhibition on family's military history. The house is set in a 286-acre (116ha) estate with ponds, trails and a bird hide. Formal and informal gardens noted for colour and diversity.

---

957 LENNOXLOVE HOUSE **6 P15**

Lennoxlove Estate, Haddington, East Lothian. On the B6369, 1 mile (2km) from Haddington. Bus from Haddington. Open Easter–Oct, Wed, Thu, Sat and Sun 1400–1630. Charge ££. Group concessions. Guided tours (available in French and German). Garden café. WC. Limited wheelchair access. Disabled WC. Car and coach parking. Telephone (01620) 823720.

The home of the Duke of Hamilton. It features a 14th-century keep originally built for Maitland of Lethington,

Secretary of State to Mary, Queen of Scots, and houses mementoes belonging to Mary, together with furniture, paintings and porcelain once part of the Hamilton Palace collection.

---

958 LERWICK TOWN HALL **1 G5**

Lerwick, Shetland. In Lerwick town centre, within walking distance from harbour and bus station. Open all year, Mon–Fri 0900–1300 and 1400–1700. Free. Guided tours. WC. Wheelchair access. Disabled WC. Car and coach parking. Telephone (01595) 744502.

Lerwick Town Hall stands on a commanding site on the ridge in the older part of the town known as Hillhead. Built between autumn 1881 and summer 1883, the chief attraction of the hall is the series of stained glass windows, gifted at the time of construction. These represent leading personalities in the early history of the islands, from Norwegian inhabitation in the 9th century to the pledging of the islands to Scotland in 1469.

---

959 LETHAM GLEN **6 N14**

Sillerhole Road, Leven, Fife. On the A915, on the outskirts of Leven. Bus from Kirkcaldy or Leven. Open all year: Nature Centre open Mon–Fri 1100–1500, Sat in summer 1400–1600, Sun 1400–1630, Sat in winter 1300–1500, Sun 1300–1530. Free. Guided tours. Explanatory displays. Picnic areas and vending machine. Pets corner. WC. Limited wheelchair access. Car parking. Telephone (01333) 429231.

The Nature Centre displays information and pictures about wildlife. Various exhibits throughout the year. Craftsmen in residence in summer. Nature trail through the Glen. Booklets and maps, pets corner. Picturesque surroundings.

---

960 LEWIS LOOM CENTRE **2 D4**

Stornoway, Lewis. In Stornoway town centre. Bus station within 0.25 miles (0.5km). Open all year, daily 0900–1800; other times by arrangement. Charge £. Shop free. Group concessions. Guided tours. Explanatory displays. Gift shop. WC. Wheelchair access. Car and coach parking. Telephone (01851) 703117.

An enjoyable introduction to the history of Harris tweed; including sheep breeds, plant dyes and demonstrations of hand spinning, looms and all aspects of producing finished cloth.

---

961 LEYDEN OBELISK AND TABLET **5 P18**

Denholm, on A698 northeast of Hawick. Access at all times. Free.

The village was the birthplace of John Leyden (1776–1811), poet, orientalist and friend of Sir Walter Scott. An obelisk was set up in 1861 and a tablet on a thatched cottage records his birth there. Another famous son of Denholm was Sir James Murray, editor of the *Oxford English Dictionary*, whose birth is commemorated on a tablet on a house in Main Street.

---

962 LIDDESDALE HERITAGE CENTRE **5 P19**

Townfoot Kirk, South Hermitage Street, Newcastleton, Roxburghshire. 21 miles (33.5km) from Hawick on B6399, 23 miles (37km) from Carlisle on A7; follow signposts to Newcastleton/Canonbie. Open Easter–Sep, Wed–Mon 1330–1630. Charge £. Residents of Liddesdale free. Group concessions by arrangement. Explanatory displays. Gift shop. WC. Wheelchair access. Car and coach parking. Telephone (01387) 375259 or 375283.

Housed in the former Congregational Church (built in 1804) within the planned village of Newcastleton (built 1793). Describes the history of Liddesdale and its people and displays a unique commorative bicentenery tapestry.

Many books and articles on the Borders region. Facilities available for genealogical research. Waverley Line railway memorabilia. Exhibitions are staged during July and August.

---

963 LIME TREE STUDIO GALLERY **2 H11**

The Old Manse, Achintore Road, Fort William. At the west end of Fort William High Street, 2 minute walk from Tourist Information Centre. Open daily except Christmas and New Year, 1030–1800. Free. Guided tours (available in French and German). Explanatory displays. Gift shop. Garden. WC. Wheelchair access. Car and coach parking. Telephone (01397) 701806.

Houses a continually changing exhibition of landscape paintings, mainly of northwest Scotland. Extensive workshop programme and stained glass exhibition.

---

964 LINCLUDEN COLLEGIATE CHURCH **5 L19**

HS. In Abbey Lane, on western outskirts of Dumfries, 1 mile (2km) from A76. Local bus service. Open at all times; contact keyholder. Charge £. Telephone 0131 668 8800.

The rich remains of a collegiate church founded in 1389 by Archibald the Grim, 3rd Earl of Douglas. The splendid chancel was probably added by his son, Archibald, the 4th Earl, and houses the exquisite monumental tomb of his wife, Princess Margaret, daughter of King Robert III.

---

965 LINDEAN MILL GLASS **5 P17**

Lindean Mill, Galashiels. On the A7, 1 mile (2km) north of Selkirk. Bus from Edinburgh or Carlisle. Open all year, Mon–Thu 0900–1200 and 1300–1700 (to 1600 Fri); closed local holidays. Free. Gift shop. Limited wheelchair access. Car parking. Telephone (01750) 20173.

Visitors can watch glassware being made by hand.

---

966 J F LINDSAY TARGEMAKER **3 K8**

Balquhidder, Main Street, North Kessock, by Inverness. 4 miles (6.5km) north of Inverness off A9, take first junction left after Kessock bridge. Bus from Inverness to North Kessock. Open all year, 0900–1900; telephone to confirm as space is limited. Free. Explanatory displays. Gift shop. Wheelchair access. Car parking. Telephone (01463) 731577.

Small workshop making high quality hand-crafted reproductions of original Jacobite targes (shields). The targemaker is happy to answer questions. Photos may be taken holding targe and sword. Targes, swords and other items for sale.

---

967 LINLITHGOW PALACE **6 L15**

HS. Kirkgate, Linlithgow, West Lothian. Nearest railway station Linlithgow, then 10 minute walk. Bus from Falkirk and Edinburgh. Open Apr–Sep, dialy 0930–1830; Oct–Mar, Mon–Sat 0930–1630, Sun 1400–1630. Charge £. Group concessions. Guided tours. Gift shop. Picnic area. WC. Wheelchair access. Car and coach parking. Telephone (01506) 842896.

The magnificent ruin of a great royal palace set in its own park and beside Linlithgow Loch. The Great Hall and Chapel (late 15th century) are particularly fine. The quadrangle has a richly-carved 16th-century fountain. A favoured residence of the Stewart monarchs from James I. Works commissioned by James I, III, IV, V and VI can be seen. Both James V and Mary, Queen of Scots were born here.

---

968 THE LINLITHGOW STORY **6 L15**

Annet House, 143 High Street, Linlithgow, West Lothian. In Linlithgow 800 yards (731m) from the station. Bus or rail from Edinburgh or Glasgow. Open Apr–Oct, Mon–Sat (except Tue) 1000–1700, Sun

1300–1600. Charge £. Group concessions. Guided tours by prior arrangement. Explanatory displays. Gift shop. Picnic area in terraced garden. WC. Car and coach parking. Telephone (01506) 670677.

A small museum of local history which tells the story, not only of the Stewart kings of Scotland who built and lived in Linlithgow Palace (see 967), but also of the ordinary people who lived and worked in the burgh. Housed in a late 18th-century merchant house.

---

969 LINLITHGOW UNION CANAL SOCIETY MUSEUM AND BOATS **6 L15**

Canal Basin, Manse Road, Linlithgow, West Lothian. In Linlithgow, 5 minute walk from station. Bus or rail from Edinburgh or Glasgow. Open Easter–Sep, weekends 1400–1700. Museum free; charge for boat trips. Explanatory displays. Gift shop. Tearoom and picnic area. WC. Wheelchair access to museum and tearoom. Disabled WC. Telephone (01506) 671215.

Historic canal basin on the Edinburgh and Glasgow Union Canal with small museum in former stable. Museum. Also trip boats *Victoria* (replica 12-seater Victorian steam packet boat, $^1/_2$ hour town stretch trips) and *St Magdalene* (50 seater, $2^1/_2$ hour trip to Avon Aqueduct).

---

970 LINN BOTANIC GARDENS AND NURSERY **6 H15**

Cove, Helensburgh, Dunbartonshire. On the B833, 10 miles (16km) from Garelochhead. Nearest railway station Helensburgh, then bus. Garden open all year dawn to dusk; plant sales daily 1100–1700. Charge £ (Garden). Children under 12 free. Group concessions. Guided tours. Car and coach parking. Telephone (01436) 842242.

A garden developed since 1971 around a listed Clyde villa in the style of Alexander Greek Thompson. Thousands of unusual, exotic and rare plants, extensive water garden, formal ponds and fountains, herbaceous borders, glen with waterfall, cliff garden and rockery. Waymarked half-mile (1km) route through garden.

---

971 LITTLE GALLERY **2 D8**

7 Portnalong, Isle of Skye. 3 miles (5km) west of Talisker distillery on the B8009. Bus service runs twice-daily Mon–Fri. Open Easter–Oct, daily 1000–1800; Nov–Easter by arrangement. Free. Explanatory displays. Wheelchair access. Car parking. Telephone (01478) 640254.

Overlooking Loch Harport, the gallery displays etchings, prints and watercolours depicting the Cuillin, Skye landscapes and its native flora and fauna.

---

972 DAVID LIVINGSTONE CENTRE **6 K16**

NTS. 165 Station Road, Blantyre, Glasgow. Off the A724 in Blantyre, within walking distance of Blantyre station. Open early Jan–Christmas, Mon–Sat 1000–1700, Sun 1230–1700. Charge £. Children free. Explanatory displays. Gift shop. Tearoom. Playground, riverside walks. WC. Limited wheelchair access. Disabled WC. Car and coach parking. Telephone (01698) 823140.

In the tenement where Livingstone was born. Displays chart his life, from his childhood in the Blantyre mills to his exploration in Africa.

---

973 LOANHEAD STONE CIRCLE **3 Q8**

HS. Near Daviot, off B9001, 5 miles (8km) northwest of Inverurie, Aberdeenshire. Nearest railway station Inverurie, bus from Inverurie, then 1 mile (2km) walk. Access at all times. Free. Car parking. Telephone 0131 668 8800.

The best known of a group of recumbent stone circles about 4000 to 4500 year old. Encloses a ring cairn and is beside a small burial enclosure.

974 LOCH-AN-EILEIN POTTERY **3 L9**

Rothiemurchus, Aviemore, Highland. 3 miles (5km) southwest of Aviemore on the Loch-An-Eilein road. Open all year, Tue–Sun 1000–1700. Free. Gift shop. Picnic area. WC. Pot-making sessions suitable for blind visitors. Wheelchair access with assistance. Car parking. Telephone (01479) 810837.

Situated on Rothiemurchus estate near Aviemore , a small rural craft pottery making terracotta domestic wares, glazed in blues and greens. Visitors make their own pot on Thursdays.

---

975 LOCH AWE STEAM PACKET **4 H13**

Loch Awe Pier, Loch Awe, Argyll. 25 miles (40km) east of Oban and 2 miles (3km) west of Dalmally on A85. Adjacent to Loch Awe railway station. Open Jun–Sep, daily 1000–1800; Mar–May and Oct, daily 1100–1800. Charge ££. Group concessions. Guided tours. Explanatory displays. Tearoom and outdoor seating. WC. Limited wheelchair access. Car and coach parking. Telephone (01866) 833333.

Steamboat rides to Kilchurn Castle and cruises around Loch Awe on the steamers *Lady Rowena* and *Flower of Scotland*.

---

976 LOCHCARRON CASHMERE WOOL CENTRE **5 P17**

Waverley Mill, Huddersfield Street, Galashiels. In Galashiels centre. Bus from Edinburgh to within 1.25 miles (2km). Open Jun–Sep, Mon–Sat 0900–1700, Sun 1200–1700. Free. Group concessions. Guided tours (charge £). Explanatory displays. Gift shop. WC. Wheelchair access with assistance. Disabled WC. Car and coach parking. Telephone (01896) 751100.

A woollen mill manufacturing cashmere from spun yarn to finished garment. Produces a huge range of pure wool tartans. Tour of mill and museum illustrating the history of Galashiels and its trade.

---

977 LOCH CENTRE **6 N15**

Well Wynd, Tranent, East Lothian. In Tranent centre. Bus from Edinburgh. Open all year (except Christmas and New Year), Mon–Fri 0900–2200, weekends 0900–1700. Charge by activity. Group concessions. Café. Crèche. WC. Wheelchair access. Disabled WC. Car and coach parking. Telephone (01875) 611081.

Swimming pool, sauna, steam room, squash courts, gym, activity hall and soft play area.

---

978 LOCH DOON CASTLE **4 J19**

HS. Off the A713, 10 miles (16km) south of Dalmellington, Ayrshire. Nearest railway station Ayr, bus from Ayr. Access at all times. Free. Telephone 0131 668 8800.

An early 14th-century castle with an eleven-sided curtain wall of fine masonry. Once known as Castle Balliol. Originally it stood on an island in Loch Doon but it was moved to its present site in the 1930s before its original site was flooded during the construction of a hydro-electric scheme.

---

979 LOCH ERIBOLL **3 J3**

Situated between Tongue and Durness in the north of Sutherland.

Reputedly the deepest sea loch or inlet in Britain. Both the loch itself and its shores are steeped in history. Despite the inhospitable landscape of today, archaeological remains indicate that people have lived here for at least the last 4000 years.

---

980 LOCH FAD FISHERY **4 G16**

Loch Fad, Isle of Bute. On the B878, 0.75 mile (1km) from Rothesay pier. Open for fly fishing Mar–late Dec and bait fishing mid Mar–early

Oct. Charge £££. Group concessions. Explanatory displays. Picnic area. WC. Limited wheelchair access. Car and coach parking. Telephone (01700) 504871.

Fishing for rainbow or brown trout from banks or boats.

---

981 LOCH FYNE MINIATURE RAILWAY **4 F15**

The Green, Ardrishaig, Argyll. 3 miles (5km) from Lochgilphead on A83. Open all year, Sat and Sun 1200–1800. Charge £. WC. Wheelchair access. Disabled WC. Car and coach parking. Telephone (01546) 603250.

Overlooking Loch Fyne, the railway has two engines; the *Flying Scotsman*, a steam replica of the original, a real enthusiast's engine, and a diesel-type shunter, yet to be named.

---

982 LOCH GARTEN OSPREY CENTRE **3 L9**

RSPB. Grianan, Tulloch, Nethybridge, Inverness-shire. Off the B970, 8 miles (13km) northeast of Aviemore. Bus from Aviemore, or Strathspey steam railway from Aviemore. Open Apr–Aug, daily 1000–1800. Charge £. RSPB/YOC members free on production of membership card. Explanatory displays in visitor centre. Gift shop. WC. Wheelchair access to centre. Disabled WC. Car and coach parking. Telephone (01479) 831694.

A public viewing facility overlooking the tree-top nest of ospreys. Direct viewing with telescopes or binoculars; CCTV transmits pictures of the nest to the centre.

---

983 LOCHINDORB **3 L8**

Unclassified road off A939, 10 miles (16km) northwest of Grantown-on-Spey.

On an island in this lonely loch stand the ruins of a 13th-century castle, once a seat of the Comyns. It was occupied in person by Edward I in 1303 and greatly strengthened. In 1371 the castle became the stronghold of the Wolf of Badenoch, the notorious Earl of Buchan who terrorised the area. The castle was dismantled in 1456.

---

984 LOCH INSH WATERSPORTS **3 L9**

Kincraig, Inverness-shire. 7 miles (11km) south of Aviemore. Nearest railway and bus stations Aviemore. Watersports from April–Oct, daily 0830–1730; Ski-ing, Dec–Apr. Charge per activity. Group concessions. Explanatory displays. Gift shop. Restaurant and picnic area. Children's adventure area, beach. WC. Wheelchair access. Disabled WC. Car and coach parking. Telephone (01540) 651272.

Watersports include sailing, windsurfing, canoeing, salmon/trout fishing and rowing. Dry ski slope skiing, mountain biking, archery. Hire and instruction. The interpretation/fun trail and stocked fishing lochan was especially designed with wheelchair users in mind.

---

985 LOCH LEVEN CASTLE **6 M14**

HS. By Kinross, Tayside. On an island in Loch Leven. Accessible by boat from Kinross. Bus service from Edinburgh to Kinross. Open Apr–Sep, daily 0930–1830. Charge £. Charge includes ferry. Group concessions. Guided tours. Gift shop. Picnic area. WC. Car parking. Telephone (0378) 040483.

A late 14th- or early 15th-century tower on one side of an irregular courtyard. The prison of Mary, Queen of Scots in 1567.

---

986 LOCH LOMOND **4 J15**

Cruises available from a number of operators, including: Sweeney's Cruises, Balloch (01389) 752376; Mullens Cruises (01389) 751481; Cruise Loch Lomond (01301) 702356.

Loch Lomond, the largest stretch of inland water in mainland Britain, and framed by lovely mountain scenery, is a popular centre for all watersports. Cruises around the banks and attractive small islands are available. See also 1003 Lomond Shores.

---

987 LOCHMABEN CASTLE **5 M19**

HS. On the south shore of Castle Loch, by Lochmaben, Dumfriesshire. Off the B7020, 9 miles (14.5km) northeast of Dumfries. Nearest railway station Lockerbie, bus from Lockerbie or Dumfries. Access at all times but view exterior only. Free. Car parking. Telephone 0131 668 8800.

The ruins of a royal castle, originally built by the English in the 14th century but extensively rebuilt during the reign of King James VI. Surrounded by extensive remains of earthworks, including a rectangular peel (timber pallisaded enclosure).

---

988 LOCH MORAR **2 F10**

Southeast of Mallaig. Rail, bus and ferry from Fort William. Car parking.

Said to be the deepest freshwater loch in Britain and the home of Morag, a monster with a strong resemblance to the Loch Ness Monster.

---

989 LOCH NAM UAMH CAIRN **2 F10**

Off A830, south of Arisaig. Car parking.

The loch is famous for its association with Bonnie Prince Charlie. The memorial cairn on the shore marks the spot from where Prince Charles Edward Stuart sailed for France on 20 September 1746, leaving Scotland as a fugitive with a price of £30,000 on his head.

---

990 LOCH NESS **3 K8**

Between Inverness and Fort William.

This striking 24-mile (38.5km-) long loch in the Great Glen forms part of the Caledonian Canal which links Inverness with Fort William. Up to 700 feet (213m) deep, the loch contains the largest volume of fresh water of any in the British Isles. Famous worldwide for its mysterious inhabitant, the Loch Ness Monster, it is also ideal for cruising and sailing.

---

991 LOCH NESS, OFFICIAL MONSTER EXHIBITION **3 J8**

The Drumnadrochit Hotel, Drumnadrochit, Inverness. In Drumnadrochit on the A82, 15 miles (24km) south of Inverness. Bus from Inverness or Fort William. Open Easter–May 0930–1730; Jun–Sep 0930–1830; Jul and Aug 0900–2030; Oct 0930–1800; winter 1000–1600. Charge £££. Disabled visitors free. Group concessions. Explanatory displays. Gift shop. Restaurant in hotel. Garden, pets corner, boat trips on Loch Ness. WC. Wheelchair access. Disabled WC. Car and coach parking. Telephone (01456) 450573.

Describes Loch Ness from the pre-history of Scotland, exploring the cultural roots of the story in Highland folklore, into the present controversy and all the phases of investigation and exploration. Includes the world's largest inflatable and one of the world's smallest submersibles. Also Loch Ness Boat Trips aboard the famous *Deepscan*, and themed shops.

---

992 LOCH NESS, ORIGINAL VISITOR CENTRE **3 J8**

Drumnadrochit. Open all year, Mar–May 0900–1900; Jun–Aug; 0900–2200; Sep–Oct 0900–2000; Nov–Feb 0900–1700. Charge ££.

Teachers and guides free. Group concessions. Explanatory displays. Cinema exhibition (in Dutch, French, German, Italian, Japanese, Spanish and Swedish). Gift shop. WC. Wheelchair access. Disabled WC. Car and coach parking. Telephone (01456) 450342.

The story of Loch Ness, the monster and other mysteries of the area is presented in a wide-screen cinema. Various gift shops.

---

993 LOCHORE MEADOWS COUNTRY PARK **6 M14**

Crosshill, Lochgelly, Fife. Lochgelly station, bus from Lochgelly or Edinburgh. Open Apr–Sep, daily 0900–1930; Oct–Mar, daily 0900–1700. Free. Explanatory displays in visitor centre. Café. WC. Braille maps for woodland trail. Wheelchair access. Disabled WC. Car and coach parking. Telephone (01592) 414300.

Green and pleasant countryside around a large loch reclaimed from coal mining waste in the 1960s. Tells the story of the reclamation by slide show, displays and ranger-guided walks. Ancient historical remains. Wildlife study, walks, picnics. Activities include fishing, sailing, windsurfing, conoeing, golf, riding. Adventure play area.

---

994 LOCH PARK ADVENTURE CENTRE **3 N8**

Drummuir Castle Estate, Keith, Banffshire. On B9014, 5 miles (7.5km) from Keith. Nearest railway station Keith. Pick-up by arrangement. Open Mar–Oct, daily 0900–2100. Charge for activities. Picnic and barbeque area. WC. Wheelchair access. Disabled WC. Car and coach parking. Telephone (01542) 810334.

Offers a wide variety of activities, including canoeing, kayaking, gorge walking and archery. Also fly fishing. Located on the Malt Whisky Trail.

---

995 LOCHRANZA CASTLE **4 G16**

HS. At Lochranza on the north coast of the Isle of Arran. Ferry from Ardrossan to Brodick, bus from Brodick. Open at all times; apply to custodian. Free. Car parking. Telephone 0131 668 8800.

A fine tower house, probably a 16th-century reconstruction of an earlier building. Reputed to be where Robert the Bruce landed on his return to Scotland in 1307.

---

996 LOCH SHIEL CRUISES **2 G10**

c/o Glenfinnan House Hotel, Glenfinnan, Fort William. On the A830, 15 miles (24km) north west of Fort William. Bus or rail from Fort William. Open Apr–Oct, daily 0900–1700 and special evening cruises. Charge ££. Children under 5 free. Group concessions. Guided tours (in French or German by special request). Explanatory displays. Refreshments and bar on boat. WC. Car and coach parking. Telephone (01967) 431706; mobile phone (07801) 537617.

Pleasure cruises from Glenfinnan and Acharacle on Loch Shiel, one of Scotland's most beautiful and historic lochs. A wide variety of wildlife, best seen from the water.

---

997 LOCH TAY POTTERY **5 K12**

Fearnan, Aberfeldy, Perthshire. Off the A827 (Fortingall Road), 3 miles (5km) from Kenmore. Open all year, 0900–1700. Free. Gift shop. Wheelchair access with assistance. Car parking. Telephone (01887) 830251.

A showroom and workshop in a former croft where Andrew Burt produces a wide variety of stoneware pots for kitchen and other domestic use and decoration. Visitors can watch him at work.

---

998 LOCHWINNOCH COMMUNITY MUSEUM **6 J16**

Main Street, Lochwinnoch, Renfrewshire. In Lochwinnoch centre, adjoining library. Bus from Glasgow. Open all year (except public holidays), Mon 1000–1300, 1400–1700 and 1800–2000, Sat

1000–1300 and 1400–1700. Free. Explanatory displays. Wheelchair access. Car and coach parking. Telephone (01505) 842615.

Portrays village life and the agricultural history of the community through various displays, objects and photographs.

---

999 LOGAN BOTANIC GARDEN **4 G21**

Port Logan, Stranraer, Wigtownshire. 14 miles (22.5km) south of Stranraer, off the B7065. Open Mar–Oct, daily 1000–1800. Charge £. Group concessions. Guided tours by arrangement (also self-guided tours). Explanatory displays. Gift shop. Licensed salad bar. WC. Limited wheelchair access. Disabled WC. Car and coach parking. Telephone (01776) 860231.

Logan's exceptionally mild climate allows a colourful array of tender plants to thrive. Tree ferns, cabbage palms, unusual shrubs, climbers and tender perennials are found within the Walled, Water, Terrace and Woodland Gardens. The Discovery Centre provides activities and information for all ages. The garden is a specialist garden of the Royal Botanic Garden, Edinburgh (see 574).

1000 LOGAN FISH POND MARINE LIFE CENTRE **4 G21**

Port Logan, Stranraer, Wigtownshire. Off the B7056, 14 miles (22.5km) south of Stranraer, 1 mile (2km) from Logan Botanic Garden (see 999). Nearest railway and bus stations Stranraer. Open Mar–Oct, daily 1200–1700. Charge £. Group concessions. Guided tours (available in Dutch, French, German and Spanish). Explanatory displays. Gift shop. Picnic area. Beach. WC. Limited wheelchair access. Car and coach parking. Telephone (01776) 860300.

A fully restored Victorian fish larder in a unique setting – a tidal pool created by a blow-hole which formed during the last Ice Age. The rock fissure through which the tide flows is now the setting for the unusual cave marine aquaruim, containing a large variety of species from the Irish Sea.

1001 LOGIE FARM RIDING CENTRE **3 L8**

Logie Farm, Glenferness, Nairn. On the A939, 10 miles (16km) from Nairn. Bus from Nairn. Open all year, daily 1000–1700. Charge for riding £££ (per hour). Group concessions. Explanatory displays. No guide dogs. Car parking. Telephone (01309) 651226.

Traffic-free riding, an extensive cross-country course, show jumping and dressage areas, outdoor arena and first class instruction. Riding holidays for adults or unaccompanied children. Stunning scenery.

1002 LOGIE STEADING **3 L7**

Forres, Moray. 6 miles (10km) south of Forres on A940. Open Easter–Christmas, Tue–Sun 1030–1700. Free. Charge £ for gardens (children free). Explanatory displays. Gift shop. Tearoom. Garden. WC. Wheelchair access with assistance. Disabled WC. Car and coach parking. Telephone (01309) 611278.

Originally built as a model farm in the 1920s, the Steading has been converted to house an unusual visitor centre where professional craftmen can be seen at work. Engraver, potter, jeweller, country furniture, dolls houses, antiquarian bookshop, gallery and textiles.

1003 LOMOND SHORES **6 J15**

Balloch, Glasgow. Nearest railway station Balloch. Telephone to confirm opening times. Telephone (01389) 721500.

Opening in April 2001, Lomond Shores will feature a visitor centre introducing visitors to Scotland's first national park, and a large format film theatre screening a specially commissioned film about Loch Lomond. Also indoor and outdoor children's play areas. Stunning views of Ben Lomond. See also 986 Loch Lomond.

1004 LOSSIEMOUTH FISHERIES AND COMMUNITY MUSEUM **3 M7**

2 Pitgaveny Quay, Lossiemouth, Moray. Bus from Elgin. Open Easter–Sep, Mon–Sat 1000–1700. Charge £. Group concessions. Guided tours (leaflets in French and German). Explanatory displays. Gift shop. WC. Wheelchair access. Disabled WC. Car and coach parking. Telephone (01343) 813772.

Exhibits on the history of fishing and the local community. Features a study of Ramsay McDonald, the first Labour Prime Minister, born in Lossiemouth.

1005 LOUDOUN CASTLE THEME PARK **6 J17**

Galston, Ayrshire. On the A719 between the A77 and the A71. Nearest railway station Kilmarnock, bus from Kilmarnock. Open on selected dates (telephone for details) from 1000. Charge £££. Charges dependant on activity. Group concessions. Guided tours for school parties. Gift shop. Restaurant, tearoom and picnic area. WC. Animals can be touched. Wheelchair access. Disabled WC. Car and coach parking. Telephone (01563) 822296.

Set in over 500 acres (202ha) of parkland and woods, in grounds of the imposing ruins of Loudoun Castle. Thrilling rides, including Galaxy Rollercoaster, road trains, woodland walks, games, stalls, go-karts and pony rides. Also gardens and farm patio.

1006 LOWER CITY MILLS **5 M13**

West Mill Street, Perth. In central Perth, just off High Street and 10 minute walk from railway and bus stations. Mill open Easter or Apr–Nov, Mon–Sat 1000–1700. Mill shop open all year: Apr–Oct, Mon–Sat 0900–1700; Nov–Mar, Mon–Fri 0900–1700. Charge £. Group concessions. Guided tours (in German by arrangement). Explanatory displays. Gift shop. Limited wheelchair access. Disabled WC. Telephone (01738) 627958.

A working Victorian oatmeal mill. Oats and wheat still processed in the traditional way. The miller will explain operations. Massive internal waterwheel and exhibition telling the story of Perth town mills. Millshop with wide selection of freshly ground flours and oatmeals.

1007 LOW PARKS MUSEUM **6 K16**

129 Muir Street, Motehill, Hamilton, Lanarkshire. Off junction 6 on the M74. Nearest railway station Hamilton, bus from Glasgow. Open all year, Mon–Sat 1000–1700, Sun 1200–1700. Free. Guided tours. Explanatory displays. Gift shop. Garden. WC. Wheelchair access. Disabled WC. Car and coach parking. Telephone (01698) 283981 or 626213.

Combines the former Hamilton District Museum with the Cameronians (Scottish Rifles) Regimental Museum. Displays on the Clyde Valley, Hamilton Estate and Cameronians. Base for tours of Hamilton Mausoleum.

1008 LUIB CROFT MUSEUM **2 E8**

Luib, Isle of Skye. On the Broadford to Sligachan road, 36 miles (57.5km) from Dunvegan in the heart of the Cuillins. Bus from Portree. Open Apr–Oct, daily 0900–1800. Charge £. Explanatory displays. Gift shop. WC. Wheelchair access. Car and coach parking. Telephone (01471) 822427.

Depicts living conditions in the early 20th century. Also the story of Bonnie Prince Charlie's escape to Skye. Exhibition of maps from 1750–2000 and information about a recently discovered Viking farm.

1009 LYTH ARTS CENTRE **3 N2**

Lyth, Wick, Caithness. 4 miles (6.5km) off the A99 between Wick and John o' Groats. Wick railway station. Exhibitions open Jul–Aug, daily 1400–1630. Open Apr–Dec for evening performances as advertised locally. Exhibitions £. Performances £££. Explanatory displays. Gift shop. Snack bar. Garden. WC. Wheelchair access. Car parking. Telephone (01955) 641270.

Up to ten new exhibitions of contemporary fine art shown simultaneously each season, ranging from local landscape to the work of established British and foreign artists. Regular performances by touring drama, music and dance companies.

1010 LYTH STABLES **3 N2**

Lyth, Wick, Caithness. 10 miles (16km) from Wick, off A99. Open all year, Tue–Sun; telephone for times. Charge £££. Car parking. Telephone (01955) 641318.

Off-road riding (and some roadwork), suitable for all levels of experience.

1011 McCAIG'S TOWER **4 F13**

On a hill overlooking Oban. Access at all times. Free.

McCaig was a local banker who tried to curb unemployment by using local craftsmen to build this tower (between 1897–1900) as a memorial to his family. Its walls are 2 feet (0.5m) thick and from 30–47 feet (9–14m) high. The courtyard within is landscaped and the tower is floodlit at night in summer. An observation platform on the seaward side was added in 1983.

1012 SIR HECTOR MACDONALD MONUMENT **3 J7**

Overlooking the town of Dingwall from the Mitchell Hill Cemetery.

This monument was erected in memory of General Sir Hector MacDonald (1853–1903) who became an outstanding soldier, starting his career in the Gordon Highlanders. Known as Fighting Mac, he was born in the nearby Parish of Ferintosh.

1013 MACDUFF CASTLE **6 N14**

East Wemyss, Fife, beside the cemetary overlooking the sea.

Reputed to be home of MacDuff of Shakespeare's *Macbeth*, now in ruins.

1014 MACDUFF MARINE AQUARIUM **3 Q7**

11 High Shore, Macduff, Banff. In Macduff close to the harbour. Bus service from Aberdeen and Elgin to Macduff. Open daily all year except Christmas and New Year, 1000–1700. Charge £. Pre-school children free, maximum of two per full-fee paying adult. Group concessions. Guided tours (available in French and German). Explanatory displays. Gift shop. Picnic area. WC. Limited sign language. Wheelchair access. Disabled WC. Car and coach parking. Telephone (01261) 833369.

A series of high quality displays covering the marine habitats of the Moray Firth, including rock pools, touch pools and splash tank. Featuring a wave machine and living kelp reef, the main display is open to the sky and is the deepest open-topped tank in Scotland. Regular programme of diving and feeding. Children's activity sheets, teacher's guides available.

1015 MACHRIE MOOR STONE CIRCLES **4 G17**

HS. 3 miles (5km) north of Blackwaterfoot on the west coast of the Isle of Arran. Ferry from Ardrossan to Brodick, bus from Brodick then 1.5 miles (2.5km) walk to site. Access at all times. Free. Telephone 0131 668 8800.

The remains of five Bronze Age stone circles. One of the most important sites of its kind in Britain.

1016 MACKINNON MILLS **6 K16**

Kirkshaws Road, Coatbridge, North Lanarkshire. Just off the A8, 10 miles (16km) east of Glasgow. Nearest railway station Whifflet, bus from Glasgow. Open Jan–Nov, daily 1000–1730; Dec, daily 0900–1800. Free. Explanatory displays. Gift shop. WC. Wheelchair access. Disabled WC. Car and coach parking. Telephone (01236) 440702.

Mackinnon Mills offers factory shopping – classic and fashion knitwear, designer label garments, co-ordinated casuals and everything for the golfer.

1017 MCLEAN MUSEUM AND ART GALLERY **6 H15**

15 Kelly Street, Greenock, Renfrewshire. At the west end of Greenock close to rail and bus stations. Nearest railway station Greenock, by bus from Glasgow. Open all year except national and local public holidays: Mon–Sat 1000–1700. Free. Guided tours by arrangement. Explanatory displays. Gift shop. Small garden with seats. WC. Wheelchair access except top floor. Disabled WC. Telephone (01475) 715624.

A museum showing local history, maritime exhibits, ethnography, Egyptology, big game mounts and fine art. Also items relating to James Watt. Programme of temporary exhibitions in the art galleries.

1018 MACLEAN'S CROSS **4 D13**

HS. On the island of Iona, off the west coast of Mull, Argyll. By passenger ferry (no cars) from Fionnphort, Mull. Day tours from Oban in summer. Nearest railway station Oban, bus service from Craignure. Parking in Fionnphort. Access at all times. Free. Telephone 0131 668 8800.

A fine 15th-century free-standing cross.

1019 MACLELLAN'S CASTLE **5 K21**

HS. Kirkcudbright. Off High Street (A711), Kirkcudbright. Bus from Dumfries and Stranraer. Open Apr–Sep, daily 0930–1830. Charge £. Group concessions. Guided tours. Explanatory displays. Gift shop. WC. Limited wheelchair access. Telephone (01557) 331856.

A handsome castellated mansion overlooking the harbour. Dating from 1577, complete except for the roof. Elaborately planned with fine detail. A ruin since 1752.

1020 MADE IN SCOTLAND **3 J8**

The Craft Centre, Station Road, Beauly, Inverness-shire. 12 miles (19km) northwest of Inverness on the A862. Regular bus from Inverness to Beauly. Open all year, Mon–Sat 0900–1730, Sun 1000–1700. Free. Gift shop. Restaurant and tearoom. WC. Wheelchair access. Disabled WC. Car and coach parking.

One of the Highland's largest craft shops, housing the best of Scotland's designer and hand-made products. Also art gallery.

1021 MAES HOWE **1 B10**

HS. Stenness, Orkney. Off A965, 9 miles (14.5km) west of Kirkwall, Orkney. Bus from Kirkwall or Stromness, tour bus from Kirkwall. Open Apr–Sep, daily 0930–1830; Oct–Mar, Mon–Sat 0930–1630, Sun 1400–1630, closed Thu pm and Fri. Charge £. Group concessions. Guided tours. Explanatory displays. Gift shop. Tearoom. WC. Wheelchair access with assistance. Car and coach parking. Telephone (01856) 761606.

The finest megalithic (Neolithic) tomb in the British Isles, consisting of a large mound covering a stone-built passage and a large burial chamber with cells in the walls. Runic inscriptions were carved in the walls by Vikings and Norse crusaders. Admission, shop and tearoom are at the nearby 19th-century Tormiston Mill (see 1429).

1022 MAGGIE'S HOOSIE **3 R7**

26 Shore Street, Inverallochy, Fraserburgh, Aberdeenshire. At the east end of Fraserburgh Bay. Open Apr–Sep, daily 1400–1630. Free.

A preserved but-and-ben fisher cottage with earth floor, box beds and original furnishings.

1023 MAGNUM LEISURE CENTRE **6 H17**

Harbourside, Irvine, Ayrshire. At Irvine harbour, 5 minutes from Irvine railway station. Open Tue, Wed and Thu 1000–2200; other days 0900–2200; closed Christmas and New Year. Charge by activity or day ticket (££). Guided tours by prior arrangement. Explanatory displays. Gift shop. Restaurant, bar and vending machine. WC. Wheelchair access with assistance. Disabled WC. Car and coach parking. Telephone (01294) 278381.

Scotland's largest indoor leisure facility set in an attractive beachpark/harbourside location. Leisure pool with flumes and Scotland's only Thunderbowl white knuckle ride. Five pools (also outdoor pool). Ice rink. Cinema. Softplay area. Boating. Ten court sports hall. Fitness/aerobic studio, steam room, sauna and spa baths. Bowling rink.

1024 MAIDEN STONE **3 Q9**

HS. Near Chapel of Garioch, 4.5 miles (7km) northwest of Inverurie, Aberdeenshire. Bus from Aberdeen, 1.5 miles (2.5km) walk from Oyne fork. Access at all times. Free. Telephone 0131 668 8800.

A 9th-century Pictish cross-slab bearing a Celtic cross on one side and a variety of Pictish symbols on the other.

1025 MAISON DIEU CHAPEL **3 P11**

HS. In Maison Dieu Lane, Brechin, Angus. Nearest railway station Montrose, bus from Montrose or Dundee to Brechin. Access at all times. Free. Telephone 0131 668 8800.

Part of the south wall of a chapel belonging to a medieval hospital founded in the 1260s, with finely-detailed doors and windows.

1026 MALLAIG HERITAGE CENTRE **2 F10**

Station Road, Mallaig, Inverness-shire. In Mallaig centre between railway station and Marine Hotel, off A830. By rail or bus from Fort William or by ferry. Open Jul–Sep, Mon–Sat 1000–1700, Sun 1300–1600; Apr–Jun and Oct, Mon–Sat 1100–1600; Nov–Mar telephone for details. Charge £. Free admission for carers accompanying disabled. Group concessions. Guided tours by appointment. Explanatory displays. Video film show and multimedia access point. Gift shop. Picnic area. Garden. WC. Large print guides for partially sighted. Wheelchair access. Disabled WC. Telephone (01687) 462085.

Exhibits and displays all aspects of the history of Mallaig and West Lochaber – social history, crofting, fishing, railway archaeology, maritime history, Knoydart clearances. Children's quizzes.

1027 MALLAIG MARINE WORLD **2 F10**

The Harbour, Mallaig, Inverness-shire. In Mallaig 100 yards (91m) from the station. By rail or bus from Fort William or by ferry from Skye. Open Jun–Sep, Mon–Sat 0900–2100, Sun 1000–1800; Oct–May, Mon–Sat 0900–1700, Sun 1000–1700 (closed Sun Nov–Mar). Charge £. Children under 5 free. Group concessions. Guided tours on request. Explanatory displays. Leaflets available in nine European languages. Gift shop. Pond garden. WC. Wheelchair access. Disabled WC. Telephone (01687) 462292.

Aquarium and exhibition featuring local marine species. A fishing display features the Mallaig fishing fleet and a video illustrates boats at work.

1028 MANDERSTON **5 Q16**

Duns, Berwickshire. Off the A6105, 2 miles (3km) east of Duns. Nearest railway station Berwick-upon-Tweed, then bus to road end at Manderston. Open from May–Sep, Thu and Sun 1400–1730. Charge £££. Group concessions. Guided tours by arrangement (available in French). Gift shop. Tearoom and picnic area. Garden. WC. Limited wheelchair access. Car and coach parking. Telephone (01361) 883450.

An Edwardian stately home set in 56 acres (22.6ha) and surrounded by formal gardens, stables, dairy, lake and woodland garden. Features include the sumptuous state-rooms, the only silver staircase in the world, a racing room and the first privately-owned biscuit tin museum. Domestic quarters in period style.

1029 MARKLE FISHERIES **5 P15**

Markle, East Linton, East Lothian. Just off the A1, 4 miles (6.5km) south of Haddington. Open all year (weather permitting) except Christmas Day and New Year's Day: 0800–dusk. Various charges £££. Group concessions. Explanatory displays. Shop. Vending machine for drinks and snacks. WC. Limited wheelchair access. Disabled WC. Car and coach parking. Telephone (01620) 861213.

Three spring-fed lakes totalling 9.5 acres (3.8ha) which are regularly stocked with trout and coarse fish. Bank fishing. Children's bait pond.

1030 MAR LODGE ESTATE **3 M10**

NTS. Braemar, Aberdeenshire. Access from the A93 on unclassified road, 5 miles (8km) west of Braemar. Bus to Braemar. Estate open all year. Mar Lodge open on special days, telephone for details. Free. Car parking. Telephone (013397) 41433.

Part of the core area of the Cairngorms, internationally recognised as the most important nature conservation landscape in Britain. The estate contains four of the five highest mountains in the UK. Outstanding wildlife, short- and long-distance walks. Ranger service.

1031 MAR'S WARK **6 L14**

HS. At the top of Castle Wynd, Stirling. Nearest railway station Stirling, bus from Glasgow and Edinburgh. Open at all times. Free. Telephone 0131 668 8800.

A remarkable Renaissance mansion built by the Regent Mar in 1570, of which the façade is the main surviving part.

1032 MARY, QUEEN OF SCOTS' HOUSE **5 P18**

Queen Street, Jedburgh. In the centre of Jedburgh. Bus from Edinburgh or Newcastle. Open Easter–Oct, Mon–Sat 1000–1645, Sun 1000–1630. Charge £. Group concessions. Explanatory displays. Booklets in European languages. Gift shop. Formal garden. Limited wheelchair access (ground floor). Telephone (01835) 863331.

A 16th-century castle which is now a visitor centre devoted to the memory of Mary, Queen of Scots, who stayed here in 1566 while she was ill.

1033 MAUD RAILWAY MUSEUM **3 Q8**

Maud Railway Station, Maud, Aberdeenshire. On the B9029, 15 miles (24km) west of Peterhead. Bus from Peterhead. Open Easter–Sep, weekends and public holidays 1230–1700. Free. Guided tours. Explanatory displays. Gift shop. Picnic area. WC. Wheelchair access. Disabled WC. Car and coach parking. Telephone (01771) 622906.

Visitors can relive the great days of steam trains at the former Maud Railway Station. Sound effects add to the nostalgia of the displays of Great North of Scotland Railway memorabilia and old photographs.

1034 MAYBOLE COLLEGIATE CHURCH 4 H18

HS. South of the A77 in Maybole, Ayrshire. Nearest railway station Maybole, bus from Ayr. Not open to the public; exterior view only. Free. Telephone 0131 668 8800.

The roofless ruin of a 15th-century church built for a small college established in 1373 by John Kennedy of Dunure.

1035 MEADOWLANDS GALLERY 3 P7

Unit 7, 83 North Castle Street, Banff. On main Aberdeen to Elgin coast road. Bus service from Aberdeen to Elgin stops within easy walking distance. Open all year, Mon–Sat 0900–1730. Free. Guided tours. Gift shop. Wheelchair access. Car and coach parking. Telephone (01261) 818535.

Housed in one of Banff's oldest buildings, the gallery has on permanent display paintings and prints by contemporary artists. Framing service and gift shop.

1036 MEADOWMILL SPORTS CENTRE 6 N15

Meadowmill, Tranent, East Lothian. Off the A198, north of the A1 and 2 miles (3km) outside Tranent. Prestonpans station, bus from Edinburgh. Open daily (except Christmas and New Year): Mon–Fri 0900–2200, weekends 1000–1700. Charge by activity. Group concessions. Café and vending machines. Crèche. WC. Wheelchair access. Disabled WC. Car and coach parking. Telephone (01875) 614900.

A general sports centre offering all kinds of activities including a gym, free weights room, soft play room, activity hall and sports pitches.

1037 MEADOW WELL 3 M2

Caithness. In Thurso.

Once a major source of the local water supply and where local fishwives gathered to sell fresh fish.

1038 THE MEFFAN 5 N12

20 West High Street, Forfar, Angus. In Forfar centre, 3 miles (5km) from A94. Nearest railway station Dundee, bus from Dundee or Brechin. Open all year (except Christmas and New Year), Mon–Sat 1000–1700. Free. Guided tours by arrangement. Explanatory displays. Gift shop. WC. Wheelchair access with assistance (ground floor only). Disabled WC. Telephone (01307) 464123.

Two art galleries with constantly changing exhibitions featuring art from contemporary Scottish artists and Angus collections. The Forfar Story features original Pictish stones from Angus, an interactive guide to the stones, a walk through an old Forfar vennel with its shoppies and a witch burning scene.

1039 MEGGINCH CASTLE GARDENS 5 N13

Megginch Castle, Errol, Perthshire. Off the A90, 10 miles (16km) east of Perth. Bus from Perth or Dundee. Open Apr–Oct, Wed 1400–1700, but every day in Aug. Charge £. Guided tours by arrangement (available in French), charge £. Wheelchair access. Car and coach parking. Telephone (01821) 642222.

Gardens around a 15th-century castle with daffodils, rhododendrons and 1000-year-old yews. Double-walled kitchen garden, 16th-century rose garden and 19th-century flower parterre. Gothic courtyard with pagoda-roofed dovecot featured in the film Rob Roy. Topiary and 16th-century physic garden with astrological garden.

1040 MEIGLE SCULPTURED STONES 5 N12

HS. Meigle Museum, Dundee Road, Meigle, Perthshire. On the A94 in Meigle, 12 miles (19km) west southwest of Forfar, Angus. Bus service from Dundee or Perth to Meigle. Open Apr–Sep, daily 0930–1830.

Charge £. Group concessions. Guided tours. Explanatory displays. Gift shop. WC. Wheelchair access. Disabled WC. Telephone (01828) 640612.

One of the most notable collections of Dark Age sculpture in Western Europe. Twenty-five sculptured monuments of the Early Christian period.

1041 MELLERSTAIN HOUSE **5 P17**

Gordon, Berwickshire. Off the A6089, 7 miles (11km) northwest of Kelso. Bus from Galashiels or Kelso. Open mid Apr–Sep, Sun–Fri 1230–1700 (restaurant 1130–1730). Charge ££. Group concessions for pre-booked tours. Guided tours by arrangement. Explanatory displays. Gift shop. Restaurant and picnic area. Award-winning garden. WC. Limited wheelchair access. Car and coach parking. Telephone (01573) 410225.

A superb Georgian mansion designed by William and Robert Adam. Features exquisite plaster ceilings, beautiful interior decoration, fine period furniture, marvellous art collection. Terraced garden and grounds.

1042 MELROSE ABBEY **5 P17**

HS. Abbey Street, Melrose. Main Square, Melrose, Roxburghshire. In Melrose, off the A7 or A68. Bus services from Edinburgh, Kelso, Jedburgh and Galashiels. Open Apr–Sep, daily 0930–1830; Oct–Mar, Mon–Sat 0930–1630, Sun 1400–1630. Charge £. Group concessions. Guided tours. Explanatory displays. Audio guide. Gift shop. Picnic area. WC. Wheelchair access with assistance. Car and coach parking. Telephone (01896) 822562.

The ruins of the Cistercian abbey founded by King David I circa 1136. It was largely destroyed by an English army in 1385 but rebuilt in the early 15th century. It is now probably the most famous ruin in Scotland because of the elegant and elaborate stonework which remains. The Commendator's House contains a large collection of on-site finds.

1043 MELVILLE GOLF CENTRE **6 N16**

South Melville, Lasswade, Midlothian. 7 miles (11km) south of Edinburgh centre, just off the city bypass. Bus from Edinburgh. Golf course open all year, daily dawn to dusk. Golf range and shop open Mon–Fri 0900–2200, weekends 0900–2000. Charge: range £, course £££. Group concessions. Golf shop. Picnic area and vending machines. WC. Wheelchair access with assistance. Disabled WC. Car and coach parking. Telephone 0131 663 8038 (range and shop) 0131 654 0224 (bookings).

Golf centre with a 9-hole play-and-pay course, driving range, 22 covered floodlit bays and 12 outdoor bays. Full equipment hire. PGA tuition. Practice area. Putting green.

1044 MELVILLE MONUMENT **5 K13**

One mile (1.5km) north of Comrie, 6 miles (9.5km) west of Crieff. Access at all times by footpath from parking place on Glen Lednock road. Free. Car parking.

The obelisk in memory of Lord Melville (1742–1811) stands on Dunmore, a hill of 840 feet (256m), with delightful views of the surrounding country. The access path is linked to the scenic 4-mile (6.5km) Glen Lednock Circular Walk, running from Comrie and back through varied woodland (waymarked).

1045 MEMSIE CAIRN **3 R7**

HS. Near Rathen, 3.5 miles (5.5km) south of Fraserburgh, Aberdeenshire. Nearest railway station Aberdeen, bus from Fraserburgh to Memsie. Access at all times. Free. Telephone 0131 668 8800.

A large stone-built cairn, possibly Bronze Age, but enlarged during field clearance in the last two centuries.

1046 MERKLAND CROSS **5 M20**

HS. At Merkland Smithy, near Ecclefechan, Dumfriesshire. Nearest railway station Gretna, bus from Gretna, Lockerbie or Dumfries. Access at all times. Free. Telephone 0131 668 8800.

A fine carved 15th-century wayside cross.

1047 MERTOUN GARDENS **5 P17**

St Boswells, Melrose, Roxburghshire. On the B6404, 2 miles (3km) east of St Boswells. Bus from St Boswells or Kelso. Open Apr–Sep, weekends and bank holidays 1400–1730 (closes 1800). Charge £. Group concessions. Guided tours. WC. Limited wheelchair access. Car and coach parking. Telephone (01835) 823236.

Gardens comprising 26 acres (10.5ha) with delightful walks and river views. Fine trees, herbaceous borders and flowering shrubs. Walled garden and well-preserved circular dovecot thought to be the oldest in the county. Dogs not permitted.

1048 METHIL HERITAGE CENTRE **6 N14**

272 High Street, Methill, Fife. 8 miles (13km) east of Kirkcaldy on A915 or A955. Bus from Kirkcaldy, Glenrothes or St Andrews. Open all year (except public holidays), Tue–Thu 1100–1630, Sat 1300–1530. Free. Explanatory displays. Gift shop. Tearoom. WC. Wheelchair access. Disabled WC. Telephone (01333) 422100.

A lively community museum, interpreting the social and individual history of the area. Permanent exhibition and a varied programme of temporary displays.

1049 MIDHOWE BROCH AND CAIRNS **1 B10**

HS. On the west coast of the island of Rousay, Orkney. Bus from Kirkwall to Tingwall, then ferry to Rousay. Access at all times. Free. Telephone 0131 668 8800.

An Iron Age broch and walled enclosure situated on a promontory cut off by a deep rock ditch. Adjacent is Midhowe Stalled Cairn, a huge and impressive Neolithic chambered tomb in an oval mound with 25 stalls. Now protected by a modern building.

1050 MILLBUIES LOCHS **3 M7**

Longmorn, 5 miles (7.5km) south of Elgin on A941 to Rothes. Open Jan–Dec (fishing Mar–Oct) daily. Free. Car parking.

The lochs are in a wooded setting with numerous walks where wildlife and flora can be seen. Four boats are available for anglers.

1051 HUGH MILLER'S COTTAGE **3 K7**

NTS. Church Street, Cromarty, Ross and Cromarty. Off A832 in Cromarty, 22 miles (35km) northeast of Inverness. By bus from Inverness. Open May–Sep, Mon–Sat 1100–1300 and 1400–1700, Sun 1400–1700. Charge £. Children free. Group concessions. Explanatory displays. Information sheets in five languages. Cottage garden. Braille guide sheets, captioned video. Limited wheelchair access. Car and coach parking. Telephone (01381) 600245.

Birthplace in 1802 of Hugh Miller, famous stonemason, geologist, writer and church reformer. Thatched cottage, built circa 1698, with restored cottage garden. Many of Miller's belongings, including fine fossil collection. Video about his life.

1052 MILL OF BENHOLM VISITOR CENTRE **3 Q11**

Mill of Benholm, Inverbervie, Kincardineshire. On the A92, 3 miles (5km) south of Inverbervie. Bus from Montrose or Stonehaven. Open Easter–Oct, daily 1100–1700. (Apr, May and Oct café open at weekends only). Charge £. Guided tours. Explanatory displays. Gift shop.

Tearoom and picnic area. WC. Wheelchair access. Disabled WC. Car and coach parking. Telephone (01561) 361969.

A restored corn mill where visitors can see the work of a rural miller come to life. Demonstrations of traditional corn milling. Woodland walk in pleasant grounds.

1053 MILL ON THE FLEET **5 K20**

High Street, Gatehouse of Fleet, Castle Douglas, Kirkcudbrightshire. In Gatehouse-of-Fleet by the river. Buses from Dumfries or Stranraer. Open late Mar–Oct, daily 1000–1630 (closes 1730). Charge £. Group concessions. Guided tours on request. Explanatory displays. Gift shop. Tearoom. Baby changing. WC. Wheelchair access (including car parking). Disabled WC. Telephone (01557) 814099.

An exhibition housed in a restored 18th-century cotton mill and telling the history of the town. Temporary and permanent exhibits. Craft shop.

1054 MILL TRAIL VISITOR CENTRE **6 L14**

West Stirling Street, Alva, Clackmannanshire. On the A91, 8 miles (13km) east of Stirling. Bus from Stirling or Alloa. Open all year (except Christmas and New Year): Jan–Jun and Oct–Dec 1000–1700; Jul–Sep 0900–1800. Free. Explanatory displays. Gift shop. Coffee shop. Children's play area. WC. Wheelchair access. Disabled WC. Car and coach parking. Telephone (01259) 769696.

An exhibition telling the story of spinning and weaving in Clackmannan (the Wee County). Features the experience of a 13-year-old working in the mills. Original weaving and knitting looms. Visitors can walk through a modern mill and watch jumpers being made. Shop sells wide variety of local craft goods, books and knitwear.

1055 MILNHOLM CROSS **5 P19**

One mile (1.5km) south of Newcastleton beside B6357. Access at all times. Car parking.

Erected circa 1320, and owned by the Clan Armstrong Trust, Milnholm Cross is a memorial to Alexander Armstrong who was murdered in Hermitage Castle some 4 miles (6.5km) away. It faces the ruin of Mangerton Castle, seat of the Armstrong chiefs for 300 years.

1056 MILTON ART AND CRAFT GALLERY **3 Q10**

Milton of Crathes, Crathes, Banchory. 15 miles (24km) west of Aberdeen and 2 miles (3km) east of Banchory on A93. Regular bus service from Aberdeen. Open all year (except 25/26 Dec and 1/2 Jan), daily 1000–1700. Free. Gift shop. Restaurant. WC. Wheelchair access. Disabled WC. Telephone (01330) 844664.

Set in a tranquil restored mill on the banks of the river Dee. The courtyard buildings have all been restored, retaining many of their original features including the water wheel. The gallery shows a wide range of art and crafts from local artists. Pottery, craft workshop and furniture shop.

1057 MINIATURE RAILWAY **5 P12**

West Links Park, Arbroath, Angus. By the seafront to the west of Arbroath. Nearest railway station Arbroath 2 miles (3km), local bus service. Open Easter–Sep, Sat and Sun 1400–1700 (Jul–mid Aug daily), weather permitting. Charge £. Disabled groups free. Group concessions. WC. Wheelchair access. Disabled WC. Car and coach parking. Telephone (01241) 879249.

Open since 1935, the small trains run from West Links Station alongside the Aberdeen to Edinburgh mainline. The station is complete with platforms, booking office, footbridge, signal box, turntable and loco-shed. The half-mile (1km) round trip includes a tunnel. There are six locomotives, two of which are coal-fired steam.

1058 MOAT PARK HERITAGE CENTRE **5 M17**

Kirkstyle, Biggar, Lanarkshire. In Biggar. Bus from Edinburgh. Open Easter–Oct, Mon–Sat 1000–1700, Sun 1400–1700. Charge £. Group concessions. Guided tours. Explanatory displays. Gift shop. Picnic area. Children's activity sheets. WC. Handling sessions by arrangement. Limited wheelchair access. Disabled WC. Car parking. Telephone (01899) 221050.

A former church adapted to display the history of the Upper Clyde and Tweed Valleys, from the days of the volcano and the glacier to the present. Fine collection of embroidery including the largest known patchwork cover, containing over 80 figures from the 1850s. Archaeology collection. Displays and models which tell the story of Clydesdale from the Stone Age to modern times.

1059 MOFFAT MUSEUM **5 M18**

The Old Bakehouse, The Neuk, Church Gate, Moffat, Dumfriesshire. In Moffat centre. Buses from Dumfries, Glasgow or Edinburgh. Open Easter and May–Sep, Mon–Sat (except Wed pm) 1030–1300 and 1430–1700, Sun 1430–1700. Charge £. Explanatory displays. Gift shop. Telephone (01683) 220868.

Located in an old bakehouse with a Scotch oven. Tells the story of Moffat and its people, border raids, Covenanters, education, sports and pastimes, famous people. A short video presentation.

1060 MOFFAT WOOLLEN MILL **5 M18**

Ladyknowe, Moffat, Dumfriesshire. Located behind the tourist information centre. Nearest railway and bus stations Dumfries, bus to Moffat. Open Apr–Oct, daily 0900–1730; Nov–Mar, daily 0900–1700. Free. Explanatory displays. Gift shop. Restaurant. Wheelchair access. Car and coach parking. Telephone (01683) 220134.

Visit the working weaving exhibition. Mill offers a good selection of cashmere, Aran, lambswool and traditional tartans and tweeds. Trace Scottish clan history and heraldry at the Clan History Centre and receive a certificate illustrating your clan ancestry.

1061 MOIRLANICH LONGHOUSE **4 J13**

NTS. c/o NTS Office, Lynedoch, Main Street, Killin, Perthshire. Off A827, 1 mile (1.5km) northwest of Killin. Open Easter Sunday and May–Sep, Wed and Sun 1400–1700. Charge £. Children free. Group concessions. Explanatory displays. Limited wheelchair access. Disabled WC. Car parking. Telephone (01567) 820988 Mon–Fri 0900–1500.

Outstanding example of a traditional cruck-frame cottage and byre dating from the mid 19th century. Inhabited until 1968, the house retains many original features and is furnished according to archaeological evidence.

1062 MONCREIFFE HILL WOOD **5 M13**

Bridge of Earn, Perthshire. South of Perth, off M90 at junction 9 or A912 at Bridge of Earn, take minor road to Rhynd following tourist sign-posting. Access at all times. Car parking. Telephone (01764) 662554.

The magnificent slopes of Moncreiffe Hill Wood occupy a prominent position about two miles south of Perth. A visit to this spectacular 333 acre (134ha) wood, which is owned and managed by the Woodland Trust, will open up outstanding views along the River Tay and Strathearn and you may also catch a glimpse of some of the wildlife which inhabits the wood, such as deer, red squirrels and birds of prey.

1063 MONIKIE COUNTRY PARK **5 P12**

Main Lodge, Monikie, Angus. Off the B962 between Dundee and Arbroath. Bus from Dundee. Open daily, May–Jul 0900–2100, Aug–Nov

0900–1700, Dec–Jan 0900–1600 (closed Christmas and New Year), Feb–Apr 0900–1700. Free. Charge for parking and watersports. Group concessions. Guided tours by ranger. Explanatory displays. Tearoom (open daily during school holidays, otherwise weekends only May–Sep). Picnic area. Barbeque area (requires booking). WC. Limited wheelchair access. Disabled WC. Car and coach parking. Telephone (01382) 370202.

Country park of 185 acres (75ha) with reservoirs, woodland and grassland. Instruction and hire for windsurfing, sailing, canoeing (May–September). Also rowing boats. Play area, orienteering trails and woodland walks.

1064 MONREITH ANIMAL WORLD AND MUSEUM **4 J11**

Low Knock Farm, Monreith, Wigtownshire. On the A747, 0.5 mile (1km) from Monreith. Bus from Newton Stewart and Stranraer. Open late Mar–Oct, daily 1000–1700. Charge £. Children under 3 free. Group concessions. Explanatory displays. Gift shop. Picnic area. WC. No guide dogs. Limited wheelchair access. Disabled WC. Car and coach parking. Telephone (01988) 700217.

Collection of animals and birds, including otters, beavers, pigmy goats, owls, waterfowl and small mammals, in natural spacious surroundings. Reptile collection. Small museum on Gavin Maxwell.

1065 MONTEVIOT HOUSE GARDENS **5 P17**

Monteviot, Jedburgh, Roxburghshire. Off the B6400, 4 miles (6.5km) north of Jedburgh (off A68). Nearest railway station Berwick-upon-Tweed 35 miles (56km). Open Apr–Oct, daily 1200–1700. Charge £. Children under 14 free. Guided tours for groups by prior arrangement. WC. Limited wheelchair access. Disabled WC. Car and coach parking. Telephone (01835) 830380.

Gardens on the bank of the River Teviot with several feature areas – river garden, rose terraces, water garden.

1066 MONTROSE AIR STATION MUSEUM **5 Q12**

Waldron Road, Montrose, Angus. At the north end of Montrose on the A92. 15 minute walk from rail station, buses from Aberdeen and Dundee. Open all year, Sun 1200–1700. Charge £. Guided tours. Explanatory displays. Gift shop. WC. No guide dogs. Limited wheelchair access. Car and coach parking. Telephone (01674) 673107.

RFC/RAF and wartime artefacts and memorabilia housed in the wartime RAF Montrose HQ, depicting the story of the historic aerodrome which opened in 1913. Various aircraft on display outside.

1067 MONTROSE BASIN WILDLIFE CENTRE **5 Q12**

Rossie Braes, Montrose. 1 mile (1.5km) south of Montrose on A92. From Aberdeen, Edinburgh and Glasgow to railway station Montrose, local bus service then short walk. Open Apr–Oct, daily 1030–1700; Nov–Mar, daily 1030–1600. Closed Christmas, Boxing Day and New Year's Day. Charge £. Group concessions. Guided tours. Explanatory displays. Gift shop. Vending machine and picnic area. WC. Touch tables. Wheelchair access. Disabled WC. Car and coach parking. Telephone (01674) 676336.

Television cameras bring the wildlife literally into the centre. Unique displays show how a tidal basin works and the routes of migrating birds. Magnificent views of wildlife on the basin through high powered telescopes and binoculars. Interactive displays.

1068 MONTROSE MUSEUM AND ART GALLERY **5 Q12**

Panmure Place, Montrose, Angus. On the Mid Links a few minutes walk from the High Street. By rail or bus from Aberdeen, Edinburgh, Dundee or Glasgow. Open all year, Mon–Sat 1000–1700. Free. Guided tours. Explanatory displays. Gift shop. WC. Wheelchair access with assistance. Car and coach parking. Telephone (01674) 673232.

Tells the story of Montrose from prehistoric times, including local geology and wildlife. On show are various Pictish stones, pottery, whaling and Napoleonic artefacts. Art gallery. See also 946 William Lamb Sculpture Studio.

1069 MONUMENT HILL **4 H13**

Off the old road to Inveraray, 2 miles (3km) southwest of Dalmally. Access at all times. Free.

Monument to Duncan Ban Macintyre (1724–1812), the Burns of the Highlands, who was born near Inveroran.

1070 MONYMUSK ARTS CENTRE **3 P9**

Monymusk, Inverurie. 18 miles (29km) west of Aberdeen, 3 miles (5km) southwest of Kemnay on the B993. By rail to Aberdeen or Inverurie, then bus to Monymusk. Open May–Sep, daily 1000–1600; telephone for other times. Free. Guided tours. Explanatory displays. Gift shop. Small garden. WC. Wheelchair access. Disabled WC. Car and coach parking. Telephone (01467) 213.

Located in an 18th-century stone-polishing mill converted to a church in 1801. Wide selection of local crafts during summer months. Art exhibition every two weeks and small educational resource centre of 18th century local social history and geography. Craft-worker often in residence.

1071 MOONSTONE MINIATURES **5 L20**

4 Victoria Street, Kirkpatrick Durham. 14 miles (22.5km) west of Dumfries, 4 miles (6.5km) east of Castle Douglas off the A75 at Springholm. Bus from Dumfries to Kirkcudbright. Open May–mid Sep, Wed–Fri 1000–1700. Weekends and winter opening by arrangement. Charge £. Children under 5 free. Guided tours. Explanatory displays. Gift shop. Wheelchair access with assistance. Car and coach parking. Telephone (01556) 650313.

Cabinets of miniature marvels at $^{1}/_{12}$th scale, including stately homes, shops and humble cottages.

1072 MORAY FIRTH DOLPHIN CRUISES **3 K8**

Shore Street Quay, Shore Street, Inverness. 10 minute walk from town centre at harbour.. Free bus service from tourist office departs 15 minutes before each cruise. Open Mar–Oct, 0900–1800, telephone for times of cruises. Charge £££. Group concessions. Guided tours. Explanatory displays. Gift shop. Refreshments. WC. Car and coach parking. Telephone (01463) 717900.

Moray Firth Dolphin Cruises operate the M.V. *Miss Serenity*, which will carry 90 passengers in comfort. The Moray Firth dolphins are the largest resident population in Britain. The company participates in the International Dolphin Watch programme.

1073 MORAY FIRTH WILDLIFE CENTRE **3 N7**

Tugnet, Spey Bay, Buckie, Moray. At the end of the B9104, 5 miles (8km) north of Fochabers on the A96. Nearest railway station Keith (12 miles/19km). Bus to Fochabers. Open daily Mar–Oct 1030–1700, Jul and Aug closes 1930; telephone to confirm times during winter. Charge £. Group concessions. Explanatory displays. Gift shop. Tearoom, picnic area and wildlife garden. WC. Wheelchair access. Disabled WC. Car and coach parking. Telephone (01343) 820339.

Housed in a former salmon fishing station built in 1768 and providing an ideal place to watch ospreys hunting, seals, dolphins, otters and many birds. Houses an exhibition about the Moray Firth dolphins and the marine environment. Hands-on activities for children. A base for research projects studying the dolphins. Environmental resource room.

1074 MORAY LEISURE CENTRE **3 M7**

Borough Briggs Road, Elgin, Moray. In Elgin, 0.25 mile (0.5km) from bus station. Elgin rail station 1 mile (2km). Open all year, daily 0700–2200, except Christmas and New Year. Various admission charges. Guided tours by arrangement. Explanatory displays. Café bar, vending machines and small picnic area. Crèche. Sports shop. WC. Wheelchair access. Disabled WC. Car and coach parking. Telephone (01343) 550033.

Ice rink, swimming and leisure pools, health and fitness suite, relaxation suite (sauna, steam room, spa pool and solarium), squash courts.

1075 MORAY MOTOR MUSEUM **3 M7**

Bridge Street, Elgin, Moray. 30 miles (48km) west of Inverness. Open Apr–Oct, daily 1100–1700. Charge £. Group concessions. Explanatory displays. Gift shop. WC. Wheelchair access. Disabled WC. Car and coach parking. Telephone (01343) 542660.

Unique collection of high quality cars and motor bikes housed in an old mill building.

1076 MORTON CASTLE **5 L18**

HS. On the A702, 17 miles (27km) north northwest of Dumfries. Beside Morton Loch. Nearest railway station Dumfries, bus from Dumfries. Closed to the public; exterior view only. Telephone 0131 668 8800.

The well preserved ruin of a fine late 13th-century hall house, a stronghold of the Douglases.

1077 MORVEN GALLERY **2 D3**

Upper Barvas, Isle of Lewis. 12 miles (19km) west of Stornoway. Bus from Stornoway. Open Mar–Oct, Mon–Sat 1030–1730. Free. Guided tours on request. Explanatory displays. Gift shop. Tearoom. WC. Wheelchair access. Car and coach parking. Telephone (01851) 840216.

Fine art by local painters and sculptors. Ceramics, tapestry, carvings and contemporary designer knitwear. Talks, slide shows and conference facility. Workshops and children's activities.

1078 MOSS FARM ROAD STONE CIRCLE **4 G17**

HS. 3 miles (5km) north of Blackwaterfoot, Isle of Arran. Ferry from Ardrossan to Brodick, bus from Brodick. Access at all times. Free. Telephone 0131 668 8800.

The remains of a Bronze Age cairn surrounded by a stone circle.

1079 MOTHERWELL CONCERT HALL AND THEATRE **6 K16**

Civic Centre, Motherwell. Off junction 6 on M74, then to Airles Road to town centre. Nearest railway station Motherwell. Telephone to confirm times and charges, dependent on performances. Bar and refreshments. WC. Wheelchair access. Disabled WC. Car and coach parking. Telephone (01698) 267515.

The refurbished Theatre and Concert Hall at the Civic Centre is the venue for performances by some of the finest and foremost stars of theatre, television and stage. Doubles as Motherwell Moviehouse showing a programme of popular films.

1080 MOTHERWELL HERITAGE CENTRE **6 K16**

1 High Road, Motherwell. Opposite library in Motherwell. Off junction 6 on M74, then to Hamilton Road to town centre. Motherwell railway station is 5 minute walk. Regular bus service. Open all year, Mon–Sat 1000–1700 (Thu, closes 1900) Sun 1200–1700; closed 25/26 Dec and 1 Jan. Free. Guided tours on request. Explanatory displays. Gift shop. Tearoom. Garden. WC. Disabled WC. Car and coach parking. Telephone (01698) 251000.

Tells the story of the Motherwell area from Roman times to the present day. Visit the Technopolis interactive media display and walk through time to see the industrial heyday of the area, social and political upheavals and the development of the modern town. Family history research room, exhibition gallery and special events programme.

1081 MOTORING HERITAGE CENTRE **6 J15**

Main Street, Alexandria, Dunbartonshire. Alexandria rail station. Open all year (closed Christmas Day and New Year), daily 1000–1800. Charge £. Group concessions. Guided tours. Explanatory displays. Gift shop. Licensed bar. WC. Wheelchair access. Disabled WC. Car and coach parking. Telephone (01389) 607862.

A motor heritage centre situated in what was once the world's largest motor car works, now Loch Lomond Factory Outlets. Display traces the history of the once-famous Argyll marque and the story of Scottish motoring. Visitors can sit in a Model T Ford, see unique archive film and fascinating carts.

1082 MOTTE OF URR **5 L20**

Off B794, 5 miles (7.5km) northeast of Castle Douglas. Access at all reasonable times. Free.

The most extensive motte and bailey castle in Scotland, dating from the 12th century, though the bailey may have been an earlier earthwork of hillfort type.

1083 MOUNT STUART HOUSE AND GARDENS **4 G16**

Mount Stuart, Isle of Bute. 5 miles (8km) south of Rothesay. By ferry from Wemyss Bay to Rothesay, bus from Rothesay. Courtesy shuttle between Reception and House. House and gardens open May–Sep, Mon, Wed, Fri, Sat and Sun 1100–1630 (house), 1000–1700 (gardens). For April and Oct please telephone. Charge £££. Group concessions. Guided tours. Explanatory displays. Visitor reception area. Gift shop. Tearoom and picnic areas. Gardens with adventure play area. WC. Induction loop. Wheelchair access. Disabled WC. Car and coach parking. Telephone (01700) 503877.

Spectacular high Victorian Gothic house, the ancestral home of the Marquess of Bute. Splendid interiors, art collection and architectural detail. Mature Victorian pinetum, arboretum and exotic gardens, waymarked walks. Three hundred acres (121ha) of ground and gardens. Audio-visual presentation.

1084 MOUSA BROCH **1 G5**

HS. On the island of Mousa, Shetland. Bus from Lerwick to Sandwick, about 14 miles (22km) south of Lerwick. By boat from Sandwick to Mousa: May–Sep, Mon–Fri pm and Sat and Sun am (and some evenings). Access at all times. Free. Telephone 0131 668 8800.

The finest surviving Iron Age broch tower, standing over 40 feet (12m) high. The stair can be climbed to the parapet.

1085 MUCKLE FLUGGA AND OUT STACK **1 G1**

Unst Island, Shetland. At the northern tip of Shetland. Depart from the pier, Mid Yell. Minibus to departure point, booking essential. Open May–Sep, Wed 1000–1700 (weather permitting). Charge £££. Group concessions. Guided tours (available in French). Explanatory displays. Fare includes picnic lunch and tea; hot drinks on boat. WC. Car parking. Telephone (01950) 422493.

All-day guided tour by motor boat to the seal islands of Yell Sound, the sensational cliffs of the west coast of Unst, around Muckle Flugga lighthouse and Out Stack and on to the Scottish Natural Heritage Centre at Hermaness National Nature Reserve (see 793) at Burrafirth. See also 1326 Shetland Wildlife Tours and 1131 Noss Nature Reserve.

1086 MUGDOCK COUNTRY PARK **6 J15**

Craigallian Road, Milngavie, Glasgow. 10 miles (16km) north of Glasgow. Nearest railway station Milngavie, bus from Glasgow. Summer shuttle to visitor centre form railway station. Open daily all year (except Christmas Day). Free. Charge for events and barbeque hire. Castle tours on request. Explanatory displays. Countryside events programme. Gift shop. Restaurant, tearoom, picnic and barbeque areas. Play areas and walks. WC. Tactile map. Wheelchair access with assistance. Disabled WC. Car and coach parking. Telephone 0141 956 6100.

Eight hundred acres (323ha) of beautiful countryside – lakes, woodland and heather. Mugdock and Craigend Castles. Countryside events – orienteering, archery. Craigend stables and Bridle routes. Also garden centre, craft shops, audio-visual displays and Victorian walled garden

---

1087 MUIRAVONSIDE COUNTRY PARK **6 L15**

The Loan, Whitecross, Linlithgow, West Lothian. On the B825, 8 miles (13km) east of Falkirk. Polmont station 4 miles (6.5km), Linlithgow station 3 miles (5km) then walk, no bus. Open Apr–Sep, Mon–Fri 0900–1700, Sun 1000–1800; Oct–Mar weekends only 1000–1600. Free. Guided tours. Explanatory displays. Tearoom at weekends Apr–Sep. Playground and children's farm. WC. Induction loop. Limited wheelchair access. Disabled WC. Car and coach parking. Telephone (01506) 845311.

Woodlands, parkland and gardens of the Muiravonside Estate, home of the Stirling family for 150 years. Exhibition in visitor centre with auditorium and ranger office. Relics of industrial past. Dovecot. Burial ground and summer house.

1088 JOHN MUIR HOUSE **5 P15**

126–128 High Street, Dunbar. In centre of town. Nearest railway station Dunbar, buses from Edinburgh and Berwick-upon-Tweed. Open Jun–Sep, Mon–Sat 1100–1300 and 1400–1700, Sun 1400–1700. Free. Explanatory displays. Car and coach parking. Telephone (01368) 862585.

The birthplace of John Muir, founding figure of the world-wide conservation movement. He was born in 1838 in this house. On the ground floor his father ran a business. His boyhood was spent in Dunbar until his family emigrated in 1849. The flat has been furnished in period style to give an impression of the circumstances in which the family lived, without gas or running water. Audio-visual tells the story of John Muir, both in Dunbar and the USA.

1089 MUIR O'FAULD SIGNAL STATION **5 L13**

HS. East of Ardunie, Perthshire. Nearest railway station Perth, bus from Perth to Crieff, then Crieff to Kinkell Bridge. Access at all times. Free. Telephone 0131 668 8800.

The site of a Roman watch tower. See also 85 Ardunie Roman Signal Station.

1090 MULL RAIL **4 F12**

Old Pier Station, Craignure, Isle of Mull, Argyll. In Craignure, 0.25 mile (0.5km) southeast of ferry terminal. By ferry from Oban to Craignure. Open Easter–mid Oct, daily 1100–1700. Charge (single) £, (return) ££. Group concessions. Gift shop. Wheelchair access and adapted coaches. Car and coach parking. Telephone (01680) 812494.

Scotland's only (narrow gauge) island passenger railway running between Craignure and Torosay Castle (see 1431). Scenic journey lasts 20 minutes. Steam and diesel locomotives.

1091 MUNESS CASTLE **1 H2**

HS. At the southeast corner of the island of Unst, Shetland. Bus from Lerwick. Open at all times; apply to keyholder. Free. Explanatory

displays. Limited wheelchair access. Car and coach parking. Telephone 0131 668 8800.

A late 16th-century tower house with fine detail and circular towers at diagonally opposite corners. The most northerly castle in the British Isles.

1092 MUSEUM OF FLIGHT **6 P15**

East Fortune Airfield, Haddington, East Lothian. 20 miles (32km) east of Edinburgh. Bus from Haddington or North Berwick. Open all year, daily 1030–1700 (closed 25, 31 Dec, 1 Jan). Charge £. Children free. Group concessions. Guided tours. Explanatory displays. Gift shop. Tearoom. Baby changing. Garden. WC. Wheelchair access and disabled parking. Disabled WC. Car and coach parking. Telephone (01620) 880308.

Scotland's national museum of aviation with a large collection of over 40 aircraft (including Britain's oldest aeroplane, a Spitfire and a Vulcan bomber) in the hangars of a wartime airfield. Special exhibitions on space flight, early aviation, air traffic control and the R34 airship. Regular events. An outstation of the National Museums of Scotland.

1093 MUSEUM OF ISLAY LIFE **4 D16**

Port Charlotte, Isle of Islay. Off A847 in Port Charlotte. Local bus service to museum. Open Apr–Oct, Mon–Sat 1000–1700, Sun 1400–1700; other times by arrangement. Charge £. Group concessions. Explanatory displays. Gift shop. WC. Wheelchair access. Car and coach parking. Telephone (01496) 850358.

The museum illustrates life on Islay from prehistoric times to the early 20th century. Also the Gordon Booth Library, where archives, photographs and books relating to island life may be consulted. In the Wee Museum of Childhood there are hands-on activities and quizzes for all ages.

1094 MUSEUM OF LEAD MINING **5 L18**

Wanlockhead, Biggar, Lanarkshire. On the B797 between Abington (A74) and Mennock (A76). Nearest railway station Sanquhar, school bus only to Wanlockhead (9 miles). Open Apr–Oct, daily 1100–1630; Nov–Mar by arrangement. Charge ££. Group concessions. Guided tours. Explanatory displays and interactive computer presentations. Visitor centre. Gift shop. Tearoom. WC. Wheelchair access. Disabled WC. Car and coach parking. Telephone (01659) 74387.

A museum tracing 300 years of lead mining in Scotland's highest village set in the dramatic Lowther Hills. Features heritage trail, beam engine, tours of a lead mine, period cottages, miners' library, displays of minerals. Gold panning centre (you can take some gold home).

1095 MUSSELBURGH LINKS, THE OLD GOLF COURSE **6 N15**

Balcarres Road, Musselburgh. At the east end of Musselburgh High Street. Nearest railway station Musselburgh, bus from Edinburgh. Open all year during daylight hours. Charge £££. Group concessions. Explanatory displays. Gift shop. Refreshments available. WC. No guide dogs. Limited wheelchair access. Car and coach parking. Telephone 0131 665 5438.

Mary, Queen of Scots is said to have played this course in 1567, although the oldest documentary evidence dates from 1672. Between 1874 and 1889 the course hosted six Open Championships and was the scene of many great matches between the leading players of the day. Today golfers can hire hickory clubs and replica balls to emulate the masters of the past.

1096 MUSSELBURGH SPORTS CENTRE **6 N15**

Newbigging, Musselburgh, Midlothian. On the A6124 to Inveresk, on the outskirts of Musselburgh. Nearest railway station Musselburgh, bus from Edinburgh. Open all year (except Christmas and New Year), Mon, Wed and Fri 0700–2130, Tue and Thu 0900–2130, weekends 0900–1700. Charge by activity. Group concessions. Café. Crèche. WC. Wheelchair access. Car and coach parking. Telephone 0131 653 6367.

A sports centre with swimming pool, sauna, steam room, squash courts, table tennis, gym and coached activities.

1097 MUTHILL CHURCH AND TOWER **5 L13**

HS. On the A822 in Muthill. 5 miles (8km) south of Crieff on A822. Nearest railway station Perth, bus service from Perth to Crieff, then bus to Muthill, also buses from Stirling. Access at all times. Free. Telephone 0131 668 8800.

The interesting ruins of an important 15th-century parish church, with a tall Romanesque tower at its west end.

1098 MUTHILL VILLAGE AND PARISH MUSEUM **5 L13**

Station Road, Muthill, Perthshire. 5 miles (8km) south of Crieff on A822. Nearest railway station Perth, bus service from Perth to Crieff, then bus to Muthill, also buses from Stirling. Open Jun–Sep, Tue, Thu and Sat 1030–1630, Sun 1230–1630. Donation. Explanatory displays. Limited wheelchair access. Car parking.

Collection of local objects from yesteryear – pictures, photographs, implements, kitchenware. Model castle and steam railway display in photographs, maps and script.

1099 MYRETON MOTOR MUSEUM **6 N15**

Aberlady, East Lothian. Off the A198 just east of Aberlady. Nearest railway station Drem or bus from Edinburgh. Open May–Oct, daily 1000–1800; Nov–Apr (except Christmas Day), 1000–1700. Charge £. Group concessions. Explanatory displays. Gift shop. Picnic area. WC. Wheelchair access. Car and coach parking. Telephone (01875) 870288.

A varied collection of road transport from 1897, including motor cars, cycles, motorcycles, commercials, World War II military vehicles and automobilia. Catalogue and children's quiz book. Period advertising, posters and signs.

1100 NAIRN FISHERTOWN MUSEUM **3 L7**

Laing Hall, King Street, Nairn. 16 miles (25.5km) east of Inverness on the A96. Open Jun–Sep, Mon–Sat 1030–1230 and 1430–1630. Charge £. Group concessions on application. WC. Wheelchair access with assistance. Telephone (01667) 453331.

The story of the fishing industry. The fisher folk and the fishertown in pictures, photographs and exhibits associated with a way of life that disappeared with the decline in the herring and line fishing.

1101 NAIRN LEISURE PARK AND SWIMMING POOL **3 L7**

Marine Road, Nairn. On the A96, 15 miles (24km) east of Inverness. Nairn station, bus from Nairn to within 0.5 mile (2km). Swimming pool open all year, Mon–Fri 0800–2100; weekends 0900–1700. Leisure park games complex open Easter–May and Sep, 1100–1700; Jun–Aug 1100–2000. Charge £. Explanatory displays. Vending machines. WC. Wheelchair access. Disabled WC. Car parking. Telephone (01667) 452061.

Leisure park with aerial runway, adventure play trails, trim trail, adventure fort, outdoor giant board games, woodland suspension bridge, toddlers' playground, swimming pool and steam room, woodland walks, outdoor games complex. Beside Nairn beaches.

1102 NATIONAL WALLACE MONUMENT **6 L14**

Abbey Craig, Hillfoot Road, Stirling. 1.5 miles (2.5km) north northeast of Stirling. Nearest railway station Stirling, local bus service. Minibus runs between car park and monument, charge £. Open all year daily; Jan, Feb, Nov, Dec 1030–1600; Mar, May, Oct 1000–1700; June, Sept 1000–1800; Jul, Aug 0930–1830. Closed 25/26 Dec and 1/2 Jan.

Charge ££. Group concessions by prior arrangement. Explanatory displays and audio-visual displays. Gift shop. Tearoom and picnic area. WC. Disabled WC. Car and coach parking. Telephone (01786) 472140.

The National Wallace Monument takes visitors back 700 years in time to the days of Scotland's first struggle for independence. The story of William Wallace, freedom fighter and national hero, is told along with background and events that shaped this period of history. Climb the 246 steps of the 220 feet (67m) high tower for superb views.

1103 NEIDPATH CASTLE **5 M17**

Peebles, Tweeddale. 1 mile (2km) west of Peebles on A72. Bus service from Peebles post office. Open Easter–Sep, Mon–Sat 1100–1700, Sun 1300–1700. Charge £. Historic House members/Great British Heritage passes accepted. Group concessions. Guided tours by prior arrangement. Explanatory displays. Gift shop. Picnic area. Grounds. WC. Limited wheelchair access. Car and coach parking. Telephone (01721) 720333.

A rare example of a 14th-century castle converted into a tower house in the 17th century. Displayed in the great hall is an exhibit of beautiful batiks depicting the life of Mary, Queen of Scots. The Laigh Hall contains informative displays and a large tartan collection. Good views from the parapet walks. Neidpath Castle is often used as a film location. Resident ghost, the Maid of Neidpath.

1104 NELSON TOWER **3 M7**

Grant Park, Forres. On A96, 11 miles (17.5km) west of Elgin. Nearest railway station Forres. Bus service from Aberdeen and Inverness. Open May–Sep, Tue–Sun 1400–1600. Free. Explanatory displays. Gift shop. Picnic area. Car parking. Telephone (01309) 673701.

Nelson Tower was built by the Trafalgar Club to commemorate Nelson's victory at Trafalgar. Displays on Lord Nelson and views of old Forres. There are also spectacular views of the Moray Firth from the tower.

1105 NEPTUNE'S STAIRCASE **2 G11**

Off A830 at Banavie, 3 miles (4.5km) northwest of Fort William. Car parking.

A series of eight locks, built between 1805 and 1822, which raises Telford's Caledonian Canal (see 258) by 64 feet (19.5 metres).

1106 NESS HERITAGE CENTRE **2 E2**

Habost (Tabost), Ness, Lewis. Towards the Butt of Lewis, 28 miles (45km) from Stornoway on the A857. Bus service from Stornoway or taxi. Open Jun–Sep, Mon–Sat 0900–1730; Oct–May, Mon–Fri 0900–1730. Charge £. Guided tours (French and German by arrangement). Explanatory displays. Gift shop. WC. Wheelchair access. Disabled WC. Car and coach parking. Telephone (01851) 810377.

The heritage centre (Comunn Eachdraidh Nis) provides a unique insight into the social and cultural heritage of the Western Isles. Over 500 artefacts and 7000 photographs illustrate the lifestyle of a people carving out an existence on the very edge of Europe. Genealogical information spanning 250 years proves an invaluable resource to visitors tracing their family histories. Also DTP services. Books, maps, videos, tapes, local knitwear and a range of items made from Harris Tweed for sale.

1107 NESS OF BURGI **1 F6**

HS. At the south eastern point of Scatness, Shetland, about 1 mile (2km) southwest of Jarlshof. Bus from Lerwick. Access at all times. Free. Telephone 0131 668 8800.

A defensive stone blockhouse, probably from the Iron Age, with some features resembling a broch.

1108 NETHER LARGIE CAIRNS **4 F14**

HS. Kilmartin Glen. Between Kilmartin and Nether Largie, Argyll. Nearest railway station Oban, then bus to Kilmartin. Access at all times. Free. Telephone 0131 668 8800.

One Neolithic and two Bronze Age cairns. There is access to the chamber in the north cairn.

1109 NEVERLAND ADVENTURE PLAY CENTRE **5 L19**

Park Lane, Dumfries. Near Dumfries Swimming Pool in the town centre. 0.75 mile (1km) from Dumfries railway station, local bus service. Open all year except Christmas and New Year's Day, daily 1000–1700. Charge £, accompanying adults free. Group concessions. Refreshments and seating area. Baby changing facilities. WC. Wheelchair access. Car parking. Telephone (01387) 249100.

Adventure play centre for ages up to ten. Themed on J. M. Barries story of *Peter Pan*, the boy who would never grow up. There are rope bridges, slides, a ball pool, Indian encampment and Captain Hook's pirate ship. Special area for under fours. Located beside the River Nith, with a pleasant seating area for adults overlooking the river. Parent/guardian supervision is required.

1110 NEVIS RANGE CABLE CARS **2 H11**

Torlundy, Fort William. On the A82, 7 miles (11km) north of Fort William. Nearest railway station Fort William, bus from Fort William. Open all year (except Nov–Dec) 1000–1700; Jul and Aug 0930–1900. Charge £££. Reduced admission for disabled visitors. Group concessions. Guided tours by prior arrangement (available in French and German). Explanatory displays. Gift shop. Restaurant, tearoom and bar. Crèche in winter. WC. Limited wheelchair access. Disabled WC. Car and coach parking. Telephone (01397) 705825.

Britain's only mountain gondolas take passengers to the slopes of Aonach Mor beside Ben Nevis. Spectacular views of the Highlands and Islands. Mountain restaurant, bar and shop at 2150 feet (655m). Mountain top gems. Walks. Interpretive slide shows, mountain bike hire and dry ski slope (July and August). Winter ski area, ski school and ski hire (December–May).

1111 NEW ABBEY CORN MILL **5 L20**

HS. New Abbey, Dumfries. On the A710, in New Abbey, 8 miles (13km) south of Dumfries. Nearest railway station Dumfries, bus from Dumfries and Dalbeattie. Open Apr–Sep, daily 0930–1830; Oct–Mar, Mon–Sat 0930–1630, Sun 1400–1630, closed Thu pm and Fri. Charge £. Group concessions. Guided tours. Explanatory displays in visitor centre, with video about milling. Gift shop. Picnic area. Limited wheelchair access. Telephone (01387) 850620.

A carefully renovated water-driven oatmeal mill in working order and demonstrated regularly to visitors in the summer months.

1112 NEWARK CASTLE **6 J15**

HS. Port Glasgow, Renfrewshire. On the A8 in Port Glasgow, Renfrewshire. Nearest railway and bus station Port Glasgow then 15 minute walk. Open Apr–Sep, daily 0930–1830. Charge £. Group concessions. Guided tours. Gift shop. WC. Limited wheelchair access. Car and coach parking. Telephone (01475) 741858.

A large turreted mansion-house in a remarkably good state of preservation, with a 15th-century tower, a courtyard and hall.

1113 NEW LANARK VISITOR CENTRE **6 L17**

New Lanark Mills, Lanark. 1 mile (2km) south of Lanark. Nearest railway station Lanark, then local bus service. Open all year, daily 1100–1700. Closed Christmas Day and New Year. Charge ££. Group concessions. Guided tours. Explanatory displays. Gift shop. Tearoom and picnic areas. Children's play area, hotel and self-catering accommodation. WC. Wheelchair access with assistance. Disabled WC. Car and coach parking. Telephone (01555) 661345.

New Lanark is the best example in Scotland of an industrial heritage village. Founded in 1785 by Scottish industrialist David Dale, it was the scene of early social experiments by Dale's son-in-law Robert Owen (1771–1858), whose far-reaching ideas on the care of his workers and the formation of man's character made New Lanark famous. The award-winning Visitor Centre gives visitors a glimpse of life under Owen's paternalistic management, especially through the Annie McLeod Experience, an innovative dark ride into 1820. Passport ticket also includes the Millworkers' House, Village Store and Robert Owen's House. New Lanark is a nominated World Heritage Site.

1114 NEWTON HILL COUNTRY SPORTS **5 N13**

Newton Farm, Wormit, Newport-on-Tay, Fife. On the B946, 4 miles (6.5km) south of the Tay Road Bridge. Leuchars station, bus from Dundee. Open all year (except Christmas and New Year's Day), daily dawn–dusk, fishing from 1000. Charge £££ by activity. Group concessions. Explanatory displays. Picnic area and snacks. WC. Limited wheelchair access. Car and coach parking. Telephone (01382) 542513.

Clay shooting, quad bikes, off-road driving and fly fishing. Tuition and equipment provided.

1115 NEWTON STEWART MUSEUM **4 J20**

York Road, Newton-Stewart, Wigtownshire. In Newton Stewart. Stranraer station, bus from Stranraer or Dumfries. Open Easter–Sep, Mon–Sat 1400–1700; Jul and Aug, Mon–Fri 1000–1230; Jul–Sep, Sun 1400–1700. Charge £. Explanatory displays. Gift shop. WC. Wheelchair access. Car and coach parking. Telephone (01671) 402472.

Contains a wealth of historical treasures and exciting and interesting displays of the natural and social history of Galloway.

1116 NIGG BAY BIRD RESERVE **3 K7**

Cromarty Firth, north of Invergordon, Ross and Cromarty.

Bird reserve. The best access is along the shore from Barbaraville.

1117 NOAH'S ARK **3 P9**

Old Schoolhouse Croft, Craigievar, Alford, Aberdeenshire. On A980 between Lumphanan and Alford, 0.5 mile (1km) past Crossroads Hotel (signposted O'Neil Corse). Local bus service passes Crossroads Hotel. Open all year except 25/26 Dec and 1/2 Jan, daily 0900–1800; telephone during winter to confirm. Charge £. Children under 4 free. Groups by advance booking. Guided tours. Explanatory displays. Gift shop. Refreshments available in shop, picnic area. Play area and pets corner. WC. No guide dogs. Wheelchair access with assistance. Car and coach parking. Telephone (013398) 83670.

A unique experience for visitors of all ages on a working farm. Guided tours let visitors feed and tend to the animals. The Information Centre is packed full of facts on farming and farm animals. Farm shop. Beautiful surroundings.

1118 NOAH'S ARK ACTIVITY CENTRE **5 M13**

Glendevon Farm, Western Edge, Perth. Off the Western Bypass (A9). Nearest railway station Perth, bus from centre to top of Burghmuir Road, then 10 minute walk. Open all year (except Christmas and New Year), daily 1000–1830. Charge children £–££; adults charge for karting only. Group concessions. Explanatory displays. Café and picnic area. Small gift shop. WC. Wheelchair access. Disabled WC. Car and coach parking. Telephone (01738) 445568.

A specially equipped and supervised children's softplay barn for under-12s. Adult lounge. Also indoor kart tracks for adults and children, no booking required.

1119 NOLTLAND CASTLE **1 B9**

HS. On the island of Westray, Orkney. Ferry from Kirkwall to Westray. Access at all times. Free. Telephone 0131 668 8800.

A fine ruined Z-plan tower built between 1560 and 1573, but never completed. Remarkable for its large number of gun loops and its impressive winding staircase.

1120 NORNOVA KNITWEAR **1 G2**

Muness, Uyeasound, Unst, Shetland. Open May–Oct, daily 0900–1700. Free. Guided tours. Explanatory displays. Gift shop. Tearoom. Garden. WC. Wheelchair access. Disabled WC. Car and coach parking. Telephone (01957) 755373.

Hand spinning, knitting and all things to do with wool. Shetland sheep – wool ready to spin – hands on. Lace knitting for shawls and stoles.

1121 NORTH AYRSHIRE MUSEUM **6 H17**

10 Glasgow Vennel, Irvine. 12 miles (19km) south of Largs on A78. Nearest railway and bus stations Saltcoats. Open all year, daily 1000–1300 and 1400–1700 (closed public holidays and Wed). Free. Guided tours. Explanatory displays. Gift shop. WC. Wheelchair access. Disabled WC. Telephone (01294) 464174.

Local history museum housed in a mid 19th-century parish church. Displays feature cottage life, Ayrshire whitework, fine art, maritime history, archaeology and natural history. Good reference and photographic collection. Children's activity and discovery area.

1122 NORTH BERWICK MUSEUM **6 P15**

School Road, North Berwick, East Lothian. Nearest railway station North Berwick, bus service from Edinburgh. Open Apr–Oct, daily 1100–1700. Free. Explanatory displays. Gift shop. Car and coach parking. Telephone (01620) 895457.

The museum, housed in the former Burgh School, offers a wide range of displays. Visitors can see the old town stocks, stroke a gannet in the Bass Rock Room or score an eagle in the Golf Room. Temporary exhibitions.

1123 NORTH BERWICK SPORTS CENTRE **6 P15**

Grange Road, North Berwick, East Lothian. On the outskirts of North Berwick near The Law. Nearest railway station North Berwick, bus from Edinburgh. Open all year (except Christmas and New year), Mon–Fri 0900–2200, weekends 0900–1700. Charge by activity. Group concessions. Café. Crèche. WC. Wheelchair access. Disabled WC. Car and coach parking. Telephone (01620) 893454.

Swimming pool, sauna, steam room, activity hall, squash courts, trampolines, body conditioning, snooker, table tennis and many coached activities.

1124 NORTHEAST FALCONRY VISITOR CENTRE **3 P8**

Broadland, Cairnie, Huntly, Aberdeenshire. 3 miles (5km) northwest of Huntly. Located just off signposted road that links the A920 to Dufftown with the A96 to Inverness. Nearest railway station Huntly. Open Mar–Oct, daily 1030–1730. Charge ££. Group concessions. Explanatory displays. Gift shop. Tearoom and picnic area. WC. Wheelchair access. Disabled WC. Car and coach parking. Telephone (01466) 760328.

The centre has almost 65 birds of prey, both indigenous and from overseas, ranging from owls to eagles. None of the birds are caged and they are all clearly visible. Regular flying displays with the amazing sight of an eagle, with a 6 foot (1.8m) wing span, gliding on the wind. Some of the birds are tame enough to be hand-held by visitors.

1125 NORTHERN LIGHTS CANDLES WORKSHOP **3 K8**

Lentran, Inverness. 5 miles (8km) west of Inverness on the A862 towards Beauly. Bus from Inverness centre. Open Easter–Christmas, Mon–Fri 1200–1800 (Jul–Sep, daily 1000–1900). Free. Gift shop. WC. Wheelchair access. Car parking. Telephone (01463) 831332.

Located in a converted crofters cowshed made from railway sleepers. Family business where a huge variety of candles are handmade using simple tools, moulds and methods. Visitors can watch candles being made.

1126 NORTHERN NATURAL HISTORY **3 L5**

Greenhill, Brora, Sutherland. On the A9, 1.5 miles (2.5km) north of Brora. Nearest railway station Brora, bus from Inverness. Open all year (except bank holidays), Mon–Fri 0830–1715. Free. Wheelchair access with assistance. Car parking. Telephone (01408) 621500.

A taxidermy workshop producing stalking and shooting trophies.

1127 NORTHFIELD FARM MUSEUM **3 Q7**

New Pitsligo, Fraserburgh, Aberdeenshire. 10 miles (16km) southwest of Fraserburgh. Nearest railway station Aberdeen, bus to Fraserburgh. Open May–Sep, daily 1100–1730. Charge £. Group concessions. Guided tours. Explanatory displays. Picnic area. WC. Wheelchair access. Disabled WC. Car and coach parking. Telephone (01771) 653504.

Vintage tractors and motorcycles, stationary engines, household and horse-drawn farm implements. Smithy, engineer's workshop, joiner's workshop. Aviary for small birds.

1128 NORTH GLEN GALLERY AND WORKSHOP **5 L20**

North Glen, Palnackie, Castle Douglas. Off A711 between Dalbeattie and Auchencairn. Nearest railway station Dumfries, bus service to Palnackie (0.6 mile/1km). Open all year, daily 1000–1800. Other times by appointment. Charge £. Free admission with purchase. Glass-blowing demonstrations. Gift shop. Picnic area. Wheelchair access. Car parking. Telephone (01556) 600200.

Gallery, workshop and home base of international artist Ed Iglehart who works with many collaborators to produce individual works of glass. Glass-blowing demonstrations. Chandeliers, experimental structures, tipis, treehouses, beach huts and bird hides. Starting point for many walks.

1129 NORTHLANDS VIKING CENTRE **3 N3**

Auckengill, Keiss, Wick, Caithness. On the A99, 10 miles (16km) north of Wick. Nearest railway station Wick, bus from Wick. Open Jun–Sep, daily 1000–1600. Charge £. Group concessions. Explanatory displays. Gift shop. Picnic area. WC. Wheelchair access with assistance. Car and coach parking. Telephone (01955) 607771.

A display explaining the heritage of Caithness including the pre-Viking kingdom of the Catti and the Norse settlers. Features models of the Viking settlement at Freswick, a Viking longship and currency.

1130 NORTH THIRD TROUT FISHERY **6 K14**

Greathill House, Stirling. 5 miles (8km) southwest of Stirling. Open Mar–Apr, daily 1000–1700; May–Aug, daily 1000–2300; Sep and Oct, daily 1000–1700. Charge £££. WC. Car and coach parking. Telephone (01786) 471967.

A rainbow trout fly-only fishery with over 120 acres (48ha) of water set in magnificent surroundings and offering both boat and bank angling. Famed for producing large numbers of fish in excess of 10lb each year. Expert advice available.

1131 NOSS NATIONAL NATURE RESERVE — 1 G5

Noss Island, Shetland. Managed by Scottish Natural Heritage (01595) 693345. On an island off the east coast of Bressay by Lerwick. By boat (7 miles) from Victoria Pier, Lerwick in M.V. Dunter II. May–Sep, Tue–Sun 1000 sailing. Charge £££. Boat charges £££. Group concessions. Guided tours (available in French). Explanatory leaflet. WC on board. Car parking. Telephone Shetland Wildlife Tours (01950) 422483.

A unique 3-hour tour of some of Europe's finest scenery and wildlife habitats. Visitors can see up to 100,000 seabirds and dozens of seals at close range. Spectacular caves, sea statues and rock arches. Entertaining commentary on geology, local history and folklore of Bressay and Noss islands. Puffins visible before second week in August. See also 1085 Muckle Flugga and Outstack, and 1326 Shetland Wildlife Tours.

1132 OBAN DISTILLERY VISITOR CENTRE — 4 F13

Stafford Street, Oban, Argyll. In centre of Oban. Within walking distance from railway station and bus stops. Open all year, Mon–Fri 0930–1700 (Jul–Sep closes 2030), also Easter–Oct, Sat 0930–1700. Dec–Feb restricted hours may operate, telephone to confirm. Last tour one hour before closing. Charge £. Children free. Guided tours. Explanatory displays. Leaflet in French, German, Italian and Spanish. Gift shop. WC. No guide dogs. Limited wheelchair access. Disabled WC. Telephone (01631) 572004.

Take a guided tour and learn about the ancient craft of distilling. Visitor centre with exhibition and audio-visual programme tells of the history of Oban. Shop with single malts, gifts and souvenirs.

1133 OBAN HIGHLAND THEATRE — 4 F13

George Street, Oban, Argyll. In centre of Oban, 0.5 mile (1km) from station. Car and coach parking nearby. Open daily in summer from 1400; in winter Mon–Fri from 1800, Sat 1400. Charge ££. Group concessions. Explanatory displays. Gift shop. WC. Wheelchair access with assistance. Disabled WC. Telephone (01631) 562444.

A complex of two cinemas, theatre and exhibition. Occasional videos focussing on Oban, Lorn and the Isles.

1134 OBAN RARE BREEDS FARM PARK — 4 F13

New Barran, Oban, Argyll. 2 miles (3km) from Oban up the Glencruitten Road. Nearest railway station Oban, bus from Oban. Open late Mar–Oct, 1000–1730. Charge ££. Wheelchair users free. Group concessions. Explanatory displays. Gift shop. Tearoom and picnic area. WC. Limited wheelchair access. Disabled WC. Car and coach parking. Telephone (01631) 770608 or 770604.

Displays rare breeds of farm animals – cattle, sheep, pigs, poultry, goats. Pets area. Woodland walk and beautiful views. Souvenir shop.

1135 OBAN SEAL AND MARINE CENTRE — 4 G12

Barcaldine, Connel, Oban, Argyll. On the A828, 10 miles (16km) north of Oban. Nearest railway station Oban, bus from Oban. Open all year, daily (except Christmas Day and New Year's Day) 1000–1800; Jul and Aug 0900–1900. Charge £££. Group concessions. Explanatory displays. Gift shop. Restaurant, coffee shop and picnic area. Adventure playground and nature trail. WC. Wheelchair access with assistance. Disabled WC. Car and coach parking. Telephone (01631) 720386.

Visitors can explore over 30 fascinating natural marine habitats, including a unique herring ring, and have close encounters with many sea creatures, including seals. In a picturesque setting among pine trees on the shore of Loch Creran.

1136 OISEVAL GALLERY **2 D3**

James Smith Photography, Brue, Isle of Lewis. Bus from Stornoway. Open all year, Mon–Sat 1000–1730. Free. Car and coach parking. Telephone (01851) 840240.

An exclusive collection of creative Hebridean landscapes by James Smith. Features the St Kilda archipelago.

1137 OLD BRIDGE HOUSE MUSEUM **5 L19**

Mill Road, Dumfries. In Dumfries town centre on the west bank of the River Nith at Devorgilla's Bridge. Nearest railway station 15 minutes walk. Nearest bus station 2 minutes walk. Open Apr–Sep, Mon–Sat 1000–1700, Sun 1400–1700. Free. Explanatory welcome in English, French and German; leaflet (also available in Dutch, Italian, Russian and Spanish). Wheelchair access with assistance. Car and coach parking. Telephone (01387) 256904.

The house, built in 1660, now has rooms furnished in period style to illustrate life in Dumfries over the centuries. Rooms include kitchens of 1850 and 1900, a Victorian nursery and a dental surgery dating from 1900. Devorgilla's Bridge was originally built circa1280 by Lady Devorgilla Balliol, who endowed Balliol College, Oxford.

1138 OLD BYRE HERITAGE CENTRE **4 E12**

Dervaig, Isle of Mull, Argyll. 1.5 miles (2.5km) southwest of Dervaig (0.6 mile/1km private road off Torloisk road at Dervaig end.). Nearest railway station Oban, then ferry to Craignure with limited bus service connecting to Dervaig. Open Easter–Oct, daily 1030–1830, last show at 1730. Charge £. Group concessions. Explanatory displays and film. Gift shop. Tearoom. WC. Limited wheelchair access. Car and coach parking. Telephone (01688) 400229.

Originally a genuine stone byre which has been converted into a museum, tearoom and gift shop. The social history of Mull has been created in miniature.

1139 OLD GALA HOUSE **5 P17**

Scott Crescent, Galashiels, Selkirk. In Galashiels, 0.25 mile (0.5km) from centre. Bus from Edinburgh or Carlisle. Open Apr–Sep, Tue–Sat 1000–1600, Jun–Aug also Mon 1000–1600 and Sun 1400–1600; Oct Tue–Sat 1300–1600. Gardens open at all times. Free. Guided tours by arrangement. Explanatory displays. Refreshments and picnic area. Garden. WC. Limited wheelchair access. Disabled WC. Car and coach parking. Telephone (01896) 752611.

Dating from 1583 and set in its own grounds, the former home of the Lairds of Gala is now an interpretive centre. Displays tell the story of the house, its inhabitants and the early growth of Galashiels. Features painted ceilings (1635), a painted wall (1988) and the Thomas Clapperton Room. The Christopher Boyd Gallery hosts an exciting programme of visual art exhibitions.

1140 OLD HAA VISITOR CENTRE **1 G3**

Burravoe, Yell, Shetland. On the island of Yell. Public transport limited. Open Apr–Sep, Tue, Wed, Thu and Sat 1000–1600, Sun 1400–1700. Donations. Explanatory displays. Gift shop. Tearoom. Garden. WC. Car and coach parking. Telephone (01957) 722339.

The oldest building on Yell, with exhibitions on local flora and fauna, arts and crafts, and local themes of historic interest. Photographs, video and sound recordings of local musicians, story telling. Genealogical information by arrangement. Craft shop and art gallery.

1141 OLD MAN OF HOY **1 A11**

Northwest coast of Isle of Hoy, Orkney.

A 450-feet (137m) high isolated stack (pillar) standing off the magnificent cliffs of northwest Hoy. The Old Man of

Hoy can also be seen from the Scrabster to Stromness Ferry. A challenge to experienced climbers.

1142 OLD MAN OF STOER **2 G4**

2 mile (3km) walk from Stoer Lighthouse, north of Lochinver, Sutherland.

This is the most westerly point of Sutherland and on a clear day it is possible to see the Hebridean Island of Lewis.

1143 OLD MANSE GALLERY **3 P11**

Old Manse, Western Road, Insch, Aberdeenshire. In Insch, 25 miles (40km) northwest of Aberdeen. Nearest railway station Insch, bus from Inverurie or Huntly. Open daily 1200–1730 but check in advance. Free. WC. Wheelchair access. Car and coach parking. Telephone (01464) 820392.

Sales display of oriental and Celtic carpets (Celtic designs can be made to customers' requirements). Permanent exhibition of work from the Royal Society of Miniature Painters, the Society of Limners and the Russian Fedoskino School. Also many local scenes in mixed media. Commissions accepted for portraits and landscapes.

1144 OLD PARISH CHURCH, HAMILTON **6 K16**

Strathmore Road, Hamilton. In the centre of town, 5 minute walk from railway and bus stations. Nearest railway and bus stations Hamilton. Open all year, Mon–Fri 1030–1530, Sat 1030–1200, Sun after the 1045 service. Evenings by appointment. Free. Guided tours. Refreshments by arrangement. WC. Induction loop. Limited wheelchair access. Disabled WC. Car and coach parking. Telephone (01698) 281905.

The oldest building in Hamilton, a Georgian masterpiece designed by William Adam between 1732–34, and the only church designed by him. The roof timbers are full of lead shot as Adam used timbers from an old man of war. Embroidery work by Hannah Frew Paterson and exceptionally detailed and engraved glass windows depicting the history of church, by Anita Pate. Well preserved and maintained 11th-century Netherton Cross and Covenanting memorials.

1145 OLD PLACE OF MOCHRUM **4 H20**

Off B7005, 11 miles (17.5km) west of Wigtown. No access to the public but can be seen from the road.

Known also as Drumwalt Castle, this is a mainly 15th- and 16th-century construction with two picturesque towers.

1146 ORBOST GALLERY **2 D8**

Dunvegan, Isle of Skye. 4 miles (6.5km) south of Dunvegan off the A863. Open Apr–Oct, daily 1000–1800; other times by appointment. Free. Explanatory displays. WC. Wheelchair access. Car and coach parking. Telephone (01470) 521207.

Paintings and prints of the landscape of Skye and adjacent highlands. Also caligraphy, wood engravings and a selection of antique prints. Picture framing service available and artist's materials on sale.

1147 ORCADIAN STONE COMPANY **3 L5**

Main Street, Golspie, Sutherland. 60 miles (96.5km) north of Inverness on A9. Nearest railway station Golspie, bus from Inverness stops nearby. Open all year, Mon–Sat 0900–1730; Apr–Oct Sun 1000–1600. Charge £ (museum). Group concessions. Explanatory displays. Gift shop. Picnic area. Garden. WC. Limited wheelchair access. Car and coach parking. Telephone (01408) 633483.

Exhibition of local geology with interpretive panels and scale model of Assynt area. Fine mineral specimens from all over the world. In the workshop, articles are made from mostly local natural stone.

1148 ORCHARDTON TOWER **5 L20**

HS. Off A711, 6 miles (9.5km) southeast of Castle Douglas, Kirkcudbrightshire. Nearest railway station Dumfries, bus from Dumfries to Palnackie. Open at all times; apply to custodian at nearby cottage. Free. Car parking. Telephone 0131 668 8800.

A charming and unique circular 15th-century tower house. Built by John Cairns.

1149 ORD OF CAITHNESS **3 M4**

At the hairpin bends on the A9, north of Helmsdale, Sutherland.

Here there are spectacular views of the Caithness coastline. At early morning or late evening, herds of red deer can often be seen.

1150 ORD SUMMIT **3 J5**

West of Lairg village, Sutherland.

Dotted with burial mounds and hut circles and topped by two chambered cairns dating back 5000 years. The view from the summit of the Ord is stunning.

1151 ORKNEY CHAIR **1 B10**

Orkney Chair Maker, Rosegarth House, St Ola, Kirkwall, Orkney. In Orphir Road (A964), 1.5 miles (2.5km) from centre. Open all year, Mon–Fri 0900–1200 and 1400–1600. Free. Gift shop. Car parking. Telephone (01856) 873521.

See craftspeople at work making Orkney chairs.

1152 ORKNEY MUSEUM **1 B10**

Tankerness House, Broad Street, Kirkwall, Orkney. Central Kirkwall, opposite St Magnus Cathedral. Open May–Sep, Mon–Sat 1000–1700, Sun 1400–1700; Oct–Apr, Mon–Sat 1030–1230 and 1330–1700. Free. Guided tours by prior arrangement. Explanatory displays. Gift shop. Garden. WC. Wheelchair access. Disabled WC. Telephone (01856) 873191.

The museum covers island life through 6000 years, with additional special exhibitions. It is housed in a merchant-laird's mansion, with courtyard and gardens, dating from 1574.

1153 ORKNEY WIRELESS MUSEUM **1 B10**

Kiln Corner, Junction Road, Kirkwall, Orkney. Near the harbour in Kirkwall. Open Apr–Sep, Mon–Sat 1000–1630, Sun 1430–1630. Charge £. Group concessions. Guided tours by arrangement. Explanatory displays. Gift shop. WC. Wheelchair access. Car parking. Telephone (01856) 871400 or 874272.

A museum explaining Orkney's wartime history which involved an intense communications network of radio and telephones to protect the home fleet in Scapa Flow. Details of a secret radar station. Also displays of domestic receivers, valves, rare equipment, gramophones, transistors. Special display of Italian POW crafts.

1154 ORMISTON MARKET CROSS **6 N15**

HS. On the B6371 in Ormiston. 2 miles (3km) south of Tranent, East Lothian. Nearest railway station at Wallyford, bus from Edinburgh to Ormiston. Telephone 0131 668 8800.

A 15th-century cross on a modern base in the main street. A symbol of the right of the inhabitants to hold a market.

1155 ORPHIR CHURCH AND THE EARL'S BU **1 B11**

HS. By the A964, 8 miles (13km) west southwest of Kirkwall, Orkney. Bus from Kirkwall to Houton. Access at all times. Free. Car and coach parking. Telephone 0131 668 8800.

Earl's Bu are the foundation remains of what may have been a Viking palace. Nearby are the remains of Scotland's only 12th-century circular medieval church.

1156 ORTAK VISITOR CENTRE **1 B10**

Hatson Industrial Estate, Kirkwall, Orkney. 10 minute walk from centre of Kirkwall. Open all year, Mon–Sat 0900–1700; winter 0900–1300 and 1400–1700. Free. Guided tours Jul–Aug. Explanatory displays. Gift shop. Complimentary refreshments. WC. Limited wheelchair access. Disabled WC. Car and coach parking. Telephone (01856) 872224.

The Ortak Visitor Centre houses a permanent exhibition with a video presentation describing how modern jewellery is made and telling the story of Ortak. In July and August visitors can watch a silversmith at work.

1157 OUR LADY OF THE ISLES **2 B7**

North of South Uist, Western Isles. Access at all reasonable times. Free.

On Reuval Hill – the Hill of Miracles – is the statue of the Madonna and Child, erected in 1957 by the Catholic community with contributions from all over the world. The work of Hew Lorimer, it is 30 feet (9m) high.

1158 OUR LADY OF THE SEA **2 A10**

Heaval, on the Isle of Barra, Western Isles.

Heaval is the highest point in Barra at 1257 feet (383m), and on the slopes of the hill is erected an attractive statue of the Madonna and Child, symbol of the islanders' faith.

1159 PAISLEY ABBEY **6 J16**

Abbey Close, Paisley, Renfrewshire. In central Paisley. Nearest railway station Paisley Gilmour Street. Open all year, Mon–Sat 1000–1530, Sun for services only (1100, 1215 and 1830). Free. Guided tours by arrangement. Explanatory displays. Gift shop. Tearoom. WC. Limited wheelchair access. Disabled WC. Telephone 0141 889 7654.

A fine Cluniac abbey church founded in 1163. Some 12th-century walls remain, but most of the nave dates from the 14th and 15th centuries. The transept and choir lay in ruins from 16th to 19th centuries, but are now fully restored. Fine medieval carvings in St Mirin Chapel. Also tombs of Princess Marjory Bruce and King Robert III in the choir. Fine stained glass and Cavaille-Coll Organ. The Abbey contains the Barochan Cross, a weathered Celtic cross attributed to the 10th century. See also 205 Brechin Cathedral Round Tower.

1160 PAISLEY MUSEUM AND ART GALLERIES **6 J16**

High Street, Paisley. In Paisley centre. Nearest railway station Paisley, Gilmour Street. Open all year Tue–Sat 1000–1700, Sun 1400–1700, public holidays 1000–1700. Free. Explanatory displays. Gift shop. WC. Limited wheelchair access. Disabled WC. Telephone 0141 889 3151.

Displays a world-famous collection of Paisley shawls. Also local, industrial and natural history of Paisley and Renfrewshire. Important ceramic collection and many 19th-century Scottish paintings.

1161 PALACERIGG COUNTRY PARK **6 K15**

Palacerigg Road, Cumbernauld, Glasgow. 3 miles (5km) east of Cumbernauld. Nearest railway station Cumbernauld, then 1.5 mile (2.5km) walk to park, bus from Glasgow to Cumbernauld, but no link to park. Visitor centre open all year, Apr–Sep 1000–1800; Oct–Mar 1000–1630. Free. Explanatory displays. Gift shop. Tearoom and picnic areas. Approx 7 miles (11km) nature trails and bridle paths. 18-hole golf course. Ranger service. WC. Disabled WC. Car and coach parking. Telephone (01236) 720047.

A 700 acre (283ha) country park with a Scottish and North European animal collection. Home to populations of roe deer, owls, bison, wildcat, lynx and moufflon.

1162 PANBRIDE CHURCH 5 P12

Panbride, Carnoustie, Angus. Nearest railway station Carnoustie.

The first mention of Panbride was in 1178 when William I gave the church and parish to Arbroath Abbey. At the church gates is a Loupin Stane, used to assist church-goers mounting horses. By the Loupin Stane there is a footpath which heads north to Muirdrum. Follow this footpath for a few hundred yards and you are at the top of the 'fairy steps'. You are supposed to make a wish on the third step.

1163 PARALLEL ROADS 2 H10

Glen Roy, unclassified road off A86, 18 miles (29km) northeast of Fort William. Free.

These parallel roads are hillside terraces marking levels of lakes dammed by glaciers during the Ice Age.

1164 RON PARKER SCULPTURE 3 L8

Beachens Two, Dunphail, Forres, Moray. 9.5 miles (15km) south of Forres on A940. Nearest railway and bus stations Forres. Open all year (except 25/26 and 31 Dec, 1 Jan), daily 0900–1800. Free. Guided tours. Sale of exhibited work. WC. Wheelchair access with assistance. Car parking. Telephone (01309) 611273.

Wood sculptor's workshop where each piece is individually handmade from managed local hardwoods. A wide range of large and small work is always available. Visitors are always welcome at the workshop and may bring their own wood to be worked to their own design.

1165 JAMES PATERSON MUSEUM, MONIAIVE 5 K19

Meadowcroft, North Street, Moniaive, Thornhill, Dumfriesshire. On the A702, 9 miles (14.5km) from Thornhill. Nearest railway station Dumfries, bus from Dumfries. Open Easter–Sep, Fri–Sun 1000–1800 (also bank holidays). Free. Explanatory displays. Gift shop. Free tea and coffee. Garden. WC. No guide dogs. Wheelchair access. Disabled WC. Telephone (01848) 200583.

An exhibition dedicated to the life and times of the artist. Memorabilia, reference library and works connected to the Glasgow Boys.

1166 PAXTON HOUSE 5 R16

Paxton, Berwick-upon-Tweed. On the B6461, 5 miles (8km) west of Berwick-upon-Tweed. Nearest railway station Berwick-upon-Tweed, then connecting bus from railway and bus station to Paxton House. Open Apr–Oct, daily 1100–1730; grounds, shop and tearoom, 1000–sunset. Charge ££. Grounds £. Group concessions. Guided tours (information in French, German, Italian, Spanish and Japanese). Explanatory displays. Gift shop. Restaurant, tearoom and picnic areas. Croquet, boat-house, museum, adventure playground, squirrel hide. WC. Tactile tour by arrangement. Limited wheelchair access. Disabled WC. Car and coach parking. Telephone (01289) 386291.

Winner of several tourism awards and one of the finest 18th-century Palladian houses in Britain. Designed by John and James Adam and built in 1758 by Patrick Home for his intended bride, Charlotte de Brandt, daughter of King Frederick the Great of Prussia. Interiors by Robert Adam. The largest collection of Chippendale furniture in Scotland,

and fine Regency furniture by Trotter of Edinburgh. Also art gallery (an outstation of the National Galleries of Scotland). Over 80 acres (32ha) of grounds and gardens, including a mile of the River Tweed.

1167 PEEBLES GALLERY **5 N17**

6 Newby Court, Peebles. In a craft centre off the High Street in Peebles. Bus from all major cities. Open daily except Sun and Wed pm, 1000–1800. Free. WC. Disabled WC. Car and coach parking. Telephone (01721) 724747.

A gallery with an artist in residence (working on the premises), specialising in miniature art work.

1168 PEEL FARM COFFEE AND CRAFTS **5 N12**

Lintrathen, by Kirriemuir, Angus. Off the B954, 20 miles (32km) north of Dundee, 6 miles (9km) from Alyth. Nearest railway station Dundee, then bus to Kirriemuir or Alyth, then walk. Open Easter–Oct, daily 0900–1700; Nov–Christmas, weekends only. Farm trail open May–Sep. Donations. Guided tours. Explanatory displays. Gift shop. Tearoom and picnic area. Play area. WC. Wheelchair access. Disabled WC. Car and coach parking. Telephone (01575) 560205.

A working farm in an unspoilt area of rural Angus close to majestic Reekie Linn waterfall. Animals include red deer, Highland cattle, horses, goats, sheep and rabbits. Craft demonstrations every Saturday (1400–1630).

1169 PEEL RING OF LUMPHANAN **3 P10**

HS. 0.5 mile (1km) southwest of Lumphanan, Aberdeenshire. Nearest railway station Aberdeen, bus from Aberdeen. Access at all times. Free. Telephone 0131 668 8800.

A major early medieval earthwork 120 feet (36.5m) in diameter and 18 feet (5.5m) high. The site of a fortified residence. Links with Shakespeare's Macbeth.

1170 PERTH LEISURE POOL **5 M13**

Glasgow Road, Perth. In Perth centre, 5 minute walk from railway station. Open daily 1000–2200 (except for two weeks in Dec). Charge ££. Group concessions. Explanatory displays. Gift shop. Restaurant, tearoom and picnic area. Crèche Mon–Fri 0900–1600 (£). WC. Wheelchair access. Disabled WC. Car and coach parking. Telephone (01738) 635454.

A tropical leisure pool with wild water cannons, flumes, outdoor pool and a training pool. Interactive play area for under-5s (admitted free). Oasis Health Suite, O-Zone Fitness Studio.

1171 PERTH MART VISITOR CENTRE **5 M13**

East Huntingtower, Perth. On the A85, 2 miles (3km) west of Perth, adjacent to the Perth Auction Market. Nearest railway station Perth, bus from Perth. Open all year, Mon–Sat 0900–1730, Sun 1000–1700. Charge £. Entry to store free. Group concessions. Explanatory displays. Leaflets in French and German. Gift shop. Restaurant. Animal farm. WC. Wheelchair access. Disabled WC. Car and coach parking. Telephone (01738) 474170.

Show presenter guides the visitor through the history of agricultural life in Scotland. Also an animal farm.

1172 PERTH MUSEUM AND ART GALLERY **5 M13**

George Street, Perth. In central Perth. Open all year (except Christmas and New Year), Mon–Sat 1000–1700. Free. Explanatory displays. Gift shop. WC. Wheelchair access. Disabled WC. Car parking. Telephone (01738) 632488.

Collections of local history, fine and applied art, natural history and archaeology. Changing programme of temporary exhibitions.

1173 PERTH SCULPTURE TRAIL **5 M13**

The Perthshire Public Art Trust, Perth Museum & Art Gallery, 78 George Street, Perth. Sculpture park in Perth (Norie-Miller Park, Rodney Gardens, Bellwood Riverside Park and Moncrieffe Island) access via Dundee Road. Nearest railway station Perth. Open at all times. Free. Guided tours. Explanatory displays. Leaflet available. Garden. Tactile sculptures. Wheelchair access. Car parking. Telephone (01738) 632488.

Perth Sculpture Trail extends through 1 mile (1.5km) of riverside parkland. Permanent public artworks have been specially created by national and international artists. Visitors may drop in to enjoy part of the trail for a few minutes or stay and enjoy the entire site.

1174 PETERHEAD MARITIME HERITAGE MUSEUM **3 R8**

The Lido, South Road, Peterhead. On the south side of Peterhead. Bus from Aberdeen. Open Apr–Oct, Mon–Sat 1000–1700, Sun 1200–1700; Nov–Mar, telephone to confirm opening times. Charge £. Group concessions. Guided tours. Explanatory displays. Gift shop. Tearoom. Children's playground. WC. Wheelchair access. Disabled WC. Car and coach parking. Telephone (01779) 473000.

Tells the story of Peterhead maritime life in sound and vision. Features audio-visual display on marine life, interactive display on fishing, whaling, navigation and the oil industry, observation box with telescope views across Peterhead Bay.

1175 PICARDY SYMBOL STONE **3 P8**

HS. Near Mireton, Insch, Aberdeenshire. Nearest railway station Inverurie, bus from Huntly or Inverurie. Access at all times. Free. Telephone 0131 668 8800.

One of the oldest and simplest Pictish symbol stones, possibly 7th century.

1176 PICTAVIA **3 P11**

By Brechin Castle Centre, Haughmuir, Brechin, Angus. Off A90 at the southerly Brechin by-pass exit. Nearest railway station Montrose, bus service from Brechin. Open Apr–Sep, Mon–Sat 0900–1800, Sun 1000–1800; Oct–Mar, Mon–Sat 0900–1700, Sun 1000–1800. Charge ££. Group concessions. Explanatory displays. Gift shop. Restaurant. Garden centre, countryside park, farmyard animals. WC. Wheelchair access. Disabled WC. Car and coach parking. Telephone (01356) 626241.

Discover Scotland's ancient past through the legacy of the ancient Picts. Pictavia offers an insight into the culture and heritage of these enigmatic people who were central to the foundation of what is now known as Scotland. Interactive exhibits, replicas and artefacts. An all-weather attraction set in the beautiful countryside park at Brechin Castle Centre.

1177 PIER ARTS CENTRE **1 B10**

Victoria Street, Stromness, Orkney. Bus from Kirkwall. By ferry from Scrabster in Caithness. Open all year (except Christmas and New Year), Tue–Sat 1030–1230 and 1330–1700. Free. Explanatory displays. Gift shop. Picnic area. WC. Limited wheelchair access. Car and coach parking. Telephone (01856) 850209.

Former merchant's house (circa 1800), coal store and fishermen's sheds which have been converted into a gallery. Permanent collection of 20th-century paintings and sculpture as well as changing exhibitions.

1178 PIEROWALL CHURCH **1 B9**

HS. At Pierowall on the island of Westray, Orkney. Ferry from Kirkwall to Westray. Access at all times. Free. Car parking. Telephone 0131 668 8800.

The ruins of a medieval church with some finely lettered tombstones.

1179 PITLOCHRY FESTIVAL THEATRE 5 L12

Port-Na-Craig, Pitlochry, Perthshire. West of the town between the River Tummel and the bypass. Nearest railway station Pitlochry, buses from Perth or Inverness, short walk from railway station. Open Jul–Oct, Mon–Sat; Sun only when there is a concert. Free. Charge for performances. Group concessions. Guided tours. Gift shop. Restaurant and tearoom. WC. Induction loop. Audio description. Wheelchair access. Disabled WC. Car and coach parking. Telephone (01796) 484626 box office.

One of Scotland's most admired repertory theatres with a resident company performing a rolling repertoire throughout the summer season. Beautifully situated overlooking the river. Sunday concerts and literary events.

1180 PITMEDDEN GARDEN 3 Q8

NTS. On A920, 14 miles (22km) north of Aberdeen near Ellon. By bus from Aberdeen. Open May–Sep, daily 1000–1730. Charge ££. Children free. Group concessions. Explanatory displays. Information sheets in four languages. Gift shop. Tearoom and picnic area. WC. Tactile map. Limited wheelchair access, wheelchairs available. Disabled WC. Car and coach parking. Telephone (01651) 842352.

Pitmedden's centrepiece is the Great Garden, originally laid out in 1675 by Sir Alexander Seton. Estate also includes the Museum of Farming Life, herb garden, wildlife garden and woodland walk.

1181 PITMUIES GARDENS 5 P12

House of Pitmuies, Guthrie, Forfar. 7 miles (11km) east of Forfar, 1 mile (1.5km) west of Friockheim on A932. Nearest railway station Arbroath (8 miles/13km), infrequent bus service. Open Apr–Oct, daily 1000–1700. Charge £. Children free. Guided tours. Explanatory displays. Picnic areas. WC. Limited wheelchair access. Car and coach parking. Telephone (01241) 818245.

Adjacent to an 18th-century house and courtyard, two walled gardens lead down to a small river with an informal riverside walk and two unusual buildings – a turreted dove cot and a Gothic washhouse. Massed spring bulbs. In summer the gardens are resplendent with old-fashioned roses, herbaceous plants and borders of blue delphiniums.

1182 PITTENCRIEFF HOUSE MUSEUM 6 M15

Pittencrieff Park, Dunfermline, Fife. On the outskirts of West Dunfermline, 10 minute walk from centre. Nearest railway station Dunfermline. Open daily, Apr–Sep 1100–1700, Oct–Mar 1100–1600. Free. Guided tours on request. Explanatory displays. Gift shop. Tearoom and picnic area in park. WC. Wheelchair access to ground floor only. Disabled WC. Car and coach parking. Telephone (01383) 722935 or 313838.

A 17th-century mansion, converted by Sir Robert Lorimer into three galleries, when the house was bought by Andrew Carnegie early this century. Displays on the history of the house and park. Art gallery with lively temporary exhibition programme.

1183 PITTENCRIEFF PARK ANIMAL CENTRE AND GLASSHOUSES 6 M15

Dunfermline. Located at the west end of Dunfermline High Street, off A994 Pittencrieff Street. Nearest railway and bus stations Dunfermline. Open all year. Glasshouses, Mon–Fri 0830–1530, Sat and Sun 1300–1600; Animal Centre, Mon–Fri 0930–1600, Sat and Sun 0930–1300. Free. Charge for parking during summer. Explanatory displays. Refreshments available during summer. Play areas, formal flower gardens. WC. Use of guide dogs may be restricted in animal centre. Wheelchair access. Disabled WC. Car and coach parking. Telephone (01383) 726313.

Visitors can see a wide range of animals, ranging from rare and endangered species of primates and birds, to domestic animals. Animal handling. The glasshouses are planted with a mixture of perennial and seasonal plants, providing a display of year-round seasonal interest.

1184 PLODDA FALLS **2 H8**

From Drumnadrochit take the A831, turning left before Cannich onto the unclassified road to Tomich.

Waterfalls 100 foot (30.5m) high, located south of the village of Tomich. They are particularly impressive when in spate.

1185 PLUSCARDEN ABBEY **3 M7**

Elgin, Moray. By the B9010, 6 miles (9.5km) southwest of Elgin. School bus only from Elgin. Open daily 0445–2045. Free. Guided tours on request (French and other languages by prior arrangement). Explanatory displays. Gift shop. Baby changing facilities. Garden. WC. Induction loop. Wheelchair access. Disabled WC. Car and coach parking. Telephone (01343) 890257.

Originally a Valliscaulian house, the monastery was founded in 1230. In 1390 the church was burned, probably by the Wolf of Badenoch who burned Elgin about the same time. It became a dependent priory of the Benedictine Abbey of Dunfermline in 1454 until the suppression of monastic life in Scotland in 1560. Thereafter the buildings fell into ruin, until 1948 when a group of Benedictine monks from Prinknash Abbey returned to restore it. Monastic church services open to the public. Visitor centre, retreats and garden.

1186 POLKEMMET COUNTRY PARK **6 L16**

Park Centre, Polkemmet Country Park, Whitburn, West Lothian. On the B7066 west of Whitburn. Nearest railway station Fauldhouse. Open all year, daily 0900–1800. Free. Charge for activities. Restaurant, bar, picnic and barbeque sites. WC. Limited wheelchair access. Disabled WC. Car and coach parking. Telephone (01501) 743905.

A public park with mature woodland, a 9-hole golf course, golf driving range and bowling green. Also barbeque site (bookable) and large children's play area (the Fantasy Forest). Rhododendrons in summer. Reception and restaurant/bar at the Park Centre.

1187 PORT EDGAR MARINA AND SAILING SCHOOL **6 M15**

Shore Road, South Queensferry, West Lothian. On the south side of Forth Road Bridge, 12 miles (19km) from Edinburgh. Bus from Edinburgh. Open Easter–Sep, Mon–Fri 0900–1930, weekends 0900–1630; Oct–Easter, daily 0900–1630. Free. Guided tours by arrangement. Explanatory displays. Tearoom. WC. Disabled WC. Car and coach parking. Telephone 0131 331 3330.

A large watersports centre and marina where visitors can learn to sail or canoe. Historic harbour and spectacular views of the Forth rail and road bridges.

1188 PORT NA CON SOUTERRAIN **3 J2**

0.5 miles (1km) north of Port na Con pier, near Durness, Sutherland.

Marked by two cairns at the east side of the road, this is a well preserved souterrain (Iron Age store room). Take extreme care and enter at your own risk.

1189 BEATRIX POTTER EXHIBITION **5 M12**

Birnam Institute, Station Road, Birnam, by Dunkeld. 15 miles (24km) north of Perth on A9. Nearest railway station and bus stop Birnam and Dunkeld then 5 minutes walk. Telephone (01350) 728970 to confirm opening times. Garden open all year, daily. Free. Explanatory displays. Gift shop. Picnic area. WC. Wheelchair access with assistance. Car and coach parking. Telephone (01350) 727674.

The Beatrix Potter Exhibition is housed in the Birnam Institute, a Victorian building erected in 1883, which stands in the centre of the historic Perthshire village. The exhibition will reopen in 2001 after extensive redevelopment and refurbishment. The garden and woodlands where the famous author walked remain open.

1190 PRAYTIS FARM PARK **6 N14**

Leven, Fife. On the A916, 3 miles (5km) north of Leven. Nearest railway station Markinch, buses from Leven, Cupar or Dundee. Open all year daily, 1000–1700 (golf range open to 2100). Charge ££. Children under 4 free. Group concessions. Guided tours. Explanatory displays. Gift shop. Café/restaurant (no entrance charge) and picnic areas. Garden and play areas. WC. Wheelchair access. Disabled WC. Car and coach parking. Telephone (01333) 350209.

Entrance fee includes animals, play barns, display rooms, farm walks, wild west fort, crazy golf, and pitch and putt. An education centre, opened in 1997, caters for school and family visits with talks on agriculture and the environment.

1191 PRESTONGRANGE INDUSTRIAL HERITAGE MUSEUM **6 N15**

Morison's Haven, Prestonpans, East Lothian. In Prestonpans, 9 miles (14.5km) east of Edinburgh, 15 minute walk from Prestonpans station. Bus from Edinburgh. Open Apr–Oct, daily 1100–1600. Free. Guided tours. Explanatory displays. Gift shop. Café and picnic area. WC. Wheelchair access with assistance. Disabled WC. Car and coach parking. Telephone 0131 653 2904.

A museum telling the story of many local industries. Displays include a historic Cornish beam engine. Special activities and steam days.

1192 PRESTON MARKET CROSS **6 N15**

HS. 0.5 mile (1km) south of Prestonpans, East Lothian. Nearest railway station Prestonpans, bus from Edinburgh to Prestonpans, then 0.5 mile (1km) walk. Access at all times. Free. Telephone 0131 668 8800.

The only surviving example of a market cross of its type on its original site. A fine early 17th-century design with a cylindrical base surmounted by a cross-shaft headed by a unicorn.

1193 PRESTON MILL AND PHANTASSIE DOOCOT **5 P15**

NTS. East Linton, East Lothian. Off A1, in East Linton, 23 miles (37km) east of Edinburgh. By bus from Edinburgh. Open Apr–Sep, Mon–Sat 1100–1300 and 1400–1700, Sun 1330–1700; weekends in Oct 1330–1600. Charge £. Children free. Group concessions. Guided tours by arrangement. Explanatory displays. Information sheets in six languages. Gift shop. Picnic area. WC. Limited wheelchair access. Disabled WC. Car and coach parking. Telephone (01620) 860426.

Picturesque mill with stone buildings dating from the 18th century. The water wheel and grain milling machinery are still intact and visitors can see them in operation. Attractive surroundings with ducks and geese on millponds and short walk through fields to 16th-century Phantassie Doocot, once home to 500 pigeons.

1194 PRESTONPANS BATTLE CAIRN **6 N15**

East of Prestonpans on A198. Access at all times. Free. Car parking.

The cairn commemorates the victory of Prince Charles Edward over General Cope at the Battle of Prestonpans in 1745.

1195 PRIORWOOD GARDEN AND DRIED FLOWER SHOP **5 P17**

NTS. Melrose, Roxburghshire. Off A6091 in Melrose. By bus from Edinburgh. Open Apr–Sep, Mon–Sat 1000–1730, Sun 1330–1730; Oct–Christmas, Mon–Sat 1000–1600, Sun 1330–1600. Charge £. Honesty box. Group concessions. Explanatory displays. Gift shop. Picnic area in orchard. Garden. WC. Wheelchair access with assistance. Disabled WC. Car and coach parking. Telephone (01896) 822493.

Unique garden overlooked by ruins of Melrose Abbey, specialising in plants suitable for drying. Visitors can watch and learn about the drying process and buy or order dried flower arrangements in the shop. The adjacent orchard includes many varieties of historic apple trees.

1196 QUEEN ELIZABETH FOREST PARK CENTRE **4 J14**

FE. Queen Elizabeth Forest Park, Aberfoyle. Open Easter–Oct, daily 1000–1800; Nov–Dec daily, 1100–1700 for Christmas tree sales. Explanatory displays. Gift shop. Tearoom and picnic area. Shop. Cycle routes, walks and forest drive. WC. Wheelchair access. Disabled WC. Car and coach parking. Telephone (01877) 382258.

The Queen Elizabeth Forest Park was first designated a Forest Park by the Forestry Commission in 1953, to mark the coronation of Queen Elizabeth II. It encompasses mountain and moorland, forest and woodland, rivers and lochs, and is home to a rich variety of animal and plant life. The visitor centre is situated on a hillside above Aberfoyle, with spectacular views in all directions, and provides information on all aspects of the forest and activities throughout the year. Resident woodcarver. Orienteering routes.

1197 QUEENSFERRY MUSEUM **6 M15**

53 High Street, South Queensferry, West Lothian. Off the A90, 12 miles (19km) west of Edinburgh. Bus from Edinburgh. Open all year, Mon, Thu, Fri and Sat 1000–1300 and 1415–1700, Sun 1200–1700. Free. Explanatory displays. Gift shop. Car and coach parking nearby. Mini induction loop. Telephone 0131 331 5545.

A museum telling the story of the town, known as the Queen's Ferry in honour of the saintly Queen Margaret (died 1093), who encouraged pilgrims to use the ferry crossing to travel to the shrine of St Andrew in Fife. Describes the development of the Queensferry Passage, the growth of the former Royal Burgh and the building of the Forth Bridges. Life, work and pastimes, including the annual Ferry Fair and a life-size model of the Burry Man.

1198 QUEEN'S OWN HIGHLANDERS REGIMENTAL MUSEUM **3 K7**

Fort George, Ardersier, Inverness. At Fort George (see 656), 14 miles (22.5km) east of Inverness. Nearest railway station Inverness, bus service from Inverness. Tour bus from Inverness. Open Apr–Sep, Mon–Sat 1000–1800, Sun 1400–1800; Oct–Mar, Mon–Fri 1000–1600. Free. Explanatory displays. Gift shop. Refreshments. WC. Limited wheelchair access. Disabled WC. Car and coach parking. Telephone (01463) 224380.

A regimental museum with collections of medals, uniforms and other items showing the history of the Queen's Own Highlanders, Seaforth Highlanders, the Queen's Own Cameron Highlanders, and Lovat Scouts.

1199 QUEEN'S VIEW, LOCH LOMOND **6 J15**

Off A809, 12 miles (19km) northwest of Glasgow. Access at all times. Free. Car parking.

From the west side of the road a path leads to a viewpoint where, in 1879, Queen Victoria had her first view of Loch Lomond.

1200 QUEEN'S VIEW VISITOR CENTRE 3 L11

FE. Tay Forest Park, Perthshire. 7 miles (11km) west of Pitlochry on B8019. Open Apr–Oct. Charge for parking £. Explanatory displays, audio-visual show. Gift shop. Tearoom. WC. Wheelchair access. Car and coach parking. Telephone (01350) 727284.

The centre, close to the viewpoint, is the focal point of the Tay Forest Park and provides an ideal introduction, describing the history of the people and forests in Highland Perthshire. The view across Loch Tummel to the mountain of Schiehallion and beyond is stunning. The viewpoint is thought to have been visited by Queen Victoria in 1866, but is more likely named after Queen Isabella, wife of Robert the Bruce.

1201 QUENDALE WATER MILL 1 G6

Quendale, Dunrossness, Shetland. 4 miles (6.5km) from Sumburgh Airport. Open May–Sep, daily 1000–1700. Charge £. Group concessions. Guided tours. Explanatory displays and video programme. Gift shop. Hot and cold drinks available. WC. Wheelchair access. Disabled WC. Car and coach parking.

A restored 19th-century over-shot water mill with displays of old croft tools. Souvenirs and local crafts.

1202 QUIRANG 2 E7

Off unclassified Staffin to Uig road, 19 miles (30.5km) north of Portree, Isle of Skye. Access at all times. Free. Limited car parking.

An extraordinary mass of towers and pinnacles into which cattle were driven during forays. A very rough track (not suitable for elderly or infirm) zigzags up to the Needle, an imposing obelisk 120 feet (36.5m) high. Beyond the Needle, in a large amphitheatre, stands the Table, a huge grass-covered rock mass. Impressive views.

1203 QUOYNESS CHAMBERED TOMB 1 C9

HS. On the east side of Els Ness on the south coast of the island of Sanday, Orkney. Ferry from Kirkwall to Sanday. Access at all times. Free. Telephone 0131 668 8800.

A megalithic tomb with triple retaining walls containing a passage with a main chamber and six secondary cells. Neolithic.

1204 RAASAY OUTDOOR CENTRE 2 E8

Raasay House, Isle of Raasay, Kyle. On Raasay, an island off Skye. Nearest railway station Kyle, bus to ferry at Sconser and by ferry to Raasay. Open Mar–Nov, Mon–Sat 0900–1900. Free. Charge by activity. Group concessions. Guided tours. Explanatory displays. Gift shop. Licensed restaurant and café. Garden, children's play area. WC. Limited wheelchair access. Disabled WC. Car and coach parking. Telephone (01478) 660266.

Qualified instruction in windsurfing, sailing, kayaking, rock climbing, abseiling, mountain biking, expeditions, forest trails, archery and orienteering. The centre, set in a Georgian mansion is surrounded by four acres (1.6ha) of woodland and lawns.

1205 RANDOLPH'S LEAP 3 L7

Off B9007, 7 miles (11km) southwest of Forres. Access at all times. Free. Car parking.

The River Findhorn winds through a deep gorge in the sandstone, and from a path above are impressive views of the clear brown water swirling over rocks or in still dark pools. Randolph's Leap is the most striking part of this valley.

1206 RAVENS ROCK FOREST WALK **3 J5**

Sutherland. At Linsidemore on the A837. Leaflet available from Forest Enterprise and tourist information centres.

A delightful walk alongside the deep gorge of the Allt Mor Burn, through old mixed woods of mature conifers and beech trees. The paths are easy and there is plenty to keep children interested. The partially suspended path leads you upward to magnificent views over the burn towards Strathoykel.

1207 RED CASTLE **5 P12**

Off A92, 7 miles (11km) south of Montrose. Access at all times. Free.

This red stone tower on a steep mound beside the sandhills of Lunan Bay probably dates from the 15th century, when it replaced an earlier fort built for William the Lion by Walter de Berkely. Robert the Bruce gave it to Hugh, 6th Earl of Ross, in 1328.

1208 RED KITE VIEWING **3 K8**

RSPB. North Kessock Tourist Information Centre, North Kessock. On the Black Isle at the north end of Kessock Bridge, Inverness, off the A9 northbound. Nearest railway station Inverness 3 miles (5km); local bus service stops at centre. Open late Apr–Jun, Mon–Sat 1000–1700, Sun 1200–1700; Jul–Aug, Mon–Sat 1000–1730, Sun 1100–1730; late Sep–late Oct, Mon–Sat 1000–1600. Free. Explanatory displays. RSPB information warden based at Tourist Information Centre. Gift shop. Picnic area. Seal and Dolphin Centre, walks. WC. Wheelchair access. Car and coach parking. Telephone (01463) 731505 or RSPB on (01463) 715000.

The red kite is one of the most beautiful birds of prey in Europe. Using a closed-circuit television camera system close to nesting sites, live pictures are beamed back to a monitor in the North Kessock Tourist Information Centre where RSPB staff are on hand to assist.

1209 RED SMIDDY **2 F6**

Poolewe, northeast of Gairloch on A832.

Poolewe was an important centre for early ironworking and the remains of Scotland's earliest blast furnace – the Red Smiddy – lies close to the village on the banks of the River Ewe.

1210 REEKIE LINN FALLS **5 N12**

Southwest of Kirriemuir on B954. Picnic area.

Spectacular waterfall in naturally gorged woodland.

1211 REELIG GLEN **3 J8**

FE. c/o Inverness Forest District, Tower Road, Smithton, Inverness. At Moniack, 8 miles from Inverness. 1 mile (0.5km) south of A862 Inverness to Beauly road. Bus service between Inverness and Beauly. Open at all times. Free. Picnic area. Wheelchair access. Car parking. Telephone (01463) 791575.

Woodland walk with viewpoint and picnic place. A feature is the number of specimen trees on the walk, with some of the tallest trees in Britain. Leaflet available from Forest Enterprise, Smithton.

1212 RENFREW COMMUNITY MUSEUM **6 J15**

41 Canal Street, Renfrew. Regular bus service from Paisley and Glasgow. Open all year except public holidays, Mon–Sat 1000–1300 and 1400–1700. Free. Explanatory displays. WC. Limited wheelchair access. Disabled WC. Car and coach parking. Telephone 0141 889 3151.

Located in the former Brown Institute building, the museum illustrates local history.

1213 RENNIBISTER EARTH HOUSE **1 B10**

HS. On the A965 about 4.5 miles (7km) west northwest of Kirkwall, Orkney. Bus service from Kirkwall or Stromness. Access at all times. Free. Telephone 0131 668 8800.

A good example of an Orkney earth house, consisting of a passage and underground chamber with supporting roof pillars.

1214 RENNIE'S BRIDGE **5 Q17**

Kelso. Access at all times. Free.

A fine five-arched bridge built over the River Tweed in 1803 by Rennie to replace one destroyed by the floods of 1797. On the bridge are two lamp posts from the demolished Old Waterloo Bridge in London, which Rennie built in 1811. There is also a fine view to Floors Castle (see 650).

1215 RESTENNETH PRIORY **5 N12**

HS. Off the B9113, 1.5 miles (2.5km) northeast of Forfar, Angus. Nearest railway station Arbroath, bus from Arbroath. Access at all times. Free. Telephone 0131 668 8800.

The ruins (chancel and tower) of an Augustinian priory church. The lower part of the tower is early Romanesque.

1216 REVACK ESTATE **3 M8**

Revack Lodge, Grantown-on-Spey, Moray. On the B970, 1 mile (2km) south of Grantown-on-Spey. Nearest railway station Aviemore, bus from Grantown-on-Spey (request stop). Coaches by appointment only. Open all year (except Christmas and New Year), daily 1000–1730. Free. Gift shop. Restaurant. Garden. WC. Limited wheelchair access. Disabled WC. Car parking. Telephone (01479) 872234.

Ten miles (16km) of woodland walks and trails, adventure playground, walled garden, ornamental lakes, exotic orchid houses, stocked fishing and a garden centre in a 350 acres (141ha) sporting and farming estate.

1217 RHUE BEACH **2 G5**

West of Ullapool.

A good family beach, with safe swimming and the possibility of catching a glimpse of seals and various sea birds.

1218 RI CRUIN CAIRN **4 F14**

HS. Kilmartin Glen. 1 mile (2km) southwest of Kilmartin, Argyll. Nearest railway station Oban, then bus to Kilmartin. Access at all times. Free. Telephone 0131 668 8800.

A Bronze Age burial cairn with the covering removed to reveal three massive cists. Axe heads are carved on one of the cist slabs.

1219 RING OF BRODGAR STONE CIRCLE AND HENGE **1 B10**

HS. Between Loch of Harray and Loch of Stenness, 5 miles (8km) northeast of Stromness, Orkney. Bus service from Kirkwall or Stromness. Access at all times. Free. Car and coach parking. Telephone 0131 668 8800.

A magnificent circle of upright stones with an enclosing ditch spanned by causeways. Neolithic. See also 1375 Stones of Stenness.

1220 RISPAIN CAMP **4 J11**

HS. Behind Rispain Farm, 1 mile (2km) west of Whithorn, Wigtownshire. Nearest railway station Stranraer, bus from Stranraer or Newton Stewart, then walk 1 mile (2km). Access at all times. Free. Telephone 0131 668 8800.

A rectangular settlement defended by a bank and ditch. First or 2nd century.

1221 RIVERSIDE GALLERY **3 K8**

11 Bank Street, Inverness. In Inverness town centre by the river Ness. Open all year, Mon–Fri 0900–1730, Sat 0930–1630. Free. Limited wheelchair access. Car parking. Telephone (01463) 224781.

Original paintings and prints by local artists. Scottish landscape, sporting, natural history and still life are all featured.

1222 RIVERSIDE GRANARY **5 M12**

Lower Mill Street, Blairgowrie, Perthshire. In Blairgowrie centre. Buses from Perth or Dundee. Open Feb–May, daily except Tue 1000–1700; Jun–Sep, daily 1000–1700; Oct–Dec, daily except Tue 1000–1700. Free. Gift shop. Restaurant and picnic area. Wheelchair access to ground floor. Disabled WC. Car and coach parking. Telephone (01250) 873032.

An art and craft gallery in a converted grain mill.

1223 ROB ROY AND TROSSACHS VISITOR CENTRE **5 K14**

Ancaster Square, Callander , Perthshire. In Callander, 16 miles (25.5km) northwest of Stirling on the A84. Nearest railway station Stirling, buses from Stirling and Edinburgh. Open Jan–Feb weekends only 1000–1700; Mar–May and Oct–Dec daily 1000–1700; Jun–Sep daily 0930–1800; Jul and Aug daily 0900–2200. Charge £. Group concessions. Guided tours (translations in French, German, Italian and Spanish). Explanatory displays. Gift shop. Play area. WC. Wheelchair access. Disabled WC. Car parking. Telephone (01877) 330342.

Discover the truth behind the remarkable life of notorious outlaw Rob Roy MacGregor in an exciting exhibition, which includes a replica blackhouse and the opportunity to dress as a Highlander. Also a spectacular cinematic introduction to the Trossachs area.

1224 ROB ROY'S GRAVE **4 J13**

West end of Balquhidder Churchyard, off A84, 14 miles (22.5km) north-west of Callander. Access at all reasonable times. Free.

Three flat gravestones enclosed by railings are the graves of Rob Roy, his wife and two of his sons. The church itself contains St Angus' Stone (8th century), a 17th-century bell from the old church, and old Gaelic Bibles.

1225 ROB ROY'S STATUE **3 Q10**

West end of Peterculter by the A93. Access at all times. Free.

Statue of Rob Roy standing above the Leuchar Burn. It can be seen from the bridge on the main road.

1226 ROCKCLIFFE **5 L20**

NTS. Dumfries and Galloway. 7 miles (11km) south of Dalbeattie, off A710. Open all year. Free. Explanatory displays. Gift shop. Restaurant and tearoom in village. WC. Car and coach parking. Telephone (01556) 502575.

The NTS owns several sites in and around the picturesque village of Rockcliffe on the Solway Firth. These include the Mote of Mark which is an ancient hill fort, Rough Island which is a bird sanctuary with access on foot at low tide, and Muckle Lands and Jubilee Path which is a beautiful stretch of coastline between Rockcliffe and Kippford.

1227 ROSEISLE FOREST **3 M7**

FE. Moray Forest District Office, Balnacoul, Fochabers, Moray. A96 west from Elgin, then B9013; turn left at College of Roseisle then 3 miles (2km). Bus route from Kinloss to Burghead then 0.5 mile (1km) walk.

Open all year, toilets closed in winter. Charge for parking. Picnic area. Guided walks and events. WC. Wheelchair access with assistance. Disabled WC. Car parking. Telephone (01343) 820223.

Pine forest giving access to the beach. Picnic tables and barbecues make this site ideal for a family picnic. Informal low level walks. Ranger service

---

1228 ROSSAL INTERPRETIVE TRAIL **3 K3**

1 mile (1.5km) from the car park at Syre, on B873 Altnaharra to Bettyhill road, Sutherland.

A pre-clearance village of great historic interest. Several displays with explanations.

1229 ROSSLYN CHAPEL **6 N16**

Roslin, Midlothian. In Roslin, 7 miles (11km) southwest of Edinburgh. Nearest railway station Edinburgh, bus from Edinburgh. Open all year, Mon–Sat 1000–1700, Sun 1200–1645. Charge ££. Group concessions. Guided tours (information in French, German, Italian and Spanish). Explanatory displays. Gift shop. Tearoom. Garden. WC. Wheelchair access (except for crypt). Disabled WC. Car and coach parking. Telephone 0131 440 2159.

A 15th-century chapel with unique carving throughout, legendary Apprentice Pillar, many references to Freemasonry and the Knights Templar. The only medieval church in Scotland used by the Scottish Episcopal Church.

1230 ROTHESAY CASTLE **4 G16**

HS. Castlehill Street, Rothesay, Isle of Bute. By ferry from Wemyss Bay on the A78. Nearest railway station and ferry Wemyss Bay, buses from Largs and Glasgow via Greenock. Open Apr–Sep, daily 0930–1830; Oct–Mar, Mon–Sat 0930–1630, Sun 1400–1630 closed Thu pm and Fri. Charge £. Group concessions. Guided tours. Explanatory displays. Gift shop. WC. Limited wheelchair access. Telephone (01700) 502691.

A remarkable 13th-century castle of enclosure, circular in plan, with 16th-century forework. Breaches made by Norsemen in 1240 are evident. A favourite residence of the Stewart kings.

1231 ROTHIEMURCHUS ESTATE **3 L9**

Rothiemurchus, Aviemore, Inverness-shire. On the B970, 1.5 miles (2.5km) from Aviemore. Nearest railway station Aviemore, bus from Aviemore. Open all year, daily 0900–1730 (except Christmas Day). Charge dependent on activity. Guided tours (in most languages with prior notice). Explanatory displays. Gift shop. Restaurant and tearoom. Buffet and barbeque lunches by arrangement. WC. Wheelchair access to limited areas. Disabled WC. Car and coach parking. Telephone (01479) 812345.

Guided walks, Landrover safari and farm tours with countryside rangers. A range of tours for groups to see Highland cattle, deer and the fishery, Loch an Eilein. Various photographic viewpoints. Loch and river fishing, clay pigeon shooting and off-road driving can be booked at Rothiemurchus Visitor Centre. Fresh and smoked trout, venison and quality foods are available from the farm shop. Quality Scottish knitwear and craftwork from the Old School Shop. Card Shop. Visitor Centre at Loch an Eilein.

1232 ROUGH CASTLE **6 L15**

HS. Off the B816, 6 miles (9.5km) west of Falkirk. Nearest railway and bus stations Falkirk. Access at all times. Free. Telephone 0131 668 8800.

The best preserved length of the Antonine Wall. Consists of a rampart and ditch, together with the earthworks of a fort, the most complete on the Wall, with a short length of military way with quarry pits. See also 62 Antonine Wall.

1233 ROXBURGH CASTLE **5 Q17**

Off A699, 1 mile (1.5km) southwest of Kelso. Access at all times. Free.

The earthworks are all that remain of the once mighty castle, destroyed by the Scots in the 15th century, and the walled Royal Burgh which gave its name to the county. The present village of Roxburgh dates from a later period.

1234 ROYAL BURGH OF STIRLING VISITOR CENTRE **6 L14**

Castle Esplanade, Stirling. Located at Stirling Castle esplanade. Nearest railway and bus stations Stirling. Open daily, Jan–Jun 0930–1700; Jul–Aug 0900–1830; Sep–Oct 0930–1800; Nov–Dec 0930–1700. Free. Guided tours. Explanatory displays. Gift shop. WC. Limited wheelchair access. Disabled WC. Car and coach parking. Telephone (01786) 462517.

The story of Royal Stirling, from the wars of independence and life in the medieval burgh, to the present day. Sound and light exhibition, multi-lingual audio-visual show.

1235 ROZELLE HOUSE GALLERIES **4 J17**

Rozelle Park, Monument Road, Ayr. In Rozelle Park, 2.5 miles (4km) from centre. Nearest railway station Ayr. Open Apr–Oct, Mon–Sat 1000–1700, Sun 1400–1700; Nov–Mar, Mon–Sat only and closed Christmas and New Year's Day. Free. Gift shop. Coffee shop and picnic area. WC. Limited wheelchair access. Car and coach parking. Telephone (01292) 445447.

Built in 1760 by Robert Hamilton, in the style of Robert Adam. Rebuilt in 1830 by David Bryce. Now a gallery for art and museum exhibitions.

1236 RUMBLING BRIDGE **6 M14**

A823 at Rumbling Bridge. Access at all reasonable times. Free. Car parking.

The River Devon is spanned here by two bridges, the lower one dating from 1713, the upper one from 1816. A footpath from the north side gives good access to a spectacular and picturesque gorge known as the Devil's Mill. Cauldron Linn is a mile downstream, whilst Vicar's Bridge is a beauty spot a mile beyond this.

1237 RUTHVEN BARRACKS **3 K10**

HS. On the B970, 0.5 mile (2km) south of Kingussie, Inverness-shire. Nearest railway station Kingussie, bus service from Aviemore then 15 minute walk. Access at all times. Free. Car parking. Telephone 0131 668 8800.

The ruins of an infantry barracks erected in 1719 with two ranges of quarters and a stable block. Captured and burned by Bonnie Prince Charlie's army in 1746.

1238 RUTHWELL CROSS **5 M20**

HS. In Ruthwell Church on the B724, 8.5 miles (13.5km) southeast of Dumfries. Nearest railway station Dumfries, buses from Dumfries, Gretna or Annan. Access at all times. Free. Car parking. Telephone 0131 668 8800.

An Anglian Cross, sculptured in high relief and dating from the end of the 7th century. Considered to be one of the major monuments of Dark Age Europe. Carved with Runic characters.

1239 RYAN LEISURE CENTRE **4 G20**

Fairhurst Road, Stranraer. In Stranraer, 1 mile (2km) from railway station and 437 yards (400m) from bus station. Open all year, Mon–Fri 0915–2315 (in winter 2200), Sat and Sun 0945–1715 (closed Christmas and New Year). Charge by activity. Group concessions. Café and vending machines. Children's soft play area. WC. Induction loop. Wheelchair access. Disabled WC. Car parking. Telephone (01776) 703535.

A multi-activity leisure centre – games hall, fitness room, dance studio, leisure pool, beach area, flume, spa bath, slides, water cannon, cascade fountain, bubble areas, health suite with sauna, steam room, children's soft play area, conference facilities. Theatres with cinema.

1240 SADDELL ABBEY **4 F17**

B842, 9 miles (14.5km) northwest of Campbeltown. Access at all reasonable times. Free.

The abbey was built in the 12th century by Somerled, Lord of the Isles, or his son Reginald. Only the walls of the original building are left, with sculptured carved tombstones.

1241 ST ABB'S HEAD **5 Q15**

NTS. Off A1107, 2 miles (3km) north of Coldingham, Berwickshire. By bus from Edinburgh, by rail to Berwick-upon-Tweed. Reserve open all year, daily. Centre open Apr–Oct, daily 1000–1700. Site free. Charge for centre and parking £. Group concessions. Explanatory displays. Tearoom. Guided walks by rangers. WC. Wheelchair access to centre. Disabled WC. Car and coach parking. Telephone (018907) 71443.

A National Nature Reserve. The most important location for cliff-nesting sea birds in southeast Scotland. Remote camera link to the centre provides glimpses of nesting birds. Spectacular walks around the headland, above 300 ft (91m) cliffs. Exhibition on wildlife.

1242 ST ANDREWS BOTANIC GARDEN **5 P13**

The Canongate, St Andrews. Nearest railway station Leuchars 4 miles (6.5km), connecting bus to St Andrews. Buses from Dundee and Edinburgh. Bus from town centre. Open May–Sep, 1000–1900; Oct–Apr and weekends all year, 1000–1600. Charge £. Reduced admission for disabled visitors and carers. Group concessions. Guided tours. Explanatory displays. Gift shop. Tea hut. WC. Wheelchair access. Car and coach parking. Telephone (01334) 476452.

Founded in 1887–8 by Dr John Wilson in St Mary's College, South Street, but removed to this site in 1960. Eighteen acres (7ha) of impressively landscaped gardens and glasshouses with a wide range of plants which have won international recognition. Peat, rock, heath and water gardens bounded by the Kinness Burn.

1243 ST ANDREWS CASTLE **5 P13**

HS. The Scores, St Andrews, Fife. On the A91 in St Andrews, Fife. Nearest railway station Leuchars 4 miles (6.5km), connecting bus to St Andrews. Buses from Dundee and Edinburgh. 10 minute walk from bus station. Open Apr–Sep, daily 0930–1830; Oct–Mar, Mon–Sat 0930–1630, Sun 1400–1630. Charge £. Group concessions. Guided tours. Explanatory displays in visitor centre. Gift shop. WC. Limited wheelchair access. Disabled WC. Telephone (01334) 477196.

The ruins of the castle of the Archbishops of St Andrews, dating in part from the 13th century. Notable features include a bottle-dungeon and mine, and counter-mine tunnelling made during the siege that followed the murder of Cardinal Beaton in 1546. These siege works are the finest of their kind in Europe. An exhibition shows the history of the castle and the cathedral.

1244 ST ANDREW'S CATHEDRAL, INVERNESS **3 K8**

Ardross Street, Inverness. On the west bank of the River Ness, below Ness Bridge, 10 minute walk from railway and bus stations. Open daily 0830–1800. Free. Donations. Explanatory displays and guide books. Gift shop. Tearoom (and other facilities) open May–Sep, Mon–Sat 1030–1530. WC. Induction loop. Car parking. Telephone (01463) 233535.

The cathedral church of the Diocese of Moray, Ross and Caithness, the first new cathedral to be completed in Britain since the Reformation. Built 1866–9 in the Gothic style to the design of Alexander Ross. Features twin towers with a ring of ten bells, octagonal chapter house, monolithic pillars of polished Peterhead granite, stained glass, sculpture, carved reredos, angel font after Thorvaldsen (Copenhagen), founder's memorial, icons presented by the Tsar of Russia. In beautiful riverside setting.

1245 ST ANDREWS CATHEDRAL AND ST RULE'S TOWER 5 P13

HS. The Scores, St Andrews, Fife. On the A91 in St Andrews. Nearest railway station Leuchars 4 miles (6.5km), connecting bus to St Andrews. Buses from Dundee and Edinburgh. 10 minute walk from bus station. Open Apr–Sep, daily 0930–1830; Oct–Mar, Mon–Sat 0930–1630, Sun 1400–1630. Charge £. Group concessions. Guided tours. Explanatory displays in visitor centre. Gift shop. Limited wheelchair access, assistance may be required. Telephone (01334) 472563.

The remains of one of the largest cathedrals in Scotland and the associated domestic ranges of the priory. The precinct walls are well preserved. A museum houses an outstanding collection of early Christian and medieval monuments and other on-site finds. St Rule's Tower in the precinct is part of the first church of the Augustinian canons at St Andrews, built early in the 12th century. Splendid views from the top of the tower.

1246 ST ANDREWS GUIDED WALKS 5 N13

Walk departs from St Andrews Pottery Shop, in centre of St Andrews. Nearest railway station Leuchars 4 miles (6.5km), connecting bus to St Andrews. Buses from Dundee and Edinburgh. Guided tours run every Wednesday throughout the year, 1100. Other tours by appointment. Charge £. Children under 12 free. Group concessions. Guided tours (available in French and German). Walks can be managed by wheelchair users and visitors with other special needs can be catered for. Telephone (01334) 850638.

Guided walks of St Andrews cover the area around the cathedral, castle, university and golf course. General and specialist tours available. Qualified Blue Badge guides.

1247 ST ANDREWS POTTERY SHOP 5 P13

4 Church Square, St Andrews, Fife. In pedestrian area in town centre next to public toilets. Nearest railway station Leuchars 4 miles (6.5km), bus station 5 minutes walk, service from Edinburgh, Dundee and Perth. Open Jul and Aug, Mon–Sat 0930–1900, Sun 1130–1630; Sep–Jun, Mon–Sat 0930–1730, Sun 1130–1630. Free. Explanatory displays. Gift shop. Wheelchair access. Car parking. Telephone (01334) 477744.

A working pottery where the public can watch the potter at work. Retail area with pottery and other Scottish crafts. Exclusive Scottish outlet for pots and pithoi Greek garden pots.

1248 ST ANDREWS PRESERVATION TRUST MUSEUM AND GARDEN 5 P13

12 North Street, St Andrews, Fife. Near the cathedral in St Andrews. Nearest railway station Leuchars 4 miles (6.5km), connecting bus to St Andrews. Buses from Dundee and Edinburgh. Open Easter, May–Sep and St Andrew's week (Nov) daily 1400–1700. Free. Guided tours by arrangement. Explanatory displays. Gift shop. Garden. Limited wheelchair access. Telephone (01334) 477629.

A charming 16th-century building with beautiful sheltered garden. Displays include old shops and businesses in the town, changing exhibitions and some of the world's earliest photographs.

1249 ST BLANE'S CHURCH, KINGARTH **4 G16**

HS. At the south end of the Isle of Bute, 8.5 miles (13.5km) south of Rothesay. By ferry from Wemyss Bay on the A78. Nearest railway station and ferry Wemyss Bay, buses from Largs and Glasgow via Greenock. Access at all times. Free. Car parking. Telephone 0131 668 8800.

The ruins of a 12th-century Romanesque chapel set within the foundations of a Celtic Monastery.

1250 ST BRIDE'S CHURCH, DOUGLAS **5 L17**

HS. In Douglas, 12 miles (19km) south southwest of Lanark. Nearest railway station Lanark, bus from Lanark. Open at all times; apply to keyholder. Free. Telephone 0131 668 8800.

The restored choir and south side of the nave of a late 14th-century parish church. The choir contains three canopied monuments to the Douglas family.

1251 ST BRIDGET'S KIRK, DALGETY **6 M15**

HS. Off the A92 at Dalgety Bay, 2 miles (3km) southwest of Aberdour, Fife. Nearest railway station Aberdour, bus from Kirkcaldy or Dunfermline. Access at all times. Free. Telephone 0131 668 8800.

The shell of a medieval church much altered in the 17th century for Protestant worship. At the west end of the building is a burial vault, with a laird's loft above, built for the Earl of Dunfermline.

1252 ST CLEMENT'S CHURCH, RODEL **2 C6**

HS. At Rodel, at the south end of the Isle of Harris (Western Isles). Ferry to Tarbert, Stornoway or Leverburgh. Bus from Stornoway to Tarbert then on to Rodel. Access at all times. Free. Telephone 0131 668 8800.

A fine 16th-century church built by Alexander MacLeod of Dunvegan and Harris. Contains his richly-carved tomb.

1253 ST COLUMBA'S CAVE **4 F15**

On west shore of Loch Killisport (Caolisport), 1 mile (1.5km) north of Ellary, 10 miles (16km) southwest of Ardrishaig. Access at all times. Free.

Traditionally associated with St Columba's arrival in Scotland, the cave contains a rock-shelf with an altar, above which are carved crosses. A large basin, perhaps a Stone Age mortar, may have been used as a font. The cave was occupied from the Middle Stone Age. In front are traces of houses and the ruins of a chapel (possibly 13th-century). Another cave is nearby.

1254 ST CORMAC'S CHAPEL **4 F15**

HS. On Eilean Mor, a small island off the coast of Knapdale in the Sound of Jura. Bus from Lochgilphead to Tayvallich, from there no public transport. Boat trips for groups from Crinan, Mon, Wed and Fri (other times by arrangement out of season) telephone Gemini Cruises (01546) 830238. Access at all times. Free. Telephone 0131 668 8800.

A chapel with a vaulted chancel containing the effigy of an ecclesiastical figure. Probably 12th century.

1255 ST DUTHAC'S CHAPEL **3 K6**

Tain, Ross and Cromarty.

Built in the 11th or 12th century and now in ruins. Robert the Bruce's wife and daughter were captured here in 1306. James IV made an annual pilgrimage to this chapel.

1256 ST FILLAN'S CAVE **6 P14**

Cove Wynd, Pittenweem, Fife. 1 mile (2km) west of Anstruther. Nearest railway station Cupar, bus from Dundee or Edinburgh. Open all year, Easter–Oct, Mon–Sat 0900–1730; Nov–Easter, Tue–Sat 0900–1730, Sun 1200–1700. Charge £. Car parking. Telephone (01333) 311495.

A cave associated with St Fillan, a 7th-century missionary to the Picts, who lived in the area. Renovated in 1935 and rededicated for worship.

1257 ST JOHN'S CHURCH, DUNOON **6 H15**

Argyll Street, Dunoon. Ferry from Greenock. Open May–Sep, Mon–Fri 1000–1200. Free. Guided tours. Refreshments. Garden. WC. Wheelchair access. Car and coach parking.

A magnificent nave and aisles church by R. A. Bryden in 1877 with Gothic spired tower. Galleried concert hall interior, raised choir behind central pulpit, organ 1895. Interesting stained glass windows, including Lauder Memorial.

1258 ST JOHN'S KIRK, PERTH **5 M13**

St John Street, Perth. In Perth centre. Open May–Sep, Mon–Sat 1000–1600, Jun–Sep, Sun 1200–1400; winter open by appointment. Free. Guided tours by arrangement. Explanatory displays in European languages and Japanese. Induction loop during services. Wheelchair access. Disabled WC. Telephone (01738) 21755.

Consecrated in 1242, this fine cruciform church largely dates from the 15th century and was restored 1923–26 as a war memorial. Here in 1559 John Knox preached his momentous sermon urging the 'purging of the churches from idolatry'. The town kirk of Perth, it is frequently a venue for musical and dramatic productions.

1259 ST KILDA **2 A1**

NTS. Western Isles. 60 miles (96.5km) west of the Isle of Harris. For details of access contact NTS Regional Office on telephone number below. Access by arrangement. Telephone (01631) 570000.

Evacuated in 1930, these remote islands are now a World Heritage Site, unrivalled for their seabird colonies and rich in archaeological remains. Each year NTS work parties carry out conservation work.

1260 ST MAGNUS CATHEDRAL, KIRKWALL **1 B10**

Broad Street, Kirkwall, Orkney. In the centre of Kirkwall. Bus from ferries or taxi from airport. Open Apr–Sep, Mon–Sat 0900–1800, Sun 1400–1800; Oct–Mar, Mon–Sat 0900–1300 and 1400–1700. Graveyard always open. Free. Explanatory displays. Wheelchair access to half the building. Telephone (01856) 874894.

Founded by Jarl Rognvald and dedicated to his uncle, St Magnus. The remains of both men are in the massive east choir piers. The original building dates from 1137–1200, but sporadic additional work went on until the late 14th century. It contains some of the finest examples of Norman architecture in Scotland, with small additions in transitional styles and some early Gothic. In regular use as a church.

1261 ST MARGARET'S CAVE **6 M14**

In Dunfermline, below Bruce Street car park, down 80 steps. By rail or bus from Edinburgh, 20 minute walk from rail station and 10 minute walk from bus station. Open Easter–Sep, daily 1100–1600. Free. Guided tours by appointment. Explanatory displays. Gift shop. Car and coach parking. Telephone (01383) 314228 or 313838.

A site of Catholic pilgrimage where Margaret, 11th-century queen and saint, sought refuge for meditation and prayer.

1262 ST MARTIN'S KIRK, HADDINGTON **6 P15**

HS. On the eastern outskirts of Haddington, East Lothian. Nearest railway station Drem, bus from Edinburgh. Access at all times. Free. Telephone 0131 668 8800.

The ruined nave of a Romanesque church, altered in the 13th century.

1263 ST MARY'S CHAPEL, CROSSKIRK **3 M2**

HS. Off the A836, 6 miles (9.5km) west of Thurso, Caithness. Nearest bus and railway stations Thurso, bus from Thurso. Access at all times. Free. Car parking. Telephone 0131 668 8800.

A simple dry-stone chapel, probably 12th-century.

1264 ST MARY'S CHAPEL, ROTHESAY **4 G16**

HS. On the A845, 0.5 mile (1km) south of Rothesay on the Isle of Bute. By ferry from Wemyss Bay on the A78. Nearest railway station and ferry Wemyss Bay, buses from Largs and Glasgow via Greenock. Access at all times. Free. Telephone 0131 668 8800.

The late-medieval remains of the chancel of the parish church of St Mary, with fine tombs.

1265 ST MARY'S CHURCH, AUCHINDOIR **3 P8**

HS. Near Lumsden, 3 miles (5km) north of Kildrummy, Aberdeenshire. Bus from Huntly. Access at all times. Free. Telephone 0131 668 8800.

The ruins of one of the finest medieval parish churches in Scotland, roofless, but otherwise complete. There is a rich early Romanesque doorway and a beautiful early 14th-century sacrament house.

1266 ST MARY'S CHURCH, GRANDTULLY **5 L12**

HS. Off the A827 at Pitcairn Farm, 3 miles (5km) east northeast of Aberfeldy, Perthshire. Nearest railway station Pitlochry, bus from Perth to Aberfeldy (request stop for St Mary's Church). Open at all times. Free. Car parking. Telephone 0131 668 8800.

A simple 16th-century parish church with a finely painted wooden ceiling illustrating heraldic and symbolic subjects.

1267 ST MARY'S CHURCH, ST ANDREWS **5 P13**

HS. Kirkheugh, St Andrews. Behind the cathedral in St Andrews, Fife. Nearest railway station Leuchars 4 miles (6.5km), connecting bus to St Andrews. Buses from Dundee and Edinburgh. Access at all times. Free. Telephone 0131 668 8800.

The scanty foundations of a small cruciform church on the edge of a cliff. It was the earliest collegiate church in Scotland. Destroyed in the Reformation.

1268 ST MARY'S COLLEGIATE CHURCH, HADDINGTON **6 P15**

Sidegate, Haddington. In Haddington. Bus from Edinburgh. Open Apr–Sep, Mon–Sat 1100–1600, Sun 0930–1630. Free. Guided tours (leaflets in many languages). Explanatory displays. Audio tapes. Tearoom and picnic area. Gift shop and book shop. Children's activity area. Brass rubbing centre. WC. Wheelchair access. Disabled WC. Car and coach parking. Telephone (01620) 823109.

A magnificent 14th-century medieval cruciform church, East Lothian's cathedral. Destroyed during the siege of Haddington in 1548, but completely restored between 1971–73. Features Burne Jones and Sax Shaw windows; Lammermuir pipe organ. The Lauderdale Chapel is a focus for ecumenical unity. A popular venue for televised services and commercial recordings, concerts and art exhibitions. In picturesque surroundings beside the River Tyne.

1269 ST MARY'S EPISCOPAL CHURCH, DALKEITH **6 N15**

Dalkeith Country Park, Dalkeith. On the A7, 7 miles (22km) southeast of Edinburgh. Bus from Edinburgh. Open most weekend afternoons in summer; telephone for details. Free. Donations. Guided tours. Explanatory displays. Garden. WC. Wheelchair access. Disabled WC. Car and coach parking. Telephone 0131 663 3359.

Built as a chapel for Dalkeith Palace in 1843 by William Burn and David Bryce. Early English style with many splendid features – double hammerbeam roof, glorious stained glass, heraldic floor tiles by Minton and the only working water-powered Hamilton organ in Scotland (recently restored).

1270 ST MARY'S LOCH **5 N17**

Off A708, 14 miles (22.5km) east southeast of Selkirk. Access at all times. Free. Car parking.

Beautifully set among smooth green hills, this 3-mile (4.5km) long loch is used for sailing and fishing. On the neck of land separating it from Loch of the Lowes, at the south end, stands Tibbie Shiel's Inn. The inn was kept by Tibbie Shiel (Elizabeth Richardson, 1783–1878) from 1823, and was a meeting place for many 19th-century writers. Beside the road towards the north end of the loch is a seated statue of James Hogg, the Ettrick Shepherd, author of *Confessions of a Justified Sinner* and a friend of Scott, who farmed in this district. On the route of the Southern Upland Way.

1271 ST MICHAEL'S PARISH CHURCH, LINLITHGOW **6 L15**

Kirkgate, Linlithgow. In the centre of the town. By rail or bus from Edinburgh. Open Jun–Sep, daily 1000–1600; Oct–May, Mon–Fri 1000–1530. Free. Guided tours by prior arrangement (available in French or German). Explanatory displays. Gift shop. Picnic area. Wheelchair access. Car parking. Telephone (01506) 842188.

A medieval parish church consecrated in 1242 on the site of an earlier church. Close association with the royal house of Stewart and Mary, Queen of Scots, born in nearby Linlithgow Palace (see 967) and baptized in the church. Sports a contemporary aluminium crown on the tower, replacing the medieval stone crown removed in 1820.

1272 ST MONANS WINDMILL **6 P14**

St Monans, Fife. 1 mile (2km) west of Pittenweem, 0.25 mile (0.5km) from St Monans. Nearest railway station Leuchars 4 miles (6.5km), connecting bus to St Andrews, buses from St Andrews or Leven. Open on request to keyholder (Hardy's newsagents in St Monans). Open Jul and Aug, 1000–1600. Free. £5 deposit for key during winter. Explanatory displays. Car and coach parking.

A windmill which served nearby saltpans.

1273 ST NINIAN'S CAVE **4 J21**

HS. At Physgill, on the shore 4 miles (6.5km) southwest of Whithorn, Wigtownshire. Nearest railway station Stranraer, bus from Newton Stewart or Stranraer, alight at junction to Cave Walk, then 4 miles (6.5km) walk. Free. Car and coach parking. Telephone 0131 668 8800.

A cave traditionally associated with the saint. Early crosses found here are housed at Whithorn Museum. Crosses carved on the walls of the cave are now weathered.

1274 ST NINIAN'S CHAPEL, ISLE OF WHITHORN **4 J21**

HS. At Isle of Whithorn, 3 miles (5km) southeast of Whithorn, Wigtownshire. Nearest railway station Stranraer, bus from Newton Stewart or Stranraer to Isle of Whithorn. Access at all times. Free. Car and coach parking. Telephone 0131 668 8800.

The restored ruins of a 13th-century chapel, probably used by pilgrims on their way to Whithorn.

1275 ST NINIAN'S CHAPEL, TYNET **3 N7**

Tynet, Fochabers, Moray. On the A98, 3 miles (5km) east of Fochabers. Nearest railway station Elgin, bus from Buckie or Elgin. Open all year, dawn–dusk. Mass at 1730 on Sat. Free. Explanatory displays. Picnic area. Wheelchair access with assistance. Car parking. Telephone (01542) 832196.

Built in 1755 by the Laird of Tynet, ostensibly as a sheepcote, but secretly as a Catholic chapel (extensively altered since). The oldest post-Reformation Catholic church still in use.

1276 ST ORLAND'S STONE **5 N12**

HS. In a field near Cossans Farm, 4.5 miles (7km) west of Forfar, Angus. Access at all times. Free.

An early Christian sculptured slab with a cross on one side and Pictish symbols and figures on the other.

1277 ST PETER'S KIRK AND PARISH CROSS **3 M7**

HS. In Duffus Churchyard in Duffus, Moray. Bus from Elgin. Access at all times. Free. Telephone 0131 668 8800.

The roofless remains of the church include the base of a 14th-century western tower, a 16th-century vaulted porch and some interesting tombstones. There is also a 14th-century cross.

1278 ST RONANS WELLS INTERPRETIVE CENTRE **5 N17**

Wells Brae, Innerleithen, Peebleshire. On the A72, 6 miles (9.5km) from Peebles. Bus from Edinburgh. Open Easter–Sep, daily 1400–1700. Free. Guided tours. Explanatory displays. Gift shop. Open-air tearoom and picnic area. Garden. WC. Wheelchair access. Disabled WC. Car and coach parking. Telephone (01721) 724820.

A site associated with a novel by Sir Walter Scott. Memorabilia of Scott, information and photographs of local festival. The well water can be tasted.

1279 ST SERF'S CHURCH, DUNNING **5 M13**

HS. In Dunning, Perthshire. Nearest railway station Perth, bus from Perth to Dunning. Exterior view only. Telephone 0131 668 8800.

The parish church of Dunning, with a square Romanesque tower and tower arch. The rest of the church was rebuilt in 1810, but contains some of the original fabric.

1280 ST VIGEANS SCULPTURED STONES **5 P12**

HS. 0.5 mile (1km) north of Arbroath, Angus. Nearest railway station Arbroath, bus services from Dundee or Montrose. Open at all times. Free. Explanatory displays. Telephone 0131 668 8800.

A fine collection of 32 early Christian and Pictish stones set into cottages in the village of St Vigeans.

1281 SAMYE LING TIBETAN CENTRE **5 N19**

Eskdalemuir, Dumfriesshire. On the B709, 16 miles (25.5km) from Lockerbie. Nearest railway station Lockerbie, bus or taxi from Lockerbie. Open all year, daily 0900–2200 (temple 0600–2200, café 0900–1700 in summer, 1200–1800 in winter and Thu–Sat evenings, shop 1330–1645. Free. Donations. Guided tours by arrangement (available in French, German and Spanish). Explanatory displays. Gift shop. Restaurant, tearoom and picnic area. Gardens, riverside walk, temple. WC. Wheelchair access with assistance. Disabled WC. Car and coach parking. Telephone (01387) 373232.

A magnificent Tibetan temple in traditional Buddhist style, in beautiful surroundings. Also guest house for visitors who attend courses on meditation, therapy, and arts and crafts.

1282 SANDAIG MUSEUM **4 B12**

The Thatched Cottage Museum, Sandaig. In Sandaig village, western Tiree. Ferry from Oban (Caledonian MacBrayne, 0990 650000) or by air from Glasgow. Open Jun–Sep, Mon–Fri 1400–1600. Free. Donations.

Guided tours. Guide booklet supplied. Restaurant adjacent. Wheelchair access with assistance. Car and coach parking. Telephone (01865) 311468.

Located in a terrace of traditional thatched buildings, the museum houses a unique collection of items illustrating life in a late 19th-century cottar's home. The adjoining byre and barn display elements of agricultural work at the croft, a testimony to the Hebridean islanders' self-sufficiency.

1283 SANDHAVEN MEAL MILL **3 R7**

Sandhaven, Fraserburgh, Aberdeenshire. On the B9031, 2.5 miles (4km) west of Fraserburgh. Open May–Sep, weekends 1400–1630. Free. Guided tours. Explanatory displays. Limited wheelchair access. Car and coach parking. Telephone (01771) 622906.

Visitors can see how oatmeal used to be ground in this typical 19th-century Scottish meal mill. Working demonstrations.

1284 SANDWOOD BAY **2 H3**

4 miles (6.5km) walk north from Kinlochbervie, northwest Sutherland.

A relatively undisturbed bay with great views. The dunes are said to be haunted.

1285 SANQUHAR TOLBOOTH MUSEUM **5 K18**

High Street, Sanquhar, Dumfriesshire. In the town centre near station. Nearest railway station Sanquhar, buses from Dumfries or Kilmarnock. Open Apr–Sep, Tue–Sat 1000–1300 and 1400–1700, Sun 1400–1700. Free. Explanatory displays and audio-visual presentation. Gift shop. Car and coach parking. Telephone (01659) 50186.

Located in a fine 18th-century tolbooth. Tells the story of Upper Nithsdale. Features world famous Sanquhar knitting, mines and miners of Sanquhar and Kirkconnel, history and customs of the Royal Burgh of Sanquhar, three centuries of local literature, life in Sanquhar jail, the earliest inhabitants, and the people of Upper Nithsdale, at home and at work.

1286 SAVINGS BANK MUSEUM **5 M20**

Ruthwell, Dumfries. On the B724, 10 miles (16km) east of Dumfries. Bus from Dumfries or Annan. Open daily (except Sun and Mon in winter), 1000–1300 and 1400–1700. Free. Guided tours (leaflets in European languages, Russian, Chinese and Japanese). Explanatory displays. WC. Touch facilities. Wheelchair access with assistance. Car and coach parking. Telephone (01387) 870640.

Housed in the original 1800 village meeting place, a museum which traces the savings bank movement from its founding here in 1810 by the Rev Henry Duncan to its growth and spread worldwide. Also displays the work of the Ruthwell Friendly Society from 1795, an early insurance scheme providing sick pay, widows pensions, funeral grants and the chance to buy staple foods at cost price. Features restoration of the 8th-century runic Ruthwell Cross (see 1238).

1287 SCALLOWAY CASTLE **1 G5**

HS. In Scalloway, 6 miles (9.5km) west of Lerwick, Shetland. Bus from Lerwick. Access at all times. Free. Explanatory displays. Car parking. Telephone 0131 668 8800.

A fine castellated mansion built in 1600 in medieval style by Patrick Stewart, Earl of Orkney. Fell into disuse in 1615.

1288 SCALLOWAY MUSEUM **1 G5**

Main Street, Scalloway, Shetland. 7 miles (11km) west of Lerwick. Bus stop nearby (limited service). Open May–Sep, Mon 1130–1630,

Tue–Thu 1400–1630, Fri 0930–1230 and 1400–1630, Sat 1000–1230 and 1400–1630. Free. Donations. Guided tours. Explanatory displays. Gift shop. WC. Wheelchair access. Car and coach parking. Telephone (01595) 880666.

Artefacts and photographs cover the history of Scalloway over the past 100 years, including its involvement with the fishing industry. A major section is devoted to Scalloway's unique role in World War II, when it was a secret base for Norwegian freedom fighters, as 16 Norwegian fishing boats ran a shuttle service to Norway carrying in weapons, ammunition and radio sets, returning with refugees. Realising the importance of this operation, the US Government donated three submarine chasers which operated between 1942 and 1945.

1289 SCAPA FLOW **1 B11**

Sea area, enclosed by the mainland of Orkney and the islands of Burray, South Ronaldsay, Flotta and Hoy.

Major naval anchorage in both wars and the scene of the surrender of the German High Seas Fleet in 1919. Today a centre of marine activity as Flotta is a pipeline landfall and tanker terminal for North Sea Oil. Interpretation Centre at Lyness, Hoy, in the old pumphouse which was used to feed fuel to ships.

1290 SCONE PALACE **5 M13**

Scone, Perth. On the A93 (to Blairgowrie), 2 miles (3km) northeast of Perth. Nearest railway station Perth, limited bus service from Perth. Open Easter–Oct, daily 0930–1645 (closes 1715). Charge £££. Group concessions. Explanatory displays. Gift shop. Restaurant, tearoom and picnic area. Adventure playground. Gardens with woodland walks and maze. WC. Wheelchair access with assistance. Disabled WC. Car and coach parking. Telephone (01738) 552300.

A castellated palace, enlarged and embellished in 1803, incorporating the 16th-century and earlier palaces. Notable grounds and a pinetum. The home of the Earl of Mansfield. Magnificent collection of porcelain, furniture, ivories, 18th-century clocks and 16th-century needlework. The Moot Hill at Scone, known in the 8th century and earlier, was the site of the famous Coronation Stone of Scone (the Stone of Destiny), brought there in the 9th century by Kenneth MacAlpine, King of Scots. In 1296, the Stone was seized by the English and taken to Westminster Abbey. In 1997 the Stone was returned to Scotland and is now in Edinburgh Castle (see 530). The ancient Abbey of Scone was destroyed by followers of John Knox.

1291 SCONE STUDIOS **5 M13**

Angus Road, Scone, Perthshire. On the A94, 2.5 miles (4km) from Perth. Open all year (except public holidays and Scottish bank holidays) Mon–Sat 1000–1700. Free. Guided tours. Explanatory displays. Garden. WC. Wheelchair access with assistance. Car and coach parking. Telephone (01738) 553662.

A fine art centre where many different artists and craftworkers exhibit their work. Sculpture/water garden.

1292 SCOTLAND'S LARDER **6 N14**

Upper Largo, Leven, Fife. (9.5km) east of Leven. Open daily Apr–Oct, 1000–late; Nov–Mar, 1100–dusk. Free. Charge for demonstrations. Explanatory displays. Garden. Gift shop. Restaurant. WC. Wheelchair access with assistance. Disabled WC. Car and coach parking. Telephone (01333) 360414.

Scotland's only visitor attraction giving information on the tradition, variety and quality of Scottish foods.

1293 SCOTLAND'S LIGHTHOUSE MUSEUM **3 R7**

Kinnaird Head, Fraserburgh, Aberdeenshire. In Fraserburgh. By bus from Aberdeen. Open Apr–Oct, Mon–Sat 1000–1800, Sun 1200–1800; Nov–Mar, Mon–Sat 1000–1600, Sun 1200–1600. Charge £. Children under 6 free. Joint ticket with Kinnaird Head Lighthouse (see 917). Group concessions. Guided tours. Explanatory displays including multi-screen projector show and touch screens. Gift shop. Tearoom. WC. Disabled WC. Car and coach parking. Telephone (01346) 511022.

A museum adjacent to a former castle which became the first lighthouse built by the Northern Lighthouse Board in 1787, now a monument to Scotland's lighthouse service. Shows the skill and dedication, the science and romance of Scotland's lighthouses. Tour to the top of the lighthouse. Special events and children's holiday activities.

1294 SCOTLAND'S SECRET BUNKER **5 P13**

Crown Buildings, Troywood, St Andrews. On the B9131, 5 miles (8km) from St Andrews. Nearest railway station Leuchars 4 miles (6.5km), connecting bus to St Andrews. Open Easter–Oct, daily 1000–1700. Charge £££. Group concessions. Guided tours. Explanatory displays. Gift shop. Café. WC. Car and coach parking. Telephone (01333) 310301.

The amazing labyrinth built 100 feet (30.5m) underground where central government and the military commanders would have run the country in the event of nuclear war. Its existence was only revealed in 1993 and it is now open to the public. Visitors can see the nuclear command centre with its original equipment. Three cinemas show authentic cold war films. There is a display of vehicles in the grounds.

1295 SCOTS DYKE **5 N19**

Off A7, 7 miles (11km) south of Langholm. Access at all reasonable times, but not easily identified. Free.

The remains of a wall made of clods of earth and stones, which marked part of the border between England and Scotland.

1296 SCOTSTARVIT TOWER **5 N14**

HS. Off the A916, 3 miles (5km) south of Cupar, Fife. Nearest railway station Cupar, bus from Cupar or Ceres. Access at all times during summer; apply to keyholder at Hill of Tarvit House. Free. Car parking. Telephone 0131 668 8800.

A handsome and well-built 15th-century tower house remodelled in the mid 16th century. Renowned as the home of Sir John Scot, author of Scot of Scotstarvit's *Staggering State of the Scots Statesmen*.

1297 CAPTAIN SCOTT AND DR WILSON CAIRN **3 N11**

In Glen Prosen on unclassified road northwest of Dykehead. Access at all times. Free.

The cairn replaces the original fountain which was erected in memory of the Antarctic explorers, Captain Scott and Dr Wilson. Early planning for the expedition took place at Dr Wilson's home in the glen.

1298 SCOTTISH AGRICULTURAL MUSEUM **6 M15**

Ingliston, Newbridge, Midlothian. By Edinburgh Airport, off A8. Nearest railway station the Gyle, bus from Edinburgh. Airport bus from Edinburgh, 10 minute walk from airport. Open Apr–Sep, daily 1000–1700; Oct–Mar, Mon–Fri 1000–1700. Free. Explanatory displays. Gift shop. Tearoom and picnic area. WC. Wheelchair access. Disabled WC. Car and coach parking. Telephone 0131 333 2674.

Scotland's national museum of country life. Interpretive displays feature tools and machinery, including tractors. Audio displays.

1299 SCOTTISH ANTIQUE AND ARTS CENTRE 5 N13

Abernyte, Perthshire. 1.5 miles (2.5km) from the A90. Bus from Dundee or Perth. Open all year, daily (except Christmas and New Year's Day) 1000–1700. Free. Guided tours. Explanatory displays. Gift shop. Restaurant, tearoom and picnic area. Creche, garden centre. WC. Wheelchair access. Disabled WC. Car and coach parking. Telephone (01828) 686401.

A large antique and arts centre with a thousand items of furniture, collectibles, new and traditional furniture, paintings, sculpture and gifts. Also at Doune.

1300 SCOTTISH CRANNOG CENTRE 5 K12

Kenmore, Perthshire. 6 miles (10km) west of Aberfeldy on A827, 14 miles (22.5km) east of Killin on A827. Nearest railway station Pitlochry, bus services from Pitlochry or Aberfeldy. Car and coach parking permitted at nearby hotel. Open Apr–Oct, daily 1000–1730. Charge ££. Group concessions. Guided tours. Explanatory displays. Gift shop. Refreshments. WC. Wheelchair access. Disabled WC. Car and coach parking. Telephone (01887) 830583.

A unique recreation of an iron age loch dwelling, authentically built from evidence obtained from underwater archaeological excavations of crannogs in the loch. Visitors can walk back in time and experience the life of crannog-dwellers. There is a wide range of ancient craft demonstrations and plenty of hands-on activities. Exhibition with information panels and a short video. This is an all-weather attraction.

1301 SCOTTISH DEER CENTRE 5 N13

Bow of Fife, Cupar, Fife. On the A91, 3 miles (5km) west of Cupar. Nearest railway station Cupar, bus from Cupar or Kinross. Open daily Apr–Oct 1000–1800; Nov–Mar 1000–1700 (except Christmas and New Year). Charge ££. Group concessions. Guided tours. Explanatory displays. Gift shop. Coffee shop and picnic areas. Adventure playgrounds. WC. Wheelchair access. Disabled WC. Car and coach parking. Telephone (01337) 810391.

Fifty-five acres (22ha) of parkland with over 160 deer (over nine species). Rangers conduct tours. Trailer rides into fields with the deer. Falconry displays three times daily. Courtyard shopping facility.

1302 SCOTTISH FISHERIES MUSEUM 6 P14

Harbourhead, Anstruther, Fife. In Anstruther, 10 miles (16km) south of St Andrews. Nearest railway station Leuchars 4 miles (6.5km), then bus to St Andrews. Bus from St Andrews or Leven. Open all year (except Christmas and New Year), Apr–Oct, Mon–Sat 1000–1730, Sun 1100–1700; Nov–Mar, Mon–Sat 1000–1630, Sun 1400–1630. Charge ££. Group concessions. Guided tours for groups by arrangement. Explanatory displays. Gift shop. Tearoom. WC. Wheelchair access. Disabled WC. Car and coach parking. Telephone (01333) 310628.

Sixteenth- to 19th-century buildings housing fishing and ships' gear, model and actual fishing boats (including *Fifie* and *Zulu* in harbour). Interior of a fisherman's cottage and extended reference library.

1303 SCOTTISH HYDRO-ELECTRIC VISITOR CENTRE 5 L12

Pitlochry Power Station, Pitlochry, Perthshire. In Pitlochry on the river Tummel. Nearest railway and bus stations Pitlochry. Open Apr–Oct, daily 1000–1730. Charge £. Salmon viewing and downstairs exhibition is free. Explanatory displays (audio-visual, in French and German) in visitor centre. Gift shop. WC. Limited wheelchair access. Disabled WC. Car parking. Telephone (01796) 473152.

An exhibition shows how Scottish Hydro-Electric's power stations are controlled and operated, and the salmon story. Visitors can also observe salmon coming upstream in the fish ladder and see into the station's turbine hall.

1304 SCOTTISH INDUSTRIAL RAILWAY CENTRE 4 J18

Minnivey Colliery, Burnton, Dalmellington, Ayrshire. 12 miles (19km) southeast of Ayr, off A713. Nearest railway station Ayr, bus service (X52) to Dalmellington. Steam days held on the last Sun of May, Jun and Sep, and then every Sun in Jul and Aug. Static display every Sat from Jun–Sep. Charge £. Group concessions. Guided tours. Explanatory displays. Gift shop. Refreshments. WC. Wheelchair access. Car and coach parking. Telephone (01292) 531144.

The centre is on the site of the former Minnivey Colliery. Steam locomotives and traditional locomotive shed. Brake van trips. Museum with extensive collection of railway relics and documents. Narrow gauge demonstration line.

1305 SCOTTISH KILTMAKER VISITOR CENTRE 3 K8

Hector Russell Kiltmaker, 4–9 Huntly Street, Inverness. In the centre of Inverness. Open May–Sep, Mon–Sat 0900–2100, Sun 1000–1700; Oct–May, Mon–Sat 0900–1700. Charge £. Group concessions. Guided tours (leaflet in French). Explanatory displays. Gift shop. Telephone (01463) 222781.

Scotland's only visitor attraction devoted to the kilt. You can learn all about its history and development, its tradition and culture, as well as how it is worn today. Audio-visual, and costume and tartan displays create a colourful, authentic and memorable experience. You can also see kilts being made in the world's largest kiltmaking workshop.

1306 SCOTTISH LIQUEUR CENTRE 5 M12

Hilton, Bankfoot, Perthshire. 7 miles (11km) north of Perth at the Bankfoot exit of the A9. Regular bus service from Perth. Open all year except Christmas and New Year, Mon–Sat 1000–1800. Free. Explanatory displays. Gift shop. Wheelchair access. Car and coach parking. Telephone (01738) 787044.

The family-run company produces original Scottish liqueurs. Free tutored tastings of products are offered, together with a brief presentation on the company's history and development. Hand-drawn postcards, paintings and local crafts for sale.

1307 SCOTTISH MARITIME MUSEUM 6 H17

Laird Forge, Gottries Road, Irvine, Ayrshire. In Irvine, at Harbourside, 5 minute walk from station. Open Apr–Oct, daily 1000–1700. Charge £. Group concessions. Guided tours. Explanatory displays. Gift shop. Restaurant and tearoom. WC. Disabled WC. Car and coach parking. Telephone (01294) 278283.

Occupies a considerable part of Irvine's harbourside. Visitors can climb aboard a Clyde puffer, tug or fishing boat or visit a 1914 shipworker's flat. Restoration underway on the former RNVR club *SV Carrick* (City of Adelaide). Development of the reconstructed 1872 engine shop of Alexander Stephen and Son of Linthouse also underway.

1308 SCOTTISH MINING MUSEUM 6 N16

Lady Victoria Colliery, Newtongrange, Midlothian. On the A7, 10 miles (16km) south of Edinburgh. Bus from Edinburgh. Open Feb–Nov, daily 1000–1700; Dec–Jan by appointment. Charge ££. Group concessions. Guided tours by prior arrangement. Printed guides in French, German and Italian. Explanatory displays. Gift shop. Restaurant. Children's play area, tourist information. WC. Wheelchair access. Disabled WC. Car and coach parking. Telephone 0131 663 7519.

The finest surviving Victorian colliery with Scotland's largest steam engine in the winding house. Visitors can follow a miner's day in the late 19th century and learn about his work. The visitor centre contains interactive displays and exhibits, and a virtual coalface.

1309 SCOTTISH OFF-ROAD DRIVING CENTRE **5 M14**

Strathmiglo, Fife. Open daily 0900–1700. Charge £££ per vehicle (holds 4). Car and coach parking. Telephone (01337) 860528.

An off-road driving range covering a 100 acres (40ha) site. Vehicle provided or visitors can bring their own vehicle for a reduced charge.

1310 SCOTTISH SEABIRD CENTRE **6 P15**

The Harbour, North Berwick. By train or bus from Edinburgh, bus from Dunbar and Haddington. Open daily during summer; telephone to confirm times and winter opening. Explanatory displays. Gift shop. Restaurant/café. WC. Wheelchair access. Disabled WC. Car and coach parking. Telephone (01620) 890202.

Visitors can discover the secret and fascinating world of Scotland's seabirds by studying the birds close up, in their natural environment – without disturbing them. Remote cameras and the latest technology provide amazing live pictures of puffins, gannets and many other seabirds. Breathtaking views across the Firth of Forth to the Bass Rock and Fife.

1311 SCOTTISH VINTAGE BUS MUSEUM **6 M15**

M90 Commerce Park, Lathalmond, Dunfermline, Fife. On the B915, 2 miles (3km) west of junction 5 on the M90 and 2 miles north of Dunfermline. Open Easter–early Oct, Sun 1230–1700. Charge £. Group concessions. Guided tours. Explanatory displays. Gift shop. Refreshments. WC. Wheelchair access (not onto vehicles). Disabled WC. Car and coach parking. Telephone (01383) 623380.

A collection of over 100 historic buses from the 1920s, mostly of Scottish origin, which can be seen in all stages of restoration. Also many artefacts depicting Scottish bus history. Visitors can observe restoration work or travel in a vintage bus around the site. Occasional special events.

1312 SCOTTISH WOOL CENTRE **4 J14**

Aberfoyle, Stirlingshire. Off Main Street in Aberfoyle. Nearest railway station Stirling, buses from Stirling or Glasgow. Open daily Apr–Oct, 0930–1800, Nov–Mar 1000–1700. Charge for live show. Group concessions. Guided tours. Show programmes in European languages and Japanese. Explanatory displays. Gift shop. Coffee shop. Kids' Farm (free). WC. Wheelchair access. Disabled WC. Car and coach parking. Telephone (01877) 382850.

Visitor centre and theatre telling the story of Scottish Wool. Farm. Traditional spinners in action. Wide range of woollens, knitwear, gifts and souvenirs.

1313 SIR WALTER SCOTT'S COURTROOM **5 P17**

Market Place, Selkirk. In Selkirk, 25 miles (40km) south of Edinburgh. Bus from Edinburgh, Carlisle or Berwick. Open Apr–Sep, daily Mon–Sat 1000–1600, also Sun, Jun–Sep 1400–1600; Oct, Mon–Sat 1300–1600. Free. Guided tours for groups by appointment. Explanatory displays. Gifts for sale. Tearoom. WC. Induction loop. Disabled WC. Car and coach parking. Telephone (01750) 20096.

The bench and chair from which Sir Walter Scott, as Sheriff of Selkirk, administered justice for 30 years are displayed, with portraits of Scott, James Hogg, Mungo Park. Watercolours by Tom Scott RSA. Audio-visual display.

1314 SCOTT'S VIEW **5 P17**

B6356, 4 miles east of Melrose. Access at all times.

A view over the Tweed to the Eildon Hills, beloved by Scott. Here the horses taking his remains to Dryburgh for burial stopped, as they had so often before for Sir Walter to enjoy this panorama.

1315 SEABEGS WOOD **6 L15**

HS. 1 mile (2km) west of Bonnybridge, Stirlingshire. Nearest railway and bus stations Falkirk. Access at all reasonable times. Free. Telephone 0131 668 8800.

A stretch of rampart and ditch of the Antonine Wall with military way behind. See also 62 Antonine Wall.

1316 SEAFOOD CRUISE **2 F8**

8 Forestry Houses, Achmore, by Kyle. Based in Kyle of Lochalsh. Nearest railway station 100 yards (90m) from departure point, bus station adjacent. Collection can be arranged from other locations. Open all year, minimum number of passengers required. Charge £££. Group concessions. Guided tours. Restaurant. Car and coach parking. Telephone (01599) 577230.

Scenic boat tours offering marvellous views of the local scenery and wildlife, and a delicious meal of freshly caught fish and seafood, prepared by the seafood restaurant based in the railway building at Kyle of Lochalsh. A unique and enjoyable experience.

1317 SEA LIFE CENTRE, ST ANDREWS **5 P13**

The Scores, St Andrews, Fife. Nearest railway station Leuchars 4 miles (6.5km), connecting bus to St Andrews. Buses from Dundee and Edinburgh. Open all year (closed Dec 25 and 26 and New Year's Day), daily, 1000–1800; Jul and Aug 0900–1900. Contact centre to confirm opening hours Sep–Jun. Charge ££. Free to wheelchair users. Group concessions. Explanatory displays. Gift shop. Restaurant, coffee shop and picnic area. WC. Limited wheelchair access. Disabled WC. Car and coach parking. Telephone (01334) 474786.

Over 30 dramatic displays of native sea creatures. Everything from shrimps and starfish to sharks and conger eels. Graceful rays nose the surface of their display to watch you watching them. Visitors can see the enchanting resident seals and watch their fluid movements underwater via a special video monitor. Magical Kingdom of the Seahorse exhibition.

1318 SELKIRK GLASS VISITOR CENTRE **5 P17**

Dunsdale Haugh, Selkirk. On the A7 to the north of Selkirk. Bus from Edinburgh or Carlisle. Open all year (except Christmas and New Year), Mon–Fri 0900–1700, Sat 0900–1700, Sun 1100–1700. Free. Explanatory displays. Gift shop. Award-winning coffee shop with patio. WC. Wheelchair access. Disabled WC. Car and coach parking. Telephone (01750) 20954.

Visitors can view the complete glassmaking process (Monday–Friday only to 1630) and can purchase quality rejects and other gifts in the shop.

1319 SETON COLLEGIATE CHURCH **6 N15**

HS. Longniddry, East Lothian. Off the A198, 1 mile (2km) southeast of Cockenzie. Nearest railway station Longniddry, bus to Seton Church road end from Edinburgh or North Berwick. Open Apr–Sep, daily 0930–1830. Charge £. Group concessions. Guided tours. Explanatory displays. Limited wheelchair access. Car and coach parking. Telephone (01875) 813334.

The chancel and apse of a fine 15th-century church. Transept and steeple added in 1513.

1320 SHAMBELLIE HOUSE MUSEUM OF COSTUME **5 L20**

New Abbey, Dumfries. On the A710, 7 miles (11km) south of Dumfries. Bus from Dumfries. Open Easter–Oct, daily 1100–1700 (grounds from 1030). Charge £. Children free. Guided tours (leaflets in French, German and Dutch). Explanatory displays. Gift shop. Tearoom and picnic area. Gardens. WC. Car parking. Telephone (01387) 850375.

A museum housed in a mid-Victorian country house designed by David Bryce. Costume displays in period room settings from the National Museums Collection. An outstation of the National Museums of Scotland.

1321 SHAPE SCAPE CERAMICS **6 P15**

The Pottery, Station Hill, North Berwick, East Lothian. In North Berwick near the station. By rail or bus from Edinburgh. Open Mon–Wed, Fri and Sat, 1000–1300 and 1400–1600. Free. Guided tours by arrangement. Gift shop. No guide dogs. Telephone (01620) 893157.

A pottery for 40 years, now occupied by a ceramicist. Visitors can buy products designed and made at the pottery.

1322 SHAWBOST SCHOOL MUSEUM **2 D3**

Shawbost, Isle of Lewis. 19 miles (31km) northwest of Stornoway. Bus from Stornoway. Open Apr–Nov, Mon–Sat 1000–1800. Donation box. Explanatory displays. WC. Disabled WC. Car and coach parking. Telephone (01851) 710212.

Created under the Highland Village Competition of 1970. The museum illustrates the old way of life in Lewis.

1323 SHETLAND CROFT HOUSE MUSEUM **1 G6**

South Voe, Boddam, Dunrossness, Shetland. On an unclassified road, east of the A970, 25 miles (40km) south of Lerwick. Bus from Lerwick to Boddam. Open May–Sep, daily 1000–1300 and 1400–1700. Charge £. Group concessions. Guided tours. WC. Wheelchair access with assistance. Car and coach parking. Telephone (01595) 695057.

A 19th-century drystone and thatched croft, consisting of inter-connected house, barn, byre, kiln and stable with water-mill nearby. Furnished throughout with period implements, fixtures and furniture. Exhibits include box beds, sea chests, working mill and quern.

1324 SHETLAND MUSEUM **1 G5**

Lower Hillhead, Lerwick, Shetland. In the town centre near the Town Hall. Open Mon, Wed and Fri 1000–1900, Tue, Thu and Sat 1000–1700. Free. Explanatory displays. Gift shop. WC. Wheelchair access. Disabled WC. Car and coach parking. Telephone (01595) 695057.

A museum covering all aspects of Shetland's history and prehistory. Archaeology from neolithic to medieval, including early Christian sculpture, Viking grave finds, medieval domestic and fishing items. Maritime displays cover fisheries, merchant marine and shipwrecks. Models, fishing gear, maritime trades. Agriculture and domestic life collection, including basketwork, peat cutting, 19th-century social history. Costume display and textiles. Temporary art exhibitions.

1325 SHETLAND TEXTILE WORKING MUSEUM **1 G4**

Weisdale Mill, Weisdale, Shetland. 7 miles (11km) west of Lerwick, take A971 and turn right on B9075 for 0.6 mile (1km). Local bus from Lerwick (not Sun) then 0.5 mile (1km) walk. Open all year, Tue–Sat 1030–1600, Sun 1200–1600. Charge £. Children admitted free. Guided tours, staff available to talk about exhibits. Explanatory displays. Café. WC. Wheelchair access. Disabled WC. Car and coach parking. Telephone (01595) 830419.

A unique collection of Shetland textiles illustrating the history of spinning, knitting and weaving in the islands from their earliest development to the present day. Augmented by a fine collection of artefacts used in the production of these items. Workshops in spinning and knitting will be arranged and visitors will have the opportunity to see demonstrations of local craft skills. Housed in the Weisdale Mill.

1326 SHETLAND WILDLIFE TOURS **1 G6**

Longhill, Maywick, Shetland. Pick-up/drop-off service available on all tours, booking essential. Telephone for details of tours. Charge £££ (dependent on tour). Group concessions. Guided tours. Explanatory displays. Telephone (01950) 422493.

Half-day to 7-day wildlife tours throughout the Shetland Islands with expert naturalist guides. See also 1085 Muckle Flugga and Out Stack, and 1131 Noss National Nature Reserve.

1327 SHIELDAIG ISLAND **1 G6**

NTS. Highland. Situated in Loch Torridon, off Shieldaig village, A896. Open all year. Free. Car and coach parking. Telephone (01445) 791368.

This 32 acre (13ha) island is almost entirely covered in Scots pine, which once formed vast forests covering much of the Scottish Highlands.

1328 SHILASDAIR **2 D7**

Carnach, Waternish, Isle of Skye. 22 miles (35km) northwest of Portree on A850, then B886. Open Easter–Oct, daily 1000–1800; other times by appointment. Free. Guided tours. Explanatory displays. Gift shop. Coffee (free). Wheelchair access with assistance. Car and coach parking. Telephone (01470) 592297.

Fleece from the owner's flock of fine wooled sheep is dyed in the traditional Hebridean manner with natural dyes augmented by indigo, logwood and cochineal. A unique range of yarns are available in kits and finished garments.

1329 SHINAFOOT ART STUDIOS **5 L13**

Shinafoot, Dunning Road, Auchterarder, Perthshire. 1 mile (1.5km) north of Auchterarder on B8062. Nearest railway station Gleneagles. Open all year, daily 1000–1700. Free. Car and coach parking. Telephone (01764) 663639.

Year-round art courses and painting holidays for all ages and abilities. Also picture framing, art materials and paintings for sale.

1330 SHOTTS HERITAGE CENTRE **6 L16**

Shotts Library, Benhar Road, Shotts, Lanarkshire. In Shotts town centre. Nearest railway station Shotts, buses from Motherwell or Wishaw. Open all year (except public holidays), Mon and Tue 0930–1900, Wed 0930–1200, Thu–Sat 0930–1700. Free. Guided tours by arrangement (telephone 0141 304 1841). Explanatory displays. Headphone sets. Wheelchair access. Car and coach parking. Telephone (01501) 821556.

Displays three life-size exhibits – Covenanters, a coal mine and 1940s shop front scene. Photographs and illustrations of local history and heritage.

1331 SILVERBURN ESTATE **6 N14**

Largo Road, Leven, Fife. On the A915, to the east of Leven. Bus from Leven. Mini Farm open Mon–Fri 0830–1630, Sat 1400–1600 (winter 1300–1500), Sun 1400–1630 (winter 1300–1530). Estate open all year. Free. Guided tours. Explanatory displays. Gift shop. Picnic areas. Garden, pets corner and mini-farm. WC. Wheelchair access. Disabled WC. Car and coach parking. Telephone (01333) 427568.

Beautiful gardens and mature woodland, with a variety of wildlife, ideal for picnics and outings. Includes several paddocks used for summer grazing for domestic animals and Shetland ponies. The Mini Farm has a collection of farm animals and farm implements. Silverburn House was opened in 1989 as a facility for youth organisations, groups and meetings.

1332 SINCLAIR AND GIRNIGOE CASTLE **3 N3**

Caithness. Noss Head, near Wick.

Built by Earl William Sinclair in the 1470s. The older part of the castle, Girnigoe, dates from between 1476 and 1486. The new wing, locally known as Castle Sinclair, was built in 1607. The castle was largely destroyed during a siege in 1690.

1333 SKAILL HOUSE **1 A10**

Breckness Estate, Sandwick, Orkney. Beside Skara Brae, 5 miles (8km) north of Stromness. No access by public transport. Open Apr–Sep, Mon–Sat 0930–1830, Sun 0930–1830. Charge £. Joint ticket with Skara Brae available from visitor centre. Group concessions. Guided tours. Explanatory displays. Gift shop. Garden. WC. Wheelchair access to ground floor. Disabled WC. Car and coach parking. Telephone (01856) 841501.

The most complete 17th-century mansion house in Orkney. Built for Bishop George Graham in the 1620s, it has been inhabited by successive lairds, who have added to the house over the centuries. On show – Captain Cook's dinner service from his ship the *Resolution*, gunroom with sporting and military memorabilia. Surrounded by spacious gardens. See also 1334 Skara Brae.

1334 SKARA BRAE PREHISTORIC VILLAGE **1 A10**

HS. Sandwick, Orkney. On the B9056, 19 miles (30km) northwest of Kirkwall. Bus from Stromness, tour bus from Kirkwall. Open Apr–Sep, daily 0930–1830; Oct–Mar, Mon–Sat 0930–1630, Sun 1400–1630. Charge ££. During summer joint ticket with Skail House. Group concessions. Guided tours. Explanatory displays. Gift shop. Restaurant, tearoom and picnic area. Limited wheelchair access. Disabled WC. Car and coach parking. Telephone (01856) 841815.

The best preserved group of Stone Age houses in Western Europe. The houses are joined by covered passages and contain stone furniture, hearths and drains. They give a remarkable picture of life in Neolithic times. See also 1333 Skail House.

1335 SKELBO CASTLE **3 L5**

Located north of Dornoch at Skelbo, Sutherland.

This site was probably chosen by invading Norsemen for the protection of the ships, beached on the shores of Loch Fleet, in the 9th century. The ruins can be seen from the roadside.

1336 SKERRYVORE LIGHTHOUSE MUSEUM **4 C12**

Hynish, Isle of Tiree. At Hynish village, western Tiree. Ferry from Oban, by air from Glasgow. Open all year during daylight. Free. Donations. Explanatory displays. Teas available during summer. Car parking. Telephone (01865) 311468.

Located in the old signal tower, the museum tells the story of the construction of the lighthouse visible for over 10 miles (16km) off shore. Skerryvore lighthouse was constructed on the infamous reef of the same name, by a team led by Alan Stevenson (uncle of Robert Louis Stevenson).

1337 SKIPNESS CASTLE AND CHAPEL **4 G16**

HS. On the coast at Skipness on the B8001, 10 miles (16km) south of Tarbert, Argyll. Bus from Tarbert to Skipness, then 0.5 mile (1km) walk. Exterior view only. Car parking. Telephone 0131 668 8800.

A fine 13th-century castle with a 16th-century tower house in one corner. Nearby is an early 14th-century chapel with fine grave slabs.

1338 SKYE ENVIRONMENTAL CENTRE

See 837 International Otter Survival Fund..

1339 SKYE MUSEUM OF ISLAND LIFE 2 D7

Kilmuir, Isle of Skye. On the A855, 5 miles (8km) north of Uig. Bus from Portree to Kilmuir, ask driver for museum stop. Open Apr–Oct, Mon–Sat 0930–1730. Charge £. Group concessions. Guided tours. Explanatory displays. Gift shop. WC. Wheelchair access. Disabled WC. Car and coach parking. Telephone (01420) 552206.

An interesting museum of rural life housed within a group of thatched cottages. It depicts the lifestyle of the crofting community of the island a century or so ago and displays a wide range of agricultural tools and implements. One house is furnished with period furniture.

1340 SKYE SERPENTARIUM 2 E9

The Old Mill, Harrapool, Broadford, Isle of Skye. On the A850, 8 miles (13km) northwest of Kyleakin. Nearest railway station Kyle of Lochalsh, buses from Kyle, Kyleakin or Armadale. Open Easter–Oct, 1000–1700, Sun in Jul and Aug and bank holidays. Charge £. Group concessions. Guided tours for groups by arrangement. Explanatory displays. Gift shop. Wheelchair access with assistance. Car and coach parking. Telephone (01471) 822209.

A unique award-winning reptile exhibition and breeding centre in a converted water mill. Visitors can watch a world of snakes, lizards, frogs and tortoises in bright natural surroundings. Also a refuge for neglected and illegally imported reptiles. Frequent informative snake handling sessions. Baby snakes for sale.

1341 SKYESKYNS 2 D7

17 Loch Bay, Waternish, Isle of Skye. On the B886, 4.5 miles (7km) from the A850, 19 miles (30km) north of Portree. Kyle station, bus from Portree or Kyle. Open Apr–Oct, daily 1000–1800. Free. Guided tours (available in French and German). Explanatory displays. Gift shop. WC. Limited wheelchair access. Car and coach parking. Telephone (01470) 592237.

Showroom visitors are offered guided tours of the tanning workshop, the only one of its kind in Scotland. They can see the traditional tools of the trade in use – the beam, paddles, drum, buffing wheel and combs. Demonstrations of rare tanning skills and hand-finishing of finest lambswool rugs. Wide range of leather goods.

1342 SKYE WOOLLEN MILL 2 E8

Dunvegan Road, Portree, Isle of Skye. 0.5 mile (2km) from Portree centre on the Dunvegan road. Bus from Portree. Open Easter–Oct, Mon–Sat 0900–1730, Sun 1100–1600; Nov–Mar, Mon–Sat 1000–1600. Free. Explanatory displays. Gift shop. Coffee shop. WC. Wheelchair access. Car and coach parking. Telephone (01478) 612889.

A woollen mill with over 100 years of history features tweeds and tartans, including the Isle of Skye tartan. Also knitwear and souvenirs.

1343 SMAILHOLM TOWER 5 P17

HS. Off the B6404, 6 miles (9.5km) northwest of Kelso, Roxburghshire. Occasional bus from Kelso and St Boswells then 1.5 mile (2.5km) walk. Open Apr–Sep, daily 0930–1830. Charge £. Group concessions. Guided tours. Explanatory displays. Gift shop. Car and coach parking. Telephone (01573) 460365.

A small rectangular 16th-century Border peel tower sited on a rocky outcrop within a stone barmkin wall. Well preserved and containing an exhibition of costume figures and tapestries relating to Sir Walter Scott's *Minstrelsy of the Scottish Borders*. Scott spent some of his childhood at nearby Sandyknowe Farm.

1344 ROBERT SMAIL'S PRINTING WORKS **5 N17**

NTS. 7–9 High Street, Innerleithen, Peebleshire. In Innerleithen, 30 miles (48km) south of Edinburgh. Buses from Edinburgh or Peebles. Open Easter and May–Sep, Mon–Sat 1000–1300 and 1400–1700, Sun 1400–1700; weekends in Oct, Sat 1000–1300 and 1400–1700, Sun 1400–1700. Charge £. Children free. Group concessions. Guided tours. Explanatory displays. Gift shop. Limited wheelchair access. Car and coach parking. Telephone (01896) 830206.

Restored printing works using machinery and methods of the early 20th century. Visitors can watch the printer at work and try setting type by hand. Victorian office with many historic items. Reconstructed water wheel.

1345 SMALL WORLD VISITOR CENTRE **3 L7**

Darnaway, Brodie, Forres. South from A96 after Brodie. Nearest railway station Forres 3 miles (5km); local bus service. Open all year, daily 1030–1630. Free. Guided tours. Explanatory displays. Gift shop. Restaurant and picnic area. Indoor children's activity area. WC. Wheelchair access. Disabled WC. Car and coach parking. Telephone (01309) 641677.

Factory manufacturing hand-painted figurines. Visitors can watch the production process and try painting a figurine themselves. Indoor and outdoor children's play areas and bouncy castle.

1346 SMA' SHOT COTTAGES **6 J16**

11–17 George Place, Paisley. By rail or bus from Glasgow. Open Apr–Sep, Wed and Sat 1300–1700. Free. Guided tours. Gift shop. Tearoom. Garden. WC. Limited wheelchair access. Car parking. Telephone 0141 889 1708.

A former 18th-century weaver's cottage, with domestic accommodation and loom shop, linked by a garden to a 19th-century artisan's house; both fully furnished. Exhibition of historic photographs and a fine collection of china and linen.

1347 SMITH ART GALLERY AND MUSEUM **6 L14**

Dumbarton Road, Stirling. In Stirling, a short walk from the bus and rail stations. On Stirling Heritage bus route. Open all year, Tue–Sat 1030–1700, Sun 1400–1700. Free. Guided tours for special exhibitions. Explanatory displays. Gift shop. Tearoom. WC. Induction loop. Wheelchair access. Disabled WC. Car and coach parking. Telephone (01786) 471917.

Displays and exhibitions on the history of Stirling. Fine art, natural history. Educational programme (telephone for details).

1348 SMITHY HERITAGE CENTRE **2 G8**

Lochcarron, Strathcarron, Ross and Cromarty. On the A896, 1 mile (2km) east of Lochcarron. Strathcarron railway station 1.5 miles (2.5km). Open Easter–Oct, Mon–Sat 1000–1730. Free. Guided tours by arrangement (available in Gaelic). Explanatory displays with video. Picnic area. Plantation. Wheelchair access. Car and coach parking. Telephone (01520) 722246.

A restored smithy with information on the history of the building, the business and the blacksmith who worked in it. Walk through plantation of native trees. Speakers, demonstrations and crafts at advertised times.

1349 SMOO CAVES **3 J2**

In Durness, Sutherland.

This impressive limestone cave has formed at the head of a narrow coastal inlet. An easy and safe access path has been made from the road above leading into the cave. With its entrance at least 100 feet (30m) wide this is arguably one of the largest cave entrances in Britain. A wooden pathway extends into the cave and allows viewing of the second inner chamber where the Allt Smoo falls from an opening in the roof above. In the outer cave there is an ancient midden which would indicate that Stone Age man once lived here.

1350 SMOO INNERCAVE TOURS **3 J2**

11 Druimbhlar, Durness, Sutherland. By train from Inverness, bus from Inverness during summer. Open Apr–Sep, daily (weather permitting). Charge £. Group concessions. Guided tours (available in Dutch, French, German, Italian and Spanish). Explanatory displays. WC. Car and coach parking. Telephone (01971) 511704.

A 15-minute boat trip to and walking tour of Smoo Innercave, featuring the cave and its natural history, archaeology and geology.

1351 SOPHIE'S PUPPENSTUBE AND DOLLS HOUSE MUSEUM **4 J20**

29 Queen Street, Newton Stewart. In Newton Stewart, 100 yards (91m) from the bus terminus. Open Apr–Oct, Mon–Sat 1000–1700; Nov–Christmas and Mar, Tue–Sat 1000–1600. Charge £. Group concessions. Explanatory displays. Guides (also available in German). Gift shop. Baby changing facilities. WC. Wheelchair access. Disabled WC. Car and coach parking. Telephone (01671) 403344.

A high quality collection of over 50 inhabited house displays which show life through the ages from home and abroad in one-twelfth scale. The displays are complemented by over 200 dolls, most of which have been specially commissioned for the individual settings.

1352 SOUTAR HOUSE **5 M13**

27 Wilson Street, Perth. In Craigie, Perth. Within 0.5 mile (1km) of Perth railway and bus station; local bus service. Open by prior arrangement. Free. Guided tours. Explanatory displays. Garden. Wheelchair access with assistance. Telephone (01738) 643687.

This is the former home of the Perth poet William Soutar. The room where he lay bedridden for 14 years, his father's wood panelling of most of the ground floor of the house and the stained glass have been meticulously preserved. Part of Soutar's library has been restored to his room, together with copies of his work, photographs and settings of some of his poems to music by contemporary composers from Benjamin Britten to James Macmillan.

1353 SOUTER JOHNNIE'S COTTAGE **4 H18**

NTS. Main Road, Kirkoswald, Ayrshire. On A77 in Kirkoswald, 4 miles (6.5km) southwest of Maybole. Buses from Ayr or Girvan. Open Easter–Sep and weekends in Oct, daily 1130–1700. Charge £. Children free. Group concessions. Explanatory displays. Cottage garden. Limited wheelchair access. Car and coach parking. Telephone (01655) 760603.

Thatched cottage, home of the souter (cobbler) who inspired the character Souter Johnnie in Robert Burns' poem *Tam o'Shanter*. Burns memorabilia and reconstructed workshop. Restored alehouse with life-size stone figures of Burns' characters.

1354 SOUTH BANK FARM PARK **4 G18**

East Bennan, Isle of Arran. 14 miles (22.5km) south of Brodick. Ferry to Brodick, bus from Brodick. Limited coach parking. Open Easter–Sep, Tue, Thu and Sun 1000–1700. Charge £. Group concessions. Maps provided.

Picnic area. Garden, pets corner. WC. Limited wheelchair access. Car parking. Telephone (01770) 820221.

A 60 acre (24ha) working farm exhibiting various rare and minority breeds of farm animals – poultry, Highland cattle, red deer, Clydesdale horses. Farm trail and superb views. Sheepdog demonstrations on Tuesday, Thursday and Sunday, 1430.

1355 SOUTH LISSENS POTTERY **6 M14**

22 Church Street, Milnathort, Kinross. In Milnathort, 2 miles (3km) from Kinross tourist information centre. Nearest railway station Perth, buses from Perth or Edinburgh. Open all year, Mon–Sat (closed Wed) 1000–1800, Sun 1200–1700 (closed Christmas and New Year). Free. Gift shop. WC. Wheelchair access. Car parking. Telephone (01577) 865642.

A pottery workshop located in an old Presbyterian church built in 1769. Traditional country pottery and contemporary pots decorated with unusual lustre effects.

1356 SOUTRA AISLE **6 N16**

Soutrahill, Midlothian. 0.5 miles (1km) south of A68 or 7 miles (11km) north of A7 on B6368, near Gilston. Bus via A68 from Edinburgh to Jedburgh/Kelso; alight at B6368 road end, then 6 minute walk to hill-top. Access at all times. Free. Guided tours by arrangement (available in French and Spanish). Wheelchair access. Car and coach parking. Telephone (01875) 833248.

Midway between Edinburgh and the magnificent Borders abbeys from the 12th century to the 17th century stood Soutra medieval hospital; a refuge for wayfarers and the needy high on the Royal Road, the main Anglo-Scottish highway. Midway, still, on modern roads, is the site of the great hospital, the spectacular viewpoint, the memorial Aisle and the unique archaeo-medical investigations.

1357 SPEAN BRIDGE WOOLLEN MILL **2 H10**

Spean Bridge, Inverness-shire. On the bridge at Spean Bridge next to Spean Bridge railway station. Bus from Fort William. Open Apr–Sep, Mon–Sat 0900–1730, Sun 1000–1630; Oct–Mar, daily 1000–1600. Free. Explanatory displays. Gift shop. Restaurant. Garden. WC. Wheelchair access. Disabled WC. Car and coach parking. Telephone (01397) 712260.

A picturesque weaving mill in a former farm steading. Angus McLeod, resident weaver, demonstrates his craft, weaving tartan and tweed. Clan Tartan Centre, whisky tasting, knitwear and gifts.

1358 SPEYSIDE COOPERAGE VISITOR CENTRE **3 N8**

Dufftown Road, Craigellachie, Banffshire. On the A941, 1 mile (2km) south of Craigellachie. Buses from Dufftown or Elgin. Open all year Mon–Fri, also Sat at Easter and Jun–Sep, 0930–1630. Charge £. Group concessions. Guided tours (available in French and German). Explanatory displays (in French, German, Italian, Spanish and Japanese). Gift shop. Light refreshments and picnic area. Baby changing facilities. WC. Limited wheelchair access. Disabled WC. Car and coach parking. Telephone (01340) 871108.

Award-winning working cooperage with unique visitor centre. Visitors can watch skilled coopers and apprentices repairing oak casks for the whisky industry. An exhibition traces the history and development of the cooperage industry. Shop specializes in quality wooden items. Highland cattle can be seen.

1359 SPEYSIDE HEATHER CENTRE **3 L9**

Skye of Curr, Dulnain Bridge, Inverness-shire. Off the A95, 9 miles (14.5km) from Aviemore. Nearest railway station Aviemore, then bus to

Dulnain Bridge. Open Feb–Dec, daily 0900–1800 (slightly reduced times in winter). Charge £. Group concessions. Guided tours (text in 12 languages). Explanatory displays. Gift shop. Tearoom/restaurant and picnic area. Play area and show garden. WC. Wheelchair access. Disabled WC. Car and coach parking. Telephone (01479) 851359.

An exhibition, craft shop, garden centre and show garden, with heather as a speciality. Includes the famous Clootie Dumpling Restaurant and a gallery and antiques shop.

1360 SPEYSIDE HORN AND COUNTRY CRAFTS **3 L9**

Rowan Tree Restaurant, Loch Alvie, Aviemore, Inverness-shire. On the B9152, 2 miles (3km) south of Aviemore. Nearest railway station Aviemore, then limited bus service (suggest taxi). Open Mar–Oct, Mon–Sat 1000–1800. Free. Guided tours and workshop demonstrations. Explanatory displays. Gift shop. Tearoom. WC. Wheelchair access. Car and coach parking. Telephone (01479) 811503.

Visitors can hear about and see the wide variety of horns still used today and see a demonstration in which craftsmen demonstrate the techniques developed by the Scottish tinkers.

1361 SPEY VALLEY SMOKEHOUSE **3 M8**

Achnagonalin, Grantown on Spey. At the outskirts of Grantown-on-Spey on the B970. Open all year, Mon–Fri 0900–1700; also Apr–Sep, Sat and Sun 1000–1300. Free. Explanatory displays and audio-visual presentation. Gift shop. Picnic area. Children's play area. WC. Wheelchair access. Disabled WC. Car and coach parking. Telephone (01479) 873078.

With a history of salmon smoking since 1888, the Spey Valley Smokehouse offers visitors the opportunity to experience the traditional smoking process in the most modern facilities: the curing and hanging of whole salmon sides. Gourmet salmon products available for purchase.

1362 SPLIT STONE, MELVICH **3 L2**

1 mile (1.5km) east of Melvich in the north of Sutherland.

Local history says that an old woman was returning from a shopping trip and was chased by the devil. She ran round and round the stone and the devil in his temper split it. The woman escaped.

1363 SPRINGBANK DISTILLERY **4 F18**

Campbeltown. In the centre of Campbeltown. Local bus service. Open Easter–Sep, tour Mon–Thu 1400 by appointment only. Charge £. Guided tours. WC. Limited wheelchair access. Car parking. Telephone (01586) 552085.

Founded in 1828, the distillery remains under the control of the great-great grandson of the original founder. Springfield Distillery is the only distillery in Scotland to carry out one hundred per cent of the process from traditional malting through to bottling.

1364 SPYNIE PALACE **3 M7**

HS. Elgin, Morayshire. Off the A941, 2 miles (3km) north of Elgin. Nearest railway station Elgin, buses from Aberdeen or Inverness, then bus to Spynie. Open Apr–Sep, daily 0930–1830; Oct–Mar Sat 0930–1630, Sun 1400–1630. Charge £. Group concessions. Guided tours. Gift shop. Picnic area. WC. Limited wheelchair access. Car and coach parking. Telephone (01343) 546358.

The residence of the bishops of Moray from the 14th century to 1686. Dominated by the massive tower built by Bishop David Stewart in the 15th century, with spectacular views of Spynie Loch.

1365 STAFFA 4 D12

NTS. Island 6 miles (10km) north east of Iona and 7 miles (11km) west of Mull, Argyll. Boat cruises from Iona, Mull or Oban. Open all year. Landing charge £. Guided tours by boat. Telephone NTS Regional Office (01631) 570000.

Romantic uninhabited island famed for its extraordinary basaltic column formations. The best known of these is Fingal's Cave, inspiration for Mendelssohn's Hebrides overture. Visitors can view the cave from a boat, or land on the island if weather conditions permit. A colony of puffins nests on the island.

1366 STANYDALE TEMPLE 1 F4

HS. 3.5 miles (5.5km) east northeast of Walls, Shetland. Bus from Lerwick to Bridge of Walls. Access at all times. Free. Telephone 0131 668 8800.

A Neolithic hall, heel-shaped externally and containing a large oval chamber. Surrounded by the ruins of houses, walls and cairns of the same period.

1367 STEINACLEIT CAIRN AND STONE CIRCLE 2 D3

HS. At the south end of Loch an Duin, Shader, 12 miles (19km) north of Stornoway, Isle of Lewis (Western Isles). Ferry from Ullapool to Stornoway, then bus service from Stornoway to Saidar Larach. Access at all times. Free. Telephone 0131 668 8800.

The remains of an enigmatic building of early prehistoric date.

1368 STENTON GALLERY 5 P15

Stenton, East Lothian. On the B6370, 3 miles (5km) from the A1 at East Linton. Transport can be arranged for groups. Open Fri–Wed, 1200–1700 during exhibitions (telephone for details). Free. Talks, lectures and demonstrations. Coffee available. WC. Wheelchair access with assistance. Car parking. Telephone (01368) 850256.

Shows the best of contemporary art from Scotland and elsewhere. Regularly changing programme of exhibitions.

1369 STEVENSON HOUSE 6 P15

Haddington, East Lothian. 2 miles (3km) from Haddington and 1.5 miles (2.5km) from the A1. Local buses to Haddington. House open daily in Jul except Fri; gardens open daily Apr–Oct. Charge £. Guided tours at 1500. Coffee and tea for parties by arrangement. Garden. Wheelchair access to garden only. Car and coach parking. Telephone (01620) 823217.

A mansion dating from the 13th century when it belonged to the Cistercian Nunnery at Haddington. Partially destroyed on several occasions and uninhabitable in 1544. Restored in 1560, with later 18th-century additions. Fine furniture and pictures.

1370 STEWARTRY MUSEUM 5 K21

St Mary Street, Kirkcudbright. In Kirkcudbright centre. Nearest railway station Dumfries, bus from Dumfries. Open May, Jun and Sep, Mon–Sat 1100–1700, Jul and Aug, Mon–Sat 1000–1800 (Jun–Sep, Sun 1400–1700); Oct–Apr, Mon–Sat 1100–1600. Charge £. Children free. Group concessions. Guided tours for groups by arrangement. Explanatory displays. Gift shop. Picnic area. WC. Limited wheelchair access. Telephone (01557) 331643.

A wide range of exhibits reflecting the social and natural history of the Stewartry of Kirkcudbright. Features illustrations, pottery and jewellery by Jessie M. King and the work of her husband, E. A. Taylor, Phyllis Bone and other Kirkcudbright artists. Special temporary exhibitions, family and local history information services.

1371 STIRLING CASTLE 6 L14

HS. Castle Wynd, Stirling. At the head of Stirling old town, off the M9. Nearest railway station Stirling, buses from Glasgow and Edinburgh. Open Apr–Sep, daily 0930–1800; Oct–Mar daily 0930–1700. Charge £££. Charge includes admission to Argyll's Lodging. Group concessions. Guided tours. Explanatory displays. Gift shop. Restaurant, tearoom and picnic area. WC. Wheelchair access. Disabled WC. Car and coach parking. Telephone (01786) 450000.

Considered by many as Scotland's grandest castle – certainly one of the most important. The castle architecture is outstanding – the Great Hall and Chapel Royal are amongst the highlights. Mary Queen of Scots was crowned here and narrowly escaped death by fire in 1561. Medieval kitchen display and exhibition on life in the royal palace. See also 88 Argyll and Sutherland Highlanders Regimental Museum.

1372 STIRLING OLD BRIDGE 6 L14

HS. In Stirling just beside the Customs Roundabout off the A9. Nearest railway station Stirling, buses from Glasgow and Edinburgh. Access at all times. Free. Telephone 0131 668 8800.

A handsome bridge built in the 15th or early 16th century. The southern arch was rebuilt in 1749 after it had been blown up during the '45 rebellion to prevent the Stuart army entering the town.

1373 STIRLING OLD TOWN JAIL 6 L14

St John Street, Stirling. At the top of the Old Town in Stirling, 5 minute walk from rail and bus stations. Nearest railway station Stirling, tour bus in summer. Open Apr–late Sep, daily 0930–1800; late Sep–late Oct, daily 0930–1700; late Oct–Mar, daily 0930–1600 (closed Christmas and New Year). Charge £. Group concessions. Guided tours (available in French, German, Italian and Spanish). Explanatory displays. Gift shop. Garden and grounds. WC. Scripts for the deaf. Limited wheelchair access. Disabled WC. Car parking. Telephone (01786) 450050.

A 150-year-old Victorian Gothic jail, once a military and a civil establishment. In summer, living history performances detail crime and punishment through the ages. Audio tour in winter.

1374 STOCKS STONES AND STORIES, EXHIBITION OF CRIEFF STOCKS AND CROSSES 5 L13

c/o Crieff Tourist Information Centre, Town Hall, High Street, Crieff. In Crieff town centre. Bus from Perth (service 15) and Stirling (service 47). Open Apr–Jun and Sep–Oct, Mon–Sat 0930–1730, Sun 1100–1600; Jun–Aug, Mon–Sat 0900–1900, Sun 1100–1800; Nov–Mar, Mon–Fri 0930–1700, Sat 1000–1400. Free. Explanatory displays. WC. Wheelchair access with assistance. Car and coach parking. Telephone (01764) 652578.

A fascinating exhibition in the basement of Crieff Town Hall, housing three of the town's conserved historical monuments: the Crieff Burgh Cross (a Pictish cross slab of the 9th century); the Drummond or Mercat Cross; and the town stocks – unique in design. Panels giving historical and conservation information for each object.

1375 STONES OF STENNESS 1 B10

HS. Between Loch of Harray and Loch of Stenness, about 5 miles (8km) northeast of Stromness, Orkney. Buses from Kirkwall or Stromness. Access at all times. Free. Car and coach parking. Telephone 0131 668 8800.

The remains of a stone circle surrounded by remains of a circular earthwork. See also 1219 Ring of Brodgar.

1376 STORR 2 E7

Two miles (3km) from A855, 8 miles (12.5km) north of Portree, Isle of Skye. Free. Car parking.

A series of pinnacles and crags rising to 2360 feet (719m). No access, but can be seen from the road. The Old Man of Storr, at the east end of the mountain, is a black obelisk, (160 feet/49m) high, first climbed in 1955. Visitors can see Storr from the main road; due to erosion it is now closed to walkers.

1377 STORYBOOK GLEN **3 Q10**

Maryculter, Aberdeen. On the B9077, 6 miles (9.5km) west of Aberdeen. Nearest railway station Aberdeen, bus from Aberdeen to Peterculter, then 1 mile (2km) walk. Open Mar–Oct, daily 1000–1800; Nov–Feb, weekends only 1100–1600. Charge ££. Group concessions. Explanatory displays. Gift shop. Restaurant and picnic area. WC. Wheelchair access. Disabled WC. Car and coach parking. Telephone (01224) 732941.

A 28 acres (11.5ha) spectacular theme park with over 100 models of nursery rhymes, old and new, set in beautiful scenic gardens. McDonald farm with all the usual animals.

1378 STRACHUR SMIDDY MUSEUM **4 G14**

The Clachan, Strachur, Argyll. On the A815 beside Loch Fyne, 20 miles (32km) north of Dunoon and 20 miles (32km) east of Inveraray. Buses from Dunoon or Inveraray. Open Easter–Sep, daily 1300–1600. Charge £. Group concessions. Guided tours. Explanatory displays. Gift shop. WC. Wheelchair access. Disabled WC. Car and coach parking. Telephone (01369) 860565.

Dating from before 1790, now restored to working order. On display are bellows, anvil, boring beam, hammers, tongs and other tools of the blacksmith and the farrier. Occasional demonstrations. Also a craft shop with a selection of modern craftwork.

1379 STRANRAER MUSEUM **4 G20**

Old Town Hall, George Street, Stranraer. In town centre, 5 minutes walk from ferry terminals. Nearest railway station Stranraer, trains from Glasgow and Ayr. Open all year, Mon–Fri 1000–1700, Sat 1000–1300 and 1400–1700 (closed on bank holidays). Free. Explanatory displays. Gift shop. WC. Wheelchair access. Disabled WC. Telephone (01776) 705088.

Permanent display on local history, archaeology, farming and polar exploration. Temporary exhibition programme throughout the year with supporting educational and family activities. Enquiry and identification service available.

1380 STRATHCLYDE COUNTRY PARK **6 K16**

366 Hamilton Road, Motherwell, Lanarkshire. 10 miles (16km) south of Glasgow on the M74, exit at junction 5 or 6. Nearest railway station Motherwell, buses from Motherwell and Hamilton. M&D's Theme Park (located in park) provide special bus service at weekends/public holidays. Park grounds open all year daily, dawn–dusk; watersports centre open daily 0800–2000. Free. Charge for watersports (group concessions by prior arrangement). Guided tours. Explanatory displays in visitor centre. Restaurant, tearoom, barbeque and picnic areas. Ranger service. WC. Wheelchair access. Disabled WC. Car and coach parking. Telephone (01698) 266155.

A 1000 acre (404ha) countryside park set in the Clyde valley. Artificial lake, mixed parkland and woodlands, and a variety of recreational facilities, including watersports. Woodland trails, countryside walks, sports pitches, sandy beaches, a caravan site, a hotel, an inn and Scotland's first theme park. Visitor centre depicts the history and wildlife of the park. Also Roman bathhouse (remains in the park).

1381 STRATHEARN RECREATION CENTRE **5 L13**

Pittenzie Road, Crieff. Adjacent to Crieff High School. Open all year (except 25/26 Dec and 1/2 Jan), daily 0700–2200. Charge £. Children under 5, carers of disabled and spectators free. Group concessions.

Explanatory displays. Vending machines. WC. Wheelchair access. Disabled WC. Car and coach parking. Telephone (01764) 653779.

Heated swimming pool, fitness suite and fully equipped sports hall offering table tennis, basketball, indoor bowls, football, volleyball, badminton and many other activities.

1382 STRATHISLA DISTILLERY **3 N7**

Seafield Avenue, Keith, Banffshire. In Keith. Nearest railway station Keith, then 5 minute walk. Bus from Aberdeen or Elgin. Open Feb–Mar, Mon–Fri 0930–1600; Apr–Nov, Mon–Sat 0930–1600, Sun 1230–1600. Charge ££. Includes shop voucher. Under 18s free; children under 8 not admitted to production areas. Guided tours. Reception centre with video presentation. Self-guided tours with coffee and shortbread (and sample whisky). Handbook. Gift shop. WC. Limited wheelchair access. Disabled WC. Car and coach parking. Telephone (01542) 783042.

The oldest working distillery in the Highlands, established in 1786, and home to Chivas Regal blended Scotch whisky. Self-guided tour of the distillery and guided tour of the fitting store and warehouses. Whisky tasting.

1383 STRATHNAVER MUSEUM **3 K3**

Clachan, Bettyhill, Thurso, Sutherland. 12 miles (19km) east of Tongue. Bus from Thurso. Open Apr–Oct, Mon–Sat 1000–1300 and 1400–1700; telephone to arrange admission during winter. Charge £. Group concessions. Guided tours. Explanatory displays. Gift shop. Limited wheelchair access. Car and coach parking. Telephone (01641) 521418.

A local museum housed in the former parish church of Farr. Shows the story of the Strathnaver Clearances and the Clan Mackay. Collection of local artefacts, including prehistoric and Pictish items, and the Ian Grimble collection of history books.

1384 STRATHSPEY STEAM RAILWAY **3 L9**

Aviemore Station, Dalfaber Road, Aviemore. 35 miles (56km) south of Inverness. Nearest railway station Aviemore, buses from Edinburgh, Inverness and Perth. Daily service Easter–Oct, but see timetable. Charge £££. Group concessions. Explanatory displays. Gift shop. Refreshments on train. WC. Wheelchair access. Disabled WC. Car and coach parking. Telephone (01479) 810725.

A steam railway, re-opened in 1978, and running between Aviemore and Boat of Garten (5 miles).

1385 STROMNESS MUSEUM **1 B10**

52 Alfred Street, Stromness, Orkney. Open May–Sep, daily 1000–1700; Oct–Apr, Mon–Sat 1030–1230 and 1330–1700. Charge £. Group concessions. Explanatory displays. Gift shop. WC. Wheelchair access. Disabled WC. Car parking. Telephone (01856) 850025.

A museum of Orkney maritime history and natural history – birds, eggs, fossils, butterfiles and moths, fishing, whaling, Hudson's Bay Company, the German fleet in Scapa Flow. Changing exhibitions.

1386 STRONSAY FISH MART INTERPRETATION CENTRE **1 C10**

Stronsay, Orkney. At ferry pier, Stronsay. By air or ferry from Kirkwall. Open all year, daily according to ferry timetable. Free. Guided tours. Explanatory displays. Gift shop. Tearoom. WC. Wheelchair access. Disabled WC. Telephone (01857) 616213.

A visual collection of herring fishing and farming memorabilia from Victorian times.

1387 STRUIE VIEWPOINT **3 K6**

South of Dornoch Firth on B9176.

Overlooking the picturesque Dornoch Firth. The Sutherland mountains are marked on an indicator board.

1388 STUART CRYSTAL **5 I13**

Muthill Road, Crieff, Perthshire. Bus service from Stirling. Open Jun–Sep, daily 1000–1800; Oct–May 1000–1700. Free. Explanatory displays. Gift shop. Tearoom. WC. Wheelchair access. Disabled WC. Car and coach parking. Telephone (01764) 654004.

Retail factory shop selling quality Stuart and Waterford crystal and Wedgwood china as well as seconds. Children's play area.

1389 JOHN MCDOUALL STUART MUSEUM **6 N14**

Rectory Lane, Dysart, Kirkcaldy, Fife. In Dysart, 2 miles (3km) east of Kirkcaldy. Bus from Kirkcaldy. Open Jun–Aug, daily 1400–1700. Free. Explanatory displays. Gift shop. WC. Telephone (01592) 412860.

An exhibition about the great 19th-century explorer of Australia, located in the house where he was born. There is a small permanent exhibition about Stuart and about the history of Dysart.

1390 STUDIO JEWELLERY WORKSHOP AND GALLERY **2 H7**

Achnasheen, Ross and Cromarty. At railway station in Achnasheen. Nearest railway station Achnasheen. Open all year, daily 0900–1730. Free. Explanatory displays. Gift shop. Café and picnic area. Children's play area. WC. Wheelchair access. Disabled WC. Car and coach parking. Telephone (01445) 720227.

Craft centre incorporating jewellery/silversmithing workshop. Viewing windows allow visitors to watch work going on, but demonstrations are not given. Silver and gold jewellery and small silverware are on sale, together with other craft items. Rare breed sheep and ducks.

1391 SUENO'S STONE **3 M7**

HS. At the east end of Forres, Moray. Nearest railway station Forres or Elgin, bus from Elgin. Access at all times. Free. Car parking. Telephone 0131 668 8800.

The most remarkable sculptured monument in Britain, standing over 20 feet (6m) high (now enclosed in glass). Probably a cenotaph dating from the end of the first millennium AD.

1392 SUMMER ISLES CRUISES **2 G5**

1 Royal Park, Ullapool, Ross-shire. 55 miles (88km) northwest of Inverness on A835. Bus from Inverness. Open Apr–Oct; 4-hour trip, Mon–Sat 1000; 2-hour trip, daily 1415 also Sun 1100. Group concessions. Limited wheelchair access. Coach parking. Telephone (01854) 612472.

An attractive group of islands, the largest of which is Tanera Mhor. Pleasure cruises give views of seals, birdlife and extraordinary rock formations. A 4-hour cruise takes in all the Summer Isles and lands on Tanera Mhor where visitors can purchase the unique Summer Isles stamp. Also a 2-hour cruise around Isle Martin.

1393 SUMMERLEE HERITAGE PARK **6 K16**

Heritage Way, Coatbridge, Lanarkshire. In the centre of Coatbridge near the stations. Nearest railway station Coatbridge, bus from Glasgow. Open daily, Apr–Oct 1000–1700; Nov–Mar 1000–1600 (closed 25/26 Dec and 1 Jan). Free. Charge for tram ride. Guided tours of mine. Explanatory displays. Gift shop. Tearoom and picnic areas. Play area and extensive grounds. WC. Limited wheelchair access. Disabled WC. Car and coach parking. Telephone (01236) 431261.

Summerlee Heritage Park is described as Scotland's noisiest museum, interpreting the history of the local steel and engineering industries and of the communities that depend upon them. It contains reconstructed miners rows, a mines and a tramway. Guided tours include the coalmine where visitors go underground and see the workings of a mine.

The Ironworks Gallery houses a programme of temporary exhibitions. Workshops and craft demonstrations also held regularly.

1394 SWEETHEART ABBEY **5 L20**

HS. New Abbey, Dumfries. 7 miles (11km) south of Dumfries. Nearest railway station Dumfries; bus from Dumfries and Dalbeattie. Open Apr–Sep, daily 0930–1830; Oct–Mar, Mon–Sat 0930–1830, Sun 1400–1630 (closed Thu pm and Fri). Charge £. Group concessions. Guided tours. WC. Limited wheelchair access. Disabled WC. Car and coach parking. Telephone (01387) 850397.

Splendid ruin of a late 13th- century and early 14th-century Cistercian abbey founded by Dervorgilla, Lady of Galloway, in memory of her husband John Balliol. Apart from the abbey, the principal feature is the well-preserved precinct wall, enclosing 30 acres (12ha).

1395 TAIGH CHEARSABHAGH MUSEUM ARTS CENTRE **2 B7**

Lochmaddy, North Uist, Western Isles. 109 yards (100m) from Lochmaddy Pier. Open Feb–Dec. Charge £. Children under 12 free. Group concessions. Explanatory displays. Gift shop. Tearoom. WC. Wheelchair access. Disabled WC. Car and coach parking. Telephone (01876) 500293.

Local museum and art gallery.

1396 TAIN THROUGH TIME **3 K6**

Tower Street, Tain, Ross and Cromarty. 1 mile (2km) off A9. Railway station and bus stations Tain. Open Easter–Oct, daily 1000–1800; Nov–Mar, Sat 1200–1600; other times by appointment. Charge ££. Carers/group leaders free. Group concessions. Guided tours. Explanatory displays. Gift shop. Churchyard with seats. WC. Wheelchair access with assistance. Disabled WC. Car and coach parking. Telephone (01862) 894089.

Part of Tain and District Museum, also St Duthus Chapel and Collegiate Church, which was an important medieval pilgrimage site with buildings dating from the 12th century. The Pilgrimage Visitor Centre has displays and audio-visual interpretation of the history of Tain as a centre of pilgrimage.

1397 TAIT AND STYLE **1 B10**

Old Academy, Back Road, Stromness, Orkney. In Stromness, short walk from centre. Open May–Sep, Mon–Fri 1100–1300 and 1400–1600, Sat 1000–1300 (closed Sun and local holidays). Free. Gift shop. WC. Wheelchair access. Disabled WC. Car and coach parking. Telephone (01856) 851186.

A workshop and showroom where visitors can see a collection of pure wool fashion and furnishing accessories hand-crafted from a specially developed felting technique.

1398 TALISKER DISTILLERY VISITOR CENTRE **2 D8**

Carbost, Isle of Skye. On the B8009, just off the A863 where it joins the A87 at Sligachan. Bus from Portree. Open Apr–Jun and Oct, Mon–Fri 0900–1630; Jul–Sep, Mon–Sat 0900–1630; Nov–Mar, Mon–Fri 1400–1630. Last tour 1600. Charge £. Guided tours. Explanatory displays. Gift shop. Picnic area. WC. Limited wheelchair access. Disabled WC. Car parking. Telephone (01478) 640314.

The only distillery on Skye. Exhibition tells the history of the distillery and its location. Shop.

1399 TAM O' SHANTER EXPERIENCE **4 J18**

Murdochs Lane, Alloway, Ayr. 2 miles (3km) south of Ayr. Nearest railway station Ayr, bus service from centre of Ayr. Open Mar–Oct, daily 0900–1800; Oct–Mar, daily 0900–1700. Closed Christmas and New

Year. Charge £. Group concessions. Explanatory displays. Gift shop. Restaurant. Children's play area. WC. Induction loop. Wheelchair access. Disabled WC. Car and coach parking. Telephone (01292) 443700.

Walk your way through history, and experience the Burns mystery and magic with two audio-visual presentations. The first tells the story of Burns and leads you on to the second presentation which is the poem *Tam o'Shanter* in the words of Burns, using the latest technology. See also 238 Burns National Heritage Park.

1400 TANGWICK HAA MUSEUM **1 F3**

Eshaness, Shetland. About 40 miles (64km) north of Lerwick via A970 and B9078. Open May–Sep, Mon–Fri 1300–1700, weekends 1100–1900. Free. Explanatory displays. Gift shop. WC. Limited wheelchair access. Disabled WC. Car and coach parking. Telephone (01806) 503389.

A museum in a restored 17th-century house built by the Cheyne family. Shows various aspects of life (agriculture, fishing, spinning and knitting) in Northmavine through the ages, using photographs and artefacts. Exhibition changed annually.

1401 TANTALLON CASTLE **5 P15**

HS. North Berwick, East Lothian. Off the A198, 3 miles (5km) east of North Berwick. Nearest railway station North Berwick, buses from North Berwick and Dunbar pass Tantallon Castle road end. Open Apr–Sep, daily 0930–1830; Oct–Mar, Mon–Sat 0930–1630, Sun 1400–1630 (closed Thu pm and Fri). Charge £. Group concessions. Guided tours. Explanatory displays. Gift shop. Picnic area, refreshments available in shop. WC. Limited wheelchair access. Car and coach parking. Telephone (01620) 892727.

Set on the edge of the cliffs looking out to the Bass Rock, this formidable castle was a stronghold of the Douglas family. It features earthwork defences and a massive 50 foot (15m) high curtain wall. Display includes replica gun.

1402 TARBET OLD CHURCH **3 L6**

Near Portmahomac, east of Tain, Ross and Cromarty.

Although statistical accounts date this church to 1756, records show that this site had a church on it as early as the 13th century. It has many points of architectural and social interest.

1403 TARVES MEDIEVAL TOMB **3 Q8**

HS. In Tarves churchyard, 15 miles (24km) northwest of Aberdeen. Nearest railway station Aberdeen, bus from Aberdeen. Access at all times. Free. Telephone 0131 668 8800.

The fine altar tomb of William Forbes, the laird who enlarged Tolquhon Castle. Remarkable carving.

1404 TAVERSOE TUICK CHAMBERED CAIRN **1 B9**

HS. On the island of Rousay, Orkney. Bus from Kirkwall to Tingwall and then ferry to Rousay. Access at all times. Free. Telephone 0131 668 8800.

A Neolithic chambered mound with two burial chambers, one above the other.

1405 TEALING DOVECOT AND EARTH HOUSE **5 N12**

HS. 0.5 mile (1km) down an unclassified road to Tealing, Angus, off the A929, 5 miles (8km) north of Dundee. Access at all times. Free. Telephone 0131 668 8800.

The dovecot dates from the late 16th century, and is an elegant little building. The earth house, of Iron Age date, consists of an underground passage, now uncovered.

1406 TEAMPULL NA TRIONAID **2 B7**

Cairinis (Carinish), close to A865, North Uist.

Ruined remains of a very important ecclesiastical site, founded in 1203 by Beatrice, daughter of Somerled, Lord of the Isles, on the foundations of an earlier place of worship. A major centre of learning in medieval times.

1407 TEDDY MELROSE, SCOTLAND'S TEDDY BEAR MUSEUM **5 P17**

The Wynd, Buccleuch Street, Melrose. 40 miles (64km) south of Edinburgh. Local and national bus services. Open all year, daily 1000–1700. Closed Christmas and New Year. Tea garden open Jun–Oct. Charge £. Group concessions. Guided tours for groups. Explanatory displays. Gift shop. Tea garden. Baby changing facilities. WC. Wheelchair access. Disabled WC. Car and coach parking. Telephone (01896) 823854.

Fascinating displays record the heritage of British teddy bears from the early 1900 Bruins through to today's artist designer bears. Visitors can meet their lifelong friends, Winnie the Pooh, Rupert and Paddington and learn their creators' stories. Contemporary Scottish designer bears alongside hundreds of teddy gifts. Teddy Bear Fairs in May and August.

1408 TEMPLE WOOD STONE CIRCLES **4 F14**

HS. 0.25 mile (0.5km) southwest of Nether Largie, Argyll. Access at all times. Free. Telephone 0131 668 8800.

A circle of upright stones about 3000 years old, and the remains of an earlier circle.

1409 TEVIOT WATER GARDENS **5 Q17**

Kirkbank House, Kelso, Borders. Midway between Kelso and Jedburgh on A698. Nearest railway stations Berwick and Carlisle, bus from Kelso. Open May–Sep, and by arrangement. Free. Guided tours by arrangement. Explanatory displays. Gift shop. Tearoom. WC. Limited wheelchair access. Disabled WC. Car parking. Telephone (01835) 850253.

The watergardens are on four levels, set amidst scenic Borders countryside. The lowest garden flows down to the River Teviot.

1410 THIRLESTANE CASTLE **5 P16**

Lauder, Berwickshire. Off A68 at Lauder. Bus from Edinburgh. Open mid Apr–Oct, Mon–Fri and Sun 1100, last admission 1615. Charge ££. Group concessions. Guided tours until 1400. Explanatory displays. Gift shop. Tearoom and picnic tables in grounds. WC. Disabled WC. Car and coach parking. Telephone (01578) 722430.

One of the seven great houses of Scotland, Thirlestane Castle was rebuilt in the 16th century as the home of the Maitland family. It became the seat of the Earls of Lauderdale and was enlarged in the 17th century by the Duke of Lauderdale, who commissioned the magnificent plasterwork ceilings in the state rooms. Still a family home, Thirlestane houses a large collection of early toys in the nursery wing, and the Border Country Life Exhibition. The old servants' hall serves as the tearoom, and there are picnic tables alongside the woodland walk.

1411 THREAVE CASTLE **5 K20**

HS. Castle Douglas, Kirkcudbrightshire. North of the A75, 3 miles (5km) west of Castle Douglas. Nearest railway station Dumfries, bus from Dumfries, then long walk to the boat over to island. Open Apr–Sep, daily 0930–1830. Charge £. Charge includes ferry. Group concessions. Guided tours. Picnic area. WC. Car and coach parking. Telephone (01556) 502575.

A massive tower built in the late 14th century by Archibald the Grim, Lord of Galloway. Round its base is an artillery fortification built before 1455, when the castle was besieged by James II. It is on an island, approached by boat.

1412 THREAVE GARDEN AND ESTATE **5 K20**

NTS. Castle Douglas, Dumfries and Galloway. Off A75, 1 mile (2km) west of Castle Douglas. Bus to Castle Douglas. Visitor centre open Apr–Oct, daily 0930–1730. Estate and garden open all year, daily 0930–sunset. Charge ££. Children free. Group concessions. Guided tours. Explanatory displays, information in four languages. Gift shop. Restaurant. Plant sales. WC. Induction loop in visitor centre. Wheelchair access, wheelchairs and batricars available. Disabled WC. Car and coach parking. Telephone (01556) 502575.

Threave Garden has a spectacular springtime display of daffodils, colourful herbaceous beds in summer, and striking trees and heathers in autumn. The visitor centre has an exhibition and delightful terraced restaurant. Threave Estate is a wildfowl refuge, with bird hides and waymarked trails.

1413 THREE FOLLIES AT AUCKENGILL **3 N2**

Auckengill, Caithness on the A9 Wick to John O' Groats road.

The first folly on the left was a boat's lantern; the second held a barometer, a log book and weather information; the third is Mervin's tower, built for a small boy who spent all his time with the workmen.

1414 THURSO HERITAGE MUSEUM **3 M2**

Town Hall, High Street, Thurso. Open Jun–Sep, Mon–Sat 1000–1300, 1400–1700. Charge £. Group concessions. Guided tours on request. Explanatory displays. Wheelchair access with assistance. Disabled WC. Car and coach parking. Telephone (01847) 892692.

A varied collection which includes historical Pictish stones, fossils, relics of the flagstone industry, local military memorabilia, and reconstruction of granny's kitchen and living room. Historical perspective of local figures in the community, and photographic history of the area.

1415 TIGHNABRUAICH VIEWPOINT **4 G15**

NTS. northeast of Tighnabruaich, Argyll on A8003.. Access at all times. Free. Explanatory displays.

A high vantage point, with explanatory indicators identifying surrounding sites, this viewpoint offers spectacular views over the Kyles of Bute and the islands of the Firth of Clyde.

1416 TIME CAPSULE **6 K16**

100 Buchanan Street, Coatbridge, North Lanarkshire. Off M8 in Coatbridge. Nearest railway stations Whifflet and Coatbridge, bus from Glasgow. Open all year (except 25/26 Dec and 1/2 Jan), daily 1000–2100. Charge ££ dependant on activity. Group concessions. Gift shop. Café/bar. WC. Wheelchair access. Disabled WC. Car and coach parking. Telephone (01236) 449572.

Swim through primeval swamps, ride the rapids, skate with a 14 foot (4m) woolly mammoth and slide down the time tunnel. Also Nardini's Water Babies park, ideal for toddlers.

1417 TIMESPAN HERITAGE CENTRE AND ART GALLERY **3 M5**

Dunrobin Street, Helmsdale, Sutherland. 70 miles (112.5km) north of Inverness, on A9 to John O'Groats. Nearest railway station Helmsdale, buses from Inverness and Wick. Open Apr–Oct, Mon–Sat 0930–1700, Sun 1400–1700 (1800 Jul and Aug). Charge ££. Group concessions. Guided tours by prior arrangement. Explanatory displays. Gift shop. Café. Art gallery. Riverside herb garden. WC. Wheelchair access. Disabled WC. Car and coach parking. Telephone (01431) 821327.

Award-winning Timespan features the dramatic story of the Highlands, from Picts and Vikings, murder at Helmsdale Castle, the last burning of a witch, the Highland Clearances, the Kildonan Goldrush, to the present day and the North Sea oilfields. Scenes from the past are re-created with life-size sets and sound effects. Audio-visual. Herb garden, beside Telford's bridge over the River Helmsdale. Art gallery with changing programme of exhibitions by leading contemporary artists.

1418 TOBERMORY DISTILLERY — 4 E12

Tobermory, Isle of Mull. By ferry from Oban to Craignure, bus from Craignure. Open Easter–Oct, Mon–Fri 1000–1700. Charge £. Guided tours. Explanatory displays. Gift shop. Limited wheelchair access. Car and coach parking. Telephone (01688) 302647.

Malt whisky is distilled using traditional methods, and guided tours and video reveal the ingredients and distilling process.

1419 TOLBOOTH ART CENTRE — 5 K21

High Street, Kirkcudbright. In the centre. Nearest railway station Dumfries, bus from Dumfries. Open May, Jun and Sep, Mon–Sat 1100–1700, Jul and Aug, Mon–Sat 1000–1800 (Jun–Sep, Sun 1400–1700); Oct–Apr, Mon–Sat 1100–1600. Charge £. Children free of charge. Group concessions. Guided tours by arrangement. Explanatory displays. Gift shop. Tearoom. WC. Wheelchair access. Disabled WC. Telephone (01557) 331556.

An interpretive centre located in the 17th-century tolbooth. Exhibition about the town's history as an artists' colony, including paintings by important Kirkcudbright artists. Audio-visual presentation. Temporary exhibitions programme.

1420 TOLBOOTH MUSEUM — 3 Q10

The Harbour, Stonehaven. In Stonehaven centre. By rail or bus to Stonehaven. Open Jun–Sep, Mon, Thu, Fri and Sat 1000–1200 and 1400–1700, Wed and Sun 1400–1700. Free. Guided tours. Explanatory displays. Gift shop. Limited wheelchair access. Car parking. Telephone (01771) 622906.

Stonehaven's oldest building, the Earl Marischal's 16th-century storehouse which served as Kincardineshire's Tolbooth from 1600–1767. Features imprisoned priests, links with the sea and local bygones.

1421 TOLLPARK AND GARNHALL — 6 K15

HS. West of Castlecary, Stirlingshire. Nearest railway station Cumbernauld, bus from Glasgow (Buchanan Street) to Castlecary. Access at all times. Free. Telephone 0131 668 8800.

A well-preserved section of the ditch of the Antonine Wall (see 62).

1422 TOLQUHON CASTLE — 3 Q8

HS. Tarves, By Ellon, Aberdeenshire. North of A920, 7 miles (11km) east northeast of Oldmeldrum, Aberdeenshire. Bus from Aberdeen to Tarves then 1 mile (2km) walk. Open Apr–Sep, daily 0930–1830; Oct–Mar, Sat 0930–1630, Sun 1400–1630. Charge £. Group concessions. Guided tours. Gift shop. Picnic area. WC. Wheelchair access. Disabled WC. Car and coach parking. Telephone (01651) 851286.

Built for the Forbes family, it has an early 15th-century tower which was enlarged in the mid 16th century with a large mansion around a courtyard. Noted for its highly ornamented gatehouse, set within a barmkin with adjacent pleasance.

1423 TOLQUHON GALLERY **3 Q8**

Tolquhon, Tarves, Ellon, Aberdeenshire. On the B999, 13 miles (21km) north of Aberdeen. Bus within 1 mile (2km). Open Mar–Dec, Mon–Sat (closed Thu) 1100–1700, Sun 1400–1700; Jan and Feb, weekends only 1400–1700. Free. Explanatory displays. All exhibits for sale. Garden. Wheelchair access with assistance. Car and coach parking. Telephone (01651) 842343.

An art gallery specialising in paintings and original prints by living Scottish artists. Also studio crafts, ceramics, jewellery, glass and wooden objects. Exhibits changed monthly. Often sculpture in the grounds.

1424 TOMATIN DISTILLERY **3 L8**

Tomatin, Inverness-shire. Just off the A9, 15 miles (24km) south of Inverness, buses from Inverness or Aviemore. Nearest bus stop 0.5 mile (1km) away. Open all year, Mon–Fri 0900–1700, Sat 0900–1200; last tour 1530. Free. Advance notice required for large groups. Guided tours (Apr–Oct available in French and German). Explanatory displays and video. Gift shop. WC. Wheelchair access. Disabled WC. Car and coach parking. Telephone (01808) 511444.

Scotland's largest malt whisky distillery – one hundred years old.

1425 TOMB OF THE EAGLES **1 B11**

Liddle, South Ronaldsay, Orkney. On South Ronaldsay, 20 miles (32km) south of Kirkwall. Ferry, then bus to Burwick in summer (to St Margaret's Hope in winter). Open Apr–Oct 1000–2000; Nov–Mar 1000–1200. Charge £. Group concessions. Guided tours with some bad weather clothing provided. WC. Personal guide and touch table for blind visitors. Limited wheelchair access. Car and coach parking. Telephone (01856) 831339.

Tour starts at museum and proceeds to 5000 year-old tomb. Also a Bronze Age house. Wildlife to see en route.

1426 TOMINTOUL VISITOR CENTRE **3 M9**

The Square, Tomintoul, Moray. In Tomintoul on the A939, 13 miles (21km) east of Grantown-on-Spey. Local bus. Open Apr and May, Mon–Fri 1000–1600; Jun–Aug, Mon–Sat 1000–1630; Sep, Mon–Sat 1000–1600; Oct, Mon–Fri 1000–1600. Closed all year 1200–1400. Free. Explanatory displays. Gift shop. Wheelchair access with assistance. Car and coach parking. Telephone (01309) 673701.

Features a reconstructed crofter's kitchen and smiddy, with other displays on local wildlife, history and the skiing industry.

1427 TOMNAVERIE STONE CIRCLE **3 P10**

HS. Near Mill of Wester Coull, about 3 miles (5km) northwest of Aboyne, Aberdeenshire. Nearest railway station Aberdeen, bus to Aboyne, then walk. Access at all time. Free. Telephone 0131 668 8800.

A recumbent stone circle about 4000 years old.

1428 TORHOUSKIE STONE CIRCLE **4 J20**

HS. Off the B733, 4 miles (6.5km) west of Wigtown. Nearest railway station Stranraer, buses from Stranraer, Newton Stewart or Dumfries, alight at Kirkcowan (5 miles/8km) or Wigton (4 miles/6.5km). Access at all times. Free. Telephone 0131 668 8800.

A Bronze Age recumbent circle of 19 boulders on the edge of a low mound.

1429 TORMISTON MILL **1 B10**

HS. On the A965 about 9 miles (14.5km) west of Kirkwall, Orkney. Open Apr–Sep, Mon–Sat 0930–1830, Sun 1400–1830; Oct–Mar, Mon–Sat 0930–1830, Sun 1400–1630, closed Thu pm and Fri. Explanatory displays. Gift shop. Tearoom. WC. Car and coach parking. Telephone (01856) 761606.

An excellent late example of a Scottish water-mill, probably built in the 1880s. The water wheel and most of the machinery have been retained. Now forms a reception centre for visitors to Maes Howe (1021).

1430 TORNESS POWER STATION **5 Q15**

Dunbar, East Lothian. Off the A1, about 6 miles (9.5km) southeast of Dunbar. Coach provided for groups. Open Mar–Sep, daily 0930–1630; Oct–Feb, Mon–Fri 0930–1630, Sat and Sun 1300–1630. Closed Christmas and New Year, telephone to confirm. Free. Guided tours. Explanatory displays. Gift shop. Complimentary refreshments. WC. Wheelchair access to visitor centre; limited access to power station. Disabled WC. Car and coach parking. Telephone (0800) 250255.

One of Scotland's two nuclear power stations which together produce half of Scotland's electricity. By means of videos, displays and models, the visitor centre explains how electricity is generated.

1431 TOROSAY CASTLE AND GARDENS **4 F12**

Craignure, Isle of Mull. 1 mile (2km) southeast of Craignure. Mull Little Railway runs from Craignure to Torosay. Open Easter–Oct, daily 1030–1730; Nov–Easter, daily 1030–sunset, garden only. Charge ££. Group concessions. Guided tours by arrangement. Explanatory displays. Gift shop. Tearoom and picnic area. Garden. WC. Wheelchair access with assistance. Disabled WC. Car and coach parking. Telephone (01680) 812421.

This Victorian family home contains furniture, pictures and scrapbooks dating from Edwardian times. Torosay is surrounded by 12 acres (5ha) of gardens, including formal terraces and a statue walk, set amidst fuchsia hedges. Woodland and water gardens, eucalyptus walk and rockery all contain many and varied plants. The gardens offers extensive views past Duart Castle and the Sound of Mull to the mountains of Arran and Lorne.

1432 TORPHICHEN PRECEPTORY **6 L15**

HS. In Torphichen village on the B792, 5 miles (8km) south southwest of Linlithgow, West Lothian. Bus from Linlithgow to Bathgate via Torphichen. Open Apr–Oct, Sat 1100–1700, Sun and bank holidays 1400–1700. Telephone 0131 668 8800.

The tower and transepts of a church built by the Knights Hospitaller of the Order of St John of Jerusalem in the 13th century, but much altered.

1433 TORR A'CHAISTEAL FORT **4 G17**

HS. 4 miles (6.5km) south of Blackwaterfoot, Isle of Arran. Ferry from Ardrossan to Brodick, bus from Brodick. Access at all times. Free. Telephone 0131 668 8800.

A circular Iron Age fort on a ridge.

1434 TORRIDON **2 G7**

NTS. Visitor Centre, Torridon, Achnasheen, Ross-shire. Off A896, 9 miles (14.5km) southwest of Kinlochewe. Estate, deer park and deer museum open all year. Visitor centre open May–late Sep, Mon–Sat 1000–1700, Sun 1400–1700. Charge £. Children free. Explanatory displays. Guided walks by rangers. WC. Wheelchair access to visitor centre and deer museum only. Disabled WC. Car parking. Telephone (01445) 791368.

Around 16,000 acres (6475ha) of some of Scotland's finest mountain scenery whose peaks rise over 3000 feet (914m).

Of major interest to geologists, Liathach and Beinn Alligin are of red sandstone, some 750 million years old. The visitor centre at the junction of A896 and Diabaig road has an audio-visual presentation of wildlife. Deer museum (unmanned) and deer park open all year. Ranger led walks in season.

1435 TORRIESTON FOREST WALKS **5 M7**

FE. Moray Forest District Office, Balnacoul, Fochabers, Moray. Off the B9010 Dallas road along the Pluscarden minor road. Torrieston car park is 2 miles (3.5km) beyond Pluscarden. Open at all times. Free. Leaflet available. Picnic area. Guided walks and events. WC. Wheelchair access with assistance. Disabled WC. Car parking. Telephone (01343) 820223.

Three varied walks of 1–2 miles (1.5–3km) on the forested hillside above Pluscarden Priory. Ranger service

---

1436 TORRYLIN CAIRN **4 G18**

HS. 0.25 miles (0.5km) southeast of Lagg on the south coast of the Isle of Arran. By ferry from Ardrossan to Brodick, bus from Brodick to Lagg. Access at all times. Free. Telephone 0131 668 8800.

A Neolithic chambered cairn with its compartments visible.

1437 TOUCHSTONE MAZE **3 J7**

Starthpeffer, west of Dingwall.

A large-scale labyrinth pathway amongst standing stones and turf walls. The maze has been built to incorporate alignments with sun and moon positions.

1438 TOY MUSEUM **2 D8**

Holmisdale House, Glendale, Isle of Skye. 7 miles (11km) west of Dunvegan. Post bus from Dunvegan. Open all year, Mon–Sat 1000–1800. Charge £. Group concessions. Guided tours. Gift shop. Garden with waterfall. Plenty of hands-on for blind visitors. Wheelchair access. Car and coach parking. Telephone (01470) 511240.

Award-winning museum, with a unique display of toys, games and dolls. Meccano's biggest ever model, the Giant Blocksetting Crane. Also on display are early examples of Pinball and Star Wars.

1439 TRAPRAIN LAW **5 P15**

Off A1, 5 miles (7.5km) west of Dunbar. Access at all times. Free.

A whale-backed hill, 734 feet (224m) high, with Iron Age fortified site, probably continuing in use as a defended Celtic township until the 11th century. A treasure of 4th-century Christian and pagan silver was excavated here in 1919.

1440 TRAQUAIR HOUSE **5 N17**

Innerleithen, Peeblesshire. 6 miles (10km) southeast of Peebles, 29 miles (46.5km) south of Edinburgh. Off A72 on B709, signposted. Nearest railway station Edinburgh, bus to Innerleithen then 1.5 miles (2.5km) walk. Open Apr–Oct, daily 1230–1730; Jun–Aug, daily 1030–1730. Last admission 1700. Charge £££. Group concessions. Guided tours. Explanatory displays. Gift shop. Cottage tearoom. WC. Limited wheelchair access. Disabled WC. Car and coach parking. Telephone (01896) 830323.

Dating back to the 12th century, this is said to be the oldest continuously inhabited house in Scotland. Twenty-seven Scottish and English monarchs have visited it, including Mary, Queen of Scots, of whom there are relics. William the Lion held court here in 1175. The well-known Bear Gates were closed in 1745, not to be reopened until the Stuarts should ascend the throne. Ale is regularly produced at the 18th-century brewhouse. Exhibitions and special events are held during the summer months. Craft workshops, brewery, woodland and River Tweed walks and maze.

1441 TREASURES OF THE EARTH **2 G11**

Corpach, Fort William. 4 miles (6.5km) from Fort William, on A830. Bus from Fort William. Open all year (except Christmas and Jan), daily 1000–1700; Jul–Sep 0930–1900. Charge £. Group concessions. Guided tours for groups by arrangement. Explanatory displays. Leaflet in French, German, Italian and Spanish. Gift shop. WC. Wheelchair access. Disabled WC. Car and coach parking. Telephone (01397) 772283.

This is a large collection of gemstones and crystals, displayed in recreated caverns and mines, just as they were found beneath the earth. Nuggets of gold and silver, aquamarines, red garnets, rubies, opals and diamonds are amongst many other gemstones and crystals on display, some weighing hundreds of kilos.

1442 TRIMONTIUM EXHIBITION **5 P17**

The Square, Melrose, Roxburghshire. Train from Berwick or Edinburgh, bus from Edinburgh. Open Apr–Oct, daily 1030–1630. Charge £. Guided tours of the site Thu 1320–1700, (£) includes tea. Explanatory displays and audio guide. Gift shop. Baby changing facilities. WC. Wheelchair access. Disabled WC. Car and coach parking. Telephone (01896) 822651.

An exhibition illustrating daily life on the Roman frontier at Trimontium fortress, the remains of which can be seen on the tour. Museum contains materials found on site.

1443 TROPIC HOUSE **4 J20**

Langford Nurseries, Carty Port, Newton Stewart. 2 miles (3km) south of Newton Stewart on A714. Bus from Newton Stewart. Open Easter–Oct, daily 1000–1700. Charge £. Group concessions. Guided tours. Explanatory displays. Gift shop. Tearoom. Baby changing facilities. WC. Wheelchair access. Disabled WC. Car and coach parking. Telephone (01671) 404050.

An extensive display of carnivorous plants here, includes the insects which they eat. In Victorian times, explorers feared that such plants would eat humans. Exotic butterflies fly amongst the tropical plants.

1444 TROSSACHS PIER COMPLEX **4 J14**

Loch Katrine, by Callander, Perthshire. 8 miles (13km) west of Callander on A821. Bus service from Callander in summer months. Open Easter–Oct, Sun–Fri 0900–1700, Sat 1000–1700. Free. Charge £ for parking. Guided tours. Explanatory displays. Gift shop. Tearoom. WC. Wheelchair access with assistance. Disabled WC. Car and coach parking. Telephone (01877) 376316.

Set in the heart of the Trossachs, the Trossachs Pier Complex has extensive loch-side walks and cycle routes, and cruises on Loch Katrine on a steam ship first launched in 1899.

1445 TROSSACHS WOOLLEN MILL **5 K14**

Kilmahog, Callander, Trossachs. 1 mile (2km) north of Callander. Open May–Sep, daily 0900–1730; Oct–Apr, daily 1000–1630. Free. Explanatory displays. Gift shop. Restaurant and tearoom. WC. Wheelchair access with assistance. Car and coach parking. Telephone (01877) 330178.

Resident weaver demonstrates skilled weaving techniques to produce the unique Trossachs Woollen Rug, available in the mill shop. Also quality knitwear, outerwear and gifts. See also 899 Kilmahog Woollen Mill.

1446 TROTTERNISH ART GALLERY **2 E6**

Kilmaluag, Duntulm, Isle of Skye. 25 miles (40km) north of Portree on the A855. Bus service from Portree. Open Apr–Sep, daily, 0900–2100; Oct–Mar, daily 0900–1730. Closed 25/26 Dec. Free. Retail gallery. Limited wheelchair access. Car parking. Telephone (01470) 552302.

Working landscape gallery set in a beautiful part of Skye with magnificent and spectacular pinnacles and cliffs. Wide selection of originals, and mounted photographic work. All artwork exclusive to gallery.

1447 TROWMILL, WOOLLEN WEAVING MILL **5 P18**

Trowmill, Hawick. On the A698, 2.5 miles (4km) northeast of Hawick. Buses from Hawick or Kelso. Factory open all year, Mon–Thu 0900–1630, Fri 0900–1130 (except local holidays). Shop open all year (except Christmas and New Year), Mon–Fri 0900–1700, Sat 0930–1700, Sun 1000–1700. Free. Self-guided tour leaflet. Explanatory leaflet. Gift shop. Refreshments and picnic area. WC. Wheelchair access. Car and coach parking. Telephone (01450) 372555.

Visitors can tour a woollen mill and see all stages of cloth manufacture.

1448 TUGNET ICE HOUSE **3 N7**

Tugnet, Spey Bay, Fochabers, Moray. Off the A96, 8 miles (13km) east of Elgin onto B9104, then 3 miles (4.5km) north. Nearest railway station Elgin, bus from Elgin. Open May–Sep, daily 1100–1600. Free. Explanatory displays. Gift shop. WC. Wheelchair access with assistance. Car and coach parking. Telephone (01309) 673701.

Scotland's largest ice house featuring displays on the local salmon fishing industry.

1449 TULLIBARDINE CHAPEL **5 L13**

HS. Off the A823, 6 miles (9.5km) southeast of Crieff, Perthshire. Nearest railway station Perth, bus from Perth to Crieff, then bus to Tullibardine. Open May–Sep only; keyholder at adjacent farmhouse. Free. Explanatory displays. Telephone 0131 668 8800.

One of the most complete and unaltered small medieval churches in Scotland. Founded in 1446 and largely rebuilt circa 1500. Good architectural detail.

1450 TURNBERRY CASTLE **4 H18**

Off A719, 6 miles (9.5km) north of Girvan. Access at all reasonable times. Free.

The scant remains of the castle where Robert the Bruce was probably born in 1274.

1451 TWEED BRIDGE **5 Q17**

A698 at Coldstream, 9 miles (14.5km) east northeast of Kelso.

The 300-feet (91m) long bridge was built in 1766 by Smeaton. In the past the bridge was a crossing into Scotland for eloping couples taking advantage of Scotland's easier marriage laws.

1452 TWEEDDALE MUSEUM AND GALLERY **5 N17**

Chambers Institute, High Street, Peebles. In the centre. Bus from Edinburgh. Open all year, Mon–Fri 1000–1200 and 1400–1700; Easter–Oct also Sat 1000–1300 and 1400–1600. Free. Guided tours. Explanatory displays. WC. Car and coach parking. Telephone (01721) 724820.

A 19th-century building housing a museum and gallery. Temporary exhibitions of art and craftwork. Gallery of local history and ornamental plasterwork.

1453 TWEEDHOPE SHEEP DOGS **5 M18**

Hammerlands Cottage, Selkirk Road, Moffat. Nearest railway stations Dumfries or Lockerbie, buses from Edinburgh, Lockerbie or Selkirk, taxi possible. Open Easter–Oct, 1100–1200 and 1500–1600. Demonstrations 1100 and 1500. Winter and weekends by appointment only. Charge £. Group concessions. Gift shop. Wheelchair access with assistance. Car and coach parking. Telephone (01683) 221471.

Border Collies work and train in a scenic environment. There are sheep dog handling demonstrations, and tuition is given most evenings.

1454 UDALE BAY **3 K7**

West of Cromarty on the north road.

The vast spread of sand and mud deposits is a National Nature Reserve. Udale Bay is a mecca for birdwatchers. Herons, greylag, geese, widgeon, teal, mallard, goldeneye and shelduck can all be found here in good numbers. A new hide has full disabled access and can comfortably accommodate ten people. Colourful display panels tell visitors about the varied birdlife.

1455 UGIE SALMON FISH HOUSE **3 R8**

Golf Road, Peterhead. At the mouth of the River Ugie opposite the golf course. Bus from centre. Open all year, Mon–Fri 0900–1700, Sat 0900–1200. Free. Guided tours. Gift shop. Picnic area. WC. Limited wheelchair access. Disabled WC. Car and coach parking. Telephone (01779) 476209.

The Fish House, 400 years old and built for the Fifth Earl Marischal for keeping game and fish, has been used by salmon fishermen for over 100 years. Visitors can see the ancient art of smoking salmon and can buy the products.

1456 UI CHURCH **2 E4**

At Aiginis, off A866, 2 miles (3km) east of Stornoway, Isle of Lewis. Access at all reasonable times. Free. Car parking.

Ruined church (pronounced eye) containing some finely carved ancient tombs of the Macleods of Lewis.

1457 UIG HERITAGE CENTRE **2 C4**

Crowlista (Cradhlastadh), Uig, Lewis. 33 miles (53km) west of Stornoway on B8011. Post bus from Stornoway. Open mid Jun–mid Sep, Mon–Sat 1200–1700. Charge £. Guided tours (French and German text). Explanatory displays. Tearoom. Access to games hall. WC. Wheelchair access. Disabled WC. Car and coach parking. Telephone (01851) 672456.

The centre contains an exhibition of local artefacts from the early to mid 20th century. Also photographs, croft histories, a turn of the century replica thatched house interior and displays of shoemaker's tools, blacksmith, fishing, weaving and agricultural implements.

1458 UIG POTTERY **2 D7**

Uig, Isle of Skye. Bus from Portree. Open Apr–Oct, Mon–Sat 0900–1800, Sun 1000–1600; Nov–Mar, Tue–Sat 0900–1800. Free. Gift shop. WC. Wheelchair access. Disabled WC. Car and coach parking. Telephone (01470) 542421.

A pottery making functional and unique pieces.

1459 UIST ANIMAL VISITOR CENTRE **2 B7**

Bayhead (Ceann A' Bháigh), North Uist. 13 miles (21km) from ferry terminal at Loch Maddy on west coast of Uist. Regular bus service. Open all year except Christmas and New Year's Day, Mon–Sat 1000–2200, Sun 1100–1900. Charge £. Group concessions. Guided tours. Explanatory displays. Gift shop. Café and picnic area. Garden, pets corner, games area. WC. Wheelchair access. Disabled WC. Car and coach parking. Telephone (01876) 510223.

An all weather attraction for the family. Hebridean sheep (and fleeces, wool, knitwear), Soay sheep from St Kilda, rare Eriskay ponies, Scottish wildcats and birds of prey. Games area, bouncy castle. Pony trekking on the beaches.

1460 UIST CRAFT PRODUCERS **2 B9**

Uist Craft Producers, Kildonan Museum, Kildonan, South Uist. 8 miles (12.5km) north of Lochboisdale. Ferry to Lochboisdale, bus from Lochboisdale, request stop. Open daily 1000–1700. Free. Explanatory displays. Gift shop. Tearoom and picnic area. WC. Wheelchair access with assistance. Disabled WC. Car and coach parking. Telephone (01878) 700483.

Crafts on view and for sale – spinning, knitting and weaving. Workshops. Photographic display of local history.

1461 ULLAPOOL MUSEUM AND VISITOR CENTRE **2 H5**

7–8 West Argyle Street, Ullapool. Bus from Inverness. Open Apr–Oct, Mon–Sat 0930–1730 (Jul and Aug closes 2000); Nov–Mar, Wed and Sat 1100–1500. Charge £. Accompanied children free. Group concessions. Explanatory displays. Gift shop. WC. Induction loop for audio-visual. Large print text. Wheelchair access. Disabled WC. Telephone (01854) 612987.

Housed in a listed building, a former Telford Parliamentary Church. The award-winning museum interprets the natural and human history of the Lochbroom and Coigach area. This includes the establishment of Ullapool by the British Fisheries Society in 1788 and the voyage of the *Hector* in 1773, the first emigrant ship to sail direct from Scotland to Nova Scotia. The museum displays objects, photographs, community tapestries and quilts, and uses audio-visual and computer technology. Maps and records are available for study. There is also a tape tour of the village.

1462 UNION CANAL **6 L15**

From the south of Falkirk to the centre of Edinburgh via Linlithgow, Broxburn and Ratho. Fishing, canoeing, etc by permit. Countryside ranger service. Guided walks and canal events during summer months. Telephone (01506) 852578.

The Forth and Clyde and the Union Canals formed an important commercial transport corridor across central Scotland for nearly two centuries. They fell victim to the roads culture of the 1960s when they were blocked at more than 30 sites and broken up into short sections. One of the biggest canal restoration projects in Europe, the Millennuim Link will bring the 69 miles (110km) of canal, from Glasgow to Edinburgh and the Forth to the Clyde, back to life by Easter 2001. See also 621 Falkirk Wheel.

1463 UNION SUSPENSION BRIDGE **5 R16**

Across River Tweed, 2 miles (3km) south of Paxton on unclassified road.

This suspension bridge, the first of its type in Britain, was built by Samuel Brown in 1820, and links England and Scotland.

1464 UNST **1 G2**

NTS. Shetland. At the northern tip of Shetland. Ferry from Aberdeen to Lerwick, then two further ferries. Open all year. Free. Car parking. Telephone (01463) 232034.

Four-thousand-acre (1619ha) estate at the northernmost tip of Britain, interesting for its geology, botany and bird life. The west coast areas are especially beautiful. The land is mostly farmed and there is an excellent Shetland pony stud.

1465 UNSTAN CHAMBERED CAIRN **1 B10**

HS. About 3.5 miles (5.5km) north northeast of Stromness, Orkney. Bus from Kirkwall or Stromness. Access at all times. Free. Telephone 0131 668 8800.

A mound covering a Neolithic stone burial chamber, divided by slabs into five compartments.

1466 UNST HERITAGE CENTRE **1 H1**

Haroldswick, Unst, Shetland. At the north end of Unst. Ferry from Mainland Shetland. Open May–Sep, daily 1400–1700. Free. Donations. WC. Wheelchair access. Disabled WC. Car and coach parking. Telephone (01957) 711528.

Local history and family trees of Unst.

1467 UP HELLY AA EXHIBITION **1 G5**

St Sunniva Street, Lerwick, Shetland. In Lerwick. Open May–Sep, Sat 1400–1600, Tue and Fri 1900–2100. Charge £. Children under 6 free. Group concessions. Explanatory displays. WC. Wheelchair access. Car and coach parking.

An exhibition of artefacts, photographs, costumes and a replica galley from the annual fire festival of Up Helly Aa. Audio-visual show.

1468 URQUHART CASTLE **3 J8**

HS. Drumnadrochit, Inverness. On the A82 beside Loch Ness, 2 miles (3km) southeast of Drumnadrochit. Nearest railway station Inverness, bus service from Inverness. Open Apr–Sep, daily 0930–1830; Oct–Mar, daily 0930–1630. Charge ££. Group concessions. Guided tours. Explanatory displays. Gift shop. WC. Wheelchair access with assistance. Car and coach parking. Telephone (01456) 450551.

The ruins of one of the largest castles in Scotland, which fell into decay after 1689 and was blown up in 1692 to prevent it being occupied by Jacobites. Most of the existing remains date from the 16th century and include a tower. Built on the site of a vitrified fort.

1469 VALLEYFIELD WOOD **5 L15**

On the north side of A985, High Valleyfield, near Culross, Fife. Open all year. Free. Wheelchair access.

Beautiful woodland walks, originally the gardens of a mansion house, landscaped by Sir Humphrey Repton.

1470 VANE FARM NATURE RESERVE **6 M14**

RSPB. Kinross, Tayside. 1 mile (2km) along the B9097 east of junction 5 off M90. Nearest railway station Lochgelly, bus service from Edinburgh to Kinross (5 miles/8km). No bus to reserve. Open Apr–Dec daily (except Christmas and New Year) 1000–1700, Jan–Mar, daily 1000–1600. Charge £. RSPB/YOC members free on production of membership card, group leaders free. Guided tours by arrangement. Explanatory displays. Gift shop. Tearoom and picnic area. WC. Wheelchair access to visitor centre, disabled parking. Disabled WC. Car and coach parking. Telephone (01577) 862355.

Vane Farm Visitor Centre overlooks Loch Leven where thousands of geese and ducks spend the winter. Two trails take visitors to hides overlooking the wetlands and loch and through woodlands to Vane Hill. There is no disabled access to the trails, but there are telescopes in the tearoom enabling visitors to see the whole reserve.

1471 VENNEL GALLERY **6 H17**

10 Glasgow Vennel, Irvine, Ayrshire. In Irvine town centre. Nearest railway and bus stations Irvine. Open all year except public holidays, Mon, Tue and Thu–Sat 1000–1300 and 1400–1700; Oct–May closed Mon. Free.

Guided tours. Explanatory displays. Gift shop. WC. Wheelchair access. Telephone (01294) 275059.

Gallery with a programme of changing exhibitions of contemporary art and crafts. The gallery includes the Heckling Shop, where Robert Burns worked, and the Lodging House where he lived in 1781.

1472 VICTORIA FALLS **2 G7**

Off A832, 12 miles (19km) northwest of Kinlochewe, near Slattadale. Access at all times. Free. Car parking.

Waterfall named after Queen Victoria who visited Loch Maree and the surrounding area in 1877.

1473 VICTORIAN FERNERY

See 98 Ascog Hall, Fernery and Gardens.

1474 VIEWPARK GARDENS **6 K16**

New Edinburgh Road, Viewpark, Uddingston. Off M74 at Bellshill exit. Open Apr–Sep, Mon–Thu 1000–1600, Fri 1000–1500, Sat and Sun 1000–1700; Oct–Easter, Mon–Thu 1000–1600, Fri 1000–1500. Free. Guided tours by prior arrangement. WC. Wheelchair access. Car and coach parking. Telephone (01698) 818269.

With its ornamental gardens and colourful displays, Viewpark Gardens includes glasshouse displays, plant collections, horticultural demonstrations, and various themed gardens including Highland, Japanese and Demonstration.

1475 VIKINGAR **6 H16**

Barrfields, Greenock Road, Largs, Ayrshire. 25 miles (40km) from Glasgow on A78. Nearest railway station Largs, bus from Glasgow. Open all year, Apr–Sep, daily 1030–1730; Oct and Mar, daily 1030–1530; Nov–Feb, Sat and Sun 1030–1530. Charge ££. Group concessions. Guided tours (language sheets available). Explanatory displays. Gift shop. Café and licensed bar. Swimming pool. WC. Braille sheet. Written tour for hearing impaired. Wheelchair access. Disabled WC. Car and coach parking. Telephone (01475) 689777.

The history of the Vikings in Scotland, including the Battle of Largs in 1263 is told here using multimedia. Other facilities include a swimming pool, sauna and health suite, as well as a 500-seat cinema. There is a Winter Garden café, children's play area and an activity room.

1476 VILLAGE GLASS **6 L14**

14 Henderson Street, Bridge of Allan, Stirlingshire. 4 miles (6.5km) north of Stirling on A9. Nearest railway station Stirling, bus from Stirling. Open all year, Mon–Fri 0900–1700, Sat 1000–1700. Free. Gift shop. WC. Wheelchair access. Car parking. Telephone (01786) 832137.

Unique glass studio. Watch the craftsman and witness beautiful glassware being created.

1477 VILLAGE STORE **3 N8**

98 High Street, Aberlour, Banffshire. 14 miles (22.5km) south of Elgin on A95. Bus service from Elgin. Open all year, Mon–Fri 1030–1700, Sun 1330–1700. Closed mid Jan–mid Feb. Free. Donations. Explanatory displays. Gift shop. WC. Wheelchair access. Disabled WC. Car and coach parking. Telephone (01340) 871243.

The Village Store is a unique time capsule of shopping and social history. It retains its original wooden counter and shelves. The shop was bought in 1922 by Mr Affie Macintyre who ran it as a general store until 1978. A canny and capable shopkeeper, he never discarded anything and the shelves are still laden with his out-dated stock. Visitors are free to open drawers and browse amongst the old accounts. Gifts, books and postcards on sale.

1478 VOGRIE COUNTRY PARK **6 N16**

Gorebridge, Midlothian. 2 miles (3km) east of Gorebridge on B6372. Open all year daily, from dawn to dusk. Free. Charge for parking. Guided tours by arrangement. Explanatory displays. Tearoom and picnic areas. WC. Limited wheelchair access. Disabled WC. Car and coach parking. Telephone (01875) 821990.

There are three route marked walks in the park which have been selected to show visitors year round interest and variety. Nature trails and wildlife information panels. Walled garden and nursery. Ponds and streams. Model railway, rookery, golf course and play area.

1479 WADE'S BRIDGE **5 Li2**

On B846, north of Aberfeldy. Access at all times. Free. Car parking.

The bridge across the River Tay was begun in 1733 by General Wade, with William Adam as architect. It is considered to be the finest of all Wade's bridges. The Black Watch Memorial is a large cairn surmounted by a kilted soldier, erected close to the bridge in Queen Victoria's Jubilee Year (1887). Easy access across lawn to river bank.

1480 MAGGIE WALLS MONUMENT **5 Li3**

1 mile (1.5km) west of Dunning, Perthshire, on B8062. Access at all times. Free. Wheelchair access with assistance. Car and coach parking. Telephone (01764) 684269.

The monument marks the spot where Maggie Wall was allegedly burned as a witch in 1657. It is constructed from rough field boulders and a plinth stone topped with a cross.

1481 WALTZING WATERS **3 K10**

Balvail Brae, Newtonmore, Inverness-shire. On A86 between Newtonmore and Kingussie. Open Feb–Dec, daily; telephone to confirm show times. Charge ££. Group concessions. Gift shop. Coffee shop. WC. Wheelchair access (except coffee shop). Car and coach parking. Telephone (01540) 673752.

Water spectacular with sound and light show.

1482 WANLOCKHEAD BEAM ENGINE **5 Li8**

HS. In Wanlockhead, Dumfriesshire, on the A797. Nearest railway station Sanquhar, buses from Sanquhar, Ayr or Dumfries. Access at all times. Free. Telephone 0131 668 8800.

An early 19th-century wooden water-balance pump for draining a lead mine, with the track of a horse engine beside it. Nearby is the privately-operated Museum of Lead Mining (see 1094).

1483 WARDLAW MAUSOLEUM **3 J8**

Kirkhill, Inverness-shire. 7 miles (11km) west of Inverness on A862, signposted from Inchmoke. Bus to centre of Kirkhill village, then 5 minutes walk. Open May–Sep, Wed–Sat 1100–1200 and 1400–1600. Free. Donations. Guided tours. Wheelchair access. Car parking. Telephone (01463) 831324.

This listed burial mausoleum was built in 1634 onto the east gable of the 13th century church. The mausoleum was altered in 1722 at which time a most exceptional bartizan tower was added and the interior was recast to allow the incorporation of a very elaborate memorial to Thomas Fraser, the 12th Baron Lovat.

1484 WARP AND WEFT VISITOR CENTRE **1 G5**

Hoswick, Sandwick, Shetland. 14 miles (22.5km) south of Lerwick. Regular bus service. Open May–Sep, Mon–Sat 1000–1700, Sun

1200–1700. Free. Explanatory displays. Presentations on request. Gift shop. Tearoom. WC. Wheelchair access. Disabled WC. Car and coach parking. Telephone (01950) 431215.

Previously a weaving shed and now an exhibition of old weaving looms and radios. The history of the area is illustrated with photographs of mining, crofting, fishing and knitting. Variety of documents on the social history of Shetland.

1485 WATERLOO MONUMENT **5 P17**

Off B6400, 5 miles (7.5km) north of Jedburgh. Open Easter–Oct. Free. No access to interior.

Prominent landmark on the summit of Penielheugh Hill. See also 782 Harestanes Countryside Visitor Centre.

1486 WATER MILL AND TEAROOM **3 L11**

Ford Road, Blair Atholl, Pitlochry. 5 miles (8km) north of Pitlochry off A9. Railway station and bus stop 200 yards (182m). Open Apr–Oct, Mon–Sat 1030–1730, Sun 1200–1730. Charge £. Group concessions. Guided tours by arrangement. Explanatory displays. Gift shop. Tearoom. Garden. WC. Wheelchair access to teagarden only. Disabled WC. Car and coach parking. Telephone (01796) 481321.

Dating from 1613, this working museum produces oatmeal and flour which is on sale in the tearoom. The stoneground oatmeal flour is an ingredient in a variety of baking on sale at the mill and locally. Also available is honey from local beehives.

1487 WATER SAMPLING PAVILION, STRATHPEFFER **3 J7**

Strathpeffer, west of Dingwall.

An opportunity for visitors to sample the sulphur waters, which made Strathpeffer Spa renowned as a destination for Victorians.

1488 GEORGE WATERSTON MUSEUM **1 F8**

Auld Schule, Fair Isle, Shetland. An island between Orkney and Shetland. By sea or air. Open May–Sep, Mon and Fri 1400–1600, Wed 1000–1230. Free. Donations. Guided tours. Explanatory displays. Gift shop. Toy corner. Telephone (01595) 760244.

Maps the social history of the island with displays of agriculture, fishing, shipwrecks, textiles, natural history and archaeology. Housed in the old school.

1489 WATLING LODGE **6 L15**

HS. In Falkirk, signposted from the A9. Nearest railway and bus stations Falkirk. Access at all times. Free. Telephone 0131 668 8800.

The best section of the ditch of the Antonine Wall (see 62).

1490 WEAVERS COTTAGE **6 J16**

NTS. Shuttle Street, Kilbarchan, Paisley. Off A737, 5 miles (8km) west of Paisley. Nearest railway station Johnstone (2 miles/3.5km); bus from Paisley, Glasgow or Johnstone. Open Easter–Sep, daily 1330–1730; weekends in Oct, 1330–1730. Charge £. Children free. Group concessions. Explanatory displays and subtitled video. Explanatory text (available in Spanish). Cottage garden. WC. Subtitled video. Car parking. Telephone (01505) 705588.

This typical cottage of an 18th-century handloom weaver contains looms, weaving equipment and domestic utensils. Displays of local, historical and weaving items. Attractive cottage garden. Weaving demonstrations (check for times). Video programme.

1491 WEAVERS COTTAGE **6 K16**

23–25 Wellwynd, Airdrie. In Airdrie town centre. Nearest railway station Airdrie, local bus service. Open all year, Mon, Tue and Thu–Sat 1000–1700. Free. Guided tours. Explanatory displays. Gift shop. WC. Wheelchair access. Car and coach parking. Telephone (01236) 747712.

Over 150 years before the industrial revolution transformed the Monklands, Airdrie became a prosperous weaving town. The cottage reflects the 1830s weaving heritage of Airdrie. Exhibition gallery and handloom demonstrations.

1492 WELL OF THE SEVEN HEADS **2 H10**

Off A82 on the west shore of Loch Oich. Access at all times. Free. Car parking.

A curious monument inscribed in English, Gaelic, French and Latin and surmounted by seven men's heads. It stands above a spring and recalls the grim story of the execution of seven brothers for the murder of the two sons of a 17th-century chief of Keppoch.

1493 WEST AFFRIC **2 H8**

NTS. Highland. 22 miles (35.5km) east of Kyle of Lochalsh, off A87. Open all year. Free. Guided walks by rangers. Telephone (01599) 511231.

Stretching over 9000 acres (3642ha), this important wild and rugged landscape adjoins the NTS property at Kintail. West Affric is magnificent and challenging walking country, and includes one of the most popular east-west Highland paths. This was once the old drove road taking cattle across Scotland from the isle of Skye to market at Dingwall.

1494 WEST HIGHLAND DAIRY **2 F8**

Achmore, Stromeferry, Kyle. 0.3 mile (0.5km) down lane towards Fernaig and Portnacullin from Achmore village. Nearest railway station Stromeferry, post bus from Kyle of Lochalsh. Parking available for small coaches only. Open all year, daily dawn to dusk. Free. Dairy shop and picnic area. Wheelchair access with assistance. Car and coach parking. Telephone (01599) 577203.

Small commercial dairy producing sheep and goat's milk cheese, an award-winning blue cheese, dairy ice cream and cranachan, a traditional Scottish dessert. A small flock of milking sheep enable the dairy to run short courses on all aspects of dairying.

1495 WEST HIGHLAND HEAVY HORSE TOURS **2 E8**

Armadale Castle, Sleat, Isle of Skye. 0.5 mile (1km) north of Armadale ferry terminal, 21 miles (34km) south of the Skye Bridge at Kyle of Lochalsh on A851. Car and passenger ferry from Mallaig to Armadale. Bus from Kyle of Lochalsh. Tours operate May–Sep, telephone to confirm times. Charge dependent on tour. Group concessions. Guided tours (available in German). Wheelchair access with assistance. Telephone (01478) 660233.

Based at Armadale Castle Gardens (see 92). Various tours in horse-drawn, traditionally built all-weather dray: around Armadale Castle Gardens; or along the stunning coastline. Private evening bookings possible. All visitor facilities available at Armadale.

1496 WEST HIGHLAND MUSEUM **2 H11**

Cameron Square, Fort William, Inverness-shire. Nearest railway station Fort William, 0.5 mile (1km). Open Jun–Sep, Mon–Sat 1000–1700; Jul and Aug, Sun 1400–1700; Oct–May, Mon–Sat 1000–1600. Charge £. Group concessions. Guided tours by arrangement. Explanatory displays.

Gift shop. WC. Limited wheelchair access. Disabled WC. Car parking. Telephone (01397) 702169.

The museum was founded in 1922, and is world renowned for its Jacobite memorabilia.

1497 WEST PORT **5 P13**

HS. In South Street, St Andrews, Fife. Nearest railway station Leuchars, 4 miles (6.5km), connecting bus to St Andrews. Buses from Dundee and Edinburgh. Ten minute walk from bus station. Free.

One of the few surviving city gates in Scotland, built in 1589 and renovated in 1843.

1498 WESTQUARTER DOVECOT **6 L15**

HS. At Westquarter, near Lauriston, West Lothian, 2 miles (3km) east of Falkirk. Bus from Falkirk. Access at all times. Free. Telephone 0131 668 8800.

A very handsome rectangular dovecot with a heraldic panel dated 1647 over the entrance doorway.

1499 WESTRAY HERITAGE CENTRE **1 B9**

Pierowall, Westray, Orkney. 7 miles (11km) from ferry terminal, minibus to Pierowall village during summer. Open mid May–mid Sep, daily 1000–1230 and 1400–1700. Charge £. Children under 5 , youth and school groups free. Group concessions. Explanatory displays. Gift shop. Tearoom and picnic area. WC. Wheelchair access. Disabled WC. Car and coach parking.

A display on the natural heritage of Westray. Many children's hands-on activities. Large collection of black and white photos. Information on local cemetaries. Local memories of wartimes, schooldays, Noup Head lighthouse, sports and kirks.

1500 WESTSIDE CHURCH **1 B9**

HS. At Bay of Tuquoy on the south coast of the island of Westray, Orkney. Ferry from Kirkwall to Westray. Access at all times. Free. Telephone 0131 668 8800.

A roofless 12th-century Romanesque church.

1501 WHALEBONE ARCH **2 D3**

Bragar, on the western side of the Isle of Lewis.

This arch is made from the huge jawbone of a blue whale that came ashore in 1920.

1502 WHALIGOE STEPS **3 N3**

At Ulbster, Caithness.

Three hundred flagstone steps descent the steep cliffs to a small quay below, built in the 18th century during the herring boom. Care should be taken in wet or windy conditions – the steps are not suitable for the very young or the infirm.

1503 WHITEASH AND ORDIEQUISH CYCLE TRAILS **3 N7**

FE. Moray Forest District Office, Balnacoul, Fochabers, Moray. Entrance 1 mile (1.5km) east of Fochabers village. Open all year except when timber harvesting – contact District Office. Free. Leaflet available. Car parking. Telephone (01343) 820223.

Three medium grade mountain bike trails through mixed forest, suitable for either a family outing or a more adventurous cycle ride. Uphill climbs are rewarded by spectacular views of Moray. Colour-coded routes.

1504 WHITHORN PRIORY AND MUSEUM **4 J21**

HS. 6 Bruce Street, Whithorn, Newton-Stewart. In Whithorn. Nearest railway station Dumfries, bus from Newton Stewart and Stranraer. Open Easter–Oct, 1030–1700. Free. Guided tours. Explanatory displays. Gift shop. WC. Limited wheelchair access. Telephone (01988) 500700.

The cradle of Christianity in Scotland, founded in the 5th century (St Ninian's Candida Casa, the Shining House). The priory for Premonstratensian canons was built in the 12th century and became the cathedral church of Galloway. In the museum is a fine collection of early Christian stone, including the Latinus stone, the earliest Christian memorial in Scotland, and the Monreith Cross, the finest of the Whithorn school of crosses.

1505 WHITHORN TRUST DISCOVERY CENTRE **4 J21**

45–47 George Street, Whithorn. Off A75 between Glenluce and Newton Stewart. Bus service from Newton Stewart, Stranraer and Dumfries. Open Apr–Oct, daily 1030–1700. Charge £. Joint ticket with Whithorn Priory and Museum (see 1504). Group concessions. Guided tours. Explanatory displays and audio-visual show. Gift shop. Picnic area. WC. Limited wheelchair access. Disabled WC. Car and coach parking. Telephone (01988) 500508.

Since 1986 archaeologists have been investigating the site of an abandoned town. 1000 years ago the Anglo-Saxons called it Hwiterne; earlier it was called Candida Casa, the Shining House. 1500 years ago St Ninian, Scotland's first saint, built a church here. Guided tour of original dig site, priory, museum and crypts, discovery centre with archaeology puzzle. Audio-visual show, exhibitions.

1506 WIDEFORD HILL CHAMBERED CAIRN **1 B10**

HS. On the west slope of Wideford Hill, 2 miles (3km) west of Kirkwall, Orkney. Access at all times. Free. Telephone 0131 668 8800.

A fine Neolithic chambered cairn with three concentric walls and a burial chamber with three large cells.

1507 WILDFOWL AND WETLANDS CENTRE **5 M20**

East Park Farm, Caerlaverock, Dumfries. 9 miles (14.5km) southeast of Dumfries. Nearest railway station Dumfries, bus from Dumfries. Open daily (except Christmas Day), 1000–1700. Charge £. Group concessions. Guided tours. Explanatory displays. Gift shop. Tearoom and picnic area. WC. Wheelchair access with assistance. Car and coach parking. Telephone (01387) 770200.

A 1350 acre (546ha) nature reserve where many birds can be seen from hides and observation towers. Trails in summer.

1508 WILDLIFE PARK, KIRKCUDBRIGHT **5 K21**

Lochfergus Plantation, Kirkcudbright. 1 mile (2km) east of Kirkcudbright, on B727. Nearest bus stop Kirkcudbright. Open Mar, Sep and Oct, daily 1000–1630; Apr, May, Jun, Jul and Aug, daily 1000–1715. Charge ££. Group concessions. Guided tours Apr–Aug. Explanatory displays. Gift shop. Tearoom and picnic areas. Baby changing facilities, children's play area. WC. No guide dogs. Wheelchair access. Disabled WC. Car and coach parking. Telephone (01557) 331645.

Over 150 animals and 32 species are found in the hillside woodland setting of this zoological park and wild animal conservation centre. On offer are guided tours of the zoo, pet-handling sessions, quizzes for children, animal sponsorship, and involvement in threatened species breeding and wildlife conservation both in the zoo and nature reserve. Also crazy golf.

1509 WILTON LODGE WALLED GARDEN **5 P18**

Wilton Park Road, Hawick. 0.5 mile (1km) from the centre. Open daily all year, 0730–1600. Free. Tearoom. WC. Wheelchair access. Car and coach parking. Telephone (01450) 378023.

107 acres (43ha) of garden with extensive shrubberies and a large selection of mature trees.

1510 WINDING WALKS FOREST WALKS **3 N7**

FE. Moray Forest District Office, Balnacoul, Fochabers, Moray. Entrance 1 mile (1.5km) east of Fochabers village. Nearest bus at Fochabers. Open at all times. Free. Leaflet available. Picnic area. Guided walks and events. Wheelchair access with assistance. Car parking. Telephone (01343) 820223.

A maze of paths winds through the magnificent trees of a dramatic steep-sided gully – choose to explore the narrow winding walks' paths or try one of the more sedate way-marked walks. Four walks from 1.5 miles (3km) to 3 miles (6km) with magnificent views over the Moray countryside. Ranger service.

1511 WINTON HOUSE **6 N15**

Pencaitland, East Lothian. 14 miles (22.5km) east of Edinburgh off A1 at Tranent. Lodge gates south of New Winton (B6355) or Pencaitland (A6093). Bus from Edinburgh to Pencaitland, then 1 mile (2km) walk. Open second and third weekends in Apr, May and Sep, 1200–1700; telephone to confirm. Other times by prior arrangement. Charge ££. Group concessions. Guided tours. Explanatory displays. Tearoom and picnic area. Garden, walks. WC. Limited wheelchair access. Disabled WC. Car and coach parking. Telephone (01875) 341309.

A 15th-century tower house restored palatially with famous stone twisted chimneys and magnificent plaster ceilings. Still a family home after 500 years, it houses many treasures which include paintings by many of Scotland's notable artists, fine furniture and an exhibition of family costumes and photographs. The grounds contain specimen trees, woodland walks and terraced gardens.

1512 WINTON POTTERY **6 N15**

Winton Estate, Pencaitland, East Lothian. 14 miles (22.5km) southeast of Edinburgh on B6355. Bus from Edinburgh to Pencaitland, then 1 mile (2km) walk. Open by arrangement all year, and during Apr, Jun and Dec. Free. Guided tours. Gift shop. Wheelchair access with assistance. Car and coach parking. Telephone (01875) 340188.

The pottery is situated in a former stable block, and specialises in thrown and hand-built stoneware for domestic use, as well as plant holders and sundials. Demonstrations are available by arrangement.

1513 WITCH'S STONE **3 L6**

In the Littletown area of Dornoch, Sutherland.

An upright slab bearing the date 1722, marking the place where the last witch in Scotland was burned.

1514 ALEXANDRA WOLFFE ANIMALS **K20**

The Tollhouse, Gatehouse-of-Fleet, Kirkcudbrightshire. At the top of the High Street. Buses from Dumfries, Castle Douglas or Newton Stewart. Open weekdays 1000–1230 and 1400–1630. Free. Wheelchair access. Car parking. Telephone (01557) 814300.

A small working ceramic studio making individual statuettes and portrait models of animals.

1515 WOLFSTONE **3 L5**

Sutherland. Situated in a lay-by, 6 miles (9.5km) south of Helmsdale at Loth.

The stone marks the spot where, in 1700, the last wolf in Scotland was killed.

1516 WOOL STONE **5 P15**

In Stenton, B6370, 5 miles (7.5km) southwest of Dunbar. Access at all reasonable times. Free. Car parking.

The medieval Wool Stone, used formerly for the weighing of wool at Stenton Fair, stands on the green. See also the 14th-century Rood Well, topped by a cardinal's hat, and the old doocot.

1517 WORKING SHEEP DOGS **3 L9**

Leault Farm, Kincraig, Kingussie, Inverness-shire. 6 miles (10km) south of Aviemore on B9152. Nearest railway station Kingussie, local bus service. Open May–Nov, daily (except Sat – times in May and Oct by arrangement): Jun 1200 and 1600; Jul and Aug 1000, 1200, 1400 and 1600; Sep 1200 and 1600. Charge ££. Group concessions. Demonstrations. Gift shop. Wheelchair access. Car and coach parking. Telephone (01540) 651310.

Displays of up to eight border collies and their skilful handlers. Traditional hand-shearing displays – visitors can participate. Also ducks, puppies and orphan lambs. Visitors can learn about the working day of a Highland shepherd.

1518 WORLD OF WOOD **2 E9**

Old Corry Industrial Estate, Broadford, Isle of Skye. Open Mar–Dec, Mon–Sat 1000–1700. Free. Guided tours. Explanatory displays. Gift shop. Picnic area. Arboretum. Wheelchair access. Car and coach parking. Telephone (01471) 822831.

The story of a tree from a seed to the various articles created from wood: the planting, harvesting and saw-milling stages, as well as many wood craft trades are displayed. General woodworking tools are on display and some are available for use by young or old – the foot powered pole lathe can be operated by even the very young. A variety of items of wood craft are on sale.

1519 YARROW **5 N17**

A708, west from Selkirk. Car parking.

A lovely valley praised by many writers including Scott, Wordsworth and Hogg. Little Yarrow Kirk dates from 1640, Scott's great-great-grandfather was minister there. Deuchar Bridge dates from the 17th century. On the surrounding hills are the remains of ancient Border keeps.

1520 YOUNGER BOTANIC GARDEN **6 H15**

Benmore, Dunoon, Argyll. 7 miles (11km) north of Dunoon, on A815. Bus from Dunoon. Open Mar–Oct, daily 0930–1800. Charge £. Group concessions. Guided tours by arrangement. Explanatory displays. Gift shop. Licensed café with indoor and outdoor seating. WC. Limited wheelchair access. Disabled WC. Car and coach parking. Telephone (01369) 706261.

Some of Britain's tallest trees can be found here, as can over 250 species of rhododendrons and an extensive magnolia collection. Other features include an avenue of giant redwoods planted in 1863, a formal garden, and a variety of waymarked trails. Younger Botanic Garden is a Specialist Garden of the Royal Botanic Garden, Edinburgh (see 574).

INDEX

Visitor attractions are indexed under the following subjects:

Abbey, cathedral or church
Aerial activity
Art gallery or museum
Art or craft centre
Castle
Castle or historic house (view from the outside only)
Country park
Distillery
Fishing
Forest trail
Garden or plant nursery
Golf course or centre
Guided tour
Historic house
Monument, notable building or antiquity
Nature reserve
Outdoor activity centre
Pleasure boat trip
Pony trekking or horse riding
Sailing
Scenic or archictectural feature
Skiing
Theatre, art or leisure centre
Visitor centre or speciality attraction
Wildlife or farm park

Abbey, cathedral or church

3 Abercorn Church and Museum
7 Aberdeen, Cathedral Church of St Machar
16 Aberdeen, Kirk of St Nicholas
20 Aberdeen, St Andrew's Cathedral
21 Aberdeen, St Machar's Cathedral Transepts
48 Alloway Old Kirk
49 Alloway Parish Church
65 Arbroath Abbey
72 Ardchattan Priory
146 Beauly Priory
164 Biggar Kirk
169 Blackfriars Chapel
192 Borthwick Parish Church
301 Castle Semple Collegiate Church
315 Church of St Magnus
316 Church of the Holy Rude
394 Croick Church
398 Cross Kirk
400 Crossraguel Abbey
410 Culross Abbey
420 Dalmeny Parish Church
429 Deer Abbey
435 Deskford Church
447 Dornoch Cathedral
458 Dryburgh Abbey
499 Dundrennan Abbey
501 Dunfermline Abbey and Palace
503 Dunglass Collegiate Church
506 Dunkeld Cathedral
529 Edinburgh, Canongate Kirk
545 Edinburgh, Greyfriars Kirk
546 Edinburgh, Holyrood Abbey
553 Edinburgh, Magdalen Chapel
566 Edinburgh, Parish Church of St Cuthbert
581 Edinburgh, St Giles' Cathedral
582 Edinburgh, St John's
583 Edinburgh, St Mary's Cathedral
584 Edinburgh, St Triduana's Chapel
604 Edrom Church
610 Elgin Cathedral
616 Eynhallow Church
661 Fortrose Cathedral
687 Glasgow Cathedral
709 Glasgow, Queen's Cross Church
745 Glenluce Abbey
812 Hilton of Cadboll Chapel
817 Holy Trinity Church, Stirling
830 Inchcolm Abbey
831 Inchkenneth Chapel
833 Innerpeffray Chapel
853 Iona Abbey
866 Italian Chapel
870 Jedburgh Abbey
882 Keills Chapel
886 Kelso Abbey
894 Kildonan Church
907 Kilmory Knap Chapel
908 Kilmun (St Munn's) Church
912 Kilwinning Abbey
914 Kinkell Church
926 Kippen Parish Church
930 Kirk of Calder
950 Largs Old Kirk
951 Lauderdale Aisle, St Mary's Church, Haddington
964 Lincluden Collegiate Church
1025 Maison Dieu Chapel
1034 Maybole Collegiate Church
1042 Melrose Abbey
1097 Muthill Church and Tower
1144 Old Parish Church, Hamilton
1155 Orphir Church and the Earl's Bu
1159 Paisley Abbey
1162 Panbride Church
1178 Pierowall Church
1185 Pluscarden Abbey
1215 Restenneth Priory
1229 Rosslyn Chapel
1240 Saddell Abbey
1244 St Andrew's Cathedral, Inverness
1245 St Andrew's Cathedral and St Rule's Tower
1249 St Blane's Church, Kingarth
1250 St Bride's Church, Douglas
1251 St Bridget's Kirk, Dalgety
1252 St Clement's Church, Rodel
1254 St Cormac's Chapel
1255 St Duthac's Chapel
1257 St John's Church, Dunoon
1258 St John's Kirk, Perth
1260 St Magnus Cathedral, Kirkwall
1262 St Martin's Kirk, Haddington
1263 St Mary's Chapel, Crosskirk
1264 St Mary's Chapel, Rothesay
1265 St Mary's Church, Auchindoir
1266 St Mary's Church, Grand Tully
1267 St Mary's Church, St Andrews
1268 St Mary's Collegiate Church, Haddington
1269 St Mary's Episcopal Church, Dalkeith
1271 St Michael's Parish Church, Linlithgow
1274 St Ninian's Chapel, Isle of Whithorn
1275 St Ninian's Chapel, Tynet
1277 St Peter's Kirk and Parish Cross
1319 Seton Collegiate Church
1394 Sweetheart Abbey
1402 Tarbet Old Church
1432 Torphichen Preceptory
1449 Tullibardine Chapel
1456 Ui Church
1500 Westside Church
1504 Whithorn Priory and Museum

Aerial activity

247 Cairngorm Gliding Club
641 Fife Airport

Art gallery or museum

1 Abbot House Heritage Centre
4 Aberdeen Art Gallery
12 Aberdeen, Gallery Heinzel
14 Aberdeen, Gordon Highlanders Museum
17 Aberdeen, Marischal Museum

18 Aberdeen, Maritime Museum
23 Aberdeen, Tolbooth
24 Aberdeen, University Zoology Museum
26 Aberdeenshire Farming Museum
45 Alford Heritage Centre
51 Almond Valley Heritage Centre
54 Alyth Museum
55 Angus Folk Museum
56 An Lanntair
66 Arbroath Museum
67 Arbuthnot Museum
88 Argyll and Sutherland Highlanders Regimental Museum
96 Arran Heritage Museum
97 art.tm gallery
100 Atholl Country Collection
104 Auchindrain Township Open Air Museum
106 Auchterarder Heritage
107 Auld Kirk Museum
110 Aviation Museum
111 Avoch Heritage Exhibition
130 Banchory Museum
131 Banff Museum
132 Bannockburn Heritage Centre
158 Bennie Museum
160 Bernera Museum
163 Biggar Gasworks Museum
167 Birkhill Fireclay Mine
173 Black House
178 Black Watch Regimental Museum
185 Bød of Gremista
189 Bonhoga Gallery
199 Brander Museum
206 Brechin Museum
212 British Golf Museum
214 Broderick, Laurence, Sculpture Exhibition
218 Broughton Gallery
222 Bruce's, Michael, Cottage
224 Buchan, John, Centre
226 Buckhaven Museum
227 Buckie Drifter
234 Burns, Robert, Centre
236 Burns House Museum
240 Burntisland Edwardian Fair Museum
241 Bute Museum
263 Campbeltown Museum
273 Carlyle, Jane Welsh, Museum
277 Carnegie, Andrew, Birthplace Museum
279 Carnegie Museum
285 Carsphairn Heritage Centre
291 Castle Douglas Art Gallery
294 Castle House Museum
300 Castle of St John
311 Childhood Memories Toy Museum
320 Clachanmore Gallery and Tearoom
322 Clan Armstrong Museum
323 Clan Cameron Museum
324 Clan Donnachaidh Museum
326 Clan Macpherson Museum
327 Clapperton's, Robert, Daylight Photographic Studio
328 Clark, Jim, Room
339 Clydebank Museum
351 Coldstream Museum
364 Cornice Museum of Ornamental Plasterwork
382 Crail Museum
389 Creetown Gem Rock Museum
391 Crichton Royal Museum
395 Cromarty Courthouse Museum
413 Cumbernauld Museum
416 Dalgarven Mill and Museum of Country Life and Costume
424 Dandelion Designs and Images Gallery
426 Davidson, Tom, Gallery
432 Denny Ship Model Experiment Tank
437 Devil's Porridge
440 Dingwall Museum
463 Duff House Country Gallery
469 Dumfries Museum and Camera Obscura
472 Dunaskin Open Air Museum
475 Dunbar Town House Museum
477 Dunbeath Heritage Centre
478 Dunblane City Cathedral Museum
490 Dundee, McManus Galleries
496 Dundee, Verdant Works
502 Dunfermline Museum
522 Edinburgh, Bank of Scotland Museum
534 Edinburgh, Dean Gallery
538 Edinburgh, Fruitmarket Gallery
549 Edinburgh, Huntly House Museum
555 Edinburgh, Matthew Architecture Gallery
558 Edinburgh, Museum of Childhood
559 Edinburgh, Museum of Fire
560 Edinburgh, Museum of Scotland
561 Edinburgh, National Gallery of Scotland
562 Edinburgh, National Library of Scotland
564 Edinburgh, Newhaven Heritage Museum
568 Edinburgh, The Peoples Story
570 Edinburgh Printmakers
572 Edinburgh, Regimental Museum of The Royal Scots
575 Edinburgh, Royal Museum of Scotland
577 Edinburgh, Royal Scottish Academy
579 Edinburgh, Russell Collection of Early Keyboard Instruments
580 Edinburgh, St Cecelia's Hall
586 Edinburgh, Scottish National Gallery of Modern Art
587 Edinburgh, Scottish National Portrait Gallery
591 Edinburgh, Stills Gallery
593 Edinburgh, Talbot Rice Gallery
596 Edinburgh University Collection of Historic Musical Instruments
599 Edinburgh, The Writers' Museum
611 Elgin Museum
612 Ellisland Farm
615 Eyemouth Museum
620 Falconer Museum
635 Fergusson Gallery
638 Fetlar Interpretive Centre
642 Fife Folk Museum
648 Flat Cat Gallery
652 Fochabers Folk Museum
668 Gairloch Heritage Museum
670 Gallery Forteviot
674 Garlogie Mill Power House Museum
680 Gladstone Court Museum
682 Glasgow Art Gallery and Museum, Kelvingrove
686 Glasgow, The Burrell Collection
689 Glasgow, Clyde Maritime Museum
690 Glasgow, Collins Gallery
692 Glasgow, Gallery of Modern Art
695 Glasgow, Heatherbank Museum of Social Work
696 Glasgow, House for an Art Lover
697 Glasgow, Hunterian Art Gallery
698 Glasgow, Hunterian Museum
700 Glasgow, The Lighthouse
702 Glasgow, McLellan Galleries
703 Glasgow, Museum of Transport
705 Glasgow, People's Palace
708 Glasgow, Provand's Lordship

711 Glasgow, Royal Highland Fusiliers Regimental Museum
712 Glasgow, St Mungo Museum of Religious Life and Art
715 Glasgow, Scotland Street School
716 Glasgow, Springburn Museum
717 Glasgow, Tenement House
727 Glencoe and North Lorn Folk Museum
733 Glen Esk Folk Museum
737 Glenfinnan Station Museum
746 Glenluce Motor Museum
747 Glen Lyon Gallery
759 Grampian Transport Museum
760 Grangemouth Museum
761 Grantown Museum and Heritage Trust
771 Groam House Museum
777 Halliwell's House Museum
779 Harbour Cottage Gallery, Kirkcudbright
786 Hastie, John, Museum
787 Hawick Museum and the Scott Gallery
799 Highland Folk Museum, Kingussie
800 Highland Folk Museum, Newtonmore
803 Highland Museum of Childhood
813 HM Customs and Excise Museum and Exhibition
822 Hoxa Tapestry Gallery
841 Inveraray Jail
842 Inveraray Maritime Museum
844 Inverbeg Galleries
847 Inverkeithing Museum
850 Inverness Museum and Art Gallery
854 Iona Heritage Centre
863 Isle of Mull Museum
871 Jedburgh Castle Jail and Museum
875 Jones, John Paul, Cottage Museum
880 Keathbank Mill Heritage Centre
895 Kildonan Museum
900 Kilmartin House Museum of Ancient Culture
904 Kilmorack Gallery
917 Kinnaird Head Lighthouse
920 Kinneil Museum
928 Kirkcaldy Museum and Art Gallery
945 Laidhay Croft Museum
946 Lamb, William, Memorial Studio
949 Largs Museum
962 Liddesdale Heritage Centre
963 Lime Tree Studio Gallery
968 Linlithgow, The, Story
969 Linlithgow Union Canal Society Museum and Boats
971 Little Gallery
972 Livingstone, David, Centre
991 Loch Ness, Official Monster Exhibition
998 Lochwinnoch Community Museum
1004 Lossiemouth Fisheries and Community Museum
1007 Low Parks Museum
1008 Luib Croft Museum
1017 McLean Museum and Art Gallery
1022 Maggie's Hoosie
1026 Mallaig Heritage Centre
1033 Maud Railway Museum
1035 Meadowlands Gallery
1048 Methil Heritage Centre
1051 Miller's, Hugh, Cottage
1058 Moat Park Heritage Centre
1059 Moffat Museum
1066 Montrose Air Station Museum
1068 Montrose Museum and Art Gallery
1075 Moray Motor Museum
1077 Morven Gallery
1080 Motherwell Heritage Centre
1081 Motoring Heritage Centre
1088 Muir, John, House
1092 Museum of Flight
1093 Museum of Islay Life
1094 Museum of Lead Mining
1098 Muthill Village and Parish Museum
1099 Myreton Motor Museum
1100 Nairn Fishertown Museum
1115 Newton Stewart Museum
1121 North Ayrshire Museum
1122 North Berwick Museum
1127 Northfield Farm Museum
1128 North Glen Gallery and Workshop
1129 Northlands Viking Centre
1136 Oiseval Gallery
1137 Old Bridge House Museum
1138 Old Byre Heritage Centre
1139 Old Gala House
1140 Old Haa Visitor Centre
1146 Orbost Gallery
1152 Orkney Museum
1153 Orkney Wireless Museum
1160 Paisley Museum and Art Galleries
1165 Paterson, James, Museum, Moniaive
1167 Peebles Gallery
1172 Perth Museum and Art Gallery
1174 Peterhead Maritime Heritage Museum
1182 Pittencrieff House Museum
1189 Potter, Beatrix, Exhibition
1191 Prestongrange Industrial Heritage Museum
1197 Queensferry Museum
1198 Queen's Own Highlanders Regimental Museum
1212 Renfrew Community Museum
1221 Riverside Gallery
1235 Rozelle House Galleries
1248 St Andrew's Preservation Trust Museum and Garden
1282 Sandaig Museum
1285 Sanquhar Tolbooth Museum
1286 Savings Bank Museum
1288 Scalloway Museum
1293 Scotland's Lighthouse Museum
1294 Scotland's Secret Bunker
1298 Scottish Agricultural Museum
1302 Scottish Fisheries Museum
1304 Scottish Industrial Railway Centre
1307 Scottish Maritime Museum
1308 Scottish Mining Museum
1311 Scottish Vintage Bus Museum
1313 Scott's, Sir Walter, Courtroom
1320 Shambellie House Museum of Costume
1322 Shawbost School Museum
1323 Shetland Croft House Museum
1324 Shetland Museum
1325 Shetland Textile Working Museum
1330 Shotts Heritage Centre
1336 Skerryvore Lighthouse Museum
1339 Skye Museum of Island Life
1346 Sma' Shot Cottages
1347 Smith Art Gallery and Museum
1351 Sophies Puppenstube and Dolls House Museum
1368 Stenton Gallery
1370 Stewartry Museum
1373 Stirling Old Town Jail
1378 Strachur Smiddy Museum
1379 Stranraer Museum
1383 Strathnaver Museum
1385 Stromness Museum
1386 Stronsay Fish Mart Interpretation Centre
1389 Stuart, John McDouall, Museum
1393 Summerlee Heritage Park
1395 Taigh Chearsabhagh Museum Arts Centre
1400 Tangwick Haa Museum

1407 Teddy Melrose, Scotland's Teddy Bear Museum
1414 Thurso Heritage Museum
1419 Tolbooth Art Centre
1420 Tolbooth Museum
1423 Tolquhon Gallery
1438 Toy Museum
1446 Trotternish Art Gallery
1448 Tugnet Ice House
1452 Tweeddale Museum and Gallery
1457 Uig Heritage Centre
1461 Ullapool Museum and Visitor Centre
1466 Unst Heritage Centre
1467 Up Helly Aa Exhibition
1477 Village Store
1488 Waterston, George, Museum
1491 Weavers Cottage
1496 West Highland Museum
1499 Westray Heritage Centre

Art or craft centre

61 An Tobar Arts Centre, Gallery and Café
63 An Tuireann Arts Centre
89 Argyll Pottery
108 Aultbea Woodcraft and Hardwood Cafe
109 Aurora Crafts
118 Balbirnie Craft Centre
126 Balnakeil Craft Village
137 Barn Gallery
138 Barnyard Studios, Gallery and Tearoom
190 Border Fine Arts Gallery
282 Carron Pottery, Craft and Art Gallery
321 Claggan Crafts
335 Clog and Shoe Workshop
354 Coll Pottery
374 Craggan Mill Restaurant, Crafts and Art Gallery
383 Crail Pottery
421 Dalton Pottery
425 Davidson, Barbara, Pottery
434 Designs Gallery and Cafe
460 Drymen Pottery
509 Dunnydeer Studio Porcelain
520 Edinbane Pottery
521 Edinburgh, The Adam Pottery
614 Embroidery Workshop
653 Fordyce Joiner's Workshop Visitor Centre
721 Glass Creations
732 Glenelg Candles Arts and Crafts Centre
764 Green Hall Gallery
780 Harbour View Gallery
784 Harris Tweed Weaving and Knitting
785 Hartmount Woodturning and Cabinet Making Studio
789 Hayward, Stephen, Wood Carving
791 Heathergems
792 Hebridean Jewellery
797 Highland Aromatics
808 Hill, Griselda, Pottery
829 Iceberg Glassblowing Studio
855 Iona Pottery and Gallery
868 Jaeger, Stephane, Knitwear
887 Kelso Pottery
915 Kin Kraft Centre for Scottish Crafts
918 Kinnaird Pottery
924 Kinsman Blake Ceramics
935 Knockan Studio and Craft Centre
965 Lindean Mill Glass
974 Loch-an-Eilein Pottery
997 Loch Tay Pottery
1002 Logie Steading
1020 Made in Scotland
1056 Milton Art and Craft Gallery
1070 Monymusk Arts Centre
1120 Nornova Knitwear
1125 Northern Lights Candles Workshop
1143 Old Manse Gallery
1151 Orkney Chair
1156 Ortak Visitor Centre
1164 Parker, Ron, Sculpture
1168 Peel Farm Coffee and Crafts
1173 Perth Sculpture Trail
1222 Riverside Granary
1247 St Andrew's Pottery Shop
1291 Scone Studios
1318 Selkirk Glass Visitor Centre
1321 Shape Scape Ceramics
1328 Shilasdair
1329 Shinafoot Art Studios
1355 South Lissens Pottery
1360 Speyside Horn and Country Crafts
1390 Studio Jewellery Workshop and Gallery
1397 Tait and Style
1458 Uig Pottery
1460 Uist Craft Producers
1471 Vennel Gallery
1476 Village Glass
1512 Winton Pottery
1514 Wolffe, Alexandra, Animals

Castle

27 Aberdour Castle
82 Ardrossan Castle
86 Ardvreck Castle
113 Ayton Castle
119 Balfour Castle
124 Balmoral Castle
128 Balvaird Castle
129 Balvenie Castle
133 Barcaldine Castle
174 Blackness Castle
180 Blair Castle
182 Blairquhan
194 Bothwell Castle
197 Braemar Castle
215 Brodick Castle
225 Bucholie Castle
233 Burleigh Castle
244 Caerlaverock Castle
271 Carleton Castle
275 Carnasserie Castle
284 Carsluith Castle
289 Castle Campbell
292 Castle Fraser
298 Castle Menzies
299 Castle of Old Wick
302 Castle Sween
303 Castle Varrich
305 Cawdor Castle
331 Claypotts Castle
363 Corgarff Castle
377 Craigievar Castle
378 Craignethan Castle
379 Craigston Castle
386 Crathes Castle
390 Crichton Castle
397 Crookston Castle
405 Cubbie Row's Castle
412 Culzean Castle and Country Park
431 Delgatie Castle
441 Dirleton Castle and Gardens
449 Doune Castle
452 Drum Castle and Gardens
462 Duart Castle
464 Duffus Castle
467 Dumbarton Castle
497 Dundonald Castle
508 Dunnottar Castle
510 Dunstaffnage Castle and Chapel
511 Dunvegan Castle
530 Edinburgh Castle
532 Edinburgh, Craigmillar Castle
605 Edzell Castle and Garden
607 Eilean Donan Castle
608 Elcho Castle
634 Fast Castle
636 Ferniehirst Castle
650 Floors Castle
666 Fyvie Castle
681 Glamis Castle
725 Glenbuchat Castle
776 Hailes Castle
795 Hermitage Castle
823 Hume Castle
826 Huntingtower Castle

827 Huntly Castle
840 Inveraray Castle
884 Kelburn Castle and Country Centre
885 Kellie Castle and Garden
892 Kilchurn Castle
896 Kildrummy Castle
910 Kilravock Castle
933 Kisimul Castle
978 Loch Doon Castle
985 Loch Leven Castle
995 Lochranza Castle
1013 MacDuff Castle
1019 MacLellan's Castle
1091 Muness Castle
1103 Neidpath Castle
1112 Newark Castle
1119 Noltland Castle
1207 Red Castle
1230 Rothesay Castle
1232 Rough Castle
1233 Roxburgh Castle
1243 St Andrew's Castle
1287 Scalloway Castle
1332 Sinclair and Girnigoe Castle
1335 Skelbo Castle
1371 Stirling Castle
1401 Tantallon Castle
1411 Threave Castle
1422 Tolquhon Castle
1431 Torosay Castle and Gardens
1450 Turnberry Castle
1468 Urquhart Castle

Castle or historic house (view from outside only)
205 Brechin Cathedral Round Tower
243 Cadzow Castle
262 Cambuskenneth Abbey
662 Foulden Tithe Barn
848 Inverlochy Castle
919 Kinneil House
987 Lochmaben Castle
1076 Morton Castle
1145 Old Place of Mochrum
1279 St Serf's Church, Dunning
1337 Skipness Castle and Chapel

Country park
39 Aden Country Park
50 Almondell and Calderwood Country Park
147 Beecraigs Country Park
195 Bowhill House and Country Park
204 Brechin Castle Centre
257 Calderglen Country Park
309 Chatelherault Country Park
341 Clyde Muirshiel Regional Park, Barnbrock Farm
342 Clyde Muirshiel Regional Park, Castle Semple Visitor Centre
343 Clyde Muirshiel Regional Park, Cornalees Visitor Centre
344 Clyde Muirshiel Regional Park, Lunderston Bay
345 Clyde Muirshiel Regional Park, Muirshiel Visitor Centre
380 Craigtoun Country Park
396 Crombie Country Park
417 Dalkeith Country Park
710 Glasgow, Rouken Glen
993 Lochore Meadows Country Park
1063 Monikie Country Park
1086 Mugdock Country Park
1087 Muiravonside Country Park
1161 Palacerigg Country Park
1186 Polkemmet Country Park
1380 Strathclyde Country Park
1478 Vogrie Country Park

Distillery
28 Aberfeldy Distillery
70 Ardbeg Distillery Visitor Centre
156 Ben Nevis Distillery Visitor Centre
159 Ben Romach Distillery
179 Blair Athol Distillery
196 Bowmore Distillery Visitor Centre
229 Bunnahabhain Distillery
267 Caol Ila Distillery
269 Cardhu Distillery Visitor Centre
347 Clynelish Distillery
418 Dallas Dhu Historic Distillery
422 Dalwhinnie Distillery Visitor Centre
526 Edinburgh, Caledonian Brewery Visitor Centre
603 Edradour Distillery
640 Fettercairn Distillery Visitor Centre
729 Glendronach Distillery
734 Glenfarclas Distillery
735 Glenfiddich Distillery
740 Glengoyne Distillery
741 Glen Grant Distillery and Garden
742 Glenkinchie Distillery
743 Glenlivet Distillery
748 Glenmorangie Distillery Visitor Centre
749 Glen Moray Distillery
753 Glen Ord Distillery Visitor Centre
754 Glenturret Distillery
805 Highland Park Distillery
858 Isle of Arran Distillery Visitor Centre
860 Isle of Jura Distillery
943 Lagavulin Distillery Visitor Centre
948 Laphroaig Distillery
1132 Oban Distillery Visitor Centre
1363 Springbank Distillery
1382 Strathisla Distillery
1398 Talisker Distillery Visitor Centre
1418 Tobermory Distillery
1424 Tomatin Distillery

Fishing
372 Cowans Law Trout Fishing and Country Sports
448 Dornoch Lochans
752 Glen of Rothes Trout Fishery
980 Loch Fad Fishery
1029 Markle Fisheries
1130 North Third Trout Fishery

Forest trail
78 Ardgartan Visitor Centre
112 Ayr Gorge Woodlands
136 Barnaline Walks
151 Ben Aigan Cycle Trails
406 Culbin Forest
423 Dalzell Park
630 Farigaig
921 Kinnoull Hill Woodland Park
1062 Moncrieffe Hill Wood
1196 Queen Elizabeth Forest Park Centre
1200 Queen's View Visitor Centre
1206 Ravens Rock Forest Walk
1227 Roseisle Forest
1435 Torrieston Forest Walks
1503 Whiteash and Ordiequish Cycle Trails
1510 Winding Walks Forest Walks

Garden or plant nursery
9 Aberdeen, Cruickshank Botanic Garden
11 Aberdeen, Duthie Park Winter Gardens and Restaurant
25 Aberdeen, Winter Gardens
32 Abriachan Garden Nursery
33 Achamore Gardens
35 Achiltibuie Hydroponicum
38 Achnacloich Gardens
69 Ardanaiseig Gardens
71 Ardchattan Gardens
74 Ardencraig Gardens
77 Ardfearn Nursery
79 Ardkinglas Woodland Garden
84 Arduaine Garden
87 Ardwell Gardens

92 Armadale Castle Gardens and Museum of the Isles
98 Ascog Hall, Fernery and Gardens
101 Attadale Garden and Woodland Walks
116 Sir Douglas Bader Disabled Garden
122 Balmacara Estate and Lochalsh Woodland Garden
150 Bell's Cherrybank Gardens
161 Biblical Garden
166 Birch House Herbs
186 Bolfracks Garden
201 Branklyn Garden
211 Brin Herb Nursery
228 Bught Floral Hall and Visitor Centre
261 Cambo Gardens
265 Candacraig Gardens, Gallery and Nursery
338 Cluny House Gardens
353 Colleonard Sculpture Garden and Gallery
355 Colonsay House Gardens
359 Colzium Estate
385 Crarae Gardens
427 Dawyck Botanic Garden
443 Dochfour Gardens
456 Drummond Castle Gardens
495 Dundee, University Botanic Garden
554 Edinburgh, Malleny Garden
574 Edinburgh, Royal Botanic Garden
592 Edinburgh, Suntrap Garden
676 Geilston Garden
685 Glasgow Botanic Garden
694 Glasgow, Greenbank Garden
755 Glenwhan Gardens
783 Harmony Garden
788 Hayes Garden Land
836 Inshriach Alpine Nursery
845 Inveresk Lodge Garden
846 Inverewe Garden
876 Jura House Garden
878 Kailzie Gardens
897 Kildrummy Castle Gardens
906 Kilmory Castle Gardens
916 Kinlochlaich Gardens
922 Kinross House
942 Lael Forest Garden
970 Linn Botanic Gardens and Nursery
999 Logan Botanic Garden
1039 Megginch Castle Gardens
1047 Mertoun Gardens
1065 Monteviot House Gardens
1180 Pitmedden Garden
1181 Pitmuies Gardens
1195 Priorwood Garden and Dried Flower Shop
1216 Revack Estate
1242 St Andrew's Botanic Garden
1409 Teviot Water Gardens
1412 Threave Garden and Estate
1473 Victorian Fernery
1474 Viewpark Gardens
1509 Wilton Lodge Walled Garden
1520 Younger Botanic Garden

Golf course or centre

362 Connachan, Jane, Golf Centre
370 Covesea Golf Course
373 Craggan Fishery and Golf Course
1043 Melville Golf Centre
1095 Musselburgh Links, The Old Golf Course

Guided tour

308 Charlestown Lime Heritage Trust
381 Crail Guided Walks
552 Edinburgh, McEwan's 80' Literary Pub Tour
573 Edinburgh, Robin's Ghost and History Tours
541 Edinburgh, Geowalks Volcano Tours
556 Edinburgh, Mercat Walking Tours
571 Edinburgh, Rabbie's Trail Burners
701 Glasgow, Literary Tour
856 Island Encounter
862 Isle of Mull Landrover Wildlife Expeditions
1246 St Andrew's Guided Walks
1326 Shetland Wildlife Tours
1350 Smoo Innercave Tours

Historic house

2 Abbotsford
13 Aberdeen, Glover House
19 Aberdeen, Provost Skene's House
47 Alloa Tower
90 Argyll's Lodging
94 Arniston House
114 Bachelors' Club
120 Ballindalloch Castle
141 Barrie's Birthplace and Camera Obscura
216 Brodie Castle
219 Broughton House and Garden
235 Burns House
260 Callendar House
270 Cardoness Castle
272 Carlyle's Birthplace
281 Carrick House
419 Dalmeny House
455 Drumlanrig's Tower
540 Edinburgh, Georgian House
542 Edinburgh, Gladstone's Land
550 Edinburgh, John Knox House
551 Edinburgh, Lauriston Castle
565 Edinburgh, Palace of Holyroodhouse
622 Falkland Palace, Garden and Old Burgh
633 Fasque
707 Glasgow, Pollok House
724 Glenbarr Abbey Visitor Centre
757 Gosford House
765 Greenhill Covenantor House
775 Haddo House
809 Hill House
811 Hill Of Tarvit Mansion House and Garden
816 Holmwood House
819 Hopetoun House
820 House of the Binns
821 House of Dun
956 Leith Hall and Garden
957 Lennoxlove House
1028 Manderston
1031 Mar's Wark
1032 Mary, Queen of Scots' House
1041 Mellerstain House
1061 Moirlanich Longhouse
1083 Mount Stuart House and Gardens
1166 Paxton House
1290 Scone Palace
1333 Skaill House
1352 Soutar House
1364 Spynie Palace
1369 Stevenson House
1410 Thirlestane Castle
1440 Traquair House
1490 Weaver's Cottage
1511 Winton House

Monument, notable building or antiquity

30 Aberlemno Sculptured Stones
31 Abernethy Round Tower
34 Achavanich Standing Stones
37 Achnabreck Cup and Ring Marks
41 Aikwood Tower
44 Alexander III Monument
62 Antonine Wall
73 Ardclach Bell Tower
76 Ardestie and Carlungie Earth Houses
85 Ardunie Roman Signal Station
93 Armstrong, Johnie, of Gilnockie Memorial
103 Auchagallon Stone Circle

121 Ballygowan Cup and Ring Marks
127 Baluachraig Cup and Ring
134 Bar Hill Fort
139 Barochan Cross
143 Barsalloch Fort
168 Bishop's and Earl's Palaces
170 Blackhall Roman Camps
171 Blackhammer Cairn
172 Black Hill
177 Black Watch Monument
183 Boath Doocot
198 Brahan Seer Plaque, Chanonry Point
200 Brandsbutt Symbol Stone
213 Broch of Gurness
217 Brough of Birsay
223 Bruce's Stone
231 Burghead Well
237 Burns Monument
239 Burnswark Hill
245 Cairnbaan Cup and Ring Marks
249 Cairn Holy Chambered Cairns
250 Cairn o' Get
251 Cairnpapple Hill
256 Calanais Standing Stones
276 Carn Ban
280 Carn Liath
290 Castlecary
295 Castle Jail
297 Castlelaw Hill Fort
304 Caterthuns
306 Chapel Finian
307 Chapel of Sand
310 Chesters Hill Fort
317 Cille Bharra
330 Clava Cairns
332 Clickimin Broch
348 Cnoc Freiceadain Long Cairns
350 Cobb Memorial
358 Columba's Footsteps
360 Commando Memorial
366 Corrimony Cairn
369 Coulter Motte
384 Crail Tolbooth
404 Crusoe, Robinson, Statue
407 Cullerlie Stone Circle
411 Culsh Earth House
414 Cunninghame Graham Memorial
415 Cuween Hill Cairn
433 Dere Street Roman Road
444 Dogton Stone
446 Doonhill Homestead
451 Druchtag Motte
453 Drumcoltran Tower
465 Dullatur
470 Dumtroddan Cup and Ring Marks
471 Dunadd Fort
476 Dun Beag Broch
479 Dun Canna
481 Dun Carloway
482 Dunchraigaig Cairn
491 Dundee, Mercat Cross
493 Dundee, St Andrew's Church and the Glasite Hall
498 Dun Dornaigil Broch
500 Dunfallandy Stone
512 Dwarfie Stane
513 Dyce Symbol Stones
514 Earl's Palace
516 Eassie Sculptured Stone
517 Easter Aquhorthies Stone Circle
536 Edinburgh, Eagle Rock
544 Edinburgh, Greyfriars Bobby
563 Edinburgh, Nelson Monument
590 Edinburgh, Scott Monument
602 Edin's Hall Broch
606 Eilach An Naoimh
643 Finavon Doocot
649 Flodden Monument
656 Fort George
663 Fowlis Wester Sculptured Stone
665 Fyrish Monument
678 Gifford, Lady, Statue
684 Glasgow, Bearsden Bathhouse
688 Glasgow, City Chambers
722 Glebe Cairn
731 Glenelg Brochs
736 Glenfinnan Monument
758 Grain Earth House
766 Greenknowe Tower
769 Grey Cairns of Camster
773 Gunn, Neil M, Memorial Viewpoint
781 Hardie, Kier, Statue
801 Highland Mary's Monument
802 Highland Mary's Statue
810 Hill O' Many Stanes
814 Hogg, James, Monument
815 Holm of Papa Westray Chambered Cairn
832 Inchmahome Priory
839 Inveraray Bell Tower
869 Jarlshof Prehistoric and Norse Settlement
889 Kempock Stone
891 Kilberry Sculptured Stones
893 Kildarton Cross
901 Kilmartin Sculptured Stones
902 Kilmichael Glassary Cup and Ring Marks
903 Kilmodan Sculptured Stones
905 Kilmory Cairns
909 Kilpatrick Dun
913 King's Knot
929 Kirkmadrine Early Christian Stones
934 Knap of Howar
937 Knocknagael Boar Stone
938 Knowe of Yarso Chambered Cairn
944 Laggangairn Standing Stones
958 Lerwick Town Hall
961 Leyden Obelisk and Tablet
967 Linlithgow Palace
973 Loanhead Stone Circle
989 Loch Nam Uamh Cairn
1011 McCaig's Tower
1012 MacDonald, Sir Hector, Monument
1015 Machrie Moor Stone Circles
1018 Maclean's Cross
1021 Maes Howe
1024 Maiden Stone
1040 Meigle Sculptured Stones
1044 Melville Monument
1045 Memsie Cairn
1046 Merkland Cross
1049 Midhowe Broch and Cairns
1055 Milnholm Cross
1069 Monument Hill
1078 Moss Farm Road Stone Circle
1082 Motte of Urr
1084 Mousa Broch
1089 Muir O'Fauld Signal Station
1102 National Wallace Monument
1104 Nelson Tower
1107 Ness of Burgi
1108 Nether Largie Cairns
1148 Orchardton Tower
1154 Ormiston Market Cross
1158 Our Lady of the Sea
1169 Peel Ring of Lumphanan
1175 Picardy Symbol Stone
1188 Port na Con Souterrain
1192 Preston Market Cross
1194 Prestonpans Battle Cairn
1203 Quoyness Chambered Tomb
1209 Red Smiddy
1213 Rennibister Earth House
1218 Ri Cruin Cairn
1219 Ring of Brodgar Stone Circle and Henge
1220 Rispain Camp
1224 Rob Roy's Grave
1225 Rob Roy's Statue
1238 Ruthwell Cross
1273 St Ninian's Cave
1276 St Orland's Stone
1280 St Vigeans Sculptured Stones
1295 Scots Dyke
1296 Scotstarvit Tower
1297 Scott, Captain, and Wilson, Dr, Cairn
1315 Seabegs Wood
1334 Skara Brae Prehistoric Village
1366 Stanydale Temple

1367 Steinacleit Cairn and Stone Circle
1375 Stones of Stenness
1391 Sueno's Stone
1403 Tarves Medieval Tomb
1404 Taversoe Tuick Chambered Cairn
1405 Tealing Dovecot and Earth House
1406 Teampull na Trionaid
1408 Temple Wood Stone Circles
1421 Tollpark and Garnhall
1425 Tomb of the Eagles
1427 Tomnaverie Stone Circle
1428 Torhouskie Stone Circle
1433 Torr A'Chaisteal Fort
1436 Torrylin Cairn
1465 Unstan Chambered Cairn
1480 Walls, Maggie, Monument
1483 Wardlaw Mausoleum
1485 Waterloo Monument
1489 Watling Lodge
1497 West Port
1498 Westquarter Dovecot
1506 Wideford Hill Chambered Cairn
1513 Witch's Stone
1515 Wolfstone
1516 Wool Stone

Nature reserve
148 Beinn Eighe National Nature Reserve
152 Ben Lawers
519 Eden Estuary Centre
623 Falls of Clyde Wildlife Reserve and Visitor Centre
629 Faraid Head and Balnakeil Bay
651 Flow Country
654 Forsinard Nature Reserve
778 Handa Island Ferry Trips
793 Hermaness National Nature Reserve Visitor Centre
835 Insh Marshes Nature Reserve
881 Keen of Hamar National Nature Reserve
939 Kylerhea Otter Haven
982 Loch Garten Osprey Centre
1030 Mar Lodge Estate
1067 Montrose Basin Wildlife Centre
1116 Nigg Bay Bird Reserve
1131 Noss National Nature Reserve
1241 St Abb's Head
1259 St Kilda
1464 Unst
1470 Vane Farm Nature Reserve
1507 Wildfowl and Wetlands Centre

Outdoor activity centre
984 Loch Insh Watersports
994 Loch Park Adventure Centre
1114 Newton Hill Country Sports
1204 Raasay Outdoor Centre

Pleasure boat trip
58 Anstruther Pleasure Trips to the Isle of May
149 Bella Jane Boat Trips
340 Clyde Marine Cruises
439 Dim Riv Norse Longship Boat Trips
659 Forth Jet
718 Glasgow Waverley Paddlesteamer
867 Jacobite Cruises
954 Leisure Marine
975 Loch Awe Steam Packet
996 Loch Shiel Cruises
1072 Moray Firth Dolphin Cruises
1085 Muckle Flugga and Out Stack
1316 Seafood Cruise
1392 Summer Isles Cruises
1444 Trossachs Pier Complex

Pony trekking or horse riding
209 Brighouse Bay Trekking Ponies
818 Homeston Farm Trail and Pony Trekking
923 Kinshaldy Riding Stables
1001 Logie Farm Riding Centre
1010 Lyth Stables

Sailing
673 Galloway Sailing Centre
1187 Port Edgar Marina and Sailing School

Scenic or architectural feature
5 Aberdeen, Bridge of Dee
6 Aberdeen, Brig O' Balgownie
40 Aigas Dam
42 Ailsa Craig
75 Ardessie Falls
115 Badbea Old Village
117 Baille An Or, Goldrush Town 1869
144 Bass Rock
153 Ben Lomond
155 Ben Nevis
162 Big Burn Walk
203 Brechin Bridge
207 Bridge of Carr
208 Bridge of Oich
220 Broughty Castle
221 Brow Well
230 Burg
258 Caledonian Canal
264 Camus a Charraig
266 Canna
268 Cape Wrath
283 Carsaig Arches
286 Cartland Bridge
288 Cassley Falls
319 Clachan Bridge
333 Click Mill
334 Cloch Lighthouse
336 Clootie Well
365 Corrieshalloch Gorge
367 Corryvreckan Whirlpool
368 Cotton Mill, Spinningdale
375 Craigellachie Bridge
393 Crinan Canal
399 Cross of Lorraine
401 Croy Hill
436 Devil's Beef Tub
442 Divach Falls
459 Dryhope Tower
466 Dulsie Bridge
473 Dunaverty Rock
480 Duncansby Head
487 Dundee, The Howf
489 Dundee Law
494 Dundee, Tay Rail Bridge
504 Dunkeld
505 Dunkeld Bridge
507 Dunnet Head
515 Eas Coul Aulin Falls
518 Eathie Burn
537 Edinburgh, Forth Rail Bridge
547 Edinburgh, Holyrood Park
598 Edinburgh, White Horse Close
609 Electric Brae
613 Embo Beach, Anchor
617 Fair Isle
619 Fairy Glen, Rosemarkie
621 Falkirk Wheel
624 Falls of Dochart
625 Falls of Foyers
626 Falls of Glomach
627 Falls of Rogie
628 Falls of Shin
639 Fettercairn Arch
655 Fort Charlotte
657 Forth and Clyde Canal
658 Forth Bridges Exhibition
660 Fortingall Yew
675 Garvamore Bridge
679 Gilnockie Tower
693 Glasgow, George Square
699 Glasgow, Hutchesons' Hall
704 Glasgow, Necropolis
713 Glasgow School of Art
719 Glasgow, Willow Tea Rooms
723 Glen Affric
726 Glencoe
738 Glenfinnan Viaduct
756 Goatfell
770 Grey Mare's Tail
774 Hackness, Martello Tower

794 The Hermitage
852 Iona
898 Killiecrankie
911 Kilt Rock
925 Kintail and Morvich
927 Kirkaig Falls
931 Kirk Yetholm
940 Kyles of Bute
941 Ladykirk
979 Loch Eriboll
983 Lochindorb
986 Loch Lomond
988 Loch Morar
990 Loch Ness
1037 Meadow Well
1050 Millbuies Lochs
1105 Neptune's Staircase
1141 Old Man of Hoy
1142 Old Man of Stoer
1149 Ord of Caithness
1150 Ord Summit
1157 Our Lady of the Isles
1163 Parallel Roads
1184 Plodda Falls
1193 Preston Mill and Phantassie Doocot
1199 Queen's View, Loch Lomond
1202 Quirang
1205 Randolph's Leap
1210 Reekie Linn Falls
1211 Reelig Glen
1214 Rennie's Bridge
1217 Rhue Beach
1226 Rockcliffe
1228 Rossal Interpretive Trail
1236 Rumbling Bridge
1237 Ruthven Barracks
1253 St Columba's Cave
1256 St Fillan's Cave
1261 St Margaret's Cave
1270 St Mary's Loch
1272 St Monans Windmill
1284 Sandwood Bay
1289 Scapa Flow
1314 Scott's View
1327 Shieldaig Island
1343 Smailholm Tower
1349 Smoo Caves
1356 Soutra Aisle
1362 Split Stone, Melvich
1365 Staffa
1372 Stirling Old Bridge
1376 Storr
1387 Struie Viewpoint
1413 Three Follies at Auckengill
1415 Tighnabruaich Viewpoint
1429 Tormiston Mill
1434 Torridon
1437 Touchstone Maze
1439 Traprain Law
1451 Tweed Bridge
1454 Udale Bay
1462 Union Canal
1463 Union Suspension Bridge
1469 Valleyfield Wood
1472 Victoria Falls
1479 Wade's Bridge
1492 Well of Seven Heads
1493 West Affric
1501 Whalebone Arch
1502 Whaligoe Steps
1519 Yarrow

Skiing

557 Edinburgh, Midlothian Ski Centre
728 Glencoe Ski Centre
828 Huntly Nordic and Outdoor Centre

Theatre, art or leisure centre

29 Aberfeldy Recreation Centre
64 Aquatec
102 Aubigny Sports Centre
278 Carnegie Leisure Centre
318 Citadel Leisure Centre, Ayr
387 Crawford Arts Centre
438 Dewars Centre
468 Dumfries Ice Bowl
474 Dunbar Leisure Pool
484 Dundee Contemporary Arts
531 Edinburgh, City Art Centre
838 International Purves Puppets
849 Inverness Aquadome and Sports Centre
955 Leisure Zone
977 Loch Centre
1009 Lyth Arts Centre
1023 Magnum Leisure Centre
1036 Meadowmill Sports Centre
1074 Moray Leisure Centre
1079 Motherwell Concert Hall and Theatre
1096 Musselburgh Sports Centre
1101 Nairn Leisure Park and Swimming Pool
1123 North Berwick Sports Centre
1133 Oban Highland Theatre
1170 Perth Leisure Pool
1177 Pier Arts Centre
1179 Pitlochry Festival Theatre
1239 Ryan Leisure Centre
1299 Scottish Antique and Arts Centre
1381 Strathearn Recreation Centre

Visitor centre or speciality attraction

8 Aberdeen College Planetarium
15 Aberdeen, Kings College Centre
22 Aberdeen, Satrosphere
36 Achiltibuie Smokehouse
43 Aldie Water Mill and the Tain Pottery
46 Alford Valley Railway
52 The Aluminium Story Library and Visitor Centre
53 Alvie Estate
57 Annan Activities
59 An Tairbeart Heritage Centre
60 Antartex Village
68 Archaeolink Prehistory Park
80 Ardnamurchan Natural History Centre
81 Ardnamurchan Point Visitor Centre
83 Ardtornish Estate
95 Aros Experience
99 Athelstaneford, Flag Heritage Centre
123 Balmichael Visitor Centre
125 Balnain House
140 Barra Heritage and Cultural Centre
142 Barry Mill
145 Baxters Visitor Centre
154 Bennachie Centre
157 Ben Nevis Woollen Mill
165 Big Idea
176 Blacksmiths Shop, Gretna Green
184 Boathouse Visitor Centre
187 Bonawe Iron Furnace
188 Bo'ness and Kinneil Railway
193 Bosta Iron Age House
202 Breadalbane Folklore Centre
210 Bright Water Visitor Centre
232 Burland Croft Trail
238 Burns National Heritage Park
242 Butterchurn and Scottish Food and Craft Centre
246 Cairngorm Chairlift
248 Cairngorm Reindeer Centre
252 Caithness and Sutherland Natural History Display
253 Caithness Glass Visitor Centre, Oban
254 Caithness Glass Visitor Centre, Perth
255 Caithness Glass Visitor Centre, Wick
259 Caledonian Railway, Brechin
274 Carmichael Heritage Centre
287 Cashmere Visitor Centre
293 Castle Garrison Encounter
296 Castle Keep
312 Children's Amusement Park
313 Chisholms Highland Dress
325 Clanland and Sealpoint
337 Cluny Clays
346 Clyde Valley Country Estate
349 Coats Observatory

352 Colfin Smokehouse
356 Colour Box Scotland
357 Columba Centre
361 Confectionary Factory Visitor Centre
388 Cream O'Galloway
392 Crieff Visitor Centre
402 Cruachan Power Station
408 Culloden
409 Culross
428 Deep Sea World
430 Dee Valley Confectioners
445 Dolphins and Seals of the Moray Firth
450 Dounreay Exhibition Centre
457 Drumpellier Country Park
461 Dualchas
485 Dundee, Discovery Point
486 Dundee, HM Frigate Unicorn
488 Dundee, Jungle Kids
492 Dundee, Mills Observatory
523 Edinburgh, Brass Rubbing Centre
524 Edinburgh, Britannia
525 Edinburgh Butterfly and Insect World
527 Edinburgh, Camera Obscura
528 Edinburgh Canal Centre
533 Edinburgh Crystal Visitor Centre
535 Edinburgh, Dynamic Earth
539 Edinburgh, Fun Park
548 Edinburgh, Hub Festival Centre
567 Edinburgh, Parliament House
569 Edinburgh, James Pringle Weavers Leith Mills
576 Edinburgh, Royal Observatory Visitor Centre
578 Edinburgh, The Royal Yacht Britannia
585 Edinburgh, Scotch Whisky Heritage Centre
588 Edinburgh, Scottish Parliament Visitor Centre
589 Edinburgh, Scottish Tartans Museum
594 Edinburgh Tartan Weaving Mill and Exhibition
595 Edinburgh, Tower Amusement Centre
597 Edinburgh, Water of Leith Conservation Trust
601 Edinburgh Woollen Mill, Jedburgh
631 Farm Buggy Trails
637 Ferrycroft Countryside Centre
644 Findhorn Foundation Community
645 Findhorn in Time and Tide
646 Finlaggan Trust
647 Flag Heritage Centre
664 Fraserburgh Heritage Centre
667 Gaelic Whiskies – Whisky Exhibition
669 Gairloch Marine Life Centre and Sail Gairloch
671 Galloway Country Style
677 Genealogy and Exhibition Centre, Co Leis Thu?
683 Glasgow, The Barras
691 Glasgow, Fossil Grove
706 Glasgow, Piping Centre
714 Glasgow, Scotkart Indoor Kart Racing Centre
730 Gleneagles Crystal
744 Glenlivet Estate
750 Glenmore Visitor Centre
751 Glen Nevis Centre
762 Grassic Gibbon Centre
763 Great Glen Fine Foods
767 Gretna Green, World Famous Old Blacksmith's Shop Centre
768 Gretna Hall Blacksmith's Shop
772 Grogport Organic Tannery
782 Harestanes Countryside Visitor Centre
804 Highland Mysteryworld
807 Highland Wineries
824 Hunter House
825 Hunterston Power Station
834 Innerpeffray Library
843 Inverawe Fisheries and Smokery Exhibition
851 Inverness, James Pringle Weavers
857 Islay Woollen Mill
859 Isle of Islay Natural History Trust
864 Isle of Mull Weavers
865 Isle of Skye Brewing Company
872 Jedburgh Woollen Mill
874 John O' Groats
877 Kagyu Samye Ling Tibetan Centre
879 Kartstart
883 Keith and Dufftown Railway
890 Kid'z Play
899 Kilmahog Woollen Mill
932 Kirroughtree Visitor Centre
936 Knockhill Racing Circuit
947 Landmark Highland Heritage and Adventure Park
952 Leadhills Miner's Library and Reading Room
953 Leighton Library
959 Letham Glen
960 Lewis Loom Centre
966 Lindsay, J F, Targemaker
976 Loch Carron Cashmere Wool Centre
981 Loch Fyne Miniature Railway
992 Loch Ness, Original Visitor Centre
1000 Logan Fish Pond Marine Life Centre
1003 Lomond Shores
1005 Loudoun Castle Theme Park
1006 Lower City Mills
1014 Macduff Marine Aquarium
1016 Mackinnon Mills
1027 Mallaig Marine World
1038 The Meffan
1052 Mill of Benholm Visitor Centre
1053 Mill on the Fleet
1054 Mill Trail Visitor Centre
1057 Miniature Railway
1060 Moffat Woollen Mill
1071 Moonstone Miniatures
1090 Mull Rail
1106 Ness Heritage Centre
1109 Neverland Adventure Play Centre
1110 Nevis Range Cable Cars
1111 New Abbey Corn Mill
1113 New Lanark Visitor Centre
1117 Noah's Ark
1118 Noah's Ark Activity Centre
1126 Northern Natural History
1135 Oban Seal and Marine Centre
1147 Orcadian Stone Company
1171 Perth Mart Visitor Centre
1176 Pictavia
1183 Pittencrieff Park Animal Centre and Glasshouses
1201 Quendale Water Mill
1208 Red Kite Viewing
1223 Rob Roy and Trossachs Visitor Centre
1231 Rothiemurchus Estate
1234 Royal Burgh of Stirling Visitor Centre
1278 St Ronans Wells Interpretive Centre
1281 Samye Ling Tibetan Centre
1283 Sandhaven Meal Mill
1292 Scotland's Larder
1300 Scottish Crannog Centre
1303 Scottish Hydro-Electric Visitor Centre
1305 Scottish Kiltmaker Visitor Centre
1306 Scottish Liqueur Centre
1309 Scottish Off-Road Driving Centre
1312 Scottish Wool Centre
1317 Sea Life Centre, St Andrews
1341 Skyeskyns
1342 Skye Woollen Mill
1344 Smail's, Robert, Printing Works

1345 Small World Visitor Centre
1348 Smithy Heritage Centre
1353 Souter Johnnie's Cottage
1357 Spean Bridge Woollen Mill
1358 Speyside Cooperage Visitor Centre
1359 Speyside Heather Centre
1361 Spey Valley Smokehouse
1374 Stocks Stones and Stories, Exhibition of Crieff Stocks and Crosses
1377 Storybook Glen
1384 Strathspey Steam Railway
1388 Stuart Crystal
1396 Tain Through Time
1399 Tam O' Shanter Experience
1416 Time Capsule
1417 Timespan Heritage Centre and Art Gallery
1426 Tomintoul Visitor Centre
1430 Torness Power Station
1441 Treasures of the Earth
1442 Trimontium Exhibition
1443 Tropic House
1445 Trossachs Woollen Mill
1447 Trowmill,Woollen Weaving Mill
1453 Tweedhope Sheep Dogs
1455 Ugie Salmon Fish House
1475 Vikingar
1481 Waltzing Waters
1482 Wanlockhead Beam Engine
1484 Warp and Weft Visitor Centre
1486 Water Mill and Tearoom
1487 Water Sampling Pavilion, Strathpeffer
1494 West Highland Dairy
1495 West Highland Heavy Horse Tours
1505 Whithorn Trust Discovery Centre
1517 Working Sheep Dogs
1518 World of Wood

Wildlife or farm park

10 Aberdeen, Doonies Farm
91 Argyll Wildlife Park
105 Auchingarrich Wildlife Centre
135 Barholm Mains Open Farm
175 Blackshaw Farm Park
181 Blair Drummond Safari and Leisure Park
191 Boreland Riding Centre and Scottish Farm Park
314 Choraidh Croft Farm Park
329 Clatteringshaws Forest Wildlife Centre
371 Cowal Bird Garden
376 Craig Highland Farm
403 Crumstane Farm Park
454 Drum Farm Centre
483 Dundee, Camperdown Wildlife Centre
543 Edinburgh, Gorgie City Farm
600 Edinburgh Zoo
618 Fairways Horse Sanctuary
632 Farmlife Centre
672 Galloway Deer Range
720 Glasgow Zoo
739 Glengoulandie Deer Park
790 Heads of Ayr Farm Park
796 Highland and Rare Breeds Farm
798 Highland Cattle Centre
806 Highland Wildlife Park
837 International Otter Survival Fund
861 Isle of Mull Angora Rabbit Farm
873 Jedforest Deer and Farm Park
888 Kelton Mains Open Farm
1064 Monreith Animal World and Museum
1073 Moray Firth Wildlife Centre
1124 North East Falconry Visitor Centre
1134 Oban Rare Breeds Farm Park
1190 Praytis Farm Park
1301 Scottish Deer Centre
1310 Scottish Seabird Centre
1331 Silverburn Estate
1338 Skye Environmental Centre
1340 Skye Serpentarium
1354 South Bank Farm Park
1459 Uist Animal Visitor Centre
1508 Wildlife Park, Kirkcudbright